To purchase additional copies of:

Gate Breakers

please contact:

Selah Publishing Group, LLC

Toll free 800-917-2665

or visit our website at

www.selahbooks.com

Copyright © 2000 by Stanley F Fleming. All Rights reserved.

Printed in the United States of America

Published by Selah Publishing Group, LLC, Arizona. The views expressed or implied in this work do not necessarily reflect those of Selah Publishing Group.

ISBN 1-58930-098-X
Library of Congress Control Number: 98-61039

DEDICATION

Dedicated to

my loyal wife, Kathy,

my loving children,

and the congregation of the House of the Lord in Oldtown, Idaho,

for their support and encouragement.

ACKNOWLEDGEMENTS

I would like to thank Dr. Ron Carlson for his continued encouragement in the creation of Gate Breakers. The Lord used him to spark the idea for my dissertation at Northwest Graduate School of the Ministry.

Further thanks goes to Dr. Bill Payne, President, and Dr. Marc Mueller, former academic Vice-President, as well as the other staff of Northwest Graduate School of the Ministry in Kirkland, Washington, for their push to excellence in ministry.

Craig Branch, former V.P. of the Watchman Fellowship, reviewed my book and encouraged me onward. Athena Dean and her family critiqued my section on Scientology. Rabbi Jacob Loren of the Congregation Shema Yisrael in Southfield, MI, reviewed my chapter on Judaism. Thanks to all of you.

I appreciate the continued support of Pastor David Minor, whom I look to as a mentor and spiritual father in the Lord. Also, Pastor Dick Iverson, of Minister's Fellowship International, has inspired me and told me that this book ought to be in every pastor's library.

A debt of gratitude is owed to the many students, both teens and adults, who have taken the Gate Breaker course and encouraged me to get it published. Their positive comments and prayers cheered me on many times when I needed strength to complete it.

I would also like to acknowledge my Mom, Joyce Fleming, for her loving support and prayers, as well as my Dad, Jackson Fleming, who challenged me to create a section on the authenticity of the Bible. My wife, Kathy, helped me tremendously with the proofing of the text. My son, Jonathan, took the course and encouraged me by suggesting the appendix on "How to Lead Someone to the Lord." My daughter, Naphtali, took the course and challenged me to make this knowledge available to all Christian high school and Bible college students. My other daughters, Amber, Susanna, and Liberty, were wonderfully supportive. Thank you, all. I could not have done this without your help. May God bless you richly!

CONTENTS

FOREWORD

We are living in an age of spiritual confusion. The market place of religion offers up a smorgasbord of "false christs" and "false gospels," each with their own truth claims. The spiritual anemia of this present generation has left it vulnerable to the spiritual counterfeits being offered by various gurus and pseudo prophets of religion.

This book provides a valuable tool in helping to equip Christians to respond to the onslaught of the Cults and Religions influencing our society today. Jude 3 commands us to "contend for the faith." This is Apologetics, a reasoned defense of one's beliefs or convictions. Our English word comes from the Greek apologia, which is found in 1 Peter 3:15 "...be ready to give a defense (or an answer) to everyone who asks."

The Cults and Religions in this book have claimed to be spokesmen for God. They are not. In fact, they assail some of the foundational doctrines of Christianity for which we are commanded to "give an answer" or in effect practice apologetics. We must answer the challenge of the Cults and World Religions according to the guidelines God has given us in His Word, the Bible.

The reader of this book will not only find the history and doctrine of the Cults and Religions laid out, but a Biblical and reasoned response to them. In our pluralistic, post-Christian society, the Cults and Religions of the World have literally become the "Mission field at our doorstep." In this volume we have practical and Biblical steps for both defending Christianity and reaching out to those ensnared in the tangled web of false teachings and practice.

Evangelism is the heartbeat of God. It is not enough to know about the Cults and Religions. We must pray that as we study this book, God would give each of us a heart of love and compassion for those lost in the false religions of today. The Gospel is truly "Good News." My prayer for you as you read this excellent work is Romans 1:16, that you will "never be ashamed of the Gospel of Jesus Christ, for it is the power of God for salvation to everyone who believes."

Dr. Ron Carlson
President, Christian Ministries International

INTRODUCTION

Samson arose at midnight and ripped off the gates of the city. The Philistines were plotting to kill him in the morning, but he anticipated their plan and overthrew it. (Judges 16:1-3). Samson had been given anointed strength from God to fight against those who worshiped pagan deities. We read about his failures as well as his victories in a morally and spiritually depraved society. His strength and cunning inspire us. He truly became a champion of the people and of God.

In some ways, this sounds like modern day America. Moral failure and paganism are on the rise. Yet, the Lord is calling for those who will champion the cause of Christianity in a society that has almost forgotten God and turned to idolatry.

In the days of ancient Israel, there were those who would worship Baal, Asherah, Nisroch, Dagon, and others. They would perform sexual rituals to the god and goddess of fertility. Then they would sacrifice their children to Molech. Others would pay homage to the Queen of heaven or get counsel from the sun, moon, and stars. It was not hard to find a fortune teller, spiritist, witch, or sorcerer. Shrines for demonic angels, wooden images of false gods, and occult symbolism were common elements in society. People would cut themselves, wear magic charms, and show off strange tattoos. There were obscene images of goddesses and altars with prostitutes. Even some professing God would embrace paganism and create a religion mixed with truth and lies. They would manipulate God's Word by adding books that gave them permission to pray for the dead and worship angels.

Today, we often think that all of these activities are things of the past. However, the rise of interest in new age angels, spiritist psychics, UFOs, and the occult are leading people into strange types of worship once again. The modern secular climate of America has made room for witches to worship the Great Mother Goddess and Satanists to exalt their master. The altar of prostitution is not hard to find, and we could easily include the sacrifice of children on the alter of "pleasure at any price." Within the cults, there are false christs, prophets, and teachers perverting the gospel of Jesus Christ and leading millions astray. Science fiction gurus teach followers bizarre myths that alter rational thinking. Secret societies worship pagan idols and conspire to dominate the world. False religions try to hold on to their captives, but Christianity is storming the gates of hell.

Indeed, Jesus Christ is on the throne! He is already victorious! He told us that the enemy gates would give way. The hour has come for champions to arise in the anointing and power of God and war on behalf of those who are in the bondages of cults and false teachings. This book focuses on the need of the Church to arise with prayer, love, and witness in this midnight hour and take the city by surprise.

HOW DOES *GATE BREAKERS* WORK?

Gate Breakers is for *individual* or *group* study. It may be taken by one or by many. It is an excellent reference book, but was designed as a course for study. There are no other books or aids necessary. It is a self-contained course on cults and religions. However, extra resources such as videos and audio cassettes related to the topic will enhance learning and benefit the student greatly. Christian book centers usually have a supply of these. Also, cult awareness ministries often provide videos, cassettes, newsletters, tracts, etc. that may be ordered to heighten learning in a classroom setting. There is a list of cult awareness ministries in the resource guide under *Appendix D* at the end of this book.

The person studying alone is encouraged *not to skip* the first two chapters on *Christian Apologetics and Doctrine* and *The Bible's Authenticity.* These are at the heart of Christianity, and it is from these that cults stray. Repetition helps us learn. Therefore, I recommend that the individual reads through a chapter two or three times and afterwards fills out the study questionnaire. Once the questionnaire is done, the one who is studying Gate Breakers may turn to the Answer Key under *Appendix B* and check for accuracy. Make any corrections necessary. Occasionally, review the chapters to maintain retention.

Below are a few suggestions for a small group or classroom setting:

Student Procedures: The format is simple. Each student reads the chapter several times *before* the class which will focus on that chapter. Prior to the class, he or she should fill in the study questionnaire which will be reviewed in the session.

Group Activities: Groups should meet once a week for one or two hours. The longer sessions allow for the elements of teaching, discussion, talking through the lessons, videos, cassettes, guest speakers, questions and answers, etc. Each session should end with a specific time for small group prayer focusing on friends, relatives, or communities caught up in the cult or religion just discussed. Praying is one of the cardinal rules of a Gate Breaker discussed in the next section entitled *"What is a Gate Breaker?"*

Leader Responsibilities: The leader's primary function is to facilitate learning. While the elements mentioned above may change, several things should remain consistent in the class time. These are: 1) A general overview of the chapter, 2) A time to score and discuss the study questionnaires, and 3) A time of prayer at the end of the class. The leader should also keep basic records such as attendance, completed lessons, grades, etc. He or she is not expected to be an expert in cults or religions. (Most aren't.) A teaching / discussion style is preferred but not mandatory. Groups can be lead by pastors, teachers, or small group leaders. If the course is being taken for a grade, the instructor can create tests. It is important for groups to first study chapters one and two, but after this the sequence can change to fit the needs of the group. It is not necessary to complete all the chapters to have a successful class season. For instance, a class may go for ten, twelve, or eighteen weeks emphasizing the various cults and religions that meet the specific needs or interests of that group. Each chapter has boxes entitled "**Thinking Through The Scripture.**" The passages included in the boxes shine the spotlight of Scripture upon a false doctrine or aspect of the cult or religion under examination. They help the class to think through that Scripture. *Appendix C* has a guide for the Scripture boxes.

WHAT IS A GATE BREAKER?

The Lord Jesus said,
*"I will build my church and the gates of Hades
shall not prevail against it."*
(Matthew 16:18)

The *Gate Breakers* course is an apologetic study to equip Christians regarding cults and world religions. A "Gate Breaker" is one who stands against the gates of deceptive bondage and helps win those caught up in cults and world religions through prayer, love, and witness.

The three cardinal rules of one who wants to be a Gate Breaker are:

PRAYER The key to mobilizing evangelism today is prayer. A *Gate Breaker* needs to develop an attitude of prayer for those in the bondage of cults and false world religions. Prayer can be individual, corporate, silent, or verbal. It can be prayer of spiritual warfare, intercession, or supplication. It can be a spontaneous prayer while driving by a Mormon temple, Kingdom Hall, etc. or a strategic prayer in a group setting. Let's believe God for breaking down the gates that hold these people in captivity.

LOVE The key to winning the right to evangelize today is love. A *Gate Breaker* needs to develop a heart of love for those in the bondage of cults and false world religions. Christ died for these people. The followers of Christ should show Christ's love and compassion. Acts of kindness and words of Agape love may cause hard, resistant hearts to soften for the gospel seed.

WITNESS The key to setting the captives free is witness. A *Gate Breaker* needs to develop his or her ability to share the Gospel with those in the bondage of cults and world religions. A Christian can plant the message of the Gospel, water what others have sown, or even reap a harvest of souls for the Kingdom of God.

The purpose of this book is to equip Christians so that they can be more effective in their witness to those caught in cults and world religions. *Appendix A* has a format for leading someone to the Lord.

Christians need to be equipped to share their faith. Wouldn't it be amazing if Christians stopped fearing the cults and slamming the door on them, and started sharing the gospel of Jesus Christ instead? *Wouldn't it be amazing if Christians became so equipped that the Mormons and Jehovah's Witnesses had to stop sending people door-to-door because they were getting converted to Christianity?* Christians should have nothing to fear. We have the truth of God's impenetrable Word and the power of God's omnipotent Spirit to help us.

CHRISTIAN APOLOGETICS AND DOCTRINE

"Christianity is unique among the religions of the world. And the reason for its uniqueness lies in the historical figure who stands at its center—Jesus Christ."[1]

I. WHAT IMPORTANT QUESTION MUST BE ANSWERED TODAY?

   A. **The Chameleon Image Factor**. Chameleons are really amazing little creatures. They show the wondrous imagination of an awesome Creator. As a child, I lived in Phoenix for a couple of years and had one of these strange lizards. It would change color to match its surroundings. If I put it on the grass, it turned green. While on the sidewalk, it was a milky sort of color. It was brown on brown and yellow on yellow. It did not turn every color, but it did turn many.

      For years I have been studying the cults and world religions and have discovered an amazing thing: they treat Jesus like a chameleon, blending His identity with their perverted doctrinal background. He becomes what they want Him to be, and in the process, He loses His Biblical identity.

      As we enter a new century and millennium, many look for the return of the Lord Jesus Christ, and many believe it will be soon. But who is this Jesus that will return? People view Him in different ways. This raises the most important question of our day—the same one Jesus asked nearly 2,000 years ago. He asked, *"Who do you say that I am?* (Matthew 16:15). Simon Peter answered that question by stating, *"You are the Christ, the Son of the Living God"* (Matthew 16:16).

B. **Who do you say that Jesus is?** Most people reading a book on this subject have already made a commitment to Jesus as Lord and Savior. However, there may be some who need to take time to examine their relationship with Jesus. If you have not yet made a personal commitment to Jesus Christ as your Lord and Savior, this chapter will give you a foundational understanding of what the Bible says about Jesus. If you are a new Christian or one who came from a cult or non Christian religion, this chapter will help you understand who the Bible says Jesus is as compared to the "Jesus" of the cults and religions.

It is vitally important that each of us has a "personal relation-ship" with Jesus Christ and not just a religious view. There are many that will try to sell you a religious view of Jesus that is actu-ally a chameleon image of the truth. The Jesus of the cults and the world religions is not the Jesus revealed in the Bible. They follow *"another Jesus"* (2 Corinthians 11:4) rather than the true One. Their concept of Jesus does not come from the Heavenly Father, but from *"the father of lies"* (John 8:44).

II. WHAT PROCLAMATION DID JESUS MAKE ABOUT HIS CHURCH?

A. **I will build My Church.** When Jesus asked His disciples who they thought He was, Peter boldly answered the question and said, *"You are the Christ, the Son of the Living God."* To this Jesus responded, *"Blessed are you, Simon Bar-Jonah for flesh and blood has not revealed this to you, but My Father who is in heaven. And I also say to you that you are Peter, and on this rock I will build My church, and the gates of Hades shall not prevail against it. And I will give you the keys of the kingdom of heaven, and whatever you bind on earth will be bound in heaven, and whatever you loose on earth will be loosed in heaven."* (Matthew 16:17-19)

B. **The Revelation.** The message that Peter received from the Heavenly Father, about the identity of Jesus, was not to be taken lightly. Jesus wanted them all to understand the significance. So he proclaimed that it was upon this very truth—of who He is—that the New Testament church would be built. Furthermore, the pro-cess of the revelation was vital because the Heavenly Father would reveal it in the heart of the believer. Jesus would build His church upon the truth of *who* He is as revealed by His Heavenly Father, and it would be confirmed in the heart of the believer. He goes on to proclaim that the gates of Hades would not be able to withstand the church and that His disciples would be given the "keys" that open the gates of Heaven.

C. **The Gates of Hades.** Ever since the days of Jesus, the church has continued to storm the gates of Hades and rescue people who were on their way to an eternity without God. The word *Hades* comes from the Greek and means "the unseen place or the place of the dead." While we recognize that there is a literal place of the dead to which people pass after this life, we should remember that many in this world are trapped in a literal place of unbelief, confusion, and darkness. They are dead because they don't know Christ and are on their way to an eternity without hope or love. It is for them that Christ died. The gates that hold them can be broken open. Jesus informed us that the power of Satan will not prevail against His church.

An insight on this verse comes from the famous commentator Adam Clarke who says, "In ancient times the gates of fortified cities were used to hold councils in, and were usually places of great strength. Our Lord's expression means that neither the plots, stratagems, nor strength of Satan and his angels should ever so far prevail as to destroy the sacred truths in [Peter's] confession."[2]

D. **The Growth of the Church.** Today, Christianity is challenging the gates of Hades all over the world. Christian evangelicals and Pentecostals are growing rapidly in the third world countries and are thought by some to be "the fastest-growing major religious grouping in the world."[3]

However, it is not easy to measure growth globally. There are many variables, and information gathering is tedious. Hence, there are differing estimates. Dr. David Barret of the Global Evangelization Movement and Research Professor of Missiometrics at Regent University, is a conservative statistician who estimates daily global church growth at about 66,000 converts. This means that over 24 million are accepting Christ as their Savior annually, and of these he told me in a recent phone conversation that 9 million are Pentecostal / Charismatic. He also expressed a great burden for the 1.7 billion (out of approximately 6 billion worldwide) who have never heard the gospel.[4]

Other estimates are higher. A few years ago one report said that 178,000 people were being added to the church daily somewhere. A further study indicates that possibly one out of every ten people in the world is a true believer in Christ.[5] This is easy to believe since one third of the world has some form of Christianity and there is no religion that equals it. Yet, there needs to be greater research to understand the actual global impact of Christianity to plot the best strategy of evangelizing the world.

There is not only growth in Christianity today, but a greater unity among believers. Movements like Promise Keepers, the March for Jesus, the Pastor's Prayer Summit, Every Home for Christ, the 10 / 40 prayer movement, and mission net-working are having a tremendous impact that unites Christians in order to complete the task of the Great Commission (Matthew 28:18-20).

E. **Salvation and Discipleship.** Even though many are getting saved, it is not enough. Jesus wants disciples not just converts. He did not commission us to get people saved but to "make disciples". Getting saved is just the first step.

Discipleship is somewhat like spiritual growth. Before Jesus comes into our lives, we are far from God because our sins have separated us (Isaiah 59:2). When we recognize our need for the Savior Jesus, we ask God to forgive us for our sins, and we invite Jesus into our lives. He always responds to a true repentant heart. This is the beginning of new spiritual birth and is often referred to as being "born again" (John 3:3). The Apostle Peter said that at this stage a new convert is like a newborn babe and must seek the pure spiritual milk of the Word of God (1 Peter 2:2). As we study the Bible, seek the Lord in prayer, and obey His ways, we begin to become disciplined in our lives (hence a disciple). There is often a stage of being infants (1 Corinthians 3:1-2) in which we struggle to overcome various things. As an infant grows, he needs solid food rather than milk. Spiritual Christian children need to cut their teeth upon the Bible thus becoming mature with better discernment (Hebrews 5:11–6:2).

This is extremely important because Christians need maturity and discernment to stand against the confusing arguments of cultists and those in non Christian religions. This is one reason that Christians need to become well informed about the issues of cults and world religions—so that they will not be deceived.

III. WHAT ARE SOME OF THE END TIME STRATEGIES OF THE ENEMY?
A. **Lawlessness and a Loss of Love.** Even though the church is rescuing people from the devil's domain, the battle wages strong. All around the world we see acts of violence happening. The media has shocked the world in the last decade as it reports on shootings in schools, day care centers, churches, and road rage incidents. Many stand by helplessly as ethnic wars annihilate people based upon race. Various racial supremacists groups twist Scripture to say that some people don't have souls, and thereby justify abuse or even

murder. As a result, people are growing cold towards God even as Jesus prophesied in Matthew 24:12. Men love pleasure, money, and self, but not God.

It should be noted that there is a debate in the Christian camp about whether certain prophecies by Jesus and the apostles have already been fulfilled. For instance, in Matthew 24 there are many prophecies by Jesus about wars, famines, earthquakes, false prophets, false christs, lawlessness, and loss of love in the end times. While many of these things did occur in the first couple centuries of the Church and throughout the ages, there is an escalation of these same things today that eclipses even what has been experienced before. Also, some of the other prophecies such as the gospel being preached to every nation (Matt. 24:14) and major cosmic disturbances (Matt. 24:29) have yet to occur, although we are getting closer. There are other prophecies in Matthew and elsewhere about the growing deception of the devil in the last days. These seem to crest just prior to the second coming of Christ.

Thinking Through The Scripture

"And a servant of the Lord must not quarrel but be gentle to all, able to teach, patient, in humility correcting those who are in opposition, if God perhaps will grant them repentance, so that they may know the truth, and that they may come to their senses and escape the snare of the devil, having been taken captive by him to do his will." (2 Timothy 2:24-26)

Questions for discussion:
1. What typically happens when people disagree over doctrine and belief?
2. Consider the word "servant" in the verse. How should it impact our attitude.
3. What does the word "repentance" mean?

B. **Spiritual Degeneration.** Many are involved in things that take them away from God and the truth of His Word. 2 Timothy 3:1-7 gives an entire list of the types of behavior we are seeing today. People are more self-oriented. Children are disobedient to parents. Men are lovers of pleasure more than lovers of God.

C. **Attention Getters.** Matthew 24:24 tells us that false christs and prophets will use signs and wonders to try and deceive even Christians. A spiritual vacuum in people's lives sets them up to be drawn into anything unusual. There is a growing interest in new age angels, psychic hot lines, UFO's, statues that weep, channeling, apparitions of Mary, and many other bizarre things. It would be naive to think that Christians aren't ever drawn to these things and are immune to their trickery. The current need for discernment by Christians is indeed great. We must be mindful of the message being taught, the character of the messenger, and the fruitfulness of the ministry being presented (Matt. 7:15-20).

In contrast to these attention-getting wonders, it is interesting to consider that most of the miracles of Jesus and the New Testament apostles came as a direct result of the need of others. The miracles of healing, deliverance, feeding, raising from the dead, even turning water into wine were all related to people's needs. They were not done for the purpose of attention-getting but out of compassion for others. People were drawn because God was meeting their needs. Christians certainly should believe that we serve a miraculous God, not only of yesterday, but of today, and forever. However, we must examine any signs and wonders under the spotlight of the Word of God because the Bible tells us that this is one of the ways the devil will try and deceive even the elect of God.

D. **False Teaching and Deception.** In 1 Timothy 4:1-6, Paul exhorts Timothy to instruct the brethren in the specific types of deception because of what will happen in the latter times. Paul says,

"Now the Spirit expressly says that in latter times some will depart from the faith, giving heed to deceiving spirits, and doctrines of demons, speaking lies in hypocrisy, having their own conscience seared with a hot iron, forbidding to marry, and commanding to abstain from foods which God created to be received with thanksgiving by those who believe and know the truth...If you instruct the brethren in these things, you will be a good minister of Jesus Christ."

He tells Timothy that there will be deceiving spirits, doctrines of demons, lies in hypocrisy, seared consciences, and dictatorial control over people getting married and what they eat. It will cause some to depart from Christianity. Today, more than ever, Christians need to learn what the Bible teaches and how it differs from the false doctrines that are leading people astray. We desperately need teachers who will instruct *"the brethren in these things"* because the number one target of cults are untrained Christians.

Once again, there is a big difference between simply being saved and becoming a disciple. A new believer brings joy to many angels in heaven, but is often prey for a well trained cultist. Although the new convert or untrained Christian believes in God and the supernatural, he or she often does not have enough knowledge about the

Bible or the deceptive doctrines of the cults in order to withstand them. They buy into the cult's view of Jesus that is actually a chameleon image of the truth.

Thinking Through The Scripture

"For the weapons of our warfare are not carnal but mighty in God for pulling down strongholds, casting down arguments and every high thing that exalts itself against the knowledge of God. (2 Corinthians 10:4-5)

"For God so loved the world that He gave His only begotten Son, that whoever believes in Him should not perish but have everlasting life." (John 3:16)

"For this is good and acceptable in the sight of God our Savior, who desires all men to be saved and to come to the knowledge of the truth." (1 Timothy 2:3-4)

Questions for discussion:
1. Considering the verses above, what are our responsibilities to those caught up in cults with regard to prayer, love, and witness?
2. Who do you personally know that is caught up in a cult or non Christian religion? What is your relationship with them now?
3. Have you ever been in a cult or non Christian religion?

IV. WHAT ARE CHRISTIAN APOLOGETICS AND POLEMICS?
   A. **Apologetics**. The word "apologetic" comes from *apologia* which means "an argument in support or justification." Apologetics is basically the branch of theology that defends and gives proofs for Christianity to those outside the faith (1 Peter 3:15). Another way of saying it is that apologetics is the systematic argumentative discourse in defense, as of a doctrine. Defense of the faith.[6]
   B. **Polemics**. This is somewhat contrasted with apologetics in that it is more of an aggressive argument that refutes someone's doctrine, principle, or opinion within Christianity. It basically denounces heresy that crosses over the lines of historic Christian doctrine. An example of this is theistic evolution, the teaching that God used evolution to create man. While this is clearly heresy according to the Scriptures, some Christians have believed it and been mislead into faulty thinking.
   C. The Bible gives some instruction to us regarding these actions.
      1) *"Beware lest anyone cheat you through philosophy and empty deceit...." (Col. 2:8)*

2) *"...there are some who trouble you and want to pervert the gospel of Christ." (Gal. 1:7)*

3) *"Dear friends,...I felt I had to write and urge you to contend for the faith that was once for all entrusted to the saints." (Jude 3) NIV*

4) *"always be ready to give a defense to everyone who asks you a reason for the hope that is in you, with meekness and fear...." (1 Pet. 3:15)*

V. WHAT IS A CULT?

A. **Definition difficulties.** Words like cult, sect, and religion are not easy to define and people often misuse them. Whereas the word religion often denotes a significance of size and a brand new development of theology, the word sect is a group within a religion that seeks to restore traditional beliefs and practices. Some say that sects are movements of religious protest within a larger religion and would include in this almost all evangelical, Pentecostal, or independent charismatic churches.[7] The word cult refers to a group that is an aberration of a religion and has novel beliefs.

B. Origin of the word. The word "cult" hasn't always had a negative connotation. Its root is found in many words such as *cult*-ured which is someone thought to be refined and intellectual. There is also the idea of *cult*-ivating a particular crop or even one's interest in a certain area. Christianity itself has been called a *cult* because of its stream of belief in the larger cultural context. Only in the last few decades has the word taken on such negative connotation.

Some experts are trying to move away from the term "cult" by using "new religious movements" or "new religions" but this then only seems to cloud the issue of what is a religion.[8] Unfortunately, whether we like the word or not, it is currently the most popular term for defining a religious group or sect thought to be false, unorthodox, and extreme.

C. **Three Types.** Cults can be of a sociological, psychological, or theological nature. Of course, there can be overlap of these three areas in any given cult, but the main emphasis of *Gate Breakers* centers on cults and world religions that theologically depart from or contrast with the main tenets of Biblical Christianity.

1) **Sociological:** Aum Shinri Kyo is an apocalyptic Buddhist sect suspected of the 1995 subway nerve gas murders in Japan. In September of 1999, one of the leaders, Masato Yokoyama was sentenced to death for murder. Shoko Asahara, the main leader, will also stand trial for murder. In October of 1999 the cult decided to change its name and image. It still has thousands of

followers in various countries and millions in assets. This cult definitely threatens society but currently only has about 40,000 members in Japan and Russia.

Another group known as the Falun Gong cult is not violent but has millions of followers and has impacted China with massive sit-in demonstrations and a counterfeit Pentecostal movement that opens up people to demonic activity. One Christian ministry in China documented 1400 deaths in the cult due to their refusal for medical treatment while trusting in Falun Gong for supernatural healing. The founder, Li Hongzhi, now runs this movement from the United States where he has resided since 1996. Falung Gong chapters have sprung up in eight countries and 21 American cities. Li teaches that extraterrestrials have secretly taken over the world and that all men have latent supernatural powers within. His movement is gaining momentum in the new century.

2) **Psychological:** The Brethren was founded by Jim Roberts in the 1970's. A report on *Prime Time* in August of 1998 revealed that this is an ultra conservative group who preys on college students and convinces them to leave everything for a higher calling to serve Christ. The strict rules demand that the individuals give all money and possessions to the group. A totalitarian method of studying the Bible robs the joy of the Lord from their lives. Smiling is restricted. All ties to family must be severed. They are told that breaking this rule will mean being disfellowshipped from the Brethren and ultimately being sent to hell by God. The women cook and sew while the men forage for food in dumpsters. They also canvass college campuses for new recruits. Those who have left the Brethren say that Jim Roberts "rules through fear" and uses "control" to bully his lieutenants and subordinates around.[9] Cults like this psychologically manipulate people into doing what the leaders want.

3) **Theological:** Many of the cults discussed in *Gate Breakers* are of this nature because they break away from the central tenets of Christianity. When considering the definition of a cult in regard to orthodox Christianity, it could be said that a cult is a group of people gathered around someone's misinterpretation of the Bible or misunderstanding of God Almighty. Their teachings deviate from the historic Biblical view of God, doctrine, or the infallibility of the Bible. Cults deny the doctrine of the Trinity and the Deity of Jesus Christ. Cult groups normally center around a strong, charismatic (not meaning spirit filled

but a popular magnetism) individual who claims to have a new revelation that has more authority than the Bible. Below are several characteristics that often help define a cult:

- New revelation that supercedes the Bible.
- Christian terminology redefined.
- Exclusivity—they are the only ones with the truth.
- Authoritarian leader—tense, strong willed, charismatic (magnetic type)
- Strict, unreasonable rules with harsh discipline for those who disobey.

D. The Bible plainly warns Christians to be on guard against false leaders and teachings:

1) *"For false Christs...will arise."* (Mt. 24:24)
2) *"Then many false prophets will rise up and deceive many."* (Mt.24:11)
3) *"For such are false apostles, deceitful workers...."* (2 Cor. 11:13)
4) *"...there will be false teachers among you. They will secretly introduce destructive heresies, even denying the sovereign Lord who bought them...In their greed these teachers will exploit you with stories they have made up."*(2 Pet. 2:1,3) NIV
5) *"Now the Spirit expressly says that in the latter times some will depart from the faith, giving heed to deceiving spirits, and doctrines of devils."* (1 Tim. 4:1)
6) *"For the time will come when men will not put up with sound doctrine. Instead, to suit their own desires, they will gather around them a great number of teachers to say what their itching ears want to hear. They will turn their ears away from the truth and turn aside to myths."* (2 Tim. 4:3-4) NIV

VI. HOW MANY MODERN DAY CULTS ARE THERE IN THE UNITED STATES?

A. No one knows for sure, but "some estimates place the number of cults in the United States alone at over 2,000."[10] There are others who say the number is much greater than that. Certainly, in the world at large there are thousands upon thousands of groups that have cult characteristics.

B. The number of bizarre cults increased dramatically as we approached and entered the new millennium.[11]

The emerging suicide cults are an example of this. For instance, in October of 1994, the Order of the Solar Temple (Temple Solaire) made headlines when 53 of its members were murdered or committed suicide at two sites in Switzerland and one in Canada.[12] Since then, others have taken their lives including 5 in March, 1997, who blew themselves up after several other unsuccessful attempts. Almost at the same time that these 5 took their lives, 39 people who belonged to a different cult known as Heaven's Gate committed suicide near San Diego, California.[13] The Solar Temple group believed that death would send them to reign on the star Sirius, while the Heaven's Gate group believed that death would place them aboard a spaceship that followed the Hale-Bopp comet. Another sad example of a suicide cult is the Movement for the Restoration of the Ten Commandments in southwestern Uganda. Hundreds were involved in suicide and murder on March 17, 2000. The leader Joseph Kibweteere preached that the world would end in 2000. It did for hundreds of his followers (between 330 - 550) after boarding themselves in a church and setting it on fire. They believed the Virgin Mary would appear and carry them to heaven.

The emerging flying saucer cults are another example of bizarre movements. Teacher Chen Tao from Taiwan founded the God Save the Earth Flying Saucer Foundation. From Garland, Texas, Chen falsely prophesied (1) that God would appear at midnight of March 25, 1998, all across the country on channel 18 in Chen's body, (2) that God would incarnate on March 31, 1998, by materializing in a body identical to teacher Chen's and then duplicate hundreds of times, and (3) that the world holocaust would occur in August of 1999.[14]

Thinking Through The Scripture

"There is a way that seems right to a man, but in the end it leads to death." (Proverbs 14:12) NIV

"For whoever finds me finds life and receives favor from the Lord. But whoever fails to find me harms himself; all who hate me love death." (Proverbs 8:35-36) NIV

Questions for discussion:
1. Why do suicide cults "seem right" to some of these people?
2. The passage from Proverbs 8 is about wisdom. How does a lack of wisdom harm people? Do people really hate wisdom and love death?

VII. HOW LARGE ARE CULTS?
   A. They can be relatively small or large. Some may only have several dozen members, while others can have memberships that range in

the thousands, tens of thousands, hundreds of thousands, or even millions. An example of a small cult might be the Heaven's Gate cult with a couple of hundred members. One example of a large cult would be the Jehovah's Witnesses, which in the United States was 892,551 by 1991; and is now nearing one million.[15] Another is the Church of Jesus Christ of Latter-Day Saints (Mormons) which claims to have a membership of millions. Some cults' membership cannot accurately be determined, such as the New Age Movement, because its borders are so elusive.

VIII. WHAT ARE THE DIFFERENT CATEGORIES OF THE CULTS?

A. **Pseudo-Christian Cults:** Organizations that claim to be Christian, but boast of some great revelation that supersedes the authority of the Bible. Examples include such groups as Jehovah's Witnesses, Mormonism, Unity, Christian Science, The Way International, and the Unification Church.

B. **Oriental Cults:** These originate from Hinduism and Buddhism. A couple examples include Hare Krishna and the Divine Light Mission.

C. **New Age Cults:** These are human potential movements. Some new age movements are Scientology, Mind Sciences, The Forum (E.S.T.), UFO's.

D. **Occult—Spiritualistic Cults:** Examples are Satanism, Witchcraft, Spiritism, and Eckankar.

E. **Apocalyptic Cults:** "End time" bizarre movements such as Solar Temple, Heaven's Gate, Aum Shinrikyo, and Movement for the Restoration of the Ten Commandments.

IX. HOW DO THE CULTS VARY IN THEIR PUBLIC IMAGE?

A. The image of these various movements are as varied as the groups themselves. Some appear friendly and some don't. There are those that warmly welcome strangers while others appear rude. The Mormons try to present a very friendly public image. They have successfully publicized themselves as a healthy, happy, family religion. They have a missionary program that goes door-to-door campaigning for their beliefs. The Jehovah's Witnesses are known for their aggressive door-to-door canvassing of neighborhoods and selling of Watchtower material. Other cults, like Christian Science or the Theosophists, appeal publicly to a rather elite group of intellectuals or celebrities. Of course, there are cults that are very secretive by design and are suspect of carrying on mischievous crimes behind closed doors.. The Branch Davidian group headed by David

Koresh was such a group. Witch covens, Satanist cults, and other Spiritism groups are also examples of this.

X. WHAT ARE SOME OF THE ESSENTIAL DOCTRINAL TRUTHS?

Note: While the following doctrines are extremely important to the Christian faith, the list is not necessarily a maximum or minimum amount of essential doctrines. They do, however, represent a significant amount of doctrines held by historic Christianity and can be used as a gauge by which to judge groups who cross over the lines.

A. **The inspiration of Scripture and the inerrancy of the Bible:** Below are some Scriptures that express the Bible's inspiration, but we will go into detail in chapter two about why we can trust the Bible and know that it is truly the Word of God.

  1) *"The Spirit of the LORD spoke by me, and His word was on my tongue." (2 Sam. 23:2)*

  2) *"All scripture is given by inspiration of God, and is profitable for doctrine, for reproof, for correction, for instruction in righteousness." (2 Tim. 3:16)*

  3) *Knowing this first, that no prophecy of the Scripture is of any private interpretation, for prophecy never came by the will of man, but holy men of God spoke as they were moved by the Holy Spirit."* (2 Peter 1:20-21)

  4) *"Brothers, the Scripture had to be fulfilled which the Holy Spirit spoke long ago through the mouth of David...." (Acts 1:16)* NIV

Other Scriptures: Rom. 16: 25-26, Luke 1:70, 1 Peter 1:25, Prov. 30:5

B. **The Trinity:** that within the nature of the ONE GOD there are Three Eternal Persons: God the Father, God the Son, and God the Holy Spirit.

The early church Fathers struggled to explain the nature of God as represented in the Scriptures by Jesus and the apostolic writers. While there was a growing understanding that the Father, Son, and Spirit were each assigned the same "substance" of God by the writers of Scripture, their thinking was still limited by their concept of unity. Since the culture had been permeated by Greek influence, their only concept for unity was "perfect oneness, excluding any internal distinctions." How could three distinct eternal persons be in one Godhead (Colossians 2:9)? And if so, were they all equal or not? Early scholars like Tertullian and Irenaeus developed a primitive form of the doctrine of the Trinity, and great thinkers advanced the concept to another level, but it was the

Capadocian Fathers (Basil the Great, Gregory of Nazianzus, and Gregory of Nyssa) who finally succeeded in understanding that the Scriptures clearly taught that God was of one substance (homousios in the Greek) and yet three distinct equal persons (hypostaseis). During these years, there was also a growing understanding that God was all powerful, all knowing, and all present. Therefore, nothing was impossible for God. So at the Councils of Nicaea (325 A.D.) and Constantinople (381 A.D.) the doctrine of the Trinity was confirmed.

Of course, there were some in those days called heretics who taught something else. There are some today who can't comprehend the concept, and so they dismiss it without really thinking it through. They say Christians have three Gods or that we have a three-headed God. Yet, in reality Christians only believe in one God. It is the sceptic's way of thinking that is the problem. The fact is that finite created man with a three and half pound brain can never truly comprehend the fullness of infinite Creator God. However, as the passages show, the doctrine of the Trinity is very Scriptural and very much in line with what Jesus and the authors of the Bible taught.

The Three Persons Of God:

1) *"Then God said, Let us make man in Our image." (Gen. 1:26)*
2) *"of the Father, and of the Son, and of the Holy Spirit." (Mt. 28:19)*
3) *As soon as Jesus was baptized, he went up out of the water. At that moment heaven was opened, and he saw the Spirit of God descending like a dove and lighting on him. And a voice from heaven said, 'This is my beloved Son, whom I love; with him I am well pleased." (Mt. 3:16-17) NIV*
Other Scriptures: Luke 1:35, 2 Cor. 13:14, Heb. 3:7-11, Isaiah 9:6, Jn. 1:1,14

The Oneness Of God:

1) *"Hear, O Israel: the LORD our God, the LORD is one !" (Dt. 6:4)*
2) *"One God and Father of all, who is above all, and through all, and in you all."(Eph. 4:6)*
3) *"Jesus answered,...Anyone who has seen me has seen the Father" (Jn. 14:9) NIV*
4) *"He [Jesus] is the image of the invisible God." (Col. 1:15) NIV*
5) *"And I will pour on the house of David, and on the inhabitants of Jerusalem the Spirit of grace and of supplication; and they will look upon Me whom they pierced. Yes, they shall mourn for Him, as one mourns for his only son...." (Zech. 12:10)*

6) *"...Ananias, how is it that Satan has so filled your heart that you have lied to the Holy Ghost...You have not lied to men but to God."* (Acts 5:3-5) NIV

7) *"Thus says the LORD, the King of Israel, and his Redeemer the LORD of hosts; I am the First, and I am the Last; Besides Me there is no God."* (Is. 44:6)

Other Scriptures: John 10:30, Phil. 2:6-7, Isaiah 9:6, 1 Tim. 2:5

C. **The Deity of Jesus Christ:** It was obvious to Jesus' disciples that He was Immanuel (God with us). They understood that He was God in the flesh (John 1:1, 14). He said He was the Messiah. He fulfilled all the prophecies regarding the birth, life, death, and resurrection of the Messiah. He said that He would be betrayed and killed and then rise on the third day, and finally He did it and so proved He was who He claimed to be. No other man who ever lived has come remotely close to doing what Jesus did. So it was not difficult for His disciples to believe He was God and to teach it to others. This they did.

However, as with the Trinity, there were some who would not buy it. They did not want to believe that Jesus was actually God, or that He was equal with God the Father. Of course, to accept that Jesus was equal with the Father was just one step away from accepting the Godhood of the Holy Spirit and thus the doctrine of the Trinity. One group in the early days of the church which taught that Jesus was not God and inferior to the Father were the Arians, whose founder was Arias. Some would debate over Scriptures such as John 14:28 in which Jesus says, "My Father is greater than I," thinking that this proved the point since even Jesus admitted it. Yet, those who held this position were misinterpreting what was being said because there is a difference between qualitative and quantitative statements. A son is quantitatively less that his father, but he is not qualitatively less than his father. He will eventually be a full grown man and a father in his own right, but still he will owe respect to the position of his own father.

The Jews certainly knew that Jesus was claiming equality with God. That's why they sought to kill Him (John 5:18; 10:33). Consider some of the many Scriptures showing the Godhood of Jesus Christ.

1) *"In the beginning was the Word, and the Word was with God, and the Word was God...And the Word became flesh and dwelt among us, and we beheld His glory, the glory as of the only begotten of the Father, full of grace and truth."* (John 1:1,14)

2) *"Jesus said to them, 'Most assuredly, I say to you, before Abraham was, I AM.'"* (John 8:58) Look up Exodus 3: 14.

3) *"God was manifested in the flesh...."* (1 Tim. 3:16)

4) *"For in Him (Jesus) dwells all the fullness of the Godhead bodily"* (Col. 2:9)

Think about the words the "Lord Jesus Christ." What do they really mean? What do they imply? Most people never realize that when they say those words they are actually supporting both the concept of the Deity of Jesus and the doctrine of the Trinity. In that name we actually see the fulness of the Godhead (Colossians 2:9). The word "Lord" represents the Jehovah or Yahweh of the Old Testament. Of course, "Jesus"' is the name given to God when he was on earth in human form. Finally, the word "Christ" is the name of the Spirit, the anointing, or the Messiah. So in essence, every time we pronounce the "Lord Jesus Christ"' we are really saying Father, Son, and Holy Spirit. Consider Acts 15:11 as an example. It says, *"But we believe that through the grace of the Lord Jesus Christ we shall be saved in the same manner as they."* In reality, you could insert Father, Son, and Holy Spirit where it says the "Lord Jesus Christ." We see in this the Trinity, and Jesus right in the center of the Godhead.

D. **The virgin birth of Jesus Christ:** The Bible is very clear that Jesus did not have a biological father. It was a miracle, pure and simple, performed by God. Both the birth and the resurrection of Jesus are beyond our natural reasoning of the physical realm. They were meant to be. If someone can't believe in the well documented, miraculous birth and later resurrection of Jesus, then how can they really believe in a God that is "big"' enough and "miraculous" enough to save them for eternity? The birth of a man or woman into the kingdom of God is also miraculous. John 3:3 says we must be *"born again"* or we cannot see God's kingdom.

1) *"Now the birth of Jesus Christ was as follows: After His mother Mary was betrothed to Joseph, before they came together, she was found with child of the Holy Spirit...for that which is conceived in her is of the Holy Spirit."* (Mt. 1:18,20)

2) *"The Holy Spirit will come upon you, and the power of the Highest will overshadow you; therefore, also, that Holy One who is to be born will be called the Son of God."* (Luke 1:35)

3) *"...The virgin will be with child and will give birth to a son, and will call him Immanuel."* (Is. 7:14) NIV

Other Scriptures: Matt. 1:23, Luke 1:27-35

E. **The substitutionary atonement of Jesus Christ's death:** Jesus was sinless. He was condemned to die but was innocent. It seemed everyone was against Him. The Jewish leaders responsible for His death used false allegations to convict Him. Judas betrayed Him, and he acted by the impulse of Satan who wanted to destroy Jesus. In His hour of need, His own disciples abandoned Him. As He hung on the cross, He even cried out and asked why His Father in Heaven had forsaken Him. Yet, it was all in God's plan (Psalm 22). The death of Jesus was foreshadowed and prophesied numerous times in the Old Testament.

Many people get confused when they read of how God commanded the Hebrews to sacrifice in the various manners prescribed in Leviticus. The sacrifices usually had something to do with the cleansing of sin. When sin was committed, the sacrifice of a bull, lamb or goat was necessary to rid that individual of sin. As the sacrifice was committed, the offense of sin was transferred from the sinner to the sacrificed animal. Sometimes the whole nation sinned and needed a sacrifice. All of those sacrifices required an animal that was "perfect" in form. It could have no defect because it represented something without sin.

That's how it was with Jesus; He was perfect and without any sin. Many don't realize this. They think He must have sinned if He were a man. Sometimes people confuse temptation with sin. Was Jesus tempted? Yes. Did He give into it and sin? No. He was perfect before His Father in heaven and before men. He was the only example of a sinless person that has ever lived.

The Old Testament Levitical laws regarding sacrifice for sin were actually a foreshadowing of His death for us. He was "the Lamb of God" that was prophesied about who would come into the world to be the substitute for our sins. He would perform the greatest act of love by laying down His life so that we might find life.

All other men and women have been sinners since the beginning. It is in our nature. We are actually born with it. David knew it and admitted that he was born in sin (Psalm 51:5). Today, in a culture of moral decay, many are saying that there are no absolutes, no definite right and wrong, thus no real sin. But that is not true. The inerrant sin nature of man can be seen in the simplest act of selfishness that a child displays to the most aggressive act of violence in society. This is sin by degree, but it all exposes the deep root problem in man.

When Jesus died on the cross, He made atonement with God for our sins. We are the sinners, not Jesus. The penalty for sin was always death. In reality, each of us is suppose to provide the sacrifice for our sin. Yet, our sin is so great that only our death and eternal separation from God would have sufficed. However, it was God's plan to provide a way for us to have our sin paid for so that we could spend eternity with Him. His plan was Jesus—the perfect sacrifice (Isaiah 53). He died for our sins on the cross. He took the penalty for each of us. If we choose to, we can accept Him as our Lord and Savior.

1) *"He himself bore our sins in his body on the tree, so that we might die to sins and live for righteousness; by his wounds you have been healed." (1 Pet. 2:24) NIV*

2) *"...the blood of Jesus Christ His Son cleanses us from all sin." (1 Jn. 1:7)*

3) *"To him who loved us and washed us from our sins in His own blood." (Rev. 1:5)*

4) *"All we like sheep have gone astray; We have turned, every one, to his own way; And the LORD has laid on Him [Christ] the iniquity of us all." (Is. 53:6) KJV*

Other Scriptures: Rom. 3:10-12, 23, 5:9, Col. 1:20, Rev. 5:9, John 1:29

F. **The literal resurrection of Jesus Christ from the dead:** Over 500 people saw Jesus after He rose bodily from the dead (1 Corinthians 15:6). He was with his disciples for forty days before He ascended into heaven, teaching them and making their understanding more perfect. Some legal scholars have said that there is enough historic evidence for the resurrection of Jesus that it would even stand up in a court of law today.

For a Christian, it is not good enough to think that Jesus might have risen from the dead; we must believe wholeheartedly. In fact, Romans 10:9 tells us that salvation comes to those who not only confess with their mouths the Lord Jesus but who also believe in their heart that God raised Jesus from the dead. When we believe that God was powerful enough to raise Jesus from the dead, it opens our understanding to His present power in our life, and gives us confidence that we too will one day be resurrected with Christ.

1) *"Jesus Himself stood in the midst of them, and said to them...Behold My hands and My feet, that it is I Myself. Handle Me and see, for a spirit does not have flesh and bones as you see I have." (Luke 24:36,39)*

2) *"...I lay down My life, that I might take it again. No one takes it from Me, but I lay it down of Myself. I have power to lay it down, and I have power to take it again...." (John 10:17-18)*

3) *"Jesus answered them, 'Destroy this temple, and I will raise it again in three days...But the temple he had spoken of was his body." (John 2:19,21) NIV*

Other Scriptures: 1 Cor. 15:42,44, John 20:26-28, John 21:4, Luke 24:16

G. **Salvation is a gift which comes through faith in Christ alone:**
Salvation cannot be earned by works. No one is good enough to
gain eternity with God by his own good works. He cannot give
enough money, time, or effort to get the precious gift. If this were
possible then it would not really be a gift.

Now faith is a different issue than works. God is pleased with
faith and anyone who comes to God must do so through faith
(Hebrews 11:6). One of the unique characteristics of Christianity is
the focus on faith. As Romans 1:17 says, *"The just shall live by
faith."* Other religions and cults place the great emphasis on works
for salvation, but this is not what the Bible teaches. Of course,
Christianity supports the practice of good works, but not as a
means of gaining salvation. Rather, any good works we might do
are out of appreciation for what Christ did for us on the cross when
He died for our sins. He redeemed us and bought us back from the
grave. We love Him because He first loved us, and we want to live
for Him. Christianity is first and foremost about relationship with
Jesus that comes through faith. Any works are a secondary issue.

1) *"For it is by grace you have been saved, through faith—and this
   not from yourselves, it is a gift of God—not by works, so that no
   man can boast."(Eph. 2:8-9) NIV*

2) *"...a man is not justified by the works of the law but by the faith of
   Jesus Christ, even we have believed in Jesus Christ, that we might be
   justified by the faith in Christ, and not by the works of the law: for
   by the works of the law no flesh shall be justified." (Gal. 2:16)*
   Other Scriptures: Titus 3:5, Gal. 3:8, Heb. 9:22, Rom. 10:9-10,
   Acts 16:31

H. **The literal return of Jesus Christ (The Second Coming):** Someday,
Jesus is coming back. 2 Peter 3:3 tells us that some scoff at this doctrine, but the Bible clearly teaches that Jesus will return. He is coming back for His people. While there are many different notions
about when and how this will occur, there is an underlying confidence among Christians that this will happen one day. Indeed! We
live in the last days that the Bible predicted, and many think that the
Lord will return soon. For Christians, this doctrine fills us with eternal hope. We know that Jesus loves us and will return for us. As John
14:1-3 tells us, Jesus went to prepare a place for us and will return.

1) *"This same Jesus, who has been taken from you into heaven, will
   come back in the same way you have seen him go into heaven."
   (Acts 1:11) NIV*

2) *"Behold, He is coming with clouds, and every eye will see Him,
   even they who pierced Him...." (Rev. 1:7)*
   Other Scriptures: Matt. 24:30, Matt. 26:63-64, 1 Thess. 4:15-17

XI. WHAT ARE THE EIGHT ESSENTIAL DOCTRINES BRIEFLY STATED?
   A. Of course, there are other scriptural truths that Christians believe.
       Some examples are the existence of Heaven (Matt. 5:12); the exis-
       tence of Hell (Matt. 25:34, 41); Eternal Judgment (Heb. 9:27, Heb.
       6:2); Repentance from Dead Works (Heb. 6:1, 2:38); Water
       Baptism (Acts 2:38, Mt. 3, Acts 10:47), the Baptism of the Holy
       Spirit (Acts 2:2-4, 8:15-17, 19:6); the Gifts of the Holy Spirit (1
       Cor. 12:1-6), and others.

       While Christians might vary regarding their view of these
       teachings, there is a general sense of agreement about the essential
       doctrines of Christianity highlighted in this lesson. Today,
       Christians need to stop divisiveness over when they think the rap-
       ture will occur, or the doctrine of predestination, or even about the
       doctrine of the baptism of the Holy Spirit. These and other beliefs
       are important; but, are they urgent? Christians need to start con-
       centrating on defending and promoting the main tenets of the
       Christian faith. They must not major on the minors.

       The various streams and schools of thought within Christianity
       were once thought to be a strength. The denominations each
       emphasized a particular historic belief that helped to define various
       aspects of Christianity. However, in today's climate of diversity the
       strength of Christianity is in what unites us rather than what sep-
       arates us. We need to once again bring to the forefront of
       Christianity the essential doctrines that make us Christians. The
       prayer of Jesus in John 17 is that we would be one so that the world
       may believe that God sent Jesus (John 17:21).

       Christians should believe in and have a healthy respect for the
       following doctrines:
       1. The inspiration of Scripture and the inerrancy of the Bible.
       2. The Trinity
       3. The Deity of Jesus Christ.
       4. The virgin birth of Jesus Christ.
       5. The substitutionary atonement of Jesus Christ's death.
       6. The literal resurrection of Jesus Christ from the dead.
       7. Salvation is a gift which comes through faith in Christ alone.
       8. The literal return of Jesus Christ (The Second Coming).

XII. WHAT IS THE GOSPEL?
   A. The word means "good message" or "to announce good news."
       When Jesus was born, the angels announced the good tidings to
       the shepherds (Luke 2:9-14). They proclaimed God's good will to
       all men. He had sent His dear son to us. Jesus would be our teacher,
       example, guide, and sacrifice for sin.

The simple gospel is spelled out for us by the Apostle Paul in 1 Corinthians 15:1-5. It shows thre basic gospel of grace which must be guarded against perversion. Paul told the Galatians that if anyone taught a different gospel, including an angel from heaven, that he should be accursed or eternally condemned (Galatians 1:8-9). He warned the Corinthians about receiving a different gospel (2 Corinthians 11:4). He also said that the message of the gospel would appear foolish to the world, but to those of us who are being saved it is the power of God (Romans 1:16; 1 Corinthians 1:18).

XIII. WHAT ARE THE MAIN DOCTRINES WHICH CULTS DENY?

A. The watershed issues for the cults are quite often the doctrine of the Trinity and the doctrine of the deity of Jesus Christ. Yet, on many of these other essential doctrines, it is often easy to see differences in teaching.

B. Another major area in which cults stray is in their acceptance of the authenticity and authority of Scripture. Many cults pay lip service to the Bible; they simply say that they have "other revelation" that now supersedes it. The Mormons, Jehovah's Witnesses, Christian Scientists, Moonies, etc. all claim that the Bible is an inspired book from God. However, they also claim that the revelation is not complete. The Mormons and Moonies have added "another testament," Christian Science says the Bible is corrupted by man, and the Jehovah's Witnesses have perverted the true Bible in hundreds of places to line up with their doctrine.

XIV. WHY DO CHRISTIANS NEED TO KNOW BIBLICAL TRUTHS TO DEFEND AGAINST THE FALSE BELIEFS OF THE CULTS?

A. Because in 2 Corinthians 11:3-4 the Bible warns us that cultists will come preaching
   1) Another Jesus
   2) Another spirit
   3) Another gospel

Thinking Through The Scripture

"But I fear, lest somehow, as the serpent deceived Eve by his craftiness, so your minds may be corrupted from the simplicity that is in Christ. For if he that comes preaches another Jesus, whom we have not preached, or if you receive a different spirit which you have not received, or a different gospel, which you have not accepted—you might well put up with it!" (2 Corinthians 11:3-4)

Questions for discussion:

1. What do you think Paul means by the "simplicity that is in Christ?" What does he fear regarding the Corinthians? Why does he think they are so gullible?
2. What are the potential dangers when someone is introduced to "another" Jesus or a "different" spirit?
3. In Galatians 1:6-9, Paul gives strong warning against any who pervert the Gospel. Why is this so important to Christianity?

B. Because many cultists manipulate Biblical terminology, Christians are at a distinct disadvantage since the Christian might think the cultist is talking about the same concept.

Example: The term *"Holy Spirit"* represents God, the third person of the Trinity to a Christian. However, to a Moonie it represents a Female or Mother Spirit,[16] to a Christian Scientist it represents divine science, and to a Jehovah's Witness it does not represent a person but an invisible active force.[17]

C. Because many cultists subtly redefine Biblical theology and capitalize on the average Christian's inability to catch the change.

Example: I was drawn into attending Kingdom Hall meetings because the Witnesses doing a Bible study in my home told me that they believed that Jesus was God. Of course, at the time, I didn't know that they only viewed Jesus as "a god'" and not the God of the Bible.

"The well-trained cultist will carefully *avoid definition of terms* concerning cardinal doctrines such as the Trinity, the Deity of Christ, the Atonement, the Bodily Resurrection of our Lord, the process of salvation by grace and justification by faith. If pressed in these areas, he will *redefine* the terms...."[18] —Walter Martin

D. Because the cultist is trained to confuse Christians by focusing on certain isolated passages of Scripture in which the meaning may be difficult and not immediately clear.

Example: Mormon missionaries will try to get Christians to consider isolated verses such as 1 Corinthians 8:5 or 15:29. Since Christians are not use to looking at these, it can give the Mormons an edge until Christians can have time to study them. In actuality, both verses are misunderstood by Mormons and have logical explanations. Christians can become equipped to share the truth.

Thinking Through The Scripture

"Now, brothers, I want to remind you of the gospel I preached to you, which you received and on which you have taken your stand. By this gospel

you are saved, if you hold firmly to the word I preached to you. Otherwise, you have believed in vain. For what I received I passed on to you as of first importance: that Christ died for our sins according to the Scriptures, that he was buried, that he was raised on the third day according to the Scriptures..." (1 Corinthians 15:1-4) NIV

Questions for discussion:
1. According to this passage, what are the three simple parts of the gospel?
2. The word gospel means "good news." Why is this such good news for men? How does this passage interact with others such as Luke 2:8 and John 3:16?
3. If this is the simple gospel, what kind of things do you think cultists might teach that pervert it? (Galatians 1:6-9)
4. Why do you think that Paul stresses "according to the Scriptures?" Which Scriptures would he be referring to in the first century?

XV. WHO IS THE JESUS TO THE CULTS?
   A. *Bahai:* He was one of nine great world manifestations. There is no Trinity. He is not God. He is a prophet beneath Baha'u'llah.
   B. *Christian Science:* He is only a divine idea.
   C. *Freemasons:* To them Christ was a mystical figure. Jao-bul-on is God, all men have divine potential.
   D. *Hare Krishna:* An enlightened vegetarian teacher of meditation, maybe Krishna.
   E. *Jehovah's Witnesses:* He is Michael the Archangel The first being God created. He came as a man, died and rose as an invisible spirit; came back invisible in 1914 to Brooklyn to head Watchtower.
   F. *Moon's Unification Church:* He was a man who failed: Moon is the Second Coming.
   G. *Mormons:* He is the spirit brother of Satan; one god in a pantheon of gods; born through physical incest.
   H. *New Age:* An ascended master, guru, and spiritual guide, but not God and not Savior.
   I. *Rosicrucian:* He is a manifestation of cosmic consciousness.
   J. *Scientology:* He is a false implanted memory in people's minds.
   K. *Spiritists:* He is an advanced medium in the 6th sphere of astral projection.
   L. *Theosophy:* No greater than other religious leaders since all men are Christs.

M. *T.M.:* He was an enlightened guru who never suffered for anyone.

N. *Unitarians:* He was a good man that followers mistakenly deified.

O. *Unity:* He was a man who perfected a divine idea.

P. *The Way:* Jesus is the Son of God, but not God the Son; they deny the Trinity.

Thinking Through The Scripture

"Beloved, do not believe every spirit, but test the spirits, whether they are from God; because many false prophets have gone out into the world. By this you know the Spirit of God: Every spirit that confesses that Jesus Christ has come in the flesh is of God, and every spirit that does not confess that Jesus Christ is come in the flesh is not of God. And this is the spirit of the Antichrist, which you have heard was coming, and is now already in the world." (1 John 4:1-3)

Questions for discussion:

1. The word "confess" comes from a Greek word meaning to assent or agree as in a convenant or strong acknowledgement. What do you think one's spirit is truly confessing in this passage?

2. Is it possible to confess with one's mouth but not one's spirit? Compare this passage to Romans 10:9 and discuss.

1. Alister McGrath, *A Passion for Truth: The Intellectual Coherence of Evangelicalism* (Downers Grove, IL: InterVarsity Press, 1996), p 25.

2. Adam Clarke, *Commentary on the holy bible,* abridged by Ralph Earle (Grand Rapids, MI: Baker Book House, 1967), p 802.

3. Bob Sjogren, Bill and Amy Sterns, *Run With the Vision* (Minneapolis, MN: Bethany House Publishers, 1995), p 49.

4. David Barrett, Global Evangelization Movement, information from telephone conversation on March 22, 2000, and from web site: www.gem-werc.org.

5. Sjoren and Sterns, p. 66.

6. Ron Carlson and Ed Decker, *Fast Facts on False Teachings* (Eugene, OR: Harvest House Publishers, 1994), p 7.

7. Irving Hexham and Karla Poewe, *New Religious Movements as Global Cultures: Making the Human Sacred* (Boulder, CO: Westview Press, 1997), p. 33.

8. Iving Hexham and Karla Poewe, *New Religions as Global Cultures: Making the Human Sacred* (Boulder, CO: Westview Press, 1997), p 36.

9. Prime Time, "The Brethren," (ABC, August 27, 1998).

10. Gary M Beasley and Francis Anfuso, *Complete Evangelism* (South Lake Tahoe, CA: Christian Equippers International, 1991), p. 137.

11. Elizabeth Gleck, "The Marker We've Been Waiting For," *Time Magazine,* April 7, 1997, p 31.

12. Richard Lacayo, "In the Reign of Fire," *Time Magazine,* October 17, 1994, p 59.

13. _____, "The Lure of the Cult," *Time Magazine,* April 7, 1997, p 45.

14. Jason Barker, "God's Salvation Church," *The Watchman Expositor*, Vol. 13, No. 2, 1998.

15. Ron Rhodes, *Reasoning From the Scriptures with Jehovah's Witnesses* (Eugene, OR: Harvest House Publishers, 1993), p9.

16. Beasley and Anfuso, p 166.

17. Ibid

18. Walter Martin, *The Kingdom of the Cults* (Minneapolis, MN: Bethany House Publishers, 1985), p24

QUESTIONNAIRE: LESSON ONE

NAME: _____ DATE: _____

1. What proclamation did Jesus make regarding the church? _____

_____

_____

2. What are some of the end time strategies of Satan? _____

_____

_____

3. Apologetics is the branch of theology having to do with the _____ and _____ of Christianity. It is the defense of the _____. The Scripture urges us "to _____ for the faith".

4. What is a cult? Use Scripture that tells us to beware of certain types of people and teachings. _____

_____

_____

_____

_____

_____

_____

5. Does any person really know how many cults there are in the U.S.? ____

6. Are all of the cults relatively small? _____

7. List three of the five different categories of cults and give one example of each:

A. _____

B. _____

C. _____

8. Do all the cults have the same public image? _____ Do any of them come across with a friendly, warm public image? _____

9. Tell about an experience you or someone you know has had with a cult. How did they come across to you? Were they friendly, aggressive, sly, etc.?

_____

_____

_____

_____

10. List the eight beliefs that the study specifically mentions that Christianity stands on:

A. Christians believe _____

B. Christians believe _____

C. Christians believe _____

D. Christians believe _____

E. Christians believe _____

F. Christians believe _____

G. Christians believe _____

H. Christians believe _____

11. After studying what Christians believe about the Deity of Christ, can you say with assurance that you know that Jesus is the Son of God, the second person of the Trinity? _____ Have you asked Jesus to be your personal LORD and Savior? _____ Take a moment and explain your relationship with Him: _____

_____

_____

12. Why is it important that Christians understand these basic Biblical truths? _____

_____

13. What are the three simple parts of the Gospel?

A. _____

B. _____

C. _____

LESSON 2

THE BIBLE'S AUTHENTICITY

*"Now there was about this time, Jesus, a wise man, if it be lawful to call him a man; for he was a doer of wonderful works, a teacher of such men as had a veneration for truth. He drew over to him both many of the Jews and many of the Gentiles: **he was the Christ.** And when Pilate, at the suggestion of the principal men among us, had condemned him to the cross, those that loved him at first did not forsake him; for he appeared unto them alive again the third day, as the divine prophets had spoken of these and ten thousand other wonderful things concerning him: whence the tribe of Christians, so named from him, are not extinct at this day."*[1] —Flavius Josephus (c. 93 A.D) Highly accurate, Jewish historian born in 37 A.D.

I. WHY STUDY THE BIBLE'S AUTHENTICITY?
   A. **Because of the need for confidence:** Knowing the proofs and truth behind the Bible makes people more confident in its accuracy. A Christian who is confident in God and the Bible can more readily defend its truth and challenge the false beliefs of others. Today, the world produces many secular humanists, evolutionists, atheists, cultists, and those of non Christian religions that seek to destroy the popularity and authority of the Scriptures. Many "scoff" at the doctrine that Christ will return as He promised (2 Peter 3:3). Many deny that the Bible is God's Word. Others add to it or subtract from it for their own gain and influence. They come up with supposedly superior revelations. However, the fact is that there is no other

28

book in the world like the Bible. Christians need not fear the criticism of skeptics or attacks by supposed intellectual giants because the Bible will always stand the tests of time. Christians can have complete confidence that God gave man His Word in the Bible. It has withstood all the tests from various experts in the fields of science, archaeology, and history. It will stand forever (Is. 40:8), but all other books from atheists, humanists, cultists and those of non Christian world religions will perish.

B. **Because of the need to share its message of Life:** The Bible is the most precious book in the world, but not everyone accepts it as God's Word. Men have an empty void in their heart that can only be filled by the Spirit of God, and the Bible has the answers for their barren souls if they will but accept it. Jesus taught people to repent because the Kingdom of God was at hand. He said, that His "kingdom is not of this world" (John 18:36) and that we need to be "born again" in order to see the kingdom of God (John 3:3). When Christians read the Bible, we do so through eyes of faith. It reveals that Kingdom to us. We receive inspiration and hope. We are like "newborn babes" who "desire the pure milk of the word" (1 Peter 2:2) and gain revelation for our lives. We are encouraged by the Spirit to diligently "study" the Bible knowing how to "rightly divide the word of truth" (2 Timothy 2:15).

II. WHAT IS MEANT BY THE STATEMENT "THE BIBLE IS THE WORD OF GOD"?

A. In his book *Is The Bible The Word of God*, author W. R. Kimball answers this question and reveals to us fullness of what it means. He says, "When we say the Bible is the Word of God, we do not mean that all the words are God's words. Some are the words of men, angels, demons, and even Satan. However, it is in its entirety the Word of God in the sense that God, through the agency of the Holy Spirit, divinely directed and inspired the writings of it and supernaturally controlled its overall construction, design, and recording of contents. In other words, it is not the product of human devising, manipulation, or imagination, but God was the author and architect behind its creation from the beginning."[2]

Thinking Through The Scripture

"All Scripture is inspired by God and profitable for teaching, for reproof, for correction, for training in righteousness; that the man of God may be adequate, equipped for every good work" (2 Timothy 3:16-17) NASB

"No prophecy in Scripture is a matter of one's own interpretation. No prophecy ever originated from humans. Instead, it was given by the Holy Spirit as humans spoke under God's direction." (2 Peter 1:20-21) GW

Questions for discussion:
1. The word "inspired" comes from a Greek word meaning *divinely breathed*. In light of this, how should we view the Bible? How does it equip us?
2. Why do you think God does not want men to interpret prophecy in Scripture to suit their own personal preferences?

III. WHY IS FAITH SO NECESSARY FOR BELIEVING THE WORD OF GOD?

    A. **Christianity is built upon faith.** It is the only religion in the world that is so centered on faith. Repentance leads to salvation as an act of faith. Confession of the mouth is an act of faith. Receiving the Lord and His atonement for our sin is an act of faith. Water baptism is an act of faith. The baptism of the Holy Spirit is an act of faith. Prayer, giving, and worship are all acts of faith. Taking the sacraments is done in faith. Faith is an aspect of why believers attend church or Christian functions. It is imperative for healing and miracles. Faith is central to Christianity. We have faith in God as omnipotent, omniscient, and omnipresent. We have faith that God could give us in a book everything that is necessary for the understanding of "salvation" (2 Timothy 3:15) and for "life and godliness" (2 Peter 1:3) in Christ Jesus our Lord.

    B. **The Bible is one long story all about faith and faithfulness** or the lack of them. Many portions of the Bible zero right in on the subject of faith. One such passage is in Hebrews chapter eleven which testifies to the historical faith and faithfulness of God's people. In Hebrews 11:6 we find out how important our faith is to God when it says, *"No one can please God without faith. Who ever goes to God must believe that God exists and that he rewards those who seek him."*

    C. **It is important to mix the Word with faith.** The reason the Israelites did not enter into the promised land was because of a lack of faith. They missed out on the blessing of God's rest because of their lack of faith. The writer of Hebrews, in an exhortation to Christians, explains why the Israelites did not enter in, when he says, *"but the word they heard did not profit them, because it was not united by faith in those who heard." (Heb. 4:2) NASB*

IV. WHY IS GOD'S WORD SO INTRICATELY LINKED WITH GOD?
  A. Because it is the record of God's activity among men.
  B. Because it describes the character and attributes of God.
  C. Because it shows God as transcendent to the Creation.
  D. Because it proclaims God's spoken word and will to man.
  E. Because it is eternal (Isaiah 40:8; Matt. 24:35; Ps. 119:152; Matt.
      5:18, 1 Peter 1:25).
  F. Because it reflects God since He represents Himself as "The Word"
      (John 1:1).

Thinking Through The Scripture

*"In the beginning was the Word, and the Word was with God, and the Word
was God. He was with God in the beginning" (John 1:1) NIV*

"The Word became flesh and made his dwelling among us." (John 1:14) NIV

*"He is dressed in a robe dipped in blood, and his name is the Word of God."
(Revelation 19:13) NIV*

Questions for discussion:
1. What is the meaning of "the Word was God?" How about "with"
    God?
2. How do the terms "flesh" and "blood" mentioned above relate to the
    Word?
3. Is the Word a physical thing or a spiritual one? Are we to read the Bible
    as though it is something more than just paper and ink?

V. WHAT ARE SOME ASPECTS THAT MAKE THE BIBLE UNIQUE?
  A. **Time span:** Written over 1,500 years and more than 40 genera-
      tions.
  B. **Writers:** Over 40 authors from every walk of life including kings,
      military leaders, fishermen, herdsmen, philosophers, peasants,
      scholars, poets, a doctor, a rabbi, a tax collector, etc.
  C. **Where and When:** Written on three different continents (Asia,
      Africa, and Europe) in the wilderness, in a dungeon, on a hillside,
      in a palace, in a cave, inside prison walls, on the road, on the isle
      of Patmos, during military campaigns, during times of war, times
      of peace, times of joy, times of sorrow, times of plenty, times of
      need, times of overcoming, and times of repentance.
  D. **Languages:** Written in Hebrew, Aramaic, and Greek.

E. **Survival:** Survived time, culture shifts, persecution, and criticism.

F. **Message:** From cover to cover it has unity and continuity expressing the story of man's fall from grace and God's redemptive plan through Jesus Christ. This it does even though it addresses hundreds of controversial topics.

G. **Popularity:** "The Bible has been read by more people and published in more languages than any other book in history...The Bible has been translated and retranslated, and paraphrased, more than any other book in existence."[3]

H. **Prophecy:** No other book on earth has a bulk of prophecies like this relating to individual nations, Israel, cities, all the people of the world, and the coming of the one who was to be the Messiah. The Bible is full of Old Testament prophecies that have already been fulfilled. Among these were over 300 that were fulfilled with the coming of Christ the first time. Many more prophecies still await fulfillment.

VI. WHAT MANUSCRIPT EVIDENCE IS THERE FOR THE NEW TESTAMENT?

A. There are more than:

5,300	*Greek Manuscripts*
10,000	*Latin Vulgate*
+ 9,300	*Other Early Versions*
Total = 24,600	Manuscript copies of portions of the New Testament in existence.

B. **A comparison to other ancient manuscripts:** The "Iliad" by Homer has the second most manuscripts at only 643. The Iliad was written 900 B.C., but the earliest complete copy we have of it is from the thirteenth century. (over 2,000 years later). This seems sufficient for historians to call it accurate. The proof of the lives, existence, and acts of Caesar, Plato, Aristotle, Herodotus, Sophocles, Pythagoras, Homer etc. are verified in several hundred books, and historians will readily confirm their authenticity. Yet, there are over 24,000 parts and complete New Testament manuscripts agreeing upon the characters and events of which they speak.

C. **Recent Discoveries:** Up until a few years ago, it was said of the New Testament that "the earliest fragment dates about A.D. 120, with about 50 other fragments dating within 150 to 200 years from the time of composition. Two major manuscripts, Codex Vaticanus (A.D. 325) and Codex Sinaiticus (A.D. 350), a complete copy, date within 250 years of the time of composition."[4] However, *today there are recent discoveries showing that portions of the Dead Sea Scrolls might actually be verses from the early Gospel manuscripts* written just a few years after Christ ascended into heaven. Also, in 1991, another scroll was revealed and is called the Crucified Messiah Scroll. Grant R. Jeffrey points out some excellent things about this scroll in *The Signature of God*. He says,

"This remarkable five-line scroll contained fascinating information about the death of the Messiah. It referred to 'the Prophet Isaiah' and his Messianic prophecy (Chapter 53) that identified the Messiah as one who will suffer for the sins of his people. This scroll provides an amazing parallel to the New Testament revelation that the Messiah would first suffer death before He would ultimately return to rule the nations. Many scholars believed that the Jews during the first century of our era believed that, when he finally came, the Messiah would rule forever without dying. The exciting discovery of this scroll reveals that the Essene writer of this scroll understood the dual role of Messiah as Christians did. This scroll identified the Messiah as the 'Shoot of Jesse' (King David's father) the 'Branch of David,' and declared that he was 'pierced' and 'wounded.'"[5]

D. **Early Church Fathers:** Further evidence of the New Testament's authenticity has been gathered from the writings of the second and third century church fathers. After careful investigation it was determined that from their writings, the entire New Testament (except for eleven verses) could be collected together if no surviving manuscript existed.[6] Speaker and author Josh McDowell adds to this:

"The text of the Bible has been transmitted accurately. In fact, there is more evidence for the reliability of the text of the New Testament as an accurate reflection of what was initially written than there is for any ten pieces of classical literature put together."[7]

"Again, based on the evidence, the conviction comes that we have in our hands a text which does not differ in any substantial particular from the originals of the various books as they came from the hands of human writers. The great scholar F.J.A. Hort said that apart from insignificant variations of grammar or spelling, not more than one-thousandth part of the whole New Testament is affected by differences of reading."[8]

VII. WHAT MANUSCRIPT EVIDENCE IS THERE FOR THE OLD TESTAMENT?

A. **The Massoretic Period** (A.D. 500 - 900). Before the discovery of the Dead Sea scrolls in 1947, the oldest complete manuscript of the old testament (Hebrew Bible) was dated A.D. 900. Since the Old Testament was completed in about 400 B.C. this gave about a 1300 year gap. The manuscript from A.D. 900 is known as the "Massoretic Text" because it was the product of the Masorrites, a group of Jewish scribes that are respected for their skills of proofreading and their highly developed system of safeguards against scribal errors. The Hebrew Massoretic Text was copied from a manuscript dating about A.D. 100. Since the A.D. 100 copy no longer existed, the question of accuracy was raised prior to the discovery of the dead sea scrolls. (Massora is the Hebrew word for "tradition")

B. **The Talmudist Period** (A.D. 100 - 500). The Talmudists were Jewish scribes that have been praised for their almost perfect accuracy of copying manuscripts to be passed on to future generations. While there are currently no known "complete" manuscripts of the Old Testament from this period, the fragments that exist from the O.T. as well as other products (copies of ancient Egyptian books, for example) show the most expert skill of the Talmudists for minor detail.

C. **The Dead Sea Scrolls** (150 B.C. - A.D. 70). In 1947 a wandering Bedouin goat herdsman discovered caves in the side of the cliffs west of the Dead Sea. It has been called the greatest archeological discovery of the century. The caves were storage units for pots containing leather scrolls. The scrolls revealed a Jewish communal society called Qumran that existed from about 150 B.C. to A.D. 70. It was much like a monastery. They farmed the land, and they spent their time studying and copying the Hebrew Scriptures. When they realized that the Romans were going to invade their land, they put the scrolls in pots and hid them in the caves. There were approximately 40,000 inscribed fragments discovered. From these fragments more than 500 books have been reconstructed. Fragments of almost every book of the Old Testament were discovered.

The most outstanding find was the earliest manuscript copy yet known of the complete book of Isaiah, dating approximately 125 B.C. The significance of this find to the authenticity of the Old Testament is dramatic. Before the discovery of the Dead Sea manuscripts, the Massoretic manuscript (A.D. 900) was being criticized for authenticity and accuracy. However, the Dead Sea scrolls—being 1,000 years earlier—proved the exactness with which the Talmudists and Massorites copied the Scriptures. The changes in a thousand years were minor and basically had to do with spelling (natural language progression) and conjunctions.

D. **The Septuagint** (c. 300 B.C). Some Jewish scribes did not copy the

Scripture into Hebrew but into Greek. Such are the scribes referred to as the LXX (70). These 70 Jewish scholars lived in Alexandria around 300 B.C. They translated the Hebrew Bible into the Greek language. The LXX appears to be a rather literal translation from prior manuscripts. This helps us know today that our Old Testaments are pretty good copies of the original translation. There exist also ancient Samaritan copies of the Pentateuch (first five books of the Old Testament) that stand as a witness to the characters and activities of the Old Testament. While there were some variations between the Hebrew manuscripts, Greek manuscripts, and Samaritan manuscripts, the differences were slight. Regarding these various texts, Paul Little tells us in *Know Why You Believe*:

"Three main types of text existed in 200 B.C. The question for us is, What is the original version of the Old Testament, in the light of these three 'families' of texts to choose from? We can conclude with R. Laird Harris: 'We can now be sure that copyists worked with great care and accuracy on the Old Testament, even back to 225 B.C. At that time there were two or three types of text available for copying. These types differed among themselves so little, however, that we can infer that still earlier copyists had also faithfully and carefully transmitted the Old Testament text. Indeed, it would be rash skepticism that would now deny that we have our Old Testament in a form very close to that used by Ezra when he taught the Law to those who had returned from the Babylonian captivity'"[9]

VIII. WHAT ARE THE THREE BASIC PARTS OF THE (JEWISH) HEBREW BIBLE?
  A. **The Law** (Torah): Genesis, Exodus, Leviticus, Numbers, and Deuteronomy
  B. **The Prophets**: Joshua, Judges, Samuel, Kings, Isaiah, Jeremiah, Ezekiel, and the Twelve Minor Prophets from Hosea to Malachi. (Both books of Samuel and Kings)
  C. **The Writings**: Psalms, Proverbs., Job, Song of Songs, Ruth, Lamentations, Esther, Ecclesiastes, Daniel, Ezra-Nehemiah, and Chronicles. (Both books of Chronicles)

IX. DOES THE NEW TESTAMENT BEAR WITNESS TO THE OLD TESTAMENT?

YES! Here are some examples:

• Matt. 21:42 "Jesus said to them, 'Have you never read in the *Scriptures*"

- Matt. 22:29 "Jesus answered…'You are mistaken, not knowing the *Scripture*"
- Matt. 26:54 "How then could the *Scriptures* be fulfilled, that it must happen thus?"
- Matt. 26:56 "But all this was done that the *Scriptures* of the prophets…. "
- Luke 24: 25-27,32 [Jesus talking to the two men on the road to Emmaus]
- John 5:39 "You search the *Scriptures,* for in them you think you have eternal life"
- John 7:38 "He who believes in Me, as the *Scripture* has said, out of his heart…."
- John 10:35 "And the *Scripture* cannot be broken"
- Acts 17:2 "Then Paul…reasoned with them from the *Scriptures*"
- Acts 17:2 "And searched the *Scriptures* daily to find out whether these things"
- Acts 18:28 "Refuted the Jews publicly, showing from the *Scriptures* that Jesus is"
- Rom. 1:2 "Which He promised before through His prophets in the *Holy Scriptures*"
- Rom. 4:3 "For what does the *Scripture* say? 'Abraham believed God,"
- 1 Cor. 15:3 "Christ died for our sins according to the *Scriptures*"
- 2 Peter 3:16 [Peter showing the equality of Paul's epistles to the O. T. Scriptures]

Other Examples: Rom. 9:17, 10:11, Gal. 3:8, 3:22, 4:30; 1 Tim. 5:18

X. DID JESUS BEAR WITNESS TO THE OLD TESTAMENT?

YES! Here are some examples:

A. In Luke 24:44 Jesus is talking to His disciples after His resurrection. He tells them *"all things must be fulfilled which were written in the Law of Moses and the Prophets and the Psalms concerning Me."*
    1. *The Law of Moses* = The Torah or Pentateuch (First five books of O.T.)
    2. *The Prophets* = All those mentioned under section VIII B.
    3. *The Psalms* = "The Writings" mentioned under section VIII C. It was common practice among Hebrews to refer to an entire section of Scripture by saying the first book of that section.
B. In Matt. 23:35 and Luke 11:51 Jesus convicts the actions of a hard hearted and rebellious people by accusing them of killing the prophets. He says, *"from the blood of righteous Abel to the blood of Zechariah, son of Berechiah."* With these two examples Jesus gives

witness to the fullness of the O. T. *Abel* was the first martyr (Genesis 4:8) and *Zechariah* was the last (2 Chronicles 24:21). The Hebrew Bible or canon was arranged differently than our O. T. Protestant canon. The Hebrew canon was arranged as displayed in Section VIII A - C. Genesis was the first book and Chronicles the last. So Jesus literally shows the authenticity from the first book to the last of the Hebrew Bible. (Note: The Apocrypha mentioned later was not included in the Hebrew Bible)

XI. WHICH PEOPLE CHOSE THE OLD TESTAMENT CANON?

Definition of canon - the word canon comes from a root meaning "reed." It signifies a standard or measuring rod. In regard to the Bible, it means those books which have been officially accepted as inspired by God.

A. The Hebrew Old Testament was completed c. 400 B.C. It contained the Torah, the Prophets, and the Writings (Section VIII). It contained 24 books. They are the same as our Bible's 39 books except for a couple of things: 1) They did not divide Samuel, Kings, or Chronicles into two books. 2) The order of the books was different.

B. It was the Hebrews themselves that determined what would be included in the canon of their Holy Scriptures. The books were received as authoritative because they were recognized by God's people as being "inspired" by God through his prophets. The first five books (Genesis - Deuteronomy) were either written by Moses, those under his authority, or collected by him. There was no question about the books by the prophets. Throughout the prophets' books are the words, "This is what the Lord says" or "The word of the Lord came to me." False prophets did not last long and their words were not regarded by the generations as inspired.

The poetical books, historical books, and other "Writings" were also accepted as canon because of their obvious authority of truth. These were the original canon of the Jewish people. Even the Septuagint written about 300 B.C in Greek by seventy Jewish scholars only included the books that we have in our Old Testament Protestant Bibles. However, other books called the Apocrypha were later added to the Septuagint. The inclusion of the Apocrypha has been debated throughout the ages. By the time Jesus came to earth, the Hebrew Bible (excluding the Apocrypha) was referred to as "the Scriptures."

XII. WHICH PEOPLE CHOSE THE NEW TESTAMENT CANON?

A. From *Eerdman's Handbook To The History of Christianity* we read:

"The example of the Old Testament 'canon' encouraged the gradual collection of a list of Christian writings which should constitute the standard or rule of the churches.... These were the books read publicly in the congregations and regarded as having special authority."[10]

B. The gathering and clarification of authenticity took place over several centuries. First, the concept for gathering the various writings had to be developed. Second, the writings had to be scrutinized for authenticity, accuracy, and inspiration. Many things were written about Jesus in the first few centuries. Some were accurate and some not. Finally, there was a process of debating by church fathers and various groups who used certain books more than others.

There were some that urged the church at large to create a canon of books in order to establish a foundation of authority and unity for the new Christian movement. By the late second century one church father, Irenaeus, had no doubt that there were only four gospels.

Around A.D. 200, a group of books, known as the Muratorian Canon, arose. These included many of our current N.T. books. By the early third century a consensus had been reached as to the authenticity of most of the canon. By A.D. 300, the only books still disputed were James, 2 Peter, 2 and 3 John, Jude, and the authorship of Revelation. By this time, the church had spread so far that there was, in a sense, an eastern church and western church. By A.D. 367 the eastern church canonized the twenty-seven books of the New Testament as we know it today. In the West, the canon lists were approved by the African Council of Hippo in A.D. 393 and then at the church council of Carthage in A.D. 397, with the exception of the book of Hebrews. This was eventually included also, but its authorship is in question. The obvious inspiration of the book and its appeal eventually overcame the dispute. Christians at Alexandria claimed that it was written by Paul; so this eventually became the accepted view.

C. The distinguishing criteria for canonization:

  1. *Apostolic Authorship:* The only two books that fell outside this realm were Luke and Mark, but they were closely related. The gospel of Mark is an account of the Life of Jesus from Peter's perspective but put in writing by Mark. Luke was a doctor who traveled extensively with Paul and others. He wrote Luke and Acts. The scriptural authority of these books was recognized from the beginning.

  2. *Recognized and used by leading churches or the majority of them:* The people of God received, collected, read, and used the various writings, confirming that these were from God. For

example: The Apostle Peter firmly acknowledged that the epistles of Paul were Scripture (2 Peter 3:15-16). Consequently, his letters were brought together first, probably around the end of the first century.

3. *A conformity to the standards of sound doctrine as from the Lord:* There was a witness in the writings that spoke with a "thus says the Lord" quality that recognized existing and accepted Scripture. There was a prophetic character about it that said this was written by God. The authenticity of it was beyond doubt. The church fathers had a standard. "If in doubt, throw it out." Once again, from *Eerdman's Handbook To The History of Christianity* we see that:

"[T]he eventual shape of the New Testament shows that the early church wanted to submit fully to the teachings of the apostles. It had been created by their preaching and now grounded itself upon their writings."[11]

Thinking Through The Scripture

"Bear in mind that our Lord's patience means salvation, just as our dear brother Paul also wrote you with wisdom that God gave him. He writes the same way in all his letters, speaking in them of these matters. His letters contain some things that are hard to understand, which ignorant and unstable people distort, as they do the other Scriptures, to their own destruction." (2 Peter 3:15-16) NIV

Questions for discussion:
1. The Apostle Peter compared Paul's letters to something. What was it?
2. What do you think the "other Scriptures" are to which he is referring?
3. What were the "ignorant" and "unstable" people doing? What's the outcome?

XIII. WHAT IS THE APOCRYPHA AND WHY IS IT REJECTED AS SCRIPTURE?
   A. The word "apocrypha" comes from a Greek word meaning hidden or concealed. The term has been applied to certain writings that have been disputed regarding their status as Scripture, primarily eleven books that have been added to the canon of the Old Testament in the Roman Catholic Bible. Some examples are the Wisdom of Solomon, Ecclesiasticus, First and Second Maccabbees, Judith, and Tobit.

B. While the *Hebrew Old Testament* did not contain any of these books, fourteen were eventually added to some manuscripts of the *Greek (Old Testament) Septuagint*; however, not when it was first created (c. 300 - 250 B.C.). Those that espouse these books as authentic Scripture, cite the fact that some of the Church fathers, notably Iranaeus, Tertullian, Clement, and Augustine accepted them and used them in public worship. They note that Jerome (A.D. 340 - 420), the great scholar and translator of the Latin Vulgate (Latin translation of the Bible), included the apocrypha. Although, the apocrypha was rejected as Scripture in the "eastern" church (A.D. 367) and then again at the African council of Hippo (A.D. 393) and Carthage (A.D. 397) as the "western" church, it was canonized as Scripture by the Roman Catholic Church at the Council of Trent (1545 - 1563). The Protestant Bible has never acknowledged these book as "inspired" by God.

C. The reasons it is rejected as authoritative and God-Inspired Scripture:
    1. Jesus never quoted the apocrypha and did not acknowledge it as Scripture.
    2. The first century apostles did not quote it or recognize it as equal to Scripture.
    3. The books were rejected by the Jewish Council of Jamnia (c. A.D. 90).
    4. It is rejected by modern day Jews and not a part of their canon.
    5. It was not originally included in the Greek Septuagint by the seventy.
    6. Jerome never regarded the apocrypha as Scripture. He only translated the books under coercion and never accepted them as Scripture. After his death, the books were added to his Latin Vulgate.
    7. Augustine did acknowledge the apocrypha in his early writings, but his later "writings clearly reflected a rejection of these books as outside the canon and inferior to the Hebrew scriptures."[12] Furthermore, he presided over the African council of Hippo that canonized the New Testament, rejecting all other books.
    8. The Roman Catholic church itself did not recognize these books until the Council of Trent (1545 - 1563), and this was done as a reaction to the Protestant Reformation and to legitimize some of their doctrinal matters. (Example: 2 Maccabees 12:45-46 gives them their doctrine of praying for the dead).
    9. The books abound in historical and geographical inaccuracies.
    10. They teach false doctrines that are at odds with other Scripture.

11. They lack the distinctive elements that give Scripture divine character.

12. The books never claim to be the Word of God or given by prophets.

XIV. WHAT SHOULD WE MEAN WHEN WE SAY THE BIBLE IS "INERRANT"?

A. **Meaning:** The word inerrant means infallible, but Christians need to be careful how they represent the Bible. When we say the Bible is "God breathed" and thus infallible, we mean at its origin. People made mistakes in copying, grammar, spelling, translation, and handing it down over the thousands of years. The mistakes are minimal, but it would be unwise not to admit them. A well trained cultist can embarrass and possibly confuse a Christian who dogmatically says "no errors." They may simply turn to an isolated verse in which an imperfection does exist and demand an explanation.

B. **Any errors?** A couple of examples will help to demonstrate the point. If you have a King James Version of the Bible, look up 2 Chronicles 22:2 and compare it to 2 Kings 8:26. You'll find a direct contradiction regarding the age of Ahaziah when he became king. A scribe must have made an error in 2 Chronicles 22:2 when he wrote that Ahaziah was "forty-two". This is impossible since his father was only forty when he died and Ahaziah became king (2 Chronicles 21:20). Another instance, probably of a scribe's error, is in 2 Samuel 15:7 regarding Absalom. It reads forty years but should read "four years."

For a New Testament example, a cultist could point out the difference between the color of Jesus' robe in Matthew 27:28 and John 19:2. Matthew records a "scarlet" robe while John says it was "purple". The Greek words for both are different. Perhaps this is a contradiction or maybe the robe had both colors. Maybe one of the Apostles was color blind. For a Christian who sees Scripture through the eyes of faith, it might even be proposed that the Lord caused this so that the representation of blood (scarlet) and royalty (purple) are connected with the same event. However, the difference must be recognized and not denied. Denial will simply make a cultist think that Christians are not rational.

C. **Reliability:** Considering the age of the Scriptures, there is overwhelming support for their reliability even with the element of human error. For instance, the Isaiah scroll found among the Dead Sea documents is almost verbatim to what was handed down from generation to generation. It is important for Christians to understand that none of the errors compromise doctrinal truth or even deal with significant issues. Almost all the imperfections have to do with spelling or grammar. Even of these, it is estimated that only one half of one percent of the New Testament is held in question.[13] That means that over 99 % of the New Testament is not considered to have any errors at all. That is an excellent track record considering the distance it has come. While we need to be sensitive in how we couch the term "inerrant" with non believers, we don't need to apologize for our allegiance to the Scriptures because they are extremely reliable.

XV. HOW DO WE DEFEND AGAINST ACCUSATIONS OF CONTRA-DICTIONS?
A. What constitutes a contradiction? Josh McDowell states it very well in his book *A Ready Defense*. He says, "The law of non-contradiction, which is the basis of all logical thinking, states that a thing cannot be both *a* and *non-a* at the same time, in the same place, and in the same manner. It cannot be both raining and not raining at the same time and in the same location"[14]

While it is easy to claim that anything—including the Bible—has inaccuracies, it is quite another to prove it. Many arrive at false conclusions based upon false assumptions. They set out to disprove the Bible but upon close investigation discover its accuracy and are converted. Praise God! One such individual was Sir William Ramsay, considered one of the greatest archaeologists to have ever lived. His deep digging only revealed truth in the Word of God. However, others don't dig deeply enough.

B. Simple mistakes in reasoning can include:
1. *The mistake of not giving the author the benefit of the doubt.* The authors were either eye witnesses or knew what they were trying to say. This isn't always obvious to the reader. He must dig and think about it.
2. *The mistake of failing to distinguish between a contradiction and a difference.* People report on what is significant to them. It might differ from what someone else reports. It also might simply be a different emphasis by the same author but at a different time. Example: The boy is telling his grandmother about how he fed the elephants at the zoo in the morning. Later, he tells his grandfather that he fed the giraffes and elephants. This is not contradictory, but it is different.
3. *The mistake of forgetting the limitations of translation.* While we hope that the Bible is translated as accurately as possible, Hebrew and Greek—as well as all languages—have peculiarities difficult to render into English.

C. Some apparent contradictions that a little digging resolves:

1. Resurrection accounts: John writes about Mary Magdalene coming to the tomb, but Luke mentions that there is a whole group. This is a difference, not a contradiction. John focuses specifically on Mary Magdalene's reaction.

2. The days of Jesus in the grave: Matt. 12:40 compares the Son of Man's death for three days and three nights to that of Jonah. Critics point out that if Jesus died on Friday and rose on Sunday then this is only two full days. Let's examine this. First, the Jews used the expression "a day and a night" as an idiom when only a part of a day was indicated. Second, the comparison is to Jonah and either does not necessarily represent the exact same amount of time that he spent in the fish, or it is exactly the same, but Jesus is giving it in a more parabolic form. Third, new evidence is showing that the crucifixion might have occurred in 31 AD rather than 30 AD as formally thought. Why is this important? Because in 31 AD, the day of Passover was on a Thursday. This would make three full days that Jesus was dead.[15]

3. Paul's experience on the road to Damacus: In Acts 9:7 the men traveling with Paul heard a voice, but in Acts 22:9 another rendition of the story says they did not hear the voice. However, upon examination, the confusion is cleared up. The Greek verb "to hear" (akouo) is constructed differently in the two accounts. In Acts 9 the emphasis is that they heard enough to know a voice was speaking, but Acts 22 indicates that they could not distinguish the words of the voice—only Paul could. Example: The radio is on in the other room. You know voices are talking, but you cannot pick out what is said.

4. How Judas committed suicide: Matt 27:5 indicates that Judas hung himself, whereas Acts 1:18 says he fell headlong on the field he had purchased and there he burst open and spilled his intestines. At first these two accounts seem to be at odds with each other. But looking more deeply reveals a few more details. First, Matthew tells how Judas dies, but does not say he didn't have a fall; nor does Peter say Judas did not hang himself. Second, Peter seems to be speaking in more symbolic terms about fulfilled prophecy since he refers to Judas buying the field, when in reality it was the chief priests (Matt. 27:6-7) using the betrayal money to buy the field. Judas had discarded the money when he learned that Jesus was to die due to his betrayal. Third, we don't have all the information about Judas after he left the priests and went on his suicide mission. Perhaps

he attempted suicide twice, or maybe he hung himself, a branch broke and he fell a great distance to the earth, bursting open.

5. The thirty pieces of silver: Matt. 27:9-10 gives credit to Jeremiah for making the prophecy regarding the thirty pieces of silver and the potter's field when it seems that Zechariah made the prediction. What do we find when we look more deeply? While it is true that Zechariah 11:12-13 makes the accurate prediction, it is equally true that Jeremiah 32:6-8 begins the entire process of the prophecy. Matthew could simply have been referring to the fulfillment of a well known combination prophecy by referring to the major prophet who started it. Also, it was acceptable for the Hebrews to refer to an entire section of Scripture by referring to the first book of that section, Jeremiah was the first book of the prophets.

XVI. WHAT ARCHAEOLOGICAL FINDINGS CONFIRM THE BIBLE STORIES?

A. **Concerning the people and places of the Bible**. There is so much archaeological evidence for the accuracy of the Scriptures that full college level courses are devoted to the subject. Anyone interested can get numerous books on the topic. Discoveries by archaeologists just continue to validate the authenticity of the Scriptures. Let us consider just a few examples: 1) Critics use to think the Hittites mentioned in the Bible were simply a myth until one day they uncovered their cities and found that the Bible accounts were true. 2) Then there were the Elba tablets discovered in 1968 which proved the existence of the five cities mentioned in Genesis 14 that Abraham defeated. These cities were also thought to be fictious before their discovery. 3) There are ancient inscriptions in the walls of the canyons and rock formations leading from Egypt to Israel that were written in a mixture of ancient Egyptian and Hebrew. These engravings speak of Moses and the many miracles God performed while the Hebrews journeyed through the wilderness.[16] 4) The seal of Governor Gedaliah that was found at Lachish. He is mentioned in 2 Kings 25:22. This validates that portion of the book of Kings. 5) The Cyrus Cylinder not only confirms the life of King Cyrus but also his directive to release the Israelites from captivity in the various countries of Babylon. This helps substantiate the books of Ezra, Nehemiah, and portions of Isaiah. 6) For another example we could use the seal of Jeremiah's scribe, Baruch. It was located in 1986 and lends strong support for the existence and words of the prophet.

There are dozens of other findings giving strong evidence for the lives of Joseph, Abraham, King David, Pontius Pilate, etc. Critics use to say that David was a simple myth that was made up by the Jews. However, a 9th century B.C. inscription was found in 1993. Words carved in a chunk of basalt by an enemy confirms the life of King David.[17] Critics also said the ancient languages did not include patriarch names. However, "as to personal names like Abraham, Isaac, Jacob, we are able to say today that these were current names in the areas referred to in the Bible."[18]

B. **Concerning the customs, laws, activities, writings, traditions, etc.** The Mari tablets confirmed numerous cities, customs, and patriarchal activities. The Nuzi Tablets give evidence for certain laws and customs. Critics said that writers of the Old Testament were wrong about camels being used around 1700 B.C. However, evidence now shows clearly that camels were in use at that time. Everywhere archaeologists investigate seem only to confirm Biblical accounts. Skeptics said that the Old Testament was not written until much later (even after Christ), however, the books of the Old Testament were found among the Dead Scrolls dating up to two centuries before Christ. Moreover, in 1979 scrolls dated c. 600 B.C. were found that revealed "a benediction from the Book of Numbers"[19]. This ancient Scripture was written centuries before the Son of God came to the earth. Another discovery in 1986, showed that some of the Old Testament was written soon after the events occurred and not centuries later, thus making the account very reliable. [20]

C. **Concerning the Flood accounts.** There are a couple of hundred flood traditions in the many cultures of the world with remarkable similarities to the Genesis account. "We cannot escape the conclusion that these flood traditions are an indisputable proof that the world catastrophe as described in Genesis is one of the greatest facts of all history."[21] Also, various sightings and explorations have many convinced that the Ark is still in existence on Mount Ararat.[22]

XVII. WHAT ARE SOME OTHER AMAZING DISCOVERIES ABOUT THE BIBLE?

A. **Hidden codes in the Bible:** Research over the past few decades is revealing that there are messages hidden within the text of the Old Testament Hebrew. Computers are now used to perform a procedure known as "equidistant letter sequencing" (ELS). For instance, the word "TORH" (Hebrew name standing for the Law and the name of first five books of the Old Testament.) is spelled out at the beginning of Genesis, Exodus, Numbers, and Deuteronomy with a skip sequence of 50 letters.[23] In other words, starting with the first "T" found in Genesis and counting to the fiftieth letter one finds the letter "O" and so on, until it spells Torh (spelled Torah in English). However, in Numbers and Deuteronomy the word is spelled backwards. Consider the following diagram:

Genesis	Exodus	Leviticus	Numbers	Deuteronomy
TORH	TORH	*YHWH*	HROT	HROT
⟶	⟶		⟵	⟵

They seem to be pointing to the center book, Leviticus.[24] Although, it does not have the word TORH hidden, it does have YHWH in seven letter increments. This is the sacred Hebrew name of God. Besides this example, there are hundreds more. There are significant historical and modern names, places, wars, and events which have been found through computer search. Books have been written on the subject exposing the various names such as "Napoleon" encoded near other words like "Waterloo" and "France." Statistical analysis shows these to be far beyond chance. No other Hebrew writings (or any other language for that matter) reveal these hidden messages. It's design shows a supernatural designer and author. However, it should be noted that not all Christian scholars accept these findings. There is a need for more research to be done in this area.

XVIII.   HOW SHOULD CHRISTIANS VIEW THE BIBLE?
   A.   As an authentic representation of what the Lord wanted to relay in writing to mankind.
   B.   As the written voice of God to man giving his purposes and plans about redemption.
   C.   As historically, scientifically, and prophetically accurate.
   D.   As a guidebook with commandments, principles, and instructions for life.
   E.   As a source for understanding the manifold character and Kingdom of God.

Thinking Through The Scripture

"For the word of God is living and powerful, and sharper than any two-edged sword, piercing even to the division of soul and spirit, and of joints and marrow, and is a discerner of the thoughts and intents of the heart." (Hebrews 4:12)

Questions for discussion:
1. How could a word be "living" and "powerful"? How is it two-edged?
2. What does the word of God pierce according to this? What is the result?
3. How should we let the word of God impact our thoughts and intents?

The Bible is true whether people believe it or not. It is accurate and inspired. As David A. Hubbard tells in *Does the Bible Really Work?*, the Bible was put together by God and says what He wants it to regardless of people's views on it:

"The Bible's inspiration is unique. There's no other book like it. It and it alone has the words of salvation, the record of what God has done, is doing, and will do to draw men and women to Himself. And the Bible's inspiration is complete. The whole Bible was spoken by God through the words of men. It says exactly what God wants it to say , and every part of it is important. But one thing more needs to be said, Briefly, the Bible is the Word of God. It does not become the Word of God. In other words, the Bible's inspiration is permanent, part of its very nature. It does not depend on how we feel about it. The Bible's inspiration is not its ability to turn me on but the fact that God has breathed His own truth in all its sentences and words. True, the message of God does not get through to me until I open my mind and heart to it in the power of the Holy Spirit. But it is God's word whether I listen to it or not. It doesn't need my vote. I need its voice. It is valid whether I respond or not. But I will not experience its validity unless I do respond. All this talk about the Bible's inspiration will be upsetting to some people. They may think it's narrow-minded and intolerant to think that only in the Bible do we find the words of salvation. A man clutching a life preserver thrown to him from the shore does not berate his rescuer for throwing only one. He's grateful that there is any way of salvation available, and so are we. Let's tell God that."[25]

End Notes

1   *Josephus: Complete Works*, trans. W. Whiston (Grand Rapids, MI: Kregel Publications, 1980), p.379
2. W. R. Kimball, *"Is The Bible The Word of God,"* a tract published by Christian Equippers International, S. Lake Tahoe, CA, 1985, p. 3.
3. Josh McDowell, *A Ready Defense* (Nashville, TN: Thomas Nelson Publishers, 1993), p.29.
4. Josh McDowell, *Answers to Tough Questions* (San Bernadino, CA: Here's Life Publishers, 1983), p. 4.
5. Grant R. Jeffrey, *The Signature of God: Astonishing Biblical Discoveries* (Toronto, Ontario: Frontier Research Publications, Inc., 1996), pgs. 99-100.
6. McDowell, *A Ready Defense*, p. 47-48.

7. Ibid. p. 24.

8. Paul Little, *Know Why You Believe* (Downers Grove, IL: Inter Varsity Press, 1988), p. 77.

9. Ibid. p. 77.

10. *Eerdman's Handbook To The History of Christianity*, ed. Tim Dowley (Grand Rapids, MI: Wm. B. Eerdman's Publishing Co., 1977), p. 105.

11. Ibid., p. 106

12. McDowell, *Answers to Tough Questions*, p. 37.

13. McDowell, *A Ready Defense*, p. 46.

14. McDowell, *A Ready Defense*, p.127.

15. David Reagan, "The Crucifixion Week in 31 AD—An Overview," *Lamb & Lion Ministries Newsletter* vol. IXX, no. 3 (March, 1998): 5.

16. Jeffrey, pgs. 48-68.

17. Ibid.

18. J.A. Thompson, *The Bible And Archaeology* (Grand Rapids, MI: Wm. B. Eerdmans Publishing), p.23.

19. Michael D. Lemonick, *"Are the Bible's Stories True?,"* *Time Magazine*, December 18, 1995, p. 67.

20. Ibid., p.65.

21. Alfred M. Rehwinkel, *The Flood in the light of the Bible, Geology, and Archaeology* (Saint Louis, MO: Concordia Publishing House, 1951), p.165.

22. John D. Morris, Ph.D., *The Search for Noah's Ark* (El Cajon, CA: Institute for Creation Research, no date), video recording.

23. David Reagan, "The Bible Code: An Evaluation," *Lamb & Lion Ministries Newsletter* vol. XVIII, no. 9 (September 1997), p. 1.

24. *Beyond Coincidence*, a tract by Koinonia House Ministry (Coeur d'Alene, ID: Koinonia House, 1994), p. 13.

25. David A. Hubbard, *Does the Bible Really Work?* (Waco, TX: Word Books, 1972), pgs. 31-32.

QUESTIONNAIRE: LESSON TWO

NAME: _____ DATE: _____

1. Who was Flavius Josephus and what was his report regarding Jesus?

_____

_____

_____

2. List the three reasons that faith is so necessary for believing the Word of God?

a) _____

b) _____

c) _____

3. Write out Isaiah 40:8 _____

_____

_____

4. List three aspects that make the Bible unique.

a) _____

b) _____

c) _____

5. How many portions of New Testament manuscripts are there? _____

6. Write a paragraph about the manuscript evidence of the Old Testament.

_____

_____

_____

_____

7. What are the three basic parts of the Hebrew Bible?

a) _____

b) _____

c) _____

8. Does the N.T. bear witness to the authenticity of the Old Testament? ____

9. In what ways did Jesus bear witness to the authenticity of the Old Testament? _____

_____

_____

10. What was the last book of the Hebrew Bible? _____

11. What is the name of the Greek Old Testament written by seventy Jewish scholars in Alexandria about 300 B.C.? _____

12. The example of the Old Testament canon encouraged the _____ of a list of Christian _____ which should constitute the _____ or rule of the churches.

13. The eastern church canonized the 27 New Testament books in A.D. ___

14. List the three distinguishing criteria for canonization.

a) _____

b) _____

c) _____

15. What is the Apocrypha? _____

_____

_____

16. Give two reasons the Apocrypha was rejected.

a) _____

b) _____

17. List the three mistakes mentioned that people make when they don't dig deeply enough.

a) _____

b) _____

c) _____

18. Circle the number that indicates how equipped you felt before this lesson regarding your knowledge to witness to someone about the Bible's authenticity, compared to now.

BEFORE 0 1 2 3 4 5 6 7 8 9 10 AFTER 0 1 2 3 4 5 6 7 8 9 10

MORMONISM

Part 1: Introduction and False Doctrines

"I think the biggest hurdle for the evangelical Church is to get past the idea that Mormons are Protestants who simply have some doctrinal problems. Nothing could be further from the truth. Mormonism is a religious system that stands in direct opposition to basic teachings of the Bible...The first step to helping Mormons is to come to terms with the fact that Mormonism is a system hatched in hell and birthed in the occult necromancies of Joseph Smith."[1]

—James Spencer, Former Mormon Elder

INTRODUCTION

I. WHO FOUNDED THE MORMON CHURCH AND WHEN DID IT BEGIN?
   A. Joseph Smith, Jr. founded the church in 1830, the same year that Smith published the *Book of Mormon* which he claims he translated from "golden plates." The plates had been supposedly hidden from mankind for about 1,400 years. Smith said he had encountered a "pillar of light." In this pillar, he saw God the Father and Jesus Christ. Later, an angel, named Moroni, revealed to him the location of the hidden plates. He claims to have had several visitations from the angel and to have spent a couple of years translating the plates. Then the plates were supposedly taken to heaven by the angel.

Thinking Through The Scripture

"for Satan himself is transformed into an angel of light." (2 Corinthians 11:14) KJV

"O Lucifer, son of the morning" [sense of brightness] (Isaiah 14:12) KJV

"But even if we or an angel from heaven should preach a gospel other than the one we preached to you, let him be eternally condemned!" (Galatians 1:8) NIV

Questions for discussion:
1. From the Scriptures above, what can we learn about angels? Are they all doing God's will? How do they sometimes present themselves?
2. How does the Bible tell us to regard an angel who comes bearing a gospel different from the one the Bible teaches?
3. Suppose that Smith really did encounter a "pillar of light." How should he have responded to an angel who brought a different gospel?

II. HOW LARGE AND INFLUENTIAL IS THE MORMON CHURCH TODAY?
    A. One report tells us that the church "has grown to almost 10 million members in more than 150 countries. That figure, however, includes children and many people, it is claimed, that no longer attend one of the 22,000 churches worldwide but are kept on the rolls."[2] A more accurate estimate is probably about four million active members worldwide.[3]

       Today, Mormonism is having a worldwide impact. They are finding acceptance in Latin America and parts of Africa. It is said that they are gaining dominance in Tonga, as well as American and Eastern Samoa islands. In 1997 I was teaching a cult seminar in the Philippines to pastors and leaders who were seeing the effects of Mormon missionaries. Last Fall I was in Hong Kong speaking with an influential pastor who showed deep concern over what the Mormons were doing there. As we enter the new millennium, Christianity has a job on its hands to answer the challenge of full-time Mormon missionaries in 160 nations.

    B. Although the influence of the Mormon church is not easy to define, it should not be underestimated. Its current assets are at least 30 billion dollars.[4] One example of their business influence can be seen in any Marriott Hotel. "If a traveler staying in a hotel of the nationwide Marriott chain searches in the dresser drawer for the usual Gideon Bible, he or she instead finds the touch of the Mormons—in the form of a paperback copy of the *Book of Mormon*."[5] The church invests large sums of money in stocks and bonds.

A serious study on the matter shows that the church owns a lot and has a lot of clout through their investments. One study on the subject was by Heinerman and Shupe called *The Mormon Corporate Empire*. In their book, written in the mid 1980's, the authors show that the church owns major interests in communication systems, colleges, nuclear power plants, computer companies, food chains, insurance companies, etc. It also bought up major land holdings in various states.[6]

The influence does not stop there. It seems that the clean-cut, all-American, authority-centered Mormon youth are likely candidates for the CIA and FBI. Utah is a place of high recruitment for these agencies. When Mormons achieve status in the agencies, they hire more Mormons. Of course, there is also political and judicial clout caused by all the interconnections of money, power, and position. This is not to say that it is unlawful or even a conspiracy. However, it does fit nicely into the Mormon "doomsday prophecy" that the U.S. will be annihilated and have to depend upon the LDS church for survival.[7]

The public does not hear these things. Rather, we hear the Mormon Tabernacle Choir singing "Christian" songs. But the average listener does not realize that the Jesus sung about by Mormons is not the "Jesus" of the Bible, and the Scriptures warn us about those who preach *"another Jesus...a different spirit...or a different gospel."* (2 Cor. 11:4)

III. WHAT IS THE OFFICIAL NAME OF THE MORMON CHURCH?

A. The Church of Jesus Christ of Latter-day Saints. Their main headquarters are in Salt Lake City, Utah. The current leader is Gordon Hinkley.

IV. WHAT IS THE REORGANIZED CHURCH?

A. The Reorganized Church of Jesus Christ of Latter-day Saints was established in 1860[8] as a result of the split in the main church after the death of Joseph Smith Jr. The Reorganized [Missouri] Church took as their leader one of Smith's sons, Joseph Smith III, whereas the more well-known church followed Brigham Young to Utah. The Reorganized Church has its headquarters in Independence, Missouri, where they believe that the second coming of Christ will happen. They reject the name "Mormon" but have many of the cultist views of the main group.

They are a major thorn to the Mormon Church since all of the court decisions have established their claim that they are the main church, but the one in Utah the schismatic. They reported approximately 200,000 members worldwide in 1985 and were growing.[9] The Reorganized Church reveres Joseph Smith and accepts many of the things he wrote as Scripture. However, they do not accept the *Pearl of Great Price* or section 132 of the *Doctrine and Covenants*.

Author Richard Kyle tells us in his book *The Religious Fringe: A History of Alternative Religions in America*, "But on several points, the Reorganized Church holds that the Utah Church has fallen into error. The Reorganized saints shun any identification with the Utah Mormons, regarding Young as a false teacher. The Reorganized Church also rejects the most controversial teachings of Joseph Smith: plural marriage, temple rites and the plurality of gods...In recent years the Reorganized Church has moved closer to evangelical Christianity, emphasizing justification by faith and deemphasizing the role of Joseph Smith. Despite these changes, the church has not joined the ranks of orthodox Christianity."[10]

V. WHAT ARE SOME OF THE POSITIVE ASPECTS OF MORMONISM?
    A. It is impossible to say that "all Mormons" do this or believe that. However, there are some positive characteristics that seem to stand out. Many are conservative, family-oriented, patriotic people who show genuine concern for others as James Coates observes in his book *In Mormon Circles: Gentiles, Jack Mormons, and Latter-day Saints*. He says, "The Mormons who live around me have been my good friends ever since childhood, and today they are fine neighbors. Observing the Mormon way of life makes me want to be a better family member, a more worthwhile citizen, or simply a friendlier person. But to be a Mormon is also to be an enigma."[11] An enigma means a person of puzzling or contradictory character. Many Mormons do not realize that the theology of Mormonism is contradictory to Christianity and collapses in the light of honest evaluation.

VI. WHAT ARE THE MAJOR EVANGELISM TACTICS OF MORMONISM?
    A. **Door-to-door witnessing by Mormon missionaries.** The Mormons encourage their most promising young people (boys aged 19 and girls aged 21) to dedicate time to missionary work on

a self-supporting basis. The young women stay for 18 months and the young men for 24 months. There are tens of thousands of Mormon missionaries worldwide spreading their false polytheistic doctrine. Recently, a Mormon missionary told me that there are approximately 60,000 Mormons on the mission field. Every week about 600 "greenies" arrive at the Mission Training Center in Provo, Utah for basic missionary boot camp.[12] This is but one of the 18 training centers for missionaries. They are trained how to approach weak and ungrounded Christians, and they have led many astray. Almost every home in the United States has had Mormons at the front door.

How Christians respond to them at those moments is very important! We should send up a quick prayer, show them the love of God, and share the truth of Jesus Christ with them. If you are on a foreign mission trip or even doing a local evangelistic event and meet Mormon missionaries, you may have an opportunity to impact them more than when they come to your home. On a short-term mission to the Philippines, a couple of us were able to impact some Mormons. They were somewhat homesick and appreciated speaking to Americans. However, more than that was their - awakening - realization that Christians did missions as well, but not from a Mormon base. Mormon missionaries sometimes come off the field not as sure about their doctrine as when they began.

Thinking Through The Scripture

"Many deceivers...have gone out into the world...Watch out that you do not lose what you have worked for...Anyone who runs ahead and does not continue in the teaching of Christ does not have God...If anyone comes to you and does not bring this teaching, do not take him into your house or welcome him" (2 John 7-10) NIV

Questions for discussion:
1. Do you think "deceivers" always know they are deceivers? What is our responsibility as Christians to those deceived?
2. What is it that the Apostle John thinks we can lose?
3. How do Mormons seem to "run ahead and not continue in the teaching of Christ? What are the implications of this that follow?
4. Consider the section below this box. How should Christians respond to Mormon missionaries? Do we have the right to be rude or slam the door?

Be cautious! The Mormons readily acknowledge that Jesus Christ has come in the flesh and that he is God. *Yet, they have perverted the true teaching [doctrine] of Christ by teaching that He is only one among a multitude of gods.* In regard to allowing them in your home, 2 John 7-10 is not a license for being rude or inhospitable. Rather, it is a warning not to accept them into your lives *in an authoritative position* (as an apostle or evangelist). Do not place them in a superior or equal role with Christian authority. This word "house" is *oikia* in the Greek. It means a residence either literally or figuratively. It implies the domestic affairs of the family.

As Christians, we are to *show the love of Christ* to the lost and *have a desire to lead them to the LORD,* but we are to do it in a wise way that will not give them an authoritative voice into our lives or compromise our families.

One time while living in Reno, Nevada, I was unwittingly drawn into a Mormon meeting aimed at converting me through a little bit of deception. (I didn't know that ever happened in Mormonism, but it did that day.) An acquaintance came by my house and asked me to go for a walk. I went along with him on what I thought was a "friendly walk." As we passed by a garage, he said he wanted me to meet some people. He quickly walked through the garage door and beckoned me to follow. I was somewhat at a loss but followed him in, not knowing any better. Within five minutes, I found myself seated before a table of five Mormons aggressively evangelizing me. They had a big book of pictures. They were leafing through the pages doing illustrative evangelism. At one point, they showed me a picture of the President of the Mormon church and told me that he was the Modern-day Prophet.

I was a recent convert to Christianity and was not informed about essential Christian doctrines, but the Holy Spirit within cautioned me. There was something wrong with this. I remember witnessing to them of my faith in Christ; He was the true authority and not their Mormon president. I probably did not show as much "grace" for them as I should have, but I was shaken and quickly departed after a few minutes. Fortunately, I had not made the mistake of letting them into a position of authority. Today, I would possibly handle something like that with more grace, but the truth of Jesus Christ as the supreme authority would be the same. The Bible tells us to be "wise as serpents but gentle as doves."

B. **A massive advertising campaign.** They spend millions of dollars every year promoting the *Book of Mormon* and the life style of

Mormonism. Slick T.V. and radio commercials encourage people to send away for the free videos and / or a King James Bible. Christian organizations could learn a lesson from the quality of Mormon advertising. Heart-melting, short dramas capture the attention of the T.V. audience and then they find out it was produced by the Church of Jesus Christ of Latter-day Saints. So, they call for the free video or book. What people don't realize is that when they call for the free items, they will also be sent a Book of Mormon and a follow up visit by the local Mormon missionaries as well.

They also publicize the Mormon lifestyle as the most beneficial way for being a happy family unit. Yet, simple research by anyone interested will show that Utah, which is currently about 76% Mormon, has its fair share of problems with murder, rape, child abuse, teen suicide, women pregnant out of wedlock, etc. Furthermore, in the early 1980's Utah was dubbed "the fraud capital of the world" because so many investors were being swindled out of their money.[13]

C. **Friendship Evangelism.** The Mormons have learned the effectiveness of kind acts. "Mormons can gradually ingratiate themselves with their neighbors (doing minor favors such as babysitting, running errands, and lending tools), selectively reveal bits of Mormon lifestyle and faith, and eventually build friendship bonds with prospective converts long before proselytizing becomes overt."[14]

There is nothing wrong with kind acts as a motivation for evangelism, and we should not criticize true friendship. Our church, for example, runs a soup kichen for the needy in order to minister to their soul after we minister to their need for sustenance. Jesus was often concerned about the needs of others around Him.

The problem is not that Mormons do kind acts in order to influence people for Mormonism. The problem is that their kind acts do not mean that they have truth in their doctrine. Many groups use friendship evangelism to sway people to their cause. The Moonies use "love bombing" but that doesn't make their doctrine any more true.

D. **Emphasis to Native Americans.** To Mormons, Native Americans are descendants from the Lamanites, an ancient Palestinian tribe that came to America before Christ. According to Mormon doctrine, many of these are to turn to Mormonism before the millennium, so much effort goes that way. Even though Mormonism throws a lot of money at recruiting and indoctrinating Native

American youth, much criticism has arisen. Heinerman and Shupe point out that Mormons are accused of deceptive campaigning and "spreading Mormon religion at the expense of native cultures."[15]

VII. WHAT IS THE MAIN HERESY OF MORMONISM?

A. There are major heresies in Mormonism, but the main one is found in their teaching about *the evolution of God.* They teach the concept "As man is, God once was, and as God is, man may become".[16] From almost the very beginning of their movement, this heretical teaching developed. Some Examples: 1) Joseph Smith, Jr. taught that "God himself was once as we are now, and is an exalted man." 2) Brigham Young formulated the Adam-God doctrine in which he taught "that Adam is our father and our God...He was the first man on the earth, and its framer and maker. He, with the help of his brethren, brought it into existence." 3) Apostle Orson Hyde taught Mormons to "Remember that God, our heavenly Father, was perhaps once a child, and mortal like we ourselves, and rose, step by step in the scale of progress, in the school of advancement; has moved forward and overcome, until he arrived at the point where He now is."[17]

It should be noted that the Adam-God doctrine is not currently taught by Mormonism, but the information is useful since most Mormons today do not realize it once was taught and has helped develop their doctrine of God.

1) The Bible teaches us that God does not change (or evolve):
    - "*I am the LORD, I do not change....*" (*Malachi 3:6*)
    - "*...even from everlasting to everlasting You are God*" (*Ps. 90:2) AMP*
    - "*Jesus Christ is the same yesterday, today, and forever.*" (*Heb. 13:8*)

2) The Bible teaches us that God is not a man:
    - "*For I am God, and not man; the Holy One....*" (*Hosea 11:9*)
    - "*God is not a man....*" (*Num. 23:19*)
    - "*Before Me there was no God formed, nor shall there be after Me.*" (*Is. 43:10*)

3) The Bible teaches us that there is only One God:
    - "*Thus says the Lord, the King of Israel, And his Redeemer, the Lord of hosts: 'I am the First and the Last; Besides Me there is no God...Is there a God besides Me? Indeed there is no other Rock; I know not one'.*" (*Is. 44:6,8*)
    - "*...the LORD is God; besides him there is no other.*" (*Deut. 4:35) NIV*

4) Even the *Book of Mormon* teaches that God does not change.
   - *"For do we not read that God is the same yesterday, today, and forever, and in him there is no variableness neither shadow of changing? And now if ye have imagined up unto yourselves a god who doth vary, and in whom there is shadow of changing, then have ye imagined up unto yourselves a god who is not a God of miracles." Mormon 9:9-10 [Book of Mormon]*
   - *"For I know that God is not a partial God, neither a changeable being; but he is unchangeable from all eternity to all eternity." Moroni 8:18*

VIII. WHAT ARE THEIR SACRED BOOKS?

A. **The Book of Mormon.** This is supposedly an account of the original inhabitants of America to whom Christ appeared after his resurrection. Smith claimed he translated it from the "golden plates" shown him by the angel Moroni. However, Smith's shady character[18] and contradictory statements lead more to the conclusion that he originally produced this scheme for money and power, and then got swept up in the delusion of being a prophet of God. In 2 Thessalonians 2:10-12, it shows how God sends strong delusion to those who do not "receive the love of the truth."

There are major problems with the accuracy of this supposed "most correct of any book on earth" since it has undergone almost 4,000 changes trying to cover up chronological, historical, and contradictory problems. It has received criticism from archaeologists and historians since its inception.

Who actually authored the book has also been long debated. It is possibly a fabrication that Smith wove together from other sources such as Ethan Smith's *View of the Hebrews; or the Ten Tribes of Israel in America* (1823),[19] Solomon Spalding's *Manuscript Found* (1812),[20] Thomas Thorowgood's *Jews in America* (1650),[21] and certain popular books of that era.[22] While there is no solid proof of this, there are many resemblances that appear to be beyond mere coincidence. Also, there are rumors of theft and plagiarism that leaves one wondering. It is amazing that Mormons sometimes think that Joseph Smith Jr. came up with a new revelation from God regarding the ancestry of the Native Americans. However, the popular theory was already well developed by his time. The theory would eventually be proven inaccurate by historians and archaeologists, but not until after Smith had fabricated various parts of people's writings on the theory and made it into a religion.

Fawn Brodie wrote a bibliography on Smith entitled *No Man Knows My History*. It is a classic and probably the most accurate bibliography ever written on the life of Joseph Smith Jr. She had this to say about Mormonism and its book: "*The moving power of Mormonism was a fable*—one that few converts stopped to question, for its meaning seemed profound and its inspiration was contagious."[23] (italics added)

B. **Doctrines and Covenants**. This book records 136 supposed revelations given mostly to Joseph Smith Jr., with a few additions by presidents of the Latter-Day Saints. As in the *Book of Mormon*, there have been thousands of changes. Some of these have been major changes of reconstruction in order to clear up contradictions between the "sacred books".

Thinking Through The Scripture

"*They perish because they refused to love the truth and so be saved. For this reason God sends them a powerful delusion so that they will believe the lie and so that all will be condemned who have not believed the truth but have delighted in wickedness.*" (*2 Thessalonians 2:10b-12) NIV*

Questions for discussion:
1. It appears that people end up believing one of two things. What are they and why does this happen?
2. Is it possible that Joseph Smith became deluded and began believing the lie?
3. What implications does this have for our lives in society today?

C. **The Pearl of Great Price**. This contains three major books called Moses, Abraham, and Joseph Smith. In this book Smith elevates himself to a Biblical position equal to Moses and Abraham. Unfortunately for Joseph, this book shows better than any of the others his great deception. In 1835, he purchased several mummies and papyri covered with hieroglyphics. Smith claimed "that one contained the writings of Abraham while he was in Egypt and that another was the work of Joseph, son of Jacob."[24] He supposedly translated the short hieroglyphic message into the greatly expanded Book of Abraham.

In 1967, the papyri that Smith used were rediscovered and no less than four expert Egyptologists examined the papyri. They all found the same thing; the papyri were nothing more than the record of an Egyptian funeral ceremony honoring the Egyptian god Osiris. "Only those who wish to preserve the fantasy that Joseph

Smith was given the ability to translate the Book of Abraham still vainly try to defend his work."[25]

In actuality, the writing of the book of Abraham probably happened as a reaction to what Smith had read in another book. Fawn Brodie shows that Smith was heavily influenced by reading the *Philosophy of a Future State* by Thomas Dick. Dick's theory was that God "organized" the universe rather than "created" it out of nothing. He held that the universe revolved around a common center - that being the throne of God. A comparison between the two works shows much similarity. Smith's imagination used Dick's theory to create the star "Kolob" near the throne of God, around which everything is centered.[26]

D. **The King James Version of the Bible**. The Mormons basically pay lip service to the Bible as being "the word of God insofar as it is translated correctly" (Articles of Faith of the Church of Jesus Christ of Latter Day Saints, Article 8.). The problem, though, is they claim that the correct translation of the Bible is impossible because the Catholic Church changed the original word of God. Mormons use to teach that the Catholic Church was the "abominable church" spoken of in 1 Nephi 13:26-29 that corrupted the gospel of the Lamb.

Although this may not be emphasized in their teaching today, it has helped to undermine Mormon trust in the Bible. So, today *the Mormons put more trust in their three other sacred books*. Also, the Mormon religion has manipulated the doctrines of the Bible and added profuse revelations which have reduced allegiance to the authority of the Scriptures.

Thinking Through The Scripture

"I warn everyone who hears the words of the prophecy of this book: If anyone adds anything to them, God will add to him the plagues described in this book. And if anyone takes away from this book of prophecy, God will take away from him his share in the tree of life and in the holy city, which are described in this book." (Revelation 22:18-19) NIV

"You shall not add unto the word which I command you, nor take from it, that you may keep the commandments of the LORD...." (Deuteronomy 4:2)

Questions for discussion:
1. How do these verses apply to the *Book of Mormon*? To what do you think the "words of prophecy" and "command" refer?

2. How could Mormons use Deut. 4:2 to refute the Christian claim that we should not add to the Bible? Consider this in regard to the New Testament.

3. Have the Mormons added "commands" and "prophecy"?

IX. WHAT WERE THE BASICS OF JOSEPH SMITH'S LIFE?

A. **Joseph Smith Jr. was a treasure seeker**: He was born in Sharon, Vermont, on December 23, 1805. The Smith family moved to Palmyra, New York, in 1816, looking to improve their financial crisis by searching for "rumored" hidden treasure in the surrounding hills. Joseph looked for gold and silver treasure through various witchcraft practices of glass-looking, incantations, occultic manipulations, divining with stakes, and "animal sacrifices".[27] He was obviously very influenced by his father, Joseph Sr., who dabbled in mysticism, followed after imaginary buried treasure, and got in trouble with the state of Vermont once for attempting to mint and counterfeit money. It made sense for young Joseph to be caught up in occultic activity and fraud since ancestry from both his mother (Lucy Mack) and his father (Joseph Smith) had a long history of it.[28]

   Another major influence in Joseph Junior's life was a fortune teller named Walters. Walters made money by pretending to know where buried treasure from ancient Indians was located. He deceived ignorant farmers by supposedly reading from an ancient Indian record which was actually a Latin copy of Caesar's Orations. He would mutter "unintelligible jargon" to hearers. He would then get money to tell them where the treasure was located. It is known that he first suggested to Joseph the "idea of finding a book."[29]

   1) The Bible tells us plainly how the LORD views those who practice such things. *"Let no one be found among you who…practices divination or sorcery, interprets omens, engages in witchcraft, or casts spells…Anyone who does these things is detestable to the LORD…."* (Deut. 18:10-12) NIV

   2) Furthermore, the Bible pronounces judgment against those who practice these things. *"Do not allow a sorceress to live."* (Ex. 22:18) NIV

B. **Joseph was well known for his storytelling**: According to his mother, he would "entertain the family for hours, describing the lifestyle of the ancient Indian inhabitants of western New York: their government, wars, dress, all in painstaking detail. And this was long before he ever suggested getting such details from a visitation of angels."[30] Unfortunately, Joseph did not keep these stories in the realm of fiction. Eventually, he would twist these fictitious accounts together with his knowledge of Christianity and invent a history of an American Indian people who never really existed. The tall tale he would spin would become the foundation for a whole new religion.

1) The Bible expresses the sad truth of what has happened to millions of people who have followed Joseph Smith in his fictitious and erroneous tales. *"And they will turn away their ears from the truth, and be turned aside to fables."* (2 Tim. 4:4)

C. **Joseph was a very controversial figure**: On the one hand he was a real trouble maker. Besides the obvious problems that he had from a childhood full of spiritism, treasure seeking, and a wild imagination, he suffered forty-seven law suits and was arrested and convicted at least five times. Most of these were for default on debts.[31] One arrest, however, was for ordering the destruction of *The Nauvoo Expositor*, an anti-Mormon publication.

Sixty-two residents of Palmyra, New York, (those who knew the Smith family) signed a complaint regarding the destitute moral character of Smith and said he was "addicted to vicious habits."[32] The late Dr. Walter Martin, who was considered a leading authority on the subject of Mormonisn, said, "The amazing fact is that there exists no contemporary pro-Mormon statements from reliable and informed sources who knew the Smith family and Joseph intimately."[33] Although Martin's statement obviously does not take into account positive comments about the Smith family by those caught up with Joseph in his scheming, it does show the general public attitude towards Smith while he lived in Palmyra.

Later on, there were serious accusations of adultery brought against Smith, one of which came in 1837 from Oliver Cowdery, one of the three witnesses to whom the angel supposedly showed the "golden plates." Furthermore, Smith practiced secret polygamy and had a harem that possibly grew to more than 50 by the time of his death. Smith did not just marry single women like many Mormons believe, but he invented a doctrine about eternal marriage of one man to many wives so that he could be wed to other men's spouses.[34]

Also, he plagiarized portions of books for his own writings, and falsely claimed support of his accurate translation work by a noted literary scholar of the time, Professor Charles Anthon of Columbia University. Professor Anthon strongly denied the claims and wrote that his support of the accuracy was "perfectly false" and that Smith's supposed translation of Egyptian hieroglyphics was "all a trick".[35]

On the other hand, Joseph Smith, was able to attract people to his cause. In his life he became wealthy, helped found a bank (which failed), became a mayor, a self-appointed general, and a candidate for the Presidency of the United States. He must have believed that the end justified the means of getting there.

1) The Bible warns us that: *"...there will be false teachers among you. They will secretly introduce destructive heresies...In their greed these teachers will exploit you with stories they have made up."* (2 Pet. 2:1-3) NIV

D. **Joseph founded a whole new religion.** According to Joseph he had a vision when he was fourteen years old while living in Palmyra, New York. After walking into the woods in the spring of 1820, he asked the Lord which Christian denomination he should join. A pillar of light (supposedly the Father and Son) appeared to Joseph and told him not to join any, that their creeds were all an abomination to the Lord.

Later on in life, Joseph claimed that the angel Moroni revealed to him the location of the hidden "golden plates". They had been hidden on the hill Cumorah 1400 years prior by Moroni, the last of the "righteous" Nephites in America who had served the Lord. These "golden plates" were written upon in ancient Egyptian hieroglyphics. He translated them by looking through the "Urim and Thummim", a large pair of miraculous spectacles that when looked through made clear the understanding of what was written. These had been provided by the angel Moroni. He translated the plates between the years 1827 and 1830. He claims to have been visited by John the Baptist on May 15, 1829, and ordained into the "Aaronic Priesthood".

In 1830, he published the book of Mormon. Smith gained a gathering that soon moved (because of unpopularity) to Kirtland, Ohio. Within six years they increased to about 16,000 followers. During this time they evangelized Jackson County, Missouri, and gained a following. The gathering moved to Nauvoo, Illinois, where Smith met his death in 1844.

E. **Joseph Smith died in a shoot out.** In Nauvoo, Illinois, the church grew large and strong, but there was much opposition. A local newspaper, The Nauvoo Expositor, adamantly opposed the cult with defaming information about Smith's true character. Smith, who was then the mayor, ordered the destruction of the press. Joseph and his brother, Hyrum were imprisoned in Carthage, Illinois. On June 27, 1844, an angry mob of approximately 200 men stormed the jail and murdered Smith and his brother. Before he died, Smith emptied a smuggled revolver into the crowd, killing two men. Soon after this, a large majority of Mormons accepted Brigham Young as the new leader. He was then forty-three. He soon led about 14,000 Mormons from Illinois to the valley of the Great Salt Lake in Utah. There he ruled the church for more than 30 years.

X. WHAT ARE SOME EFFECTS OF FREEMASONRY ON MOR-MONISM?

   A. **Joseph was a member of Freemasonry** and used many of the secret signs and rituals in his formation of Mormonism. Some of Mormonism today comes from a direct influence by Freemasonry. Even the fabricated story of the discovery of the "Golden Plates" parallels a step in Freemasonry. John L. Brooke points this out in *The Refiner's Fire* when he states, "The Enoch myth of Royal Arch Freemasonry, in which the prophet Enoch, instructed by a vision, preserved the Masonic mysteries by carving them on a golden plate that he placed in an arched stone vault marked by pillars, to be rediscovered by Solomon."[36]

   The secret signs and blood oath rituals of freemasonry were used as Mormon temple rituals until 1990 at which time they were "reportedly dropped."[37] Smith helped establish the lodge in Nauvoo and then confiscated many of their rituals for use in Mormonism. He became so interested in masonry that many of the elders of the church quickly followed his lead.

   B. **Occultic influence on the creation of Mormon temples.** Most people do not understand the occultic and Satanic influence that resides in the origin of Freemasonry. This same influence casts a shadow over the construction of the various Mormon temples. The Mormon Temple in Salt Lake, Utah, for instance, is full of pictures, reliefs, design, and architecture that exhibit occultic and Satanic symbolism. For example, there are planetary stones, Saturn stones, reliefs of pentagrams, the star of Seth, the Big Dipper, the All-Seeing Eye, icons of secret handclasps, and the symbol of the bee-hive, but there is no cross representing what Jesus did for us at Calvary. These others are all symbols used in occultic rituals.

   There is a controversy today between Christian apologists of Mormonism about how deeply the occult has been an influence. Some experts seem to disregard the impact of Smith's Freemasonry and occultic experience on the church while others believe the influence has trickled down to every level of modern day Mormon life. In their book entitled *Whited Sepulchers*, authors Schnoebelen and Spencer go so far as to say that the "sharp, needle-like spires on the LDS temples and meeting houses" are known as the 'sign of the nail' and represent Satan himself.[38]

Whatever the truth is about the occultic influence on Mormonism, it must be understood by Christians that most Mormons are totally oblivious to the Freemasonry roots and more blatant Satanic symbols seen in the construction of the temples. The fact remains, however, that they are present and that the rituals inside the temples still include secret rites.

XI. WHAT IS THE CORE OF MORMON DOCTRINE?

While there are many contradictions in Mormonism thus differences as to the core, it is important for Christians to gain a basic understanding as to how all their doctrines flow together. In the movie, *The God Makers*, Ed Decker gives perhaps the simplest and clearest perspective of their core doctrine.

"Mormonism teaches that trillions of planets scattered throughout the cosmos are ruled by countless gods who once were human like us.

They say that long ago on one of these planets, to an unidentified god and one of his goddess wives, a spirit child named Elohim was conceived. This spirit child was later born to human parents who gave him a physical body.

Through obedience to Mormon teaching, death, and resurrection, he proved himself worthy and was elevated to godhood as his father before him.

Mormons believe that Elohim is their heavenly Father and that he lives with his many wives on a planet near a mysterious star called Kolob. Here the god of Mormonism and his wives, through endless celestial sex, produced billions of spirit children.

To decide their destiny, the head of the Mormon gods called a great council meeting. Both of Elohim's eldest sons were there, Lucifer and his brother Jesus.

A plan was presented to build planet Earth, where the spirit children would be sent to take on mortal bodies and learn good from evil. Lucifer stood and made his bid for becoming savior of this new world. Wanting the glory for himself, he planned to force everyone to become gods. Opposing the idea, the Mormon Jesus suggested giving man his freedom of choice, as on other planets. The vote that followed approved the proposal of the Mormon Jesus, who would become savior of the planet Earth.

Enraged, Lucifer cunningly convinced one-third of the spirits destined for Earth to fight and revolt. Thus Lucifer became the devil and his followers the demons. Sent to this world in spirit form, they would forever be denied bodies of flesh and bone.

Those who remained neutral in the battle were cursed to be born with black skin. This is the Mormon explanation for the Negro race. The spirits that fought most valiantly against Lucifer would be born into Mormon families on planet Earth. These would be the lighter skinned people, or "white and delightsome," as the Book of Mormon described them.

Early Mormon prophets taught that Elohim and one of his goddess wives came to Earth as Adam and Eve to start the human race. Thousands of years later, Elohim in human form once again journeyed to Earth from the star base Kolob, this time to have physical relations with the Virgin Mary in order to provide Jesus with a physical body.

Mormon Apostle Orson Hyde taught that after Jesus Christ grew to manhood he took at least three wives: Mary, Martha, and Mary Magdalene. Through these wives the Mormon Jesus supposedly fathered a number of children before he was crucified. Mormon founder Joseph Smith is supposedly one of his descendants.

According to the Book of Mormon, after his resurrection Jesus came to the Americas to preach to the Indians, who the Mormons believe are really Israelites. Thus the Jesus of Mormonism established the church in the Americas as he had in Palestine. By the year 421 A.D., the dark-skinned Israelites, known as Lamanites, had destroyed all of the white-skinned Nephites in a number of great battles. The Nephites' records were supposedly written on golden plates buried in the Hill Cumorah by Moroni, the last living Nephite.

About 1400 years later a young treasure-seeker named Joseph Smith, who was known for his tall tales, claimed to have uncovered the same gold plates near his home in upstate New York. He is now honored by Mormons as a prophet because he claimed to have had visions from the spirit world in which he was commanded to organize the Mormon Church because all Christian creeds were an abomination. It was Joseph Smith who originated most of these peculiar doctrines which millions today believe to be true.

By maintaining a rigid code of financial and moral requirements, and through performing secret temple rituals for themselves and the dead, the Latter-day Saints hope to prove their worthiness and thus become gods. The Mormons teach that everyone must stand at the final judgment before Joseph Smith, the Mormon Jesus, and Elohim."[39]

FALSE DOCTRINES OF MORMONISM

XII.   WHAT DOES THE BIBLE TEACH ABOUT THE MORMON DOC-
       TRINE THAT GOD THE FATHER HAS A BODY OF FLESH AND
       BONE.?

A. The Bible teaches that God the Father is Spirit.
    "But the hour is coming, and now is, when the true worshipers will worship the Father in spirit and truth; for the Father is seeking such to worship him. God is a Spirit...." (Jn. 4:23-24)
B. The Bible teaches that spirit does not have flesh and bone.
    "Behold My hands and My feet, that it is I Myself. Handle Me, and see, for a spirit does not have flesh and bones as you see I have." (Lk. 24:39)
C. The Bible teaches that the Father is not flesh and blood.
    "And Jesus answered and said to him, 'Blessed are you, Simon Bar-Jonah: for flesh and blood has not revealed this to you, but my Father who is in heaven." (Matt. 16:17)

XIII. WHAT DOES THE BIBLE TEACH ABOUT THE MORMON DOCTRINE OF POLYTHEISM AND MALE MORMONS STRIVING TO BECOME GOD?

Polytheism = Belief in the existence of more than one God.

A. The Bible teaches that there is only one Lord and God.
    "Hear, O Israel: the LORD our God, the LORD is one" (Deut. 6:4)
    "There is...One Lord, One God and Father of all...." (Eph. 4:4-6) KJV
    Other Scriptures: Isaiah 45:5, 6, 14, 21-22; 46:9
B. The Bible teaches that there has been and only ever will be one God.
    "You are My witnesses, says the Lord, and My servant whom I have chosen, that you may know Me, believe Me and remain steadfast to Me, and understand that I am He. Before Me there was no God formed, neither shall there be after Me. I, even I, am the Lord, and besides Me there is no Savior." (Is. 43:10-11) AMP
C. The Bible teaches that the deception of becoming god was a part of Satan's plot.
    "Then the serpent said to the woman, 'You will not surely die: For God knows that in the day you eat of it your eyes will be opened, and you will be like God, knowing good and evil." (Gen. 3:4-5) KJV

XIV. HOW DO THE MORMONS REPRESENT "JESUS" AND HOW DOES THE BIBLE REFUTE THEM?
A. They teach that there was a time when the spirit of Jesus Christ did not exist. After his spirit was begotten (by God the Father and mother in heaven) and raised to maturity in a pre-mortal state, he obtained a body and was resurrected, just as his father before him. But the Bible teaches that Jesus Christ remains the same.

"Jesus Christ is the same yesterday, today, and forever." (Heb. 13:8)
NIV

B. They teach that Jesus is but one god in a pantheon of gods.
However, the Bible teaches that there is only one God, and He has
revealed Himself to us as the Triune Father, Son, and Holy Spirit.
The Bible tells us that Jesus Christ is the everlasting Father and
only true God.
*"For to us a child is born...And he will be called...Mighty God,
Everlasting Father...."* (Is. 9:6) NIV
*"We know also that the Son of God has come and has given us under-
standing, so that we may know him who is true. And we are in him
who is true—even in his Son Jesus Christ. He is the true God and eternal life."* (1 John 5:20) NIV

C. They teach that his spirit brother is Satan. However, the Bible does
not teach this. It teaches rather that Jesus was the only Son of God.
"For God so loved the world that he gave his one and only Son...." (Jn.
3:16) NIV
*"For God so greatly loved and dearly prized the world that He [even]
gave up His only-begotten (unique) Son...."* (Jn. 3:16) AMP

D. They teach that he was born through the physical act of sex
between the Mormon Father God and Mary. However, this is contrary to the Scriptures that teach that Jesus was conceived by the
Spirit of God.
*"This is how the birth of Jesus Christ came about: His mother Mary
was pledged to be married to Joseph, but before they came together, she
was found to be with child through the Holy Spirit."* (Matt. 1:18) NIV
*"Then the angel said to her, The Holy Spirit will come upon you, and
the power of the Most High will overshadow you (as a shining cloud);
and so the holy (pure, sinless) Thing which shall be born of you, will
be called the Son of God."* (Lk. 1:35) AMP

E. Some of the early leaders taught that blood atonement was required
by sinners for certain sins. Although this is not currently taught in
Mormonism, it is important for Christians to understand the confusion that has existed in the history of Mormon doctrine over the
issue of blood. Author James Spencer in his excellent book *Have
You Witnessed to a Mormon Lately?* shows us that Smith and Young
taught that the blood of Jesus was not sufficient for some sin.

"Blood atonement in Mormon doctrine says it is sometimes
necessary to 'shed a man's blood to save his soul.' The idea is that
he can commit sins that are so grievous that he can only go to
heaven if his own blood is shed, that is, if he is killed...This doctrine...was birthed in a vision of Joseph Smith's in which he said he

(Peter) had killed Judas—that he had hung him for betraying Christ...Brigham Young, as usual, carried the doctrine to its logical ultimate conclusion. He said if he found a brother in bed with his wife he would: 'Put a javelin through both of them, [and be] justified, and they would atone for their sins, and be received into the kingdom of God...I would do it with clean hands...There is not a man or woman, who violates the covenants made with their God, that will not be required to pay the debt. *The blood of Christ will never wipe that out, your own blood must atone for it'*...So widespread was the knowledge of the doctrine of Blood Atonement that the Utah Capital punishment law was written to include a form of death that would shed blood...Even to this day [prior to 1990] all participants in Mormon temple ceremonies place their right thumbs under their left ears and draw the thumb quickly across the throat to the right ear to 'symbolize the penalty' for revealing the temple ceremony."[40] [italics added]

Thinking Through The Scripture

"And the blood of Jesus Christ His Son cleanses us from all sin...If we confess our sins, He is faithful and just to forgive us our sins, and to cleanse us from all unrighteousness." (1 John 1:7,9)

"For you know that it was not with perishable things such as silver or gold that you were redeemed from the empty way of life handed down to you from your forefathers, but with the precious blood of Christ." (1 Peter 1:18-19) NIV

Questions for discussion:
1. How many of our sins are cleansed by Christ's blood when we confess? Are there any examples of sins that are not covered if we confess and repent?
2. Consider the note below. How does Mormon doctrine collide with the Scriptures? Also, look up Heb. 9:11-14 and Col. 1:20 and compare.

Note: Today, the Mormon church does not teach the taking of life to atone for one's sins, nor do they make participants in temple rituals do blood oaths, however, they do teach that some sins are not forgivable either in this world or the next. An example of this would be in Doctrine and Covenants, section 42:18-19, 79 in regard to killing. In their system, one who kills cannot find forgiveness in God either now or in the future. The whole issue shows that the Mormons have still not worked out the concept of how complete and sufficient the shed blood of Christ is for every single sin. Also, notice that you *never see a cross* on Mormon churches and that *they don't use grape juice or wine for a communion element to represent the blood of Christ.* Rather, they use water which takes the emphasis off of the blood of Christ.

XV.   HOW DO THE MORMONS REPRESENT "SALVATION" AND HOW DOES THE BIBLE REFUTE THEM?

A.   Mormon Salvation = faith + baptism + obedience to the laws and ordinances + membership in the Mormon church. But the Bible teaches that salvation is strictly a faith issue with God because we can't become "good enough" to earn it.

"Knowing that a man is not justified by the works of the law, but by faith in Jesus Christ, even we have believed in Christ Jesus, that we might be justified by faith in Christ and not by works of the law...." (Gal. 2:16)

"For by grace you have been saved through faith; and that not of your-selves: it is the gift of God, not of works, lest any one should boast." (Eph. 2:8-9)

Other Scriptures: John 6:28-29; 1 John 5:11-13

B.   Mormons keep genealogies to proxy salvation and baptism for the dead. But the Bible tells us that taking note of endless genealogies is unproductive.

"As I urged you when I went into Macedonia, stay there in Ephesus so that you may command certain men not to teach false doctrines any longer nor to devote themselves to myths and endless genealogies. These promote controversies rather than God's work—which is by faith." (1 Tim. 1:3-4) NIV

"But avoid foolish controversies and genealogies and arguments and quarrels about the law, because these are unprofitable and useless." (Tit. 3:9) NIV

C.   In order to obtain the highest exaltation in the Celestial Kingdom and become gods, Mormonism teaches that couples must be married in the Temple. The ceremony involves them being sealed for time and eternity by taking vows in a secret ritualistic ceremony. According to Ed Decker and David Hunt in the new edition of their book, *The God Makers*, this is causing thousands of divorces today. Why? Because Mormon authorities influence those married to non Mormons. They convince them to get divorced and marry a Mormon who willing submits to the Temple ceremony. Decker and Hunt say, "The amazing thing is that there is not one verse in either the Bible or the Book of Mormon that teaches celestial marriage for eternity involving secret or even sacred rituals in a Temple, much less that says it is essential for eternal life."[41]

In the Fall of 1999, I toured the new Temple just outside of Spokane, Washington, with a friend. This was but one of thirty that was to be built around the world that year as Mormonism expanded. The new Temples are smaller, less expensive, and easier to build. When I got into the room of "sealing" where couples say vows for time and eternity I decided to ask a question. People were standing around with badges for tourists who had questions. So I simply ask a young woman, "Why would God hear and accept the vows said in this room but not the same vows proclaimed in a different place?" I am still learning about Mormonism, so I figured that she would have an answer for me. Yet, she could not answer this simple question. So I asked her, "Where is this taught in the Bible?" She went and got a superior who gave me a bad time and who also could not answer the questions. Her suggestion was that the missionary by the front door could answer it. However, his answer simply referred to "new revelation." In other words, we are back on the subjective issue. They do it because some authority got a supposed revelation. The weird thing today is that the practices of Mormonism contradict its own Book of Mormon.

XVI. WHAT'S THE SAD TRUTH ABOUT MORMONISM?
   A.   They have turned away to fables. 2 Timothy 4:3-4
   B.   They have exchanged the truth of God for a lie. Romans 1:22-25
   C.   They have been working hard, but not for God's righteousness. Romans 10:1-3

End Notes

1. James R. Spencer, *Have You Witnessed to a Mormon Lately?* (Grand Rapids, MI: Fleming H. Revell, 1993), p. 26, 33.
2. Andy Butcher, "Penetrating the Mysterious World of Mormonism," *Charisma and Christian Life*, August, 1996, p. 53.
3. Josh McDowell, *The Best of Josh McDowell: A Ready Defense* (Nashville, TN: Thomas Nelson Publishers, 1993), p. 343.
4. David Van Biema, "Kingdom Come," *Time Magazine*, August 4, 1997, p. 52.
5. John Heinerman and Anson Shupe, *The Mormon Corporate Empire* (Boston, MA: Beacon Press, 1985), p. 1.
6. Ibid., pgs. 109-127.
7. Ibid., p. 22.
8. John L. Brooke, *The Refiner's Fire* (New York: Cambridge University Press, 1994), p. 225.
9. Walter Martin, *The Kingdom of the Cults* (Minneapolis, MN: Bethany House Publishers, 1985), p. 166.
10. Richard Kyle, *The Religious Fringe: A History of Alternative Religions in America* (Downers Grove, IL: Inter Varsity Press, 1993), p. 90.

11. James Coates, *In Mormon Circles: Gentiles, Jack Mormons, and Latter-day Saints* (Reading, MA: Addison-Wesley Publishing Company, Inc., 1991), p. ix.

12. Ibid., p. 142.

13. Spencer, p. 27.

14. Heinerman and Shupe, p.31.

15. Ibid., p. 226

16. Ron Carlson and Ed Decker, *Fast Facts On False Teachings* (Eugene, OR: Harvest House Publishers, 1994), p. 165.

17. Martin, p.203.

18. Walter Martin, *The Maze of Mormonism* (Ventura, CA: Vision House, 1984), pgs. 33-38.

19. Fawn M. Brodie, *No Man Knows My History* (New York: Alfred A. Knopf, 1946), pgs. 46-49.

20. Spencer, pgs. 201-210.

21. Brooke, p. 35.

22. Brodie, p. 45.

23. Brodie, preface ix.

24. Harry L. Ropp, *Are the Mormon Scriptures Reliable?* (Downers Grove, IL: Inter Varsity Press, 1987), p. 80.

25. Ibid., p. 95

26. Brodie, pgs. 171-172.

27. Spencer, p. 41.

28. Brooke, p. 129.

29. Brodie, pgs. 19, 409.

30. Ibid., p. 40.

31. Martin, pgs. 33-40.

32. E. D. Howe, *Mormonism Unveiled* (Zanesville, Ohio, 1834), p. 261.

33. Martin, *Kingdom of the Cults*, p. 175.

34. Brodie, pgs. 334-347.

35. Ibid., p. 181.

36. Brooke, p. 157.

37. Coates, p. 216.

38. William J. Schnoebelen and James R. Spencer, *Whited Sepulchers* (Boise, ID: Triple J. Publishers, 1990), pgs. 14-20, 25.

39. Carlson and Decker, p. 167.

40. Spencer, pgs. 148-150.

41. Ed Decker and David Hunt, *The God Makers* (Harvest House Publishers, Eugene, OR, 1997), p. 64.

QUESTIONNAIRE: LESSON THREE

NAME: _____ DATE: _____

1. What are some of the words that Joseph Smith Jr. used to describe his first impression of the angel that he encountered? _____
_____ What Scripture warns us about Satan coming as "an angel of light"? _____

2. Do all angels that come to men necessarily represent God? Yes No

3. Explain in a few sentences what the Reorganized Church is: _____
_____
_____
_____

4. List three main evangelistic strategies that Mormons use today:

a) _____

b) _____

c) _____

5. Even though Mormons admit that Jesus came in the flesh, the passage in 2 John 7-12 applies to them. Explain why: _____
_____
_____

6. In the 1980's Utah was dubbed _____ because so many investors were being swindled out of their money.

7. What is the main heresy of the Mormon religion? Write out two Scriptures to refute it. _____
_____
_____

8. Do Mormons believe that the King James Bible is more important than their other sacred books? Yes No

9. List the five basic parts of Joseph Smith Jr.'s life according to the study.

a) _____

b) _____

c) _____

d) _____

e) _____

10. What is one thing you learned from reading about the core of Mormon belief that you did not know they believed. _____

_____

_____

11. Tell about an experience that you have had with Mormonism. Perhaps it was your involvement, someone you knew, or an encounter. _____

_____

_____

_____

_____

_____

12. Does the heavenly Father have a body of flesh and bone? _____

Write out one Scripture from the study to prove your answer. _____

_____

_____

13. How can we know that God did not evolve from man? _____

_____

_____

14. Mormon Salvation = faith + _____ + _____

+ _____

According to the Scriptures, the Mormon view of salvation is false. Explain why. _____

_____

_____

15. What are two sad truths about Mormonism:

a) _____

b) _____

MORMONISM

Part 2: Arguments, Problems and Witnessing to Mormons

"I feel cheated, deceived, and spiritually raped by a doctrine and philosophy that I embraced and trusted. It has been more than difficult to break away from the hold that Joseph Smith and his Book of Mormon have on me"[1]
—Kathryn, a former Mormon

DECEPTIVE ARGUMENTS OF MORMONISM

A Mormon term for non-Mormons is "Gentile." They teach that all non-Mormons are gentiles including Christians. They are taught that Joseph Smith was given a revelation that all Christian sects are wrong, "that all of their creeds were an abomination in his [God's] sight, and that all their teachers were corrupt" (From *The Pearl of Great Price*, book of Joseph Smith, Chapter 2, verses 15-19). In 1990, Mormon leadership did make some diplomatic revisions eliminating from its temple endowment ceremonies "several controversial passages that cast all other religions...as the direct work of Satan."[2] However, they are still basically brain washed with the myth and fiction of Mormonism to believe that Christianity is an abomination to Christ.

They are tutored in how to win souls to Mormonism by confusing weak and ungrounded Christians. Below are some of the arguments that you might hear Mormons bring up in conversation. The best thing for Christians to do is 1) educate themselves about the arguments and what the real issues are, 2) not get shaken up by calculated attacks but put on the whole armor of God, and 3) let the love of Christ shine through you to them so that the Holy Spirit might show them the error of their way.

I.   WHAT SEVEN BASIC APPROACHES DO MORMON MISSIONARIES USE?
     A.   Restoration: Story of mirrors. The Catholic church perverted the true words of God.
     B.   Progression: All life has always existed and is working towards exaltation.
     C.   Revelation: God reveals answers to life's most difficult questions.
     D.   Ordinances: The Catholic church corrupted baptism by immersion and priesthood.
     E.   Patriarchy: Happiness comes through obeying the Living Prophet (LDS president).
     F.   Jesus Christ: Only Mormons know Him and His true history.
     G.   Heavens: Each "worthy male" is striving for exaltation and god-hood through works.[3]

II. WHAT ARE SOME TYPICAL QUESTIONS THEY MAY ASK?
     A. They may say, "Don't you know the Bible is very inaccurate?"
     Mormons do not recognize the Bible as the infallible Word of God. Their Eighth Article of Faith states "We believe the Bible to be the Word of God, as far as it is translated correctly; We also believe the *Book of Mormon* to be the Word of God". The Bible takes second place to the *Book of Mormon* because Mormons are taught that the Bible has been "mutilated, changed, and corrupted" (From *The Bible Alone, an Insufficient Guide*, pgs. 44-47 by the Mormon prophet Orson Pratt).
     The *Book of Mormon* also tears down the Bible in 1 Nephi 13:26-29 when it accuses the "great and abominable church" of removing "many plain and precious things" regarding "the gospel of the Lamb" from Scripture. Christians need not run from any argument about the Bible's accuracy - they must simply become well informed and be able to present the truth. Here are some questions to ask Mormons if the subject comes up.
          1.   Do you know that there is more overwhelming support for the accuracy of Scripture than any other book ever written in the history of mankind - over 24,000 original manuscripts of the New Testament from Greek, Latin, etc.?
          2.   Do you know that the Dead Sea Scrolls unearthed within the last few decades undeniably confirm the accuracy of the Old Testament?
          3.   Have you ever read *Evidence That Demands a Verdict*, by Josh

McDowell or any of the other hundreds of books that confirm the Bible's accuracy? (You might want to have a copy of Josh McDowell's book on hand.)

4. Do you know that history, archaeology, science, and the fulfillment of Biblical prophecy also support and confirm Biblical accuracy?

5. Do you know that Jesus quoted from the Old Testament verifying its accuracy?

6. Do you think that it is logically consistent that God would give us His Word and then not keep it and preserve it? Have you ever read through the Bible?

7. Have you considered that 2 Nephi 29 does not deny the accuracy of the Bible?

B. They may ask, "Where did you get your authority?"

Mormonism teaches that they have the only true priesthood. One rationale is this: Jesus chose twelve apostles. When Judas died, it took all eleven apostles to choose a new one. After Jesus' death they were separated and killed. Since the quorum of apostles chose no other apostles, the priesthood died out - that is until Smith came along. Author James R. White explains in his book *Letters To A Mormon Elder* that "supposedly the Aaronic priesthood was conferred on Joseph Smith and Oliver Cowdery on May 15, 1829, and then, sometime in June of the same year, Peter, James, and John supposedly appeared and conferred the Melchizedek priesthood upon them...Joseph did not claim to hold the priesthood until after the founding of the church in 1830, and that he was more than willing to 'edit' previously written revelations to 'insert' the concept of the priesthood so that it appeared to have been a part of his original teachings (i.e., Section 27 of the D&C being a prime example)."[4] Smith named eleven other apostles.

Today, there are twelve apostles in the church. When one dies, all the others must meet to fill the vacancy. Also, the elders of the church consider themselves of the Melchizedek priesthood. Mormons will ask, "Who gives your pastor the priesthood right to marry, bury, and baptize?" Here's some questions to ask Mormons if the subject comes up.

1. Do you think it is logically consistent that Joseph Smith could choose eleven apostles by himself and yet one of the original apostles could not.?

2. Did you know that the New Testament calls other people apostles besides the twelve? 1) Barnabas (Acts 14:3-4, 14); 2) Andronicus & Junias (Romans 16:7); 3) Silas & Timothy (1 Thess. 1:1, 2:6); 4) James, the Lord's brother (Gal. 1:19); 5) Paul (Rom. 1:5, 1 Cor. 1:1, 2 Cor. 1:1).

3. Did you know that the Apostle Peter calls all those that believe a royal priesthood? *"Therefore, to you who believe, He is precious;...But you are a chosen generation, a royal priesthood...."* (1 Peter 2:7,9)

4. Did you know that the Apostle Paul had no quorum of apostles to make him an apostle? *"Paul, an apostle, (not from men nor through man, but through Jesus Christ, and God the Father, who raised him from the dead)"* (Gal. 1:1)

5. Are you of the tribe of Levi? Have you done the rites necessary to be ordained in the Aaronic priesthood? Exodus 29; Leviticus 8.

C. **They may ask, "Why do you challenge our good works? Don't you know that faith without works is dead?**

Note: We shouldn't criticize the "good works" of Mormons, and many do good works. The real problem is this: 1) Why they do good works, and 2) In whom they have faith.

WHY THEY DO GOOD WORKS: Mormon doctrine of salvation includes works as a prerequisite to Celestial Heaven. This is missing the truth in a couple of ways. First, their view of heaven is inaccurate, which will be discussed later on. Second, their view of what it takes to get to heaven is in error. Two prominent verses in the *Book of Mormon* show their view that the grace of God is not enough, but that works are needed. By these, they deny the sufficiency of the grace of God. Nevertheless, this is simply not accurate. Ephesians 2:8-9 clearly shows that it is by grace and not works that we are saved. Salvation through works would only let us boast. The thief on the cross who repented had no chance to do good works, obey the laws and ordinances, get baptized, or join the Mormon church, and yet he got saved and went to heaven. The reason the Mormons work is to gain exaltation in heaven, whereas, the reason Christians work is out of a heart of love and appreciation for what Christ did for them at Calvary.

IN WHOM THEY HAVE FAITH: Mormons will say they have faith in Jesus Christ. Perhaps some do, but if they have swallowed the lie that some of them are evolving into gods, then their faith is in *"another [false] Jesus"*—2 Cor. 11:4. Here are some questions to ask Mormons if the subject comes up!

1. What do you think you will gain by good works? Consider who should get the glory for your works by looking at Ephesians 2:10 and Philippians 2:13.

2. Do you know that Jesus told us what work God wants us to work? *"Then they said to Him, 'What shall we do, that we may*

work the works of God?' Jesus answered and said to them, 'This is the work of God, that you believe in Him He sent." (John 6:28-29)

3. In what are you placing your faith for salvation?

D. **They may ask, "Why do you oppose our idea of becoming gods? Don't you know that the Bible says there are many gods and lords?"**

Actually, they may avoid this topic with Christians because they know it is controversial. However, it is important to establish that this is what they believe. A couple of local Mormon missionaries (young men) were trying to convert a teenage girl who drifted from youth group to youth group. Her home life was messed up because of broken relationships, and it caused her faith to waver. Since she was hurting, she was looking more for attention than truth. They gave it to her and soon she was attending the Mormon church and preparing for baptism. I had some influence in the girl's life, and so I was able to get together with her and the missionaries in my office. Although I tried to be cordial, I also knew that this was possibly the only chance I would have to expose what Mormonism teaches regarding men becoming gods. The missionaries tried to avoid my direct questions but eventually had to admit that they did believe they could become gods. I would like to say that the girl immediately responded to this and gave up Mormonism, but it took a little while for her to come to grips with the truth. After a few weeks, she came to see that what they taught was wrong and she did leave. Hallelujah!

Most Mormons have been taught just enough of the Scripture to be dangerous. They might refer you to 1 Cor. 8:5 where Paul refers to many gods and lords. But they single this verse out, thus taking it out of context. In the passage, Paul is addressing the issue of whether or not Christians should eat food sacrificed to demons (idols) in the pagan marketplace. When you read the verse before and after, it becomes clear that Paul is saying that while there are so called "gods", Christians believe there is only one God. Therefore the meat has not been defiled because someone put it in a pagan temple. Read the passage below.

"Therefore concerning the eating of things offered to idols, we know that an idol is nothing in the world, and *that there is no other God but one.* - verse 4

For even if there are so-called gods, whether in heaven or in earth, (as there are many gods and lords), - verse 5

yet to us there is one God, the Father, of whom are all things, and we for him; *and one Lord Jesus Christ,* through whom are all things, and through whom we live." - verse 6

Here are some questions to ask Mormons if the subject comes up!

1. Have you read the verse before and after 1 Cor. 8:5?
2. Why do you think Paul says there is but one God? Who taught you this meaning?
3. Have you considered the use of the word "god" in Jeremiah 10:11, Psalm 82:6-7, or Exodus 7:1? It is obvious that the word does not refer to supernatural beings.

E. **They may ask, "Why don't you believe in baptism for the dead like the Bible says?"**

The Mormons have formed a major doctrine around a single, isolated verse in 1 Corinthians 15:29. They teach that they can be baptized for dead unbelievers, purchasing for the dead a place in Mormon heaven. They spend vast amounts of time and money investigating their dead ancestors in order to be baptized for them. Although the motivation is not wrong, the action is a vain work The verse in question states:

"Now if there is no resurrection, what will those do who are baptized for the dead? If the dead are not raised at all, why are people baptized for them?" (1 Cor. 15:29) NIV

Commentators indicate that this is probably the most difficult verse to understand in the entire New Testament. However, the true meaning lies no where near what the Mormons contrived. Much of chapter fifteen is written by Paul to cause critical thinking about the resurrection of the dead. In verse 12 he asks, "How can some of you say there is no resurrection of the dead?" His purpose is to convince the reader through various arguments that there is a resurrection. The true meaning of the verse lies closer to one of the following views:

•   Paul often liked to use cultural views to prove his points, so some commentators believe he was referring to the pagans' ritual of being baptized for the dead to prove that even they believe in the resurrection. Therefore, so ought we to believe. This argument is based on the pronoun change. Notice that in the verses surrounding verse 29 Paul uses "we," but in the verse itself he uses "they."

•   Just as plausible is the idea that Paul is arguing that Christians have symbolically entered into Christ's death through water baptism and a life of sacrifice—and that "our" baptism into "our" death would all be in vain if there was no literal resurrection of the dead. This idea of symbolic death makes sense when you consider that in verse 31 Paul states that he [symbolically] dies daily.

•   Another thought expressed later in the chapter is that the perishable or mortal body will be changed in the resurrection to a body imperishable and immortal. Verse 29 could simply be referring to the two different states of the same person before and after resurrection.

Here are some questions to ask Mormons if the subject comes up!

1. If this is so important, why isn't it mentioned anywhere else in the Bible?
2. Where in the verse does it say that the act produces salvation for the dead?

F. **They may ask, "Have you prayed about whether or not the book of Mormon is true?**

This is a subtle way of getting a Christian off track and making him consider that he has a moral responsibility to seek God subjectively regarding every matter.

It is amazing to me that Mormon missionaries constantly base their view of truth on subjective feeling alone. For instance, they will say, "This is my testimony that Joseph Smith was a true Prophet of God and that the Mormon Church is the only true Church on the earth." There are a billion Muslims that would disagree because they have been taught to chant "There is no god but Allah and Muhammad is Allah's Apostle." Both of these statements condition people's thinking based upon feelings rather than objective truth.

Mormons say, "Pray about all this and ask God if it is true and you will receive a burning in the bosom to confirm it." This comes from Doctrine and Covenants 9:8. It says, "your bosom shall burn within you; therefore, you shall feel that it is right." However, people feel a lot of things but that does not make it right. New Age cults teach people to feel the divine power within and become God. Feelings are simply emotions that are easily triggered by what we believe. If one wants to believe Joseph Smith for whatever reason than he goes into the prayer with a preconditioned mind set which then mentally stimulates an experience of a burning in the bosom. Hypnotists use this form of auto suggestion all the time. It is nothing new, and it proves nothing.

In all of this, notice that there is no testimony about Jesus as personal Savior. The outcome is not based upon reason, right or wrong, or agreement with the Bible, but upon an experience. As Christians, we do not need to seek God about whether lies and heresies are true.

Ask the Mormons to consider 1 Thessalonians 5:21, 1 John 4:1, and Proverbs 28:26 regarding the need for testing the spirit of a thing. There are many inconsistencies with the *Book of Mormon* so here are some questions to ask Mormons to help them see the errors of the book.

1. Why is it translated in 16th century King James English rather than the dialect of 19th century New England English?

2. Why is use of the magnetic compass found in 1 Nephi 16:10; 16:26-30; 18:12,21; 2 Nephi 5:12, etc. when it wasn't even invented until 1000 A.D.?

3. Why is the word "church" (1 Nephi 4:26) so common throughout the book when the word is actually from the New Testament Greek "ekklesia"?

4. Do you know that it has an abundance of quotations from the New Testament even though it was supposedly written 600 years before?

5. Do you know that there is much evidence showing that Smith borrowed heavily from a previous book entitled *View of the Hebrews; or the Ten Tribes of Israel in America* by Ethan Smith.[5]

6. Why did young Joseph use a dream his father had as a vision Lehi had in 1 Nephi 8? Lucy Smith recorded it in her biographical sketches. Check *No Man Knows My History: The Life of Joseph Smith*, by Fawn Brodie, p. 58.

7. Do you understand that Smith borrowed many stories from the Bible? Some examples are "The daughter of Jared, like Salome, danced before a king and a decapitation followed. Abinadi, like Daniel, deciphered handwriting on a wall, and Alma was converted after the exact fashion of St. Paul. The daughters of the Lamanites were abducted like the dancing daughters of Shiloh; and Ammon, the American counterpart of David, for want of a Goliath slew six sheep-rustlers with his sling."[6]

8. "How could Joseph carry the golden plates around so easily, and how could the witness have 'hefted' the plates without (a recorded) difficulty when the plates had to weigh at least 230 pounds? (The plates are said to have been 7" X 8" X 6" high, and gold weighs 1204.7 pounds per square foot...)"[7]

9. Doesn't it make you suspicious that Joseph wrote in 2 Nephi 3:15 that a great seer named Joseph would one day arise?

10. Since God is logically consistent, why would God variate people's skin color according to sin and righteousness in places like 2 Nephi 5:21 and 3 Nephi 2:15 and not today?

11. Since Jacob 2:21-27 condemns having more than one wife, how do you justify Joseph Smith who had over 50?

12. How do you explain a modern word like "machinery" (book of Jarom, v. 8) in a book supposedly several thousands of years old?

13. Did Smith make a mistake when he wrote that Jesus was to be born in Jerusalem rather than Bethlehem in Alma 7:10?

14. How could the "gift of the Holy Ghost" (Alma 9:21) be given in 82 B.C., long before the day of Pentecost pictured in Acts 2?

15. How could there be "Christians" (Alma 46:13) long before the Christ came?

16. The book of Helaman (3:25-26) tells us about a great church in America and tens of thousands of believers getting baptized before Christ was even born, but there is no real evidence of that. Why?

17. Since 3 Nephi 15 and 16 state that Jesus went to visit "other sheep" and "tribes" besides America and Israel, why is there no accounting of it?

18. Mormon chapter 6 tells of a horrific battle near the hill Cumorah in which over a quarter of a million Nephite soldiers fought against a greater force of Lamanites. All the Nephites were killed. Compare this to the following: There were 38,000 casualties at Gettysburg, 204,000 battlefield casualties in all of the Civil war, 126,000 Americans died in WWI and 405,000 in WWII. How is it that such a battle, as the *Book of Mormon* describes, could occur without a shred of evidence?

19. Why do you think God would take such great care to keep the golden plates and allow only one man - a scoundrel - to see them before taking them to heaven?

20. Do you really think that the God of Love would hide something like this for so long and then expose it in such a suspicious manner that it makes honest seekers skeptical of its authenticity?

G. **They may ask, "Do you know the Bible confirms the Mormon view of three heavens?"**

Some Mormons think 2 Corinthians 12: 2 verifies their doctrine of three heavens. In this verse the Apostle Paul is referring to a man he knew [himself, it is believed] who had been "caught up to the third heaven". Throughout the Scriptures there are three different words for heaven as expressed below:

- "rekia" - the firmament or expansion: the Atmosphere.
- "shamayim" - the two heavens or expansions: the starry heaven
- "hashshamayim" - the heaven of heavens: the throne of His divine Glory

As you can see, the three levels of heaven simply refer to 1) The atmosphere or sky, 2) The universe containing the sun, moon, and stars, and 3) God's Dwelling Place. This last heaven is the one to which Paul was referring when he said the third heaven. It was simply his way of saying he got caught up into God's Glory. Mormon heaven is not really based upon this premise at all. Its three levels are as follows:

- *Celestial* - The highest level where Mormons will be exalted to varying degrees. There are actually three degrees or levels of the Celestial kingdom. Those who go to the highest level will be exalted as gods. "The inhabitants of this kingdom dwell in the very presence of God...In this heaven exclusively, Mormons are able to live with their spouses and children and possess the ability of continual procreation."[8]

- *Terrestrial* - This "will be the domain of 'honorable men of the earth' who either did not hear the Mormon gospel or who rejected it on the earth, but received it in the spirit world before the resurrection. This also will be the domain of lukewarm Mormons. Those who inhabit the terrestrial kingdom 'receive the presence of the Son, but not the Father,' and never get to marry and continue in exaltation."[9]

- *Telestial* - This is for the vast majority of people who have lived on planet earth. After the millennium and the second resurrection, any who are not sent to the outer darkness will go to the Telestial kingdom. It will be comprised of most of the wicked of the earth and yet it is not a bad place to live. Its glory surpasses anything here on earth, and those in it will serve the Most High but cannot go where God dwells.

Here are some questions to ask Mormons if the subject comes up!
1. In light of what you believe, which level will a Christian go to?
2. In light of what Christians believe, where will you go if we are right?
3. Would you like to hear what the Bible has to say about salvation and eternal life?

Thinking Through The Scripture

"And I will pour on the house of David and on the inhabitants of Jerusalem the spirit of grace and supplication: then they will look on Me whom they pierced. Yes, they will mourn for Him, as one mourns for his only son, and grieve for Him, as one grieves for a firstborn." (Zechariah 12:10)

Questions for discussion:
1. How does this verse show the concept of the Trinity?
2. How does it display the omnipresence of God?

H. They may ask, "How did Jesus pray to himself in the garden of Gethsemane?"

To Mormons Jesus is just one of many gods. As author Anthony A. Hoekema says in his book *Mormonism*, "The Christ of Mormonism is a far cry from the Christ of Scriptures."[10] Neither do they have a true concept of the Trinity (The Father, The Son, and The Holy Spirit); nor do they have a true concept of a God who is omnipotent, omniscient, or omnipresent. They think of God's nature in terms of human reasoning and cannot conceive how he can be in more than one place at once. Of course, to the Christian there is only one True God, but within the nature of that one God, there are three eternal Persons who exist without confusion and without separation. God is much bigger than Mormon theology allows.

EXPOSING PROBLEMS

III. WHY IS THERE A PROBLEM IN THE BOOK OF MORMON WITH ARCHAEOLOGICAL AND HISTORICAL ACCURACY?

   A. Because archaeologists firmly deny the existence of any such cultures as the Lamanites or Nephites in America at the time described in the book. From author Peter Bartley in *Mormonism: The Prophet, the Book, and the Cult,* we learn that "No iron, steel, or brass, no chariots, swords, shields, breastplates or any form of armour have ever been recovered from pre-Columbian archaeological sites...The ox, the horse and the ass which the Nephites, and the Jaredites before them, are said to have possessed were introduced into America by Europeans, as were the cattle, sheep and swine which the Jaredites are supposed to have domesticated."[11] Furthermore, there is no evidence for gold and silver coins, compasses, wheeled vehicles, tents, linen, or shipbuilding.

   B. Because the language and terminology expressed in the book display modern day concepts and cultural experiences rather than those of the sixth century B.C.

   C. Because American Indians could not possibly have descended from the "Laminites" (a fictitious Semitic race of Jewish origin) as the book contends, since physical anthropologists, who specialize in genetics, have proven that the blood factors and apparent characteristics make it impossible.

   D. In his book *Are the Mormon Scriptures Reliable?*, Harry Ropp tells us of a false claim that is made sometimes. He says, "Mormon missionaries have often claimed that the Smithsonian Institution uses the Book of Mormon as a guide to its archaeological research. This claim is untrue."[12]

   In actuality, the National Museum of Natural History refutes that claim as well as any evidence for the legitimacy of the Book of Mormon. The Department of Anthropology at the Smithsonian Institute prepared the following statement regarding the Book of Mormon on behalf of the National Museum of Natural History.

Statement Regarding The Book Of Mormon

1. The Smithsonian Institution has never used the Book of Mormon in any way as a scientific guide. Smithsonian archaeologists see no direct connection between the archaeology of the New World and the subject matter of the book.

2. The physical type of the American Indian is basically Mongoloid, being most closely related to that of the peoples of eastern, central, and northeastern Asia. Archaeological evidence indicates that the ancestors of the present Indians came into the New World—probably over a land bridge known to have existed in the Bering Strait region during the last Ice Age—in a continuing series of small migrations from about 25,000 to 30,000 years ago.

3. Present evidence indicates that the first people to reach this continent from the East were the Norsemen, who briefly visited the northeastern part of North America around 1000 A.D. and then settled in Greenland. There is no evidence to show that they reached Mexico or Central America.

4. None of the principal Old World domesticated food plants or animals (except the dog) occurred in the New World in the pre-Columbian times. This is one of the main lines of evidence supporting the scientific premise that contacts with Old World civilizations, if they occurred, were of very little significance for the development of American Indian civilizations. American Indians had no wheat, barley, oats, millet, rice, cattle, pigs, chickens, horses, donkeys or camels before 1492. (Camels and horses were in the Americas, along with the bison, mammoth, and mastodon, but all these animals became extinct around 10,000 B.C. at the time the early big game hunters traveled across the Americas.)

5. Iron, steel, glass, and silk were not used in the New World before 1492 (except for occasional use of unsmelted meteoric iron). Native copper was worked in various locations in pre-Columbian times, but true metallurgy was limited to southern Mexico and the Andean region, where its occurrence in late prehistoric times involved gold, silver, copper, and their alloys, but not iron.

6. There is a possibility that the spread of cultural traits across the Pacific to Mesoamerica and the Northwestern coast of South America began several hundred years before the Christian era. However, any such inter-hemispheric contacts appear to have been the results of accidental voyages originating in eastern

and southern Asia. It is by no means certain that such contacts occurred; *certainly, there were no contacts with the ancient Egyptians, Hebrews, or other peoples of Western Asia and the Near East.*

7. No reputable Egyptologist or other specialist on Old World archaeology, and no expert on New World prehistory, has discovered or confirmed any relationship between archaeological remains in Mexico and archaeological remains in Egypt.

8. Reports of findings of ancient Egyptian, Hebrew, and other Old World writings in the New World in pre-Columbian contexts have frequently appeared in newspapers, magazines, and sensational books. *None of these claims has stood up to examination by reputable scholars.* No inscriptions using Old World forms of writing have been shown to have occurred in any part of the Americas before 1492 except for a few Norse rune stones, which have been found in Greenland. (underline added)

Note: While there is a dispute over certain dates that the Smithsonian proposes in the statement above (i.e. 25,000 to 30,000 years), the other evidence seems clear that the entire account of the *Book of Mormon* has no scientific or archaeological validity according to the Smithsonian Institute. (Copies may be requested from the Smithsonian Institute in Washington, D.C. 20560).

IV. WHY IS THERE A PROBLEM IN THE BOOK OF MORMON WITH PLAGIARISM?

A. Because as Walter Martin tells us, "it contains at least *25,000 words from the King James Bible...*The comparison of Moroni chapter 10 with 1 Corinthians 12:1-11, 2 Nephi 14 with Isaiah 4, and 2 Nephi 12 with Isaiah 2 reveals that Joseph Smith made free use of his Bible to supplement the alleged revelation of the golden plates. The book of Mosiah, chapter 14 in the *Book of Mormon*, is a reproduction of the fifty-third chapter of Isaiah the prophet; and 3 Nephi 13:1-18 copies Matthew 6:1-23."[13]

Thinking Through The Scripture

"There will be false teachers among you...In their greed these teachers will exploit you with stories they have made up." (2 Peter 2:1-3) NIV

"For the time is coming when [people] will not tolerate (endure) sound and wholesome instruction, but having ears itching [for something pleasing and gratifying] they...will turn aside from hearing the truth and wander off into myths and man-made fictions." (2 Timothy 4:3-4) AMP

Questions for discussion:
1. How do these verses apply to Mormonism with regard to archaeological findings?
2. In your opinion, what are the basic myths of Mormonism?
3. What are other modern-day myths that people often entertain?

B. Because, the alleged translation of *"reformed Egyptian Hieroglyphics"* came out in perfect *King James English* over one thousand years before it was spoken.

C. Because as James Spencer tells us, "The only passages spelled correctly and correct grammatically, are the chapters of Isaiah Joseph [Smith] lifted whole out of the King James Bible. The King James passages are, in fact, verbatim, proving that Joseph did not translate them from reformed Egyptian hieroglyphics as he claimed. Joseph so faithfully plagiarized the King James passages that *he even included the italicized words in the text—the transitional words the King James translators added for clarity, but which were not in the Hebrew text.*"[14]

D. Because at the end of Jacob's chapter, he bids farewell and says, *"Brethren, adieu"* (Jacob 7:27). This word adieu is a modern day *French word* that Joseph Smith is saying was translated from reformed Egyptian hieroglyphics.

V. WHY IS THERE A PROBLEM IN THE BOOK OF MORMON WITH AUTHENTICITY?
A. Because the testimony of the three witnesses which appears at the front of the Book of Mormon (Oliver Cowdery, David Whitmer, and Martin Harris) that "...an angel of God came down from heaven, and he brought and laid before our eyes, that we beheld and saw the plates, and the engraving thereon..." was later denied by Martin Harris, who admitted that he had not seen them with his natural eyes but spiritual only.[15] All three quarreled with Smith, left the Mormon faith, and were described by Mormon contemporaries as thieves and counterfeits. However, two of them, Cowdery and Harris, did eventually return and get rebaptized.

B. Because there is great probability that the bulk of the Book of Mormon came out of several sources from which Joseph heavily borrowed. Consider the following:
1. **View of the Hebrews:** There are striking similarities between the book of Mormon and Ethan's Smith's earlier book *View of the Hebrews; or the Ten Tribes of Israel in America.* Even B. H. Roberts (a deceased Mormon scholar) found no less than 18

major parallels between the *View of the Hebrews; or the Ten Tribes of Israel* and the *Book of Mormon*.[16] These are stated in his book entitled *Studies of the Book of Mormon*.

2. **Spaulding Theory:** There is controversy over this theory. Certain adversaries to Smith's authorship of the Book of Mormon use a manuscript written in 1812 by Solomon Spaulding. He was a Congregational preacher and graduate of Dartmouth College who wrote a book entitled *Manuscript Found*. It is about the intrigue of a lost important document found even as the *Book of Mormon* purports to be.

   Solomon Spaulding knew Sidney Rigdon and thought he stole the manuscript.[17] Proponents of this theory say that after Spaulding died in 1816, there were eye witnesses that substantiated Spaulding's premonition about Rigdon's thievery. Joseph Smith and Sidney Rigdon eventually met, and Rigdon became an important part of Mormonism. Also, contemporaries of Spaulding, who had both seen and heard Spaulding read out of the manuscript, claim that the Book of Mormon was in fact Spaulding's stolen manuscript.[18]

   On the other hand, the theory has some major holes in it. The account of the eye witnesses is weak and the memory of the friends and relatives was proven to be unreliable. They were trying to remember what Spaulding had read aloud from twenty years prior. Also, the only original of *Manuscript Found* that can be located today is substantially different from the *Book of Mormon*. However, the supporters of the Spaulding theory say that the writer actually created two manuscripts and that the one Smith plagiarized from differs from the copy we have today.

3. **Other Possible Sources:** These might include *American Antiquities* by Josiah Priest, various newspaper articles, and sermons by leading preachers of that day.[19] The belief that the Hebrew-Indian tribe theory originated with Joseph Smith is fantasy.

Thinking Through The Scripture

"For nothing is secret, that will not be revealed, nor anything hidden that will not be known and come to light." (Luke 8:17)

"Therefore do not fear them. For there is nothing covered that will not be revealed, and hidden that will not be known." (Matthew 10:26)

Questions for discussion:
1. How do these apply to the *Book of Mormon*? When God brings something to light, is it a quick thing or does it take time?
2. How will the issues most troubling Mormonism come to the light?
3. Why should Christians not fear Mormon apologetics regarding the *Book of Mormon*? How can we best uncover the truth for Mormons?

VI. WHY IS THERE A PROBLEM WITH CHANGES IN THE BOOK OF MORMON?
   A. Because this alleged "most correct of any book on earth" has undergone about 4,000 major and minor changes since the 1830 edition.
   B. Because many of the changes had to take place since the original version showed itself to be the work of a very uneducated, human source rather than a translation by the "gift and power of God." Consider the following *lack of clarity*. The first two are from the 1830 edition and the last three are current.
       1) "Yea, if my days could have been *in them days*...But, behold, I am consigned that these are my days." (Helaman 7:8-9)
       2) "He went forth among the people, waving the rent of his garment in the air, that all might see the writing which he had wrote upon the rent." (Alma 46:19)
       3) "They being shielded from the more vital parts of the body, or the more vital parts of the body being shielded from the stokes of the Laminites." (Alma 43:38)
       4) "There were no robbers, nor murderers, neither were there Laminites, *nor any manner of ites*; but they were one, the children of Christ." (4 Nephi 1:17)
       5) Here is a major mistake that is still in modern day versions of the Book of Mormon. "And it came to pass, that when Coriantumur had leaned upon his sword, that he rested a little, he smote off the head of Shiz. And it came to pass that *after he had smitten off the head of Shiz, that Shiz raised upon his hands and fell; and after that he had struggled for breath, he died.*" (Ether 15:30-31) *Now how can someone with his head cut off rise up on his hands to take a breath of air?*

Thinking Through The Scripture

"God is not the author of confusion but of peace." (1 Corinthians 14:33)

"Heaven and earth will pass away, but my words will never pass away" (Mark 13:31) NIV

Questions for discussion:
1. What are the most confusing things about Mormonism's claims to you?
2. What weakness is found in the Mormon's claim that Smith translated the plates under the inspiration of the Holy Spirit?
3. How many mistakes "is too many mistakes" for claiming divine authorship?

VII. WHY IS THERE A PROBLEM BETWEEN MORMONISM AND ITS BOOK?
   A. Because the *Book of Mormon* is clearly *not polytheistic* but Mormonism is.
   B. Because the *Book of Mormon* denounced *polygamy* but Smith encouraged it.
   C. Because the original book cast Afro-Americans in an inferior status, but Mormons, under pressure of *the Civil Rights Movement changed the book* (2 Nephi 30:6) after a supposed revelation in 1978 that Afro-Americans could now hold the priesthood.
   D. Because even Mormon professors and theologians have questioned the authenticity of the Book.
      1) "No evidence has been found in the new world for a ferrous metallurgical industry dating to pre-Columbian times. And so this is a king-size kind of problem, it seems to me, for the so-called *Book of Mormon* archaeology. This evidence is absent."— BYU Anthropology Professor Ray T. Matheny[20]
      2) Another BYU anthropology professor, John L. Sorensen, told the Latter Day Saints that American Indians did not descend from the Hebrews, the Indian languages have no Hebrew root, the biological characteristics are completely different, and that the supposed geography of the Book of Mormon stretching from South America to New York state is inaccurate. He says that Mormons are going to have to *revise their concept of truth* about the *Book of Mormon*.[21]

Thinking Through The Scripture

"For although they knew God, they neither glorified him as God nor gave thanks to him, but their thinking became futile and their foolish hearts darkened. Although they claimed to be wise, they became fools and exchanged the glory of the immortal God for images made to look like mortal man...." (Romans 1:21-23) NIV

Questions for discussion:
1. What kind of image has Mormonism made of God?
2. Why is it so hard for people to glorify the one true God?
3. How is our thinking affected when we have the wrong image of God?

---

3) One of the Mormon's greatest theologian, historian, and apologist spent the last few years of his life concerned about the unexplainable problems in the book. As mentioned earlier, Brigham H. Roberts saw parallels between the *Book of Mormon* and the *View of the Hebrews* by Ethan Smith. However, it should also be noted that Roberts argued before the Twelve Apostles of the Mormon church that the Book of Mormon was of human origin, that the revelations of Joseph Smith were merely human productions, that Smith's visions were psychological, and that the gold plates "were not objective"—meaning they did not exist.

VIII. WHY IS THERE A PROBLEM WITH MORMONISM'S PROPHETIC ACCURACY?
   A. Because of the 70 or so prophecies by Smith only six came to pass and Mormon missionaries are unable or unwilling to give out a list of prophecies by Smith or any of the other leaders. One simple example would be Doctrine and Covenants # 132 by Smith regarding plural marriage. V. 6 says it is eternal, but it only lasted until about 1890. Those not living in plural marriage were to be damned. That would include most modern day Mormons then. Also, his wife Emma was to be destroyed if she fought plural marriage. She did, but lived to a ripe old age.
   B. Because while Joseph Smith did predict the Civil War (he "drew heavily upon published articles both in newspapers and magazines"[22]) he was incorrect in that England did not become involved in war against the U.S. and slaves did not rise up against masters.
   C. Because Smith's prophecy that he and his descendants would live from generation to generation in the house he built at Nauvoo was false (Doctrine and Covenants 124:22, 23, 59).
   D. Because Brigham Young falsely prophesied that men inhabit the sun (Journal of Discourses, Vol. 13, p. 271), that the earth is alive (Jour. of Discourses, Vol. 6, p. 36), and that the Civil War would not free the slaves (Journal of Discourses, Vol. 10. p. 250). There are many other false prophecies as well.

Thinking Through The Scripture

*"A prophet who presumes to speak in my name anything I have not com-
manded him to say, or a prophet who speaks in the name of other gods, must be
put to death. You may say to yourselves, 'How can we know when a message
has not been spoken by the Lord?' If what a prophet proclaims in the name of
the Lord does not take place or come true, that is a message the Lord has not
spoken. That prophet has spoken presumptuously. Do not be afraid of him.
(Deuteronomy 18:20-22) NIV*

Questions for discussion:
1. Is there a difference between ignorance in prophecy and falsehood in
   prophecy?
2. Should Smith and Young assume the same responsibility for their mistaken prophecies if they did them out of ignorance as compared to
   deception?
3. Should they receive the same penalty as false prophets?

WITNESSING TO MORMONS

IX. WHAT ARE FOUR BROAD CONTRASTING VIEWS IN MOR-
    MONISM TODAY?
    Note: As in any large group, Mormons have their share of people
    pushing their views. The following simply shows that within
    Mormonism today there are various competing beliefs that exist from
    historical movement within or modern social pressure without.
    A. **Neo-orthodox:** There is a group who wants to reemphasize the fall
       of Adam, original sin, Christ's atonement, and God's saving grace.[23]
       This would help their theology line up more with mainline
       Christianity.
    B. **Fundamentalists:** This group rejects any changes this century and
       wants to return to polygamy. Some 50,000 Mormons now practice
       polygamy.[24]
    C. **Feminists:** Those who want to break down the doctrinal walls
       excluding women from the priesthood, and thus giving them dual
       divinity in eternity.
    D. **Hermetic:** There are those who embrace the occultic and alchemic
       traditions of Joseph Smith and want them to emerge as
       Mormonism's unashamed heritage and future focus.[25]

X. WHAT ARE SOME THINGS TO REMEMBER ABOUT MORMONS?
   A. They are deceived, but God loves them.
       *"For God so loved the world that He gave His only begotten Son" (Jn.
       3:16) KJV*
   B. Those that come to your door are striving to gain heaven and
       please God through works of righteousness.
       *"For by grace you have been saved through faith; and that not of your-
       selves, it is the gift of God; not as a result of works, that no one should
       boast" (Eph. 2:8-9) NASB*
       *"I bear them witness that they have a [certain] zeal and enthusiasm for
       God, but it is not enlightened and according to [correct and vital] knowl-
       edge. For being ignorant of the righteousness that God ascribes (which
       makes one acceptable to Him in word, thought and deed), and seeking to
       establish a righteousness (a means of salvation) of their own, they did not
       obey or submit themselves to God's righteousness." (Rom. 10:2-3) AMP*
   C. They might be nice people, but without salvation through Jesus
       Christ, they are doomed.
       "I am the Vine...without me you can do nothing." (Jn. 15:5) KJV
   D. Those that come to your door are prepared to talk about God. Seize
       the moment, if possible, to introduce them to the real Lord and
       Savior of all, Jesus Christ.
       "[Strive to] save others, snatching [them] out of [the] fire" (Jude 23) AMP

XI. WHAT ARE THE DON'TS OF WITNESSING TO MORMONS?
   A. Don't get uptight and on the defensive or criticize their motives or
       works.
   B. Don't forget to smile.
   C. Don't be afraid to take "leadership" of the conversation.
   D. Don't be afraid to acknowledge something if they are right.

XII. WHAT ARE THE DO'S OF WITNESSING TO MORMONS?
   A. Do be polite throughout the conversation. Shake their hands. Ask
       their names, their occupations, and their place of residence.
   B. Do pray quietly to the Holy Spirit and ask His assistance.
   C. Do explain that you are a Christian and that your concept of God
       according to the Scriptures is much different than theirs.
   D. Do share the love of Christ with them by sharing your own per-
       sonal testimony.

XIII. WHAT ARE SOME PRACTICAL TIPS FOR STARTING TO WITNESS?
   A. Begin with the cardinal rules of a Gate Breaker:
       1) **Prayer:** Start with prayer. Even if you are caught off guard at the
           door, take time to silently pray for them as you begin to listen

to what they have to say. The Holy Spirit is powerful. Pray that they would be open to receive what you say. Pray that God would give you a heart of compassion. Pray against the lies and confusion of the devil's trickery. Many of us have been impacted and brought into the kingdom by someone's prayer.

The girl that I mentioned near the beginning of this chapter was being prayed for by many Christians. Her need, however, was not just that she should be open to doctrinal truth; it was for emotional healing. She had grown up with somewhat of a rejection problem and felt drawn to the attention and strokes that the Mormon young men were giving her. As she got drawn into the cult, a network of Christians began praying for her. The prayers were focused on her getting her emotional needs met by Jesus. Miraculously, a few days later, she felt the Holy Spirit touch her, warn her about Mormonism, and then guide her to the safety of Christian friends. The problem with rejection seemed to be totally gone, and her determination to follow Christ was resolved. I point this example out so that we remember that people get caught up in cults for all kinds of reasons. Therefore, our prayers need to be open to the inspiration and guidance of the Holy Spirit since He knows the deep issues that hold people in bondage.

2) **Love:** Don't close the door on them or end the conversation in anger. You might be the only person willing to take the time and share the love of Jesus with them. Don't be phony in an attempt to just witness, but really take the time to be interested in them and their personal life. If you can't do it at the moment, make another appointment. Remember that it is people seeing *"the goodness of God"* that leads them to repentance (Romans 2:4).

So often, Christians want to take on a Mormon like David took on Goliath and put another notch on their belt. I've been guilty of this before. We need to remember that Goliath was an enemy of God's people. Mormons are not enemies. Are they confused? Yes. Are they lost? Most often. There are some that appear to have a relationship with Jesus Christ. Yet, if this is so, they are in the wrong place doing the wrong thing and need to get free from the bondage of Mormonism. But let us not treat them like enemies. Nor should we just bombard them with truth without showing them any love. Someone once said that people don't care how much you know until they know how much you care. In John 1:14-17, we see that Jesus is *"full of grace and truth."* Notice that the grace is first and then the truth. Be gracious. When you show Christian kindness, people will normally be open to what you have to say.

One time our church was putting on an evangelistic drama for the community. A couple Mormon missionairies attended and were impressed by the Spirit of God that they felt at the event. Afterwards, some well meaning Christians from another church began to aggressively evangelize the Mormons. As I walked up to them, I felt the need to just be friendly. I chatted with them about where they were from, how they liked this area of the country, and so forth. Then I started getting into the doctrinal problems about Mormonism. After a while, one of them confessed to me that he had been offended by the aggresiveness of the Christians but appreciated what I had to say even though I had driven home some points fairly aggressively myself. What was the differnce? It was in the approach. An attitude of grace will make a place for truth to come and dwell.

3) **Witness:** Chances are you are going to be planting seeds or watering someone else's seeds rather than reaping the harvest yourself, but that is a part of the process. Don't be discouraged if you don't see a conversion. If possible, strike up a relationship. Invite them to church. Make another appointment. Get them some good literature on Mormonism.

B. You may begin to witness by starting with the Bible. Get right to the heart of the issue and ask, "How reliable do you think the Bible is? Get them to specify any areas of Scripture they think are unreliable and then avoid those. Use Titus 3:5 regarding "works of righteousness" to begin witnessing, or walk through Isaiah 43 - 46 and consider the places where God identifies Himself as the One and only God. This strikes at the heart of their doctrine of polytheism.

C. You may begin to witness by starting with the *Book of Mormon*. Use Alma 11:22-31 to show that the *Book of Mormon* is monotheistic (belief in only one God). Since modern-day Mormons are polytheists (belief in many gods) this is a contradiction. If Mormons want to be true to their book, they need to abandon their church beliefs. If they want to be true to current church teachings, they need to abandon the *Book of Mormon*. Another starting point could be Moroni 8:18 which speaks of God being unchangeable. This contradicts Mormon teaching that God was once a man. Also, Alma 34:32-35 teaches that man must choose God and His ways before he dies. Once he dies his fate is "sealed." This contradicts the Mormon church teaching that people can proxy for those who have died, and by baptism for the dead rescue them from their choice in this life.[26]

End Notes

1. James R. Spencer, *Have You Witnessed to a Mormon Lately?* (Grand Rapids, MI: Fleming H. Revell, 1993), p. 56.
2. James Coates, *In Mormon Circles: Gentiles, Jack Mormons, and Latter-day Saints* (Reading, MA: Addison-Wesley Publishing Company, 1991), p. 216.
3. Ibid., pgs. 145-146.
4. James R. White, *Letters To A Mormon Elder* (Minneapolis, MN: Bethany House Publishers, 1993), p. 243.
5. Harry L. Ropp, *Are the Mormon Scriptures Reliable?* (Downers Grove, IL: Inter Varsity Press, 1987), p. 40.
6. Fawn Brodie, *No Man Knows My History: The Life of Joseph Smith* (New York: Alfred A. Knopf, 1946), pgs. 62-63.
7. Walter Martin, *The Maze of Mormonism* (Ventura, CA: Vision House, 1984), pgs. 319-320.
8. Mather and Nichols, *Dictionary Of Cults, Sects, Religions, And The Occult* (Grand Rapids, MI: Zondervan Publishing House, 1993), p. 51.
9. Spencer, pgs. 173-174.
10. Anthony A. Hoekema, *Mormonism* (Grand Rapids, MI: Wm. B. Eerdman's Publishing Company, 1978), p. 58.
11. Peter Bartley, *Mormonism: The Prophet, the Book, and the Cult* (Dublin: Veritas Publications, 1989), p. 50.
12. Ropp, p. 55.
13. Walter Martin, *The Kingdom of the Cults* (Minneapolis, MI: Bethany House Publishers, 1985), p. 187.
14. Spencer, p. 121.
15. Brodie, p. 78.
16. B. H. Roberts, *Studies Of The Book Of Mormon* (Salt Lake City, UT: Signature Books, 1992), pgs. 320-344.
17. Spencer, p. 206.
18. Ropp, p. 38.
19. Brodie, pgs. 45-58.
20. Spencer, p. 125.
21. Ibid., pgs. 126-127.
22. Martin, p. 190.
23. John L. Brooke, *The Refiner's Fire* (New York: Cambridge University Press, 1994), p. 296.
24. Ibid., p. 298.
25. Ibid., p. 302.
26. Ronald Enroth, ed. *Evangelizing The Cults: How to Share Jesus with Children, Parents,Neighbors, and Friends Who Are Involved in a Cult*, chapter by Wesley P. Walters (Ann Arbor, MI: Servant Publications, 1990), pgs. 84-89.

QUESTIONNAIRE: LESSON FOUR

NAME: _____ DATE: _____

1. List the three best things that the lesson says a Christian can do to withstand the deceptive arguments of Mormons:

a) _____

b) _____

c) _____

2. Mormon missionaries are taught seven basic _____ to witness.

3. The lesson refers to a number of deceptive questions that Mormons may ask. On the lines below, list two of them and then refute it with the Bible or alternative questions.

a) Deceptive Question _____

_____

   Refutation: _____

_____

b) Deceptive Question _____

_____

   Refutation: _____

_____

4. List three questions to ask Mormons to help them see the errors in their book:

a) _____

b) _____

c) _____

5. List two reasons why the *Book of Mormon* is in error according to archaeology.

a) _____

b) _____

6. List two reasons why the *Book of Mormon* is obviously plagiarized.

a) _____

b) _____

7. Although Joseph Smith might have authored the *Book of Mormon*, history seems to indicate that he got his ideas from _____ Smith who authored *View of the Hebrews* and Solomon _____ who wrote *Manuscript Found*. Also, it is obvious that he simply wrote out much of the King James _____ in various places.

8. List two reasons why Mormonism contradicts the Book of Mormon.

a) _____

b) _____

9. For God is not the author of "_____ " (1 Cor. 14:33)

10. List three false prophecies that Mormon leaders have given.

a) _____

b) _____

c) _____

11. List two don't's and tell why they are important.

Don't _____

Don't _____

12. List two do's and tell why they are important.

Do _____

Do _____

13. Take a moment to pray for deliverance and salvation for those caught up in this cult.

14. Consider your knowledge of Mormonism before and after these lessons. Circle the number below that indicates how equipped you felt before taking the course to witness to a Mormon as compared to how equipped you feel now. Please be honest.

BEFORE 0 1 2 3 4 5 6 7 8 9 10 **AFTER** 0 1 2 3 4 5 6 7 8 9 10

JEHOVAH'S WITNESS

Part 1: Introduction and False Doctrines

"Don...began reading standard versions of the Bible instead of the New World Translation and the Lord 'turned on the light' in his life. 'What I found, or rather, what I was shown by the Holy Spirit, was that **the New Testament is a Jesus book**. I was flabbergasted. Everywhere I looked I saw Jesus.'"[1] [emphasis added] —Don Nelson, former Jehovah's Witness

INTRODUCTION

I. WHO FOUNDED THE WATCHTOWER AND WHEN DID IT BEGIN?
   A. Charles Taze Russell. In 1884 Russell formerly incorporated Zion's Watchtower Tract Society in Pittsburgh, Pennsylvania. The Society, however, officially looks to the year 1896 that the Watchtower Bible and Tract Society was founded.

II. HOW LARGE AND INFLUENTIAL IS THE CHURCH TODAY?
   A. There are almost 1 million members in the U.S. and 4.5 million worldwide[2] in at least 212 countries.[3] Four to six new Kingdom Halls are constructed every month somewhere in the U.S. using their "quick-building system" of 300 workers completing buildings in only four days.[4] Another influence is the aggressive distribution of their literature throughout the world. The main headquarters are in Brooklyn, New York, but there branch offices are all over the world.

Like many other cults, this one lost no time making an impact on the former Soviet Union after the Berlin Wall came down. When I lectured about cults at Moscow Bible College in 1998 on behalf of Campus Crusade, the students all had things to say about the Jehovah's Witnesses. Between 1991 and 1997, the Witnesses grew at a rate of 30 percent per year and claimed to be the fifth largest Christian group in Russia. They currently distribute 5,000 tons of literature in Russia each year. Some say that in Spain there are as many Witnesses as Protestants, and that in Poland they outnumber the Protestants.

B. While their organization continues to grow, it has not always been preceived as healthy as M. James Penton points out in *Apocalypse Delayed: The Story of the Jehovah's Witnesses:*

"Even despite their growth, it can be argued that Jehovah's Witnesses are members of a sick religion. They are wracked with internal problems which their leadership is unwilling to recognize, let alone deal with satisfactorily. And most serious for them, they continue to experience a tremendous turnover in membership— something that the society refuses to talk about and a fact largely unrecognized by most Witnesses. Furthermore...Jehovah's Witnesses continually lose most of their best-educated and most intelligent people. Hence, after many years of organizational 'brain drain,' the upper echelons of the Watch Tower hierarchy are largely an intellectually arid group with few persons of any real ability to call on for assistance."[5]

III. WHAT GROUPS SPLINTERED OFF FROM THE SOCIETY?

A. After Russell's death in 1916, several factions responded to the new leadership of Judge Joseph Franklin Rutherford. Some names were the Dawn Bible Student Association, the Standfast Movement, Paul Johnson Movement, Elijah Voice Movement, Eagle Society, and Pastoral Bible Institute of Brooklyn. Altogether, there are about a dozen "Russellite" groups among which the Jehovah's Witnesses are the most prominent.[6]

Thinking Through The Scripture

"A good tree cannot bear bad fruit, nor can a bad tree bear good fruit. Every tree that does not bear good fruit is cut down and thrown into the fire. Therefore by their fruits you will know them. Not everyone who says to Me, 'Lord, Lord,' shall enter the kingdom of heaven, but he who does the will of My Father in heaven." (Matthew 7:18-21)

"For such are false apostles, deceitful workers, transforming themselves into the apostles of Christ. And no marvel; for Satan himself is transformed into an angel of light. Therefore it is no great thing if his ministers also be transformed as the ministers of righteousness: whose end shall be according to their works." (2 Corinthians 11:13-15) KJV

Questions for discussion:
1. The passage from Matthew is speaking of false prophets and in Corinthians it warns Christians about false apostles. How could people like this get into positions of authority within the church?
2. Are there apostles and prophets today who are true and others false?
3. What kind of fruit would you expect from a false prophet or apostle?
4. How do Satan and his ministers trick people?
5. Who enters the kingdom of heaven according to Jesus' words?

IV. WHEN DID THE NAME JEHOVAH'S WITNESSES ORIGINATE?
    A. In 1931, at a convention in Columbus, Ohio. In order to distinguish themselves from the other various groups that had splintered off, the Watchtower Society coined their new name based upon **Isaiah 43:10** *"Ye are my witnesses, saith the LORD [Jehovah], and my servant whom I have chosen." (KJV)* One author says, "These people are not 'Christians, but 'witnesses'—according to their own interpretation."[7]

V. WHAT ARE SOME OF THE POSITIVE ASPECTS OF JEHOVAH"S WITNESSES?
    A. As with Mormons, it is impossible to say that "all" witnesses do this or believe that. However, there are some practical discipleship things they do from which Christians could learn. In example, they give new converts constructive discipleship, and then train them how to witness. In contrast, many Christians never receive the instruction necessary to defend their faith. Furthermore, the Watchtower has a slick publishing approach that is second-to-none. Also, they have mapped out every home in many countries and send witnesses to these at least once a year. We could certainly learn from their ability to organize, but we would want to do so without coming into the bondage of legalism, as they have.

        Most witnesses are nice people who think they are doing things that please God. Not all of their door-to-door visitation is motivated by fear of Jehovah or hope of reward. Some have a genuine desire to see others come to truth. They care for their family and neighbors just like Christians. Unfortunately, they have bought into the Watchtower's world view and are trapped into a belief system of unbiblical rules, penalties, works, and authoritarian control.

VI. WHAT ARE THE MAJOR EVANGELISM TACTICS OF THE SOCIETY?
   A. **Door-to-Door Witnessing**. Every member is a missionary. They are trained to go door-to-door and equipped to debate doctrine with Christians. They often do not identify themselves as J.W.'s and are tactful in their approach. As with the Mormons, there are normally two that witness, one experienced and one an apprentice. "The Jehovah's Witnesses have mapped out the entire United States so that every residence will be contacted at least once or twice a year by a team of door-to-door workers. They claimed recently that in one year over 3.6 million members spent over 835 million hours of door-to-door witnessing for the Watchtower! Out of sheer grueling persistence they have been able *to harvest many people who have not been grounded in God's Word* and were easily led astray by this counterfeit religion."[8]

   William J. Schnell, a former Jehovah's Witness, explains the Watchtower's strategy regarding ungrounded Christians in his book *Thirty Years A Watchtower Slave*. He says, "The Watchtower leadership sensed that within the midst of Christendom were millions of *professing Christians who were not well grounded in the truths once delivered to the saints, and who would rather easily be pried loose from the churches and led* into a new and revitalized Watchtower organization. The Society calculated, and that rightly, that this lack of proper knowledge of God and the widespread acceptance of half-truths in *Christendom would yield vast masses of men and women*, if the whole matter were wisely attacked, the attack sustained and the results contained, and then reused in an ever-widening circle."[9]

Thinking Through The Scripture

"*For that day will not come except the apostasy comes first—that is, unless the [predicted] great falling away of those who have professed to be Christians has come*" (2 Thessalonians 2:3) AMP

Questions for discussion:
1. There are various views on the end times, but what is the one thing we can know from this verse about those who profess Christianity?

2. Have you known someone who professed to be a Christian but was not very committed? (They talked the talk, but did not walk the walk.)
3. Have you ever seen someone taken away in a cult or false religion?

B. **Massive Publications.** The Watchtower Organization is the largest publisher in the free world, printing billions of pieces of literature each year. Their two main magazines are published twice a month in most of the known countries of the world. The *Watchtower* magazine is produced in over 100 languages, and the *Awake* magazine is produced in over 60 languages. "More than ten million copies of the Watchtower magazine alone are printed each edition."[10] They also produce millions of books each year such as *Let God Be True* and *You Can Live Forever In Paradise on Earth*. These books deceive millions.

VII. WHERE DO THE JEHOVAH'S WITNESSES MEET?
A. In Kingdom Halls. As of 1993, there were 8,220 such congregations in the United States. Within these congregations are overseers and servants. There are traveling ministers that visit the various congregations for about a week and then move on in the circuit. "Where possible each congregation holds meetings three times a week, for a total of 4 hours and 45 minutes."[11] A special group entitled "pioneers" dedicate 100 hours per month to the society. No tithes are taken, but each member is expected to sell the publications.
B. One of the main meetings is on Sunday and consists of two significant parts. First there is a lecture and then a study of the Watchtower material. One ex-Jehovah's Witness, Gordon E. Duggar, in his book *Jehovah's Witnesses: Watch out for the Watchtower,* says that the lectures are spoken by someone who is "rarely a skilled speaker, and most of the talks are monotonous, low key and, as a matter of fact, dull." Although, they do sing a couple of songs, he says that there is "no music servant, and the singing is often disastrous...It is evident that music is not important—a striking testimony to the absence of joy in this religion. Although the word 'worship' is popular in their books, and they agree that the word means to bend before God, there is no kneeling and never any show of emotion."[12]

Thinking Through The Scripture

"See to it that no one carries you off as spoil or makes you yourselves captive by his so- called philosophy and intellectualism, and vain deceit (idle fancies and plain nonsense), following human tradition—men's ideas of the

material [rather than the spiritual] world—just crude notions following the rudimentary and elemental teachings of the universe, and disregarding [the teachings of] Christ, the Messiah. For in Him the whole fullness of Deity (the Godhead), continues to dwell in bodily form...And He is the Head of all rule and authority...." (Colossians 2:8-10) AMP

"He [Jesus] is the head of the body, the church, who is the beginning, the firstborn from the dead, that in all things He may have the preeminence." (Colossians 1:18)

Questions for discussion:
1. Why are we to regard the teachings of Christ? What dwells within in Him?
2. Who is to be the head of the church? What have Jehovah's Witnesses made to be the head? What does this do to their concept of the church and of God?
3. How has philosophy and intellectualism affected their reasoning?

VIII.   WHY DOES THE WATCHTOWER ORGANIZATION MEAN SO MUCH TO JEHOVAH'S WITNESSES?
    A. They have accepted the Organization as the prophet of God.
    B. They have accepted the Organization as God's sole channel for His truth.
    C. They believe that to reject the Organization is to reject God.
    D. They believe that only the Organization can interpret the Bible, not individuals.
    E. They believe the *Watchtower* magazine contain's God's truth, directed by Him, through the Organization.[13]

IX. WHAT IS THE MAIN HERESY OF THE WATCHTOWER?
    A. The most cultic teaching is their denial of the Trinity and the Deity of Christ. Traditional Christianity has had to put up with such cultic twists almost since the time of Christ. Arius (AD 250 - 336) denied the deity of Christ by teaching that Jesus was not coeternal with the Father. Arianism influenced many people including Eusebius, the first century historian. Arianism was condemned at the Council of Nicaea (AD 325) because it failed to recognize the authority of numerous Scriptural references affirming the deity of Christ (Isa. 7:14; 9:6; Mic. 5:2; John 1:1; 5:18; 5:21- 24; 8:58; 10:30; 17:5; Phil. 2:11; Col. 2:9; 1 Tim. 3:16; Heb. 1:3; 1 John 5:20, etc.).
    However, even though Christianity has warded off attacks of heretics in the past, the Watchtower has become a powerful voice

because of its publications. Their "supposed" translation of the Bible, *New World Translation*, has erroneously changed many verses that oppose their doctrine, but they weren't able to change them all.

Thinking Through The Scripture

"*For unto us a Child is born, unto us a Son is given; and the government will be upon His shoulder. And His name will be called Wonderful, Counselor, Mighty God, Everlasting Father, Prince of Peace.*" (Isaiah 9:6)

"*All this took place to fulfill what the Lord spoke through the prophet: The virgin will be with child and will give birth to a son, and they will call him Immanuel—which means, God with us.*" (Matthew 1:22-23) NIV

Questions for discussion:
1. This verse from Isaiah reads much the same in the *New World Translation*. How does this help illustrate the doctrine of the Trinity? Which of the titles assigned to the child, best refutes the J.W.'s view of Jehovah and Jesus?
2. Matthew uses a verse from Isaiah 7:14 to begin his Gospel. He walked with Jesus and knew Him firsthand. What kind of message was he trying to share with the reader? Who were the people of his day he was trying to convince?

X. WHAT ARE SOME OF THE WATCHTOWER PUBLICATIONS?

Note: There are a great deal of books and publications by the Watchtower Society. The following are just a few of their arsenal of propaganda.

A. **Magazines:** *The Watchtower Announcing Jehovah's Kingdom* and *Awake* were discussed under Roman Numeral V "Major Evangelism Tactics." In 1874, Russell began publishing *The Herald of the Morning* which eventually became the Watchtower magazine. These magazines have been used by the Jehovah's Witnesses as God's modern day word to people. However, the magazines have made major mistakes regarding the fulfillment of Biblical prophecy. The last great mistake was in 1975. It was to be the end of human history and the beginning of Armageddon. Hundreds of thousands of J.W.'s left the Organization between 1976 and 1978 as a result of this false prophecy.[14] However, "the Watchtower Bible and Tract Society continues to grow in the 1990's despite the fact that its predictions concerning end-time events have failed to come to pass...Many new converts simply are not aware of or told the history of the organization."[15]

B. **Studies in the Scriptures**: A seven volume set of books written by Russell. The first was written in 1886 and was then called *The Millennial Dawn*. The seventh volume was a collection of Russell's writings published in 1917 after his death.

Unfortunately, *Russell was just egotistical enough to believe that no one could understand the Bible without these volumes.* He said that "people cannot see the divine plan in studying the Bible by itself...[if he] goes to the Bible alone, though he has understood his Bible for ten years, our experience shows that within two years he goes into darkness. On the other hand, if he merely read the Scripture Studies with their references, and had not read a page of the Bible, as such, he would be in the light at the end of two years."[16]

C. **Reasoning from the Scriptures**: This 1985 Watchtower Society book teaches J.W.'s how to argue their peculiar doctrines. The Witnesses are basically brainwashed into believing that only their Society has the truth. They anticipate Christian responses and debate their theology. They believe Christians are completely deceived and under Satanic influence. They are taught to cast off the most influential Christian insight as Satanic trickery.

D. **Jehovah's Witnesses: Proclaimers of God's Kingdom**: Published in 1993, this book gives the history and worldwide impact of Witnesses from their perspective. It is a good resource for certain aspects of history, doctrine, and growth. Of course, it is heavily biased and overlooks significant character flaws, false prophecies, and both sides of doctrinal controversies.

E. **The New World Translation of the Holy Scripture**: Produced in 1950 under the Watchtower leadership of Nathan H. Knorr. Regardless of their claims that five Greek scholars did this translation, in truth the Organization simply manipulated the Scriptures to line up with their own misguided doctrines. Under a veneer of supposed intellectual honesty, they have unsuccessfully tried to quote world renowned Greek scholars as agreeing with their translation.

However, their deceptive ways have been exposed time and again as the truth was manifested. One example of this can be seen in their defense of rendering John 1:1 "the Word was a god." They cite this as proof that Jesus was not God Almighty, but a lesser god. In doing this, they cited a number of Biblical authorities: Johannes Greber, Julius R. Mantey, Dr. Philip B. Harner, and Dr. John L. McKenzie. However, much to the Watchtower's chagrin and displeasure, all of these citings fell into shambles. Greber, who did render the latter part of John 1:1 "a god" was no Biblical scholar. In fact, he was a spiritist who claimed spirits helped him translate the New Testament. Even the Watchtower eventually denounced Greber in the Watchtower magazine, April 1, 1983. After that, they cited him no more as a reference.

What about the other three citations? Of the three, not one of them was quoted correctly by the Watchtower. Dr. Harner was misquoted and emphatically argues against the Watchtower's position.[17] Dr. McKenzie's words were taken totally out of context. In context, his words argue against the Watchtower position. And what of Julius R. Mantey who authored *A Manual Grammar of the Greek New Testament*? He has had several things to say over the years regarding his viewpoint of the Watchtower Translation:

1) "Out of all the Greek professors, grammarians, and commentators they [the Watchtower] have quoted, only one (a Unitarian) agreed that 'the word was a god'."[18]

2) "When they do meet certain passages of Scripture that seem to be against their viewpoint, to my great disappointment, they mistranslate them deliberately and deceptively—deliberate deception—in some cases and, to me, that is unpardonable. It's dishonest and, to a certain extent, it's diabolical."[19]

Thinking Through The Scripture

"When he, the Spirit of truth, comes, he will guide you into all truth." (John 16:13) NIV

"I am writing these things to you about those who are trying to lead you astray. As for you, the anointing you received from him remains in you, and you do not need anyone to teach you. But as his anointing teaches you about all things and as that anointing is real, not counterfeit—just as it has taught you, remain in him." (1 John 2:26-27) NIV

Questions for discussion:

1. Who guides us into the truth? How does this contrast with the Watchtower teaching that one must read *Studies in the Scriptures* to really understand?

2. The verse above mentions "anointing" three times. What is real anointing? From whom do you receive the anointing? Read 1 John 2:22-23 and consider this: Who are "those" who are trying to lead Christians astray?

XI. WHAT WERE THE BASICS OF CHARLES TAZE RUSSELL'S LIFE?

A. **Russell was led astray**: He was born on February 16, 1852, to Joseph L. and Anna Eliza Russell in Allegheny (now Pittsburgh), Pennsylvania. By age 15, he became a partner in his father's haberdashery (men's clothing and accessories) business, and by 25, managed several stores. He was raised Presbyterian, but became dissatisfied and changed to Congregationalism in his mid teens. Before long, however, Russell recoiled from this denomination as well, being disturbed by the Calvinistic doctrine of Predestination and eternal damnation.

Russell became skeptical of Christianity and chanced upon a meeting of a group who called themselves "Second Adventists", led by Jonas Wendell. This group had a history of predicting Christ's return. They were predicting that Christ would return in 1874. Russell became convinced they were right and formed a Bible study that met regularly for the next few years and *actively taught that Christ would return in 1874. Rather than admitting that Christ did not return in 1874, he became convinced that Christ had returned invisibly and spiritually to the earth.* He then began publishing his magazine, *The Herald of the Morning* (later changed to The Watchtower), and by 1880 he had a sizable following, about thirty congregations in seven states.

He married Maria G. Ackley in 1879. She worked hard with him, spreading his teachings, until 1897 when she left him. At one time, Maria taught others that her husband was the "faithful and wise servant" spoken of in Matthew 24:45 until she became disillusioned with him. After she left him, she taught that he was rather the "evil servant" spoken of in Matthew 24:48.[20] Russell *eventually changed the year of Christ's return to 1914.*

When 1914 came and went without Christ's return, he taught that this—rather than 1874—was the legitimate invisible and spiritual return of Christ's Kingdom. Russell died on October 31, 1916, having made two major predictions both of which were wrong. The Bible warns Christians of false prophets. In Deuteronomy 18:22, we are told that if a prophecy does not happen then God was not in it in the first place. Also, the Apostle Peter tells us these false prophets introduce destructive heresies and deny the Lord (2 Peter 2:1).

B. **Russell taught heresy**: Unfortunately, Russell was not only a false prophet but a false teacher as well, straying far from mainline Christian doctrine. Some of the heresy he taught were 1) that the concept of the Trinity was nonsense and a plot of Satan, 2) that Jesus was not God, 3) that the physical body of Jesus was destroyed after crucifixion and that Jesus simply "created and assumed such a body of flesh and such clothing as he saw fit for the purpose intended,"[21] and 4) that Christ would not return again in physical form but only spiritual. He also taught against any concept of judgment or the existence of hell.

Admittedly, interpretation of Scripture is not always an easy thing and Christians often disagree over exact interpretation. Some are given more to a literal view of everything while others spiritualize the Scriptures beyond reason. However, Russell did not just misinterpret; he manipulated Scripture so that it supported his doctrine. It is hard to understand why anyone would conspire to do such a thing, but it is important that we leave judgment in the hands of the Lord. However, if he were purposefully distorting the truth to deceive others then 2 Thessalonians 2:10-12 has strong judgment that addresses his actions and outcome.

C. **Russell's honesty was challenged** publicly: Russell's life was tattered with assaults on his character. He was in and out of court battles and the news for allegations of his conduct. Two of these episodes are briefly summarized here.

1) Russell brought suit against *The Brooklyn Daily Eagle* for making fun of the Watchtower's "Miracle Wheat" fund raiser. The Watchtower had advertised this wheat to grow five times as much wheat as any other brand. The government stepped in and tested the wheat. It was a very low grade wheat. The Eagle won the suit and continued to expose Russell's cult as a money making scheme for himself, since he owned 99 percent of the Organization.

2) Russell brought suit against Pastor J.J. Ross for publishing a pamphlet entitled "Some facts about the Self-Styled 'Pastor' Charles T. Russell." The pamphlet exposed Russell's lack of theological education, ignorance of Greek and Hebrew, and false doctrines. Russell was eventually sorry for the law suit because he perjured himself (got caught lying before the jury) in court and then was publicly humiliated as he had to confess that he could not translate the letters of the Greek alphabet and knew nothing of Latin or Hebrew. Ross won the case and then wrote another scorching pamphlet regarding Russell.

Thinking Through The Scripture

"The LORD detests lying lips, but he delights in men who are truthful." (*Proverbs 12:12*) NIV

"Everyone who does evil hates the light, and will not come into the light for fear that his deeds will be exposed. But whoever lives by the truth comes into the light, so that it may be seen plainly that what he has done has been done through God." (John 3:20-21) NIV

Questions for discussion:
1. Look up the word "detests". What other adjectives illustrate the feeling?
2. When people live by the truth, why don't they have to fear the light?

XII. WHO WAS JOSEPH FRANKLIN RUTHERFORD?
   A. He took over the Watchtower Organization in 1917 after Russell's death and remained the leader until his own death in 1942. There emerged a split as Rutherford held to only some of Russell's views. Rutherford was the lawyer who defended Russell in the suit against Ross. He was popularly called Judge because he had briefly served as a special judge in Missouri. His charisma and organizational talent matured the cult from infancy into a major organization. Under his influence, the Society began to be seen as Jehovah's theocratic kingdom on earth. It became God's "supposed" voice to the world. It was under Rutherford's leadership that the name Jehovah's Witnesses was coined.
   B. His personal life proved embarrassing for the society. His drinking problem, vulgar language, and possible promiscuity lead to Watchtower humiliation as well as a divorce from his wife.[22] Another major embarrassment for the Watchtower occurred under Rutherford, because of false prophecy.

      He taught that in 1925, Abraham, Issac, Jacob, and the Old Testament prophets would return as "princes" and live in an estate in San Diego, California, known as Beth-Sarim ("House of Princes"). Of course, large sums of money were solicited to build the spectacular home for the prophets' return and Watchtower leadership took full advantage of the situation while waiting for their return. Many Jehovah's Witnesses were once again disappointed when the prophecy failed.

XIII.   WHO WERE THE OTHER LEADERS OF THE WATCHTOWER?
   A. Nathan H. Knorr lead the Watchtower from 1942 until his death in 1977. He started the Gilead Missionary Training School in South Lansing, New York, produced the Watchtower's erroneous translation of the Bible, *New World Translation,* in 1950, and pushed for strong missionary involvement around the world. He prophesied

that 1975 would be the end of the age and that Armageddon would occur at that time. Close to one million Jehovah's Witnesses left the Organization after this failed prophecy. Under Knorr, the society became a "collective oligarchy."[23]

B. Frederick Franz lead the Watchtower from 1977 until 1992. As the chief translator of *The New World Translation*, his integrity was called into question in the case of Douglas Walsh vs. The Right Honorable James Latham Clyde in 1954 when he could not even translate an "elementary passage of Hebrew from Genesis" after claiming he could read Hebrew.[24] Franz brought a new era of authoritarian control within the organization. Intellectual honesty and debate was not allowed. His form of leadership did not allow for any questioning about the way things were done by the Watchtower elite.

C. Milton G. Henschel currently leads the Organization.

FALSE DOCTRINES OF THE WATCHTOWER

XIV. WHAT DOES THE BIBLE TEACH ABOUT THE WATCHTOWER'S DENIAL OF THE TRINITY?

Watchtower Doctrine = They believe that Jehovah is God Almighty, Jesus is only a god, and the holy spirit is simply an active force. *But Christians believe* that within the nature of the one God, there are three eternal and co-equal persons: God the Father, God the Son, and God the Holy Spirit.

A. The Bible teaches that the Father is God (2 Peter 1:17), the Son is God (John 20:28; Col. 2:9), and that the Holy Spirit is God (Acts 5:3-4; Acts 13:2).

  1) *"He received honor and glory from God the Father." (2 Pet. 1:17) NASB*

  2) *"Thomas said, 'My Lord and my God.'" (John 20:28) NIV*

  3) *"You have lied to the Holy Spirit...to God." (Acts 5:3-4) NIV*

B. The Bible also teaches there is only ONE GOD (1 Tim. 2:5; Gal. 3:20; Deut. 6:4; Is. 44:6) Therefore; the doctrine of the Trinity is substantiated by the Bible.

  1) *"For there is one God." (1 Tim. 2:5)*

  2) *"I am the first and the last; there is no other God." (Isaiah 44:6) LIV*

XV. WHAT DOES THE BIBLE TEACH ABOUT THE WATCHTOWER'S DENIAL OF CHRIST'S DEITY?

Watchtower Doctrine = They believe that Jesus was Michael the Archangel, the first created being, only a man when on earth, not God. *But Christians believe* that Jesus Christ is God and part of the Trinity.

A. The Bible clearly teaches that Michael is the archangel of God and never implies that he is Jesus Christ. He is a created being just as is Gabriel, the angel. Lucifer was an archangel, but fell. Jesus Christ is not the same as the angels (Heb. 1:4) and is to be worshipped by all the angels of God (Heb. 1:6). Michael was / will be present when the voice from heaven proclaims Jesus Christ (Rev. 12:7, 9).

B. The Bible teaches that Jesus is the Second Person of the Trinity.

1) *"...in the name of the Father, and of the Son, and of the Holy Ghost." (Mt. 28:20) KJV*

XVI. WHAT DOES THE BIBLE TEACH ABOUT THE WATCHTOWER'S DENIAL OF THE HOLY SPIRIT'S DEITY?

Watchtower Doctrine = They believe that the "holy spirit" (NWT) is only an active force, that it has no personality, and not part of the Trinity. **But Christians believe** that the Holy Spirit is God, the third person of the Trinity.

A. The Bible clearly teaches that the Holy Spirit (Holy Ghost) is the Third Person of the Trinity and has always been.

1) *"...of the Father, and of the Son, and of the Holy Ghost" (Mt. 28:20) KJV*

2) *"...and the Spirit of God was hovering over the waters" (Gen. 1:2) NIV*

3) *"Then God said, 'Let us make man in our image.'" (Gen. 1:26) NIV*

B. The Bible also teaches that the Holy Spirit has a personality that can comfort us (Jn. 14:26), give us righteousness, peace, and joy (Rom. 14:17), sanctify us (Rom. 15:16), give us spiritual gifts (1 Cor. 12:4-10), and give us direction (Luke 12:12, Acts 16:6). In Acts 5, we are told that Ananias and Sapphira died because they lied to the Holy Ghost. We can commune with the Holy Ghost (2 Cor. 13:14).

XVII. WHAT DOES THE BIBLE TEACH ABOUT THE WATCHTOWER'S DENIAL OF THE BODILY RESURRECTION OF JESUS CHRIST?

Watchtower Doctrine = They believe that Jesus was not resurrected in the same physical body which was sacrificed on the cross. He was resurrected a spirit being who simply created various bodies with which to represent himself to those who saw and touched him. **But Christians believe** in the bodily resurrection of Jesus Christ.

A. The Bible teaches that Jesus Christ physically rose from the dead in the same body. It never insinuates that Christ's spirit inhabited various bodies.

1) *"See My hands and My feet, that it is I Myself; touch Me and see, for a spirit does not have flesh and bones as you see that I have."* (Luke 24: 39) NASB

2) Other Scriptures: Jn. 2:19-21; Jn. 20:28; 1 Cor. 15:17; Matt. 24:30

XVIII. WHAT DOES THE BIBLE TEACH ABOUT THE WATCHTOWER'S DENIAL OF THE FULL ATONEMENT BY THE SHED BLOOD OF CHRIST?

Watchtower Doctrine = They believe that atonement is half by God and half by man and will not be "fully completed until the survivors of Armageddon return to God through free will and become subject to the Theocratic rule of Jehovah."[25] **But Christians believe** in the all-sufficient cleansing power of the shed blood of Jesus Christ for all sins, to any who appropriate it, through repentance and confession of faith in Christ.

A. The Bible teaches that the atonement blood of Jesus cleanses us from sin.

1) *"...and the blood of Jesus Christ his Son cleanses us from all sin."* (1 Jn. 1:7)

2) *"...and they overcame him [the devil] by the blood of the Lamb."* (Rev. 12:11)

3) *"...we have confidence to enter the holy place by the blood of Jesus."* (Hebrews 10:19) NASB

XIX. WHAT DOES THE BIBLE TEACH ABOUT THE WATCHTOWER'S DENIAL OF THE PHYSICAL RETURN OF CHRIST?

Watchtower Doctrine = They believe that Christ returned invisibly to earth in 1914, in secret, and specifically to the Watchtower Organization. According to them, he will not return physically to earth. **But Christians believe** in the physical Second Coming of Christ.

A. The Bible teaches that all the nations will see His return. It will not be done in secret as the Witnesses imply. This was merely a whitewash to cover up Charles Russell's failed prophecy predicting the return of Christ in 1914.

1) *"At that time the sign of the Son of Man will appear in the sky, and all the nations of the earth will mourn. They will see the Son of Man coming on the clouds of the sky, with power and great glory."* (Matt. 24:30) NIV

B) The Bible teaches that Jesus will physically return just as He physically departed.

1) *"This same Jesus, who has been taken from you into heaven, will come back in the same way you have seen him go into heaven."* (Acts 1:11) NIV

2)   *"Lo, He is coming with the clouds, and every eye will see Him,
     even those who pierced Him; and all the tribes of the earth shall
     gaze upon Him." (Rev. 1:7) AMP*

XX.   WHAT DOES THE BIBLE TEACH ABOUT THE WATCHTOWER'S
      DENIAL OF THE IMMORTALITY OF THE SOUL?

Watchtower Doctrine = They believe that people do not possess an
immaterial nature (soul or spirit) that goes on existing after death,
when it ceases its association with the body.[26] Man's spirit is interpreted
as the "life-force" within him, and at death, the life-force wanes: "After
breathing, heartbeat, and brain activity stop, the life-force gradually
ceases to function in body cells."[27] **But Christians believe** in the awareness of the immortal soul, that people will spend eternity with God or
without Him.

A)   Although the subject of the soul, the spirit, and the physical body
     may be viewed differently according to interpretation, it is clear
     that the Bible often makes a distinction between soul and physical
     body. This then denies the Witnesses' claims that the body and soul
     have no difference and that the soul ceases after death.

     1)   *"Do not be afraid of those who can kill the body but cannot kill the
          soul." (Matt. 10:28) NIV*

     2)   *"Why are you in despair, O my soul? And why are you disturbed
          within me?" (Psalm 43:5) NASB*

     3)   *"And as the murderous stones came hurtling at him, Stephen
          prayed, 'Lord Jesus, receive my spirit." (Acts 7:59) LB*

B)   Furthermore, the Bible teaches that there is eternal awareness of
     the soul.

     1)   *"Multitudes who sleep in the dust of the earth will awake: some to
          everlasting life, others to shame and everlasting contempt." (Dan.
          12:2) NIV*

     2)   *"And these will go away into everlasting punishment: but the righ-
          teous into life eternal." (Matt. 25:46)*

XXI. WHAT DOES THE BIBLE TEACH ABOUT THE WATCHTOWER'S
      DENIAL OF HELL AND ETERNAL PUNISHMENT?

Watchtower Doctrine = They believe hell simply means the grave
and that there is no awareness of punishment because there is no existence for those not saved. **But Christians believe** that hell is a real place
of eternal suffering that people choose by rejecting Christ and His plan
of Salvation.

A)   The Bible teaches that hell was created for the devil and his angels.
     It is a real place and not just another name for the grave. Those

who reject Christ choose eternity without God in a place of suffering and torment.

1) *"Depart from me, you who are cursed, into everlasting fire prepared for the devil and his angels."* (Matt. 25:41) NIV

2) *"The rich man also died and was buried. In hell, where he was in torment, he looked up and saw Abraham far away, with Lazarus by his side."* (Lk. 16:22-23) NIV

3) *"And the smoke of their torment goes up forever and ever; and they have no rest day and night...."* (Rev. 14:11) NASB

XXII. WHAT DOES THE BIBLE TEACH ABOUT THE WATCHTOWER'S DOCTRINE OF SALVATION?

Watchtower Doctrine = They say they believe in salvation by grace through faith in Christ, but they pollute the idea of true grace by claiming that one must identify with the Watchtower and do its works in order to receive eternal life. **But Christians believe** that salvation is by grace through faith in Christ alone. Works are not done in order to secure salvation, but as a result of changed lives and appreciation for what Christ has done.

A) While the Watchtower might talk the talk, they don't walk the walk when it comes to salvation through grace, as Duane Magnania, a former Jehovah's Witness explains in his book *The Watchtower Files:*

"What the Watchtower means by 'free grace' is that Christ's death only wiped away the sin inherited from Adam. They teach that without this work of atonement, men could not *work their way toward salvation.* But the 'gift' of Christ's ransom sacrifice is freely made available to all who desire it. In other words, without Christ's sacrifice, the individual wouldn't have a chance to get saved. But in view of His work, the free gift which removed the sin inherited from Adam, the individual now has a chance."[28]

B) Although Christians will be commended for their "good works," the Bible is very clear that salvation is not earned as a result of works, but is a "free gift" for any who repent and turn to Christ in faith.

1) *"the free gift of God is eternal life in Christ Jesus our Lord."* (Rom. 6:23) NASB

2) *"For it is by grace you have been saved, through faith—and this not from yourselves, it is the gift of God—not by works, so that no one can boast. For we are God's workmanship, created in Christ Jesus to do good works, which God prepared in advance for us to do."* (Eph. 2:8-10) NIV

3) *"Repent, and let each of you be baptized in the name of Jesus Christ for the forgiveness of your sins; and you shall receive the gift...."* (Acts 2:38) NASB

XXIII. WHAT ARE SOME OF THE OTHER PECULIAR DOCTRINES OF
        THE WATCHTOWER?
   A. THE 144,000 ELECT (ANOINTED CLASS) AND THE OTHER
       SHEEP. Watchtower theology teaches that only 144,000 J.W.'s will
       go to heaven. The other sheep must remain on earth, but in par-
       adise. The first J.W. pioneers to embrace the Society as the true way
       became the 144,000 elect. All of these slots were filled by 1935.
       After this, the most one could hope for was to work one's way into
       paradise on earth.

       Of the original 144,000 Jehovah's Witnesses, just a few thou-
       sand are still alive as the world enters the new millennium. This
       anointed class is truly the elite according to Watchtower theology
       and have many privileges. Among these distinct privileges they
       only are born again, conformed in Christ's image, members of the
       New Covenant, partakers of the Lord's Supper, justified by faith,
       receive glorified bodies, enjoy life in heaven, and rule with Christ.

       Of course, contrary to Watchtower theology, the Bible classifies
       the 144,000 as literal Jews (Rev. 7:4-8), makes mention of an innu-
       merable amount of believers in heaven (Rev. 7:9), and makes avail-
       able all the riches of glory to any who choose Christ (Eph. 1:13-14,
       18), but somehow this has escaped the eyes of the Jehovah's
       Witnesses.
   B. THEY REFUSE BLOOD TRANSFUSIONS. Because Jehovah's
       Witnesses believe that references to the Old Testament Scriptures
       of "eating blood" prohibit receiving blood through transfusions,
       they forbid it even in cases of life and death. The following is by
       authors Leonard and Marjorie Chretien in *Witnesses of Jehovah*:

       "[One man talked about] the heartrending decision he was
       forced to make between his religion and the life of his child. His
       baby was born with a serious hernia. An immediate operation was
       required to save the child's life, but that would require a blood
       transfusion. Jehovah's Witnesses taught that this is against God's
       Law, and the penalty for not obeying this rule is removal from the
       organization and isolation from all friends and family members
       who are Witnesses. The heartbroken father chose to obey 'God's
       Law,' and two days later his baby died."[29]
   C. THEY FORBID THE CELEBRATION OF BIRTHDAYS. Because the
       Bible only mentions the celebration of birthdays with regard to
       Pharaoh and King Herod (both evil), they teach that it affronts God.
   D. THEY FORBID THE CELEBRATION OF CHRISTIAN HOLIDAYS.
       "Christmas, Good Friday, Easter, and family birthdays are not
       observed because they are regarded as pagan."[30]

E. THEY ARE NOT PERMITTED TO SERVE THEIR COUNTRY. As Mather and Nichols tell us in their *Dictionary Of Cults, Sects, Religions, And The Occult,* "Watchtower members do not salute the flag of whatever nation they reside in and refuse to participate in war and military activity because they think they have a singular responsibility to show allegiance to the Watchtower society."[31] The society, they believe, is God's government on earth.

F. THEY ARE NOT PERMITTED TO WEAR CROSSES. Although the Watchtower once taught that Christ was crucified on a cross, they now teach that it was a straight stake and so deny the wearing of crosses. However, Scriptures like John 20:25 that speaks of nails needed as compared to a single nail, John 21:18-19 that show the need for Jesus to outstretch his hands (not above his head), as well as other Scriptures have convinced Greek Scholars down through the centuries that Jesus was crucified on a cross and not a stake.

XXIV. WHAT IS THE SAD TRUTH ABOUT JEHOVAH'S WITNESSES?

A. That as hard as they work and as organized as they are, none of the Witnesses that knock on your door believe that they are going to heaven. They are simply trying to earn paradise on earth because they believe that only a hundred and forty-four thousand will be with Jehovah in heaven and those spots were all earned in the beginning of the Society. They have no hope of eternity with God in heaven. They have enclosed themselves in literary deception and believe that any book outside of their Society, including the Bible, is under Satanic influence and not to be trusted.

Thinking Through The Scripture

"'Is not My word like fire?' declares the LORD, 'and like a hammer which shatters a rock? Therefore behold I am against the prophets,' declares the LORD, 'who steal My words from each other. Behold, I am against the prophets,' declares the LORD, 'who use their tongues to declare, The Lord declares. Behold I am against those who led My people astray by their falsehoods and reckless boasting; yet I did not send them, nor do they furnish this people the slightest benefit,' declares the LORD." (Jeremiah 23:29-32) NASB

Questions for discussion:

1. What does God compare His word to and why?
2. What three types of people does this say the Lord is against?
3. How do these declarations apply to the Watchtower's doctrines?
4. How do these declarations apply to the New World Translation?

Testimony

A part of my testimony has to do with the Jehovah's Witnesses. I was drawn into attending Kingdom Hall meetings through their door-to-door evangelism in Reno, Nevada. It happened back in the mid 1970's. However, before explaining that, let me give you a little background. Prior to that time, I had gone through a deep personal search for the truth. This had turned into a search for God. Like so many other "hippies" of the late sixties and seventies, I had explored various eastern religions and philosophies of life. There were many cultic and occultic concepts that I waded through in my search. This is probably not so strange since I had not grown up in a Christian family that regularly attended church. Of course, I had little-to-no understanding of the deceptive darkness into which I was being drawn. However, whereas some simply skimmed the surface of such things, I jumped deeply into the mire and then sank. Fortunately, God hears the cries of those truly searching for Him, even if they are calling from the depths of miry darkness.

One of my favorite Scriptures is Jeremiah 29:13 which says, *"And you will seek Me and find Me when you search for Me with all your heart."* That's what happened to me! I discovered that Jesus was Lord. He healed my shattered mind, delivered me from demonic strongholds, helped me see the emptiness in drugs, free love, new age, occult, etc. Unfortunately, however, I wasn't in a church, and I had no mentor. I did find out later that my aunt Lyla had prayed regularly for me, but at the time, there was no consistent Christian influence in my life - except for the Lord.

There came a time when I knew that I needed to read the Bible. My best friend, Phil Van de Veer, who had gone through similar experiences, had sent me one, so I began to read and study. After about a year, I got into the New Testament. As I did, the Lord started tugging on me to get involved with His people - somewhere. But where? Since I didn't have a clue as to what distinguished one church from another, I was open prey. Then there came a knock-at-the-door. Guess who? That's right, the Jehovah's Witnesses. These nice people said they were interested in doing Bible studies. I asked them if they believed in Jesus. "Oh yes," they said. So we started having weekly home Bible studies. The "fellowship" felt good because I was going through a broken relationship at the time. My life consisted of work, college, and now this. It was late spring when we first started meeting, and by mid Summer, I was attending Kingdom Hall meetings. We had little green and red books from which we would practice arguing doctrine with others (I didn't know at the time that those "others" were Christians).

As I started into my Senior year of college, I was on work study at the University in Reno. On the first day, there were several students standing around the station where I was working. So I thought that I would see if any were Christians by proclaiming, "Praise the Lord!" When I did, a young man named David quickly walked over and said, "Did you say, 'Praise the Lord?'" I said, "Yes." He replied, "Are you a Christian?" I told him, "Yes." He said that he was also, and we both started jumping up and down with excitement saying, "Praise the Lord." He then asked me where I went to church. When I told him that I attended the Kingdom Hall, he turned a shade of green. After a few minutes, he said, "You sure sound like a Christian." I was a little offended and said, "Of course, I'm a Christian. Isn't that what I just told you?" He stammered, "But—you go to the Kingdom Hall. Don't you know that they aren't Christians?" I argued, "Sure they are; we talk about Jesus all the time." Then he looked at me for a moment and said, "You need to understand that they don't believe Jesus is God." I couldn't accept it, but he sounded so convincing. He challenged me to ask them at the next meeting.

Well, the next Sunday morning, I did just that. After the service, I went up to the senior elder and politely asked him if they believed that Jesus was God. He told me that they believed Jesus was "a god." This got my attention, and I started to realize that David might be right. It was time to get to the bottom of it. So, I opened to the passages of John 1:1 and John 8:58 to prove to the elder that Jesus really was God. In a way, I felt bad for him. There had been a time during my search for God that I had thought the same thing - that Jesus was the son of God, but not God himself. In fact, prior to that, I had thought that He was just one of many gods. I could get more bizarre and confess that at one time I was crazy enough to think that I was Jesus. However, fortunately for me, I found the real Jesus and he healed my demented mind. I knew that if Jesus had revealed Himself to me, then He could do it for anyone. The central teaching of the Bible is that Jesus Christ is God. So, I didn't mind pointing this guy to the "Truth." As we talked, I began to notice that his Bible said different things than the one I had. I thought we were having a nice discussion, and that I was even making some good points. Suddenly, I realized that we weren't alone anymore. Several men of the Kingdom Hall had surrounded us. They were eyeing me suspiciously. After another short discourse, this group seemed to instantly respond to a command by the senior elder. I found myself being bodily forced to the front doors of the Kingdom Hall. Then they gave me "the left foot of fellowship" right out the front.

Well, David was right! They didn't believe Jesus was God. He and I went back to the couple, with whom I had been doing the weekly studies. I thought for sure that they would be open to this most important truth, but they would not listen. They had already been warned about us, and said we were deceived. I left - disappointed. After that experience, I got involved in a "real" Christian church, as well as the InterVarsity Christian Fellowship on campus. God had spared me from the snare of that cult and brought me into a Bible-believing, Jesus-loving body of believers. Thank You, Lord!

End Notes

1. Ron Rhodes, *Reasoning From The Scriptures With Jehovah's Witnesses* (Eugene, OR: Harvest House Publishers, 1993), p. 12.
2. Ibid., p. 9.
3. Ronald Enroth, ed. *Evangelizing The Cults* (Ann Arbor, MI: Servant Publications, 1990), p. 122.
4. Ruth Tucker, *Another Gospel: Alternative Religions and the New Age Movement* (Grand Rapids, MI: Zondervan Publishing House, 1989), p. 137.
5. M. James Penton, *Apocalypse Delayed: The Story of Jehovah's Witnesses* (Toronto: University of Toronto Press, 1986), p. 124.
6. Richard Kyle, *The Religious Fringe: A History of Alternative Religions in America* (Downers Grover, IL: Inter Varsity Press, 1993), p. 156.
7. Richard E. Wentz, *Religion in the New World: The Shaping of Religious Traditions in the United States* (Minneapolis, MN: Fortress Press, 1990), p. 305.
8. Ron Carlson and Ed Decker, *Fast Facts On False Teachings* (Eugene, OR: Harvest House Publishers, 1994), pgs. 117-118.
9. W. J. Schnell, *Thirty Years A Watchtower Slave* (Grand Rapids, MI: Baker Book House, 1956), p. 19.
10. Tucker, p. 135.
11. *Jehovah's Witnesses: Proclaimers of God's Kingdom* (Brooklyn, NY: Watchtower Bible and Tract Society, 1993), p. 236.
12. Gordon E. Duggar, *Jehovah's Witnesses: Watch Out for the Watchtower!* (Grand Rapids, MI: Baker Book House, 1993), p. 11.
13. Carlson and Decker, pgs. 121-122.
14. Leonard and Marjorie Chretien, *Witnesses of Jehovah* (Eugene, OR: Harvest House Publishers, 1988), p. 58.
15. Mather and Nichols, *Dictionary Of Cults, Sects, Religions, And The Occult* (Grand Rapids, MI: Zondervan Publishing House, 1993), p. 158.
16. From *The Watchtower*, September 15, 1910, p. 298 as reported in Walter Martin, *Kingdom of the Cults* (Minneapolis, MI: Bethany House Publishers, 1985), p.46.
17. Robert M. Bowman, *Jehovah's Witnesses, Jesus Christ, and the Gospel of John* (Grand Rapids: Baker Book House, 1989), pgs. 70-73.
18. Julius Mantey; cited by Walter R. Martin, "The New World Translation," *Christian Research Newsletter*, 3:3, p. 5.
19. Michael Van Buskirk, *The Scholastic Dishonesty of the Watchtower* (Santa Ana, CA: CARIS, 1975), p. 13; cited by Mather and Nichols in *Dictionary of Cults, Sects, Religions and the Occult*, p. 152.
20. Penton, pgs. 33, 37.
21. Charles Taze Russell, *"Studies in the Scripture,"* 7 vols. as quoted by Martin, p. 59.
22. Penton, pgs. 48, 72.
23. Kyle, p. 157.
24. Heather and Gary Botting, *The Orwellian World of Jehovah's Witnesses* (Toronto: University of Toronto Press, 1984), p. 98.

25. Martin, *Kingdom of the Cults*, p. 99.
26. *Reasoning from the Scriptures* (Brooklyn: Watchtower Bible and Tract Society, 1989), p. 383.
27. Ibid., p. 98.
28. Duane Magnani, *The Watchtower Files* (Minneapolis: Bethany House Publishers, 1985), p.232.
29. Chretien, p. 14.
30. Mather and Nichols, p. 151.
31. Ibid.

QUESTIONNAIRE: LESSON FIVE

NAME: _____ DATE: _____

1. Who was the founder of the Watchtower Society? _____

2. From what Scripture did they claim the name of Jehovah's Witnesses?

_____

3. What are the two main evangelistic strategies of the Watchtower?

a) _____

b) _____

4. Briefly explain what W. J. Schnell wrote regarding the Watchtower's strategy. _____

_____

_____

_____

5. List the three reasons that the Watchtower means so much to the Jehovah's Witnesses.

a) _____

b) _____

c) _____

6. Whom does Colossians 2:8-10 say we should look to for headship?

_____

7. What is the main heresy of the Jehovah's Witnesses? _____

_____

8. Write out one Scripture that refutes this heresy. _____

_____

_____

9. What claims did Russell make about his *Studies in the Scriptures* that should cause Christians to be cautious of the volumes? _____

_____

_____

10. How does the New World Translation expose the dishonesty of this cult? _____

_____

11. Russell falsely predicted that Christ would return to the earth in 18____ and then in 19____. Rather than admit that he was incorrect in his calculations, he argued that Christ had returned _____ and _____ to the earth, not physically.

12.Under Rutherford's influence, the Society began to see itself as Jehovah's _____ kingdom on earth. The society was embarrassed by his _____ problem.

13. Write out the definition of the Trinity: _____

_____

14. The Bible clearly teaches that _____ is the 2nd Person of the Trinity and that the _____ _____ is the 3rd Person of the Trinity.

15. In regard to the bodily resurrection of Jesus Christ, Jesus said, "See My hands and My feet, that _____ ; touch Me and see, for a spirit does not have flesh and bones as you see that I have." Luke 24:39 NASB

16. In regard to the atonement of our sins through the blood of Jesus, we know that the Bible says, "the blood of Jesus Christ his Son cleanses us from _____ sin" 1 Jn. 1:7

17. Explain the problem with the Watchtower's view of "salvation through grace." _____

_____

_____

18. List Four of the Peculiar Doctrines of the Watchtower:

a) _____

b) _____

c) _____

d) _____

19. Tell about an experience you've had with a Jehovah's Witness. Perhaps you were involved in it, or a relative, or someone you knew. _____

_____

_____

JEHOVAH'S WITNESS

Part 2: Arguments, Problems and Witnessing to J.W.'s

"All those years as Jehovah's Witnesses, the Watchtower organization had taken us on a guided tour through the Bible. We gained a lot of knowledge about the Old Testament, and we could quote a lot of Scripture, but we never heard the gospel of salvation in Christ. We never learned to depend on Jesus for our salvation and to look to him personally as our Lord. Everything centered around the Watchtower's works program, and people were expected to come to Jehovah God through the organization."[1]

—David Reed, former Jehovah's Witness

DECEPTIVE ARGUMENTS OF THE WATCHTOWER

As we consider their deceptive arguments, it must be remembered that they speak these things because they believe them. The Watchtower is not some terrorist gang of thugs simply out to confuse and destroy. Rather, in their minds, they are serving Jehovah and working their way to Paradise. They are under constant pressure to distribute the Watchtower literature so that they don't forfeit eternal life.[2]

Because their religion can come across to a nominal Christian as very authoritative, these are often easy prey. The Witnesses are strategic. They go out in groups of two or three; there is always one skilled Witness with an apprentice. Don Nelson, a former Jehovah's Witness, gives some insight as to how easy it is to win nominal Christians. After just a few weeks training, he states, "The first day I went witnessing door-to-door, I defeated two

Baptists, a Lutheran, and three Presbyterians in dialectic combat! I was genuinely shocked by the Biblical illiteracy of most Christians."[3] While the Witnesses do receive training in their religion, the Christian should not fear. J.W.'s are confused and lost in a system of works. They need to know the "GOOD NEWS" of Jesus Christ just like everyone. *Wouldn't it be incredible if the J.W.'s and Mormons had to cease their door-to-door witnessing because too many of their workers were getting saved by well-equipped, loving Christians at home?*

The Witnesses come with a weakness—an Achilles' heal—in that each one has an emptiness that can only be filled by a personal salvation relationship with the LORD JESUS CHRIST. A humble Christian, who knows the Word and has confidence in his relationship with God, should be more than a match for a J.W. When you talk with J.W.'s, keep three things in mind: 1) They are very confused about basic doctrines because their erroneous translation of the Bible (*New World Translation*) has been perverted in thousands of places. 2) Although they use Christian terminology, the meanings have been carefully redefined (manipulated) to fit into their system of religion. 3) Let the love of Christ shine through you to them so that the Holy Spirit might show them the error of their way.

I. WHAT ARE THREE MYTHS ABOUT THE JEHOVAH'S WITNESSES?

A. **They never get saved or leave the organization.**[4] Actually, many do leave it, even those born into the society.[5] Also, scholars who discover the Watchtower's true history and perversion of doctrine are often forced to leave.[6] In her book *Another Gospel*, Ruth Tucker gives the following insight:

"The truth is that there are vast numbers of Jehovah's Witnesses who do not come to your door, who struggle to witness their minimum of one hour a month. And those who are more faithful in witnessing are not necessarily as self-assured about their beliefs as they might appear."[7]

B. **They know their Bible well.** Actually, they frequently know only the Watchtower viewpoint of certain doctrines they are taught to argue. Also, they are kept so busy reading Watchtower information that they have little time for Bible study.

C. **They are always antagonistic.** Actually, they are trying to upgrade their image by being more friendly at the door. This makes witnessing to them more possible.

II. WHAT ARE SOME TYPICAL THINGS THEY MAY SAY?

A. **They may say, "Don't you know it is essential for one's salvation to use the correct name of God, Jehovah"?**

In their *New World Translation,* the name Jehovah appears numerous times throughout Scripture emphasizing that this is the name of God the Father. Even though thousands of original Greek manuscripts of the New Testament never include the name, the Watchtower took liberty to put it in any place they felt referred to the Father. While the name "Jehovah" is included in some legitimate translations in the Old Testament (American Standard Version, King James, etc.), it is not included to the extent of the Watchtower's translation. The amazing thing is that the name "Jehovah" is not actually included in the majority of the Hebrew or Greek manuscripts from which English translations of the Bible are derived. While a select few translations do use the name of God as Jehovah, the overwhelming majority of what are considered reliable translations know nothing of that name. The King James only uses the name four times.

The original Hebrew (Old Testament) includes the name "Yahweh"—or more literally, YHWH (only consonants, no vowels). Since the Hebrew scribes had a superstitious dread of pronouncing the name of God, they would say "Adonai" (Lord) instead. Eventually, scribes inserted the three vowels of "Adonai", a-o-a, into YHWH and produced Yahowah, or Jehovah. Most modern scholars believe "Yahweh" is the correct rendering. However, we should not criticize anyone for using the name "Jehovah" but rather understand it is not necessarily the most accurate. Here are some questions to ask J.W.'s if the subject comes up.

1. Can you give me proof of one of the original Greek New Testaments—out of all of the thousands—that used this name?
2. Have you ever considered that the majority of modern day Hebrew scholars think that YHWH is actually rendered "Yahweh"?
3. Do you know that the disciples in Acts 11:26 came up with a good name that followers of Christ should be called—Christians? Since that was right for the first century believers, don't you think you should reconsider being labeled by a name (Jehovah's Witness) that is less than a century old?

There are a number of passages in the New Testament that lift up the name of Jesus, not Jehovah. Since we want to exalt the name of Jesus and point the Witnesses in His direction, take time to help them consider these following passages.

1. In whose name should we meet together? (Matt. 18:20; 1 Cor. 5:4)
2. Demons are subject to whose name? (Luke 10:17; Acts 16:18)
3. Repentance and forgiveness should be preached in whose name? (Luke 24:47)

4. In whose name are you to believe and receive the forgiveness of sins? (John 1:12; 3:16; Acts 10:43; 1 John 3:23; 5:13)

5. By whose name, and no other, do we obtain salvation? (Acts 4:12)

6. Whose name should be invoked as we bring our petitions to God in prayer? (John 14:13,14; 15:16; 16:23,24)

7. In whose name is the Holy Spirit sent? (John 14:26)

8. Whose name and authority was invoked by the disciples in healing the sick and lame? (Acts 3:16; 4:7-10, 30)

9. Whose name did Paul tell us to call upon? (1 Cor. 1:2) Whose name is above every name? (Eph. 1:21; Phil. 2:9-11)[8]

The answer to all of these questions is—you guessed it—JESUS!!!

B. They may say, "The term Trinity is not in the Bible."

This is accurate. The word is not in the Scriptures, but the concept is throughout the Scriptures. There are many terms that have been created to simply describe a concept. These terms are not actually in the Bible. The word "rapture" is an example. Someday, we will be "caught up together...in the clouds to meet the Lord in the air" as 1 Thess. 4:17 tells us. The name simply refers to a Biblical concept.

Another name not specifically mentioned in the Bible is "theocracy" (government by officials divinely inspired). Israel was a theocracy. The Watchtower Society claims to be a theocracy. They believe they are God's government on earth. This is one of the reasons that their members cannot pledge allegiance to any country. Here are some questions to ask if the subject comes up.

1. Since the Watchtower considers itself a theocracy, do you think this is a Biblical concept? Doesn't it make sense then that the word "Trinity" is simply describing a concept found in the Bible?

2. Since the name of Jehovah does not appear as such in any legitimate Hebrew or Greek manuscripts, does this mean that it should not be used?

C. They may say, "The concept of the Trinity is not reasonable. It is not something anyone can understand."

The doctrine of the Trinity and of the Deity of Christ are the watershed issues that theologically divide main stream Christianity from the cults. It certainly is the case with the Witnesses. These are the main areas that Jehovah's Witnesses will attack. In their reasoning, they attempt to make the concept of the Trinity appear illogical, and even ridicule the teaching of it. While the doctrine of the Trinity (Father, Son, and Holy Spirit) might not be easy for our three pound brains to understand, it does not make the concept unreasonable.

There are many concepts in life that are not easily understood, but they are true. No one doubts the truth of electricity even though science admits that it has not yet fully understood it. Eternity, past and future, is accepted, but who can grasp it? Infinity in space is taught, but who can comprehend it?

The Watchtower has erred in believing that they can reason out everything about God with their minds. But faith in the concept of the Trinity, and the numerous Scriptures supporting it, can only be done in the heart. Also, be careful about definitions and terminology when talking about the Trinity because, once again, there is confusion on their part. They are often taught that what Christians mean by the word "Trinity" are three separate Gods, or some three-headed god. Make sure that you let them know that you believe the Bible teaches that there is only One God. Here are some questions if the subject comes up.

1. What have you been taught that the concept of the Trinity means?
2. Since men cannot even fully grasp the concept of electricity, the quantum theory of physics, the laws of relativity, the infinity of time, space, and matter, do you really think it is reasonable that we will fully understand the Creator of it all?

D. **They may say, "Jesus tells us 'The Father is greater than I'. Therefore, Jesus is not God Almighty."**

There are many verses that they will zero in on, that at first appearance, seem to justify their position. But when these Scriptures are truly considered in context, it becomes obvious that the Witnesses are trying to manipulate the Scriptures for their beliefs. This Scripture is found in John 14:28. Jesus is telling His disciples that He will soon depart to the Father and that the Holy Ghost will be sent to them. The Witnesses use this verse to contend that Jehovah was greater than Jesus not only in regard to office or position but also in regard to His person. While it is admitted that God the Son in human flesh did not have the advantageous position of God the Father in Spirit condition which made Him *quantitatively* inferior, there is no implication here upon Jesus' part that He is *qualitatively* inferior.

The Jehovah's Witnesses, who place so much emphasis on human reasoning, should see that a son is not intrinsically inferior to a father. There is simply a difference in position of respect. The ancient Athanasian Creed says it well, Christ is "equal to the Father as touching his Godhood and inferior to the Father as touching his manhood".[9] Here are some questions to ask if the subject comes up.

1. Since the Creator designed the Creation in such a way that sons are intrinsically equal to their fathers, although not in position or respect, why do you strain to take Jesus as the only exception

to the rule? Don't you see that He is God the Son showing respect for the position of God the Father?

2. Will you please consider John 5:18 and tell me how it is that Jesus could tell the Jews that He was equal to God the Father if, in reality, He thought of Himself as inferior?

3. Ask them to explain John 1:18; 5:22-23; 10:30; and 20:28.

Thinking Through The Scripture

"For the Father judges no one, but has committed all judgment to the Son, that all should honor the Son just as they honor the Father. He who does not honor the Son does not honor the Father who sent Him." (John 5:22-23)

Questions for discussion:
1. This Greek word for "honor" is to *prize*. By implication, it means to *revere*. How are we to prize or revere the Son according to this verse?
2. How will our relationship with the Son affect our relationship with the Father?

The deceptive arguments that the Watchtower will teach its members are numerous and too cumbersome to include here. The Christian who takes time to understand what the Bible teaches regarding the essential doctrines of Christianity should be well equipped to meet the challenge of the Witnesses' deceptive arguments. The Bible tells us to "speak the truth in love."

Don't be afraid to challenge the Witnesses on what they believe. The best defense is often a good offense. Although Witnesses will often just quote a portion of a verse to make their point, slow them down by having them read aloud the whole passage. They are not normally challenged to consider the context in which something is being written, and this can be a real advantage for the Christian. *Although their arguments will be many, the best thing you can do is keep pointing them back to the Lord Jesus Christ and His Deity.*

EXPOSING PROBLEMS

Although Jehovah's Witnesses are well versed in how to contend with Christians regarding what they believe, you may get the opportunity to expose them to some legitimate problems which they should consider concerning their roots and their organization. Remember, they are caught in a deceptive web of false conclusions based upon a perverted text and the Lord might use you to set the captive free.

III. WHY IS THERE A PROBLEM WITH THE WATCHTOWER'S PROPHETIC ACCURACY?

   A. Because the prophecy of the second coming of Christ in 1874, of which Charles Russell had a part, failed to occur.

   B. Because Russell's prophecy that Armageddon would occur in 1914 failed.

   C. Because Watchtower's prophecy that Christ would return to earth in 1918 failed.

   D. Because Russell's prophetic teaching - that the Great Pyramid of Egypt was "God's Bible in Stone" showing us God's prophetic time table - was later contradicted by a Watchtower teaching that the Great Pyramid was rather Satan's Bible in Stone.

   E. Because Judge Rutherford's prophecy of the earthly resurrection of Abraham, Isaac, Jacob, and the prophets of old between 1925 and 1929 failed to occur.

   F. Because Watchtower's prophecy of Armageddon in 1954, forty years after Christ supposedly returned in 1914, never came to pass. Then they began to teach that 1958 was Armageddon.

   G. Because Watchtower's prophecy that the world would end in 1975 failed. *Over a million disillusioned J.W.'s left the organization in 1976 and 1977.*

IV. WHY IS THERE A PROBLEM WITH THE WATCHTOWER'S ACCURACY AND INTEGRITY REGARDING ITS NEW WORLD TRANSLATION?

   A. Because the five men who translated it were not scholars, were not very educated, had no Hebrew or Greek language expertise, and thus no authority to do such a thing.

   B. Because the vast majority of scholars totally disagrees with the Watchtower interpretation. One scholar, Dr. Julius R. Mantey says:

   > "Out of all the Greek professors, grammarians, and commentators they [the Watchtower] have quoted, only one (a Unitarian) agreed that 'the word was a god'...Ninety-nine percent of the scholars of the world who know Greek and who have helped translate the Bible are in disagreement with the Jehovah's Witnesses. People who are looking for the truth ought to know what the majority of scholars really believe."[10]

   C. Because of the three Greek scholars that the Watchtower cited as verifying their interpretation, Julius R. Mantey, Philip B. Harner, and John L. McKenzie, all three were misquoted and adamantly disagree with the Watchtower's interpretation.

D. Because for years the Watchtower cited Johannes Greber as the authority that verified some of their New Testament interpretation, but eventually it was discovered that Greber was a spiritist who called on the spirits to help him interpret. However, the Bible tells us plainly, that we should never *"ask ghosts or spirits for help, or consult the dead. Whoever does these things is disgusting to the Lord"* (*Deut. 18:10-12*). Embarrassed by this, the Watchtower ceased using him as a source, but did not repent of their translation.

E. Consider Luke 23:43 as an example of a subtle change the Watchtower made which emphasizes their doctrine. From Heather and Gary Botting in *The Orwellian World of Jehovah's Witnesses*, we learn the subtle way that the Watchtower manipulates Scripture. They write, "The change at Luke 23:43 is significant in terms of the Witnesses' view of the earthly resurrection as a future event—the resurrection to heaven did not commence until this century. Therefore, the Witnesses argue, the thief hanging on the torture stake beside Jesus could not have been promised that he would be with Christ in paradise on 14 Nisan AD 33. *By placing the comma after 'today' instead of before it*, the implication becomes that Jesus was merely telling the thief that some day they would be together in paradise, not that particular day."[11] [italics added]

"And Jesus said unto him, Verily I say unto thee, Today shalt thou be with me in paradise." (Luke 23:43) King James Version

"And he said to him: 'Truly I tell you today, You will be with me in Paradise'." (Luke 23:43) *New World Translation*

V. WHY IS THERE A PROBLEM WITH THE WATCHTOWER'S VIEW THAT THE HOLY SPIRIT IS ONLY AN ACTIVE FORCE AND NOT A PERSON?

Example: *The New World Translation* has been twisted in many places to represent the Holy Spirit as simply an active force. "Now the earth proved to be formless and waste and there was darkness upon the surface of [the] watery deep; and God's active force was moving to and fro over the surface of the waters" (Gen. 1:2) NWT. Notice how it says *"God's active force"* rather than the words *"Spirit of God"* found in an accurate translation. They have reduced the third person of the Trinity, the Holy Spirit, to an active force that is of itself devoid of personality. This is error. We see why there is a problem with this stand in the following ways:

A. Because the Watchtower has violated one of the basic rules of translation by translating the Hebrew word *ruwach* as an "active force" in some places, but as "spirit" in other places.

B. Because the Hebrew word *ruwach* (7307 in Strongs) means wind as in resemblance of breath or resemblance of spirit and is always translated spirit by scholars.

C. Because the Watchtower failed to change all of the Scriptures that give evidence for the person of the Holy Spirit even in their *New World Translation*. Examples of their translation are below. Notice that they do not capitalize holy spirit. How can an active force feel hurt, speak, bear witness, and hear?

1) In Isaiah 63:10 the holy spirit feels hurt.
2) In Acts 13:2 the holy spirit speaks.
3) In John 15:26 the spirit bears witness of the truth.
4) In John 16:13 the spirit hears and speaks.
5) In Acts 20:28 the holy spirit appoints overseers.

Thinking Through The Scripture

"*Unless one is born again of water and the Spirit, he cannot enter the king- dom of God.*" (*John 3:5*)

"*Now the Lord is the Spirit; and where the Spirit of the Lord is, there is lib- erty.*" (*2 Corinthians 3:17*)KJV

"*When the Spirit of Truth comes, he will guide you into the full truth. He won't speak on his own. He will speak what he hears and will tell you about things to come. He will give me glory, because he will tell you what I say. Everything the Father says is also what I say. This is why I said, 'He will take what I say and tell it to you'.*" (*John 16:13-15*) GW

Questions for discussion:
1. What are some of the important things that John 3:5 and 2 Corinthians 3:17 tell us about our relationship with the Holy Spirit?
2. What are the characteristics of the person of the Holy Spirit mentioned in John 16:13-15? The Watchtower says it is only an active force with no personality. Can an active force hear, speak, guide, or give glory?

VI. WHY IS THERE A PROBLEM WITH THE WATCHTOWER'S OVEREMPHASIS ON THE NAME JEHOVAH?

A. Because Jesus never addressed the Father as Jehovah.
B. Because Jesus taught us to pray, "Our Father who art in heaven...."

C. Because the Watchtower has inserted the name Jehovah throughout their New Testament translation despite the fact that it blatantly goes against thousands of Greek Manuscripts of the New Testament in which the Greek word *kurios* is always rendered "Lord" or "God" but never Jehovah. In *The Jehovah's Witnesses New Testament: A Critical Analysis of the New World Translation of the Christian Greek Scriptures*, author Robert H. Countess points out the motive of the Watchtower in doing this:

"The translators of the NWT were not merely intending to restore to the pages of the New Testament God's name, which name, it is alleged, was perhaps excised due to anti-semitism or ignorance on the part of the early Christian scribes. NWT has introduced "Jehovah" into the Greek Scriptures for the sole purpose of wiping out any vestige of Jesus Christ's identity with Jehovah."[12]

D. Because the name of Jesus is found in hundreds of Scripture verses in contrast to Jehovah which is used in a very limited fashion. The King James has it in only four places: Ex. 6:3; Ps. 83:18; Is. 12:2; and Is. 26:4.

E. Because most modern scholars believe that "Yahweh" is the correct rendering of the Hebrew consonants YHWH and not "Jehovah."

Thinking Through The Scripture

"By the name of Jesus Christ the Nazarene, whom you crucified, whom God raised from the dead—by this name this man stands here...And there is salvation in no one else; for there is no other name under heaven that has been given among men, by which we must be saved" (Acts 4:10,12) NASB

"This, then, is how you should pray; 'Our Father in heaven, hallowed by your name, your kingdom come, your will be done on earth as it is in heaven..." (Matthew 6:9-10) NIV

Questions for discussion:
1. What does Acts 4 tell us is the most important name for salvation under heaven? How did Jesus tell us to address God when praying? Did Jesus use the name Jehovah when he prayed?
2. Why do you think that the Watchtower is so adamant about using the name "Jehovah" as compared to Yahweh or even Jesus?

VII. WHY IS THERE A PROBLEM WITH THE WATCHTOWER'S STATEMENTS REGARDING THE PERSON OF JESUS CHRIST?

The Watchtower has demoted Jesus to a second class position. They have twisted their translation to make it appear that Jesus is not God Almighty, but that he was simply "a god". In some of their current literature "The Witnesses now teach that Jesus was only a perfect man."[13] But there are serious *contradictions* in their own Bible regarding this.

A. Because while their translation says that Jehovah will judge us (Is. 33:22), it also says "I solemnly charge you before God and *Christ Jesus*, who is destined to judge the living and the dead." (2 Tim. 4:1) NWT

B. Because while the NWT says that Jehovah is the Shepherd (Ps. 23:1), it also has Jesus saying, "I am the fine shepherd." (John 10:11) NWT

C. Because while the NWT says that Jehovah is the light (Ps. 27:1), it also has Jesus saying, "I am the light of the world." (John 8:12) NWT

D. Because while the NWT says that Jehovah is the King of the Jews (Is. 33:22), it also states that "This is Jesus the King of the Jews." (Matt. 27:37) NWT

E. Because while the NWT says that Jehovah God is the Father, it says "For there has been a child born to us...And his name will be called Wonderful Counselor, Mighty God, Eternal Father, Prince of Peace." (Is. 9:6) NWT

F. Because of the many other attributes that (supposedly) only Jehovah should have, their translation shows: Jesus sitting on the judgment seat (2 Cor. 5:10); baptism in the name of Jesus (Acts 2:38); Jesus sending the Holy Spirit (John 16:7); Jesus raising himself from the dead (John 2:19); Jesus as Lord (1 Cor. 8:6); Jesus as the Savior (1 John 4:14; Acts 4:10,12); Jesus being worshipped (Heb.1:6; Rev.5:11-14).

Thinking Through The Scripture

"Then Moses replied to God, 'Suppose I go to the people of Israel and say to them, The God of your ancestors has sent me to you, and they ask me, What is his name? What should I tell them?' God answered Moses, 'I Am Who I Am. This is what you must say to the people of Israel: I Am has sent me to you'." (Exodus 3:13-14) GW

"Jesus told them, 'I can guarantee this truth: Before Abraham was ever born, I am'. Then some of the Jews picked up stones to throw at Jesus." (John 8:58-59a) GW

Questions for discussion:
1. How did God reveal Himself to Moses?
2. What was the significance of Jesus statement to the Jews?
3. How did they respond to Him? Why?

VIII. WHY IS THERE A PROBLEM WITH THE WATCHTOWER'S STAND ON HOLIDAYS?
   A. Because the Society originally promoted the celebration of Christmas up through 1926.
      1) Watchtower, Jan. 15, 1919: President Rutherford thanks his followers for Christmas gifts.
      2) Watchtower, Dec. 15, 1926: "The event [Christmas] is so important, that it is always appropriate to call it to the minds of the people, regardless of the date."[14]

IX. WHY IS THERE A PROBLEM WITH THE WATCHTOWER'S STAND ON NO BLOOD TRANSFUSIONS?
   A. Because as David A. Reed states in *Jehovah's Witnesses Answered Verse by Verse* the Watchtower has "a history of introducing other medical prohibitions and then later changing their mind. In 1967, for example, they prohibited organ transplants. Followers were expected to choose blindness rather than accept a cornea transplant, or to die rather than submit to a kidney transplant. But then, in 1980, the leaders reversed the teaching and allowed transplants once again."[15]
   B. Because the verses in Leviticus 7:26-27 upon which the Watchtower builds this rule has to do with eating blood, not transfusions.
   C. Because even the "Orthodox Jews of today, who still scrupulously observe the regulations for kosher butchering and bleeding of meat, have no religious objection to blood transfusions."[16]
   D. Because Leviticus 3:17 says, "You must not eat any fat or any blood at all," yet the J.W.'s have no objection to eating fat.

X. WHAT ARE SOME PROBLEMS THEY HAVE HAD WITH REVERSALS?
   A. **Divorce** - Until December 1972, they held that "adultery" (Matt. 19:9) was the only valid reason for divorce. But then they decided that the word "pornea" used by Jesus referred to all types of illicit sexual intercourse. This was positively accepted by many Witnesses, but after several years the teaching was reversed because the true boundaries for divorce were now fuzzy.
   B. **Transplants** - Until 1967, the Society had no problem with people getting certain types of transplants such as cornea, kidney, and bone. The Watchtower issue of November 15 now called it a type of cannibalism. That caused many hardships for Witnesses for the next thirteen years until it was reversed in 1980 when it decided that it was a matter for personal conscience.

C. **Acts 20:20** - In this verse Paul states that he has taught from house to house. The Society used this for many years as justification of going door-to-door. However, for several years in the 1970's it admitted that this verse was not really talking about going door-to-door. Then in 1979, it reversed itself again and used it for their purposes of pushing members to go door-to-door selling publications.[17]

Thinking Through The Scripture

"God saved you through faith as an act of kindness. You had nothing to do with it. Being saved is a gift from God. It's not the result of anything you've done, so no one can brag about it." (Ephesians 2:8-9) GW

"Therefore by the deeds of the law no flesh will be justified in His sight." (Romans 3:20)

Questions for discussion:
1. The people of the Old Testament were required to fulfill many laws and ceremonies but always fell back into sin. Why do you think this was so?
2. If fulfillment of the deeds of the law does not justify us then would disobedience disqualify us from God's mercy? What is the gift of God to us?
3. If something is a gift, can it be earned? Can someone refuse a gift?

XI. WHY IS THERE A PROBLEM WITH UNITY WITHIN THE WATCHTOWER'S ORGANIZATION?

The organization was having internal problems in the early 1990's with unity among leadership, as Gordon Duggar tells us in *Jehovah's Witnesses: Watch Out for the Watchtower:* "There is strong and growing evidence that there is much discord at Bethel and that more than a few members of the Bethel family are challenging the errors and organizational procedures. The press has become interested and numerous articles are appearing in newspapers and magazines. A recent article in Newsweek magazine reported about Raymond Franz, a life-long member of the society, author of major books such as *Aid to Bible Understanding*, a member of the governing body, said to be in line to replace the present leader, Frederick Franz, Raymond's uncle.

Raymond Franz, during Bible research for some of the books he authored, discovered that Scripture did not agree with certain doctrine of the society. He tried to reason with the hierarchy about these problems with no success. In fact, he was removed from his position at

Bethel and later was disfellowshipped from the organization because he was 'seen eating' in a restaurant with another disfellowshipped witness, Peter Gregerson, who also had been a ranking officer in the society. Mr. Gregerson has appeared on radio, and the things he tells are hardly congruent with a 'loving' organization."[18]

WITNESSING TO JEHOVAH'S WITNESSES

XII. WHAT ARE SOME THINGS TO REMEMBER ABOUT JEHOVAH'S WITNESSES?

A. Remember that they don't think they will ever get into heaven. They have been told that only 144,000 will make it to heaven and that all those slots are full. The most they can hope for is life on an improved earth someday. They are even confused in this because their doctrine is somewhat inconsistent.

Ex-Jehovah's Witnesses, Heather and Gary Botting write: "the average Witness believes—has been told many times—that he will survive Armageddon into God's New World. For him, the attainment of paradise is a simple matter of hanging on to the faith until he gets through Armageddon. He lives in expectation of 'the Millennial Hope.' Clearly, this is a naive hope if Armageddon survivors are still to be considered 'dead in God's sight' and must wait another thousand years of 'Judgment Day' before qualifying for 'everlasting human life in Paradise.' Most Witnesses do not understand the implications of this long wait."[19]

B. Remember that most of them are not coming door-to-door because of some driving force to see people won over to Jehovah, but rather it is a work-out-salvation ethics that is required of them. Their eternal life in Paradise is connected to their obedience to spread the Watchtower word. The moment they cease to be an active part of selling the publications and going door-to-door is the moment that the other Witnesses question their eternal life in Paradise.

C. Remember that many of them have no experience of God's saving grace. Therefore, their conversion—if it can be called as such—is more of a cognitive agreement than a decisive turning point that is normally associated with religious conversion.[20]

D. Remember that they have been brainwashed to believe that anything outside of the Watchtower Organization is from the devil. In their eyes, the devil probably wants to use you to lead them astray. It is sad, but "the average Witness is so preoccupied with the evils of this 'dying old world' and involvement in proselytizing his neighbors that he usually has little time or desire to examine his faith or community objectively."[21]

E. Remember that they are lost souls who still have an empty place in their life that only Jesus Christ can fill. They might be deceived into thinking they have all the right answers, but the truth is, that somewhere deep down inside, they know they don't. Be sensitive to God using you in a special way.

F. Remember that when you speak the Word of God, it will look for fertile ground in the hearts of those who hear. You may think the J.W.'s are not really listening, but don't be too sure. Robert Passantino gives encouraging testimony of one occasion when he and his wife thought no one was affected by what they said:

"My wife and I once shared the gospel with a roomful of Jehovah's Witnesses, some of whom were in positions of congregational leadership. We spent hours talking about the Watchtower, the doctrine of the Trinity, the deity and resurrection of Christ, and Biblical salvation. None of the Witnesses seemed to be affected at all. On the way home, my wife and I were discouraged. Nothing had seemed to penetrate the Watchtower mentality. The next morning, one of the Witness couples called us. They told us, 'When you were talking last night, it was like bright sunshine filled the room. The Jesus you talked about is the Jesus we really believe in. We were tricked by the Watchtower, but now, no matter what, we have to follow the Jesus God showed us last night through what you said."[22]

XIII. WHAT ARE THE DON'T'S OF WITNESSING TO THE JEHOVAH'S WITNESSES?

A. Don't become defensive or argumentative even at the cost of loosing the debate. A strong confrontational spirit might win the battle, but patience can win the war.

B. Don't engage in a conversation about present world events.[23]

C. Don't unwittingly answer their leading questions. William J. Schnell tells us that "These probes by the JW are to discover whether you are a person who has fear about the troubles in the world; or whether you are a person who is lonely; or whether you are a person who has gripes against the establishment. If you give so much as a hint of such attitudes, you are immediately categorized by the Jehovah's Witnesses...."[24]

D. Don't stray too far from the focal issue that can set the captive free. Walter Martin warns, "The Deity of Christ...is a prime answer to Jehovah's Witnesses, for if the Trinity is a reality, which it is, if Jesus and Jehovah are 'one' and the same, then the whole framework of the cult collapses into a heap of shattered disconnected doctrines incapable of even a semblance of congruity."[25]

E. Don't try to correct every error and notion of a Witness. The simple words of truth will have a penetrating effect beyond what you can see with your physical eyes. The Holy Spirit will continue to minister truth even after the conversation.

F. Don't forget to be friendly. If time permits, ask them where they are from, where they work, and how many children they have. Most witnesses have received much verbal abuse and very little politeness. Let the love of Christ shine through you.

G. Don't forget to follow the *Golden Rule of Apologetics*. In other words, don't push them or ridicule them if you don't want the same in return. Matt. 7:12 should guide us as we witness to those bound up in the cults and world religions.[26]

XIV. WHAT ARE THE DO'S OF WITNESSING TO JEHOVAH'S WITNESSES?

A. Do pray quietly to the Holy Spirit and ask Him to lead your discussion.

B. Do encourage an examination of beliefs.

C. Do try to find common ground.

D. Do take your time.

E. Do ask leading questions. Jesus used questions to draw people to conclusions.

F. Do undermine the authority of the Watchtower Organization. Author Ron Rhodes gives the reason in *Reasoning from the Scriptures with the Jehovah's Witnesses*:

"If you can lovingly demonstrate that the Watchtower Society has been wrong time and time again in terms of its many predictions—as well as changed its position on key doctrines back and forth over the years—this will serve to call into question everything else the Society teaches. As you continue to *chip away at the Witness's confidence in the Watchtower Society*, you will find it easier to make doctrinal points with him or her."[27] (italics added)

G. Do ask them to share their testimony and be willing to share yours.

H. Do share the gospel story. David Reed makes an interesting observation:

"Jesus was a shepherd—not a cowboy! He did not ride herd on the sheep, shooting guns and cracking whips like cowboys do in a cattle drive. No. He gently led the flock. Jesus called, and his sheep heard his voice and followed him. We can do the same by *kindly presenting the gospel from the Word of God, confident that the sheep will hear and follow without our having to bully them* into it. Jehovah's Witnesses are accustomed to being bullied by their elders; we should stand out in contrast."[28] (italics added)

XV. WHAT ARE SOME PRACTICAL TIPS FOR STARTING TO WITNESS?

   A. **Prayer:** Let the Holy Spirit guide you while witnessing. He is concerned about protecting you but also using you to tell the truth to others. If you suddenly find yourself in a conversation with Witnesses, take a moment to pray in your heart and gain the peace that you know you have in Christ Jesus. If you sense sudden tension, it might be the stress of being abruptly pushed into a witnessing experience, or it might be your spiritual antennae perceiving an attack by the devil. Be sure to stay humble and resist the devil (James 4:6-7). Depending on the situation, it might even be appropriate to have prayer together. However, they will be focusing on Jehovah and not Jesus. When preparing for a prearranged meeting, ask the Lord for the best approach to the issues. If the Lord is for you, who can stand against you? Also, develop a habit of prayer on behalf of those that you personally know who are caught up in this cult.

   I mentioned in the other chapter on Jehovah's Witnesses that my Aunt Lyla prayed consistently for me. She prayed for me as I walked through many cultic and occultic practices. She helped pray down the strongholds that held me in prison. Prayer is often warfare against an enemy that holds people in cultic bondage. S. D. Gordon once said, "The greatest agency put into man's hands is prayer. And to define prayer one must use the language of war. Peace language is not equal to the situation. The earth is in a state of war and is being hotly besieged. Thus one must use war talk to grasp the fact with which prayer is concerned."[29]

   B. **Love:** Unfortunatley, the Witnesses are use to a generation of Christians who are not well equipped and who react in fear rather than love. As 1 John 4:18 implies, we should strive for that *"perfect love"* that casts out all fear. The lyrics of an old song say, "They will know we are Christians by our love." *This is what will help melt the cold legalism of the Watchtower organization.*

   Consider the following testimony of Chuck Love, a former Jehovah's Witness and consider what the impact of a Christian's testimony and agape love could be:

   "My wife and I have probably called on thousands of homes between the two of us. Not once did we encounter anyone who shared their testimony or their faith in Christ with us. Lots of people would say something like, 'Oh, you're that group that doesn't believe in hell' or, 'You don't believe in the Trinity.' Most people spoke to us in negative terms, telling us our beliefs were wrong but never bothering to tell us what was right. Nobody ever said anything about the love of Jesus Christ. No one ever tried to witness to us at the door."[30]

C. **Witness:** If you have time to sit and discuss the Bible, you can talk through many of the scriptural topics already mentioned. Make sure that you point out the inaccuracies in their *New World Translation*. Also, they need to see the entire passage and not just isolated verses. If your time is short, one of the following approaches might work. Write them in your Bible or memorize them so as to be ready at a moment's notice:

1) **Walk them through Revelation** regarding the Alpha and Omega. They can use their own translation if they would like. I did this one day with a couple of Witnesses going door-to-door. It can be quite effective and make them stop and think. Focus on the Witness that is being trained and ask the following:

   a. **Rev. 1:8** - Ask them who the verse says "Alpha & Omega" is. They will respond that it is Jehovah God.

   b. **Rev. 21:5-7** - Ask them if this also refers to Jehovah God? They will agree that this does refer to the Lord God Jehovah.

   c. **Rev. 22:13** - Ask them if this refers to Jehovah. They will agree.

   d. **Rev. 1:17-18** - Ask them to read this aloud. Then ask them, "When did Jehovah die?" They will not know how to respond because it is obvious that Jesus is the one who died and this clearly means that Jesus and Jehovah are one and the same.

2) **Walk them through the Great I Am.** When Moses asked God for his name, God told Him "I AM WHO I AM". Jesus revealed that this was His name also in John 8:58, but the Witness's translation is perverted, so walk through the following steps.

   a. **Exodus 3:14** - Ask them to read this from their NWT. Part of it will read:
      - "I SHALL PROVE TO BE WHAT I SHALL PROVE TO BE."

      Now ask them to read it from your Bible. It should read:
      - "I AM WHO I AM"

   b. **John 8:58** - Ask them to read this from their NWT. Part of it will read:
      - "Before Abraham came into existence, I have been."

      Now ask them to read it from your Bible. Part of it should read:
      - "Before Abraham was born, I am!"

   c. Now tell them that the Greek words here are "Ego eimi" = I am. Tell them someone has messed with their Bible in both these verses. Tell them to look it up in their own Kingdom Interlinear Translation and they will see it in the footnote.

3) **Walk them through True God or False God.**
   a. **John 17:3** - Ask them (based on this verse) how many true Gods there are?
       They should answer that there is only one true God.
   b. **John 1:1** - Ask them (based on this verse) if they believe that Jesus was "a god". They will agree with this. So then ask whether Jesus was a true God or a false God. "This will cause a dilemma for the Jehovah's Witness. If he or she says Jesus is a false god, he is contradicting the New World Translation of Scripture...If he says Jesus is a true God, he is also contradicting the Watchtower understanding."[31]

4) **Plant Seeds.** It is unlikely that Christians will see Jehovah's Witnesses or Mormons converted at the door. The real key is to witness to them and plant seeds which the Holy Spirit can later nurture, water, and grow. Tell them of your faith, your love for Jesus, and the witness of the spirit of Christ within you.

   Witnesses are not taught that the spirit of Jesus abides within the true believer. Have them turn to 2 Corinthians 13:5 and let them know that the Bible gives us a test as to whether we are really in the right faith. Those who have Jesus Christ "in" them are in the faith. Of course, their version, the NWT, says "in union with" because they don't believe that the spirit of Jesus Christ resides in His followers. However, you just take the time and let them know that their version is mistranslated. Let them know that they can have Jesus in their lives as well. Below is the testimony of Jean Eason, a former Jehovah's Witness, who got a hunger for God's Word and discovered that this was true.

   "No longer was I interested in reading all those different opinions about what the Bible taught - now I just wanted to know the Word! I wanted to read and read and read - for the love of God from deep within me was nourished for the first time! I started in the New Testament and read straight through. I noticed something I never saw before. Jesus was on every page! I always thought the Kingdom was the theme of the New Testament!

   I did something I've never done before. I got on my knees and prayed a prayer that went something like this: 'Dear Jehovah—Father of Jesus—with the aid of the Holy Spirit—if there is such a thing of inviting Jesus into my heart—I now open the door—come in—come in today—come in to stay.' For the first time I knew what all those 'religionists' had when I knocked at their door, telling them I wanted to share the good news of the Kingdom - no wonder they didn't want it - THEY ALREADY HAD IT!"[32]

End Notes

1. David A. Reed, *Jehovah's Witnesses Answered Verse by Verse* (Grand Rapids, MI: Baker Book House, 1994), pgs. 126-127.
2. Heather and Gary Botting, *The Orwellian World of Jehovah's Witnesses* (Toronto: University of Toronto, 1984), p. 107.
3. Don Nelson, "That Hideous Strength: The Watchtower Society," *Christian Research Newsletter*, March/April 1991, p. 1.
4. Ruth Tucker, *Another Gospel: Alternative Religions and the New Age Movement* (Grand Rapids, MI: Zondervan Publishing House, 1989), p. 145.
5. Botting, p. 120.
6. M. James Penton, *Apocalypse Delayed: The Story of Jehovah's Witnesses* (Toronto: University of Toronto, 1985), preface.
7. Tucker, p. 145.
8. Marian Bodine, *Christian Research Newsletter*, "Bible Answer Man" column, May/June 1992, p. 3.
9. Robert M. Bowman, *Why You Should Believe In The Trinity* (Grand Rapids, MI: Baker Book House, 1989), pgs. 14-15.
10. Julius Mantey; cited by Walter R. Martin, "The New World Translation," *Christian Research Newsletter*, 3:3, p. 5.
11. Botting, p. 99-100.
12. Robert H. Countess, *The Jehovah's Witnesses New Testament: A Critical Analysis of the New World Translation of the Christian Greek Scriptures* (Phillipsburg, N.J.: Presbyterian and Reformed Publishing Company, 1982), p. 33.
13. Gordon E. Duggar, *Jehovah's Witnesses: Watch Out for the Watchtower* (Grand Rapids, MI: Baker Book House, 1993), p. 34.
14. Ibid., p. 107.
15. Reed, p. 23.
16. Ibid., p. 30.
17. Penton, pgs. 110-116.
18. Duggar, p. 98.
19. Botting, p. 101.
20. Ibid., pgs. 76-77.
21. Penton, p. 304.
22. Ronald Enroth, ed. *Evangelizing the Cults: How to Share Jesus with Children, Parents, Neighbors, and Friends Who Are Involved in a Cult* (Ann Arbor, MI: Servant Publications, 1990), p. 138.
23. William J. Schnell, *30 Years A Watchtower Slave* (Grand Rapids, MI: Baker Books, 1984), p.190.
24. Ibid., p. 191.
25. Walter Martin, *The Kingdom of the Cults* (Minneapolis, MN: Bethany House Publishers, 1985), p.84.
26. Enroth, p. 136.
27. Ron Rhodes, *Reasoning from the Scriptures with the Jehovah's Witnesses* (Eugene, OR: Harvest House Publishers, 1993), p.20.
28. Reed, pgs. 114-115.
29. David Shibley, *A Force in the Earth: The Charismatic Renewal Worldwide* (Altamonte Springs, FL: Creation House, 1989), p. 74.
30. "I Was an Elder with the Jehovah's Witnesses: Personal Testimony of Chuck Love," interviewed by Dan Kistler, *Christian Research Newsletter*, 2:3, p.1.
31. Rhodes, pgs. 19-20.
32. Jean Eason, *A Jehovah's Witness Finds The Truth* (College Press, Joplin, MO, 1999), pgs. 51-52.

QUESTIONNAIRE: LESSON SIX

NAME: _____ DATE: _____

1. What are three myths about the Jehovah's Witnesses?

a) _____

b) _____

c) _____

2. The lesson refers to some deceptive questions that Witnesses may ask. On the lines below, list two of them and then refute them with the Bible or alternative question.

a) Deceptive Question _____

_____

    Refutation: _____

_____

b) Deceptive Question _____

_____

    Refutation: _____

_____

3. List two reasons why there is a problem with prophetic accuracy in the Watchtower.

a) _____

b) _____

4. List two reasons why there is a problem with accuracy and integrity concerning the NWT.

a) _____

b) _____

5. Why is there a problem with the Watchtower's view of the Holy Spirit?

_____

6. Jesus taught us to pray, "Our _____ who art in heaven...."

7. Exodus 3:13-14 "God answered Moses, 'I _____ Who ____ ____. This is

what you must say to the people of Israel: I Am has sent me to you'."

John 8:58 *"Jesus told them, 'I can guarantee this truth: Before _____ was born, ____ ____'."*

8. Give an example of one major reversal in Watchtower doctrine.

_____

9. Remember that a sad truth about the Jehovah's Witnesses that come to your door—They don't think there is any chance of them ever going to _____. Also, they have been brainwashed to think that you are totally deceived by the _____ and will have a hard time receiving from you.

10. List two don't's and tell why they are important.

Don't _____

_____

Don't _____

_____

11. List two do's and tell why they are important.

Do _____

_____

Do _____

_____

12. List in order the four verses that walk through Revelation regarding Alpha & Omega:

a) _____ b) _____ c) _____ d) _____

13. Why does Revelation 1:17-18 prove that Jesus is Jehovah? _____

_____

_____

14. Consider your knowledge of Jehovah's Witnesses before and after these lessons. Circle the number below that indicates how equipped you felt before taking the course to witness to a Jehovah's Witness as compared to how equipped you feel now. Be honest.

BEFORE 0 1 2 3 4 5 6 7 8 9 10 **AFTER** 0 1 2 3 4 5 6 7 8 9 10

THE EVOLUTION DECEPTION

"One of the reasons I started taking this anti-evolutionary view, or let's call it a non- evolutionary view, was last year I had a sudden realization for over twenty years I had thought I was working on evolution in some way. One morning I woke up and something had happened in the night, and it struck me that I had been working on this stuff for twenty years and there was not one thing I knew about it. That's quite a shock to learn that one can be so misled so long. Either there was something wrong with me or there was something wrong with evolutionary theory. Naturally, I know there is nothing wrong with me, so for the last few weeks I've tried putting a simple question to various people and groups of people. Question is: Can you tell me anything you know about evolution, any one thing, any one thing that is true? I tried that question on the geology staff at the Field Museum of Natural History and the only answer I got was silence. I tried it on the members of the Evolutionary Morphology Seminar in the University of Chicago, a very prestigious body of evolutionists, and all I got there was silence for a long time and eventually one person said, 'I do know one thing—it ought not be taught in high school.'" —Dr. Colin Patterson (Senior Paleontologist, British Museum of Natural History, London). Keynote address at the American Museum of Natural History, New York City, November 5, 1981

I. WHO WAS CHARLES DARWIN?
   A. Charles Robert Darwin was the man more responsible than any other for bringing about the publicity of the theory of evolution. He

built his theory upon the work of such men as Lamarck (a lecturer of the late eighteenth century), Hutton (propounded the theory of uniformitarianism in 1795), and Lyell (wrote Principles of Geology).

Darwin, who at one time was preparing for the Christian ministry at Cambridge, lost his faith and became an atheist somewhere in the years 1836-1839 as he came to believe in evolution and natural selection. He took a voyage to the Galapagos Islands off the coast of South America and observed many types of wildlife. Through observation, he thought he saw examples of evolution and natural selection at work together. In 1859 he published *The Origin of Species by Means of Natural Selection*.

Through the push of a scientist named Thomas Henry Huxley the world began to accept Darwin's theory of evolution, the theory that man evolved from apes. While natural selection (the survival of the fittest) had merit, it now took on a new role of proving man's ancestral leaps from ape to modern man. It was obvious that even though Darwin professed Christianity at one time and claimed support for the truth and authority of Scripture that he never had a really firm grasp on the Special Creation in the book of Genesis. He thought, until age fifty-two, that Genesis specifically stated that God created the world in 4,004 B.C.[1] (Date proposed for creation by the Archbishop Ussher several hundred years before Darwin).

Thinking Through The Scripture

"For since the creation of the world His invisible attributes are clearly seen, being understood by the things that are made, even His eternal power and Godhead, so that they are without excuse, because, although they knew God, they did not glorify Him as God, nor were thankful, but became futile in their thoughts, and their foolish hearts were darkened. Professing to be wise, they became fools, and changed the glory of the incorruptible God into an image made like corruptible man—and birds and four-footed animals and creeping things. Therefore God also gave them up to uncleanness, in the lusts of their hearts, to dishonor their bodies among themselves, who exchanged the truth of God for the lie, and worshiped and served the creature rather than the Creator, who is blessed forever. Amen." (Romans 1:20-25)

Questions for discussion:
1. The word "attribute" means an inherent characteristic or quality. What are some of God's invisible attributes that manifest themselves for us to see?

2. Why are people without excuse? What is their so called "wisdom" in reality?
3. What does this passage imply about Darwin's theory of evolution?
4. What problems do men heap on themselves when they turn from the Creator?

II. WHY IS EVOLUTION BEING CONSIDERED IN A BOOK ON THE CULTS?

A. **Because the deception of evolution has created a foundation for humanism** to invade our education, entertainment, social events, and governmental philosophy. Sir Julian Huxley, one of the founders of the American Humanist Association and promoter of neo-Darwinism tied the connection to humanism and evolution when he wrote:

> "I use the word 'humanist' to mean someone who believes that man is just as much a natural phenomenon as an animal or plant; that his body, mind, and soul were not supernaturally created but are products of evolution, and that he is not under the control or guidance of any supernatural being or beings, but has to rely on himself and his own powers."[2]

B. **Because many false religions accept the deception of evolution.** Furthermore, the deception of evolution has invaded and perverted the belief system of some professing Christians, thus damaging their faith in the Genesis account of real Divine Creation.

One perversion of faith is called **Theistic Evolution.** It is the view that both the Bible and evolution can work together - that God created the first protozoa and evolution took over from there. Another perversion of faith is called **Progressive Creation.** This variant view of theistic evolution teaches that God inserted special creative acts at certain strategic stages of evolutionary history. For instance, He created the first protozoa, later a different phyla, and eventually the first man.

In October of 1996, the Pope shocked the Christian world by sending a papal bull (solemn document) to the Vatican's Pontifical Academy stating that "Fresh knowledge leads to recognition of the theory of evolution as more than just a hypothesis." This was an attempt to build a bridge between the Catholic Church and modern science.[3] The Pope needs to read the Bible again because this view is an aberration from historic Christian doctrine and compromises the sincere Creationist stand by teaching that most of life evolved according to evolution.

In his comprehensive book *The Biblical Basis for Modern Science*, Dr. Henry Morris, the president of the Institute for Creation Research, show the relationship of false religions to evolution and acknowledges the impact of the heresy of theistic evolution:

"Modern Buddhists, Hindus, Confucianists, Shintoists, Lamaists, and advocates of other great ethnic religions, as well as Taoists and other Eastern mystics, all maintain that their religions are 'scientific' because they harmonize so well with modern evolutionism. In fact, the only world religions that assume a primeval special creation of all things, including that of the universe itself, are those based on the Bible and thus, ultimately on the first chapter of the Bible, namely Christianity, Judaism, and Islam. Even these, of course, are now mostly 'liberalized,' with large segments of each of these faiths now promoting theistic evolution rather than real creation."[4]

C. **Because many atrocities have occurred by the deception of evolution.** Of course, man's sin nature is the underlying force fueled by Satan. But evolution simply provided a license and justification for evil without guilt. Dr. Morris also says,

"Untold damage has been wrought, especially during the past century, by the dismal doctrine that man is merely an evolved animal. Racism, economic imperialism, communism, Nazism, sexual promiscuity and perversions, aggressive militarism, infanticide, genocide, and all sorts of evils have been vigorously promoted by one group or another...since they were based on evolution."[5]

Ken Ham gets even more specific showing the connection between evolutionist teaching and the atrocities of WWII in his book *The Lie: Evolution:*

"To see evolutionary measures and tribal morality being applied vigorously to the affairs of a great modern nation, we must turn again to Germany of 1942. We see Hitler devoutly convinced that evolution produces the only real basis for a national policy...The means to be adopted to secure the destiny of his race and people were organized slaughter, which has drenched Europe in blood."[6]

D. **Because evolution actually comes across as a religion.** Although evolutionists might resent being classified among religions, many of their advocates have made the very same comparison. Furthermore, one must have a certain amount of faith in evolution to be an evolutionist. Ken Ham states:

"All the evidence a scientist has exists only in the present. All the fossils, the living animals and plants, the world, the universe—in fact, everything, exists now—in the present. The average person (including most students) is not taught that scientists have only the present and cannot deal directly with the past. Evolution is a belief system about the past based on the words of men who were not there, but who are trying to explain how all the evidence of the present (that is fossils, animals and plants, etc.) originated. (Webster's Dictionary defines religion as follows: '...cause, principle or system of beliefs held to with ardor and faith.' Surely, this is an apt description of evolution.) Evolution is a belief system—a "religion."[7]

Thinking Through The Scripture

"As you therefore have received Christ Jesus the Lord, so walk in Him, having been firmly rooted and now being built up in Him and established in your faith, just as you were instructed, and overflowing with gratitude. See to it that no one takes you captive through philosophy and empty deception, according to the tradition of men, according to the elementary principles of the world, rather than according to Christ." (Colossians 2:6-8) NASB

Questions for discussion:
1. Consider the words root, build, and establish. What does it mean to be firmly rooted, built up, and established in your faith in Christ Jesus?
2. According to this passage, what are the traps we must avoid? How do these traps try to neutralize a Christian's faith?

III. WHY IS GENESIS SO IMPORTANT TO THE CHRISTIAN FAITH?
   A. **Because it is the foundation that adds meaning to our lives.** From *Genesis and the Decay of the Nations* by Ken Ham, we learn:
      "The meaning of anything is related to its origin. The meaning of marriage, for instance, is based in the book of Genesis, the book which gives us the first historical account of marriage. This is also true of death, sin, the seven-day week, why we wear clothes, and why Jesus died on a cross—all doctrine ultimately has its foundation in the book of Genesis, some more directly than others...Logically then, the Christian framework (like its doctrine) can stand only when the foundation exists. But if the foundation is removed, then the entire Christian structure will ultimately collapse."[8]
   B. **Because The Book of Genesis gives the only true and reliable account** of the origin of all the basic entities of the universe and of life.[9] Dr. Morris expresses which origins are depicted in Genesis in his book entitled *The Genesis Record.*
      1) Origin of the universe
      2) Origin of order and complexity
      3) Origin of the solar system

    4) Origin of the atmosphere/hydrosphere
    5) Origin of life
    6) Origin of man
    7) Origin of marriage
    8) Origin of evil
    9) Origin of language
    10) Origin of government
    11) Origin of culture
    12) Origin of nations
    13) Origin of religion
    14) Origin of the chosen people

IV. HOW HAS SATAN USED THE DECEPTION OF EVOLUTION TO ATTACK THE WHOLE STRUCTURE OF CHRISTIANITY?

A. Evolution is the foundation upon which humanism has built its stronghold. From this structure the societal plagues of euthanasia, abortion, divorce, racism, homosexuality, pornography, etc. spread and increase against the Christian church.

B. While Christians have been busy battling the plagues of humanism that Satan is casting forth, they have often overlooked the foundational battle that must take place between evolution and creationism. We must solidly proclaim the fallacies of the theory of evolution. There can be no compromise. The theory of evolution has many, many holes in it that must be exposed by Christians.

    The collapse of evolutionism will bring humanists face to face with the reality of creation because there are only two choices through which life could have come into existence: 1) Life happened by accident and somehow spread to the organized state it is today, or 2) Life was created by an Intelligent Supreme Being. There are no third choices. Once evolution collapses through the weight of its many absurdities, the only choice left is Special Creation.

V. WHY DOES GENESIS 1:1 PROVE SUCH A THREAT TO SO MANY FALSE PHILOSOPHIES AND RELIGIONS?

"In the beginning God created the heaven and the earth"

A. *Atheism*, the belief that there is no God, is threatened because this teaches the universe was created by God.

B. *Pantheism*, the doctrine that equates God with the forces and laws of the universe, is threatened because this states that God was outside of the universe He created.

C. *Polytheism*, the belief in many gods, is threatened because this teaches that only one God created it all.

D. *Materialism*, the theory that everything can be explained as being or coming from matter, is threatened because this teaches that matter had a beginning.

E. *Dualism*, the belief that the earth and all flesh is evil and distinctly always at war with the spirit which is good, is threatened because God is good and He alone created the heavens and the earth and later called them "good".

F. *Humanism*, the doctrine that places man's self importance at the center of everything, is threatened because it is God and not man that is the ultimate reality.

G. *Evolutionism*, the theory that life happened accidentally and evolved into higher forms of intelligence, is threatened because this teaches that God created all things.[10]

VI. WHAT ARE SOME OF THE PROBLEMS WITH THE THEORY OF EVOLUTION?

A. **The Problem of Spontaneous Generation.** This theory teaches that life somehow came from non-living matter. In *Fast Facts on False Teachings*, Carlson and Decker explain the evolutionists believe "that some 3.5 billion years ago there was a large inorganic soup of nitrogen, ammonia, salts, and carbon dioxide bubbling away. Out of this noxious caldron arose the first single-cell alga."[11]

One problem is that *Biogenesis* (life comes only from life) is a basic axiom of biology and is taught as fact to biology students. This completely contradicts spontaneous generation and supports the concept of everything yielding seed and fruit after its own kind as presented in the first chapter of Genesis.

Another problem for spontaneous generation is that it has been disproved by eminent scientists, time and time again, starting with Louis Pasteur. Scientists have tried to create life in test tubes many times. Dr. Stanley Miller and Dr. Sidney Fox tried, but the most that they have accomplished was combining some atoms to form amino acids which are the simplest compound units out of which proteins can be assembled. However, this did not strengthen their case for spontaneous generation but weakened it because "The mixture of amino acids and other simple chemicals [were] not right for producing life."[12] There are some combinations of amino acids that will build life and some that will destroy it. These were the latter.

The odds of scientists actually constructing a full DNA molecule from non living matter in a test tube are literally astronomical, but if they did—what would it prove?—only that life was created in a supervised, highly organized laboratory by an intelligent being.

B. **The Problem of Reproduction.** There is in every cell of plants, animals, and humans a complex metabolic motor. This enables the cell to draw or extract energy from its surrounding environment in order to give enough energy for the reproduction of the cell and other functions. This metabolic motor is required for life to exist and reproduce. Since there was no metabolic motor present, it would have been impossible for the nonliving "inorganic soup" that the evolutionists propose to create life. Also, DNA (deoxyribonucleic acid) could only be spawned by life containing DNA and every living thing must have DNA.

C. **The Problem of Probability.** The probability of life arising from non life and then upgrading through evolution is so slight that evolutionists have turned creationists after studying it themselves. The following give some kind of idea of the chances:

1) One chemist calculated the chances of amino acids combining in the necessary arrangement by coincidence to be 1 against 10 with 67 zeros, and this he said would need to be in an ideal atmosphere, with an ideal mixture of chemicals, and with 100 billion years.[13]

2) Sir Fred Hoyle, English astronomer and professor of Astronomy at Cambridge University compared the probability the same as a tornado whipping through a junk yard and creating a Boeing 747 from the junk. Furthermore, he said,

   "The likelihood of the formation of life from inanimate matter is one to a number with 40,000 noughts after it...It is big enough to bury Darwin and the whole theory of Evolution. There was no primeval soup, neither on this planet nor on any other."[14]

D. **The Problem of the Second Law of Thermodynamics.** All energy and matter are governed by the physical laws of thermodynamics. The Second Law states that everything in the universe slowly runs out of energy and disorganizes. It tends towards chaos and breakdown.

The idea of things going from new to old or from complex to disorganized is clearly seen in life. Cars rust, wood rots, buildings fall down, hair falls out, rooms get messy, people die, and no genuine perpetual motion machine keeps going indefinitely. Everything loses energy at a gradual rate. This is called entropy. The problem the theory of evolution has with this, is that evolution is built upon the assumption that chaos turns into order, that basic life forms move in an upward progression into complex life forms.

Thinking Through The Scripture

"And God said, 'Let the land produce living creatures according to their kinds: livestock, creatures that move along the ground, and wild animals, each according to its kind.' And it was so. God made the wild animals, according to their kinds, the livestock according to their kinds, and all the creatures that move along the ground according to their kinds. And God saw that it was good." (Genesis 1:24-25) NIV

"When You send forth Your Spirit and give them breath, they are created; and You replenish the face of the ground." (Psalm 104:30) AMP

Questions for discussion:
1. Read Genesis chapter one and consider the complexity of the earth and heavens. What are some of the awesome aspects of Creation that can be derived from the verses above?
2. What do you think it means "according to their kinds"?
3. In Psalm 104:30 what is the importance of the Spirit of God?

E. **The Problem of the Fossil Record.** Darwin told us that evolution was a slow, gradual change which the fossil record would eventually prove with millions of transitional forms. However, after more than a hundred years of digging and countless numbers of fossils unearthed, the fossil record bears practically nothing. The best that evolutionists have come up with (actually the only thing) is Archaeopteryx which they claim is the transitional intermediate of a reptile changing into a bird. It did have teeth and claws like a reptile and wings and feathers like a bird, but no transition was taking place. All of these things were fully formed. Dr. Henry Morris makes the following statement regarding the fossil record:

"Now even if we take the geological ages at face value, all the way from the Cambrian period of the Paleozoic era to the Pleistocene epoch of the Cenozoic era, the remarkable fact is that there is still not the slightest evidence for evolution in the fossil record. That is out of all the billions of fossils known and documented in the rocks of the earth's crust—fossils in tremendous variety, representing both extinct and living kinds—there is not a single true transitional evolutionary form that has yet been excavated anywhere in the world."[15]

VII. WHAT ARE THE PROBLEMS WITH THE MISSING LINKS—APE MEN?

A. **Ramapithecus:** A few bones found in India created for some evolutionists the missing link in man's climb from an ape. The specimen was named after Rama, one of the Indian gods. Someone's wild imagination created an entire Ramapithecus walking upright from only jaws and teeth. Millions of textbooks crowned it the missing link. Convinced that it was of human ancestry, paleoanthropologist David Pilbeam of Harvard University promoted it for years on the flimsiest fossil evidence.

   Finally, in the late 1970's Pilbeam came to the shocking realization that the specimen was that of an extinct ape and not that of a man. It was not the missing link.

B. **Australopithecus:** (southern ape) africanus, robustus, and afarensis. The best known of these is afarensis, affectionately known as "Lucy," a three-foot-tall australopithecine found by Don Johanson in Ethiopia in 1974. Lucy is assumed to be three million years old by evolutionists and considered by many of them the missing link. However, various evolutionist including the famous, Richard Leakey, have concluded that there is no good evidence that Lucy was the missing link. Many eminent evolutionists believe Australopithecus are just another group of extinct apes.

   Also, it has been discovered that the modern pygmy chimpanzee (Pan paniscus) is remarkably similar to the skeletal remains of Australopithecus casting serious doubt on the age factor or missing link theory. Indeed, one of England's top scientists, Lord Zuckerman (an evolutionist) carried out a number of examinations, tests and measurements on these australopithecine bones. His research team concluded that they were not related to man, did not walk upright, and were more like the orangutan than any other living animal. "Lord Zuckerman himself had the following to say about the evidence for human evolution…'[If man] evolved from some ape-like creature…[it was] without leaving any fossil traces of the steps of the transformation.'"[16]

C. **Homo Habilis** (Handy Man): Some evolutionists still stick to their theories that Australopithecus evolved into Homo habilis, who evolved into Homo erectus, who evolved into Homo sapiens and modern man. The absurdity in this is that even according to their own reckonings, Homo habilis, Homo erectus, and Homo sapiens existed at the same time. This means no evolution because there was no transition from one to the other. Another difficulty for evolutionists to explain is that H. habilis is only half as tall as H. erectus.

   Louis and Mary Leakey brought to light another confusing issue in that they found "primitive" Oldowan-type tools with a group of H. habilis thought to be 2 million years old but then found the same tools in Kanapoi Valley, northern Kenya of very recent origin. This throws great doubt upon the age. The crushing blow to H. habilis, however, is that bones of modern man have been found alongside the H. habilis showing that evolutionists have been mixing human with monkey bones. A current theory now is that H. habilis is another extinct type of ape or chimp.

D. **Homo Erectus** (erect man): Some evolutionists hold that this was the precursor to modern man, but even among evolutionists there is much controversy because much of what has been discovered simply shows it to be modern man. H. erectus has been found with tools, the use of fire, and understanding of burial or cremation. One scientific Creationist, Marvin L. Lubenow in his book *Bones of Contention: A Creationist Assessment of Human Fossils* writes, "the differences between Homo erectus and Homo sapiens are not the result of evolution but instead represent genetic variation within one species."[17]

Two of the most famous cases are as follows. "Peking Man" was supposedly a missing link. Skulls and teeth found in China were described and then mysteriously lost. What was not publicized, however, was that evidence of ten humans, fire, and tools were discovered at the same site. Circumstantial evidence indicates the men to be hunters who brought ape skulls to the site to eat. "Java Man" discovered by Eugene Dubois and propounded as the missing link. Later, it was found to be a modern-type human leg bone along with a very ape-like skull cap. A whole group of evolutionist scientists on the Selenka-Trinil Expedition in 1907 studied the area located by Dubois. They concluded that Java man was not related to modern man. Apparently, even Dubois eventually said the same.

E. **Nebraska Man:** Supposedly the genuine missing link and the evidence used against creationists at the famous Scopes "Monkey Trial." A vivid reconstruction was commissioned of Nebraska man based on a single tooth and a few tools. Eventually, it was found that the tooth was not that of ancient man, but a wild pig.

F. **Piltdown Man:** Based on skull fragment found in a gravel pit at Piltdown, East Sussex, England. For forty years it was held up as classic proof of evolution. Then it was discovered that the whole thing was a fraud based upon altered orangutan bones mixed with human ones.

G. **Neanderthal Man:** The classic textbook example of Neanderthal sends pictures of primitive man through our minds. Evolutionist like to add grotesque features based upon very few bone fragments and speculation. In actuality, it appears that Neanderthal was simple

100 percent human, perhaps suffering from the disease of rickets. This information has been available from the beginning when in 1872 Rudolf Virchow, a professor of pathology at the University of Berlin, discoverer of embolism and leukemia, "published a carefully argued and factual diagnosis that the original Neanderthal had been a normal human who suffered from rickets in childhood and arthritis in adulthood."[18]

The evolutionists did not want to regard Virchow's analysis because he questioned Darwin's theory to begin with. Today, further evidence by Francis Ivanhoe is showing Neanderthal people as a group to be those who suffered from rickets. However, evolutionists are still not regarding this information. Dr. Lyall Watson made an interesting observation regarding the actual number of bones that might be considered legitimate examples of the evolution process. He said:

"The fossils that decorate our family tree are so scarce that there are still more scientists than specimens. The remarkable fact is that all the physical evidence we have for human evolution can still be placed, with room to spare, inside a single coffin."[19]

Thinking Through The Scripture

"And God created man in His own image, in the image of God He created him; male and female He created them." (Genesis 1:27) NASB

"Then the Lord God formed man of dust from the ground, and breathed into his nostrils the breath of life; and man became a living being." (Genesis 2:7) NASB

Questions for discussion:
1. What does dust plus God's breath of life equal?
2. Consider the word image. Do you think this is a literal or figurative image? Is it a spiritual or physical one, or both? How does this contrast with the image that evolutionists see as man's origin?
3. Suppose man became so technologically advanced that he could create life in a test tube. What would this really prove or suggest? Why would this actually support the need for a Supernatural Intelligence as the Creator?

VIII. WHAT ARE THE PROBLEMS WITH THE CAVE MEN THEORY?
   A. Evolutionists treat the concept of people living in caves and drawing on walls as though this is how men used to live but no longer.

The fact is, people living in caves proves nothing about when they lived. People still live in caves. The Tarahumara Indians of Mexico often dwell in caves. Indians of South America live in caves. People all over the world can be found living in caves even today. The absurdity of connecting cave dwelling with ancient man is the same faulty reasoning that connects stone tools with ancient man, yet these same tools are found among modern day tribes and peoples.

B. The Bible refers to numerous occasions upon which people fled to caves and used them for fortresses or hideouts. Lot and his two daughters dwelt in a cave according to Gen. 17:30. In Joshua 10:16, five kings hid themselves. David, his household, and many of his men dwelt in a cave in 1 Samuel 22:1. In 1 Kings 18:4, Obadiah hid fifty prophets. Israel fled to the caves in Judges 6:2.

Thinking Through The Scripture

"Their strength is gone. Shriveled up from need and hunger, they gnaw at the dry and barren ground during the night. They pick saltwort from the under-brush, and the roots of the broom plant are their food. They are driven from the community. People shout at them in the same way they shout at thieves. They have to live in dry riverbeds, in holes in the ground, and among rocks. They howl in bushes and huddle together under thornbushes. Godless fools and worthless people...." (Job 30:2-8) GW

Questions for discussion:
1. Certain scholars think that Job is the oldest book in the Old Testament. What do you think the phrase "holes in the ground" means? What type of people did these appear to be? Why were they driven from communities?
2. Sometimes caves are found with child-level paintings or drawings on the walls. What does this suggest regarding the inhabitants of the dwellings. Is there any possible correlation between the above passage and these people?

IX. WHY IS CIRCULAR REASONING A PROBLEM IN THE THEORY OF EVOLUTION?
A. A foundation stone of evolution is called *the uniformitarian view of geology.* It was created by an atheist named Charles Lyell in the nineteenth century. Lyell, a lawyer who was influenced by Hutton, divided the earth into twelve geologic age-layers of earth, based upon the philosophical assumption of evolution over millions of

years. Lyell did not witness these twelve layers with his eyes because they don't exist. Even today, only five of the layers have been found and in order, and they are upside down from Lyell's configuration. Lyell proposed that the twelve layers each represented an earth age and he dated the layers. Therefore, he concluded, fossils found in those layers could be dated according to the layer.

B. The evolutionist's problem with circular reasoning is this: *They date the fossils based upon the age of the geologic layer the fossils are found in on the one hand. But then on the other hand, they date the geologic layer based upon the known fossils found in that layer.* They have no absolute. Each dates the other and so all dates are only assumption and speculation. There are simply no facts to verify any of it.

X. WHAT IS THE EVIDENCE OF A WORLD WIDE FLOOD?

A. There are numerous cultures that have accounts, stories, or traditions of a great flood back near the beginning of their cultures. Although these traditions have been modified through the ages, as should be expected, and though there are vast differences across the traditions, there are certain similarities that make these traditions more than a coincidence. They show all the stories origination from one source and being modified from it.

   As one author points out, "There is almost complete agreement among them all on the three main features: 1. There is a universal destruction of the human race and all other living things by water. 2. An ark, or boat, is provided as the means of escape. 3. A seed of mankind is preserved to perpetuate the human race. To these might be added a fourth, which, though not occurring in all the traditions, occurs very frequently, namely, that the wickedness of man is given as the cause of the Flood."[20]

   The following are some of the cultures, tribes, and peoples in both past and present that have a flood tradition:

   Athapascan tribe on the West Coast of the U.S.A, The Papago Indians of Arizona, The Arapaho Indians, The Algonquin Indians, Primitive Brazilians, Ancient Indians of Peru, Mexican Indians, The Natives of Alaska, The Natives of Sudan, The Hawaiians, The Mongols, Sumatra, Polynesia, Micronesia, Tahiti, New Zealand, New Guinea, Melanesia, Wales, Lithuania, India, China, Persia, The Chaldeans, The Egyptians, The Greeks, The Romans, and The Babylonians.

B. The Babylonian flood account is well written out on clay tablets. The story has similarities to the Biblical account, including birds being sent forth to discover dry land, an altar, and a sacrifice. However, there are "many differences between the two stories despite the resemblances, and it is more likely that both stories reach back to an original event than that the Hebrew story is a modification of the ancient myth."[21] Also, the Babylonians have a list of kings before and after the flood.

C. Fossil graveyards including those of dinosaurs indicate a quick and violent death. Many dinosaur graveyards have signs stating that the dinosaurs were killed by a flood.

D. Tree fossils can be found extending through various strata of earth signifying a quick burial as a flood would produce.

E. Sylvia Baker writes a fascinating account: "Along the coastline of Northern Siberia and into Alaska are buried the remains of about five million mammoths...the mammoths are entombed in ice...The mammoths died so quickly that in one or two cases food is preserved undigested in their stomachs and in their mouths."[22]

XI. WHAT ARE SOME OF THE MANY EVIDENCES OF A YOUNG EARTH?

A. **Carbon 14 dating** - It shows the earth to be several thousand years old.

B. **Earth's Magnetic Field** - The rate of current degeneration would have made the earth with a magnetic field greater than a star if it is even ten thousand years old.

C. **The Sun** - If the earth were really billions of years old, the sun would have been so large as to kill everything on the surface of the earth.

D. **Meteorites** - If the earth is so old, there should be many more meteorites.

E. **Space Dust** - If the moon is billions of years old, the astronauts should have found between 50 and 180 feet of space dust instead of less than an inch as they did.

F. **The Oldest Written Records** - None were found older than 3,000 B.C.

G. **The Red Woods** - Some of the oldest living things only 4,000 years old.

H. **Oxygen** - The present level of atmosphere could be produced by plants in 5,000 years.

I. **Population Growth** - Some people wonder how this many people could arise from Adam and Eve in just six thousand years, but even conservative population estimates give us the present world population in just 4,000 years. The real question to evolutionists is: WHERE ARE ALL THE BONES OR PEOPLE? The fact is, that if man has been around as long as they claim, then there should have been (conservatively) 3,000 billion people who have lived. Our earth should be much more crowded, the fossils of human bones should be everywhere, and there should be much more evidence of ancient culture everywhere. Where are all the bones?

XII.   DID JESUS TEACH US THAT GENESIS WAS AUTHENTIC?

YES! here are some examples.

Matt. 19:4 *"'Haven't you read,' he replied, 'that at the beginning the Creator made them male and female'."*

Jn. 8:58 *"'I tell you the truth,' Jesus answered, 'before Abraham was born, I am!'"*

Matt. 10:15 *"I tell you the truth, it will be more bearable for Sodom and Gomorrah on the day of judgment than for that town."*

XIII.   DID THE NEW TESTAMENT AUTHORS TEACH US LIKEWISE?

YES! here are some examples.

Matt. 1:2 *"To Abraham was born Isaac; and to Isaac, Jacob; and to Jacob...."*

Lk 3:38 *"...son of Enoch, the son of Seth, the son of Adam, the son of God."*

1 Cor. 15:45 *"The first man, Adam, became a living soul...."*

2 Peter 2:4-5 *"For if God did not spare angles when they sinned, but cast them into hell and committed them to pits of darkness, reserved for judgment; and did not spare the ancient world, but preserved Noah, a preacher of righteousness, with seven others, when He brought a flood upon the world of the ungodly."*

XIV.   WHAT IMPACT CAN WE HAVE AS CHRISTIANS?

A.   **Prayer:** Even though many are caught up in the strongholds of humanism and evolution today, we must remember who the true enemy is and the mighty weapons of our warfare. As the following passage indicates, we need to take a stand of prayer.

"Finally, be strong in the Lord, and in the strength of His might. Put on the full armor of God, that you may be able to stand firm against the schemes of the devil. For our struggle is not against flesh and blood, but against the rulers, against the powers, against the world forces of this darkness, against the spiritual forces of wickedness in the heavenly places. Therefore, take up the full armor of God, that you may be able to resist the devil in the evil day, and having done everything to stand firm." (Ephesians. 6:10-13) NIV

B.   **Love:** It is easy to become infuriated at those who profess that we ascended from apes, but it is our responsibility to show them the love of Christ. Remember that we are to respond with a spirit of power, love, and a sound mind (2 Timothy 1:7). Sometimes, all the

reasoning in the world will not change the mind of an evolutionist, but love will soften his heart so that he can hear the message of
the gospel.

C. **Witness:** Don't think that you know too little to reason with an
evolutionist regarding our origins. While it is good to be equipped
as Christians with the most information, we must also remember
that most evolutionists have very little solid information of their
own. Witness to them about the truth of God in Creation. Show
them that what makes the most sense is a Supernatural Creator.

End Notes

1. Marvin L. Lubenow, *Bones of Contention: A Creationist Assessment of Human Fossils*
    (Grand Rapids, MI: Baker Book House, 1994), p. 95.
2. Sir Julian Huxley writing in a promotional pamphlet by the American Humanist
    Association. Quoted by Henry M. Morris, *The Biblical Basis for Modern Science* (Grand
    Rapids, MI: Baker Book House, 1993), p. 391.
3. Mike Gendron, "The Pope and Evolution: The drift from truth continues," *Lamplighter
    Newsletter,* produced by Lamb & Lion Ministries 18, 10 (October, 1997): 6.
4. Morris, p. 107-108.
5. Ibid., p. 403.
6. Ken Ham, *The Lie: Evolution* (Colorado Springs, CO: Master Books, 1987), p. 85.
7. Ibid., pgs. 16-17.
8. Ken Ham, *Genesis and the Decay of the Nations* (El Cajon, CA: Master Books Publishers,
    1991), pgs. 12-13.
9. Henry M. Morris, *The Genesis Record* (Grand Rapids, MI: Baker Bood House, 1995), pgs.
    18-20.
10. Ibid., adapted from a concept presented by Morris on p. 38.
11. Carlson and Decker, *Fast Facts On False Teachings* (Eugene, OR: Harvest House
    Publishers, 1994), pgs. 53-54.
12. Paul S. Taylor, *The Illustrated Origins Answer Book* (Mesa, AZ: Eden Productions, 1990),
    p. 22.
13. A.J. White, "Uniformitarianism, Probability and Evolution," *Creation ResearchSociety
    Quarterly* 9, 1 (June 1972): 32-34.
14. Sir Fred Hoyle, "Hoyle on Evolution," *Nature,* 12 November 1981, p. 148.
15. Morris, p. 337.
16. Ibid., p. 399.
17. Lubenow, p. 137.
18. Ibid., p. 150.
19. Dr. Lyall Watson, "The water people," *Science Digest,* 90 (May 1982): 44.
20. Alfred M. Rehwinkel, *The Flood* (Saint Louis, MO: Concordia Publishing House, 1951),
    p. 128.
21. J. A. Thompson, *The Bible and Archaeology* (Grand Rapids, MI: Wm. B. Eerdmans
    Publishing Co., 1977), pgs. 14-15.
22. Sylvia Baker, "Just What do the fossils prove", *Bone of Contention: Is EvolutionTrue?*
    (Resource Center, P.O. Box 302, Sunnybank, Queensland 4109, Australia: Creation
    Science Foundation, 1994), p.12.

QUESTIONNAIRE: LESSON SEVEN

NAME: _____ DATE: _____

1. Who was Charles Darwin? _____
_____
_____

2. List three reasons why the evolution deception is considered in a course on the cults.

a) _____

b) _____

c) _____

3. Were you taught to believe evolution or creation in your education?
_____

4. What is theistic evolution? _____
_____
_____

5. Do either theistic evolution or progressive creation line up with the Bible's account? _____

6. Give a list of religions that accommodate and harmonize with evolution:
_____

7. Why is the accuracy of Genesis so important for Christians? _____
_____
_____

8. List and explain three philosophies or religious beliefs that Genesis 1:1 threatens:

a) _____ : _____

b) _____ : _____

c) _____ : _____

9. Briefly explain why the theory of evolution has a problem with each of the following:

a) Spontaneous generation: _____

_____

b) Reproduction: _____

_____

c) Probability: _____

_____

d) 2nd Law of Thermodynamics: _____

_____

e) Fossil Record: _____

_____

10. Consider the supposed missing links. Tell about the problems they present to evolution. _____

_____

_____

_____

11. Write out Genesis 1:27. _____

_____

12. List three reasons that are evidences of a world wide flood:

a) _____

b) _____

c) _____

13. Did Jesus teach us that Genesis was authentic? _____. Did the authors of the New Testament teach us that Genesis was authentic? _____ Write out a scripture showing that Jesus did teach and authenticate the book of Genesis. _____

_____

_____

14. Consider your knowledge of the evolution deception issues before and after this lesson. Circle the number that indicates how equipped you felt before taking the course to witness to someone on this issue as compared to how equipped you feel now. Be honest.

BEFORE 0 1 2 3 4 5 6 7 8 9 10 AFTER 0 1 2 3 4 5 6 7 8 9 10

THE NEW AGE MOVEMENT

"Several years ago actress Shirley MacLaine cried out, 'I am God!' on a TV special based on her best-selling book, Out on a Limb. Almost overnight, it seemed, 'New Age' became a household term in America. Today the New Age movement represents what I believe is the greatest counterfeit spiritual revival the world has ever known. Satan, in a last-ditch effort as the return of Christ approaches, is attempting to imitate the tremendous explosions of evangelism and genuine Holy Spirit revival we have seen around the world over the last decade. A sort of satanic 'Pentecost' or New Age, occultic, cultic and Eastern mystical ideas is sweeping the globe. I was personally involved in the New Age movement for more than a decade before being converted to Christ. I experienced firsthand 'cosmic consciousness,' 'seeing the great white light,' 'mental telepathy' and other psychic phenomena. I know how dangerous the New Age is - and how deeply it is rooted in demonic deception...The fact is that Eastern mysticism, the occult and counterfeit religions have infiltrated every single sector of our society. It is now ingrained in our culture, and interest in psychic power and false spirituality is at an all-time high."[1] —Paul McGuire*

I. WHAT IS A DEFINITION FOR THE NEW AGE?
   A. *In Understanding the New Age,* author Russell Chandler gives this definition: "New Age is a hybrid mix of spiritual, social, and political forces, and it encompasses sociology, theology, the physical sciences, medicine, anthropology, history, the human potentials

movement, sports, and science fiction. New Age is not a sect or cult, per se. There is no organization one must join, no creed one must confess. Identifying individuals as 'full-blown' New Agers is baffling. Some subscribe to certain portions of New Age, some to others; some dissociate themselves from the movement altogether, though they embrace core aspects of its thinking. The New Age influence touches virtually every area of life, and thousands of New Age activists seek to transform society through New Age precepts. Millions more have adopted the movement's view of reality, though they may simply think of it as a pragmatic, humanistic philosophy of life."[2]

II. WHAT ARE THE ROOTS OF THE NEW AGE?
   A. Chandler also says, "Although 'new' in style and vocabulary, the movement is in many ways as old as the Eastern religions of Hinduism and Buddhism, Western occultism, and the mystical oracles of ancient Greece and Egypt. New Age has simply recast the theory of reincarnation into the language of Western humanistic psychology, science, and technology."[3]
   B. Some of the earliest roots are:
      1. Astrology (c. 2000 B.C)
      2. Hinduism and Yoga (c. 1800 B.C.)
      3. Buddhism (c. 500 B.C.)
      4. Witchcraft and shamanism (prehistoric)
      5. Gnosticism (c. 160 A.D.)
      6. Taoism (c. 400 A.D.)
   C. Some of the more recent roots are:
      1. *Swedenborgianism* (c. 1792) Emmanuel Swedenborg's followers began a movement based upon his writings that emphasize a) communication with the dead, b) spiritual evolution, and c) denial of the Trinity.
         Script. Refuting: 1 Sam. 28:7-14; 1 Chr. 10:13; 2 Cor. 5:17; Mt. 28:19
      2. *Mormonism* (c. 1830) Joseph Smith began a movement that teaches a) man can become a god, b) pre-existence of the soul, c) salvation through secret knowledge, and d) confusion between matter and spirit.
         Script. Refuting: Is. 44:10-11; Ps. 104:29-30; Rom. 6:23; 1 Cor. 15:44
      3. *Spiritualism* (1848) The Fox sisters revived old teachings. The movement emphasizes a) communication with the dead, b) mediums communicating with spirits, c) the ministry of angels, and d) reincarnation.

Script. Refuting: Dt. 18:10-12; Heb. 1:6-7,14; Heb. 9:27; Eccl. 3:20

4. *Evolution* (1859) Charles Darwin's theory a) reshaped how people viewed their origins, and b) paved the way for the merging of spiritual evolution and progressive human reincarnation.
   Script. Refuting: Gen. 1 - 3; Matt. 19:4; 1 Cor. 15:45; Rom. 5:12

5. *The Mind Sciences* (c. 1862) The various originators of this movement taught that a) God is a force and not a person, b) mind can control reality, and c) sin and death are not real.
   Script. Refuting: Matt. 3:16-17; Dt. 18:10-12; 2 Thess. 2:10-12

6. *Theosophy* (1875) Helena Petrovna Blavatsky began a movement that teaches a) Christianity as de-evolutionary, b) belief in the Ascended Masters who guide the earth, c) an evolutionary "plan" for mankind, and d) "spiritual racism" and anti-Semitism.
   Script. Refuting: Jn. 3:3; Is. 44:6,8; Jn. 11:25; Gal. 3:28-29

Thinking Through The Scripture

"'You will not surely die,' the serpent said to the woman...'when you eat of it your eyes will be opened, and you will be like God'...she took some and ate it." (Genesis 3:4-6) NIV

"What has been will be again, what has been done will be done again; there is nothing new under the sun." (Ecclesiastes 1:9) NIV

Questions for discussion:
1. How did the serpent trick Eve? What lie did she swallow? How is this lie still being used by Satan to lure people into the New Age Movement?
2. The book of Ecclesiastes implies that there is nothing new. What kind of things do you think the author is referring to here? Why are people the same now as in the days of the Garden of Eden?

III. WHO ARE SOME OF THE NAMES IN THE NEW AGE MOVEMENT?
Note: The following list represents only some of the prominent people caught up in the current New Age Movement. It helps show the pervasiveness of the problem in the American society. Do you recognize any of these names?
   A. *Marilyn Ferguson:* author of "Aquarian Conspiracy"
   B. *Shirley MacLaine:* actress, author of "Out on a Limb", and seminar leader
   C. *Fritjof Capra:* physicist, philosopher, and author of "The Tao of Physics"

D. *J. Z. Knight:* channeler of "Ramtha", a 35,000 year old ascended master
E. *Al Gore:* politician and eco-crisis propagandist
F. *Dr. James Lovelock:* biologist, promoter of "Gaia", Greek goddess of the earth
G. *John Kenneth Galbraith:* economist, part of the "Iron Mountain" team
H. *Maurice Strong:* secretary general of the earth summit
I. *Teilhard de Chardin:* mystic, father of spiritual globalism
J. *Barbara Marx Hubbard:* low key author opposed to Christianity
K. *Helen Schucman,* author of "A Course in Miracles"
L. *Brad Steiger,* author of numerous books on UFOlogy
M. *Betty Jean Eadie:* author of "Embraced By The Light"
N. *Carl Jung:* psychologist, promoter of a "collective unconsciousness"
O. *Oprah Winfrey:* uses her talk show to promote many New Age teachers
P. *Marianne Williamson:* Promoter of *A Course in Miracles*
Q. *Deepak Chopra:* New Age physician
R. *David A Lee:* Creator of New Age Web Works in 1995.

Thinking Through The Scripture

"Enter through the narrow gate, for wide is the gate and spacious and broad is the way that leads away to destruction, and many are those who are entering it. But the gate is narrow—contracted by pressure—and the way is straightened and compressed that leads away to life, and few are they who find it. Beware of false prophets, who come to you dressed as sheep, but inside they are devouring wolves." (Matthew 7:13-15) AMP

Questions for discussion:
1. How many find the way that leads to life? Why do you think that is? In what way does the New Age Movement typify the wide gate?
2. Why do Christians need to be concerned about the mixing of New Age teaching with that of Christian doctrine? How can we protect Christians and yet still reach out with love to those who are lost and on the wrong path?

IV. WHAT ARE SOME OF THE MAJOR BOOKS OF THE NEW AGE?
   A. **Aquarian Conspiracy:** (1980) Marilyn Ferguson was "catapulted into the New Age limelight."[4] In the book, Ferguson claims scientific support for a theory that an evolution of world wide consciousness is about to take place. She believes that there will be an awakening of "godlike potential" in many human beings.

B. **Out on a Limb**: (1983) Shirley MacLaine's first New Age book made a sensation and promoted her to a chief spokesman of the New Age. In the book, MacLaine tells about her "out-of-the-body experience, triggered by her friend, David, while she is meditating on the flame of a candle in a mineral spring bath high in the Peruvian Andes."[5] Through certain aspects of the experience, MacLaine and her friend came to the conclusion that reincarnation must be true. In a later book, "Dancing in the Light", she relates another out-of-body experience which shows her that she has a "Higher Self" that is God.

C. **A Course in Miracles**: (1975) Helen Schucman was an atheist psychologist teaching at a university in New York when she claims that a spirit entity (declaring himself to be Jesus) gave her visions and spoke to her. She recorded notes from the "voice inside of her brain" for ten years and then created a three volume do-it-yourself New Age course. Its popularity has increased dramatically in the last decade, and according to author Texe Marrs "is also now being taught in many New Age churches throughout America as well as Europe.

Its influence is especially deeply felt in Unitarian churches and such New Age-oriented denominations as the Church of Religious Science, Unity, and others. However, the course has also caught on with such liberal Christian denominations as the Methodists, Episcopals, Disciples of Christ, and some Lutheran groups."[6] The course's subtle underlying messages are that 1) the world is an illusion, 2) Jesus is Christ but not the only Christ, 3) Jesus was *not* punished for our sins, 4) salvation comes individually through works and holiness, 5) we are all a part of God, 6) sins are only bad dreams, and 7) there is no death. Today, one of the chief promoters is Marianne Williamson.

D. **Embraced By The Light**: (1992) In this book, Betty Jean Eadie recounts an experience that she claims occurred one night in November of 1973 at Riverton Hospital (now Highline Specialty Center) in Seattle, Washington. "There at approximately 9:30 p.m., 31-year-old Betty Jean Eadie allegedly began hemorrhaging as she lay recovering from a routine hysterectomy."[7] Betty died, met with Jesus, and returned to life some five hours later. Betty gives the clearest account ever it seems of what death is like and what life is all about.

People flocked to buy the book and hear Betty at conventions. However, some problems arose for Betty. First, it was strange that not one of Seattle's newspapers reported such a startling event. Second, Betty's length of death has changed from five hours to two hours to four. Third, Betty's refusal to name the attending physician has added much speculation against her story. Fourth, her Mormon background comes through clearly in the false doctrines and peculiar wording of the book and was highlighted by her early refusal to admit that she was a Mormon. Fifth, her book released in Utah (Mormon central) was written in such a way to add credence to Mormon doctrine and acceptance, whereas her book released in other places, altered the story enough to put emphasis on New Age views.

E. **The Nag Hammadi Library in English:** (2000) This is an update of the library first published in 1978 and includes new research. The texts were unearthed in 1945 near Nag Hammadi in Upper Egypt and they helped promote the modern Gnostic Movement. Gnosticism was the first cult of Christianity. New Agers say that these texts bring a balance to the distorted concept of God presented in the Dead Sea Scrolls. The Nag Hammadi teaches that Eve was created first, that there are two Gods in the universe—a good one of truth and light and an evil one of ignorance and darkness, and that men are really gods trapped in the material world. (See chapter on Mind Science)

F. **Other Books:** Because New Age encompasses so many areas, a browser section would include sections like Astrology, Chakras, Channeling, Divination, Feng Shui, Mysticism, New Thought, Urantia, etc. I remember that in my search for the truth I read many books that are now considered New Age classics like *Jonathan Livingston Seagull, The Teachings of Don Juan: A Yaqui Way of Knowledge, The Tibetan Book of the Dead, The Uranita,* etc. We would take drugs like peyote or magic mushrooms and search for inner truth. But the answers found only created larger questions in the mind which eventually challenged the existence of reality itself. Add to these the reading of philosophy and eastern religion books, as well as many other sub-culture drug books and it shapes a mind to have a very mystical, disconnected view of reality. This unwittingly can open the door for demonic activity and blatant deception.

Another area of books is on angels. Just walk into any major bookstore and ask for books on angels. There will be an entire section. The New Age has a plethora of books on the subject. These are not books on Biblical angels, although they might be included, but these are on a host of other angels sometimes referred to as spiritual guides to which the writers give names, attributes, and supernatural powers. The fascination with the New Age angels has produced an unhealthy worship of demonic angels who disguise themselves as angels of light and ministers of righteousness (2 Corinthians 11:14-15) by which they deceive people. This camouflage is nothing new. The Apostle Paul even had to warn the Colossians saying, *"Let no one cheat you of your reward, taking delight in false humility and the worship of angels, intruding into those things which he has not seen, vainly puffed up by his fleshly mind, and not holding fast to the Head* [which is Jesus]" (Colossians 2:18-19).

V. WHAT ARE SOME DIFFERENCES BETWEEN NEW AGE AND CHRISTIANITY?

TOPIC	NEW AGE	CHRISTIANITY
God	Impersonal, amoral evolving force	Personal, moral being; omnipotent
Jesus	One of many avatars; God-guru	Unique God - Man, only Lord & Savior
Creation	Always existed	Created by God out of nothing
Nature	All is (one) consciousness; monistic	Interconnected, but not monistic
Man	Spiritual being; a sleeping God	Made in God's image; now fallen
Truth	Through mysticism and spirit guides	Through natural & Scriptural revelation
Sin	Failure to recognize one's own deity	Moral evil; willful violation of God's ways
Death	Illusion; entrance to reincarnation	Entrance to eternal heaven or hell
Ethics	Situational and relative	Based on God's will; absolute
Salvation	Revelation of one's own deity	Repentance & Faith in Jesus' atonement
Judgment	No personal judgment	Everyone judged before the seat of Christ
Angels	Highly evolved guides; non biblical	Created by God; servants, others are fallen

VI. WHAT ARE THE TWO MAJOR SCHOOLS OF NEW AGE THOUGHT?

　A. **Consciousness Renaissance:** Mankind is at a point where certain individuals are stepping beyond certain self-imposed limitations of the mind and uniting with a utopian universe full of perfection, divinity, and highly evolved guides. For decades, books and speakers have been pushing "a separate reality" that seekers can find. Some have referred to it as "Mind at Large" (Aldous Huxley). James W. Sires tells what some of the names for this are in his book *The Universe Next Door:*

　　"Mind at Large is a sort of universe next door, alternately called 'expanded consciousness' or 'alternative consciousness' (MacLaine), 'a separate reality' (Castaneda), 'Clairvoyant Reality' (LeShan), 'other spaces' (Lilly), 'other realities' (Leonard), 'another order of reality' (Brodie), 'supermind' (Rosenfeld) or 'Universal Mind' (Klimo)."[8]

　B. **Quantum Leap of Consciousness:** Mankind is at a point in which the whole world must ready itself to take a quantum leap into a higher evolutionary dimension of consciousness. "In contrast to Consciousness Renaissance, this explosion into the New Age will come as we ready ourselves to accept the gift of new life from powers beyond us. This giant step into cosmic reality will take place in a moment of time. It sees mankind on the edge of a massive evolutionary explosion in which we all wake up one morning in a new world where we are all one with divinity and power and goodness."[9]

　　One backlash of this view has come against Christianity because we don't adhere to this New Age view and believe that they are deceived. In the *Spiritual Counterfeit Project Journal*, Brooks Alexander gave an example of what one "extremist" New Ager is saying about it:

　　"Barbara Marx Hubbard is both influential and controversial. Yet she is also surprisingly obscure. She is influential because she has a great deal of money to put behind her passionate New Age convictions...She is controversial because she has clearly stated that classical Christianity and its believers are unfit to enter the New Age, and that both will therefore have to be extinguished before the New Age can properly begin. In support of that belief, she serves up a high-octane mixture of evolutionary mysticism and her own 'inner voice' of revelation from 'Christ' Himself."[10]

　　Troy Lawrence was a Theosophist who worked for an elite New Age organization known as the Tara Center. His job was to locate and promote the New Age Messiah (the antichrist of the Bible). However, Troy met the real Messiah in the process and got saved.

In his book, *New Age Messiah Identified: Who Is Lord Maitreya?* he tells us how the New Age elite feels about Christianity:

"Christianity! Most Christians are just now aware of the hatred and anger that word elicits in the hearts and minds of the New Age elite. After all, to a devoted New Ager, the Christian Community is the last great hurdle between an old and decaying age of superstition and ignorance and a New Age of brotherhood, tolerance, and happiness for all - a hurdle that New Agers intend to overcome in a most brutal fashion."[11]

VII.WHAT IS "HARMONIC CONVERGENCE"?

A. It is built upon the "Quantum Leap of Consciousness" myth. The founding father of Harmonic Convergence, Jose Arguelles, is a New Age social-change leader who has already attempted one world wide rally that would draw people together in such a harmonic way that it would jettison the world into a new age order. Arguelles requested that 144,000 'rainbow' humans come together on August 16 and 17 of 1987 at various places in the earth. He believed that if a 144,000 convergers came together that several things would take place: 1) That there would be massive UFO sightings and extraterrestrial activity, 2) That the 'resonant attunement' of the convergers would be like human voltage affecting 550 million persons on the planet (11% of earth's population), and 3) that 550 million people represent the minimum critical mass of humanity necessary to propel us into a new world order. Only 20,000 convergers showed up and no UFO's. Disappointed representatives have warned that Gaia (mother earth) will possibly respond with wrath due to lack of converger support, thus bringing about cataclysmic destruction as a way of blowing off negative steam.

VIII. WHAT ARE SOME OF THE INFLUENCES NEW AGE HAS HAD ON SOCIETY?

A. **Holistic Health:** Healing for the total person: mind, soul, and body. While this view has some merit to it, those who espouse it have often taken it to an extreme (monistic: all is one in the universe) position. Promoters of holistic health have created many approaches to health based almost solely on assumption without verifiable data to confirm the approach. Among these is 1) Reflexology (assumes the foot is the window into internal body parts), 2) Iridology (the eye is the mirror of the soul), 3) Etheric Electromagnetic Color Fields (the reading of auras), and 4) Cymatic therapy (transmits the correct "sound" of health to ailing body parts. There are many more. Here are some things for Christians to beware of when considering health needs:

1) Beware of psychic diagnosis and healing
2) Beware of therapies claiming to manipulate "life energies"
3) Beware of therapies grossly at odds with known biological mechanisms
4) Beware of therapists with only one answer[12]

B. **Transpersonal Psychology:** This relatively new field is being dubbed the "fourth force" with behaviorism, classical psychoanalysis, and humanistic psychology considered the first three respectively. With a monistic worldview that sees people as one with the universe, it stresses self worth, freedom to choose (relativism), and power to change one's reality. Furthermore, it emphasizes unitive consciousness, peak experiences, mystical experiences, self-actualization, oneness, awareness, and transcendental phenomena.

C. **Education:** Evolutionism, values clarification, Eastern mysticism, intolerance for Christian heritage, humanistic psychology, and New-Age-sensitive curriculum has flung the doors of public education wide open to embrace New Age thinking. Teachers who want to teach traditional values are more and more pressed to conform. In some places, the "three R's" are being pushed aside for visualization exercises. It is not too difficult to find colleges which offer courses emphasizing self-hypnosis, parapsychology, telepathy, clairvoyance, out-of-body experiences, etc.

D. **Science:** There is a modern day attempt to shift science from "objective" reality into one of "subjective" reality. We will consider two of them. First, in Capra's influential book "The Tao of Physics" he tries to make parallels between new physics and mysticism by comparing statements of physicists to those of Buddhists, Taoists, and Hindus. Capra concludes that quantum theory basically reveals the oneness of the universe (monism). He had a visionary experience in which he saw the atoms of his body participating in the cosmic dance of energy. He perceived that this was "the dance of Shiva, the Lord of Dancers" who is worshipped by Hindus.[13] Of course, something is lost in it all because Capra was very familiar with the Bhagavad Gita which describes the dance. In response to his conclusions, one might ask him, "how did you know your vision represented Shiva's dance? Would you have drawn the same conclusion if you had not read the Bhagavad Gita which explains the dance?"

Second, a Belgian physical chemist named Ilya Prigogine won the Nobel prize for his theory of dissipative structures. He hypothesizes that *entropy* (the second law of thermodynamics which makes evolution impossible) is counteracted by a higher law which he calls *syntropy*. This, he claims , accounts for evolution of higher and more intricate levels of organization. Although it is only a hypothesis—that has as yet no proven support—New Agers have grabbed hold of it and used it to support all forms of social evolutionary concepts. They say it proves man is evolving socially and at a point where we are monistically ready to join with the universe. However, this doesn't make any sense as Chandler points out:

"The New Age variety of social evolution assumes that human nature is innately good—the precise opposite of the view held by the Judeo-Christian Scriptures. The Prigogine hypothesis, when applied to belief in inherent and ever ascending social improvement, is also contradicted by the record of history. India is a good case in point. One would think that a land dominated for thousands of years by a holistic worldview (the same worldview the New Agers now say science has verified) would have long ago synergistically eliminated hunger, violence, overpopulation, and the institutionalized racism of its caste system...There is no essential connection between social evolution and biological evolution. Neither a holistic worldview nor mystic enlightenment can erase the stubborn stain of individual and corporate sin and bring personal salvation."[14]

E. **Ecology:** Is there an eco-crisis? One would certainly think so listening to all of the bad things that the news and certain politicians say about it. While it is important to stress that Christians should be good stewards of the earth (Gen. 1:28), it is also important to understand that there is much evidence denying the alleged crisis of certain issues such as global warming, ozone depletion, the spotted owl issue, as well as many other areas.

New-Age extremists have mixed mysticism with science to create a cult like atmosphere around environmental issues. New-Age advocates call the earth Gaia and say she is alive. In the midst of this mystical fervor, clear evidence disputes erroneous claims:

1) *Global Warming Crisis?* Satellite data and tree ring analysis show no warming in the past twenty-five years. 90% of all warming this century occurred prior to 1940. Substantial evidence also shows that a variety of natural causes increased all of the temperature.[15]

2) *Ozone Depletion?* Ultraviolet radiation reaching the earth is at an all time low. CFC's (chlorofluorocarbons) decompose in weeks rather than a century. Ozone thinning occurs only in polar regions. All ozone depletion occurs in hemispheric winter, not summer. There is a natural annual variation of 50 percent but

CFC's and other man made depleters account for 10 percent at the most.[16]

3) *Spotted Owl Problem?* In 1986 the National Audubon Society reported that a minimum of 1,500 pairs of spotted owls in California, Oregon, and Washington would be enough to preserve the species. Current evidence suggests that there may be 8,500 owls in northern California alone.[17] Michael S. Coffman states in *Saviors of the Earth?*:

"The assumption [the] earth is being destroyed is not open for discussion. It is already presumed. Through intimidation and ever more restrictive laws, environmental leaders are in effect willing to risk destroying the American economy and shatter perhaps millions of lives on a unproven and highly questionable premise. Yet this premise goes unchallenged while they demand that everyone else in America go through major upheavals to conform to their view of reality. And that view of reality is to stop or transform our economy rather than find solutions within our existing economic system."[18]

F. **Politics:** Certain advocates of the New Age want to see national sovereignty and property rights cease in order to help usher in a one world monistic unity. The push towards a global economy and global peace force is on the agenda of certain factions of the New Age because they see it as necessary for the "quantum leap of consciousness". Other factions have a similar agenda but for different reasons. While many new agers are not caught up in politics at all, there is an undercurrent mixing of philosophies, cultures, religions, science, education and other issues that is trying to merge the various sovereignties of the earth into a global community.

One group who is possibly instrumental in pushing this agenda is the Theosophical Society. Some have called it the religion of the counterculture, peace, and environmental movements. The mystical world viewpoint of theosophy believes that nature is sacred and that true harmony between man and nature will only occur in a civilization that is simple and shamanistic. In the last century the society has been successful in enlisting the aid of the rich and the influential to carry out its agenda. It has also been successful at camouflaging itself and being secretive.

There is speculation that the society was at the heart of the Iron Mountain group. This secretive elite group of fifteen experts in various scientific and social fields met in secret for two years beginning in August of 1963. They first met at Iron Mountain, New York. There goal was to determine what problems would face the U.S. if "permanent peace" should arrive. After two years of meeting, they anonymously issued a report stating that "war" unified a people and stabilized a nation. Without war, the U.S. would have disunity and instability. The group focused on various substitutes for war— a substitute that would eliminate war but unite the world against a common enemy to keep stability.

The report concluded that an eco-crisis was the best alternative and that environmental catastrophes could be "invented" to begin the process of world globalization. Incredibly, the report also emphasizes a nation's need for a class system (poor and rich) for internal incentives and the national good. No wonder the group wished to remain anonymous. Coffman gives the following insight:

"Whereas we really do have some manageable environmental problems, it is now apparent the eco- catastrophe was manufactured to further a much larger agenda. By 1990, about a generation and a half later, just about everything in the Iron Mountain Report had come true. The attack on our Constitution and national sovereignty was well under way. The environmental movement was draining our financial resources dry. Many Americans had been whipped into a state of raw terror—in fear of global ecological collapse. And President Johnson's Great Society had created a welfare system that was effectively locking the poor into chains of poverty."[19]

Thinking Through The Scripture

"Behold, the Lord is riding on a swift cloud, and is about to come to Egypt; The idols of Egypt will tremble at His presence, and the heart of the Egyptians will melt within them. So I will incite Egyptians against Egyptians; and they will each fight against his brother, and each against his neighbor, City against city, and kingdom against kingdom. Then the spirit of the Egyptians will be demoralized within them; And I will confound their strategy, so that they will resort to idols and ghosts of the dead, and to mediums and spiritists. Moreover, I will deliver the Egyptians into the hand of a cruel master, and a mighty king will rule over them, declares the Lord God of hosts." (Isaiah 19:1-4) NASB

Questions for discussion:
1. The Lord will judge a nation that turns away from truth to idols. From this passage, what are some of the signs that show a nation drifting from the truth?
2. What are some of the signs that indicate the direction of our modern society? If we are moving away from the truth and into idolatry, what kind of action can we expect the Lord to take? Are there any indications of His judgment today?

IX. IS THERE A CONSPIRACY AND HOW SHOULD CHRISTIANS
    RESPOND?

A. Douglas R. Groothuis gives Christians something to think about in
   his book *Unmasking the New Age* when he says, "Much Christian
   interest in the New Age has centered around various conspiracy theories. Because of the pervasiveness and influence of New Age ideas,
   it would not be unnatural to assume that some level of conspiracy
   was afoot. But we must keep in mind that conspiracy theories of all
   shapes, styles and sizes have been crisscrossing the planet throughout history. Any group that has transnational allegiances (such as
   Freemasons, Jews, Roman Catholics and international bankers) has
   been targeted as the elite conspirators plotting world takeover. New
   Age conspiracy charges simply transfer this thinking into a more
   modern context.

   Levels of conspiracy are natural to like-minded people and
   groups. The New Age makes much of networking—linking ideas
   and people together for greater influence and creativity. This is nothing new. Christians work together to further the kingdom of God.
   Communists work together to expand their regime. Those linked by
   ideology want to implement a common agenda...While levels of
   cooperation and organization exist between various groups and
   individuals, the New Age movement is better viewed as a worldwide shift than a unified global conspiracy."[20]

B. Scripture casts the definitive light on conspiracy theorizing: The
   problem is as old as Eden. *The Fall itself was a serpentine plot*—the
   serpent enlisted a naive Eve on behalf of his hidden agenda.
   Conspiracy theories soon ensued: The first were Adam's and Eve's
   explanations of their bungle (see Genesis 3:9-13). As author Karen
   Hoyt tells us in *The New Age Rage*, the pattern of primal tragedy
   tells us three things:
   1. There really is a conspiracy.
   2. Theories about it generally begin in fear and end in rational-
      ization.
   3. The theories tend to be diversions, even when factually accu-
      rate.[21]

C. The Lord gave some instruction to the prophet Isaiah regarding
   conspirators and how he should react to conspiracy theories in
   Isaiah 8:10-14:
   *Make plans for battle, but they will never succeed. Give orders, but
   they won't be carried out, because God is with us! For thus the Lord
   spoke to me with mighty power and instructed me not to walk in the
   way of this people, saying, "You are not to say, 'It is a conspiracy!' In
   regard to all that this people call a conspiracy, And you are not to fear*

what they fear or be in dread of it. It is the Lord of hosts whom you should regard as holy. And He shall be your fear. And He shall be your dread. Then He shall become a sanctuary....."

X. CHANNELING—WHAT IS IT AND WHAT IMPACT IS IT HAVING?
  A. It is similar to Spiritism's mediums invoking departed spirits for the purpose of communication, but whereas this was primarily personal for a loved one left behind, the New-Age channelers receive messages by unrelated spirits that speak guidance, knowledge, and direction.
  B. Many channelers have arisen in the last decade proclaiming profound truths from disembodied entities and selling these truths for top dollar. J. Z. Knight of Yelm, Washington, claims to channel Ramtha, a 35,000 year old Cro-Magnon warrior and ascended master from the lost continent of Atlantis. Various Hollywood stars have been influenced by Knight. Hundreds of Knight's followers have moved to the rural Northwest to survive the destruction that Ramtha predicts after the millennium. In Knight's school (New Age Ramtha School of Enlightenment), people are trained in various mystical and psychological aspects of New Age thinking.

  One individual, Gregory May, who has been very influenced by the Human Potential Movement of the 1970's and now by Ramtha, was hired by the Federal Aviation Administration to put employees through various training sessions. FAA has now been sued by former employees and is under Congressional investigation. May abused employees' rights by having people tied together (sometimes the opposite sex) during showers and bathroom times, as well as using abusive language and forcing disclosure of personal matters.[22]

  Other examples of channeling are Lazarus through Jach Pursel, and Mafu who was supposedly a leper in A.D. 79 in Pompeii through Penny Torres-Rubin. The channelers sometimes are booked years in advance for private (costly) consultations. Their influence is growing in a mystic-seeking culture.

Thinking Through The Scripture

"You must never...practice black magic, be a fortuneteller, witch, sorcerer, cast spells, ask ghosts or spirits for help, or consult the dead. Whoever does these things is disgusting to the Lord." (Deuteronomy18:10-12) GW

Questions for discussion:
1. Why are these things disgusting to the Lord? In what way do they hurt and hinder people? Why do they draw people?

2. How do they separate people from God? What is their source of power and information? Do you know anyone who has practiced these things?

XI. WHAT ABOUT CRYSTAL CONSCIOUSNESS AND POWER?
   A. The New Age mixes mysticism with science. New Agers—as well as many who are not—like crystals. People hang them in cars, make necklaces and earrings, meditate upon them, and basically idolize them. Supposedly, their mystical properties were known to Hindus thousands of years ago. They are used to reveal past lives and future events. Health and happiness (they say) are transmitted because crystals molecularly can develop shapes in harmony with the internal structure of the human body, helping us to balance our energy fields. Some espouse that the knowledge of the planet is stored in crystal. Scientifically speaking, it is the most common mineral on the planet composing approximately 12 percent of the Earth's crust.

   There is a minute electrical charge called the piezoelectric effect that can be produced by tapping or squeezing crystal because the compression forces positive and negative ions to interact. Quartz crystal has been used for radios, computers, watches, lasers, etc. because its vibration is constant. With the modern day craze of people assigning metaphysical properties to crystals, it appears that scientific objectivity has not had enough impact to stop people from drifting back into "dark age" paganistic thinking.

XII. ARE THERE POSITIVE ASPECTS OF THE NEW AGE MOVEMENT?
   A. It would be unfair to say that there are no positive aspects of the New-Age movement. It draws people from many backgrounds (including Christians) because there are certain areas of agreement. Some of these are listed below along with other aspects of it that might be indirectly positive. However, some elements of liberal Christianity are promoting "companionship"[23] between the Bible and the New Age, while at the same time admitting that there is a fundamental difference between our viewpoint of God; namely monism (the belief that all is one; therefore each is divine) versus monotheism (the belief that there is one God).[24] This type of approach must be avoided because it dilutes irreconcilable differences and lowers standards of Christianity that must be held high.

   However, this is not to say that there are no positive aspects of the movement. As Christians we need to respect "Truth" with whomever it is found. The New Age shares these common views with Christians:

1) An increasing awareness of man's impact upon the environment.
2) The desire to be proper steward's of the world's many forms of life.
3) An emphasis upon the nutritional health of the human body.
4) The realization that mankind has deep spiritual needs not being met.
5) The revelation that the new millennium is bringing dramatic spiritual changes.

As Christians, we need to accept truth wherever we find it, even hiding in the New Age Movement. However, as Groothius states, we must also be ready to confront the things that are not true:

"All truth is God's truth, whether it be from the Bible or from the mouth of a New Age follower. Nevertheless, Christians must learn to witness to the truth of their faith and to expose the weaknesses of the New Age. Effectively confronting the New Age will take a humble, loving spirit and conscious effort at reaching out to those in the movement. We need to look for legitimate common ground with the New Age. We've noted that the New Age raises crucial issues for the modern world. This can be used as a springboard in communicating Christ to the New Age. We can agree on some things...At the same time we affirm the common ground between the New Age and Christianity we must clearly specify and define the differences between the world views. Because the New Age generally believes that all roads lead to God, Christians must clearly explain how Christianity contradicts the One."[25]

XIII. HOW CAN WE HELP THOSE CAUGHT UP IN THE NEW AGE?

A. **Prayer:** It is easy to get overwhelmed by an onslaught of New Age philosophy. When that happens, we need to remember the story of Elisha and his young servant in 2 Kings 6:16-17. The young man was afraid of the visible enemies. However, Elisha comforted him and said, *"Do not fear, for those who are with us are more than those who are with them."* He then prayed for the Lord to open his servant's eyes, and He did. Behold, he saw a heavenly host of angelic warriors surrounding them. Today we need to pray down the strongholds of the New Age, and we need to pray for those caught up in it. There are mighty testimonies of God meeting people who were lost in this cult. Many of today's young Christians at one time were influenced by this, but escaped because of friends or relatives who prayed for them.

B. **Love:** Even though men swallowed the lie in the Garden of Eden about becoming gods, the Lord God loved people enough to send

His Son to die for all our sins on the cross. By this act, He once again makes open the way to any who are willing to have fellowship with God in the Garden. Since we as Christians have received this and have been given such a great gift, shouldn't we also show the love of Christ to all others?

Each person, whether in the New Age or not, has certain low times in life in which he can be impacted by those who care. Through the sensitivity of the Holy Spirit, we can be led to those who are in need and shine the love of Christ. A new-age advocate who is deathly ill from aids or cancer, facing a divorce, looking at financial chaos, feeling the impact of an empty soul, or some other calamity is simply someone who is lost that needs a Savior. At times like this, a Christian's love can help heal and inspire. It can lead someone out of darkness into God's perfect light.

C. **Witness**: People today are often drawn into the New Age because the church is failing to provide a certain element of experience that their souls need. A dry, thirsty soul does not just need theology and doctrine, it needs the life giving power of the Holy Spirit. It needs to be immersed in the presence of God as an active, daily, vital source. One of the best witnessing tools that you have for those in the New Age is your testimony of God's power, love, and impact upon your own life. How does He minister to you daily? How does He speak to you? What are some miraculous testimonies you have to share?

1) *Some tips for witnessing:*
   a. Read Acts 17:16-34 - Discover Paul's techniques for common ground.
   b. Listen to them: Ask them to share their spiritual journey.
   c. N.A.M. says man is "asleep." We say he's worse—dead without Christ.
   d. Share your salvation story with them. Personal experience is hard to refute.
   e. Ask them how they explain blatant examples of sin with New Age philosophy.
   f. Explain to them that Christ taught redemption, not reincarnation.
   g. Ask, "If we are all evolving into gods, who created the first God"?

End Notes

1. Paul McGuire, "Hooked on Hollywood Religion," *Charisma & Christian Life Magazine* (November 1996): 60.

2. Russell Chandler, *Understanding the New Age* (Grand Rapids, MI: Zondervan Publishing House, 1993), p. 17.
3. Ibid.
4. Karen Hoyt, *The New Age Rage* (Old Tappan, NJ: Fleming H. Revell Company,1987), p. 19.
5. James W. Sire, *The Universe Next Door* (Downers Grove, IL: Inter Varsity Press, 1988), p. 193
6. Texe Marrs, *Texe Marrs Book of New Age Cults and Religions* (Austin, TX: Living Truth Publishers, 1990), pgs. 87-88.
7. Richard Abases, *Embraced By The Light and the Bible* (Camp Hill, PA: Horizon Books, 1994), p. 13
8. Sire. p. 173.
9. Carlson and Decker, *Fast Facts on False Teachings* (Eugene, OR: Harvest House Publishers, 1994), p. 188.
10. Brooks Alexander, "Last Exit Before Judgement: Barbara Marx Hubbard And The 'Armageddon Alternative'," *S C P Journal* 19,2/3 (Spring / Summer 1995):.32.
11. Troy Lawrence, *New Age Messiah Identified: Who Is Lord Maitreya?* (Lafayette, LA: Huntington House Publishers, 1991), p. 2.
12. Hoyt, pgs. 64-67.
13. Chandler, p. 228.
14. Ibid., pgs. 232-233.
15. Michael S. Coffman, *Saviors of the Earth?* (Chicago, IL: Northfield Publishing, 1994), p. 40.
16. Ibid., p. 54.
17. Ibid., pgs. 124-125.
18. Ibid., p. 104.
19. Ibid., p. 209.
20. Douglas R. Groothuis, *Unmasking the New Age* (Downers Grove, IL: Inter Varsity Press, 1986), pgs. 33, 35.
21. Hoyt, pgs. 200-201.
22. ABC News Nightline #3587, "A Cult and Its Influence Within the FAA" (Journal Graphics, Inc. 1535 Grant Street, Denver, CO 80203, Air Date: February 21, 1995), p.3
23. Ronald Quillo, *Companions in Consciousness: The Bible and the New Age Movement* (Liguori, MO: Triumph Books, 1994), p. 166.
24. Ibid., p. 156.
25. Groothuis, pgs. 173-174.

QUESTIONNAIRE: LESSON EIGHT

NAME: _____   DATE: _____

1. Is New Age an organization that one joins? _____

2. Consider the section on more recent roots of the movement. Tell about one of the roots and then use one or more of the Scriptures to refute the particular teaching of that cult. _____

_____

_____

_____

_____

_____

3. Which of the four New Age books mentioned in the lesson clearly teaches Mormon doctrine?_____

4. Look at section five (V.) and fill in the blanks: To the New Age, God is an impersonal, amoral _____ force. Jesus is just one of many _____ . Creation has always existed. Nature is (m)_____ . Man is a sleeping _____ . Death is an (i)_____ . Salvation is just the revelation of one's own _____ . Angels are not like the Biblical ones but are highly _____ _____ .

5. What are the two main schools of New Age thought and what do they mean?

a) _____ : _____

_____

_____

b) _____ : _____

_____

_____

6. Jose Arguelles is called the founding father of _____

7. Healing for the total person is called _____ health.

8. The new "fourth force" psychology is called _____ .

9. Explain how India is a good example that the Prigogine hypothesis is not accurate in regard to social evolution: _____

_____

_____

_____

_____

_____

10. What was the name of the group that began having secret meetings in 1963 to determine what would happen to the U.S. in case permanent peace arrived? _____

11. What are the three things we learn about conspiracy from Adam and Eve's example?

a) _____

b) _____

c) _____

12. Who does J.Z. Knight channel? _____

13. Write out Deut. 18:10-12 _____

_____

_____

_____

_____

14. Regarding crystals, the New Age mixes _____ with _____.

15. List two tips that can help you witness to someone entangled in the New Age.

a) _____

b) _____

16. Consider your knowledge of the New Age Movement before and after this lesson. Circle the number that indicates how equipped you felt before taking the course to witness to someone on these issues as compared to how equipped you feel now. Be honest.

BEFORE 0 1 2 3 4 5 6 7 8 9 10 **AFTER** 0 1 2 3 4 5 6 7 8 9 10

THE MIND SCIENCES

"Doug and Rita Swan had watched their sixteen-month-old baby convulse and scream with pain for twelve days. When they finally rushed him to the hospital, it was too late. Little Matthew died six days later. As devout Christian Scientists, Doug and Rita had tried to follow their faith. Their church 'practitioner' had told them to stop praying, tell no one, and ignore Matthew's anguished condition. After all, 'Mother' Mary Baker Eddy had declared that sin, illness, and disease are all illusions of the mind to be corrected by right thinking."[1]

INTRODUCTION

I. WHAT ARE THE MIND SCIENCES?
    A. The Mind Sciences are "A general classification for religious groups that relegate religious truths (love, self-worth, etc.) to aspects of the mind or toward the latent divinity that resides in every individual...Generally, mind sciences are religions that emphasize the use of metaphysical science in order to prescribe therapy necessary to the aid and betterment of an individual."[2]

II. WHAT IS GNOSTICISM?
    A. From the Greek word *gnosis* meaning knowledge. Gnosticism was one of the cults of the early church period because they taught that Jesus and the Christ were not the same. The early church fathers

fought against gnosticism because it taught that Jesus refers to the man and Christ refers to the divine influence. *To the gnostics, Jesus was a human man who reached the higher Christ consciousness* available to all of us. He was but one of many angelic intermediaries between God and man. In gnosticism, God is impersonal and the eventual goal is to reach oneness with it.

According to *Eerdmans' Handbook To The History of Christianity,* Gnosticism views "the material creation as evil. Sparks of divinity, however, have been encapsuled in the bodies of certain 'spiritual' individuals destined for salvation. These 'spirituals' are ignorant of their heavenly origins. God sends down to them a redeemer [Jesus] who brings them salvation in the form of secret knowledge of themselves, their origin and their destiny. Thus awakened, the 'spirituals' escape from the prison of their bodies at death and pass safely through the planetary regions controlled by hostile demons, to be reunited with God."[3]

B. Gnosticism forms the foundation for many modern day cults including the Mind Science cults. In essence, they believe that Jesus was simply a man who achieved Christ consciousness but was not Christ uniquely himself. Jesus Christ, they say, was not God Almighty.

Thinking Through The Scripture

"For this reason the Jews tried all the harder to kill him; not only was he breaking the Sabbath, but he was even calling God his own Father, making himself equal with God." (John. 5:18) NIV

"Who is a liar but the one who denies that Jesus is the Christ?" (1 John. 2:22) NASB

Questions for discussion:
1. Why were the Jews trying to kill Jesus? How does this refute the Gnostics?
2. What are people denying when they say that Jesus is not the Christ?

III. WHAT IS THE METAPHYSICAL MOVEMENT?
A. The word metaphysics is a philosophical term concerned with the ultimate causes and underlying nature of things. The religious movement began in the nineteenth century based upon this philosophical idealism mixed with Eastern religions, Biblical doctrines and some Christian concepts.

IV. HOW DID SO MANY MIND SCIENCE CULTS BEGIN?

    A. The Mind Sciences are interesting from the aspect that we can see how a twisted concept promoted by a certain individual can spread like a disease and multiply into other cults who differ only slightly in definition but find a whole new niche of people who can be deceived. Below is a diagram of how *Phineas Parkhurst Quimby's* (1802 - 1866) views spread and eventually infected millions. Quimby, called the Guru of Mind Sciences, was a clock maker in Belfast, Maine. He had been an early student of mesmerism and animal magnetism and had promoted a theory of mental healing that he called 'The Science of Man' in the mid nineteenth century. He is indirectly considered the father of at least three cults (Christian Science, Unity, and New Thought) because his teachings impacted others who started these cults.

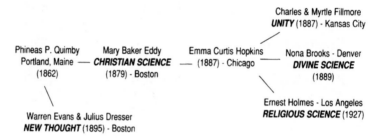

V. HAS THE MOVEMENT HAD ANY POSITIVE IMPACT ON CHRISTIANITY?

    A. Overall the effect has been negative because of the false teachings and heresy. However, it would be unfair to say there was no positive impact. The emphasis on certain areas such as healing, prophecy, positive faith, etc. are areas that certain cults emphasized that Christendom had generally either forgotten or neglected. Furthermore it would be unfair to say that there were no Bible-believing Christians involved in some of these groups. Unfortunately, however, whatever influence these Christians had, was not enough to keep the groups from forsaking the main doctrines of Christianity. In reference to this, Walter Martin makes this statement:

    "Within the theological structure of the cults there is considerable truth, all of which, it might be added, is drawn from Biblical sources, but diluted with human error as to be more deadly than complete falsehood. The cults have also emphasized the things which the Church has forgotten, such as divine healing (Christian Science, Unity, New Thought), prophecy (Jehovah's Witnesses and Mormonism), and a great many other things...."[4]

CHRISTIAN SCIENCE

VI. HOW DID CHRISTIAN SCIENCE BEGIN?
   A. It's founder was Mary Ann Morse Baker, known as Mary Baker Eddy.
   B. **Mary Baker** (1821 - 1910) was born in Bow, New Hampshire and raised on a farm. Her parents were Congregationalists. She was married three times in her life and had one son. The last man she married was named Eddy. She kept that name after he died. Her childhood and adult life was full emotional and physical ailments. As a child she was exposed to the practice of healing mesmerism. In 1862 she was healed by Phineas P. Quimby of spinal inflammation. Quimby used healing techniques derived from his theory of mental healing. She was heavily influenced by Quimby's beliefs.

   She claims that Christian Science began as the result of an accident she had on February 1, 1866. She slipped on a sidewalk and was laid up for three days. According to Mrs. Eddy the doctor reported that her case was hopeless because of internal injuries. She was to die. As the story goes, Mrs. Eddy was miraculously healed on the third day when she asked for a Bible and opened to Matt. 9:2. This she claims is where she received her revelation of Christian Science and Health. In 1875 she published *Science and Health with Key to the Scriptures*. In 1879 she founded the Church of Christ, Scientist in Boston and it grew from there.
   C. Several things should be noted regarding the character of her life:
      1) The doctor who treated her for her slip on the sidewalk was Alvin M. Cushing. He eventually denied under oath in a 1,000 word statement that he ever believed that she was in a life-threatening condition or gave her reason to think that she was going to die.
      2) She plagiarized major portions of Quimby's book, *Science of Man*, and also Lindly Murray's book, *The English Reader*, but claimed them as her own revelation. The New York Times plainly exposed her plagiarism when it ran parallel columns of Quimby's words alongside hers.
      3) Throughout Mary Baker Eddy's life, she repeatedly used the drug morphine as a medication for her ailments.
      4) Her own father, Mark Baker, tried to talk Dr. Patterson, a dentist, out of marrying Mary because of her emotional instability. However, he married her anyway (he was her second husband) but years later wished he had not. She divorced him because she said he abandoned her.
      5) Mary Baker Eddy died with no small fortune. She had amassed

about three million dollars from her followers' donations and book selling. It is no hidden fact that she continually urged Christian Scientists to sell her books. In 1897 she even went so far as to command that they read nothing else during the year except the Bible and her books and that they continuously sell her books. The penalty for disobedience was dismembership. (Christian Science Journal, March, 1897)

Thinking Through The Scripture

"Not everyone who says to Me, 'Lord, Lord,' will enter the kingdom of heaven; but he who does the will of My Father who is in heaven. Many will say to Me on that day, 'Lord, Lord, did we not prophesy in Your name, and in Your name cast out demons, and in Your name perform many miracles? And then I will declare to them, 'I never knew you; Depart from Me, you who practice lawlessness'." (Matthew 7:21-23) NASB

Questions for discussion:
1. What does this passage tell us about some who think they will go to heaven?
2. Upon what are they basing their right to enter heaven? Why is knowing Jesus so important? Why is the will of the Father connected to knowing Jesus?
3. The word lawlessness means illegality or wickedness referring to a heart problem. Why does Jesus use this in response to the so called "good" works that the people use for a defense?

VII. WHAT HAPPENED TO THE CULT AFTER EDDY'S DEATH?
   A. There was a power struggle. A self perpetuating board of directors ended up in charge of the fortune and the followers. No one has ever risen to the level of control that Mary Baker Eddy had even though she predicted someone would within fifty years and that Christian Science would be the dominant religious belief of the world. The last three decades have brought a major decline to the movement. The cult will not publish the number of its membership, but it now ranges from a quarter to a half million people. The number of practitioners has dropped nearly 50 percent.
   B. In 1991, a major controversy broke out when the church published Bliss Knapp's book *The Destiny of the Mother Church* that deified Mary Baker Eddy. The Knapps left about 90 million dollars to the church if they would publish the book.

VIII. WHAT IS A PRACTITIONER?
   A. "Lay member who serves as a full-time minister in Christian Science and Religious Science. A practitioner's main area of service and responsibility is to pray and minister healing to other members of the church."[5]

IX. WHAT IS A CHRISTIAN SCIENCE CHURCH SERVICE LIKE?
   A. The members appear to be "conservative, well-educated, upper socio-economic types." The services do not resemble "mainstream Christian practices." While there is no clergy, there are people who read portions of Christian Science books. The Sunday services are normally based around pre-planned "Bible Lessons" put forth in the Christian Science Quarterly. Practitioners administer healing. "No ordinances are recognized and the service is ended with a reading of the Lord's Prayer (the verses interspersed with Mrs. Eddy's interpretations)."[6] The Wednesday evening services are for testimonials of spiritual healing.

X. WHAT ARE SOME OTHER ASPECTS OF THE ORGANIZATION?
   A. They produce many publications:
      1) *Christian Science Sentinel*, a weekly publication.
      2) *The Christian Science Journal*, a monthly magazine.
      3) *The Herald of Christian Science*, a magazine.
      4) *Science and Health with Key to the Scriptures*, the main text book by Eddy
      5) *Christian Science Monitor:* This daily newspaper in metropolitan areas has over half a million subscribers and has gained great prominence among the intellectual, economic, and political circles of today for superior journalism.
      6) Various other writings of Eddy and others.
   B. They produce radio programs:
      1) Monitor radio broadcasts on shortwave giving news and feature programs throughout many nations and in many languages.
   C. They open Christian Science Reading Rooms in communities for people to come, read, study, and practice spiritual healing.

XI. WHAT DO THEY THINK OF THE BIBLE?
   A. Christian Scientists openly read the Bible and profess belief in it. However, the average Christian Scientist views the Bible as having hundreds of thousands of mistakes, as well as metaphors, allegories, myths, and fables. They have spiritualized away much of the Scriptures and have a very non-literal view. Because of its many

errors, they believe, it took a divinely inspired Mrs. Eddy to look through the maze of confusion in the Bible and interpret it accurately. Through this, they think, she rediscovered the true healing principles of Jesus lost to us for centuries. Through this supposed "final revelation" she discovered Christian Science—the Divine Comforter.

However, as we learned in the chapter on the Bible's authenticity, it stands on its own as the authoritative Word of God. It is inspired by the Spirit of God and was inerrant as given to man. All the words of Mrs. Eddy will fade, but of the Bible it says, *"The grass withers and the flowers fall, but the word of our God stands forever"* (Isaiah 40:8). Jesus also said, *"The earth and the heavens will disappear, but my words will never disappear"* (Mt. 24:35).

XII.   WHAT IS THE CORE OF CHRISTIAN SCIENCE TEACHING?
    A.   That illness, disease, and problems with our bodies are strictly illusions of the mind and that healing becomes possible when one grasps this revelation.
    B.   That Mrs. Eddy discovered this divine truth and healed many by her own acknowledgements. She claims that Christ didn't really do supernatural miracles, but simply showed people their illusion. However, it must be noted that:
        1)   She never gave the names or identifications of any she healed so that it could be verified.
        2)   She refused to answer the challenge of Dr. Charles A. L. Reed, a prominent Cincinnati physician, who offered every opportunity to prove her claims by healing any of his patients who had identical cases to those she said she healed. (*New York Sun*, January 1, 1899)
        3)   According to her close associate, Mr. Alfred Farlow, chairman of the Publications Committee and President of the Mother Church in Boston, he knew of no healing that Mrs. Eddy ever made in her entire life of any organic disease, but that of a stiff leg which is hardly a major illness and could be psychological in nature.
        4)   Just because she healed anyone does not mean it was through God. The magicians of Pharaoh performed miracles through satanic power.

Thinking Through The Scripture

   "Then Jesus said to him, 'Get up! Pick up your mat and walk.' At once the man was cured; he picked up his mat and walked." (John 4:8-9) NIV

"He spit on the ground, made some mud with the saliva, and put it on the man's eyes. 'Go,' he told him, 'wash in the Pool of Siloam'...So the man went and washed, and came home seeing." (John 9:6-7) NIV

"But Jesus said, Someone touched me; I know that power has gone out from me.' Then the woman, seeing that she could not go unnoticed, came trembling and fell at his feet. In the presence of all the people, she told why she had touched him and how she had been instantly healed. Then he said to her, 'Daughter, your faith has healed you'...." (Luke 8:46-47) NIV

Questions for discussion:
1. These passages represent just a few of the many healing miracles of Jesus. What are some things that stick out about them? For instance, was there any doubt that these were miracles? Were they done secretly? Who was Jesus concerned about when healing?
2. Can you think of any time in which Jesus healed someone by having them deny the reality of their illness, sickness, infirmity or death? How does this pose problems for the Christian Science view?

XIII. WHAT ARE THE FALSE TEACHINGS OF CHRISTIAN SCIENCE?
  A. That Mary Baker Eddy received a superior revelation to traditional mainline Christianity and the Scriptures.
      1) In *Science and Health* on page 107, Eddy quotes Gal. 1:11-12 in which Paul testifies that the Gospel was revealed to him by God and not man, that it was a revelation of Jesus Christ. Then she writes this next statement alluding to her belief that a greater "Good News" has been revealed to her.
          "In the year 1866, I discovered the Christ Science or divine laws of Life, Truth, and Love, and named my discovery Christian Science. God had been graciously preparing me during many years for the reception of this final revelation of the absolute divine Principle of scientific mental healing."[7] —Mary Baker Eddy
  B. That the Christian concept of the Trinity (The Father, Son, and Holy Spirit) is false and that the true trinity is Life, Truth, and Love. —*Science and Health*, p. 115
      Scriptures refuting: Gen. 1:26; Is.6:8; John 1:1; John 1:14; Mt. 28:19, etc.
  C. That Jesus was simply a human man, (Gnosticism) that "Christ is the divine idea," and that "Jesus Christ is not God"—*Science and Health*, p. 473:9-16; p.361:12
      1) One pamphlet produced by the Christian Science says...

"Christian Science draws a distinction between the Savior's divine title of Christ and his human history as Jesus...There is a legitimate theological difference, to be sure, between Christian Scientists and those denominations which believe Jesus to be God."[8]

Scriptures refuting: Isaiah 9:6; 1 John 2:22; John 1:1; John 1:14; John 5:18; John 8:58; Col. 1:15; Col. 2:9; 1 John 5:1; Luke 2:11;

D. That Jesus did not die and that his resurrection was only in a spiritual sense. —*Science and Health*, p. 45:31-46:1; p. 34:24:27.

    Scriptures refuting: Mt. 27:58-60; Rom. 5:6; 1 Cor. 15:20-22; Luke 24:39.

E. That Satan, sin, and evil are only unreal beliefs of the human mind. —*Science and Health*, p. 458 in glossary "Devil"; p. 472:27-30; 473:5-6.

    Scriptures refuting: Rom. 3:23; Rom. 6:23; 1 John 1:10; Luke 4:3-6.

F. That the Christian sense of eternal salvation is not necessary because "Man as God's idea is already saved with an everlasting salvation" —Miscellaneous Writings, p. 261.

    Scriptures refuting: John 3:16; Acts 16:31; John 3:3; 2 Cor. 5:17.

G. That "Man is not matter; he is not made up of brain, blood, bones...Man is idea, the image, of Love; he is not physique" — *Science and Health*, p. 475:6,13.

    1) From an article in one Christian Science Sentinel we read, "God, being ever present Spirit, never created anything unlike Himself called matter. Like produces like. Therefore, matter was never created and consequently does not exist...The material senses, which tend to present life in mortal terms, would lead us to think of matter instead of Spirit, as reality."[9]

        Scriptures refuting: Gen. 2:7; Psalm 100:3; 1 Cor. 15:47

    2) It is worth noting here some remarks that Walter Martin gave regarding this view by Christian Scientists that physical matter is not real. He says,

        "Without fear of contradiction all rational persons will admit the reality of their physical existence. There are three principal reasons for this admission, which, briefly stated are these:

        1. Man is capable of perceiving his corporeal form.

        2. The demands of the body, such as food, clothing, etc., prove that it has a material existence.

        3. The human mind is capable of discerning the difference between concrete and abstract ideas, the body being easily discerned as a concrete proposition."[10]

H. That God would never send disease, nor death, nor any type of destructive force against man because he is good and good could never do that.

   1) Although the Bible does confirm that God is wholly good, He is also holy just, but man is sinful and there have been times when God has dealt with man's sin. Here are some examples of God's judgment for man's sin:

      a. Example of the flood (Genesis 6).
      b. Example of God sending pestilence (2 Samuel 24).
      c. Example of the tower of Babel (Genesis 11).
      d. Example of Babylon (Jeremiah).
      e. Example of Jesus dying as our atonement (Isaiah 53).
      f. Example of God's wrath against unrighteousness (Romans 1:18).

XIV. WHAT IS THE SAD TRUTH ABOUT CHRISTIAN SCIENCE?

A. The unhappy reality for those caught up in this cult is that it is not even Christian. Authors Josh McDowell and Don Stewart say it very well in their book, *Understanding the Cults*:

   "*Christian Science is neither Christian nor scientific* because every important doctrine of historic Christianity is rejected by Christian Science. The claim of divine revelation by Mrs. Eddy is contradicted by the facts that clearly attest she does not represent the God of the Bible. Although she speaks in the name of Jesus, her teachings conflict with His in every respect."[11] (italics added)

UNITY SCHOOL OF CHRISTIANITY

XV. HOW DID THE UNITY SCHOOL OF CHRISTIANITY BEGIN?

A. Its founders were Charles Sherlock Fillmore and his wife, Mary Caroline (Myrtle).

B. **Myrtle (1845 - 1931)** was raised a Methodist in New England where she made her living as a school teacher. She was stricken with tuberculosis much of her life. She married Charles in 1881 and moved to Kansas City, Missouri, in 1884. In 1886 they went to a lecture where a man named E. B. Weeks proclaimed, "I am a child of God and therefore I do not inherit sickness".[12] Myrtle, who claims she contracted malaria and was given only six months to live, said she repeated those words over and over again and then was miraculously healed of all maladies.

She became a Christian Scientist and was probably very influenced by one Emma Curtis Hopkins. Hopkins had been a chief disciple of Mary Baker Eddy and had served as her general editor. They had a falling out and Hopkins left, but started teaching her own strain of Mind Science. Myrtle picked up the cause and began having two weekly meetings.

C. **Charles** (1854 - 1948) did not readily accept his wife's techniques for healing. He had seen many financial ups and downs in life and failed as a real estate agent. He had a withered leg because of a touch of tuberculosis in the hip. After extensively studying eastern religions, including Hinduism and Buddhism, Spiritualism, and the Mind Sciences he gave his wife's technique of continued meditation a try and his leg was healed. They began publishing magazines in the late 1880's that launched their new religion which was a mixture of Christian Science and the eastern religions, including a heavy emphasis on reincarnation.

The name Unity was adopted in 1891 as a theme for uniting the best things from all religions. By 1922 Unity far exceeded Christian Science and New Thought for membership. After their death, their sons continued to lead the movement. Today, it has grown into what Dr. Walter Martin calls, "the largest gnostic cult in Christendom".[13] Some estimates say it has close to 4 million adherents worldwide.

XVI. WHERE ARE THE MAIN HEADQUARTERS LOCATED?
A. Unity Village, Lees Summit, Kansas City, Missouri, 64065. From this village millions of books, magazines, and tracts are published and distributed.

XVII. WHAT CORRESPONDENCE AND MEDIA AVENUES DO THEY USE?
A. They receive "an average of fifteen thousand calls a week and two and one half million letters annually...All calls and requests are answered."[14]
B. Also, "more than one thousand radio and television stations broadcast two hundred fifty Unity programs a week."[15]

XVIII. WHAT ARE SOME OF ITS PUBLICATIONS?
A. *Unity; Unity Daily Word*
B. *Wee Wisdom*, a periodical for Sunday School children.
C. *Good Business; Progress*
D. *Weekly Unity*, as well as books, tracts, and pamphlets.

XIX. WHY IS UNITY SOMETIMES CALLED AN INOFFENSIVE CULT?

A. From Walter Martin's study on the subject, he states: "Unity, as it is known to millions of persons, is probably the most inoffensive of all the cults, since *its adherents usually retain their membership in the church of their choice*, while at the same time subscribing to the Unity publications, thus giving them a direct access to many churches and many congregations where the Unity cult teachings are subtly disseminated under the guise of a higher plane of Christian experience."[16] (italics added)

B. Unity also has a number of churches and ministers throughout the main cities of the United States proclaiming *Christian truth mixed with non-Christian religions*. But one must dig a little to see the underlying eastern religious and non-Christian concepts.

C. *Unity resists making creeds, doctrines, or statements* because it wants to include all religions and sects whether they are Christian or not. One of their tracts states, "Unity believes that there is good in every religion and that we should keep our minds open...Unity has no strict creed or dogma. One might describe Unity as a religious philosophy with an 'open end'."[17] It is easy to see from this that Unity does not make a legitimate distinction between Christian and heathen. But because it does not require anyone to give up their religion, it is called an inoffensive cult.

Thinking Through The Scripture

"Do not be bound together with unbelievers; for what partnership have righteousness and lawlessness, or what fellowship has light with darkness? Or what harmony has Christ with Belial, or what has a believer in common with an unbeliever?...Come out from their midst and be separate, says the Lord." (2 Corinthians. 6:14-15, 17) NASB

Questions for discussion:
1. In what way are the various mind sciences mixing Christian beliefs with that of heathen beliefs? Why will this not work in God's economy of things?
2. What type of impact is Gnosticism having upon modern-day culture? What is our responsibility regarding these things in our personal lives?

XX. HOW DOES UNITY BELIEF DIFFER FROM CHRISTIAN SCIENCE?
A. Unity believes matter is real; Christian Science believes it is illusion.
B. Unity believes sin and illness are real (matter) but that sickness is an unnatural state of existence, and therefore denies their existence

by positive thinking. They emphasize spiritual healing, but do not deny medical treatment. Christian Science maintains that illness is illusion and thereby discourages medical attention.

Thinking Through The Scripture

"No one can serve two masters. Either he will hate the one and love the other, or he will be devoted to the one and despise the other. You cannot serve both God and Money." (Matthew 6:24) NIV

"Godliness with contentment is great gain. For we brought nothing into the world, and we can take nothing out of it. But if we have food and clothing, we will be content with that. People who want to get rich fall into temptation and a trap and into many foolish and harmful desires that plunge men into ruin and destruction. For the love of money is a root of all kinds of evil. Some people, eager for money, have wandered from the faith and pierced themselves with many griefs." (1 Timothy 6:6-10) NIV

"Give me neither poverty nor riches, but give me only my daily bread. Otherwise, I may have too much and disown you and say, 'Who is the Lord?' Or I may become poor and steal, and so dishonor the name of my God." (Proverbs. 30:8-9) NIV

Questions for discussion:
1. Many prosperity cults have risen up as a result of mind science teaching. How do these passages balance an unhealthy focus on money? What is the root of evil? How does the passage from Proverbs tell us to approach riches? What does it tell us about the danger of poverty? Who is to be our true master?
2. What are a Christian's responsibilities regarding personal debt? Giving? Tithing? Generosity? How many people in the Bible were actually rich?

C. Unity teaches reincarnation as the means to Christ Consciousness.
D. Unity emphasizes financial prosperity as one of its main tenants. Below is an example of the length that Charles Fillmore would go to emphasize "brutal materialism". He reworded the twenty-third Psalm as follows:
  "The Lord is my banker; my credit is good. He maketh me to lie down in the consciousness of omnipotent abundance; He giveth me the key to His strong-box. He restoreth my faith in His riches, He guideth me in the paths of prosperity for His name's sake. Yea, though I walk through the very shadow of debt, I shall fear no evil,

for Thou art with me; Thy silver and gold, they secure me. Thou
preparest a way for me in the presence of the collector; Thou fillest
my wallet with plenty; my measure runneth over. Surely, goodness
and plenty will follow me all the days of my life; And I shall do
business in the name of the Lord forever."[18]

XXI. WHAT ARE SOME OF THE FALSE TEACHINGS OF UNITY?

A. That we can gain eminent spiritual truths from other sacred writings along with the Bible. They believe that "the Scriptures are the
testimonials of men who have, in a measure, apprehended the
divine Logos, but that their writings should not be taken as final."
(Unity's Statement of Faith, part 27) It was Charles Fillmore's notion
to be open to the truth of all religions. It should be noted that Unity
claims the Bible as their basic textbook. They regard it historically,
morally, ethically, and as a literary work. However, the deception is
that they interpret it metaphysically, thus spiritualizing away many
of the basic literal truths clearly taught in the Scriptures.
Scriptures refuting: 2 Peter 1:20-21; 2 Peter 3:16; 1 Thess. 2:13; 2
Tim. 3:16-17

B. That God is not a personal being but a thing: Principle, Love, Life,
in everything, etc.
Scriptures refuting: Rom. 1:18-25; Gen. 1:1,4; Ex. 2:24; 3:14; 2
Tim. 2:19

C. That Jesus and Christ are different. (Similar to Christian Science)
Scriptures refuting: 1 Jn. 2:22; 1 Jn. 5:1; Luke 2:11,26

D. That "Being born again or born from above is not a miraculous
change that takes place in man; it is the establishment of that
which has always existed as the perfect man, ideas of divine
Mind."[19] They say that Christian born-again salvation is unnecessary.
Scriptures refuting: Jn. 3:3; 5:24; Rom. 3:23-24; Eph. 2:1; Jn. 8:24

E. That immortality and ultimate salvation comes through reincarnation

1) One Unity tract reads: "Many Unity students accept the concept of reincarnation (re-embodiment after a period of soul-
rest) as an opportunity for man to attain new understanding in
a new life experience, so that he can more nearly express perfection and demonstrate eternal life, which is the ultimate goal.
When he achieves that goal, as Jesus did, it will no longer be
necessary for him to reincarnate."[20]

2) Another Unity tract reads: "You are really a glorious spiritual
being, but in this world we know only a certain fraction of that

being, and we call that fraction John Smith and think it is the whole man. That great being is the real you and is your true self. In this incarnation a fraction of him appears on this earth to learn certain lessons, but it is only a fraction, and not the whole being. In the last incarnation you put a different fraction of yourself into this world to learn other lessons."[21]

Scriptures Refuting: Phil. 1:21-24; 1 Cor. 15:54-56; Ps. 49:15; Luke 16:19-31

F. That there is no personal return of Jesus Christ to judge the earth.
    Scriptures refuting: 2 Thes. 1:7-10; 1 Thess. 4:13-18; Rev. 1:7; Matt. 25:31-46

Thinking Through The Scripture

"People die once and after that they are judged." (Hebrews. 9:27) GW

"We are confident, yes, well pleased rather to be absent from the body and to be present with the Lord. Therefore we make it our aim, whether present or absent, to be well pleasing to Him. For we must all appear before the judgment seat of Christ, that each one may receive the things done in the body, whether good or bad." (2 Corinthians 5:8-10)

Questions for discussion:

1. Reincarnation originated from a Hindu concept called transmigration. However, the Bible does not support it. How many times do people die?
2. After people die, what happens to them? When our spirit is absent from the body, where is it? What happens at the judgment?
3. Consider the passages in Matthew 16:27; Acts 10:42; Romans 2:16; and Romans 14:10, 12. How do they focus on the issue of judgment and limit the possibility of any thought of reincarnation?

XXII. WHAT IS ONE SAD TRUTH ABOUT UNITY?

A. Some of what Unity teaches is scripturally accurate. However, much of it is tainted with eastern mysticism and religion so that they have overlooked the most important aspects of what makes one a Christian. One perceptive comment puts it this way:

"The positive faith in God's provision which Unity encourages would be commendable were they [Unity Writers] born-again Christians. However, not having believed in the atoning power of the blood of Christ, they have not entered into God's new covenant (Heb. 9:13-15)...Unity interprets Scriptures that are specifically addressed to the redeemed as though they were meant for everyone."[22]

DIVINE SCIENCE

XXIII. WHAT IS THE HISTORY AND TEACHINGS OF DIVINE SCIENCE?
   A. **History.** Divine Science was founded by Nona Brooks in 1889 in Denver, Colorado. Brooks was influenced by Mrs. Frank Bingham's lectures. Bingham lectured on the teachings of Emma Curtis Hopkins who had distanced herself from Christian Science because of dispute with Mary Baker Eddy. Brooks, who had experienced a healing of a throat condition, began treating others in Pueblo, Colorado. Eventually, she moved to Denver where she teamed up with Melinda Cramer to begin a Divine Science college in 1898.

   The following year the first Divine Science church opened with Sunday services. Although Divine Science never became prominent like Unity and Christian Science, it grew enough to form a Divine Science Federation International in 1957. In the 1970's the churches numbered approximately twenty with twenty-six practitioners.[23]

   B. **Teachings.** Like most of the other Mind Sciences, this one teaches that God is perfect mind and that he is the only real presence in the universe. Therefore, every sin and sickness are illusions and only occur because of wrong thinking. In Divine Science, the Father is simply the source and cause of all good, the Son or "Christ" is an indwelling principle to which we can all attain, and the Holy Spirit imparts divine illumination for self-realization. *Accordingly, we are not sinners in the Christian sense and do not need the cross of Christ for eternal sin atonement and salvation.*

   They say salvation is to learn the knowledge of the unity that we have with the universe and the perfection that is ours simply through the understanding of these truths. Healing is possible when we cure our mind of the false belief we have about the reality of sin, sickness, and evil. However, the Bible tells us that *"the message of the cross is foolishness to those who are perishing, but to us who are being saved it is the power of God"* (1 Corinthians 1:18). For Christians, salvation is much more than just the acquisition of knowledge. In John 17:3, the Lord tells us that eternal life comes through knowing Jesus Christ, not just knowledge about Him or the universe.

RELIGIOUS SCIENCE

XXIV. WHAT IS THE HISTORY AND TEACHINGS OF RELIGIOUS SCIENCE?
   A. **History.** Religious Science was started by Ernest Holmes (1887-1960). He and his brother, Fenwicke, were heavily influenced by

the teachings of Emma Curtis Hopkins who also influenced a couple of the other cult origins. In 1917 they started the Metaphysical Institute in Los Angeles and began a publication entitled "Uplift". Holmes published a couple of books (Creative Mind, The Science of Mind) in the next several years and then in 1927 founded the Institute of Religious Science in Los Angeles. In 1949 the International Association of Religious Science Churches was formed after many of Holmes followers began churches of their own.

Some noted individuals in Religious Science have been actor Robert Young (Father Knows Best), actor Robert Stack (Elliot Ness, and more recently Unsolved Mysteries), and Norman Cousins (Saturday Review).

Today, there are two main branches of the movement: The United Church of Religious Science and Religious Science International. In 1988 there were 125 chartered churches. A worship service will actually resemble many mainline Protestant services, but with a heavy emphasis on the goodness of humanity, positive thinking, and health.

B.   **Teachings**. As with the other Mind Science movements, this one claims that the evil of life is only due to the ignorance of mind. The power of positive thinking brings about union with God who is the impersonal primary mind of the universe. The only sin is ignorance. Hell is a part of man's ignorance and not a real place. It cannot exist in a God-inhabited universe.

Salvation in the Christian sense is unnecessary because the only breach between God and man is man's ignorance of his oneness with God. Man is inherently good. Jesus learned this by mastering the mind and the laws of the universe. He is differentiated from the Christ who inhabits all. Spirit, Soul, and Body form the Trinity of Religious Science of which we are all a part.

Thinking Through The Scripture

"But your wrongs have separated you from your God, and your sins have made him hide his face so that he doesn't hear you. Your hands are stained with blood, and your fingers are stained with sin. You speak lies, and mutter wicked things." (Isaiah 59:2-3) GW

"Behold, I was brought forth in iniquity, and in sin did my mother conceive me." (Psalm 51:5) NASB

"But God demonstrates His own love toward us in that while we were yet sinners, Christ died for us. Much more then, having now been justified by His

blood, we shall be saved from the wrath of God through Him." (Romans 5:8-9)
NASB

Questions for discussion:
1. How do these Scriptures contrast with the Gnostic view that men are born inherently good? What separates us from God? In what was David born?
2. What is the difference between a sin and sin nature? Does a child's innocence mean that there is no sin nature? What types of things do children all around the world do without being taught? How do these actions show us the problem that we have with sin nature?

NEW THOUGHT

XXV. WHAT IS THE HISTORY AND TEACHINGS OF NEW THOUGHT?
   A. **History.** The cult movement known as New Thought was started by a former Methodist minister, Warren Felt Evans (1817-89), and Julius Dresser (1838-93). Evans received a healing through the practice of Phineas Quimby in 1863. Evans authored various books (The New Age and Its Messenger, The Mental Cure, and others) espousing the views of the mind sciences.
       Julius Dresser was a spokesman who really added momentum to the movement. Dresser communicated well the thoughts of Evans and Quimby in Boston and challenged Mary Baker Eddy's rights to exclusiveness of the mind science concepts. Dresser established the Church of Higher Life. A periodical called *New Thought* was begun in 1890 and organized branches of New Thought were founded in 1895, 1899, and 1915. In 1915 the (INTA) International New Thought Alliance began.
       Today, New Thought's primary adherents are intellectuals and those who approach religion philosophically. It has an open door policy and puts emphasis on wealth and prosperity as does Unity.
   B. **Teachings.** Although it is not easy to give boundaries to what adherents of New Thought believed because the followers were from mixed backgrounds (Christian, Eastern Religions, Occult, etc.), the Alliances Constitution gives us understanding regarding their erroneous view of God and man's position to Him. It reads as follows:
       "...to teach the Infinitude of the Supreme One, the Divinity of Man and his Infinite possibilities through the creative power of constructive thinking and obedience to the voice of Indwelling

Presence, which is our source of Inspiration, Power, Health, and Prosperity."[24]

C. As with the Christian Science, all evil is illusion, and salvation, unnecessary.

D. Jesus is not uniquely the Christ because God is in everything. He is the creation. Christ consciousness is within everyone and everything.

XXVI. HOW DOES NEW THOUGHT COMPARE TO THE NEW AGE MOVEMENT?

A. Author William DeArteaga makes an interesting observation in his book entitled *Quenching the Spirit* regarding a comparison between the two:

"Both New Age and New Thought originated with a Gnostic-demonic component. However, New Thought began in an age when the Bible and Christian doctrine influenced everything in the culture. This factor is missing in today's society where the New Age movement flowers. The Gnostic-demonic powers that rule over the New Age movement have no restraining hand and proclaim witchcraft, paganism, and anti-Christian beliefs openly...the Metaphysical movement had pagan and demonic elements from the beginning. However, they were accompanied by elements of philosophical idealism and healing...After the 1950's, what Christian influence existed within New Thought dwindled away, and what was left in the Metaphysical movement was the spiritualist, Gnostic and pagan elements which would become the New Age movement of today."[25]

XXVII. HOW CAN WE HELP THOSE CAUGHT UP IN THE MIND SCIENCES?

A. **Prayer:** In a sense, the Mind Science cults mentioned here overlap with the New Age Movement, and at times there seems to be no significant difference. However, there is a key element in these cults that will help us know how to pray. Each of the groups referred to in this lesson has a major doctrine that zeros in on the mind. For instance, the teaching that evil is only due to ignorance of the mind, or that God is an impersonal mind force, or even that reality is simply an illusion of the mind are all "mind-centered" doctrines. The big emphasis in these cults is on intellectualism. If we change our mind perspective, they think, we will be on the right track.

Yet the Bible teaches that the real need is to put on the mind of Christ (1 Corinthians 2:16) and to be transformed by the renewing of our carnal minds (Romans 12:2) in order to gain His heavenly perspective. Those engrossed in these cults do need a new change of mind, but it goes even deeper than that; they need a change of heart. It is not enough to change thoughts; they must change belief, and this comes from the heart center. As Christians, we have powerful weapons in our arsenal of prayers that can be waged against the enemy strongholds in their minds. These are the areas in which we should pray for them. The Bible plainly tells us of the true warfare in the following passage:

"For the weapons of our warfare are not carnal but mighty in God for pulling down strongholds, casting down arguments and every high thing that exalts itself against the knowledge of God, bringing every thought into captivity to the obedience of Christ." (2 Corinthians 10:4-5)

B. **Love:** The Bible tells us that *"God is Love."* This is different than saying that "God is mind." The mind is simply a thing often filled up with empty vanity and useless imaginings. Yet, love is more than just a thing: it is an action, a movement of caring and compassion employed in a deed. God allows us to identify Him not only as the essence (or thing) of love but as the very movement (or action) of love. When we have Agape (godly) love, we show forth the truth of God to their deluded minds.

Love, the Bible tells us, is the greatest gift. When we willingly give that gift, it will have an impact. We might not always see it at first. It might be like the pebble in the pond. Yet, it will have an influence upon an empty soul. When the heart cries out because of thirst, the mind will stop trying to rationalize with grandiose arguments and allow the heart to drink. The God of love is a match for any thick-minded man.

C. **Witness:** Since the Mind Science cults are so big on publications, get Christian tracts, books, videos, etc. to share with those to whom you are witnessing. Challenge their intellects by asking them to read books like *Evidence That Demands A Verdict* by Josh McDowell or *The Signature of God* by Grant Jeffrey. Use questions from the sections entitled "Thinking Through The Scripture" or some of the following to contest their views:

1) If God is omnipotent, couldn't He create an accurate Bible?
2) If sin, sickness, and evil are not real, then who started them all in the beginning?
3) If matter isn't real, how do you know anything is, including Mary Baker Eddy?

    4) Did Jesus heal anybody by having them deny the reality of their sickness?

    5) If ignorance is the only sin, then why are smart people sometimes evil?

End Notes

1. Bob Larson, *Larson's Book of Cults* (Wheaton, IL: Tyndale House Publishers, Inc., 1988), p. 130.

2. Mather and Nichols, *Dictionary of Cults, Sects, Religions and the Occult* (Grand Rapids, MI: Zondervan Publishing House, 1993), p.185.

3. *Eerdmans' Handbook To The History of Christianity*, ed. Tim Dowley (Grand Rapids, MI: Wm. B. Eerdman's Publishing Co., 1977), p. 98.

4. Walter Martin, *The Kingdom of the Cults* (Minneapolis, MN: Bethany House Publishers, 1985), p. 17.

5. Mather and Nichols, p. 223.

6. Larson, p. 132.

7. Mary Baker Eddy, *Science and Health with Key to the Scriptures* (Boston, MA: The First Church of Christ, Scientist, 1971), p. 107.

8. "What Makes Christian Science Christian?" a pamphlet published by the Christian Science Publishing Society, 1982, p. 12.

9. J. W. Humbert, "Disasters are not inevitable," *Christian Science Sentinel,* 9 October 1995, p. 7.

10. Martin, p. 159.

11. Josh McDowell & Don Stewart, *Handbook of Today's Religions: Understand the Cults* (San Bernardino, CA: Here's Life Publishers, 1982), p. 174

12. Ibid., p. 177.

13. Martin, p. 279.

14. Mather and Nichols, p. 291.

15. Ibid.

16. Martin, p. 279.

17. Charles R. Fillmore, "The Adventure Called Unity" (Unity Village, MO: Unity Publishers, 1993), p. 6-7.

18. J.K. VanBaalen, *The Chaos of Cults* (Grand Rapids, MI: Wm. B. Eerdman's Publisnigh Company, 1975), p. 137-138. Quoting Fillmore, Prosperity, p. 60.

19. Dwain C. Wolfer, *God And One Make A Majority (You)* (Portland, OR: Wolfer, 1984), p. 50. Quoting from Charles Fillmore, Christian Healing, p. 24.

20. Phil and Mary Stovin, "Twenty Questions About Unity" (2102 So. 23rd, Tacoma, WA. 98405), p.9.

21. Emmet Fox, "Consciousness" (Unity Village, Missouri: Unity School of Christianity), p. 10.

22. Elliot Miller, "Unity School of Christianity," in Walter Martin, ed., *Walter Martin's Cult Reference Bible* (Santa Ana, CA: Vision House, 1981), p. 69.

23. Mather and Nichols, p. 93.

24. Sydney Ahlstrom, *A Religious History of the American People,* 2 Vols. (Garden City, NY: Image Books, 1975), p. 537.

25. William DeArtega, *Quenching the Spirit* (Lake Mary, FL: Creation House, 1992), p. 160.

QUESTIONNAIRE: LESSON NINE

NAME: _____ DATE: _____

1. Mind sciences are religions that emphasize the use of _____ science in order to prescribe therapy necessary to the aid and betterment of the individual.

2. Gnostics were one of the _____ of the early church period. Gnosticism forms the foundation for many modern day cults including the _____ _____ cults.

3. Who has been called the Guru of Mind Sciences? _____

4. On the blanks below, place the name of the founders and the dates or origin.

	Founder	Date
a) Christian Science:	_____	_____
b) Unity:	_____	_____
c) Divine Science:	_____	_____
d) Religious Science:	_____	_____
e) New Thought:	_____	_____

5. What book did Eddy publish in 1875? _____

6. List three things that would make one cautious of her character?

a) _____

b) _____

c) _____

7. They view the Bible as having _____ of _____ of mistakes.

8. Jesus never healed anyone by having them deny the _____ of their disease.

9. All of these cults emphasize, in varying degrees healing, mental health, and financial prosperity. In your own words tell 1) why you think these concepts have been so widely embraced by people, and 2) how these teachings have been used by the cults to cover up their blatant differences with mainline Christianity.

_____

_____

_____

_____

_____

_____

_____

_____

_____

_____

10. Some of the false teachings of Unity are listed below. Fill in the blanks and then write out the Scripture refuting the cult's teaching.

a) That we gain eminent (prominent) spiritual _____ from other sacred writings along with the Bible.

2 Timothy 3:16 _____

_____

_____

b) That God is not a _____ being but a thing.

Exodus 2:24-25 _____

_____

_____

c) That Jesus and Christ are different.

1 John 2:22 _____

_____

_____

11. Consider your knowledge of the Mind Sciences before and after this lesson. Circle the number below that indicates how equipped you felt before taking the course to witness to someone in these cults as compared to how equipped you feel now. Be honest.

BEFORE 0 1 2 3 4 5 6 7 8 9 10 **AFTER** 0 1 2 3 4 5 6 7 8 9 10

THE UNIFICATION CHURCH

"They are under great pressure to win new recruits like me so the day will be blessed by Reverend Moon. Now, though I do not realize it yet, I am being manipulated in another way. The lack of sleep, the poor food, the ceaseless noise and commotion, the isolation, the chanted prayers and songs weaken my resolution and make me desperately afraid of trying to break free. I never wake without wondering what I am doing here, but by the time the determinations are hollered out, I am thinking only of how to sell enough flowers to meet my quota. If we don't sell more, the Captain says Reverend Moon will fail to win this country, and Satan will triumph. Like the others, I lie. The money goes for drug rehabilitation programs, I tell some people, or for Christian youth projects. Few ask for details. Sun Myung Moon says it is okay to lie to achieve your goal; he calls it heavenly deceit."[1] —a former Moonie

I. WHAT IS THE UNIFICATION CHURCH AND WHAT ARE ITS ROOTS?
   A. The complete name is Holy Spirit Association for the Unification of World Christianity. It was founded in 1954 by Sun Myung Moon in Seoul, Korea. Missionaries were sent to Japan in 1958 and one year later to the United States. Young Oom Kim established the first American Unification commune on the West Coast. In 1972 it gained momentum in the U.S. after Moon himself moved from Korea. It became officially incorporated in 1976. The main headquarters are at the New Yorker Hotel right across from Madison

Square Garden in New York City. This is designated the world mission center. Membership is considered to be about 2 million with influence in Asia, South America, and the United States. The participation of some 30,000 U.S. followers in the 1980's has dropped significantly to about one tenth of that number as we enter the new millennium. The hard core, full-time members work 18 to 20 hours per day raising money and witnessing. The church is considered a new religion because its theology represents an interpretation of the Bible and Christian tradition that is new.

B. Cult historian Richard Kyle says, "The Unification movement was a product of the social, economic and religious climate of post-World War II Korea. The removal of the religious restrictions that had been imposed by the occupying Japanese and the post war political and economic chaos provided the context for a stream of religious innovations. The country was in the grips of a serious economic depression, and communists and anticommunist forces were polarizing the Korean people. As a consequence, Korean society witnessed the rise of a number of religious groups led by charismatic leaders who combined elements from folk, Christian and Confucian traditions…these new religions had a popular appeal in that their doctrines had a distinctively this-world focus. They offered not only the hope of salvation and human perfectibility but also the hope of 'achievable prosperity.' It is important to understand that Moon's movement was only one of many such religious groups in Korea at this time."[2]

II. WHAT ARE SOME OF THE ORGANIZATIONS OF THE CHURCH?

A. In 1993 there were fifty-five worship centers throughout the U.S. These worship centers network together with the main headquarters at the New Yorker Hotel and the Unification seminary campus in Tarrytown, New York. The church hosts a number of conferences and symposiums for scientists, philosophers, and theologians through a Unification front organization called NEW ERA. Its purpose is to create successful events in order to increase positive publicity.

In *Cults: Faith, Healing, and Coercion,* author Marc Galanter says, "An annual conference on the Unity of Sciences was begun in 1972, and attracted at least 25 Nobel Prize winners in the following twelve years. In this venture, the sect was successful in obtaining positive press coverage while expending relatively little capital, since speakers and attendees were attracted by leading scholars who had agreed to participate."[3]

Not all of its ventures have been successful, however. In 1982 the church spent 48 million dollars producing *Inchon*, an anti-communist World War II movie. The movie received bad reviews, low attendance, and criticism over funding and distribution.[4] The church has poured massive amounts of money into various religious, political, business, and social organizations in order to make an impact and gain acceptance. Some of them are as follows:

1) **Religious Organizations:** Washington Institute for Values in Public Policy, International Religious Foundation, International Clergy and Laity, and International Cultural Foundation.

2) **Political Groups:** International Federation for Victory Over Communism, CAUSA—USA, CAUSA—International, and American Constitution Committee.

3) **Businesses:** One up Enterprises, International Oceanic Enterprises, News World Communications (a New York newspaper), World Media Association, Washington Times News Paper, and Free Press International.[5] Add to these Bridgeport University in Connecticut, a recording studio and travel agency in New York, a cable network—the Nostalgia Channel, and a couple hundred more businesses worldwide, and it suggests a financial kingdom.

4) **Other:** New Hope Singers International is a singing publicity front for the organization, and Collegiate Association for the Research of Principles (CARP) is a front used to recruit member and funds from college areas.

III. WHO IS SUN MYUNG MOON AND HOW DID HE BEGIN THE MOVEMENT?

A. He was born on January 6, 1920, as Yong Myung Moon (Shining Dragon Moon) in Pyungan Bukdo, a providence in Korea (now North Korea). At ten years of age, his family was converted to Christianity and joined the Presbyterian church. While attending high school, he got involved with an underground Pentecostal church which had cultist beliefs—namely, that Korea was the New Jerusalem of the Bible and that the future Messiah would be Korean-born.

B. As a youth, Moon had a strong interest in clairvoyance and spiritist practices. He claimed to be able to see through people into their spirits. McDowell and Stewart write, "At age 16 young Moon experienced a vision [on Easter of 1936] while in prayer on a Korean mountainside. Moon claims that Jesus Christ appeared to him in the vision admonishing him to carry out the task that Christ had failed to complete. Jesus supposedly told Moon that he was the only one who could do it. Finally, after much repeated asking by Jesus, Moon accepted the challenge."[6]

After Moon finished high school, he went to Japan for a time to study electrical engineering and do independent Bible study. He claims to have had regular contact with Buddha, Krishna, Jesus, Moses, John the baptist, and other prophets. In 1944, Moon married the first of several wives. One year later, he began what would later become the Unification church.

Kyle notes that it was in 1946 when "Moon claims, he came upon the key to all of humankind's problems: Satan had sex with Eve in the Garden of Eden. Moon became convinced that he was God's chosen instrument to reverse the fall of humanity caused by Eve's sin. In line with this new commission and his conviction that he was divinity, a new Messiah, Moon changed his name to Sun Myung Moon (meaning Shining Sun and Moon)."[7]

C. Many significant events occurred in Moon's life in the next decade: In 1948 the Presbyterian Church of Korea excommunicated him for his heretical teachings, so he became a self-ordained and independent preacher. He was imprisoned twice by the North Korean communists for capitalistic pursuits and bigamy, although his followers claim that he simply was persecuted for preaching his faith. The United Nations liberated the prison camp in 1949, and he fled to Pusan in South Korea where once again he started to preach.

He officially started his church, the Holy Spirit Association for the Unification of World Christianity in 1954 in Seoul, South Korea. This same year his wife divorced him. In 1955, Moon was arrested by South Korean police for immorality and draft evasion. He was released after three months, however, and the charges were dropped, possibly because he had success in a variety of business ventures and his support of General Park Chung Hee, the leader of South Korea. The Unification Bible, "Divine Principle" was published in 1957. It should be noted that the immorality charge for which Moon was arrested was based around a blood-cleansing sex ritual called Pikaruna. Richard Kyle tells about this:

"Pikaruna is based on the belief that because original sin came through Eve's sexual intercourse with Satan, a woman could have sex three times with Moon (the perfect man) and thus liquidate her original sin. After intercourse with Moon a woman achieved a perfected status, and male church members could have sexual relations with her and liquidate their own sin. Couples experiencing this blood cleansing [could] produce perfect children. If practiced widely enough, such a ritual could save the world."[8]

D. The development of Moon's theology lead him to conclude that he was chosen to find a woman who would be the perfect mother for humanity. Three marriages failed before he married Han Ja Han in 1960. Over the next twenty years she bore him twelve children, thus creating the "perfect family" and completing what Moon considered was a part of the unfulfilled physical aspect of Christ's mission, namely, to marry and have a family.

However, Moon's "perfect family" is having abnormal problems and causing alarm even at Unification headquarters. The eldest son, Hyojin Moon, has had problems with the law over the past several years regarding drugs, alcohol, and physical abuse. His wife, Nansook, has now divorced him and said that the supposed perfect family values of Moon are more like the seven deadly sins: gluttony, lust, avarice, sloth, anger, envy and pride.[9] Furthermore, Moon's fidelity is a joke. His theology, based upon the 1936 vision, also includes the divine need for him to have sexual relations with 70 married women, 70 widows, and 70 virgins.

It seems that sorrow is now filling Moon's family as the true fruit of his religion is becoming revealed. One of the children, Young Jin Moon, committed suicide by jumping from the seventeenth floor of Harrah's Hotel/Casino complex in Reno, Nevada, in October of 1999. This is an unfortunate jolt for a man who has proclaimed that he was sent to save the world by creating the "perfect family."

Thinking Through The Scripture

"Dear friends, I had intended to write to you about the salvation we share. But something has come up. It demands that I write to you and encourage you to continue your fight for the Christian faith that was entrusted to God's holy people once for all time. Some people have slipped in among you unnoticed. Not long ago they were condemned in writing for the following reason: They are people to whom God means nothing. They use God's kindness as an excuse for sexual freedom and deny our only Master and Lord, Jesus Christ." (Jude 3-4) GW

"The wrath of God is being revealed from heaven against all the godlessness and wickedness of men who suppress the truth by their wickedness...Therefore God gave them over in the sinful desires of their hearts to sexual impurity for the degrading of their bodies with one another." (Romans 1:18,24) NIV

Questions for discussion:
1. Over nineteen hundred years ago, Jude exhorted us to fight for the faith because of people's ulterior motives. How does this passage typify the character and teachings of Sun Myung Moon today?

2. Why is the wrath of God being revealed? How do these people's actions cause God to respond? What is the end result?

E. During the 1960's, Moon began making trips to the United States. On one such trip in 1964, he attended a seance with a spiritualistic medium named Arthur Ford. Ford claims that his spirit guide indicated Moon to be a New Age leader. Ben Alexander states in his book *Out of Darkness*:

"Arthur Ford's spirit guide, Fletcher, proclaimed that Mr. Moon was the voice of the creative mind and that he would be the front runner of the New Age Movement. He said, 'Mr. Moon in deep meditation can project himself and be seen just as Jesus has been able to project himself and be seen by the saints. This is one of the marks of the messiahs always...He is one of those who will be the human instrument through whom the World Teacher will be able to speak. And he was chosen because the New Age can be ushered in only through the eastern gate of the City of God.'"[10]

But the Lord speaks plainly against those who *"turn to mediums or spiritists"* (Lev. 19:31). He says, *I will also set My face against that person and will cut him off"* (Lev. 20:6). Moon needs to repent of gross sin, immorality and spiritism or face God's wrath.

F. In late 1971, Moon received a supposed revelation to move headquarters to New York. He launched a series of support rallies across the U.S. His public support of Richard Nixon during the Watergate investigations, anti communist rallies, and non-traditional American methods brought him quick notoriety.

Good business and investment sense brought the church increased holdings and assets, but unethical, mind-manipulating methods of recruiting brought governmental investigation. The focus on the cult increased, and tax evasion became an issue. In 1983, he faced tax fraud charges and received an 18 month prison term on July 20, 1984. He appealed, but unsuccessfully, and so spent 11 months in a minimum security federal prison.

Since his release in 1985, Moon has worked at establishing a positive public image for the church. He hosts large media events to draw prominent speakers, sometimes even noted evangelical Christians, and then tries to have his photo taken with them. These in turn will then be splashed all over the pages of his newspaper, *The Washington Times*. In 1996, at Moon's World Convention of the Family Federation for World Peace, he drew such noted people as Dr. Robert Schuller, Pat Boone, Ralph Reed, Beverly LaHaye, and

Jack Kemp.[11] The money that his recruits have brought in, as well as his many business dealings, has made him a multimillionaire. Authors Ron Carlson and Ed Decker tell us the following about some of Moon's financial holdings:

"Sun Myung Moon is a multimillionaire, with assets of over 30 million dollars in South Korea, 20 million dollars in Japan, and over 30 million dollars in the United States. He has gained his wealth through a variety of manufacturing enterprises, producing cosmetics, rifles, instant tea, titanium, and pharmaceuticals, and more. In the last few years Sun Myung Moon has been buying up much of the commercial fishing industry in the United States. This has become a great concern to the fishing fleets along the Gulf of Mexico, the Eastern Seaboard, the West Coast, and Alaska. In the average year, Moonies selling flowers, candy, and peanuts on street corners take in close to 20 million tax-free dollars. In New York state alone they own over 25 million dollars in property."[12]

G. While many of his followers espoused that Moon was the Messiah, he would only hint this was the case, but in the background he was creating a theology that pointed at him being the Korean Messiah (the third Adam). However, his hints at being Messiah have now turned into bold claims as the August 17, 1990 headlines of the San Francisco Chronicle read "Rev. Moon Says He's The Messiah". In the midst of swamis, scholars, lamas, and imams, Moon declared that he was the new world Messiah.[13]

H. In the past few years, Moon has spent much time in Latin America where he has been spreading his gospel and business empire. In Uruguay alone, the Unification Church has an estimated 200 million dollars worth of investments in shipyards, meat-packing plants, printing companies, and hotels.[14]

One of the disciples of Sun Myung Moon told me that he felt Moon had tried to unite the Christians of United States behind him but was unsuccessful. As a result, he has seceded the United States to Satan's domain and has turned his focus to South America where some Mormons in the Church of Jesus Christ of Latter-Day Saints think Jesus may return one day.

His South America connection is becoming stronger with the purchase of hundreds of square miles of land in southern Brazil, Paraguay, and Uruguay. One venture he calls "New Hope East Garden" and proclaims it as "a kingdom of heaven on earth, a new Garden of Eden." However, his popularity is waning in the region even though he has poured millions into the economy. Recent complaints about manipulative recruitment and indoctrination, as well as heresy charges by both Protestants and Catholics, are bringing the same type of pressure the Unification Church received in the United States.

Thinking Through The Scripture

"Be careful that no one misleads you—deceiving you and leading you into error. For many will come in (on the strength of) My name—appropriating the name which belongs to Me— saying, I am Messiah, the Christ; and they will lead many astray." (Matthew 24:4-5) AMP

Questions for discussion:
1. What does Jesus warn us about? Where will these false messiahs lead people?
2. What do they use to trick or deceive people? Why are people so easily duped and deceived? How does Sun Myung Moon fit into this picture?
3. Read Matthew 24:3 in your Bible. What do the disciples ask that prompts Jesus to give the above reply? Since there are many today that claim to be the Messiah, what implications does this have upon the return of Christ?

IV. WHAT IS DUALISM?
  A. Dualism is a belief in a universe of opposites and dualities. All of existence is dual. According to dualists, flesh and spirit are not harmoniously conjoined but are at war with each other. Furthermore, the flesh is considered evil and counterproductive to the spirit or soul.
      Gnosticism is based upon the concept of dualism—namely, that The Supreme Father God emanated from the 'good' spirit world. From him proceeded successive finite beings (AEONS), one of which (Sophia) gave birth to the Demiurge (creator - God). The creator - God, or the Demiurge, created the material 'evil' world together with all the various organic and inorganic things that constitute it."[15]
      Many modern day cults embrace the concept of dualism, but it is rejected by traditional Christianity as being heretical to the Bible's view that all of God's creation is good because God created it that way (Gen. 1). Rather than the body or flesh being evil, the Apostle Paul tells us that it is sin which is actually evil (Rom 7:17).
  B. "Basic to Moon's world view is the concept of dualism. All of existence is dual: Father God and Mother God; Male and Female; Light

and Dark; Yin and Yang; Spirit and Flesh. Each part of existence has its dual aspect. Moon's God (with dual male / female aspects) always acts in a dual manner with his dual creation."[16]

V. WHAT IS THE MAIN BOOK OF THE UNIFICATION CHURCH?

A. **The Divine Principle.** Moon published this in 1957. In The Divine Principle, Moon gives his interpretation of Scripture. The Moonies consider it as high a source as the Bible. In essence, they don't have a bible; they have two bibles. "Moon's theological scheme is based on a scope of history divided into an Old Testament Age, a New Testament Age, and the present Completed Testament Age. The latter requires a new revelation of truth to supplant the Bible, and Moon's 536-page Divine Principle fills the bill.

It was dictated, he explains, by God to him through the process of automatic writing. Its 'truths' were compiled only after Moon had conferred in the spirit world with Buddha, Jesus, and other notable religious figures. All bowed in acquiescence to Moon, imploring him to bring humanity the unuttered revelations supposedly mentioned by Jesus in Jn. 16:13. Moon also reserves the option of continuing to add supernatural revelation or adjusting his 'divine principle' at a future date."[17]

B. The book places much emphasis on the number 2,000 between the first Messiah (Jesus) and the coming of the second Messiah. The Messiah will be born in Korea, the 'Third Israel'. The book does not state that Moon is the Messiah, it simply sets him up for it. The so called "completed testament" lists some requirements for his life: "He must be born a complete human being, conquer sin and evidence God's masculine nature. Moreover, he must marry a woman who manifests God's feminine characteristics. The Lord of the Second Advent will thus complete the half of the messianic mission that Jesus did not."[18]

VI. WHAT ARE SOME OF THE FALSE TEACHING OF THE CULT?

A. **Moon's Teaching That the Divine Principle is the "completed testament:"** They think it takes precedence over the Bible: (The Old and New Testaments)

1. But the Bible says: *"I testify to everyone who hears the words of the prophecy of this book; if anyone adds to them, God shall add to him the plagues which are written in this book."* (Deut. 4:2) NASB.

2. Also, the Bible tells us that the faith has been *"once for all delivered to the saints"* (Jude 3). Therefore, any new revelation must

be examined against the Bible. If it contradicts, it is thrown out as false. It works like this:

    a) God is immutable: (Mal. 3:6 and Heb. 6:17-18): He does not change, He is consistent in Truth, and He won't contradict Himself.

    b) Thus, any new revelation must be judged against previous scriptural revelation.

    c) The Bible is our ultimate authority: 1 Thess. 5:21; Heb. 4:12; Eph. 6:17

B. **Moon's doctrine that Eve had sex with Satan in the garden of Eden**: He teaches that Eve had sex with the devil in the garden of Eden. This caused the *spiritual fall* of man. She received spiritual insight and saw her mistake, so she had sex with Adam trying to regain her relationship with God; this caused the *physical fall* of humanity (dualism). Eve's affair with Lucifer produced Cain and the ultimate ramification upon humanity was the political force of *communism*. However, the fruit of her love for Adam produced Abel. This symbolized humanity's relationship with God and resulted in the political force of *democracy*.

    1. But the Bible gives absolutely no support of any of this in Genesis.

        a) Eve did not have sex with Satan and Cain was not his biological son.

        b) The fall of man did not happen in two stages, but one.

        c) The political connections are unsubstantiated.

    2. Furthermore, the Genesis account is to be taken literally. It was written along with the other first five books of the Bible by Moses. It is an account of history but it is also prophetic for its impact upon all creation. The Bible tells us..."*No prophecy in Scripture is a matter of one's own interpretation.*" (2 Pet. 1:20) GW. God included in Genesis all the necessary information for us to understand the basics of what happened. There is no secret information (Gnosticism) to which we must attain in order to understand it.

Thinking Through The Scripture

"Now the man had relations with his wife Eve, and she conceived and gave birth to Cain, and she said, 'I gave gotten a manchild with the help of the Lord.' And again, she gave birth to his brother Abel. And Abel was a keeper of flocks, but Cain was a tiller of the ground." (Genesis 4:1-2) NASB

Questions for discussion:
1. Who was Eve's husband? Look up the word "relations" in various translations. According to the passage, who did she have relations with in order to conceive Cain? In order to conceive Abel?
2. Consider Moon's personal sex life. How does it impact his theology? How is it reflected in his misinterpretation of Scripture?

C. **Moon's false teachings regarding Jesus Christ:**
   1. *That there was no virgin birth:* Moon continues to teach that Jesus' parents were Zechariah and Mary[19] even though it is ludicrous.
      Scriptures Refuting: Isaiah 7:14; Mt. 1:18-25; Lk. 1:26-38; 2:1-21
   2. *That the cross portrays failure because it was not essential for the redemption of mankind and not a part of God's perfect plan:* Moon says that God had prepared the world for Jesus the Messiah by sending Malachi to the Jews, Confucius and Buddha to the Asian world, and Socrates to the Hellenistic world so that under Jesus all religions and cultures would unite. John the Baptist, who was suppose to prepare the way for Jesus, lost faith. This caused people to abandon Jesus and eventually murder him. Jesus was suppose to come and find his perfect "Eve", make the perfect family, and usher in the Kingdom of God. But under the circumstances, Jesus had to choose the cross which defeated Satan, but this only brought spiritual salvation to the world, and not physical. He denies that the cross was necessary and planned.
      Scriptures Refuting: Ps 22; Isaiah 53; Zech. 12:10; 1 Jn. 2:2; Heb. 1:3
   3. *That Jesus was not uniquely God:* Moon denies the unique deity of Christ while he does hold that Jesus was without original sin. Although it is easy for Moon to make a statement like this, it falls far short of explaining the extraordinary life of Jesus while on earth. Indeed, there is no one in recorded history who has ever done the things that Jesus did. Furthermore, there are not even any stories about others who have come close to doing the many miracles that are reported of Jesus. The following paragraph by the late Dr. Walter Martin from his book *The Kingdom of the Cults* makes the strong point:
      "The Lord Jesus, while on earth, was both God and man and indicated this on numerous occasions by forgiving sins (Mark 2:5), raising the dead (Jn. 11), casting out demons (Mk. 5:7-13), and affirming to the Jews who challenged his identity

that He was indeed the eternal Being who spoke with Moses at the burning bush (Ex. 3:14,15; cr. John 8:58)."[20]

   Scriptures Refuting: Mt. 1:23; Jn. 1:4; Col. 2:9; Heb. 1:3, 8

   4. *That Jesus was resurrected as a spirit only and not in the physical body.*

   Scriptures Refuting: Mt. 8:26; Mr. 8:31; Lk. 24:36-39; Jn. 20:27

D. **Moon's doctrine that he is the new chosen Messiah:** He teaches that he is commissioned to bring physical salvation to the world: He claims to be the third Adam, the Lord of the Second Advent. But the Bible says: *"That by the name of Jesus Christ of Nazareth, whom you crucified, whom God raised from the dead, by Him this man stands here before you whole. This is the stone which was rejected by you builders, which has become the chief corner stone, Nor is there salvation in any other, for there is no other name under heaven given among men by which we must be saved."* (Acts 4:10-12)

E. **Moon's doctrine that the Holy Spirit is the feminine counterpart to the Father:** "For a family of children to exist, there must be a 'true father' and a 'true Mother.' The true Mother is the Holy Spirit coming as the second Eve. She is the mother of the fallen children who are reborn. Because the Holy Spirit is essentially a female spirit, we cannot become the bride of Jesus unless we receive the Holy Spirit."[21]

   1. But the Bible teaches that the Holy Spirit came upon the virgin Mary and planted within her the seed of the holy offspring that would be called the Son of God (Luke 1:35). In this action, He clearly portrays male characteristics.

   2. While it must be remembered that God created both male and female in his image (Gen. 1:27) and that the qualities of each are thereby found in Him, it is equally important to remember that He represents Himself as "his" (Gen. 1:27) and that the church is to become the bride of Christ. (Rev. 19)

Thinking Through The Scripture

"'And behold, you will conceive in your womb and bring forth a Son, and shall call His name Jesus. He will be great, and will be called the Son of the Highest; and the Lord God will give Him the throne of His father David. And He will reign over the house of Jacob forever, and of His kingdom there will be no end.' Then Mary said to the angel, 'How can this be, since I do not know a man?' And the angel answered and said to her, 'The Holy Spirit will come upon you, and the power of the Highest will overshadow you; thereafter, also, that Holy One who is to be born will be called the Son of God." (Luke 1:31-35)

Questions for discussion:
1. Who did Mary say that she had not known? How does this contrast with Moonie doctrine that Zechariah was the father of Jesus?
2. Who does the angel say will come upon Mary in order to conceive Jesus? Who is the "Highest"? What gender does the Highest portray in this passage? How does this show the inaccuracy of Moonie doctrine?

F. **Moon's doctrine that Hell exists only now on earth:** He teaches that it will one day be done away with as the kingdom of heaven is established on earth: Moonies place much emphasis on serving Sun Myung Moon so that the kingdom of heaven will be established and Satan ultimately defeated. They believe that "your works can save you and other people who have died before you" and that "all humanity will ultimately be saved".[22]
   1. But the Bible indicates that the concept of eternal hell should be taken quite literally. In Rev. 20:13-15 we see the "lake of fire" for all who deny Christ. Jesus taught about hell on various occasions. Examples: He taught it as a real place in Matt. 5:22 when speaking about what is in our hearts, and as a final place for some when giving the parable of Lazarus and the rich man (Luke 16)

VII. WHAT IS INDEMNITY?
   A. The church teaches its members that people "also play a role in the salvation of humanity. They take part in the world's restoration by positioning themselves with the Messiah. Such an alignment can be achieved by participating in a process called indemnity. Through the indemnity process, people prepare themselves for entrance into the restored kingdom. Indemnity is a form of salvation by works in which individuals must atone for their sins through specific acts of penance...During the time of indemnity people observe absolute celibacy and perform sacrificial work. At the conclusion of this period, [often many years] Moon matches each 'Moonie' with an appropriate mate. The couple is then married in a ceremony performed by Moon and his wife. Involved in the consummation of the marriage is a ritual that dramatically reenacts the process of indemnity and restoration."[23]
   B. Moon performs massive weddings. Beginning in 1969 with 777 couples, he shocked traditional mainstream America with a new approach to mating. These weddings bring much publicity because of their size. In 1992, 20,000 couples were married at once, and in February of 1999, 40,000 couples exchanged vows in Seoul, South

Korea. The last mass wedding in the United States at the time of this writing was in June of 1998 in which 1,500 couples were married in Madison Square Garden. These weddings bring much publicity because of their size—in 1992, 20,000 couples were married at once. The process of getting married as a Moonie is not a quick one. Members apply for engagement to the Blessing Committee. If they are selected, chances are they will not even know the person to whom they will be engaged until the mass engagement occurs.

At this time, the members are matched and quite often with someone of a different ethnic origin, culture, or nation. They are allowed to speak for fifteen minutes to determine if there is any reason they should not marry. "Kodak matches" are common because sometimes Moon uses pictures of foreigners who were unable to attend. He matches these with someone present. After an engagement consecration, the couples remain separated often for three years of time. The mass wedding is performed with all the brides dressed in modest white gowns and the grooms in dark blue suits with maroon ties. The music of Mendelssohn's Wedding March plays in the background. After the ceremony, "sexual relationships were still not allowed, a period that would end a half year later, and then only if each spouse had brought into the church three new members".[24] This is the Indemnity.

VIII. WHO DOES THE CULT TARGET FOR RECRUITMENT?
  A. **Lonely college students**. They look for new students who are away from home for the first time and have no friends.
  B. **Idealistic people who are dissatisfied with the world** and who want to help build a utopia on earth. These they recruit from various rallies. The rallies are often disguised as ecology or world peace gatherings.

IX. WHAT ARE THEIR EVANGELISM TECHNIQUES?
  A. **They invite people to workshops:** They approach young people on the street or on college campuses and ask them to visit the church headquarters for an informal discussion or lecture. The process of induction works like this:
    1. Attend a workshop at the church or other location.
    2. Attend a two-day workshop (weekend) at a retreat location.
    3. Continue on for an extended workshop of one week.
    4. Continue on for a final workshop of two weeks.
    5. Join the group permanently. Marc Galanter gives the results of one study:

One study done on this induction method followed 104 "guests" through the five steps mentioned above to determine drop out rate: 71 percent stayed through the weekend workshop, 29 percent stayed through the extended one week workshop, 17 percent stayed beyond the first week, and 9 percent joined the group. They knew they were joining an uncompromising communal living situation but did it anyway. Each step took the candidates deeper into Moonie theology and lifestyle. Also, there was the chance that those who left early might return at a later date.[25]

B. **They use "heavenly deception":** The church gives its members the right to deceive others if it will benefit or promote the causes of the church. This is used in *selling* and *recruiting*. In selling flowers, candles, etc., the members have been known to tell customers that the money is going for a "drug rehabilitation program" or to "feed starving children".

In recruiting, it is used as a cloak for the group's real purpose. There will be advertisements for creative community workshops, ecology issues, world peace crusades, rallies for improved race relations, workshops on extrasensory perception, etc. People who attend these events do not realize that it is run and heavily infiltrated by Moonies looking for candidates. They do everything they can to make candidates feel welcome, to have an identity with the group, and a desire to know more. They are invited to get to know the group more, and plans are made for other encounters. These are quickly scheduled and much follow up is done until the candidates are invited to a weekend *retreat*. It is not until part way through the weekend, in a location a distance from home, that they come to find out who the group represents. They are told the group must take these deceptive actions in order to get out their real message because negative publicity has smeared the truth about the organization. By this time, emotional ties have grown and many stay.

C. **They use love-bombing:** This is a manipulation technique of bombing someone with love. Lonely people are looking for love, acceptance, and purpose. Moonies saturate a candidate with approval and friendship, making them feel important. That's the love aspect of it. The bomb is hidden, however, because their real agenda is to convert someone to serve Sun Myung Moon, "the True Father," for their entire life.

X. WHAT FOUR-POINT PROGRAM OF CULTS MEETS PEOPLES' BASIC NEEDS?

A. For an individual to reach maturity and establish himself / herself in life, four things must take place: 1) Independence from family,

2) Successful relationship to the opposite sex, 3) An occupation for personal support, and 4) A meaningful and workable philosophy of life. The cults satisfy these things for some people.

1. Independence from family is gained by dependence upon the cult and its leaders.
2. Successful relationship with the opposite sex is gained by strict moral codes.
3. Personal support is gained as converts succeed at the simple tasks assigned.
4. "[T]he philosophy of the cult or the cult leaders is overlaid on top of the individual thought process. Instead of building a meaningful philosophy of life for themselves, these individuals become dependent and accept the philosophy given them by the cult leaders."[26]

XI. WHAT IS THE LIFE STYLE OF THE PEOPLE IN THE CULT?

A. Since it is an authoritarian commune system, the lives of the people are controlled extensively. The church determines living locations, jobs, marriage, schedules, clothing, eating, and basic lifestyle. There are even pressures to put children in full- time communal day care centers. The daily schedule often includes singing, reading the Bible and the Divine Principle, recording thoughts, and prayer to Moon. While there is freedom to leave the cult, they are put under great psychological and mental pressure to stay—they are told that those who leave fall prey to Satan and also that Sun Myung Moon needs them if America is to be won against Satan.

B. There is a "central figure" for each area who acts as leader and counselor. People may earn their way, through loyalty and hard work, from recruiting and selling to working at one of the many businesses (voluntarily) owned by the church. These people work approximately 67 hours per week, while new recruits out on the streets might easily put in more than a hundred. But the "earned" positions of the long time members can be disrupted for massive crusades. During these times, jobs change and families are divided for the duration of the crusades.

C. A typical Sunday morning service, according to cult expert Bob Larson, would be as follows: "Sunday mornings are set aside to pay homage to the True Parents. Rising at 5:00 A.M., the Church Family bows three times before a picture of Rev. and Mrs. Moon. A pledge follows in which members vow to do whatever necessary to bring about Moon's will on earth. At times, prayer sessions (with petitions directed to Moon himself) become loud, frenzied affairs.

Observers report seeing some devotees sob and wail, pounding their fists on the floor in explosive outpourings of grief and exclamations of victory. Moonies were described by one reporter as jerking spasmodically 'in spiritual transport like participants in a voodoo ceremony.' Such traumas of self-evaluation are better than receiving a humiliating tirade from Moon. To those who fail his goals, the True father is merciless. He scathingly attacks slothful members, accusing them of not helping to build the kingdom of heaven on earth."[27]

XII. WHAT ARE SOME POINTS TO REMEMBER IN WITNESSING TO A MOONIE?
   A. **Prayer:** The Unification church not only messes up people's theology, but it messes up their thinking. It "brain washes" its victims with mind manipulation techniques and causes a psychological meltdown so that the individual does not think clearly. A part of the technique is to keep the individuals so preoccupied and tired that they do not have time to think about the strange life they live or the bizarre things they are taught. They trade away their individual goals and identity in order to feel secure and have their daily needs met. However, there are deeper needs, and like seeds, they are hidden under the exterior of what appears to be an impenetrable rocky surface. This is where a Christian should aim prayer.

   I met a Moonie named Shinji who was getting divorced from his second or third wife. He was hurting but trying to rationalize the situation by thinking that the marriage would work out because it was somehow represented as a principle in the Bible and thus meant to be. He had a hard time just recognizing his own sin and the problems cast upon their marriage by the organization. He had a real need that was beginning to emerge from that rocky soil, and so I prayed with him about his need. It wasn't harvest time, but it did start to melt his heart and make a way to share the truth about Christ. He even came to a Christian meeting and admitted that he had doubts about the Reverend Sun Myung Moon.

   Like Shinji, these people often harbor heart-felt needs under the surface. Maybe they have loved ones that they have forsaken because of the organization, parents or even children that they haven't seen in years. Take time to ask them about their biological family and then invite them to pray with you on their behalf. Somewhere under the surface, there usually beats a heart that feels concern, and quite possibly, shame.

B. **Love:** Moonies need to know the love of the *True Father in Heaven.*
Let the love of God shine through you so that they may know His
love and by this realize that Sun Myung Moon falls far short of the
glory of God (Romans 3:23). Moonies can be intense and intimi-
dating. They are manipulated to work, work, work. Inviting one of
them over for a meal might produce some stress on your end, but
it will put them in an environment of home life that they seldom
see. Ask what their favorite meal is and try to fix it for them. The
act of generosity will not go unnoticed. True Christian love will not
fail to soften the ground of their rocky heart so that the seeds of
truth can be watered in order to grow.

C. **Witness:** Here are a couple of ideas for starters:

1) In many Scriptures, the Apostle Paul shows how Jesus came to
deliver us from sin but also from the "dead works" of a code of
legalistic standards. The Moonies need to know the "freedom"
which is theirs in God, not the bondage of an authoritarian
commune.

Examples: Galatians 3:1-14 Colossians 2:1-17, 2023; Romans
10:1-12.

2) The many Scriptures cited in this lesson can be used to witness
the truth to them about their false doctrine, but for a quick witness, consider using the concept that *"salvation comes from the
Jews" (John. 4:22) GW.* This quickly counteracts their doctrine
of a New Messiah arising from Korea. Also, you can show them
that there is no savior other than the God of the Bible (Hosea
13:4), and Jesus is His name (Acts 4:12). Hallelujah!

3) Don't be afraid to invite them to church. They may come just
because they think you are a prospect. They will thrive off of a
good Bible discussion.

End Notes

1. Ron Carlson and Ed Decker, *Fast Facts on False Teachings* (Eugene, OR: Harvest House
Publishers, 1994), p. 156.
2. Richard Kyle, *The Religious Fringe: A History of Alternative Religions in America*
(DownersGrove, IL: Inter Varsity Press, 1993), pgs. 333-334.
3. Marc Galanter, *Cults: Faith, Healing, and Coercion* (New York: Oxford University Press,
1990), p. 132.
4. Walter Martin, *The Kingdom of the Cults* (Minneapolis, MN: Bethany House Publishers,
1985), p. 342.
5. George A. Mather and Larry A. Nichols, *Dictionary of Cults, Sects, Religions and the
Occult* (Grand Rapids, MI: Zondervan Publishing House, 1993), p. 282.
6. Josh McDowell and Don Stewart, *Understanding the Cults* (San Bernadino, CA: Here's
Life Publishers, Inc., 1982), p. 133.

7. Kyle, p. 333.
8. Ibid., p. 334.
9. "National News in Perspective," *Vantage Point: A Mini Expositor*, produced by Watchman Fellowship (March 1998): 7.
10. Ben Alexander, *Out From Darkness* (Joplin, MO: College Press Publishing Company, 1986), pgs. 157-158.
11. Bob Waldrep, "Unification Church Influence in America," *The Watchman Expositor* 13, 6 (1996): 10.
12. Carlson and Decker, pgs. 151-152.
13. Ibid., p. 147.
14. *Latin Trade*, (July 1997): 35.
15. Mather and Nichols, p. 111.
16. Josh McDowell, *A Ready Defense* (Nashville, TN: Thomas Nelson Publishers, 1993), p. 357.
17. Bob Larson, *Larson's Book of Cults* (Wheaton, IL: Tyndale House Publishers, Inc., 1988), pgs. 227- 228.
18. Kyle, p. 339.
19. Larson, p. 225.
20. Martin, p. 343.
21. Mather and Nichols, p. 284.
22. Francis Anfuso, A tract called "Who's That Knocking at My Door?" (2100 Eloise Avenue, South Lake Tahoe, CA 96150: Christian Equippers International, 1981), pgs. 15 and 21.
23. Kyle, p. 339.
24. Galanter, p. 153.
25. Ibid., pgs. 140-141.
26. Carlson and Decker, p. 158.
27. Larson, p. 230.

QUESTIONNAIRE: LESSON TEN

NAME: _____ DATE: _____

1. In which country did the Unification Church begin? _____. How many current members are in the U.S.A.? _____. Where are the main headquarters located? _____.

2. Who is the founder of the movement? _____. What was the name given to him at birth? _____. At what age was he when he received the vision that changed his life? _____.

3. Explain what Pikaruna is and what it had to do with Moon? _____

_____

_____

_____

4. What is the supposed name of Arthur Ford's spirit guide and what did it tell Moon? _____

_____

_____

5. Write out Lev. 19:31: _____

_____

_____

6. Briefly explain what dualism is: _____

_____

_____

7. What is Moon's "completed testament" called? _____

8. Regarding the false teachings of the cult, give one reason why each false teaching mentioned below is not scriptural. You may use Scripture if you like.

a) The Divine Principle: _____

_____

_____

b) Moon's "fall of man in the garden": _____

_____

_____

c) Moon's view of "the cross of Christ": _____

_____

_____

d) Moon's view "of Christ's divinity": _____

_____

_____

g) Moon's view of himself: _____

_____

_____

h) Moon's view "of the Holy Spirit": _____

_____

_____

9. The group's form of salvation by works, in which individuals must atone for their sins through specific acts of penance, is called _____.

10. List the two types of evangelism techniques they use:

a) _____

b) _____

11. List two of the four basic needs to maturity that the cults try and provide.

a) _____

b) _____

12. What are Moonies doing on Sunday morning? _____

_____

_____

13. Consider your knowledge of the Moonies before and after this lesson. Circle the number below that indicates how equipped you felt before taking the course to witness to a Moonie as compared to how equipped you feel now. Be honest.

BEFORE 0 1 2 3 4 5 6 7 8 9 10 **AFTER** 0 1 2 3 4 5 6 7 8 9 10

LESSON 11

FREEMASONRY

"I do not want to go into all the details of what transpired at that time except to say that they had me remove my suit coat, my shoes and socks, and my tie. I was then told to take off my trousers and slip my left arm out of my shirt so that my arm and breast were bare. They gave me a pair of baggy pants to wear that had one leg cut off at the knee and then blindfolded me and put a noose around my neck.... I guess that while I was expecting it to be a bit 'fraternity' in nature, I hadn't prepared myself to be in such a state. I became quite upset when they required that I remove my wedding ring from my finger. You know, I wanted to stop it all right then, because that ring was the symbol of my love and my fidelity to my wife, Jennifer. But I let it go rather than make a scene, and I allowed myself to fall one step deeper into deception. Then there was a knock on the door, the person asked who was there, and the man with me said that I was a poor, blind candidate who had long been in darkness and was seeking the light of that worshipful Lodge."[1] —Book character, Jeff Moore

I. WHAT IS FREEMASONRY?
    A. It is the world's largest secret organization of men. It cloaks itself in "good works" but inside it is perverting into a paganistic religion. Many good people, including Christians, join the Masons thinking it is like a fraternity. If they don't advance very far into it, they won't realize that the inner circles are simply using them to propel its New Age occultic agenda. In a little booklet called *Masons*, Harold Berry tells us:

232

"While researching the beliefs of the Masons, I came into contact with an Air Force officer who had been *a fourth generation Mason*. By age 23, he was a 32nd Degree Scottish Rite Prince of the Royal Secret, a York Rite Knight Templar, the Senior Deacon of a Blue Lodge that he attended and unofficial Tyler of another lodge he frequently attended. He had been to lodges in New Hampshire, Arkansas, Oklahoma, Maine, Nebraska—even Japan and the Philippines. He not only attended but was active in most of these lodges. *Of his own free will and accord he came to see that Jesus Christ was the true Light and chief cornerstone that the builders had rejected* (1 Peter 2:6,7). When he became a Master Mason, he was given a Masonic edition of the Bible. When he opened it, his eyes fell on Matthew 6:24, where he read that it is impossible to serve two masters. This caused him to think seriously about the conflicts that he knew existed between Freemasonry and Christianity. He eventually realized he had to forsake Masonry...*he believes that there is no possibility that a knowledgeable and committed Christian can also be a Mason.*"[2] [italics added]

II. WHY IS FREEMASONRY BEING CONSIDERED IN A STUDY ON THE CULTS?
   A. Because it uses *deception* to get men involved and entraps them by *secret ritual rites and secret blood oaths.*
   B. Because it opposes the Christian faith by:
      1) Teaching a salvation based upon works through the lodge.
      2) Purposely removing the name of Jesus Christ from its Scripture quotations.
      3) Blaspheming the true name of God.
      4) Reducing the Holy Scriptures to nothing but symbolism.
   C. Because it worships and gives honor to *Jabulon, Abbadon, and Baphomet* in the upper degrees of masonry.[3]
   D. Because its own writers teach *paganism, spiritism, and the occult.* In his book *The Truth About Masons*, Robert Morey states:
      "Hundreds of Masonic books which attack Christianity and openly teach *paganism* are published, supported, and recommended by high officials, states Lodges, and supreme councils. We are told that this is proper because the Lodge should be universal in appeal and each mason can interpret the word 'God' and the symbols of the Craft any way he wants. But when a Christian Mason attempts to give a Christian interpretation of the rituals and symbols of the Craft, he is forbidden to do this! That this is true can be seen if we ask when was the last time that a Christian interpretation of the

Craft was published, supported, and recommended by high officials, state Lodges, and supreme councils. *We have seen hundreds of Hindu, Buddhist, Gnostic, druid, occultic, New Age, Hermetic, etc. interpretations of the Craft but not one Christian interpretation!* If Masonry is truly universal and open to all religions, then why is it closed to Christianity? "[4] [italics added]

III. WHAT ATTRACTS MEN TO FREEMASONRY ?
    A. Many things attract prospects to it. Some are as follows: 1) Relatives or friends are involved. 2) Some are searching for God, purpose, or mystical insight. 3) The secrecy itself is a drawing card. 4) The mason's organization is well known and has some measure of respect in society. 5) Some see the Shriners parading around in their red fezzes and doing good deeds for children. 6) A desire for social fellowship and respect. 7) Belonging to an exclusive men's lodge. 8) Business connections.

IV. WHEN AND WHERE DID "SPECULATIVE" MASONRY BEGIN?
    A. **Definitions:** 1) *Operative* means the actual craft of stone masonry. 2) *Speculative* means *the symbols, degrees, and secrets* of modern masonry.
    B. **The formal beginning** of speculative Masonry is considered to be June 24, 1717. The Grand Lodge of London was organized at the Goose and Gridiron Tavern.[5] The word "grand" simply means governing lodge. Other lodges formed prior to this time did not have the distinction of being based solely upon speculative principles. Scotland established a Grand Lodge in 1736 but holds the oldest known lodge meeting minutes (business records) dating July, 1599, from the lodge of Edinburgh known as Mary's Chapel.[6] There certainly is controversy over when non-operatives (speculatives) first became the dominant force of Freemasonry. Scotland can also document "the first authentic instance of a non-operative mason appearing as a member of a lodge"[7] on June 8, 1600, however, it appears that the meeting of 1717 in London is the first one in which the entire membership was made up of non-operatives.
    C. **A great controversy** over the actual origins of speculative Freemasonry is given fuel by the numerous Masonic historians that theorize the beginnings of speculative Freemasonry as: 1) The religion of Atlantis or the lost land of Mu, 2) The original religion of all people, 3) The religion of Stonehenge and ruins like it, 4) That it came from the ancient occult, 5) That it came from ancient India, China, Egypt, Assyria, Palestine, Greece, Italy, France, 6) That it

was started by Emmanuel Swedenborg, 7) That it goes back to the Druids, and 8) That its from the ancient American Indians.[8]

Thinking Through The Scripture

"But false prophets also arose among the people, just as there will be false teachers among you, who will secretly introduce destructive heresies, even denying the Master who bought them, bringing swift destruction upon themselves." (2 Peter 2:1) NASB

Questions for discussion:
1. How does this verse relate to the actions and teachings of freemasonry?
2. Why do false teachers introduce heresies secretly?
3. Do they know they are destructive? How do they deny the Master?

V. WHAT IS A BRIEF HISTORICAL OUTLINE OF AMERICAN FREEMASONRY?
   A. 1730's: Masonic lodges established. Clubs, mostly upper class. Christian influence.
   B. Revolutionary Period: Masons gain some secret political, economic and social clout.
   C. Post Revolution: Movement shifts from upper class to middle class.
   D. 1826: William Morgan murdered for exposing masonic secrets in his book.
   E. 1826 - 1843: The Antimasonic Political Party swells to oppose masonry.
   F. 1860 - 70's: Albert Pike rewrites Scottish Rite degrees *to de-Christianize freemasonry.*
   G. 1920's: Increase in Christian membership attempts to reclaim masonry.
   H. Twentieth Century: Inner struggle between Christian, pagan, and occultic influences.
   I. 1990's: Worldwide membership = 6 million; U.S.A. membership = 4 million, but in decline as the true inner circle agenda is being exposed. Christians are reevaluating their membership. Some are fighting for a return to Christian emphasis.

VI. WHAT WERE SOME OF THE ASPECTS OF EARLY FREEMASONRY?
   A. **Beginnings:** "Freemasonry originated in London in the early 1700's. Founded as a stonemason's trade guild, the order became a club for tradesmen, merchants, and a few much-celebrated noblemen."[9] The

first grand lodge in London was established for the upper class aristocracy. The masonic lodges made their way to America and were established in the coastal towns by the 1730 - 1740's. "During the early decades the order experienced little growth, met infrequently, and functioned chiefly as a drinking and eating club."[10]

B. **Cultural Differences**: The Masonry movement was very much influenced by the country and culture in which it originated. It was shaped by the surrounding climate of the times. In England, for instance, it has always been associated with the upper class. In the U.S., it began with the upper class but became a middle-class organization after the American Revolution. Germany has always had a strong military membership. The occultic influence of Emanuel Swedenborg helped shape Sweden's Masonry movement. France's Masonry became a hotbed of every antisocial and antireligious group. *Anti-Catholics* bedded together with occultists, Rosicrucians, magicians, and others. The anti-Catholic Masonry of France eventually *infected the Masonry movements of Italy, Spain, Mexico, Central America, and South America.*

C. **Masonic Influence In Early America**: The true influence that Freemasonry had upon the shaping of America is very much a subject of debate. There is no doubt that *many of the early Masons were Christians.* The emphasis of Masonic brotherhood possibly played a significant role in America's fight for independence since many Masons were men of political influence. However, other Masons (Benedict Arnold for one) were loyal to the King of England and worked against the Revolution.

Many of America's well-known and well-loved founders were Masons. Some of the names are *George Washington, Thomas Jefferson, Benjamin Franklin, Paul Revere, and John Hancock.* The influence of Masonry upon these men is unknown, but there is currently no hard evidence that they were in any way controlled by the society. In fact, according to Morey, "Washington became a Mason in his youth but never attended much. His prominence in the Revolution and the presidency gave Masons the chance to boast about his being a Mason. But this does not erase the fact that he had not attended a Lodge meeting more than once or twice in 30 years! He rejected his election to the office of Supreme Grand Master of all Lodges. *In short, he was not a faithful Mason.*"[11]

This is not to say, however, that the secret society did not have some profound shaping influences upon the United States. It is an interesting thing to look below the surface regarding some of the historical events of America. Quite often, one will find masonic influence. For instance, few Americans know that the Statue of Liberty was actually given by the French masons to the American masons. A more graphic illustration of masonic involvement in the shaping of America, in regard to the design of Washington D.C., is found in *What You Need To Know About Masons* by Ed Decker:

"Take any good street map of downtown Washington D.C. and find the Capitol Building. Facing the Capitol from the Mall and using the Capitol as the head or top of the Compass, the left leg is represented by Pennsylvania Avenue and the right leg by Maryland Avenue. The Square is found in the usual Masonic position with the intersection of Canal Street and Louisiana Avenue. The left leg of the Compass stands on the White House and the right leg stands on the Jefferson Memorial. The circle drive and short streets behind the Capitol complete the picture to form the head and ears of what Satanists call the Goat of Mendes or Goat's head. *On top of the White House is an inverted five-pointed star, or pentagram, which is one of the highest-level symbols of witchcraft and Satanism.* The point rests squarely on the White House and is facing south in true occult fashion. It sits within the intersections of Connecticut and Vermont Avenues, north to Dupont and Logan Circles, with Rhode Island and Massachusetts going to Washington Circle to the west and Mount Vernon Square on the east. The center of the pentagram is 16th Street where, 13 blocks due north of the very center of the White House, the Masonic House of the Temple sits at the top of this occult iceberg. The Washington Monument stands in perfect line to the intersecting point of the form of the Masonic Square, stretching from the House of the Temple to the Capitol building. Within the hypotenuse of that right triangle sit many of the headquarter buildings for the most powerful departments of government, such as the Justice Department, the U.S. Senate, and the Internal Revenue Service...do you realize that most federal buildings, from the White House to the Capitol Building, have had a cornerstone laid in a Masonic ritual and had specific Masonic paraphernalia placed in each one?"[12] [italics added]

Thinking Through The Scripture

"But there is nothing covered up that will not be revealed, and hidden that will not be known. Accordingly whatever you have said in the dark shall be heard in the light, and what you have whispered in the inner rooms shall be proclaimed upon the housetops. And I say to you, My friends, do not be afraid of

those who kill the body, and after that have no more that they can do. But I will warn you whom to fear: fear the One who after He has killed has the authority to cast into hell; yes, I tell you, fear Him!" (Luke 12:2-5) NASB

Questions for discussion:
1. The Lord Jesus spoke these words over nineteen hundred years ago. What secret things do you think He is referring to in this passage? When He says "covered up," does he mean literally or figuratively?
2. How will the secret words be made manifest? Who hears the things spoken in darkness or whispered in the inner rooms?
3. Why should Christians not fear those who secretly plan and plot against them?

D. **The Murder of William Morgan in 1826**: This "triggered a national movement—the first mass movement in American history—to destroy Freemasonry."[13] William Morgan worked in Batvia, New York, as a stone mason. Having been initiated as a Royal Arch Mason, he understood the workings of the lodge and the rituals within. He became disgruntled at his Masonic brothers for refusing to start a Masonic chapter in Batvia where he hoped to be given the contract for building the Hall[14] and decided to publish a book entitled *Illustrations of Masonry, exposing all the rituals, secrets, handshakes, and oaths*. The Masons retaliated by kidnapping and murdering Morgan.

There was a grass-roots movement that rose up against the Masons, because not only was a man murdered but the conspiracy of kidnapping and murder exposed a network of Masons within the political and judicial systems. Court trials drug on for five years until 1831. There were a few convictions, but all the prison sentences were light. *The Antimasonic Party* rose up in politics and wielded significant influence for over a decade. Many masons left the organization as a result of the murder and society's opposition. The Mason's membership declined and many lodges closed down, but it did not put an end to the secret society.

E. **The Influence of Albert Pike** (1809 - 1891). While only 16 percent of today's Grand Lodges in the United States consider Albert Pike's books as authoritative for Masons,[15] it would be a mistake to say his life did not have a major impact upon the entire society. Albert Pike, probably more than any other Mason, was responsible for shaping modern-day masonry. He was given *the honorary thirty-third degree* of the Scottish Rite in 1857 and became the Grand

Commander of the Supreme Council in 1859 and reigned as the undisputed head until his death in 1891. His life was colored by many influences. He was a writer, fur trapper, teacher, lawyer, lecturer, and brigadier general. He studied Hinduism and occultism. *He is most remembered for rewriting the Scottish Rites in which he tried to de-Christianize the whole movement.* His famous masonic book entitled *Morals and Dogma* is basically just the doctrines of classical Hinduism mixed with astrology, magic, and reincarnation. He opened the door for many occultic and pagan forces to influence masonry.

Thinking Through The Scripture

"A scoffer seeks wisdom and does not find it...Go from the presence of a foolish man, when you do not perceive in him the lips of knowledge." (Proverbs 14:7-8)

"Those who reject me by not accepting what I say have a judge appointed for them. The words that I have spoken will judge them on the last day. I have not spoken on my own. Instead, the Father who sent me told me what I should say and how I should say it." (John 13:48-49) NIV

Questions for discussion:
1. Since Albert Pike was a scoffer of Christianity, did he end up finding what he thought he would? According to Proverbs, how should Freemasons - many who consider themselves Christians - respond to the teachings of Albert Pike?
2. Can someone reject the teachings of Jesus and not reject Jesus Himself? What will people be judged by on the last day? Why?

VII. WHAT IS THE BLUE LODGE?
    A. It is the local meeting place of the Masons. They call it a *Temple.* There are currently 33,700 lodges in 164 countries with 15,300 of them in the U.S.[16] Each state has a Grand Lodge that presides over the state and is autonomous.
    B. The head of the Blue Lodge is the *Worshipful Master.* He has the responsibility of running business and initiation meetings. The first three degrees on initiates are:
       1) Entered Apprentice
       2) Fellow Craft
       3) Master Mason

VIII. WHAT ARE THE OPTIONS FOR ADVANCEMENT AFTER THE BLUE LODGE?

    A. **Scottish Rite:** In this branch, the Mason may move up to the thirty-second degree called Master of the Royal Secret. There is a *thirty-third honorary degree* which cannot be earned, but is given for outstanding service to the masons.

    B. **York Rite:** In this other major branch, Masons move through various Chapter, Council, and Commandery degrees ending with the degree of Knights Templar.

IX. WHAT ARE THE OTHER GROUPS ASSOCIATED WITH FREEMASONRY.

    A. The Order of the Eastern Star: for women 18 years and older. In their book *The Secret Teachings of the Masonic Lodge*, authors John Ankerberg and John Weldon give us a perspective on the women's side of Freemasonry:

        "When one reads through the ritual of the Order of the Eastern Star, the claim is made that 'the Order is no part of that Ancient Institution' (i.e., Masonry). Yet there can be no doubt that the Order of the Eastern Star supports both the causes and doctrines of Masonry. This is evident throughout the ritual itself where the Order is stated to uphold Masonry. In addition, a similar emphasis is laid upon various Masonic beliefs: 1) faith in (the Masonic) god; 2) secrecy and solemn oaths; 3) personal character building and the immortality of the soul which presuppose salvation by works. However, these are not as forcefully or clearly stated as in the rituals of Masonry itself. It is as if the Order of the Eastern Star exists to introduce the daughters, wives and other relatives of Master Masons to a basic Masonic world view with the understanding that the Master Mason himself as head of the household will fill in any remaining gaps."[17]

    B. The Shrine: for members of the Scottish Rite or Knight's Templer of the York Rite.

    C. DeMolay: for young men ages 13 - 21.

    D. Rainbow: for young girls ages 13 - 20.

    E. Some Others: Acacia (college fraternity); Order of Amaranth (women), Daughters of Mokanna, Daughters of the Nile, Job's Daughters, Desoms (deaf), Grotto, High Twelve International, Ladies' Oriental Shrine of North America, National Sojourners, Inc., Philalethes, Royal Order of Scotland, Tall Cedars of Lebanon, White Shrine of Jerusalem, Co-masonry, and Prince Hall.

X. WHAT OUTSIDE GROUPS REFLECT MASONIC INFLUENCE?
    A. **The Animal Lodges**: The Fraternal Order of Eagles, the Benevolent
        and Protective Order of Elks, and the Loyal Order of the Moose.
    B. **Others**: The Odd Fellows, the Woodsmen of the world, the Knights
        of Pythias, the Mystic Order of Veiled Prophets of the Enchanted
        Realm, the Knights of the Red Cross of Constantine, etc. These
        reflect certain elements of Freemasonry, but each has its own initi-
        ation process and degree system. For instance, the Odd Fellows
        confer eight degrees compared to the Mason's thirty-two Scottish
        Rite degree.

XI. WHAT ARE SOME OF THE SYMBOLS AND THE CLOAKED DECEP-
     TION?
    A. **Some of the Symbols** and their supposed meanings:
        1) Three Great Lights:
            a) The Bible: God's Will.
            b) The Square: Morality.
            c) The Compass: Spirituality.
        2) Three candles: the sun, moon, and Masonic Worshipful Master.
        3   "G": God or geometry. "All seeing eye": God.
        4) Cable tow (rope around neck): Masonic brotherhood.
        6) White apron: innocence, purity, and honor.
        7) The Sword pointing to naked heart symbolizes justice and
            God's reward to men according to their deeds.
        8) Many words are symbolic: The Grand Architect of the Universe
            (G.A.O.T.U.) is God the Father or the generating principle.
    B. **The Cross**: At first, the symbols seem like things that a Christian
        could feel comfortable with, but beneath the surface paganistic
        meanings change everything. For instance, many lodges used to
        have crosses. One investigator of secret rituals, Mark C. Carnes,
        tells of the subtle deception in *Secret Rituals and Manhood in
        Victorian America*:
            "The cross itself figured prominently in many fraternal rituals,
        but initiates gradually learned that it did not refer to Christ. The
        cross, Pike wrote, was a sacred symbol among the druids, Indians,
        Egyptians, and Arabians 'thousands of years before the coming of
        Christ.' The obvious Christian meaning of these symbols merely con-
        cealed a deeper association with ancient—and pagan—religions."[18]
    C. **The Bible**: While it sounds noble to call it one of the three great
        lights, it is deceptive at best. They consider the Bible only to be
        symbolic lodge furniture that can be replaced by the Koran, the
        Vedas, the Book of Mormon, any "religious" book .

D. **Communion:** The following quote by Mark Carnes shows how the symbols lure Christians and then slowly change the heart of the individual about the Christian faith:

"Lodge members and clergymen, reassured of the propriety of their rituals by the familiar symbols of the church, created and repeatedly practiced rituals which *altered the context—and the meaning—of those symbols.* Christians who joined orders were likely to have believed that the rites posed no challenge to their religious convictions. Symbols linked the lodge and the church, and what is more, the professed purpose of the rituals—to make men mindful of ethical principles—accorded with the teachings of Christianity. *With each successive degree, however, the context of the symbols changed.* By the time a Mason came to the point of performing the revised version of the thirtieth degree of the Scottish Rite (Knight Kadosh), *in which he drank wine and broke bread, the likelihood of his perceiving a Christian significance in that act had diminished considerably. Rather, in a setting of coffins and skulls, bloody oaths and frightening scenery, the symbols of chalice, wine, Bible, and candles connoted antithetical ideas about the past, death, and divinity.*"[19] [italics added]

Thinking Through The Scripture

"Whoever eats this bread or drinks this cup of the Lord in an unworthy manner will be guilty of the body and blood of the Lord. But let a man examine himself, and so let him eat of the bread and drink of the cup. For he who eats and drinks in an unworthy manner eats and drinks judgment to himself, not discerning the Lord's body." (1 Corinthians 11:27-29)

Questions for discussion:
1. How does the Bible say that a person should approach the communion table?
2. How does one become "guilty" of the body and blood? How can a person prevent that guilt? Who brings judgment on himself? Why?

XII. WHAT ARE EXAMPLES OF SOME OF THE RITUALS OF FREEMASONRY?

A. The general teachings of the degrees and rituals is that the candidate 1) Is in darkness without the light of Masonry that reveals hidden mysteries, 2) The true name of God has been lost but must be searched for, 3) That it is found in the deeper rituals of Masonry, and 4) That religion is only symbolical of hidden truth.

B. **Entered Apprentice**—Candidate is blindfolded, left arm and breast naked, wears blue pajamas with one leg missing, noose around the neck, led around from darkness to light. It is here that they are given the white apron. This represents purity and the covering of sin and will save them at judgment day. Masons wear this when buried.

C. **Master Mason**—*The Legend of Hiram Abiff.* Candidate pretends to be Hiram Abiff, the builder of King Solomon's Temple (1 Kings 7:13). Their legend teaches that Hiram was privileged to know the name of the one true God. He was killed and the name was lost to men. The initiate acts all of this out. However, in the end of the ritual the initiate is raised back to life with the strong grip of the Lion's paw by "King Solomon". This grip is very important to secret societies. It is used in the witchcraft rituals of Wicca and is known as the "Strong Grip of the Lion of the Tribe of Judah."

D. **Royal Arch Degree**— Candidate stands before someone dressed in a high priest outfit and has revealed to him "the lost word"—the "lost name of God" that *Hiram Abiff* knew. This is the name that the Mason has been searching for throughout the rituals of Masonry. *He is told that the true name of God is Jabulon.*

E. Others—Every degree has its own ritual to go through offering secret revelation to the candidate. In one ritual the candidate may be learning secret information about Adam. In another, he is drinking communion wine from a skull or driving a dagger through it. Each degree has blood oaths that must be taken.

XIII. WHAT ARE EXAMPLES OF SOME OF THE OATHS OF FREEMASONRY?

A. **Entered Apprentice**—"having my throat cut across, my tongue torn out from its roots, and my body buried in the rough sands of the sea."

B. **Master Mason**—"my body severed in two, my bowels taken from thence and burned to ashes...."

C. **Past Master of the York Rite**— "binding myself under no less penalty than to have my tongue split from tip to root."

Thinking Through The Scripture

"If a person swears, speaking thoughtlessly with his lips to do evil or to do good, whatever it is that a man may pronounce by an oath, and it is hidden from him—when he realizes it, then he shall be guilty in any of these matters, that he shall confess that he has sinned in that thing; and he shall bring

his trespass offering to the Lord for his sin which he has sinned." (Leviticus 5:4-6)

Questions for discussion:
1. What is the significance of an oath? What if the person doesn't realize it?
2. Does the Bible give a way out of a foolish oath? What is it? What type of offering do you think the Lord would want from a repentant Freemason today?

   D. **The Royal Arch Degree of the York Rite**— "I would sooner have my skull struck off than divulge any of the secrets of this degree unlawfully...and have my brain exposed to the scorching rays of the noonday sun."

   E. **Tenth Degree of the Scottish Rite**— "I do promise and swear upon the Holy Bible...To keep exactly in my heart all the secrets that shall be revealed to me. And in failure of this by obligation, I consent to have my body opened perpendicularly, and to be exposed for eight hours in the open air, that the venomous flies may eat of my entrails, my head to be cut off and put on the highest pinnacle of the world."

XIV. WHO ARE THE GODS OF FREEMASONRY?

   A. **Jabulon** (or Jaobulon) - The seeking Mason discovers the "lost" name of God in the Royal Arch degree. Three Masons reveal the name to the candidate by speaking their part of it, Jao - bul - on. The name is held so sacred that one Mason is not suppose to speak it; it takes three. Each of the three parts reveals a name of God.

     1) Jao = Jah meaning Yahweh or Jehovah. God of Israel.
     2) Bul = Baal or Bel. God of Canaan.
     3) On = Osiris. (Egyptian sun god). God of Egypt.

   B. **Abbadon** - In the 17th degree of the Scottish Rite the candidate is taught that this is a sacred name to be honored. This is the king over the demons in the pit of hell.

   C. **The Hindu Trinity** - Albert Pike substituted a triangle for the cross and said that it referred to Shiva, Krishna, and Brahma.[20]

Thinking Through The Scripture

"The Israelites did evil in the eyes of the Lord; they forgot the Lord their God and served the Baals." (Judges 3:7) NIV

"They had as king over them the angel of the Abyss, whose name in Hebrew is Abaddon, and in Greek, Apollyon." (Revelation 9:11) NIV

"You shall have no other gods before Me." (Exodus 20:3)

Questions for discussion:
1. Who does the Bible say the Israelites served instead of God? What does this imply regarding the name ascribed as God by Freemasons? Who do Masons honor in the 17th degree ritual of the Scottish Rite?
2. What is the first of the Ten Commandments? Who are the gods of Masonry?

D. **Allah** - The Shriners take an oath to Allah, the god of Arabs and Moslems.[21]
E. **Baphomet** - Manley P. Hall, one of the highest level Masonic authors, claims that the key demon of the Masons is Baphomet, known as the satanic Goat of Mendes.
F. It should be noted that there are many references to Jehovah and Adonai also in the Masonic rituals, but the names are blasphemed because they are perverted to represent something other than the God of the Holy Bible. Furthermore, the Masons have *systematically removed the name of Jesus* from their verses or literature.

XIV. WHO ARE THE SHRINERS AND HOW DO THEY FIT INTO ALL OF THIS?
A. **The Shriners do good works.** They provide hospitals for children, put on a circus, and march in parades wearing their funny red fezzes (hats). They strive to be the face of the Masonic brotherhood to the public. Public image is what they are all about. Certainly, they have kindness in their hearts towards people, but is there something not quite up front? If you look carefully at the red fezzes, you'll see an Islamic sword and crescent encrusted with jewels on the front. That's a strange thing to wear—seeing that the city of Fez represents a bloody slaughter of 50,000 Christians in the eighth century by Islamic barbarians. The Muslim murderers dipped their caps in the blood of the Christians as a testimony to Allah.
B. **Initiation.** In order to become a Shriner, a man must have risen through all the degrees of either the Scottish or York Rites. After an initiation rite into the Shriners that is obscene, the candidate swears a blood oath that is four and half pages long, agrees that it is nonrevocable, and then takes an oath in *the name of Allah.* This

is not just another name for God, as some Christians have mistaken, this is a pagan deity of the Muslims.

C. **The Money.** "Several years ago, a daily newspaper in Florida, the Orlando Sentinel, published a report on the Shrine hospital program. Ninety-eight percent of the money the Shriners raise in these circuses wasn't going to the hospitals; it went to the Shriners for their parties. Ninety-eight percent went to their little cars and their little boats and their temples and their little hats. Two percent went to the hospitals."[22]

XVI. WHAT ARE SOME OF THE OCCULTIC INFLUENCES IN FREEMASONRY?

A. **Alice Bailey,** renowned as the reigning queen of the occultic New Age movement until her death in the 1970's, wrote many books through the help of her spirit guide, the Tibetan master Dwjhal Khul. She taught that Freemasonry would be one of three channels used to usher in the New Age Christ Consciousness. The other two channels are the liberal neo-orthodox (dead) church and the educational field. She wrote:

"The Masonic Movement when it can be divorced from politics and social ends and from its present paralysing condition of inertia, will meet the need of those who can, and should, wield power. It is the custodian of the law; it is the home of the Mysteries and the seat of initiation. It holds in its symbolism the ritual of Deity, and the way of salvation is pictorially preserved in its work. The methods of Deity are demonstrated in its Temples, and under the All-seeing Eye the work can go forward. *It is a far more occult organization than can be realized, and is intended to be the training school for the coming advanced occultists.*"[23] [italics added]

B. Thirty-third degree Manley P. Hall, considered Masonry's greatest philosopher, teaches that the three degrees of the Blue Lodge actually represent the Trinity of God displayed in each man. He explains in his book *The Occult Anatomy of Man* that Masonry is helping man realize his godhood.

"It is only when this builder is raised that the symbols of mortality can be changed into those of immortality. Our bodies are the urn containing the ashes of Hiram, our lives are the broken pillars, crystallization is the coffin, and disintegration is the open grave. But above all is the sprig of evergreen promising life to those who raise the serpent power, and that showing under the debris of the temple is buried the body of the builder, who is 'raised' *when we liberate the divine life which is locked within our material natures.*" [24]

C. This secret society has influenced many and has been influenced by many occultic groups and individuals overs the years. Among these are the Illuminati, the Rosicrucians, the Ku Klux Klan, Helena Petrovna Blavatsky - founder of the Theosophical Society, and Aleister Crowley - thirty-third degree Mason and the father of modern Satanism.

XVII. WHAT ARE SOME OF THE OBVIOUS FALSE TEACHINGS OF MASONRY?

A. *That Masonry is the light in the world*, but the Bible shows that Jesus is the Light of the world. (Jn. 1:9; Jn. 3:19; Jn. 8:12; Jn. 9:5; 2 Cor. 4:4; Eph. 5:13-14)

B. *That the name of God was lost and is only revealed along the path of Masonry*, but the Bible plainly tells us that Jesus Christ was God incarnate (in the flesh) and that at the name of Jesus every knee shall bow and tongue confess that he is Lord. (Matt. 1:23; Phil. 2:11; Titus 2:13; Jn. 1:1, 14; Jn. 8:58; Jn. 14:9; Isaiah 9:6; Zech. 12:10)

C. *That salvation is through works of service to Masons and our fellowman - that the apron will cover them at judgment*, but the Bible teaches that salvation is a gift of God through faith in Jesus Christ alone. (Rom. 6:23; Eph. 2:8-9; Rom. 10:9-10; Acts 4:12)

D. *That the Bible is only symbolic*, but there is more evidence for the authenticity of the Bible and all of its events as recorded than any other book ever written. It claims to be the inspired word of God (2 Tim. 3:16). Christians accept this in faith, believing that God gave to men the Word (Jn. 1:1) of life to be taken literally as authentic.

E. *That truth is mysterious and hidden*, but the Bible teaches that Jesus is the Truth (Jn. 14:6), that abiding in His word will produce truth (Jn. 8:31), that the Holy Spirit leads us into truth (Jn. 16:13), that his word is truth (Jn. 17:17).

XVIII. ARE THERE CHRISTIANS WITHIN THE ORGANIZATION?

A. Yes. Although many denominations have publicly denounced Masonry, there are still Christians caught up in the deception of it. For many of the Masons at the local Blue lodge level, they would be somewhat naive about the inner circle of occultic Masonry. Some Christian Masons are fighting for the organization, wanting to drive out the pagan and occultic influences. However, it is difficult to understand how a Christian can rationalize staying in an organization that denies praying in Jesus' name but will allow prayer to any other god. Christian Masons often react to the strong stand that the church is taking against the Masonic movement, but they need to beware that they are ultimately compromising and being deceived. Perhaps the best place to currently help change it is from without, rather than within.

XIX.   IS THERE ANY HOPE FOR FREEMASONRY TO CHANGE?
   A.   Perhaps. It is hard to say. There is some movement within the orga-
       nization to remove the blood oaths from the rituals, but at this
       point the impact is negligible. Robert Morey, sets a significant and
       yet hopeful challenge before the Masons:
           "There is no just reason under God's heaven why modern
       Freemasonry cannot remove those elements in its symbols and rit-
       uals which are blatantly anti-Christian, pagan, and occultic which
       are offensive to Christians. If Freemasonry is to be saved, a grand
       conference should be called in which leading anti-Masons and
       Masonic leaders will sit down and calmly talk about the issues and
       try to resolve things in such a way that everyone is satisfied. But
       what if the present leadership of the Fraternity is not interested in
       resolving the issues which deeply offend its Christian members?
       The leadership should be changed. But what if this cannot be
       done? Then the Christians must leave the Craft. On this point
       there can be no middle ground. Either Masonry will change or
       Christians must leave it."[25]

Thinking Through The Scripture

"According to the grace of God which was given to me, as a wise master builder I have laid the foundation, and another builds on it. But let each one take heed how he builds on it. For no other foundation can anyone lay than that which is laid, which is Jesus Christ. Now if anyone builds on this foundation with gold, silver, precious stones, wood, hay, straw, each one's work will become clear; for the Day will declare it, because it will be revealed by fire; and the fire will test each one's work, of what sort it is." (1 Corinthians 3:10-13)

Questions for discussion:
1.   What does the Apostle Paul mean by he "laid the foundation"? Are the
     Masons trying to lay another foundation? Is it possible?
2.   What is the foundation of Christianity? Can the Masons honestly say
     they have the same foundation? If not, then what are they building on?
     If they are building on Christ, is it with gold, silver, and precious stones
     or something else? In light of this Scripture, what name might repre-
     sent them better?

XX.   HOW CAN WE BRING TRUTH TO THE FREEMASONS?

  A. **Prayer:** Let's suppose that within Freemasonry there are those who
      attend a Bible- believing church on a regular basis. This must be so
      since some churches still have Freemasons as members and even
      leaders. Furthermore, the fact is that the Freemasons maintain a
      significant strength within the Southern Baptist Convention. This
      is obvious since they were able to defeat a denominational vote in
      opposition to them in the early 1990's.[26] Now let's suppose that of
      these Freemasons who attend a Christian church, there is a rem-
      nant that are actually born-again, Bible-believing, God-fearing
      Christians. What should our response be? It should be one of
      prayer. We should pray that they will come into the full revelation
      of God's truth.

      I have met quite a few Christians who carry burdens for rela-
      tives or friends who are Masons but who also say they believe in
      Jesus. Often they don't know what to do with the burden. So we
      will stop and pray on behalf of their relative or friend, and it brings
      a release to the burden. That's the thing about burdens. When God
      brings a burden, He has a reason. We should pray and then give it
      to Him. He might want to use you, as an intercessor, to break open
      the gates and bring truth into that person's life. If you are a
      Christian Freemason reading this, then you should be praying for
      those within the organization.

      There is a story in Isaiah of when King Hezekiah exhorted the
      people to *"lift up prayer for the remnant"* (Isaiah 37:4). If there is a
      remnant of Christians within Freemasonry, and *if* there is still hope
      for the Christian Freemasons to change the organization, then *it
      must begin with groups of intercessors.*

  B. **Love:** The Bible admonishes Christians to be *"speaking the truth in
      love"* (Ephesians 4:15). This has two parts. First, we are to speak
      the truth. We do not have to ignore the fact that there are many
      things about Freemasonry that are clearly occultic and perverse.
      We are told to *"have no fellowship with the unfruitful works of dark-
      ness, but rather to expose them"* (Ephesians 5:11).

      The manner by which we go about "exposing" brings us to the
      second part; we are to do it in love. How we expose the unfruitful
      works of others can actually test whether we are doing it with true
      love or not. What do we have in mind when we expose unfruitful
      works? It should not be our craving to be right, and it should not
      be a desire to devastate the individual in question. It should be to
      bring glory to God, but it should also be for the benefit of the indi-
      vidual who is captured in that darkness. When speaking the truth,

one should consider some of the rudimentary characteristics of love such as *"love is patient, love is kind."* (1 Corinthians 13:4). This will help in the timing and the manner by which truth is presented. If this person is a work mate or neighbor, you might need to take time to build a relationship of trust before launching into the things you know about Freemasonry. If this is someone that you may only get one chance to speak to then you seek the guidance of the Holy Spirit for that particular situation.

C. **Witness:** Here are a couple ideas for approach:

1) If the Mason is a Christian, then just explaining to him the deception of Freemasonry can help. Thousands of Christians have left the organization in the last few years as the pagan agenda of the inner circles has been exposed.

2) If the Mason is not a Christian then consider doing some of the following:

    a. Share the Gospel, your testimony, and your church with him.

    b. Regarding the blood oaths, share 1 John 1:9 and Lev. 5:4-6,10.

    c. Get him a good book or cassette about the problems of Masonry.

    d. Look in the resource guide of this book and send for the *Saints Alive in Jesus* newsletter. It is a ministry to Freemasons and Mormons.

3) Use Acts 4:11-12 to show the Freemason that Jesus is the stone which the Jewish builders rejected, but He is now become the Chief Cornerstone whose name brings salvation to those who follow Him. Now explain that the Freemasons are doing the same thing—rejecting Him—by removing His name from all of their prayers, passage readings, and books. Ask him, "When is the last time the name of 'Jesus Christ' was spoken and exalted in your secret meetings?"

End Notes

1. Ed Decker, *What You Need To Know About Masons* (Eugene, OR: Harvest House Publishers, 1992), pgs. 167 - 168.

2. Harold J. Berry, *Masons* (Lincoln, NE: Back To The Bible, 1990), pgs. 39-40.

3. Ed Decker, *The Dark Side of Freemasonry* (Lafayette, LA: Huntington House Publishers, 1994), pgs. 18-20.

4. Robert Morey, *The Truth About Masons* (Eugene, OR: Harvest House Publishers, 1993), p. 116.

5. Ibid., p. 73.

6. James Paton, editor, *Scottish History and Life* (Glasgow, Scotland: James Maclehose and Sons, 1902), p. 289.

7. Ibid., p. 260.

8. Morey, pgs. 60-64.

9. Mark C. Carnes, *Secret Ritual and Manhood in Victorian America* (New Haven and London: Yale University Press, 1989), p. 22.

10. Ibid.

11. Morey, p. 99.

12. Decker, *What You Need To Know About Masons*, pgs. 15 -16.

13. Paul Goodman, *Towards a Christian Republic* (New York: Oxford University Press, 1988), preface.

14. William Preston Vaughn, *The Antimasonic Party in the United States* (Lexington, Kentucky: The University Press Of Kentucky, 1983), p.3.

15. John Ankerberg and John Weldon, *The Secret Teachings of the Masonic Lodge* (Chicago: Moody Press, 1990), p. 16.

16. Ron Carlson and Ed Decker, *Fast Facts on False Teachings* (Eugene, OR: Harvest House Publishers, 1994), p.73.

17. Anderberg and Weldon, p. 27.

18. Carnes, p. 63.

19. Ibid., p. 62.

20. Morey, p. 48.

21. Decker, p. 24.

22. Ibid., p. 25.

23. Alice A. Bailey, *The Externalisation of the Hierarchy* (New York: Lucis Publishing Company, 1972), p. 511.

24. Manly P. Hall, *The Occult Anatomy of Man* (Los Angeles, CA: The Philosophical Research Society, Inc., 1957), p.35.

25. Morey, p. 127.

26. Decker, The Dark Side of Freemasonry, pgs. 217-218.

QUESTIONNAIRE: LESSON ELEVEN

NAME: _____ DATE: _____

1. Freemasonry is the world's largest _____ organization.

2. Give three reasons why Freemasonry is being discussed in the cults.

a) _____

b) _____

c) _____

3. What date is considered the formal beginning of Freemasonry? _____

4. How many Masons are there in the world? _____ in the U.S.? _____

5. Tell briefly some of the influence that Freemasonry had upon the beginning of the U.S. _____

_____

_____

_____

6. The murder of William Morgan spawned which political party?

_____

7. Albert Pike is most remembered for rewriting the _____ Rites in which he tried to _____ the whole movement.

8. What is another name for the Blue Lodge? _____

9. What is the title of the leader of the lodge? _____

10. What three degrees are earned at the Blue Lodge level?

a) _____

b) _____

c) _____

11. The highest honorary degree of the Scottish Rite is the _____ degree.

12. Do you have any relatives or friends that are or have been Masons?

_____

13. Briefly explain what is deceptive about the symbolism of Masonry?

_____

_____

_____

14. Candidates are taught that the true name of _____ was lost when _____ Abiff was killed and they must search for it.

15. In the Royal Arch degree, they are taught the name of God is _____.

16. List three examples of the bloody oaths of Masonry.

a) _____

b) _____

c) _____

17. Tell what the following mean:

Jao = _____   Bul = _____   On = _____

18. Write out the Scripture about Abbadon from Rev. 9:11 _____

_____

_____

19. The Shrines wear red _____ with the emblem of an Islamic _____ and crescent signifying the slaughter of 50,000 Christians in the city of _____ in the 8th century by _____ barbarians. The candidate swears an extensive blood oath in the name of _____.

20. Which false teaching disturbs you the most about Masonry? Explain why and give a Scripture that refutes the teaching. _____

_____

_____

_____

21. Consider your knowledge of Freemasons before and after this lesson. Circle the number below that indicates how equipped you felt before taking this course to witness to someone in the Freemasons as compared to how equipped you feel now. Be honest.

BEFORE 0 1 2 3 4 5 6 7 8 9 10 AFTER 0 1 2 3 4 5 6 7 8 9 10

SCIENTOLOGY

"My friend went on to explain he was now a strong Christian and no longer a Scientologist. He was obviously deeply troubled by my news but he wished me well. As I questioned him he explained that Scientology had all the earmarks of a cult and because of his experiences, he no longer agreed with anything they were doing. I was shocked. He was the first person I had ever met who could tell me, from experience, what I needed to know. There were questions I had been afraid to ask. Now I had to know. Later Carol and I gave ourselves permission to ask ourselves about all of the fears and unresolved problems we had been compelled to ignore about the Scientology organization. Now they flooded to the surface. We suddenly realized we were about to become absorbed into a cult that had kept us in the dark about many things. We had known all along it worked that way, but we had refused to look at it. What followed were days of confusion and doubt. The disappointment was almost unbearable. The one truth I was sure of was Christ. I had almost forgotten Him but now I prayed. Finally things started to fall into place...Through Christ, the joy of my life quickly returned to me and my family."[1] —Tom Hutchinson

I. WHAT ARE SOME SIGNIFICANT WORDS IN SCIENTOLOGY?

Analytical Mind - That mind which computes—the "I" and his consciousness.[2]

Auditor - Scientologist counselors who administer tests and therapy.

Clear - An individual who has had all engrams removed from his or her life.

Dianetics - Method employed in Scientolgy for probing into a person's past.[3]

E-Meter - Electropsychometer.[4] Used somewhat like a lie detector for confessional aid.

Engram - Mental Blocks caused by negative events in one's life at a subconscious level.

Erase - The removal of an engram.

MEST - Matter, energy, space, and time.

Potential Trouble Source - (PTS) Anyone associated with a suppressive person.[5]

Reactive Mind - Portion of the mind in which engrams are stored and will surface at times.

Registar - One who sells the Scientology courses.

Suppressive Person - A marked enemy of Scientology.

Thetan - Ancestors of the human race who are gods. A "clear" can awaken his godhood.

II. WHAT IS THE SIZE AND SIGNIFICANCE OF SCIENTOLOGY TODAY?

   A. Although Scientology claims "over 8 million members with 2,318 churches and missions in 107 countries,"[6] many former Scientologists have pointed out over the years that the number of actual active members is much less, perhaps several hundred thousand to a couple of million.[7] Worldwide, there are at least 12,000 church staff members, many of whom are located in Los Angeles. Of these, over 3,000 belong to the elite, zealous faction known as the Sea Organization (Sea Orgs).[8]

   B. The International headquarters are in Los Angeles, but there are other major branches in places like Clearwater, Florida, Washington D.C., New York, as well as cities in England, Italy, Japan, Australia, South America, Africa, etc. The president is the Reverend Herbert Jentzsch. However, the real power, the chairman of the board, is David Miscavige. David Miscavige is a second-generation church member who runs the organization with an iron hand. "Defectors describe him as cunning, ruthless and so paranoid about perceived enemies that he kept plastic wrap over his glass of water."[9] Nevertheless, he directs the activities of this pseudo-scientific religious cult that has large amounts of money to print enormous amounts of influential reading materials and to bring suit against critics of the organization in order to keep them quiet.

III. WHO IS DRAWN TO SCIENTOLOGY AND WHY?

   A. Scientology has positive aspects in that it helps people with com-
       munication skills and gives them personal attention.[10] It appeals to
       those who have normal problems with loneliness, finances, mar-
       riage, interpersonal conflict, psychological, or physical illness.[11] It
       has a drug rehabilitation program called Narcanon, as well as a pro-
       gram with prisoners and the mentally retarded. These things draw
       people into Scientology.

   B. One survey showed that converts were mostly young people under
       thirty years of age who had abandoned a Protestant or Roman
       Catholic heritage. Almost forty percent of these had a university
       education.[12]

   C. It also draws those looking for the answers to life in science, tech-
       nology, or science fiction. Many of these have New Age concepts
       which oppose the idea of One Creator God and think that men are
       gods. Authors Bromley and Hammond make an insightful predic-
       tion in *The Future of New Religious Movements:*
           "In an age of religious transformation, we can predict that
       many people will join Scientology or other techno-scientific reli-
       gions, *seeking to be God rather than to find Him*...we must suspect
       that some religion very much like Scientology will be a major force
       in the future of our civilization."[13] [italics added]

Thinking Through The Scripture

*"Before Me there was no God formed, Nor shall there be after Me. I, even
I, am the Lord, and besides Me there is no savior."* (Isaiah 43:10-11)

*"I am the First and the Last; Besides Me there is no God...Is there a God
besides Me? Indeed there is no other Rock; I know not one."* (Isaiah 44:6,8)

Questions for discussion:
1. How do these Scriptures confront the idea of men becoming gods?
2. How has science fiction played a part in creating techo-scientific reli-
    gions like Scientology? How has it impacted men's thinking? Has it
    influenced science?

IV. WHO WAS L. RON HUBBARD AND WHAT IS THE HISTORY OF THE
     CULT?

   A. **His personal life.** Lafayette Ron Hubbard rewrote much of his life
       to include glamorous events that never occurred and eliminated

darker events that did occur. He was born in Tilden, Nebraska, in 1911. His father was in the U.S. Navy and eventually became an officer; some of his time was served in China and Japan.[14] Hubbard spent some of his childhood at his grandparents' ranch in Helena, Montana. Although, it is debatable how much time. He had trouble in high school, spending time at two different institutions in Seattle, Washington. After moving to Washington D.C., he graduated from Woodward, a school mainly run for difficult students and slow learners. He spent two years at George Washington University in Washington D.C. in engineering, though Scientologists will say it was nuclear physics.

He was a zealous reader and writer of science fiction. He became an expert in hypnotism, navigation, and organization. After serving in WWII, he started writing for *Astounding Science Fiction* magazine where he gained notoriety. While speaking at a science fiction convention in 1949, he reportedly said, "Writing for a penny a word is ridiculous. If a man really wanted to make a million dollars, the best way would be to start his own religion."[15] So, with his interest in scientific methods that would cure mental illness, he published Dianetics in 1950 and began a new religion.

His first two marriages to Margaret Louise Grubb and then Sara Northrup ended in fiery divorces. During Sara's divorce, she placed a letter from Margaret in the court records. It said, "Ron is not normal. I hoped you could straighten him out. Your charges probably sound fantastic to the average person—but I've been through it—the beatings, threats on my life, all the sadistic traits which you charge—12 years of it."[16] Hubbard's third wife, Mary Sue, bought into her husband's strange religion and quest for power. She was arrested and sent to prison in the early 1980's, along with other top Scientologists, for infiltrating, burglarizing and wiretapping more than 100 private and government agencies.[17] Of his seven children, many have tried to distance themselves from Hubbard and Scientology. One of his sons, Quentin, committed suicide at age 22 while another, L. Ron Hubbard Jr., changed his name to Ronald DeWolfe and has written against Scientology (See *L. Ron Hubbard: Messiah or Madman?* by Brent Corydon and L. Ron Hubbard, Jr.).

Hubbard became paranoid and went into hiding in 1980, roaming the Northwest and finally settling on a ranch in Creston, California. He died at age 74 on January 24, 1986.

B. **His exaggerations and delusions.** Apparently, he had a hot temper and in the 11th grade got into a brawl with his vice principal.

He left to be with his parents in the Far East. It was possibly during this trip to the Far East that he toured China and later wrote, "My basic ordination for religious work was received from Mayo in the Western Hills of China when I was made a lama priest after a year as a neophyte." Mayo was supposedly the last in a long line of magicians of Kublai Khan. However, Hubbard's diary of that period doesn't verify this and shows an intolerance for their culture and race.[18]

It was from this point in Hubbard's life that it appears his great imagination and ego combined together to cause excessive exaggeration. For instance, he did attend George Washington University, but he did not graduate as he claimed. After only two years (1931-32), he was placed on probation for low grades in his science classes. He dropped out and never returned.[19] His supposed Ph.D. from Sequoia University in California was a sham. The "school" was nothing more than a nonaccredited diploma mill that sells degrees. According to Hubbard, he was a WWII navy hero with 21 medals and many artillery type wounds of which he eventually "cured himself through techniques that would later form the tenets of Scientology and Dianetics." But in actuality, he received only four medals given to many of the servicemen who served where he did in the South Pacific, and his hospitalization was not due to battle injuries, but to chronic hip infection, conjunctivitis, and an ulcer.[20] This twisting of the truth caused one Los Angeles Superior Court judge to say that Hubbard was "virtually a pathological liar."[21]

Of course, the Church of Scientology backs Hubbard's many tales of his life and claims that the Navy and government have falsified documents and information. There is no doubt that he was a well-read individual and prolific writer, but his vain imagination lead him to believe that he twice visited heaven,[22] even though he later denied the existence of heaven and Christ. He told associates that in previous reincarnated lives he had been many people including Cecil Rhodes, the British-born diamond king of southern Africa, a marshal to Joan of Arc, and Arpen Polo, the original musician of three million years ago.[23] However, perhaps the most outlandish exaltation of Hubbard comes from his followers because some teach that he is Maitreya Buddha, the modern day spiritual guide prophesied by Guatama Buddha 2,500 years ago. Accordingly, Guatama said that a great spiritual Buddha would come to usher in a new spiritual and world order.[24]

It is sad that so many today will follow someone like Hubbard at the cost of their own souls. In 2 Thessalonians 2:10-12, it talks about people who refuse to love and accept the truth, and so all that is left for them is strong delusion and condemnation.

Thinking Through The Scripture

"Watch out for false prophets. They come to you in sheep's clothing, but inwardly they are ferocious wolves. By their fruit you will recognize them. Do people pick grapes from thornbushes, or figs from thistles? Likewise every good tree bears good fruit, but a bad tree bears bad fruit." (Matthew 7:15-17) NIV

Questions for discussion:
1. This passage gives us parables. What are they? What type of people do they represent? How does a false prophet influence people's lives.
2. Was Hubbard a false prophet? Do you think he was disguised or misguided or both? What kind of fruits did he bear? What fruit does a thornbush or thistle produce? In examination of our own lives, are we given to fantasies (like Hubbard) that produce bad fruit? Read Galatians 5:22. What is the fruit of the Spirit? How can this help us stay on the right track?

C. **His creation of a religion.** For over thirty years, Hubbard worked at changing the perception of his followers from that of a new kind of mental health approach into that of an accepted religion. With the publication of his book, *Dianetics: The Modern Science of Mental Health* in 1950, Hubbard was jettisoned into the limelight as the founder of a whole new approach to dealing with mental health. Hubbard claimed that many of man's basic problems were due to mental blocks caused by negative events in one's life at a subconscious level. These he called engrams. Accordingly, he could help erase these engrams (for a lot of money) by acting as an auditor for the troubled individual. Once the engrams were removed, the person could achieve a state of being a Clear. At this level, the person could raise his I.Q., take almost supernatural charge of his whole being and environment, but most importantly, he could now audit others for money.

The book went even further; it began to propose a new rationale for the modern state of man and his origins. Later books and magazines would develop this theme into a finely-tuned, science fiction type of outlook on life. The early development of Dianetics was supported by several wealthy businessmen. However, there soon arose controversy over who was in control and Hubbard distanced himself by moving to Phoenix, Arizona, in 1952. It was in Phoenix that Dianetics transformed into Scientology. In *The Road to Total Freedom: A Sociological Analysis of Scientology*, author Roy Wallis states:

"Scientology was a new revelation entirely transcending the limitations of Dianetics. While Dianetics had been a form of psychotherapy concerned with eradicating the limitations on the achievement of full human potential, Scientology was heralded as the 'Science of Certainty' concerned with rehabilitating the thetan [the Scientology god within us] to its full spiritual capacity...On the basis of this new doctrine, Hubbard began to organize his following as a congregation responsive to his charismatic authority. He had transformed himself from a magician, to a mystagogue. His extraordinary character was transformed into charismatic authority by a process of subordinating other potential leaders, and expelling those who refused to accept his sole authority. Through control of the movement's publications he determined what was to be represented as correct doctrine and practice, and hence secured a virtual monopoly on the means of revelation. In these publications he skillfully promoted an image of himself as a superior human being."[25]

It was in Phoenix that the Hubbard Association of Scientologists (HAS) was incorporated as a religious fellowship. In 1955, Hubbard established the Founding Church of Scientology in Washington D.C. and New York. As the church grew internationally, he needed an international headquarters. So in 1959, Saint Hill Manor in East Grinstead, Sussex, England, became the international headquarters.

The Sea Orgs was a unique concept established in 1967. Because of rising controversy over Scientology's methods of induction and aggressive illegal covert activities, Hubbard took several hundred of his followers to the sea in three ships to escape the spreading hostility. Eventually, Hubbard returned to land, but the Sea Orgs continued. Today, Los Angeles is the international headquarters.

Over the years, the cult got into trouble with government because of their aggressive espionage. They would conspire, bug telephones, burglarize government agencies, frame their enemies on trumped up charges, bribe, and lie to get what they wanted. The cult's practice of *"Fair Game"* has given it much negative publicity over the years. Their Fair Game policy tells Scientologists that a *suppressive person* (enemy of the cult) "may be deprived of property or injured by any means by any Scientologist without any discipline of the Scientologists. May be tricked, sued, lied to or destroyed."[26]

In the last few years the church has tried to put on more of a positive public image to cover their dubious deeds. As one author says, "Scientologists have tried to keep a clean image, publicly eschewing drugs, adultery, and premarital sex. Members are usually well-scrubbed, respectable, middle-class types. Church ministers wear the conventional black priest suit and white collar, and even sport crosses, though they point out it isn't representative of Christ's crucifix. Scientologists talk at length about their anti drug abuse program called Narcanon, and their efforts with prisoners and the mentally retarded."[27]

However, despite their appearance of good works, they still employ their Fair Game edict with deceit and ruthlessness. Recently, the Church of Scientology attacked the *Cult Awareness Network* (C.A.N.) and tried to punish its executive director, Cynthia Kisser, for standing up against the cult. In 1991, Kisser had said, "Scientology is quite likely the most ruthless, the most classically terrorist, the most litigious and the most lucrative cult the country has ever seen." Scientology proved Cynthia Kisser's statement correct when they: 1) set up a smear campaign to defame her character, 2) bombarded C.A.N. headquarters with applications for membership by Scientologists seeking to gain control, 3) brought suit against C.A.N. forcing the network into bankruptcy, and 4) bought C.A.N. outright as a result of the bankruptcy. Now when you call the *Cult Awareness Network* for any kind of help, guess who you will probably be talking to? That's right, a Scientologist! On December 28, 1997, 60 Minutes investigated the story. Interviewer Leslie Stahl asked Cynthia Kisser (no longer with C.A.N.) if she still felt her statement about Scientology was accurate. Kisser replied, "Oh, more than...everything they've done since just proves that quote."[28]

Thinking Through The Scripture

"The righteousness of the blameless will direct his way aright, but the wicked will fall by his own wickedness. The righteousness of the upright will deliver them, but the unfaithful will be caught by their lust. When a wicked man dies, his expectation will perish, and the hope of the unjust perishes. The righteous is delivered from trouble, and it comes to the wicked instead. The hypocrite with his mouth destroys his neighbor, but through knowledge the righteous will be delivered." (Proverbs 11:5-9)

Questions for discussion:
1. According to this, what characteristic will deliver the upright? Does this mean that the upright will never have trouble? How should

Christians act in the midst of those who persecute or trouble them?
Have you been persecuted?
2. What happens to all the plans of the wicked in the end? How is it that
the "righteous" are delivered from trouble and it comes on the
3. How does Scientology come across to you - doing right or doing

V. WHAT IS THE WORLD VIEW OF SCIENTOLOGY?
A. Scientology teaches that L. Ron Hubbard has unlocked the secrets of
the universe and the true meaning of life. Each man, Hubbard
taught, is actually a god, but we fooled ourselves in a "big game"
over a space of time and forgot that we were gods. How foolish to
think that omniscient gods could forget that they were gods, but as
author John Weldon emphasizes in the following report, they think
that we are hypnotically trapped by the illusionary reality around us:

"Scientology maintains that in his true nature, man is not the
limited and pitiful body and ego he mistakenly imagines himself to
be. He is a thetan whose fundamental nature is basically good and
divine. He is not morally fallen; rather he is simply ignorant of his
own perfection. His only 'Fall' was into matter, not sin. How did
this Fall come about? Apparently, trillions of years ago thetans
became bored, so they emanated mental universes to play in and
amuse themselves. Soon, however, they became more and more
entranced in their own creation until they were so conditioned by
the manifestations of their own thought processes that they lost all
awareness of their true identity and spiritual nature. They became
hypnotized and trapped by MEST. Compounding the problem was
the accumulation of endless engrams throughout trillions of years
of existence. The final result was a pitiful creature indeed—a mate-
rially enslaved entity existing as a mere stimulus-response
machine. Today, only slavery to the reactive mind and bondage to
the MEST universe (i.e., the physical body and environment) are
what remain of once glorious spiritual beings."[29]
B. Hubbard supposedly discovered that we are all gods trapped in a
hypnotic state of illusion and that our true potential of godhood is
stifled by negative experiences in the many reincarnated lives that
we had lived. These negative experiences caused engrams to be
deeply embedded within our reactive mind without being apparent
to our analytical mind. Through the intensive counseling of people
that Hubbard referred to as auditors, each of us can rid ourselves

of engrams and move up the scale towards full-fledged thetans once again. The first level is to become a *Clear*, one who has had all engrams erased. After that, it is possible to move on to various levels of "operating thetans." According to Hubbard, "Operating Thetan has not before been known as a state of being on Earth. Neither Lord Buddha nor Jesus Christ were OTs according to the evidence. They were just a shade above Clear."[30] Thanks to Hubbard, many people are now on the track to becoming gods, or so they think. Of course, it costs a lot of money to become a god. In fact, one former operating thetan, Jon Atack, spent many years and much money in Scientology before he realized it was all a scam. He has since written about Hubbard's true agenda for creating the religion. He writes in *A Piece of Blue Sky*:

"It was 1950, in the early, heady days of Dianetics, soon after L. Ron Hubbard opened the doors of his first organization to the clamoring crowd. Up until then, Hubbard was known only to readers of pulp fiction, but now he had an instant best-seller with a book that promised to solve every problem of the human mind, and the cash was pouring in. Hubbard found it easy to create schemes to part his new following from their money. One of the first tasks was to arrange 'grades' of membership, offering supposedly greater rewards, at increasingly higher prices. Over thirty years later, an associate wryly remembered Hubbard turning to him and confiding, no doubt with a smile, 'Let's sell these people a piece of blue sky.'"[31]

VI. WHAT ARE THE ROOTS OF SCIENTOLOGY?

A. **Science Fiction**: Dianetics was somewhat patterned after a novel by A. E. Van Vogt entitled *The World of Null-A*.[32] Vogt, a writer that Hubbard respected, wrote his book in 1948, two years prior to when Dianetics was published. Vogt centered on linguistic therapy rather than engram removal, but had many similarities to Dianetics including a new religion, the Church of General Semanticists.

B. **Psychology**: Hubbard was most likely a very well read individual on the subject of mental illness and the various approaches. Who he exactly borrowed from is a subject of debate. The fact is, however, that he claimed that Dianetics was a whole new approach to viewing mental illness and dealing with it. This is not accurate. Much of what Hubbard wrote can be found in the work of others. For instance, Pavlov theorized that certain human behaviors were due to trauma (negative events) long before Dianetics taught it. The approach of Dianetics to auditing is strikingly similar to Freud's approach with hypnotism, expanding the memory, and searching for repressed negative thoughts. On the subject of taking a person back to the traumas caused at birth, Dr. J. Sader wrote that sometimes patients had to be taken back to their existence as sperm or ovum, and Grace W. Paithorpe, M.D. argued that patients should be psychoanalyzed more deeply about the trauma of birth nine years before Dianetics emphasized it. Also, Hubbard claimed to have discovered man's ultimate goal: survival. He created eight dynamics about it. However, the idea of man's ultimate purpose being survival actually comes from an English philosopher in 1600, Thomas Hobbes.[33] Even the word "engram" was not new; it was a common term that Richard Semon and a number of psychologists used thirty years prior to *Dianetics*.

There are similarities and differences, of course, between the Dianetic view and those of others mentioned above. However, the similarities appear to be much more than a coincidence. Hubbard has been accused of plagiarism, but Scientologists defend Hubbard and his supposed discovery.

C. **Religion:** Hubbard does not deny that he was influenced by such things as the Vedic Hymns or Buddhist writings. Rather, he claims them. The "Bodhi" (the moment of complete harmony with the Absolute all) of Buddhism is said to be like the "release" of Dianetics. The "Lila" (Divine Play) of Hinduism is like the game of life that the thetans play. The "maya" (illusion of reality) of Hinduism is like the view of life in Scientology.

Yoga also parallels with Scientology in a number of ways. The idea of rebirth and karmic transmigration (carrying subconscious negative events in the next reincarnated lives) is found in Yoga. Furthermore, gnosticism must be compared to it, as it is a system of "secret knowledge" revealed to men so that they can escape from the material world of evil into the spiritual world of good. There were also occultic connections from which Hubbard received some of his thoughts.

D. **The Occult.** He was a member of the Rosicrucians (AMORC) in 1940 for a while, and in 1945, he was connected to the satanic group called Order Templi Orientis (OTO). It is well documented that Hubbard acted as a scribe for a sex magic ritual lasting eleven consecutive nights between his friend Jack Parsons, a leader in the satanic movement, and his wife-to-be, Cameron. Hubbard was robed, chanted incantations, and recorded the events. Eventually, he tried to cover his tracks by saying that he had been doing undercover work for Naval Intelligence to break up black magic in America, but Cameron disputed Hubbard's story.[34]

It should also be noted that Hubbard said he received his insight for writing Dianetics from automatic writing, speaking, and clairvoyance; these are all occultic activities.[35] Hubbard met Sara Northrup through Jack Parsons and married her a full year before he divorced Margaret. His relationship with Parsons came to an abrupt end after Parsons took legal action to retrieve the money of which he had been swindled.

It was during another court case in the 1980's that Hubbard was exposed as one who spent his life in service to the occultic dark side. He claimed Hathor, the Egyptian goddess of Love as his guardian angel. She supposedly gave him the information for his writings. He would be induced by this demonic power to "automatically" write down the words that millions have read since then.

It should also be noted that Aleister Crowley's views impacted Hubbard. Crowley (1875 - 1947), a man who greatly influenced twentieth century witchcraft and Satanism, saw a direct connection between the Egyptian goddess, Hathor, and the patroness of witchcraft, Diana. This same Diana has been known by many names thoughout history and is the same as the Greek goddess, Diana, referred to in Acts 19:24-35. Hubbard, who seemed infatuated by this goddess, named his own daughter, Diana, and changed the name of the first Sea Org yacht from *Enchanter* to *Diana*.[36] I am curious about the similarity between the name "Diana" and that of "*Dianetics*" itself. Supposedly, the word is derived from the Greek *dia*, meaning "through," and *nous*, meaning "mind," altogether denoting "through the mind." Perhaps this is so. However, the resemblance is striking.

VII.   WHAT ARE SOME OF THE PUBLICATIONS OF SCIENTOLOGY?
   A. The main text book is *Dianetics: The Modern Science of Mental Health*.
   B. *Source,* published by Scientology's Flag Organization; *The Auditor, International Scientology News,* and *Celebrity* published by the Church of Scientology in California—the Saint Hill Organization; and *Advance,* published by the Church of Scientology in California, Advanced Organization of Los Angeles.

VIII.   WHAT ARE SOME OF THE ENTITIES OF SCIENTOLOGY?
   A. **The Sea Orgs.** From just three ships and several hundred people in 1967, Hubbard's sea organization has grown to include many ships and thousands of people. What Jules Verne only fantasized about

in his book *Twenty Thousand Leagues Under the Sea* with Captain Nemo and the Nautilus became somewhat of a reality in the Sea Org. Navy style uniforms, strict discipline, hard work, authoritarian control, little pay, but respect from other Scientologists, is what the elite Sea Org branch of Scientology has become today. But whereas, the sailors of the fictitious Nautilus only served Nemo for life, the Sea Orgs have committed themselves to serve a billion years of future lifetimes as well, that they might help secure this sector of the galaxy.

B. **FLAG.** Another noted branch of Scientology is the Flag Service Organization in Florida. Scientologists refer to FLAG as "the Mecca of Scientology." It is at FLAG that training occurs for advancement within the organization and ultimately into higher levels of operating thetan (godhood). Training for the Sea Orgs, staff positions at various churches and missions, and other training occurs at Flag.

Thinking Through The Scripture

"'Moreover you see and hear that not only at Ephesus, but throughout almost all Asia, this Paul has persuaded and turned away many people, saying that they are not gods which are made with hands. So not only is this trade of ours in danger of falling into disrepute, but also the temple of the great goddess Diana may be despised and her magnificence destroyed, whom all Asia and the world worship.' Now when they heard this, they were full of wrath and cried out, saying, 'Great is Diana of the Ephesians!' So the whole city was filled with confusion, and rushed into the theater with one accord, having seized Gaius and Aristarchus, Macedonians, Paul's travel companions." (Acts 19:26-28)

Questions for discussion:
1. In the above passage, Demetrius, a silversmith, rallies the people into action against Paul. Why? What was Paul teaching? Why were people confused?
2. What was Demetrius' trade? What was L. Ron Hubbard's trade? Are there any similarities? Why are Christians such a threat to Scientology?

C. **Other Facets of Scientology:** Some other parts of the organization include 1) The Way to Happiness Foundation which has distributed 3.5 million copies of a Hubbard booklet to school children, 2) The Citizens Commission on Human Rights which fights against psychiatry, 3) Narconon, a chain of alcohol and drug rehabilitation centers, 4) The Church of Spiritual Technology which appears to be a parent organization for storing away cash, and 5) Religious Technology Center which collects information about *suppressive persons* and *potential trouble sources* and acts out against them as seems appropriate. Although some of the entities within Scientology appear to be beneficial for society, there are other parts of it that have been labeled dangerous and subversive by various countries and judicial systems. The organization's manipulative ways of drawing people in, brainwashing them, and sucking up their money has come under constant attack. The way that they attack ex-members and critics of Scientology, as well as their plots of conspiracy, wire tapping, and burglarizing have made them the subject of many law suits and investigations. From Jon Atack's information we find that one judge, Justice Latey, ruling in the High Court in London in 1984 said this:

"Scientology is both immoral and socially obnoxious...it is corrupt, sinister and dangerous. It is corrupt because it is based upon lies and deceit and has as its real objective money and power for Mr. Hubbard, his wife and those close to him at the top. It is sinister because it indulges in infamous practices both to its adherents who do not toe the line unquestioningly and to those who criticize or oppose it. It is dangerous because it is out to capture people, especially children and impressionable young people, and indoctrinate and brainwash them so that they become the unquestioning captives and tools of the cult, withdrawn from ordinary thought, living and relationships with others."[37]

The facet of Scientology that concerns their children must be mentioned. The living conditions of the youngsters within the organization is suspect and quite possibly deplorable. Reports surface from time to time of the way in which parents are separated from children and only allowed minimal contact. The Computer *Internet* is full of stories that I have seen by former Sea Orgs and other Scientologists. Some of the reports come from parents who unwittingly allowed their children to be taken from them and placed in supposedly "high quality" children's centers. They found out later that the living conditions were abominable and that the children were neglected and abused. The horror stories that emerged during the 1970's and 1980's makes one wonder "if the accounts are true then why hasn't social services done something about it?" Some of the accounts (even affidavits) come from children themselves who grew up in the intolerable conditions of neglect, harsh treatment, menial labor, unsanitary living conditions, and abuse. According to one account about a Sea Org nursery, there was no furniture, no toys, no books, and the children stunk of urine. They were considered of little importance since they were not yet productive members of the church of Scientology.[38] I hope these reports are not true.

IX. WHO ARE SOME OF THE CELEBRITIES OF THE CULT?
   A. **David Miscavige**. Although Miscavige keeps a low profile, he is the man in control of Scientology. He grew up in the cult and at age 14 joined a select group of trusted young people called the "Commodores messengers." He would deliver messages for Hubbard. He grew in service and position and eventually became the key figure when Hubbard went into hiding. After, Hubbard's death a power struggle ensued between Miscavige and Pat Broeker, another close associate of Hubbard, but Miscavige won out. Today, Miscavige works hard, demands perfection, but keeps a low profile.
   B. **Hollywood Stars and Celebrities**. Scientology uses its stars to promote their cause. Some of the better known names that embrace the church and its teachings are John Travolta, Kirstie Alley, Tom Cruise, Nicole Kidman, (the late) Sonny Bono, and Geoffrey Lewis. How involved these celebrities are and how much they really know about the dubious inner operations of Scientology are debatable. They are probably treated like royalty among the elite ranks because of their popularity, and the church takes full advantage of these movie idols for its publicity purposes.

X. WHAT ARE SOME OF THE TEACHINGS OF SCIENTOLOGY?
   A. **Reincarnation and Evolution**. Since Hubbard believed in these concepts, his teachings on thetans getting trapped in physical bodies reflected them. He taught that we have all been embodied in numerous life forms at one time or another and that many of our engram hang ups are due to bad experiences we had. For instance, in his book the *History of Man*, Hubbard claims that many of man's inhibitions and bad habits spring from his past lives in the form of clams, sloths, apes, Piltdown man, and cave men. He does not believe in heaven or hell, nor eternal consequences for choice.
      Refutation: The theory of a soul progressing through successive bodies to eventually reach godhood is important in a lot of cults. The fact that there is no proof doesn't seem to bother those who espouse it. The luring temptation to believe that we can become God is the same one that the serpent used in the garden of Eden (Gen. 3:4). In deed! It is this very type of thinking that caused man to fall from grace in the first place. The thrust of the Bible is that man is dead and lost until he is *"born again"* (Jn. 3:3)

into the Kingdom of God, that comes through accepting the free gift (Rom. 6:23) of eternal life by placing our trust in Jesus Christ alone (Eph. 2:8-9). Heb. 9:27 tells us that we only die once [physically] before facing the judgment, and in Heb. 6:2 we find that the judgment is eternal. Christians believe in resurrection freedom not reincarnation bondage. The theory of evolution is disproved by the Scriptures, but also has major scientific problems. Gen. 1:27 and 2:7 show us that man was created completely in God's image. The theory of evolution has so many inconsistencies that many scientists are bailing out of it today. Furthermore, the Piltdown man that Hubbard supposedly had secret knowledge about was found to be a hoax.

B. **Levels of Perfection.** Scientologists are taught to be experts at drawing people into their courses. *They offer free personality tests* and tell the people that a particular course in Scientology will meet their need for any problem named. New students on the *Preclear* level must take courses to learn about the inner workings of Dianetics. It is the function of registars to sell people on these courses. The courses are extremely expensive, but through pressure and manipulation the registars get people to sign up.

Along with courses are sessions in which the Preclears receive auditing to remove all their hidden engrams. The use of E-Meters are employed somewhat like lie detectors to find hidden areas of engram blockage. When the supposed engrams are removed, they become Clears. Once this is attained, they take higher level classes to become Thetans and then move on through the eight levels of "Operating Thetans." Supposedly, at the upper levels, they have much psychic ability and powers and are close to becoming gods. Of course, new levels of operating thetans are being created so that the cycle of growth and money exchange continues.

Refutation: A system of salvation through works is that of Scientology. Like every other cult in the world, the people must do something to gain salvation from earthly bondage. Of course, those works mean big dollars for the people at the top of Scientology. The Bible teaches that there is salvation in no other name under heaven than that of Jesus Christ (Acts 4:10-12). Jesus came to show us the way to salvation. He offers us the free gift of eternal life (Rom. 5; 6:23) that comes through faith in Christ alone (John 3:16; Eph. 2:8-9).

No one is good enough to be saved. That's why we need a Savior. No works we can do are good enough (Eph. 2:8-9). If we could work our way to salvation then we could boast and look down upon others, but we have no reason to boast. Our boasting is to be in Christ because of who He is and what He did for us. Jesus Christ was God in the flesh (Matt. 2:23) and willingly gave Himself that we might find life. Scientologists teach that we become perfect through their courses and auditing. They say that people must become cleared of engrams in order to have perfect memory and recall, but the proof is in the pudding, as the old expression goes. Kurt Van Gorden tells in *Evangelizing the Cults* of the fiasco that Hubbard faced when he proclaimed the world's first "clear," Sonia Bianca:

"Dr. Winter, who claimed that Hubbard was 'absolutistic and authoritarian' gave several reasons for leaving the movement. His most important reason was that no one had become a clear through dianetics. He may have been referring to the grandiose event held at Shriner's Auditorium in Los Angeles, August 10, 1950, when Hubbard announced Sonia Bianca as the world's first clear. The event failed miserably. Miss Bianca, a physics major from Boston, was paraded before a full auditorium of press representatives and curiosity seekers. When questions were put to her, she could not remember a basic physics formula or the color of Hubbard's necktie, which she had seen moments before. The total recall of the clear floundered so badly that Hubbard did not announce another cleared person until 1966."[39]

Since then, there have been thousands of "cleared" persons, but they could not do any better than Sonia, so the new levels of *Thetans* were created as steps of advancement towards perfection. In reality, however, it's a delusion; they never reach it.

C. **Man is Basically Good.** Scientology teaches that deep down inside, men are actually good. The problem is not sin, they say. Our dilemma has occurred as a result of suppressed engrams and forgetting that we were once thetans playing a game.

Instead of just admitting that we are sinners who need God's saving grace, L. Ron Hubbard concocted a doctrine which states that much of mankind's problems originated some 70 million years ago when Xenu, the President of the Galactic Confederation, forced people to come to earth and be placed near volcanos. He then dropped nuclear bombs on us. Afterwards, he then spent 36 days implanting false religious and technological images in us (or should I say the thetans that we once were). Xenu was eventually caught after six years by Rawl - none other than L. Ron Hubbard in a past life - and then imprisoned in a mountain. However, humans have had significant hang-ups ever since because of the engrams, implants, and forgetfulness.

Refutation: Every culture in the world has a problem with sin. People steal, murder, rape, plunder, covet, and lie. Little ones fight over toys. No one has taught them to be selfish; they are too young. Of course, man has his good moments also. The Bible teaches us that in the Garden we ate of the tree of the knowledge of good and evil (Gen. 3:6), and so today we see the good and the evil. The problem is sin which we all have (Rom. 3:23). It has nothing to do with Xenu or nuclear bombs exploding on us. Like white and black paint being mixed, we are all colored by our sin nature to some extent. The punishment for our sin was death and eternal separation from a Holy, Righteous God of perfection. But because He loved us and did not want us to be punished forever, He sent His own Son, Jesus, to be our sacrifice for sin by dying on the cross. Jesus rose again on the third day and now sits at the right hand of the Father. If we repent of our sins and ask His forgiveness, He does forgive us and also gives us eternal life.

Man is not basically good, however God is totally good and in that goodness, he made a way for man to return to Him, but we must humble ourselves and do it His way. We cannot work our way by going through levels of perfection. It will not work for us to rationalize our sin nature away by saying that it wasn't our fault, Xenu made us do it. That sounds strangely familiar to the Eden account when Adam blamed his sin on Eve and she, in turn, blamed it on the devil.

Thinking Through The Scripture

"See, the Lord is coming with thousands upon thousands of his holy ones to judge everyone, and to convict all the ungodly of all the ungodly acts they have done in the ungodly way, and of all the harsh words ungodly sinners have spoken against him. These men are grumblers and faultfinders; they follow their own evil desires; they boast about themselves and flatter others for their own advantage." (Jude 14-16) NIV

Questions for discussion:
1. According to this passage, what is one thing we can expect some day? How many will be judged? For what kind of things will the ungodly be judged?
2. Which ungodly acts should the church of Scientology be concerned about?
3. Will blame shifting be effective? Can they blame Hubbard or Xenu?
4. Scientology has sued a lot of people in the human court of law. What

are the positive aspects of the fact that all will appear before the judgment seat of Christ in the Lord's court of Law? What are the negative aspects?

XI. WHAT ABOUT GOD AND JESUS CHRIST?

    A. **God the Creator**. Scientologists say that new comers are free to believe in whatever God they want. They purposely leave the term "Supreme Being" undefined. However, brainwashing occurs through the teachings of reincarnation and the thetan scam. This leaves one with a panentheistic concept (believing that all finite entities are within, but not identical to, God.)

    Hubbard believed that there are many gods and gods over those gods. But this view is completely contradictory to the Bible which teaches that there is only one God (Deut. 4:39; 6:4) and that He is transcendent, not being a part of what He created. In other words, we are not all gods, but we and everything that is had to be created by one Supreme Creator God. He represents Himself to us in the form of the Trinity: God the Father, God the Son, and God the Holy Spirit, three persons intrinsically united in the one Godhead (Gen. 1:26; Zech. 12:10; Matt. 28:19; 2:9).

    B. **Jesus Christ**. There is very little said in Scientology about Jesus. It has been stated that He was a shade above Clear but not an operating thetan. Hubbard challenged the orthodox view of Christ. Although Scientologists use a type of cross as a symbol for betrayal, Hubbard stated that Jesus was a false dream or implanted picture put into our minds between the time when we die and are born into a new body.[40]

    This sounds like science fiction to me. It doesn't take much research—for anyone interested—to find out that there is more evidence for the life of Jesus Christ the way that it is represented in the Bible than any other man who has ever lived, including L. Ron Hubbard. The sad truth is that these people buy into a science fiction lie and give all their money to an organization based on a fantasy. It's strange that they look for made up stories when the real ones are so magnificent.

XII WHAT CAN CHRISTIANS DO FOR THESE PEOPLE?

    A. **Prayer:** The late Reverend Gordon Linsay, a prayer warrior for God, once said, "Every man ought to pray at least one violent prayer every day."[41] He based this statement on Matthew 11:12: *"And from the days of John the Baptist until now the kingdom of heaven suffers violence and the violent take it by force."*

Scientology will not ultimately be defeated through legal victories in the court system. Nor can we expect simple reasoning power to be the main weapon against this coming-of-age, techo-scientific religion. These things may help and ought to be done, but the primary battle must be waged through "violent prayers" (Ephesian 6:12 prayers) in the heavens against demonic strongholds that have tricked people into believing science-fiction fantasy rather than down-to-earth reality.

The "escapism" mentality of this age has made possible delusions of fantasy that go far beyond mere intellectual stimulus and entertainment, way down into the core of where people think they came from, where they think they are going, and why they think they are here. The church needs to stand up against this science-fiction cult and nemesis with prayers of intercession on behalf of its victims. We should pray deliverance for the children and the "potential trouble sources" within the cult. We should pray protection for the "suppressive" marked Christians who oppose Scientology. We should pray for the Hollywood stars that they would escape the snare of the cult and become truly "clear" in Christ Jesus.

B. Love: "God hates sin but loves the sinner." How many times this expression has been used - and with good reason - to show what our view should be towards those who are not yet Christians! God's love can permeate the most wretched soul and bring healing and health. The warmth and charity of the Holy Spirit can unravel the deepest of mental and emotional bondage and bring true clarity to our minds.

People are drawn into Scientology for many reasons and people leave Scientology for many reasons. Those who are drawn into Scientology are looking for something to fill a void or a need in their life. The wise Christian will seek the Lord in how to best show the Scientologist who only can fill that void or who only can really meet that need. Proverbs 11:30 tells us *"He who wins souls is wise."* The mind set of most Scientologist is such that it will take real wisdom to win them. However, we are called to be "fishers of men" and to learn to cast with the right bait, at the right time, and in the right place. There is an old adage that says, "You have to love them before you can lead them." If you want to lead someone out of Scientology, then let God's love shine through you on behalf of their children, their spouse, their situation, etc.

Those who have escaped from Scientology have not necessary come to Christ yet. In fact, they may be weary of anybody trying to lead them into anything. It is important that they don't just perceive you as another "auditor" type or "Operating Thetan" - whatever - just trying to woo them into another scam. The focus needs to be on Christ and His sacrificial love for them. Don't come across as the perfect one or they will never listen to you. They have had enough of people telling them that "they have arrived." They know it's just not true.

C. **Witness:** Here are some possible things to do:

1) Ask how long he or she has been a Scientologist. Be careful not to ridicule their experiences. Ask if they have ever had anything come up during auditing which made them question the experience or what was being taught.

2) Show them the evidences for the reliability of the Bible. If they have been told confusing things about the Bible, then clear it up. One couple, Keith and Shawn Scott, rejected Scientology after many years of trying to rid themselves of negative energy. It took a couple of years to shed the emotional scars but then the breakthrough came when they read God's Word.[42] Praise the Lord! The Scotts gave their lives to Jesus and went on to form the Cults Awareness Ministry, dedicated to warning others about Scientology.

3) Get books for those in the cult on the subject such as *Understanding Scientology* by Margery Wakefield and Bob Penny or *A Piece of Blue Sky* by Jon Atack

End Notes

1. Tom Hutchinson, "Deliverance from Scientology," *Biblical Literacy Today*, Winter 1987-1988, p. 12.

2. L. Ron Hubbard, *Dianetics: The Modern Science of Mental Health* (Los Angeles, CA: Bridge Publications Inc., 1978), 423.

3. Mather and Nichols, *Dictionary of Cults, Sects, Religions And The Occult* (Grand Rapids, MI: Zondervan Publishing House, 1993), p. 90.

4. John A. Saliba, *Understanding New Religious Movements* (Grand Rapids, MI: William B. Eerdmans Publishing Company, 1995), p.150.

5. Ruth Tucker, *Another Gospel: Alternative Religions and the New Age Movement* (Grand Rapids, MI: Zondervan, 1989), p. 313.

6. Craig Branch, "Scientology Part One: Hubbard's Religion," *The Watchman Expositor* Volume 13, No. 2, 1996, p. 9.

7. Kurt Van Gorden, "Scientology," *Evangelizing The Cults: How to Share Jesus with Children, Parents, Neighbors, and Friends Who Are Involved in a Cult*, Ronald Enroth, ed., (Ann Arbor, MI: Servant Publications, 1990), p. 155.

8. Robert W. Welkos and Joel Sappel, "Work: Former Adherents Recount Harsh Conditions," *Los Angeles Times*, June 26, 1990, p. A16.

9. Richard Behar, "The Thriving Cult of Greed and Power," *Time Magazine*, May 6, 1991, p. 33.

10. Dr. Christopher Evans, *Cults of Unreason* (New York: Dell Publishing Company, 1973), pgs. 127-128.

11. Roy Wallis, *The Road to Total Freedom: A Sociological Analysis of Scientology* (New York: Columbia University Press, 1977), p. 170.

12. Tucker, p. 318.

13. David G. Bromley and Phillip E. Hammond, ed., *The Future of New Religious Movements* (Macon, GA: Mercer University Press, 1987), p. 74-75.

14. Richard Kyle, *Religious Fringe: A History of Alternative Religions in America* (Downers Grove, Illinois: InterVarsity Press, 1993), p. 305.

15. Van Gorden, p. 155.

16. Welkos and Sappel, June 24, 1990, p. A37.

17. Behar, p. 32.

18. Welkos and Sappel, June 24, 1990, p. A39.

19. Wallis, p. 21.

20. Welkos and Sappel, p. A38.

21. Ibid.

22. Evans, p. 28.

23. Welkos and Sappel, p. A36.

24. Wallis, p. 250.

25. Ibid., p. 91, 249.

26. Tucker, p. 317.

27. Bob Larson, *Larson's Book of Cults* (Wheaton, IL: Tyndale House Publishers, Inc., 1988), p. 314.

28. *60 Minutes*, "The Cult Awareness Network," (CBS, December 28, 1997).

29. John Weldon, "Scientology: From Science Fiction to Space-Age Religion," *Christian Research Journal*, Summer, 1993, p. 23.

30 Wallis, p. 104.

31. Jon Atack, *A Piece of Blue Sky: Scientology, Dianetics and L. Ron Hubbard Exposed* (New York: Carol Publishing Group, 1990), forward.

32. Bromely and Hammond, p. 60.

33. Jeff Jacobsen, "The Hubbard is Bare: Exposing L. Ron Hubbard's Grandiose Claims," Jesus People USA, P.O Box 3541, Scottsdale, AZ, pgs. 14-15.

34. Welkos and Sappel, p. A36.

35. Jacobsen, p. 16.

36. Atack, pgs. 89-102

37. Atack, forward.

38. Margery Wakefield, "The Road to Xenu," *Internet*, Newsgroups: alt.religion.scientology, swhitlat@nmt.edu (Steven Whitlatch), August 19, 1995.

39. Van Gorden, p. 158.

40. Welkos and Sappel, p. A36.

41. Cindy Jacobs, *Possessing the Gates of the Enemy: A Training Manual for Militant Intercession*, (Grand Rapids, MI: Chosen Books, 1995), p. 73.

42. Ken Walker, "Escape From Spiritual Deception: California Dreaming," *Charisma & Christian Life Magazine* (August 1996): 59-60.

QUESTIONNAIRE: LESSON TWELVE

NAME: _____ DATE: _____

1. Give one reason why people are drawn to Scientology today: _____

_____

_____

2. The founder of Scientology was _____, and the current leader of the group is _____ Miscavige.

3. Hubbard had a very controversial life because he rewrote much of what actually happened to him. Give some examples of his exaggerations and delusions. _____

_____

_____

_____

_____

4. In 1950, L. Ron Hubbard wrote _____: *The Modern Science of Mental Health* which has turned into the modern day religion of _____. The international headquarters are located in _____ but there are various branches and missions from it around the world. One of the strangest groups of Scientologists are those who live on board ships and sail the seas. They are known as Sea _____. They have signed up for a billion years of service to the organization. While this sounds far fetched to the average person, it makes sense to them because of what they have come to believe. Scientology teaches that all men are actually gods which they call _____; at least we were at one time, before we started playing a big mind game and trapped ourselves in _____, meaning matter, energy, space, and time. Like Hinduism, they teach that everything around is actually an illusion and that we spend countless lives of death and rebirth playing the game of life. Over these lifetimes we have been impacted by negative events which have caused mental blocks so that we have forgotten that we are really gods. These mental blocks they call _____. Scientology teaches that L. Ron Hubbard discovered these truths and the method of getting back to godhood. We must get rid of these engrams, he says, through intensive sessions with _____ who occasionally use a device called an E-_____ to locate hidden engrams. When all engrams are removed, we become _____. After this, we move on

into levels of becoming an operating thetan. The whole system is called Dianetics because it helps people probe into their past and then discover the omniscient and omnipotent power that can be theirs.

5. Matthew 7:16 tells us that we will know people by their _____. How should we apply this to Hubbard's life? Give examples. _____

_____

_____

_____

_____

6. List three of the four roots of Scientology and explain a little about each one:

a) _____

_____

b) _____

_____

c) _____

_____

7. Consider Genesis 3:4. What is the lie that Eve bought into and the same one that Scientology espouses? _____

8. Hebrews 9:27 tells us that it is appointed for men to die _____ and after that we face the judgment. Hebrews 6:2 informs us that the judgment is _____.

9. In regard to a system of salvation through becoming clear of engrams and then becoming gods, what does Ephesians 2:8-9 tell us about grace and works? _____

_____

_____

_____

10. Consider your knowledge of Scientology before and after this lesson. Circle the number below that indicates how equipped you felt before taking this course to witness to a Scientologist as compared to how equipped you feel now. Be honest.

BEFORE 0 1 2 3 4 5 6 7 8 9 10 **AFTER** 0 1 2 3 4 5 6 7 8 9 10

THE OCCULT

Part 1: Spiritism and Ufology

"And I really believe it was the providence of God that led me to the eighteenth chapter of Deuteronomy. I opened up the Word and I was shocked as I read about Moses warning the Children of Israel as they were about to enter the Promised Land, that they must not follow after the ways of the Canaanites. Moses said, 'When you enter the land which the Lord your God gives you, you shall not learn to imitate the detestable things of those nations. There shall not be found among you anyone who makes his son or daughter pass through the fire, one who uses divination, one who practices witchcraft, or one who interprets omens, or a sorcerer, or one who casts spells, or a medium, or a spiritist, or one who calls up the dead; for whoever does these things, the Lord your God will drive them out before you.' (Deut. 18:9-12) I was shocked at what I was reading because we had been doing the very things which were disgusting in the eyes of God. Then I began to look at the concordance and I was amazed as I went through the Scriptures to find well over 100 verses that condemned these things that we thought were of God. This certainly was a new understanding, but it was not difficult for me to realize how true the Bible was, especially after the experiences I had in Spiritualism."[1]

—Ben Alexander, a former spiritist and medium

I. WHAT IS THE OCCULT?
    A. The word "occult" comes from the Latin word *occultus* which refers to hidden or secret things. It is beyond the realm of empirical knowledge and centers around a fourth dimension, the spirit realm, which

impacts our three dimensional life. Typically, it refers to any secret or mysterious supernatural powers derived through witchcraft, Satanism, neo-paganism, or certain types of psychic perception.

B. In his book, *The Religious Fringe: A History of Alternative Religions in America*, author Richard Kyle speaks of the reemergence of interest in the occult arts in the last few decades. He mentions some of many areas that are today considered a part of the occult subculture in the United States:

"The reappearance of the occult in the seventies was not limited to the United States. It was a world-wide phenomenon. It had never declined in much of the Third World, and Europe also witnessed an increased interest in the occult. Did all of this activity indicate an explosion of the occult? There is a widely held view that in the seventies America experienced an occult revival...The occult has had a substantial presence in America for the last century and a half. What happened in the 1970's in respect to the occult was an unprecedented peak in public attention, publishing and organizational activity. Of greater importance, the occult worldview is becoming widely accepted in the 1970's and 1980's, far more than in previous years and perhaps to a degree unprecedented since the seventeenth century.

This so-called occult explosion entails two tendencies, one focusing on specific phenomena, and the other on a world-view. These two emphases are not mutually exclusive; they entail considerable overlap. First is the renewed interest in certain occult practices (the occult 'arts'). Most popular are astrology and the many forms of divination (cartomancy, crystal-gazing, palmistry, Ouija boards, prophetic dreams and visions, psychometry, numerology, I Ching and others). Other familiar occult practices and focuses that one might encounter include witchcraft, Satanism, spiritualism (necromancy), magic, paranormal experiences, unidentifiable flying objects and perhaps an occasional monster."[2]

Thinking Through The Scripture

"If anyone acknowledges that Jesus is the Son of God, God lives in him and he in God. And so we know and rely on the love God has for us. God is love. Whoever lives in love lives in God, and God in him. In this way, love is made complete among us so that we will have confidence on the day of judgment, because in this world we are like him. There is no fear in love. But perfect love drives out fear, because fear has to do with punishment. The one who fears is not made perfect in love." (1 John 4:15-17) NIV

Questions for discussion:

1. Sometimes Christians get the idea that contemplating certain topics like this study will make them vulnerable to enemy attack. However, when someone acknowledges that Jesus is the Son of God, where does the Bible say that God lives? Since this is so, what kind of confidence should this give Christians?

2. In what manner is fear cast out? The word "fear" comes from the Greek *phobos* and is where we get our English word "phobia." It means alarm or fright. The author of this passage, John, is informing Christians that they can have confidence about a certain coming event. What is that event?

3. How can the revelation of "perfect love" assist us as we consider the occult and the bizarre things that occur within it? How can it help those who are delivered from the occult? Should they fear the coming judgment?

II. WHAT IS THE ATTRACTION OF THE OCCULT?

A. **It attracts a large variety of adults:** People basically look the same on the outside, but inside they are vastly different. They are complex creatures that are motivated towards and moved into the occultic lifestyle through a wide variety of reasons: superstition, curiosity, loneliness, boredom, rebellion, power seeking, psychically inclined, bad religious experience, sadness over the lost of a loved one, or as the offspring of an occultist. Women in mid life are often attracted to the occult because of its subjective emphasis, a dissatisfaction with their role in a "man-dominated" world, menopause, or the need to find a meaning to life in a confusing world. Authors Josh McDowell and Don Stewart point out in their book *Understanding the Occult* that there is also the aspect of secretive knowledge and the supposed hidden answers to life's questions that lure a number of people who later are filled by dark things and ultimately deceived:

"There is a reality in the occult experience which attracts many people to it. All of us desire some sort of ultimate answer for life's basic questions. The astrologist will chart your future. The Ouija board promises you direction, and the medium talking to the spirit of your dead relative, informs you that things are fine in the next world. Since these occultic practices do reveal some amazing things, the practitioner is lulled into thinking that he has experienced ultimate reality and no longer needs to continue his search for truth. The spiritual vacuum is filled by means of a spiritual experience, not with God, but often from the very pit of hell."[3]

B. **It attracts the young:** These last couple of decades have seen a substantial number of teens drawn toward dark areas. One of those is called *Goth*. Some say it started among young, educated, but rebellious, types who were frustrated and bored by their parent's culture. Different movements within it drew some to the arts and philosophy, while others were more bent on pleasure seeking and even self destructive actions. In the 1990's it has taken on the character of drugs, sex, black clothing, white face-paint, and black lipstick, with an interest in cemeteries, vampires, death, and dark mood music.

Not too long ago, we had a teenage girl come to one of our Christian youth meetings. She attended the Christian school, but her relationship with the Lord was questionable as she sometimes manifested some of these characteristics. Her clothes were usually black and there was an unhealthy interest in death. There was concern because she had spoken of suicide. People had been praying that the Lord would touch her. He did! An emptiness within her life drew her to the youth meeting. During the worship time, some of the young prayer warriors began doing battle against dark principalities and powers. As the meeting proceeded, the teenage girl kept moving farther away from the group. When this was noticed, she was approached with love and concern but responded with fear and hate. Her voice changed and became demonic. It was suddenly apparent to the Youth Pastor and young leaders what was happening. After a time of interceding on behalf of the teen and then a confrontation with the demons, the young woman was delivered.

Praise Jesus! Afterwards, she revealed that her life had been one of deception. She had faked being a born-again Christian because of the pressure by her Mom to live for Jesus. In actuality, she was caught up in the occult and even prayed to the dark powers. Her thoughts were constantly dark. But the mighty Lord led her out of the darkness and into His marvelous light. Her countenance, thoughts, and choices of clothing were immediately impacted in a positive way.

However, many of the young people today are not so fortunate. They are being deceived into believing even fantasy roles about themselves and others. One recent outcome of Gothic influence has been the so called "vampire cults." These demented individuals file their teeth and prey on harmless animals. In their book *Fast Facts on False Teachings*, Ron Carlson and Ed Decker depict the sad tragedy that is happening today among the youth as a result of the many problems within the American culture:

"Young people are getting more involved in satanic activity than ever before. With the increase of dysfunctional families, many young people are into alcohol abuse, drug abuse, and sexual abuse, and are also seeking new kinds of energy and personal control through satanic activity. They believe Satan will give them power or dominion over their lives and over the lives of those around them.

Many kids go from the dabbling aspect into becoming obsessed with the world of the occult. Soon they begin to take on the characteristics of occult influence, such as wearing occult and satanic jewelry, buying occult books, dressing in black, and wearing white makeup. They begin to practice the occult rituals they read about or are shown by their friends. They begin to play fantasy role-playing games, such as Dungeons and Dragons. They begin to watch occult movies and videos. They immerse themselves in heavy metal and acid rock music. "They openly go into the occult, seeking to take charge somehow in a world they feel alienated from. They step through a veil of darkness, not knowing the evil awaiting them.[4]

What are some of music groups in the last couple of decades delivering Gothic messages that young people should be warned about? Here are just some of them: Southern Death Cult, Sex Gang Children, Christian Death, Creaming Jesus, Front 242, Gangwar, Marilyn Manson, AC/DC, Iron Maiden, Merciful Fate, Black Sabbath, Slayer, Motley Crue, Anthrax, Danzing, Exodus, Grim Reaper, Halloween, Mega Death, Metal Church, Metallica, Celtic Force, Satan, Sodom, and Possessed. The names and album covers make it obvious what message these groups are sending through their music.

III. WHAT IS DIVINATION?
   A. It is an attempt to foretell the future or gain "secret knowledge" from occultic methods such as astrology, crystal balls, dreams and predictions by secular prophetic figures, I Ching, numerology, omens, Ouija board, palm reading, tarot cards, etc.
   B. **Astrology** is considered to be the largest area of the occult today. It also "vies with Spiritism for the honor of being the most ancient cult."[5] It was possibly first practiced by the Chaldeans in Babylon but also has ancient roots in Greece, China, India, and others. It was thought to be science until the time of Copernicus who discovered that the earth was not the center of the universe but revolved around the sun. His discovery was the basis for modern astronomy.

Astrology is based upon the twelve signs of the Zodiac. It reemerged in popularity in the 1970's and even found its way into council at the White House in the 1980's. It is estimated that one in five adult Americans tend towards astrology, eight out of ten know their sign, and that nearly 2,000 newspapers carry daily horoscopes.[6] It comes across so factual that even Christians are sometimes caught up in it, unaware of its falsity. Astrologers try to make some connection between our time of birth and our future, justifying it by saying that we are just a small reflection of the cosmic universe. However, they have some real problems objectively for any who investigate:

1. The science of astronomy totally disputes any accuracy of astrology.
2. Astrologers are not objective; they are caught up in the system.
3. It was based upon the faulty assumption of earth at the universe's center.
4. There are billions of celestial bodies outside our galaxy that they overlooked.
5. Some use 8, 12, 14, or even 24 Zodiac signs. It is inconsistent.
6. Horoscopes computed by a Hindu would be much different than by a Buddhist.
7. Since heredity factors are determined at conception, it's off by nine months.
8. The constellations have shifted 30 degrees in the last 2,000 years.
9. Most astrological charts are based on the 7 planets known at its origin.
10. The Bible warns us against any form of divination in Deut. 18:9-13. There are specifc warnings against it. Some are in Isaiah 47:13-15, Jer. 10:2; Deut. 4:19, and Acts 7:41-45. A part of Josiah's reformatory work was to remove the astrologers (2 Kings 23:5).

Thinking Through The Scripture

"Disaster will come upon you, and you will not know how to conjure it away. A calamity will fall upon you that you cannot ward off with a ransom; a catastrophe you cannot foresee will suddenly come upon you. Keep on, then, with your magic spells and with your many sorceries, which you have labored at since childhood. Perhaps you will succeed, perhaps you will cause terror. All the counsel you have received has only worn you out! Let your astrologers come forward, those stargazers who make predictions month by month, let them save you from what is coming upon you. Surely they are like stubble; the fire will

burn them up. They cannot even save themselves from the power of the flame.
Here are no coals to warm anyone; here is no fire to sit by. That is all they can
do for you—these who have labored with and trafficked with since childhood.
Each of them goes on in his error; there is not one that can save you." (Isaiah
47:11-15) NIV

Questions for discussion:
1. The passage above was prophesied against Babylon. Where is that civilization today? What happened to it? Do you see any of these activities occurring in this country? What are some examples? What judgment may come?
2. What will happen to the astrologers that lead the people? From what are they unable to save themselves? Are they able to save anyone else?

C. **Crystal ball** gazing is also called crystalomancy or skrying. The diviner supposedly enters a trance and sees a series of pictures regarding someone's future. Today it has become a sideline business by gypsy types and has taken a step down in stature.

D. **Dreams and Predictions** by people such as Edgar Cayce and Jeane Dixon come under the category of divination. Cayce formed a foundation in 1931, called the Association of Research and Enlightenment (A.R.E.). Today, it aggressively proclaims his false teachings regarding God and the Bible, and it promotes his some 15,000 "readings" on medical questions as well as his many predictions. While many of his trances regarding medical issues were astonishingly accurate, his predictions have fallen far short of accuracy. Fortunately for Californians, the state did not fall into the Pacific in the early 1970's. Cayce taught that Jesus Christ was the reincarnation of Adam, Mary was virgin born like her son, God does not know the future, salvation is through works, as well as other false doctrines.

Dixon has been heralded for her fulfilled prophecies, but many are not aware of her false prophecies. Contrary to her predictions, World War III did not begin in 1954, the Viet Nam War did not end in 1966, and Jacqueline Kennedy did get married on October 19, 1968, to Aristotle Onassis, even though Dixon predicted otherwise! There are many others. Also, her predictions were normally quite vague and could be construed in different ways to make it appear that she was accurate.

E. **I Ching** ("Book of Changes") is an ancient Chinese manual of divinations based upon gaining guidance through coin tossing and sticks. It is based upon the Ying & Yang.

F. **Numerology** is closely related to astrology but holds that the heavenly bodies are each associated with a number and its qualities. People's birth dates and the letters in their names align them with a significant number revealing secret knowledge.

G. **Omens** are supposed to be events or objects that act as signs of things to come. There are good omens and bad omens. Examples of superstitious omens are a black cat walking across one's path or someone walking under a ladder.

H. **Ouija boards** are one of the most popular occultic devises in the world today. They are used by spiritists and sometimes in a game-board party style to contact the dead. Numbers, letters, and a "yes" and "no" answer are at various places. A pointer on the board is moved by the hand of a user who is under the influence of a "spirit."

I. **Palm reading** "or chronancy, is the art of divination from the shape and markings of the hands and fingers."[7]

J. **Tarot cards** consist of a pack of twenty-two cards inscribed with symbols that vary from pack to pack. These symbols are used in combination to foretell the future.

IV. WHAT IS MAGIC?

A. One type of magic deals with the art of illusion and is used to entertain people. This type of magic uses various tricks and deceptions such as sleight of hand, psychological principles, a stooge, unseen devices, mathematical principles, physics, physical and mechanical deception, optical illusion, and probability. Many of these deceptive forms are also used in seances with spiritists who trick people.

B. "However, the magic we are concerned with is none of the above. It is occultic in nature, an attempt to master supernormal forces in order to produce visible effects. This magic is a secretive art, and it is difficult to give a precise definition of all it includes. Arthur S. Gregor defines magic in the following manner: 'Magic is an attempt to gain control over nature by supernatural means. It consists of spells, charms, and other techniques intended to give man what he cannot achieve with his normal human powers'."[8]

Thinking Through The Scripture

"The sin of Black Magic is rebellion" (1 Samuel 15:23) GW

"So Moses and Aaron came to Pharaoh, and thus they did just as the Lord had commanded; and Aaron threw his staff down before Pharaoh and his servants and it became a serpent. Then Pharaoh also called for the wise men and

the sorcerers, and they also, the magicians of Egypt, did the same with their secret arts. For each one threw down his staff and they turned into serpents. But Aaron's staff swallowed up their staffs." (Exodus 7:10-12) NASB

Questions for discussion:
1. Who created the Laws of Nature? If we consider that Black Magic is the attempt to gain control over nature by self-imposed supernatural means, why does the Bible call this rebellion?
2. Some people think that there is no real power in magic. However, who did Pharaoh call upon to demonstrate the power of their secret arts? What were they able to do?
3. What did Aaron's staff do to the others? What does this tell us about God's power and authority? Is any thing too difficult for Him?
4. Look up Exodus 7:22; 8:7; and 8:18-19. How many of the Ten Plagues were the magicians able to counterfeit? When they could not conjure up any more, what did they realize? What should this imply for those involved in today's occult? What should they realize about God's power and authority?

V.   WHAT IS PARAPSYCHOLOGY?
   A.   One defintion of parapsychology is this: It is "the pseudoscientific study of phenomena of the human psyche that are not accounted for through normal empirical means. Such studies are directed toward mental telepathy, clairvoyance, esp, psychokinesis, etc."[9]
   B.   Is it wrong? To consider that some type of latent potential might reside in certain individuals or in all of us is not necessarily a wrong thing. There may be types of power associated with individuals in varying degrees that are not necessarily evil nor from demonic sources. Some people have better vision, hearing, or physical strength. Power—in and of itself—is not evil. Atomic energy is neither good nor evil.

   However, its moral value depends on how it is used. Having power does not mean we are in right relationship with God as the magicians of Pharaoh's court discovered. People who experience strange phenomena need to line it up against Scripture, for it is the authority of the Word of God that judges our experiences rather than our experience superseding the Word of God.
   C.   Is it a science? McDowell and Stewart say, "The demand for scientific investigation is a valid quest and should and must be made. This responsibility lies with Christians too. However, in the consideration of parapsychology as science, one must be willing to

embrace the most accurate explanation of the data, whether it be fraud, the occult or a valid paranormal experience. *For in most cases, one fruit in the study of parapsychology is an increasing lack of motivation to study the Scriptures.* In fact, it often leads one in a direction of the paranormal or supernatural totally apart from a biblical base."[10]

This then should be a warning for Christians and those seeking the truth of God's Word to be extremely careful regarding the subject of parapsychology or the experience of strange phenomena. [italics added]

VI. WHAT IS ROSICRUCIANISM?

A. **History.** One rather obscure group that is involved in mysticism and the occult are the Rosicrucians. The fraternity of the "Rose Cross" was allegedly founded in 1408 by Christian Rosenkreutz. The name Rosenkreutz means rose cross, hence the name of the fraternity. However, some believe that this name is merely symbolic for the alchemic symbols of "ros" which is the solvent for gold and "crux" (cross) which represents light. Supposedly, Rosenkreutz was an alchemist, as well as a student of Hinduism, Judaism, Hermetism (ancient Greek and Egyptian writings of alchemy), the occult, and medicine. He searched the world over for truth—so to speak—and came up with magic and medicine.

Most scholars agree the story is mythical.[11] As the story goes, he died in 1484 but left instructions for his followers to open his tomb in 120 years which would signal a new epoch in European history. When opened in 1604, it was reported that his body was in tact and that the manuscripts of his teachings were beside the body. The names of the manuscripts were Fam Fraternitatis and The Confession of the Order.

Yet, it is believed that Joann Valentin Andrea really wrote the manuscripts and created the fictitious story of Rosenkreutz. However, even with the confession of Andrea, the order continued to flourish. In 1694 Rosicrucianism came to America through the teachings of Johann Kelpius, but the real awakening happened near the turn of the twentieth century.

B. **The Symbol.** To one modern day branch of Rosicrucian "the cross represents 'the body of man' with the rose symbolizing 'man's soul unfolding and evolving.'"[12] This symbol does not represent the cross of Christianity, one of suffering but also one of overcoming. There is some attempt by people to see these two symbols representing the same, but at best, this is mystical Christianity.

C. **Modern.** Today, two locations in California claim to be the true representative of the teachings of Christian Rosenkreutz. Each claim their true origins go far back to ancient times. The Rosicrucian Fellowship in Oceanside claims ancient Chaldea as its origin, but the Ancient Mystical Order of the Rose Cross (AMORC) in San Jose embraces ancient Egypt. Dr. H. Spencer Lewis founded AMORC in 1915 and was heavily influenced by Aleister Crowley (see Satanism) and the occultic group Order Templi Orientis (OTO).

D. **Beliefs.** Their teachings basically echo *New Thought* and *New Age*. Even though the use of Christian terms are employed, the underlying theme is one of pantheism. God is not distinct from the creation. They do not consider themselves a religion, but a secret society who use metaphysical and physical philosophy to awaken sleeping power within individuals. Some of their false teachings:
   1) The Father is the highest initiate among humanity of the planet Saturn.
   2) The Holy Spirit (Jehovah) is the highest initiate of the Moon.
   3) The Son is the highest initiate of the Sun.
   4) Jesus had Aryan blood.
   5) He didn't die on the cross but ended up in a monastery.
   6) He didn't ascend to heaven.
   7) The Bible is not unique, just one of many books with truth.

Thinking Through The Scripture

"For the word of the cross is to those who are perishing foolishness, but to us who are being saved it is the power of God. For it is written, 'I will destroy the wisdom of the wise, and the cleverness of the clever I will set aside.' Where is the wise man? Where is the scribe? Where is the debater of this age? Has not God made foolish the wisdom of the world? For since in the wisdom of God the world through its wisdom did not come to know God, God was well-pleased through the foolishness of the message preached to save those who believe." (1 Corinthians 1:18-21) NASB

Questions for discussion:
1. What do the Rosicrucians teach about Jesus' death on the cross? In what way then are they represented in this passage?
2. Why is the "word of the cross" considered the power of God by Christians?
3. In the end, what will be revealed about the wisdom of those who refused the gospel story? Why does the gospel seem like foolishness to

the world? What did the world fail to do through its wisdom? Why is belief so important?

VII. WHAT IS THEOSOPHY?

A. **History.** Theosophy comes from the Greek word *theosophia* meaning "divine wisdom." To some, Theosophy should be ranked among the Mind Sciences. However, it is distinguished from them by its emphasis on the mystical and occult teachings. The Theosophical Society was the creation of one Helena Petrovna Blavatsky who founded it in 1875, in New York, with the aid of Colonel Henry Olcott.

Helena P. Hanh was born in the Ukraine in 1831. At age seventeen, she married a much older man, a Czarist general named N. V. Blavatsky. The unhappy marriage only lasted a couple of months, but she kept the name and began a deep search for occult wisdom that lead her into many countries over the next several decades. Although Helena - known as H.P.B. to her friends - was involved in Spiritualism, she finally came to reject some of its tenets and mixed its teachings with those of other religions. In his book, *The Chaos of Cults*, J. K. Van Baalen cleverly points out that Theosophy "is the apostate child of Spiritism mixed with Buddhism."[13] One could also throw Gnosticism and Hinduism into that mixture. In 1879, after only limited success in the United States, Blavatsky and Olcott left. They established the international headquarters in Adyar, India, in 1882. Eventually, she was accused of being a fraud in India and then later by the London Society for Psychical Research. Regardless of the attacks, she continued on in her life's work and wrote extensively until her death in 1891. Some of Blavatsky's books included *Isis Unveiled, The Secret Doctrine, The Voice of Silence*, and *The Key to Theosophy*.

The greatest successor to Blavatsky was Mrs. Annie Besant (1847 - 1933), the daughter of an English minister. She became the president of the international movement after Olcott's death in 1907 and then became a prolific writer expressing theosophical ideas until her death.

Alice Baily (1880-1949) and her husband, Foster, emerged from Theosophy and formed the Arcane School in New York in 1923. It was kin to Theosophy but grew into what came to be called "Full Moon Meditation" groups which focused on the second advent (of a New Age Messiah) and One World Idealism.[14] Alice Baily has heavily influenced various political, environmental, and social groups through her emphasis on *"The Plan"* for a one world system. Today, Theosophical headquarters are located in such places as Wheaton, Illinois, Los Angeles, and Covina, California. This is the result of the various competing factions.

B. **Impact.** Like the Mind Sciences, Theosophy supposedly never got off the ground or became significant. If you merely consider registered members, there are only about 6 thousand in the United States and maybe only forty thousand in the world.

Yet, whenever we consider occult groups who wish to be veiled in secrecy, it is important to remember that all-is-not-as-it-seems. Let me give a couple of examples. First, Theosophy was pivotal for the creation or impact of other movements. Author and historian, Richard Kyle, points out that Theosophy should be considered "one of the most important occult movements in America,"[15] and the reason is because of its influence on New Thought, Rosicrucianism, New Age Movement, The "I Am" Ascended Masters, and many other Spiritualistic movements.[16] These groups were initiated or transformed through theosophic thinking. Second, it is somewhat bizarre where the influence of Theosophy shows up: There is the assassin, Sirhan Sirhan who was purported to have killed Robert Kennedy, and then requested *The Secret Doctrine* by Blavatsky after he was locked up.[17] There is Adolph Hitler who was drawn to the same book and used a variation of the theosophical symbol representing Thor's hammer to create the swastika.[18] There is the strange coincidence between the environmental agenda of the Iron Mountain meetings (see "Politics" in the chapter on New Age) and the Theosophical doctrine regarding man's impact on nature.

What are the implications of this? Well, these could just be isolated instances and coincidence, and perhaps they are. However, there are some who believe that Theosophy is much more secretive and powerful than most imagine. In his book *Saviors of the Earth*, author Michael S. Coffman makes a case for this view:

"The evidence of this religion is everywhere. Yet most of those who subscribe to it in one form or another call it something besides Theosophy. Many have never even heard the word *Theosophy*. So how could it be so prevalent in such a short period of time? Because Theosophy depends on secrecy, even within its own circle of believers. It is not important to theosophical leaders whether this belief system is called Theosophy or something else, as long as its initiates believe in its general precepts. That is the way of the occult and esoteric religions. The initiates never know what the higher 'truths' are until they have been prepared (preconditioned) to receive them, at which time they are initiated into the next secret level."[19]

C. **Beliefs.** Theosophy has a pantheistic view of God as an impersonal divine source expressed in the forces of nature and the laws of the universe. They believe that all people have latent divinity within them, and that people go through successive reincarnations. As people are reincarnated and become more aware of the deep and hidden knowledge within themselves, they ascend the ladder of divinity to occupy an astral body.

There is a basic focus in Theosophy on the Mahatmas or Ascended Masters that are supposedly guiding the world into a better place. Blavatsky claims that many of her writings were actually revelations delivered from these masters. This has emerged into the concept of today's New Age guides. There is also the teaching that above all these masters is the *"One Supreme Teacher.* When he becomes incarnated, we have a Christ among us."[20] According to Theosophy, there have been a number of these Christs already, and they expect another one soon who will come as the New Age Messiah.

VIII. WHAT IS SPIRITISM?
A. **History.** Spiritism (sometimes called *Spiritualism* or Necromancy) is considered by some to be mankind's oldest religion. There are traces of it in ancient Chinese, Hindu, Babylonian, Egyptian, and Roman culture. It stems from two desires: 1) to gain information about life after death and, 2) to contact deceased loved ones.

The more recent interest began in 1843 with a cobbler from New York named Andrew Jackson Davis who claimed to be a medium for the spirit world. This caused a sensation. Then later, in 1848, the Fox sisters, Kate, Margaret, and Leah claimed to have heard spiritual rapping noises in their home in Hydesville, New York. They claimed to be able to communicate with Mr. Splitfoot, the supposed ghost of Charles B. Roena, a peddler who had been murdered in the house years before. Even though the Fox sisters eventually admitted that the rapping noises were an artificial gimmick, the movement of Spiritism had emerged in America with many claiming similar experiences.

In 1967 the famous medium, Arthur Ford, held a seance for Episcopal Bishop James A. Pike on Canadian television. Pike was trying to establish contact with his dead son, Jim. It was a media circus that drew much interest.
B. **Impact.** In general, Spiritism is more popular in Brazil, France, and England than in the U.S.A. Brazil has approximately 10 million (1993 estimates) adherents and other Latin American countries

one million. Estimates in the U.S. vary, but there are up to 150,000 Americans that claim spiritualism as their religion. There are nearly twenty Spiritualist denominations.[21]

The Universal Church of the Master (UMC) began in 1908, in Los Angeles and currently boasts of approximately 300 congregations that total about 10,000 people. Church services seek to resemble Christian style services, but there are differences also. Words of hymns are changed, spirit greetings replace pastoral blessings, psychic readings replace prayer, and the minister may deliver the sermon while in a trance.

C. **Beliefs**. Spiritists claim that certain passages of the Bible support seeking the dead. Proponents use the story from 1 Samuel 28 in which King Saul sought the aide of a medium (spiritists) at Endor in order to communicate with Samuel who was deceased. They say that the Transfiguration in Matt. 17 was spirit materialization, that Pentecost was the greatest seance in history, and that Jesus was the master medium of all time, levitating the stone from his tomb and materializing before his disciples. Spiritists deny the deity of Jesus Christ and assert the deity of mankind. They do not hold to original sin, miracles, the virgin birth, or hell. They teach around their seven principles and nine articles.

The Seven Principles of Spiritism:

1) The Fatherhood of God
2) The Brotherhood of Man
3) Continuous Existence
4) Communion of Spirits and Ministry of Angels
5) Personal Responsibility
6) Compensation and Retribution Hereafter for Good or Evil Done on Earth.
7) A Path of Endless Progression.[22]

The Nine Articles of Spiritism:

1) We believe in Infinite Intelligence.
2) We believe that the phenomena of Nature, both physical and spiritual, are the expression of Infinite Intelligence.
3) We affirm that a correct understanding of such expression and living in accordance there with, constitute true religion.
4) We affirm that the existence of personal identity of the individual continues after the change called death.
5) We affirm that communication with the so-called dead is a fact scientifically proven by the phenomena of Spiritualism.

6) We believe that the highest morality is contained in the Golden Rule: "Whatever ye would that others should do unto you, do ye unto them."

7) We affirm the moral responsibility of the individual, and that he makes his own happiness or unhappiness as he obeys or disobeys Nature's physical and spiritual laws.

8) We affirm that the doorway to reformation in never closed against any human soul here or hereafter.

9) We affirm that the precept of Prophecy contained in the Bible is a divine attribute proven through Mediumship.[23]

D. **Seances:** This is a gathering with one or more mediums (channelers) in order to contact the dead. The vast majority of these are deceptive shams put on by tricksters to dupe people out of their money. But there are cases in which legitimate meetings with "spirits" take place. Many bizarre and unnatural things can occur by demonic forces which deceive people into thinking that they are in contact with the dead.

A friend of mine, Doug Sheaffer, experienced a power encounter one time between a Christian and a Satanist at a seance. Doug grew up in a family that attended a "Christian" Spiritualist church in Portland, Oregon. He practiced power games, tarot cards, aura studies, numerology, phrenology, palmistry, and Ouija boards, and yet he thought he was a Christian. Doug even carried around a Bible. He didn't read it, but he carried it around because they were supposedly Christians, and they had been told that what they practiced was in the Bible. Having the Bible around kind of gave more authority to what they did, or so they thought. What Doug didn't know, however, is that the spiritualistic practices they performed were in the Bible's list of abominations. Because of his position in the generations, he was slated to carry on the traditions and preside over the seances.

At the seance mentioned above, a Christian friend (they had dubbed "Crazy Louie") came into the seance unnoticed and sat in the background. When a known Satanist started chanting, the Christian jumped up and rebuked Satan in the name of Jesus. The Satanist was shocked. He stood up in anger and opened his mouth to yell back, but then something unexpected happened. He closed his mouth without saying a word, went over to the couch, lay down, and promptly fell asleep.

This so impressed Doug that he started searching the Scriptures. He was given Christian tracks about the abominations of Spiritism. Eventually, he came to see the truth about the activities of Spiritism and was, himself, convicted of sin. As he asked Jesus Christ to forgive him of the sin of Spiritualism, he was miraculously delivered from a demonic stronghold. Jesus became his Lord and Savior that day.[24] Today, he serves the Lord Jesus!

IX. WHAT DOES THE BIBLE SAY ABOUT SPIRITISM AND ITS BELIEFS?
  A. **Regarding the Ability to Communicate with the Dead:** The Bible actually gives very little—if any—support for communication with the dead. In Luke 16:19-31, Jesus tells the parable of two men who die. We find in this parable that the dead are limited in their movement because there is a great gulf fixed between heaven and hell that cannot be passed over. Furthermore, the rich man is refused permission to contact his living relatives in order to warn them of pending doom. Also, while Jesus did speak with Moses and Elijah on the mount of transfiguration (Matt. 17), it must be remembered that the Son of God has unlimited power not available to the whim of human will, and also that He had purpose in the divine plan of redemption that was unique for the occasion.

  We do see in the case of 1 Samuel 28:15 that Saul was able to communicate with Samuel, but this seems to be the exception rather than the rule, seeing how the medium herself was shocked (verse 12) when she actually saw Samuel appear. Perhaps God, uniquely on this occasion, brought forth the spirit of Samuel to rebuke Saul. In any case, the overall picture of the Old and New Testament gives the picture that communication with the dead is impossible unless God supernaturally intercedes for His own purposes.

Thinking Through The Scripture

  "Do not turn to mediums or spiritists, do not seek them out to be defiled by them." (Leviticus 19:31) NASB

  "So do not listen to your prophets, your diviners, your interpreters of dreams, your mediums or your sorcerers who tell you, 'You will not serve the King of Babylon.' They prophesy lies to you that will only serve to remove you far from your lands...." (Jeremiah 27:9-10) NIV

Questions for discussion:
1. Can there be any doubt that these activities are forbidden by the Bible? Who do mediums and spiritists actually contact? How does one become defiled?

2. In the last decade, there has been a swelling interest in the psychic hot-line. People call psychics for advice. How do these psychics fit into the passages above? Can psychics tell the future? Are they necessarily evil or wrong?

3. In the passage from Jeremiah, what is the Lord warning His people about? Are these prophets and diviners foretelling the truth or a lie? What does God say will be the result of listening to them?

4. Now consider some of the New Testament prophets of God: Ananias who ministered to Paul (Acts 9:10-18); Agabus who prophesied a great famine (Acts 11:28) and who foretold Paul's future (Acts 21:10); and the prophets who selected Paul and Barnabas. Why is it appropriate and right to listen to God's prophets as compared to those who are not? In what ways can Christians discern if a prophet is from God or not? How can we judge?

B. **Regarding the Act of Trying to Communicate with the Dead:** The Bible specifically speaks against mediums (New Age channelers) and their activities in Scriptures such as: Lev. 19:26, 31; Lev. 20:6, 27; Deut. 18:9-12; Isa. 8:19, etc. Perhaps one reason that God does not want people to seek out mediums is to protect them from the deception of "familiar spirits" which were actually demons. The Hebrew word for *witch* actually represents a woman that has a familiar spirit. In other words, this was a possessing spirit very familiar to the woman.

C. **The New Testament gives accounts of people working in the occult.** Look up the following two passages and read the accounts for yourself. As you read these, consider the many New Age channelers and psychics of today. These elements of the New Age Movement are not new at all. *They are actually just Spiritism in disguise.* They are the deceptions of the devil tricking people into believing things that are not true and things that lead them away from God.

    1) Acts 13:6-12 - In this account we find a magician, Elymas, whom the Bible tells us is a) a false prophet (v. 6); b) one who is trying to turn men from the faith (v. 8); and c) full of deceit and fraud, a son of the devil, and an enemy of righteousness. Paul, through the Holy Spirit, rebuked the magician.

    2) Acts 16:16-19 - In this account we find a woman possessed by a spirit (demon) of divination (v. 16) who was being used by her masters to predict people's fortunes. The spirit had to con-fess the superior position of the disciples in God by crying out (v. 17). Paul, through the name of Jesus, cast out the demon.

X. WHAT IS THE HISTORY OF UFOLOGY?

A. **The modern study and history of unidentified flying objects**
    began on June 24, 1947, when a pilot named Kenneth Arnold
    sighted nine bright disks in the skies of Washington state as he was
    flying his plane. He called them "saucers". In 1952 George
    Adamski began writing books about his supposed encounter with
    an alien. Since then, thousands of people around the world have
    claimed to have seen UFO's or met ETI's (extraterrestrial intelli-
    gences), communicated with them, and ridden in their spaceships.
    These "flying saucers" appear to break all the laws of our known
    physics. They appear and disappear, and they speed quickly up to
    thousands of miles per hour and suddenly make ninety degree
    turns or stop. They are often described as luminescent circular,
    cylindrical, or spherical shapes with flashing lights. Many minor
    cults have grown up around the concept of a UFO or an individ-
    ual's experience with an ETI.

B. **Speculation of ancient UFO's** has been birthed by the modern
    study. Theories of aliens planting inhabitants on earth, building
    the pyramids, and posing as pagan gods have been proposed.
    Some look to the Old Testament and speculate that Ezekiel's vision
    was in reality flying saucers or that Elijah's chariot of fire was a
    spaceship.

XI. WHAT IS AN EXAMPLE OF A UFO CULT?

A. **Heaven's Gate** is a cult that has grown up around the concept of
    UFO's. The tragic mass suicide of thirty-nine adults in March, 1997,
    was the group's supposed exit from their human "containers" to join
    with a spaceship following the famous Hale-Bopp comet. The
    group, located in Rancho Santa Fe mansion near San Diego,
    California, was led by sixty-five year old Marshall Herff Applewhite.
    He had a long history of mixing apocalyptic Christian heresies with
    New Age philosophy, science fiction dramas, computer technology
    and UFO's. Applewhite, had formerly been known as "Bo" of the Bo
    and Peep cult. He and "Peep," Bonnie Lu Nettles, considered them-
    selves the Two Witnesses in the book of *Revelation*. They taught that
    Bo had been Jesus, Elijah, and Moses in his former reincarnated
    lives.

    They believed that their group was not going to die a physical
    death, but be whisked away by a spaceship which would carry them
    to a planet where they would be coequals with the King of Kings.
    The cult almost fell apart in 1985 when Peep died of cancer rather
    than being taken away by a spaceship. However, the group did not

cease completely. Applewhite continued to convert people to his strange doctrines which became even more twisted as he began centering on suicide as a means to exit. Many were convinced that they were actually aliens sent here to show men the way to the higher source. When Applewhite realized that he was dying of cancer, he convinced his group that the time was right to enter Heaven's gate by departing through suicide to join up with a UFO.[25]

B. There are many bizarre things that this cult teaches which the Bible clearly refutes. For instance, Hebrews 9:27 refutes the concept of reincarnation when it tells us that men only die once and then are judged. Hebrews 6:2 tells us this judgment is eternal. The concept of being coequals with the King of Kings is faulty and goes back to the deception that Satan fed Eve in the garden of Eden (Gen. 3:5). Of course, the idea of Applewhite being Jesus is heresy, and we know that Jesus Himself prophesied that "false christs" would arise in the last days (Matt. 24:24).

But a growing issue that needs to be addressed is this idea of suicide being an acceptable means to exit into a better place. Although the Bible is somewhat silent on the subject of suicide, the weight of Scripture does not come out in favor of such an act. In the suicide of Judas, we see someone running away from his responsibility and dying with guilt (Matt. 27:3), and in the case of King Saul, we see someone totally out of the will of God (1 Samuel 31:4). Also, 1 Corinthians 3:17 speaks against anyone hurting himself when it says, "If anyone destroys God's temple, God will destroy him; for God's temple is sacred, and you are that temple." It could further be contented that the commandment "Thou shalt not kill" applies to ourselves also. Suicide produces death which results in judgment. Each one will have to give account of what he did in this life (2 Cor. 5:10).

XII. WHAT IS SOME OF THE INFORMATION REGARDING SIGHTINGS OF UFO'S?

A. **The experiences and information** gathered from those claiming abduction fits a similar pattern. Reports of people, even those under hypnosis, have similarities in them that should be considered: 1) A person sights a UFO and then investigates it out of curiosity, 2) A humanoid-type of creature (ETI) appears which is very similar to the *"familiar spirit" looking creatures of Spiritism* , 3) The person is frightened at first but then calmed through the reassuring gestures of the alien, 4) The communication is normally telepathic and nonverbal, 5) The person receives a physical examination by a probe passing over the body, 6) At this point, there is sometimes a sexual encounter with the alien, 7) The aliens insist that they are advanced, benevolent beings only trying to help mankind understand truth and nature.

B. **Are UFO's for real?** Author Bob Larson addresses that issue and says, "Most are not and are easily dismissed as mistakenly identified planets, rocket launchings, weather balloons, and atmospheric phenomena. The Air Force Project Blue Book was able to provide a rationale for all but 700 out of 12,600 cases of sightings between 1947 and 1969. Other reports are not so easy to dismiss. *What of the cases where UFO's have torn off treetops, ricocheted bullets, and razed thousands of acres of forest (in the Soviet Union)? What about the hundreds of reports from responsible citizens claiming to have seen and heard unexplainable objects zooming across the sky?* Why do these flying machines often hover near power lines, bodies of water, and military installations? Can such diversity of situations with striking similarities be dismissed as hallucinatory speculations or imaginations run wild?"[26] [italics added]

XIII. WHAT ARE SOME OF THE VIEWS AND CONSIDERATIONS OF UFO'S?

A. **That it is all a hoax.** However, there seems to be too many sightings for this.

B. **That it is natural phenomena and poor eyesight.** (weather balloons, satellites, etc.) This explains much but not all; there are still the abduction reports.

C. **That it is a super-secret weapon.** However, all the countries seem to be baffled by the influx of information and the technology seems too far beyond what we know.

D. **That it is an unknown earth civilization perhaps subterranean.** However, we have no evidence of this even with the photographs of over 200 satellites that constantly circle the earth taking pictures with highly accurate ability. Also, why would a subterranean civilization have flying capability beyond us?

E. **That it is aliens from either our galaxy or another.** However, our probes to Venus, Mars, Jupiter and beyond have turned up nothing. Our advanced radio signals and photographs of space reveal no signs of life. To this point astronomers cannot even locate a planet capable of sustaining life as we know it.

F. **That it is a parallel reality.** This view enters into the realm of spirit beings and is possible considering the Biblical account of the Lord's angels and the demons. But the thought that a percentage of the sightings and meetings are with the angels of the Lord, must be balanced with a couple of thoughts: 1) True angels of the Lord direct man to God and glorify God (this does not seem to be happening), and 2) Why would true angels of the Lord need the restrictions of a spaceship?

XIV. DOES THE BIBLE DENY THE EXISTENCE OF EXTRATERRES-TRIAL LIFE?
A. No. There is no verse in the Bible prohibiting the existence of life on other planets. This omission causes some to speculate that God did create life on other planets but gave us the Bible to meet our unique needs as a world gone astray. However, this view seems incompatible for the following reasons:
   1) Adam's sin apparently affected the entire cosmos not just the earth.
   2) If sin halted our technological advance, why not the other worlds?
   3) If they are sinless, why would God allow them exposure & contamination?
   4) If they do exist, why didn't the Lord tell us?

XV. WHAT ABOUT THE POSSIBILITY OF AN END TIME SATANIC PLOT?
A. While there is no conclusive evidence, this view makes some sense because:
   1) The world is looking for a technological savior rather than Jesus.
   2) Some abductions include sexual encounters.
   3) The similar form of the alien's appearance to a medium's spirit guide.
   4) ETI's encourage participation in a wide variety of occultic activities, including suicide. There seems to be a wide variety of activity in things that are not Christian. However, there is no focus on man's sin, the coming judgment, man's need for redemption, and even the glorification of the Lord Jesus Christ is ignored. Certainly, if these UFO's were sent from Christ there would be sufficient mention of these issues so that Christians would not be left unsure.
   5) The world is left in confusion about the whole subject because there is very little proof of life outside of this planet. *It emphasizes the occult and deemphasizes Christianity.* Since the Bible tells us that "God is not the author of confusion" (1 Cor. 14:33), we have good reason to believe that it is an end time satanic plot.

End Notes

1. Ben Alexander, *Out From Darkness* (Joplin, MO: College Publishing Company, 1986), pgs. 48-49.
2. Richard Kyle, *The Religious Fringe: A History of Alternative Religions in America* (Downers Grove, IL: Inter Varsity Press, 1993), pgs.258-259.
3. Josh McDowell and Don Stewart, *Understanding the Occult* (San Bernadino, CA: Here's Life Publishers, Inc., 1982), pgs. 21-22.
4. Ron Carlson and Ed Decker, *Fast Facts on False Teachings* (Eugene, OR: Harvest House Publishers, 1994), pgs. 235-236.
5. J.K. Van Baalen, *The Chaos of Cults* (Grand Rapids, MI: Wm. B. Eerdmans Publishing Company, 1975), p. 18.
6. Bob Larson, *Larson's Book of Cults* (Wheaton, IL: Tyndale House Publishers, Inc.,1988), p. 254.
7. McDowell and Stewart, p. 73.
8. Ibid., p. 89.
9. George A. Mather and Larry A. Nichols, *Dictionary of Cults, Sects, Religions, and the Occult* (Grand Rapids, MI: Zondervan Publishing House, 1993), p. 219.
10. McDowell and Stewart, p. 101.
11. Ibid., p. 116.
12. Larson, p. 310.
13. Ibid., p. 62.
14. Kyle, p. 113.
15. Ibid., p. 107.
16. Mather and Nichols, p. 275.
17. Larson, p. 326.
18. Michael S. Coffman, *Saviors of the Earth?* (Chicago: Northfield Publishing, 1994), p. 245.
19. Ibid., pgs. 231-232.
20. Van Baalen, p. 70.
21. Ibid., p. 323.
22. Mather and Nichols, p. 264.
23. Larson, p. 322.
24. Doug Sheaffer, "Christian Spiritualism," a message on audio tape, (Illwaco Community Church: Illwaco, WA) September 12, 1987.
25. *Time Magazine*, April 7, 1997, pgs. 28-46.
26. Larson, p. 344.

QUESTIONNAIRE: LESSON THIRTEEN

NAME: _____   DATE: _____

1. The word occult refers to _____ or _____ things.

2. How or why does the occult attract adults? _____
_____
_____

How or why does the occult attract the young? _____
_____
_____

3. Write out the definition of divination: _____
_____
_____

4. List two reasons astrology has real problems with credibility:

a) _____

b) _____

5. Choose one of the divinations listed and tell about it. _____
_____
_____
_____

6. Have you had any experience with occultic activities? Tell about it.
_____
_____
_____
_____
_____

7. What happened to the serpents of Pharaoh's magicians? _____
_____

8. Why should Christians be cautious regarding involvement with para-psychology? _____
_____

9. Does the Rosicrucian cross represent the Christian cross? _____
Explain: _____

_____

10. Why should we be careful about underestimating the influence and power of Theosophy? _____

_____

_____

11. What did the Fox Sisters finally confess? _____

12. In which countries is Spiritism the most popular? _____

13. Which Old Testament story do Spiritists use to claim that contact with the dead is possible?_____

14. Write out Leviticus 19:31 _____

_____

_____

_____

15. What are the three things we learn about Elymas in Acts 13:6-12?

a) _____

b) _____

c) _____

16. The woman in Acts 16:16-19 was being used by her masters to do what?_____

17. List three of the views mentioned about UFO's:

a) _____

b) _____

c) _____

18. Does the Bible deny the existence of extraterrestrial life? _____

19. List three reasons that indicate a possibility of an end time satanic plot:

a) _____

b) _____

c) _____

THE OCCULT

Part 2: Satanism and Witchcraft

"Twice he freed his arms from our hold. Once, he grabbed the man's (Durian's) throat and began choking him. We immediately forced his hands loose. He then grabbed the forehead of the man and shouted in that guttural tone, 'I'll crush his head! I'll crush his head!' His strength was phenomenal. With great effort we again pulled his hands away and held him even tighter. He banged the back of his head on the concrete floor several times before we were able to restrain him. As we continued commanding Beezlybub [the name of the demon] to come out, Pastor Manguiat asked if he had an anting-anting (amulet). 'No!' he replied. We searched the man's body but found nothing. As we shouted at him with growing intensity, he began shouting in my face all kinds of vulgarities one after the other. I shouted at him, 'Do not talk to me like that! In the name of Jesus come out, Beezlybub!' He still defiantly resisted, and the man's body twisted in pain. We felt as though the demon was getting weaker and could not resist much longer, so we shouted and rebuked the demon with even greater intensity. I told Durian (the man) to help us and pray for Beezlybub to come out. Durian began praying and crying vehemently, 'Beezlybub, come out...in the name of Jesus, Beezlybub, come out!' He said this over and over, and we were doing the same. As Durian began shouting this, he grabbed his stomach in severe pain. The demon shouted, 'I'll destroy him! I'll kill him!' Durian cried out, 'Please, Jesus, help me! Come out, Beezlybub!' After several minutes of this last shouting match and Durian's intense pain, suddenly Durian relaxed and became very still. Then be began

weeping and cried out, 'I'm free...I'm free...I'm free! Praise Jesus, I'm free!" He
sat up and lifted his hands and continued praising the Lord, weeping as he did.
The deliverance was complete! Beezlybub had been cast out! Durian was
free!"[1]

I. WHAT SNARES DO CHRISTIANS NEED TO BE AWARE OF AND
    AVOID?

    A. **The Snare of Blame Shifting:** Christians, at times, have unwit-
        tingly played into the enemy's trap by thinking that demons are
        "behind every bush" and responsible for every problem of
        mankind. This is not so and gives the enemy an "imagined" place
        of authority in people's lives. Men are perfectly capable of causing
        their own dilemmas without demons or the devil being involved.
        Remember, that all men have *"sinned and fall short of the glory of*
        God" (Romans 3:23). If a Christian has not submitted himself fully
        to the Lordship of Jesus Christ and fails to pay a bill on time thus
        getting in trouble for it, or if he gets involved in a fleshly sin,
        whose fault is that?

        Some will blame the devil for their own lack of character. They
        will blame the devil for a problem with their family, church, com-
        munity, etc. without ever shining the spotlight on their own free
        will choices to do good or bad. While there is nothing wrong with
        seeking to discern if the devil is attacking some individual or
        group, we must also be willing to take responsibility for our own
        fault if there is any. For instance, if a church falls into financial
        chaos because many of the members refuse to tithe even after
        being taught the concept from Scripture, that is not the devil's
        fault. The Apostle Peter informs us to be mindful that judgment
        begins with the family of God. If the non tithing church blames
        the devil for the financial struggles, then it is the same as Eve
        blaming the serpent for tempting her in the Garden of Eden. She
        still sinned. She had the free will choice to not give in to that
        temptation. God held her accountable as well as Adam and the
        serpent.

        The Holy Spirit is very interested in honesty and truth. He
        wants us to be as well. When we blame shift, we are deceiving our-
        selves with confusion and may be giving place to the devil
        (Ephesians 4:27). However, when our hearts are right before the
        Lord, there will be no confusion and we will more accurately be
        able to discern if there is an enemy attack or satanic involvement
        of any kind.

Thinking Through The Scripture

"You, dear children, are from God and have overcome them, because the one who is in you is greater than the one who is in the world. They are from the world and therefore speak from the viewpoint of the world, and the world listens to them. We are from God, and whoever knows God listens to us; but whoever is not from God does not listen to us. This is how we recognize the Spirit of truth and the spirit of falsehood. Dear friends, let us love one another, for love comes from God. Everyone who loves has been born of God. Whoever does not love does not know God, because God is love." (1 John 4:4-8) NIV

Questions for discussion:
1. This passage tells Christians that through God they have overcome the spirits that do not testify that Jesus has come in the flesh and also the spirit of the antichrist (1 John 4:1-4). But what does this mean, "the one who is in you is greater than the one who is in the world?' What does it mean by the word "spirit?" What confidence should this give Christians?
2. To whom are worldly people most likely going to listen? What viewpoint will they most likely have?
3. What is John's test? How does he recognize the Spirit of truth and the spirit of falsehood? What does it have to do with listening? Consider John 10:2-3. How does it relate to the idea of listening?
4. What is the power of love in Christian birth? What is another sign that John tells us to look for regarding whether someone is from God or not?

B. **The Snare of Extremism:** Christians should be balanced in their thinking and reasoning regarding the strongholds of evil. On the one hand, we should not under estimate enemy activity and strength. It is not wise to blindly ignore that many are deceived by the enemy and that there are dark spiritual strongholds. On the other hand, we should not give ourselves to exaggeration about the enemy's power nor sensationalize evil as though it has ultimate victory. It does not; God does!

For a Christian, this life is somewhat like walking on a high wire. We are to stay focused on Jesus, the author and finisher of our faith (Hebrews 12:2) who is on the other side of the wire. As we walk forward towards Him, we should balance ourselves with the power and authority of the Word of God (Hebrews 4:12). It is like a pole that keeps us centered on the high wire. The Word gives us a proper and balanced perspective on life. Since a part of our Christian walk has to do with discerning whether the devil or demonic powers are involved in a particular situation or not, we need to keep an open mind and be guided by the Holy Spirit. C. S. Lewis gave an excellent admonishment regarding a person's perspective of demonic activity:

"There are two equal and opposite errors into which our race can fall about the devils. One is to disbelieve in their existence. The other is to believe, and to feel an unhealthy interest in them. They themselves are equally pleased by both errors and hail a materialist or a magician with the same delight." [2]

II. WHAT ARE DEMONS?
  A. One dictionary definition is this: "An evil spirit or, as it is sometimes translated, a devil. In some circles demons are considered to be beneficial in that they guide humans in making decisions. Demons in Christian traditions are the agents of Satan."[3] As Christians, we definitely do not see any redeeming qualities in demons or their supposed guidance. When they do give guidance, it is not towards God nor His ways. Many Spiritists and even witches are deceived into thinking that demons are often acting on behalf of humans, but they have ulterior motives. Satanists often understand that these powers are agents of Satan bent on doing his will.
  B. The Bible has a lot to say about the subject of demons, possibly more than people really want to hear. The idea of demons is certainly not a fun topic. Neither are the subjects of witchcraft and Satanism something that the average person often wants to ponder. However, the reality of them is certain and we must not ignore their existence unless we succumb to the subtle deception of the serpent. There are certain aspects of warfare that are ugly, and we don't like to consider them much. Yet, there are times when the designs and make up of the enemy must be frankly discussed. Otherwise, the troops are at a disadvantage because of a lack of information.

     In the early 1980's, authors Josh McDowell and Don Stewart did an excellent job making a list of things that the Bible says about demons. I have modified it in the following section. Consider what the Bible says we can know about demons, and then look at our authority as Christians:[4]
  1) **They fell out of fellowship with God.**
     "And the angels who did not keep their positions of authority but abandoned their own home." (Jude 6) NIV

2) **They are many, one-third of the original angels.**

"*For Jesus had said to him, 'Come out of this man, you evil spirit!'
Then Jesus asked him, 'What is your name?' 'My name is Legion,'
he replied, for we are many.*" (Mark 5:8-9) NIV

"*His tail swept [across the sky] and dragged down a third of the
stars, and flung them to the earth.*" (Rev. 12:4) AMP

3) **They are spirits without bodies roaming the earth to torment
unbelievers.**

"*Now when the unclean spirit goes out of a man, it passes through
waterless places, seeking rest, and does not find it...Then it goes
and takes along with it seven other spirits more wicked than itself,
and they go and live there; and the last state of that man becomes
worse than the first.*" (Matt. 12:43-45) NASB

4) **They are an organized enemy force to oppose God's people
and God's Kingdom.**

"*This is not a wrestling match against a human opponent. We are
wrestling with rulers, authorities, the powers who govern this
world of darkness, and spiritual forces that control evil in the
heavenly world.*" (Eph.6:12) GW

Other Scriptures: Matt. 12:24 1 Peter 5:8

5) **They are allowed certain supernatural powers:**

"*They are spirits of demons that do miracles.*" (Rev. 16:14) GW

a. They can sometimes inflict sickness.

"*And when the demon was driven out, the man who had been
mute spoke.*" (Matt. 9:33) NIV

b. They can sometimes possess animals.

"*The demons begged Jesus, 'Send us among the pigs';...and the
evil spirits came out and went into the pigs.*" (Mark 5:13) NIV

c. They can sometimes cause mental disorders.

"*...a man with an evil spirit came from the tombs to meet
him...Night and day among the tombs and in the hills he
would cut himself with stones.*" (Mark 5:2-5) NIV

d. They can sometimes possess or control people.

"*Mary (called Magdalene) from whom seven demons had
come out.*" (Luke 8:2) NIV

6) **They teach false doctrines.**

"*But the (Holy) Spirit distinctly and expressly declares that in latter times some will turn away from the faith, giving attention to
deluding and seducing spirits and doctrines that demons teach.*" (1
Tim. 4:1) AMP

7) **They are knowledgeable of God.**

"*And behold, they cried out, saying, 'What do we have to do with*

You, Son of God? Have You come here to torment us before the
time?" *(Matt. 8:29) NASB*

8) **They know that Jesus Christ is the Holy One.**
   "What do we have to do with You, Jesus of Nazareth? Have you
   come to destroy us? I know who You are—the Holy One of God!"
   (Mark 1:24) NASB

9) **They tremble before God.**
   "You believe that God is one; you do well. So do the demons believe,
   and shudder [in terror and horror such as make a man's hair stand
   on end and contract the surface of the skin]! (James 2:19) AMP

10) **God's people do not need to fear demonic possession.**
   "You are from God, little children, and have overcome them;
   because greater is He who is in you than he who is in the world."
   (1 John 4:4) NASB
   "In him the whole building is joined together and rises to become
   a holy temple in the Lord. And in him you too are being built
   together to become a dwelling in which God lives by his Spirit."
   (Eph. 2:21-22) NIV

   Note: There is somewhat of a controversy among
   Christians as to whether a Christian can be demon possessed.
   It would be easy to write one or more chapters on this subject,
   but that is not the object of this book. So let me just say this:
   The Bible gives little or no support for the view that a Christian
   can be demon possessed. If it were possible for a child of God
   to be possessed by demons then the Lord Jesus would have
   made it extremely clear to His followers because of what the
   whole concept implies. Yet, He did not even address the subject. His silence on the subject - as well as the silence of the rest
   of the Bible on the topic - speaks volumes: a Christian cannot
   be demon possessed. When someone accepts Jesus Christ as
   his Lord and Savior, that individual is "ransomed" or bought
   with a high price, even the blood of the Lamb. God now owns
   that individual, and it is His Spirit that comes to take up resi-
   dency. We become the "temple of God" and "the Spirit of God
   dwells" in us (1 Cor. 3:16).

   However, this is not to say that Christians should not be on
   guard. While Christians cannot be demon possessed, they can
   certainly be attacked, tempted, and even oppressed by the devil
   and his demons. The Bible warns us that it is possible for
   Christians to "give place to the devil" (Eph. 4:27) through sinful behavior. The real issue for Christians is not one of possession but one of control. People can let others control them, and

they often do. Even so, Christians can let sinful things into their lives to which they submit. Unrepentant sin can "give place" to demons which then gain control. This is why it is so important for Christians to be honest before God and let the Holy Spirit have control over their lives. We are to draw near to God in humility, submission, and purity. We are to resist the devil, and he will flee from us (James 4:7-8).

11) **God takes advantage of demons to accomplish His divine purposes.**

"Then God sent an evil spirit between Abimelech and the men of Shechem; and the men of Shechem dealt treacherously with Abimelech." (Judges 9:23) NASB

12) **God will judge demons at the last judgment.**

"God didn't spare the angels who sinned. He threw them into hell, where he has secured them with chains of darkness and is holding them for judgment." (2 Peter 2:4) GW

"He held angels for judgment on the great day. They were held in darkness, bound by eternal chains. These are the angels who didn't keep their position of authority but abandoned their assigned place." (Jude 6) GW

13) **God created hell for the devil and his angels.**

"Then He will also say to those on the left, 'Depart from Me, accursed ones, into the eternal fire which has been prepared for the devil and his angels." (Matt. 25:41) NASB

Thinking Through The Scripture

"And He said to them, 'I see Satan fall like lightning from heaven. Behold, I give you authority to trample on serpents and scorpions, and over all the power of the enemy, and nothing shall by any means hurt you. Nevertheless do not rejoice in this, that the spirits are subject to you, but rather rejoice because your names are written in heaven." (Luke 10:18-20)

Questions for discussion:
1. How does Satan come down from heaven? What does this imply?
2. To whom does Jesus give authority? What do you think "serpents and scorpions" represent? Are they literal or figurative or both? What does it mean to have authority over all the power of the enemy? If you had authority over the forces of an enemy army, what would you be able to accomplish?
3. What shouldn't we rejoice in? What should we rejoice in?

III. WHAT IS THE HISTORY, BELIEF AND PRACTICE OF SATANISM?

   A. **History.** Satanism grew out of a reaction to Christianity. Basically, it is the worship of the devil, also called Lucifer and Satan (Gen. 3:1-15; Isaiah 14:12). Its history before the seventeenth century is hard to find. Devil possession was the initial charge leveled against the women of the Salem Witch trials of 1692. Voodoo magic and a pact with the devil by several people brought about the hysteria of the witch hunt.

   B. **Modern Satanism** was propelled by the life of Aleister Crowley (1875-1947). Although he never considered himself a Satanist, his writings and teachings on magic highly influenced twentieth century Satanism. He belonged to various secret occultic groups in his life such as the Order of the Golden Dawn, the Secret Chiefs of the Hermetic Order, and the Ordo Templi Orientis (OTO). He taught that powerful magic could be harnessed through sex and drugs. As these were employed, the consciousness of any sense of morality was destroyed opening the individual to influence of powerful supernatural spirit beings. "Crowley was a homosexual, murderer, and practitioner of black sex-magic. He sought to violate every moral law possible, and actually renamed himself 'Beast 666'".[5] He claims that revelation came to him while in Cairo, Egypt, he was visited by a guardian angel named Aiwaz. Crowley wrote the revelations which turned into the *The Book of the Law* with the central theme being, *"Do what thou wilt shall be the whole of the Law."* This book and his other, *The Equinox*, became the basis for modern Satanism.

   C. **Types.** Among modern Satanist there are those who function as individual sorts and those who group together for common purpose. Of those that group together, there are four basic groups:

      1) Authentic Satanism (white Satanism) is probably the least common. It believes in the existence and worship of the fallen angel and probably comes from the gnostic tradition.[6]

      2) Sex club Satanism celebrates the sexual aspects of the black mass but does not put as much emphasis on the other occultish aspects.

      3) Gang club Satanism, such as the notorious Charles Manson and his group, grew out of the acid culture of the 1960's and focuses on narcotics more than occultism. These groups are more rare than sensationalized headlines would have us believe.

      4) The Satanic Church in America is the largest and most publicized of the satanic groups.

D. **The Satanic Church** was started by the late Anton LaVey in 1966 in San Francisco, California. By the mid 1970's they had more than 10,000 members involved in public Satanism. LaVey published his book "The Satanic Bible" in 1969. Other books included "The Satanic Rituals" and "The Complete Witch". Strangely enough, the Church of Satan embodies little of true Satanism. "In fact, these Satanists do not believe in Satan or the devil in any real sense. They believe in magic, but define it simply as obtaining changes in accordance with one's will. The power of magic comes not from without, but from within. The purpose of Satanism is to acquire control, and one does this by openly admitting and accepting one's passions."[7]

As Christians, we probably sometimes wonder if there is any hope for people who have lived the life of Satanism. I was at a Christian Conference lately and met a pastor who shared some wonderful news with me; two of Anton LaVey's children have come to accept Jesus Christ as Lord and Savior. For the sake of privacy and protection, I will not mention any names, but the awesome thing is that one of the kids is living with a Christian family. Mentoring and discipleship is happening. The prophet Jeremiah said, *"Through the Lord's mercies we are not consumed, because His compassions fail not. They are new every morning; Great is your faithfulness"* (Lamentations 3:22-23).

What seems impossible for us is not impossible for God at all. He is generous and forgiving to all who seek Him in repentance and faith. There is no one too lost which the arm of the Lord cannot rescue. I can testify of that! He saved me out of the occult, madness, and many cultic philosophies. It is God's desire that none should perish but that *"all men should come to repentance"* (2 Peter 2:9). For He *"desires all men to be saved and to come to the knowledge of the truth"* (1 Timothy 2:4). That is the wonderful Lord and Savior we serve. We have a Savior who wants to save all!

It is so sad that some not only reject the Lord Jesus, but taunt Him as well. This appears to be what Jose Luiz Howarth Silva was doing according to a *Charisma* article in January, 2000. Silva says he was drawn to the dark side as a boy. He has written a book entitled *Devil"s Bible* and leads a growing group of followers in southeastern Brazil. There he intends to build a satanic cathedral shaped like a huge coffin called the Lucifer cave. When asked about the second coming of Jesus, he responded: "I'm here waiting for him."[8] Silva might not realize it, but he is only a heartbeat away from standing before the judgment seat of Christ that will result in eternal consequences.

E. **Beliefs.** "There is a list of nine Satanic statements to which all
    members must agree. These are that Satan represents 1) indul-
    gence, 2) vital existence, 3) undefiled wisdom, 4) kindness only to
    those who deserve it, 5) vengeance, 6) responsibility only to those
    who are responsible, 7) the animal nature of man, 8) all the 'so-
    called sins', and 9) 'the best friend the church has ever had, as he
    kept it in business all these years.'

    The Satanic Church is strongly materialistic as well as being
    anti-Christian. Pleasure-seeking could well describe their philoso-
    phy of life. What9 the world has to offer through the devil is taken
    full advantage of in the Church of Satan."[9] LaVey's "Satanic Bible"
    encourages Satan followers that a new millennium is coming in
    which they shall reign on earth. Unfortunately for Anton, he went
    to meet His Maker before the new millennium arrived.

    One of the things Satanists often do is to collect a wide variety
    of occultic books that cover their beliefs and practices. When
    someone gets saved out of Satanism, witchcraft, or some other
    major occult group, it would be a wise idea to consider burning all
    of the magical sorcery books that they have. In Acts 19:19 we see a
    burning party taking place among those who had been saved out of
    the occult. It says, *"many of those who had practiced magic brought
    their books together and burned them."*

    I think this is a good thing to do for a couple of reasons. First,
    it makes a definitive break from the occult in the mind and heart
    of the one making the commitment. This is done before the sight
    of God and man, and it will have an impact in the spiritual realm
    as well. A release will come and the yoke of bondage will be bro-
    ken. Second, the books will no longer be available for others to use.
    I had a personal experience with this.

    Shortly after I gave my life to Jesus, I made the mistake of not
    burning a lot of books on Satanism and Witchcraft that had been
    left in my possession. I didn't even know the books were hidden in
    some boxes that somebody had asked me to keep for them. They
    said they would return shortly. They never did. I tried to contact
    them, but they had disappeared. A year later, I graduated from col-
    lege and was rummaging through things for a yard sale as I pre-
    pared to move to another state. I discovered the books, but I was
    not alone. Others saw them also, including people I did not know.
    One rather overbearing man wanted them badly, but I said, "No."
    That night I threw them in the garbage can for the garbage truck
    to pick up the next day. I poured bleach and detergent all over

them thinking to destroy them, but I should have burned them. The next morning they were gone. Someone had watched me do it all. He came in the night and got all but two of the most damaged ones.

Thinking Through The Scripture

"But the cowardly, the unbelieving, the vile, the murderers, the sexually immoral, those who practice magic arts, the idolaters and all liars—their place will be in the fiery lake of burning sulfur." (Revelation 21:8) NIV

Questions for discussion:
1. What is the fiery lake of burning sulfur? Why do you think their place will be one of burning sulfur? If this isn't the same as hell then what is it?
2. What is the sad truth about those who practice the magic arts and don't repent? What is the one thing all these groups have in common? Do you think the people who commit horrendous crimes against others know what awaits them? What should our attitude be towards them?

F. **Practices.** Depending on how steeped a person is in Satanism, the occult, and evil, will determine the depth of involvement in activities of crime. There are cases of animal and human sacrifice among various extremist satanic groups, but many of the practices of satanists tend more towards occultic and mystical experience, as well as sensual pleasure. The Church of Satan observes two major holidays, Halloween and Walpurgisnacht (April 30).

The Church of Satan only symbolically celebrates the black mass. However, other satanic groups perform it quite literally. The black mass specifically focuses on violating the Lord's Supper. Since classical Satanism vents its hatred towards Christianity, the black mass is a gross celebration of the devil and degradation of the Lord Jesus Christ and His sacrifice on the cross. Although its rare, participants may actually drink the blood of animals and eat human flesh in mock communion ritual.

Another practice of Satanism, which is mixed with witchcraft, is that of casting spells or placing curses on others. It is kind of like the idea of sticking a Voodoo doll - that represents some person - with pins and praying to the dark powers that calamity will befall the victim. Fortunately, Christians have nothing to worry about when it comes to people putting spells or curses on them. Of course, we do battle the dark forces and we do need to keep our "swords" sharp and our "shields" always ready (Ephesians 6).

Yet, Christians need not fear because we have been redeemed by Jesus Christ. Of Him, John the Baptist said, *"Behold the Lamb of God who takes away the sin of the world"* (John 1:29). Jesus was the perfect sacrifice for our sin. When someone repents and places his faith in Christ and His substitutionary atonement on his behalf, then his sins are completely forgiven and forgotten. This is why the Father sent His Son into the world (John 3:16). Furthermore, the Bible says, *"the blood of Jesus Christ His Son cleanses us from all sin"* (1 John 1:7). His blood over our lives is so powerful that every vestige of sin is cleansed. This means that every claim that the devil has on a person's life is broken and shattered at the time of salvation. That is a part of what salvation is all about. There is an old hymn that says, *"There is power, power, wonder working power in blood of the Lamb."*

There have been several cases over the years in which Satanists realized that they did not have the power to cast spells over Christians. Sometimes, even Satanic leaders know this. One example happened years ago at the State Fair in Puyallup, Washington. Both the Jesus People and the Church of Satan had booths set up at this event. A dialogue broke out between Warren, one of the leaders of the Jesus People, and one of the elders of the Church of Satan. The Satanist got upset and said he wanted to put a spell on Warren to demonstrate his power.

The Satanist said that he wished he had some of Warren's hair for the spell. Warren, who was a strong Christian, was undaunted. He cut off some hair, gave it to the Satanist, and said, "Go ahead." So the Satanist went back to his booth and started casting the spell. One of his superiors asked him what he was doing. When he told the leader of the Church of Satan what he was doing, the man said, "Don't bother. You can't put a spell on a born-again Christian. If that person has a living relationship with Jesus Christ; it won't work."[10] Hallelujah! There is power in the blood of the Lamb that covers the children of the most high God, the Lord Jesus Christ.

G. **Balance Regarding Sensationalism.** Abduction of children by satanic cults has worried parents for decades. While it is always good to be cautious, it should be understood that the large majority of children abducted have to do with domestic disputes between parents or relatives. The actual activity of satanic groups has been grossly exaggerated. It has been claimed that between

50,000 and 2 million children per year are kidnapped and sacrificed. David Alexander, who writes for a magazine points out the indisputable nonsense of some of the claims:

"Think about the logistics required to kill two million people a year. A recent example will provide us with some perspective. During World War II, millions of Jews, Gypsies, Slavs, Poles, and others considered 'subhuman' by the Nazis were rounded up and systematically exterminated...The Nazis ran six major killing centers and sixteen hundred smaller camps. Researchers estimate that there were over one hundred fifty thousand people involved in running and servicing the death camps, from railroad clerks to the guards who ran the gas chambers. It was a large operation which ran at its peak from 1941—1944. It takes a large and efficient organization to exterminate two million people a year...Could an organization of crazed baby killers—an organization a hundred times larger than organized crime—exist without any of us catching on?

Where is the evidence for such an operation in this country?...Even the low estimate of fifty thousand ritual victims a year is little less than the total number of Americans killed in Vietnam during the entire war. Virtually everyone in the United States over the age of thirty knows someone who was killed in Vietnam or knows someone who knew someone who was killed. How many people do you know who have been ritually sacrificed? Moreover, the Federal Bureau of Investigation compiles statistics about crime in the United States. If, as some 'experts' claim, there are fifty thousand unreported ritual sacrifice murders being committed, then we must have a nation of very inefficient police and sheriffs' departments, as the figure is two and one-half times the twenty thousand murders annually recorded by the FBI."[11]

IV. WHAT DOES THE BIBLE SAY ABOUT SATAN?
   A. He is the god of this age. 2 Cor. 4:4
   B. He is the deceiver of the human race. Gen. 3:4-13
   C. He is the archenemy of God. Matt. 4:6; John 8:44; 2 Cor. 2:11
   D. He reigns over sinners. Acts 26:18
   E. He attempts to reclaim Christians. Eph. 6:12; Matt. 24:24
   F. He creates deceptive & lying wonders. 2 Thess. 2:9
   G. He was defeated in plan by Jesus' birth. Gen. 3:15
   H. He could not tempt Jesus to sin. Matt. 4:1-11; 16:21-23
   I. He was defeated in power by Jesus' death. Heb. 2:14-15
   J. He is doomed to eternity in a lake of fire. Rev. 20:7-10

Thinking Through The Scripture

"Then I heard a loud voice in heaven say: 'Now have come the salvation and the power and the kingdom of our God, and the authority of his Christ. For the accuser of our brothers, who accuses them before our God day and night, has been hurled down. They overcame him by the blood of the Lamb and by the word of their testimony; they did not love their lives so much as to shrink from death." (Revelation 12:10-11) NIV

"Then the devil who had led them astray—deceiving and seducing them— was hurled into the fiery lake of burning brimstone where the beast and false prophet were; and they will be tormented day and night forever and ever— through the ages of the ages." (Revelation 20:10) AMP

Questions for discussion:
1. The loud voice from heaven said that several things came as a result of the accuser being hurled down? What are they? When Christians cast down the enemy from their life, do they also appropriate these things in a spiritual sense?
2. Who is the accuser of the brothers? How do Christians overcome him?
3. Is the last part of Revelation 12:11 speaking of martyrdom?
4. Where will the devil ultimately end up? Who else will be there?
5. How long will he be tormented? How long will hell last? Why?

V. WHAT IS THE DIFFERENCE BETWEEN SATANISM AND WITCHCRAFT?
   A. Although many people confuse these two occultic groups by combining them, they are actually two very distinct groups. They are often lumped together because 1) They both share magical world views, and 2) Some Satanist openly identify with witchcraft and practice it. But as the following authors point out, Satanism stands in opposition to Christianity, whereas "modern" witchcraft is more of an alternative world-view religion like many others.
      "The basic distinction between witchcraft and Satanism lies in their relationship to Christianity. Modern neopagan witches do not consider themselves to be a Christian heresy or breakoff. Conversely, Satanist see themselves as in an alliance with Satan, either literally or symbolically (many Satanist are atheists). Witchcraft exists as an independent religion, much like other non-Christian religions. It stands as an alternative to the Christian faith, as do Hinduism and Buddhism. Yet Satanism could be described as a kind of inverted Christian sect. It draws on Christianity, but aims

to overthrow the Christian deity in favor of his adversary. Satanism stands in a polemical relationship to Christianity in both belief and ritual, using Christian elements but changing them and giving them different meanings."[12] —Richard Kyle

"Satanism should not be confused with witchcraft, though both are part of the occult. There is evidence that links the two in some instances. Witchcraft, however, can only be classified as Satanism insofar as the former understands itself as practicing its craft over and against the Judeo-Christian God. Many witchcraft groups are aligned with non-Christian, pre-Christian, or pagan deities. Satanism is distinguished from witchcraft in that it is dedicated to the antithesis of the God of the Christian Bible."[13] — Mather and Nichols

VI. WHAT IS THE HISTORY, BELIEF, AND PRACTICE OF WITCHCRAFT?

A. **History.** Witchcraft is sometimes called the "Old Religion". The ancient Biblical story of King Saul approaching the witch of Endor (1 Samuel 28) illustrates not only its antiquity but also its long-standing occultic world view. The word witchcraft is derived from the English word *wiccian* meaning "practice of magical arts." "In the past it has most often referred to the human harnessing of supernatural powers for the malevolent purpose of practicing black Magic. For this reason, 'witchcraft,' 'sorcery,' and 'magic' are very nearly synonymous."[14]

Since it predates Christianity, there is no basis for saying that it grew out of opposition to Christianity. However, during the medieval revival of witchcraft, one of the requirements of being a witch was worship of the devil.[15] This, along with the casting of magical spells and anti social behavior, helped produce widespread hysteria that reigned in European society for approximately 300 years. The "witch hunts" of those days, spawned out of an irrational fear, took the lives of hundreds of thousands of people (most of them innocent). People were accused of being witches or warlocks (male witches) and had no right to defend themselves in a court of law.

The witch hunts of Salem, Massachusetts, in 1692, claimed the lives of twenty-two others even though the clergy of those days "continually cried out for mercy to be extended to the many who were being accused." [16] However, within a few years, the mood of New England had changed and it was determined that much innocent blood had been shed. A public apology from the governing officials was issued, but a scar remained reminding us that irrational fear must be tamed with equitable standards of justice.

B. **Modern Witchcraft.** Today, witchcraft bears little resemblance to that of medieval times, especially the concept of an old hag in black, wearing pointed hats, brewing up spells in a cauldron, and flying on a broom. This is folklore and myth. In today's society, the craft is not limited to the illiterate or ignorant. Most witches are relatively well educated. There seems to be an appeal to white, middle class, women ranging in age from teens into their thirties. There are approximately twice as many women as men. Worldwide appraisals are hard to figure because of its secretive image, but a conservative estimate would be under 100,000.

The craft is coming out of the closet today, however, in the United States and is gaining acceptance. It is being popularized by movies such as *Practical Magic, The Craft,* and *The Blair Witch Project,* as well as T.V. shows like *Sabrina: The Teenage Witch* and *Charmed.* Sales are up on books such as *Teen Witch: Wicca For A New Generation* and *The Little Book of Hexes.* Today, in Salem, Massachusetts, and other cities witchcraft is openly celebrated. In 1999 even the Pentagon affirmed the right of military personnel to practice the religion on military bases.

The rise of modern witchcraft received its impetus from various people. However, a few stand out as the originators. Gerald Gardner (1884-1964) is considered the father of modern witchcraft. Gardner's life was influenced by extensive occultic involvement in Southeast Asia, Freemasonry in Ceylon, and Rosicrucianism in England. A couple of his books that spawned the movement were Magic's Aid (1949) and Witchcraft Today (1954). He popularized the concept that witches should worship the Mother Goddess. His books actually built upon the work of Margaret Murray (1863-1963). Her influential books and writings argued that witchcraft predated Christianity and was simply an ancient religion of nature worship. Another name of influence was the notorious magician and occultic guru, Aleister Crowley (1875-1947), who had a direct impact upon the work of Gardner. As with Satanism, modern witchcraft is sometimes done by individuals, but there is more of an emphasis with witchcraft to come together since it is taught that magic works better in groups.

C. **Beliefs.** Modern witchcraft is a conglomeration of influence from many sources thus making borders of belief hard to define. It would be a misnomer to try and categorize the belief system of all witches. Since the core of witchcraft has to do with one's own ability to create magical power to influence the world around, it follows that all other beliefs would normally revolve around this central ego and position themselves in various strata of importance or acceptance according to the individual. The following list of beliefs simply shows what many witches believe:

1) The most obvious characteristic of witchcraft is an appreciation and love for nature. It produces in witches almost a pure pantheistic world view that God exists in nature and in all of us. He is not transcendent to His creation.

2) The main deity of modern witchcraft is the Great Mother Goddess. Throughout the ages she has been represented as Artemis, Astarte, Aphrodite, Diana, Kore, Hecete, Isis, the Magna Mater, etc.

3) The main male deity in Wicca is known as Pan (the horned god), Adonis, Apollo, Baphomet, Cernunnos, Dionysius, Lucifer, Osiris, Thor, etc.

4) Beyond the above deities, witches often believe in a wide variety of others.

5) Wiccan groups firmly reject the teachings of the Bible. The concept of sin and the need for salvation is considered foolish and archaic to them. Since many of them do not believe in the God of the Bible, they also reject the Satan of the Bible. This, of course, is not true of all witches. Some witches combine their witchcraft with Satanism. Others, believe in God—only not in the way that Christians revere Him—and actually begin their magic liturgies by addressing their invocations to "God the Father, God the Son, and God the Holy Spirit."[17]

6) Witches are taught to have the ethics of Wiccan Rede, a principle that states, "That ye harm none, do what you will." This implies the notion of witches seeking to have harmony with the world, nature, and other people.

7) White witchcraft (white magic), they believe, is practiced in order to bring about "good", and black witchcraft (black magic) is conducted to bring harm. Even among witches, however, those who pursue doing evil towards others are shunned.

8) Among modern witches there is also a growing belief in reincarnation because of Gardner's teaching, although it differs from eastern religion in that witches simply believe that the soul returns to the earth instead of advancing or dropping backwards in its progression towards nirvana (state of bliss).

I once witnessed to a male witch (warlock) who considered

himself a "white" witch as compared to a "black" one. We spent perhaps an hour sharing world views. Of course, I kept trying to bring Jesus into the conversation. At one period in our talk, I asked him what the specific difference was between a white witch and a black one. This was his answer and does not necessarily represent that of all other white witches. He talked about the difference between white witches doing "good" and black ones putting evil spells on people. He didn't like that.

However, he made an interesting point regarding the Lordship of Jesus Christ. He told me that white witches knew that Jesus might possibly be the Lord and return someday; yet, they weren't banking on it. They figured He wasn't really coming back, and if He did return then they would fall down and repent gambling on His mercy. He then went on to tell me that black witches did not believe Jesus was truly Lord, but if He did return then they would fight Him.

What a joke! I could hardly believe my ears. What would they do - try to cast spells on God Almighty? Not a chance! I spent the remainder of the conversation trying to convince him that when Jesus does return - and He will return - there won't be time for repentance. It will be all over. Even thought they try to manipulate will power and demonic forces, they won't be able to control God's mercy.

D. **Practices.** The following are a list of some of their practices:
1) Covens - These are witch groups of approximately 13 members ruled by a high priest or priestess. The practices of covens vary greatly. Many have three degrees of initiation. First, one becomes a member. Second, one becomes a trainer. Third, one becomes a high priest or priestess. The majority of covens operate independently. However, some belong to major witchcraft groups. Many covens have achieved tax-exempt status.
2) Rituals and Festival Days - Their rituals have to do with worshipping nature. There is much sexual symbolism employed in the rituals to exemplify the female and male forces of nature. Sometimes the act of sex is performed in ritual ceremonies. Certain tools are used. The most important is the athame, a black-handled, double-edged dagger which is used to consecrate a circle of worship and invoke the gods. This symbolizes the male component of certain ceremonies while the shape of a cup of wine symbolizes the female.

Wiccans celebrate eight festival days known as sabbats

each year. Four are recognized as greater sabbats while the four seasonal changes are considered lesser sabbats. The eight are: 1) Imbolg—February 2; 2) Spring Equinox—March 21; 3) Beltane—April 30; 4) Midsummer Solstice—June 22; 5) Lugnasad—July 31; 6) Autumn Equinox—September 21; 7) Samhain—October 31; and 8) Winter Solstice—December 22.

The day most celebrated is Samhain known to us as Halloween. Samhain was the ancient Druid god of the dead. It is on this night that witches believe they have their greatest power as the spirits of the dead come forth to their homes to visit the living. At one time Halloween was called "All Hallows Eve" to honor the saints of church history. It was created to off-set the tradition of the Druids. However, the pagan celebration eventually corrupted the Christian celebration. Today, it is a secular holiday in which children dress up and go door-to-door requesting treats or they will pull a "trick" on the household. Other meeting times for covens are called esbats, and they vary from coven to coven.

3) Magic - This, of course, is the center of witchcraft. It is their craft. It overlaps and includes almost every form of occultic activity such as divination, spiritism, sorcery, spells, astral projection, clairvoyance, etc. As explained earlier, there is a different intention for white and black magic, *however neither of them honor the Lord Jesus Christ because they are based upon the individual's own will power, self exaltation, and manipulation of the spiritual and natural realm outside of the Lord's design.*

There are various forms of magic. Sympathetic magic is based upon things having resemblance or relationship with each other.[18] High magic sometimes deals with healing through natural medicines such as herbs and spells. A liturgy of magic (magic ceremony) will include the four elements: invocation, charm, symbolic action, and fetish. Other forms and methods of magic exist and can be quite devious depending upon the beliefs, character, and intentions of the witch.

E. **Witchcraft Praying:** Galatians 5:19-21 gives a list of the works of the flesh. One of those works of the flesh is "witchcraft" or "sorcery" depending on which translation you read. This type of praying enters into the sphere of manipulation and control. It centers on the individual's own will as compared to God's will. Jesus said to His Father in heaven, "...*if it is possible, let this cup pass from Me; nevertheless, not as I will but as You will*" (Matthew 26:39). This shows us that it is appropriate to ask permission for something; yet at the same time we should acknowledge the need for God's sovereign will to be done. He knows what's best for any given situation. In James 4:13-17, there is an exhortation along these lines. James refers to a man who says he is going to go to a city for a year and buy and sell and make profit. However, this man is wrong because he is doing it in his own will power without consideration for the will of God.

Christians need to be careful about praying manipulative or controlling prayers that try to force a response in the spiritual realm. All of our prayers should be submitted to the sovereign will of God. Although sometimes His will is obvious, there are many situations in which Christians need to listen to the leading of the Holy Spirit before launching out into prayer. For instance, prayers of salvation, deliverance, spiritual warfare, mercy, etc. are going to line up with Scripture. God wants all people to be saved, therefore He is already in agreement with those types of prayers.

However, what if someone asks you to pray that God will supernaturally bring the money for a certain debt that he owes but it is not God's will? You start to pray for it, but there is a check in your spirit. Maybe the Lord is dealing with that individual to get a job, but they are being lazy. If you persist in prayer - even against the check of the Holy Spirit - you have just prayed outside of His will for their life.

Author and speaker Cindy Jacobs is the president of Generals of Intercession and one of today's leaders in worldwide prayer. In her book *Possessing the Gates of the Enemy*, she talks about this subject. She warns Christians to always be open to the will of God or it can bring confusion into the camp:

"This is the basis of what witches do in their unholy intercession: They produce curses and false bindings on those for whom they pray. This is why witchcraft is listed as a work of the flesh in Galatians 5:20. These are actually psychic prayers out of our own human minds and not ones prayed from the mind of Christ. The psychics and witches sometimes call this mind control…When someone prays a prayer out of his own mind, will or emotion, he is releasing tremendous psychic (and many times demonic) forces to work against the one for whom he is praying. Proverbs 18:21 says: 'Death and life are in the power of the tongue…' Words are powerful. Consider the words of the Hebrew spies in the book of Numbers. The evil report given by the spies defiled the whole camp.

Our words spoken in prayer can work in much the same way; if the plan prayed for others is not God's will for their lives, they can find themselves confused...If you have been praying wrong prayers, repent and ask the Lord to remove the deception from your life. Ask God to show you any wrong praying you have done. Then, in the name of Jesus, release each one for whom you have prayed amiss and manipulated in prayer.

If you sense that you have had intercessors pray manipulative prayers over you, consider this: Are you experiencing confusion or heaviness for no known reason? If the problem is not physical or related to sin or strife, then pray in this manner: Father, in the name of Jesus, I now break the power of every work prayed for me that is contrary to Your will for my life. I thank You now that all bondage is broken from any manipulating prayers."[19]

VII. WHAT DOES THE BIBLE SAY ABOUT THE PUNITIVE ASPECTS?
  A. **Regarding Israel in the Old Testament:** In the days of Israel the laws of government were based upon a theocratic (God-ruled) system. Because of this, any forms of rebellion against God were treated much like treason is today. Therefore, the practice of witchcraft including sorcery, astrology, divination, spiritism, etc. was punishable by death.
  1) *"Thou shall not suffer a witch to live."* (Ex. 22:18) KJV
  2) *"A man or a woman who is a medium, or who has familiar spirits, shall surely be put to death; they shall stone them with stones. Their blood shall be upon them."* (Lev. 20:27)
  B. **Regarding Involvement Today:** There is no longer any theocratic governments on earth and so there are usually no legal penalties for such activities. However, the Word of God clearly forbids involvement in any of these activities:
  1) *"Do not turn to mediums or spiritists; do not seek them out to be defiled by them. I am the Lord your God."* (Lev. 19:31) NASB
  2) *"There shall not be found among you anyone who makes his son or daughter pass through the fire, one who uses divination, one who practices witchcraft, or one who interprets omens, or a sorcerer, or one who casts a spell, or a medium, or a spiritist, or one who calls up the dead...For those nations, which you shall dispossess, listen to those who practice witchcraft and to diviners, but as for you, the Lord your God has not allowed you to do so."* (Deut. 18:10-11,14) NASB
  3) *"Now the works of the flesh are evident, which are: adultery, fornication, uncleanness, lewdness, idolatry, sorcery, hatred, contentions,*

jealousies, outbursts of wrath, selfish ambitions, dissensions, here-sies, envy, murders, drunkenness, revelries, and the like; of which I tell you beforehand, just as I also told you in time past, that those who practice such things will not inherit the kingdom of God." (Gal. 5:19-21)

VIII. WHAT ARE SOME THINGS FOR PARENTS TO CONSIDER?
  A. **Signs of a troubled teen:** The following is not an exhaustive list but is included to help parents understand some of the indications of problems. Proverbs 20:11 says, *"Even a child is known by his deeds, whether what he does is pure and right."*
      1) A loss of a sense of humor.
      2) Avoidance of family members.
      3) Change in sleeping habits.
      4) Loss of touch with reality.
      5) Increase in fear or anxiety.
      6) Seem uncommunicative or aloof.
      7) Preoccupation with death and suicide.
      8) The possession of ritualistic items for witchcraft, Satanism, or other pagan religions.
  B. **Responsibility:** Parents must realize the positive impact that they can have upon their children. This is not to ignore the fact that some children have more difficult temperaments than others. Yet, parents are to do their best by seizing the opportunity in a timely manner.
      1) Proverbs 22:6 *"Train up a child in the way he should go, and when he is old he will not depart from it."*
      2) Ephesians 6:4 *"And you, fathers, do not provoke your children to wrath, but bring them up in the training and admonition of the Lord."*
  C. **Prevention from joining cults:** Here are some ideas for parents who see signs of trouble in their teens and are taking responsibility to help them.
      1) Communication: I have found that parents can unknowingly loose contact when their kids reach ages 10 to 13. Stay in touch, talk daily, and be a friend and confidant.
      2) Prayer: Lift your children up to the Lord every day. He hears your prayers.
      3) Resources: Get Christian books on cults and read them together.
      4) Security: Help them build their assurance in Christ.

5) Love: A child needs to know the "unconditional" love of the parents. Acceptance should not be based on performance but on family membership.

6) Restrictions: Discipline should be age appropriate and balanced with affection.

7) Humility: Teens see through parents who say one thing but live another way. Be real with your children about your own struggles as a youth, and your need for a Savior.

IX.   HOW CAN WE HELP PEOPLE IN THE OCCULT?

A. **Prayer:** In the last two chapters, we have seen that there are many levels of occult activity and some are so secretive that the average Christian may never have the opportunity to share with them about Jesus. For instance, while it may be possible to witness to someone drawn into a UFO cult, Spiristism or Theosophy, the chances of knowing that someone is active in a witch coven is minimal. But through prayer, every Christian can help pull down the strongholds (2 Corinthians 10:4) and do spiritual warfare against the demonic forces that hold these people in darkness (Ephesians 6:10-18).

There may be times when a Christian is called to help cast out a demon. In this case, a Christian needs to be strong in the Lord. Jesus tells us in Matthew 17:21 that it is sometimes necessary to pray and fast in order to accomplish this. We can also learn from Acts 19:13-16 that exorcists (those casting out demons) had better have a personal relationship with Jesus Christ before attempting to free the person from a demon. In this story, seven Jewish men, who had no saving relationship with the Lord Jesus Christ, were using His name to cast out a demon because they saw that Christians were able to do it. The demon jumped on them and beat them severely.

In regard to rebuking the devil or demons, Christians need to understand their authority in Christ. God has given us authority over the devil and his workers, not because of how strong we are, but because we belong to God. The Spirit of God within us is greater than any demonic power that exists in the universe. However, this is not based upon some superior physical, mental, or spiritual strength that we as humans possess; rather, it is solely because of whose we are, that being the Lord's children. In two places, Old and New Testament, the Bible tells us to use the words, *"The Lord rebuke you"* when dealing with the devil. The verse in

Jude 9 shows that this is the way Michael the archangel dealt with the devil, and in Zech. 3:2 the Lord Himself shows us that this is the proper method.

Our authority is in the name of the Lord Jesus Christ Himself. Our part is to have a humble attitude knowing that in and of ourselves we do not have the ability to win such a match, but through the supremacy of the name of the Lord, we can defeat our opponent. Nor are we to have a cocky attitude about this authority. We are to understand who gives us the authority and represent Him accordingly. The following story of the authority of a police officer is a good illustration of how a Christian's badge of power works over the enemies:

"Out in the center of the intersection was a platform, on which stood a uniformed policeman. About 20 of us waited at the corner to cross. All of a sudden, he blew his whistle and put out his hand. As he lifted his hand, all those cars came to a screeching halt. With all of his personal power he couldn't have stopped one of those cars, but he had something far better; he was invested with the authority of the police department. And the moving cars and the pedestrians recognized that authority."[20]

B. **Love:** Christians should not fear those who are caught up in occultism. We have access to a love from God that has power over fear. We must also remember that God loves the sinner but hates the sin. Those snared by the occult need to be saved, and Jesus is the only way for salvation. There is authority in love to overcome fear. Agape love has authority to pierce the hardest heart. Remember that the Bible teaches that *"God is Love"* (1 John 4:16).

There are tremendous testimonies of how the love of Christians have softened the hardest and most wicked of hearts. Many have been saved from the occult by Christians showing love or telling about the love of Jesus. The Bible says: *"Keep yourselves in God's love as you wait for the mercy of our Lord Jesus Christ to bring you to eternal life. Be merciful to those who doubt; snatch others from the fire and save them; to others show mercy, mixed with fear—hating even the clothing stained by corrupted flesh."* (Jude 21-23) NIV

C. **Witness:** There is power in the Word of God. Someone took time to share Jesus with me when I was caught up in occult thinking. Tad, a fellow employee, told me - at a critical moment in my life - that *"Jesus is the Light of the World."* He made me read those words from the Bible. Even though I was lost and spaced out, he wouldn't leave me alone. The Lord used him to plant a seed. God knew that it would take someone bold in my case, so he had his servant speak those words to me over and over again. Every day at lunch, he made me say those words aloud. I was so crazy that I almost never spoke at that time in my life. This man even shouted those words to me from across the warehouse where we worked in Reno, Nevada. In front of others, he yelled, "I'm telling you, Stan, that Jesus is the Light of the World."

I could not remain working there very long, but those words stuck. Several weeks later, as I was astral projecting on my bed trying to escape from the madness of life, I remembered those words. My mind was crazy, demented, and full of demonic strongholds, but I remembered those words. I cried out, "If there is a God in heaven, please come and save this man because I'm going over the edge." God heard that prayer and led me to the answers for which my soul longed. He led me, by His Light, to the truth that set me free. He healed my mind of great paranoia and deception.

Never underestimate the power of the Word of God in the life of one caught in cults and the occult. God can free someone from the deepest deception and darkest place.

End Notes

1. Michael W. Andress, "An Experience with Demon Possession: A Case Study," vol. 2 of *Philippine Journal of Religious Studies: The Demonic, Evil and Suffering* (Baguio City, Philippines: Philippine Baptist Theological Seminary, 1996), pgs. 8-9.
2. C. S. Lewis, *The Screwtape Letters* (New York: MacMillian Company, 1961), preface.
3. George A. Mather and Larry A. Nichols, *Dictionary of Cults, Sects, Religions and the Occult* (Grand Rapids, MI: Zondervan Publishing Company, 1993), p.89.
4. Josh McDowell and Don Stewart, *Understanding the Occult* (San Bernadino, CA: Here's Life Publishers, 1982), pgs. 47-49.
5. Bob Larson, *Larson's Book of Cults* (Wheaton, IL: Tyndale House Publishers, Inc., 1988), p. 307.
6. Richard Kyle, *The Religious Fringe: A History of Alternative Religions in America* (Downers Grove, IL: Inter Varsity Press, 1993), p. 277.
7. Ibid., p. 278.
8. Mauricio Zagari, "Pop Satanist Known as 'Devil's Pope' Attracts Huge Following in Brazil," *Charisma and Christian Life*, January 2000, pgs. 26-27.
9. McDowell and Stewart, p. 141.
10. Doug Sheaffer, "Christian Spiritualism," a message on audio tape, (Illwaco Community Church: Illwaco, WA) September 12, 1987.
11. David Alexander, "Giving the Devil More Than His Due, The Humanist" March/April, 1990), p. 6, as cited by George A. Mather and Larry A. Nichols, *Dictionary of Cults, Sects, Religions and the Occult* (Grand Rapids, MI: Zondervan Publishing House, 1993), pgs. 246-247.

12. Kyle, p. 276.
13. George A. Mather and Larry A. Nichols, *Dictionary of Cults, Sects, Religions and the Occult* (Grand Rapids, MI: Zondervan Publishing Company, 1993), p. 241.
14. Ibid., p. 312.
15. McDowell and Stewart, p. 173.
16. Mather and Nichols, p. 314.
17. McDowell and Stewart, p. 91.
18. Ibid., p. 91.
19. Cindy Jacobs, *Possessing the Gates of the Enemy: A Training Manual For Militant Intercession* (Grand Rapids, MI: Chosen Books, 1995), pgs. 137-139.
20. Josh McDowell, *A Ready Defense* (Nashville, TN: Thomas Nelson Publishers, 1993),p. 396.

QUESTIONNAIRE: LESSON FOURTEEN

NAME: _____ DATE: _____

1. There are two snares that Christians need to avoid. One is the snare of _____ and the other the snare of _____.

2. Have you ever experienced demonic activity in your own life or someone else's? Please explain. _____

_____

_____

_____

3. Write out five things you learned or found interesting regarding what the Bible teaches about demons.

a. _____

b. _____

c. _____

d. _____

e. _____

4. Who did God create hell for? _____

_____

5. Briefly tell about Aleister Crowley and how he influenced modern Satanism. _____

_____

_____

_____

6. List the four basic types of Satanism:

a. _____

b. _____

c. _____

d. _____

7. Who started the Satanic Church and wrote the Satanic Bible?_____

8. The purpose of Satanism is to acquire _____, and one does this by openly admitting and accepting one's passions.

9. According to Rev. 12:10-11 we will overcome the devil by what two things:

a. _____

b. _____

10. For what two reasons are Satanism and witchcraft normally lumped together, even though they are very distinct occultic groups?

a. _____

b. _____

11. The basic distinction between witchcraft and Satanism lies in their relationship to _____. Witchcraft exists as an _____, much like other non-Christian religions. It stands as an alternative to the Christian faith, as do Hinduism and Buddhism. Yet _____ can be described as a kind of inverted Christian sect. It draws on Christianity, but aims to overthrow the Christian deity.

12. Who is considered the father of modern witchcraft? _____

13. Who do most witches consider the main deity to be? _____

14. Witches are taught to have the ethics of _____ a principle that states, _____

15. What is the center of witchcraft? What is their craft? _____

16. Write out Leviticus 19:31 _____

_____

17. What is witchcraft prayer and why is it wrong? _____

_____

18. How can we help these peope? _____

_____

19. Consider your knowledge of the occult before and after these lessons. Circle the number below that indicates how equipped you felt before taking this course to witness to someone in the occult as compared to how equipped you feel now. Be honest.

BEFORE 0 1 2 3 4 5 6 7 8 9 10 AFTER 0 1 2 3 4 5 6 7 8 9 10

ROMAN CATHOLICISM

"*I was born and raised Roman Catholic, attending parochial schools and a Benedictine monastery in high school. I was thoroughly catechized in Roman Catholic theology. I was an altar boy in the days when the Latin Mass was still used. I used to pray earnestly for souls in purgatory and was thoroughly devoted to Mary. But as a teen I followed in the path of many young people in turning from the church to a life of sin and rebellion. By the time I was nineteen years old I was a disillusioned alcoholic. At twenty-four, through the witness of evangelical Protestants, I was converted to Jesus Christ. I joined a Protestant church, not because of an anti-Catholic attitude, but because it was through this church I had come to know Christ, and now I had a deep desire to know more of God's Word. I was completely ignorant of major differences between Roman Catholicism and Protestantism. Over a number of years, exposure to God's Word deepened my understanding of salvation and fueled a desire to share it with others, particularly Roman Catholic friends.*"[1]

—William Webster

Note: Many Catholics are Christians who love and follow Jesus as Lord. This is not written to cause them grief, but to teach Christians about the system of Romanism which has added a standard of works to the Gospel for salvation. This was never intended by our Lord. I hope Christian Catholics understand my motives by including Catholicism in this study. I pray for them to be a light from within.

I. WHAT IS THE SIZE AND INFLUENCE OF THE ROMAN CATHOLIC
    CHURCH?
    A. Approximately 620 million world wide and 50 million in the U.S.
        Many countries worldwide are dominated by Catholic influence
        and thought.
    B. The Pope and Vatican at Rome are so strong that nations send
        ambassadors to them.
    C. Catholic schools, hospitals, orphanages, and other community
        centers are spread around the world in major cities.
    D. Catholic thought has influenced centuries of art: music, painting,
        sculpture, architecture.
    E. The Church stands strong on certain moral issues such as the sanc-
        tity of human life, marriage, no birth control, traditional family val-
        ues, etc.

II. WHAT ARE THE SIMILARITIES BETWEEN CATHOLICS AND
    PROTESTANTS?
    A. We all believe in the truth and spirit of the ancient *Apostle's Creed:*
            I believe in God the Father Almighty, Maker of heaven and
        earth; and in Jesus Christ His only Son, our Lord, who was con-
        ceived by the Holy Spirit, born of the virgin Mary, suffered under
        Pontius Pilate, was crucified, dead, and buried; He descended into
        hell; the third day He rose from the dead; He ascended into heaven,
        and sitteth on the right hand of God the Father Almighty; from
        thence He shall come to judge the living and the dead. I believe in
        the Holy Spirit; the holy catholic Church, the communion of
        saints; the forgiveness of sins; the resurrection of the body; and the
        life everlasting. Amen. (Note: "catholic" here means "universal")
    B. Protestants and Catholics sometimes sing the same songs, pray the
        same prayers, teach the same Bible passages, and fight the same
        secular humanistic giants.
    C. There are certain essential doctrines that we both hold sacred. Ron
        Carlson and Ed Decker point some of these out in their book *Fast
        Facts on False Teachings:*
            "Let us assure you that it is not with all the essential, basic
        issues of theology that we disagree, because Catholics do affirm
        some of the central doctrines of Christianity. Catholics affirm belief
        in the Trinity, the deity of Jesus Christ, the Virgin Birth, the sinless-
        ness of Christ, and the atonement of the cross. Rather, what disturbs
        us is what Catholics have added to Scripture over the years, so that
        many Catholics can no longer see the teachings of God's Word in
        their faith. What they see instead are the ritual and tradition that

have been piled on top of God's Word over hundreds of years by the Catholic Church."[2]

III. WHAT IS A BRIEF HISTORY OF THE EARLY CHURCH AND THE REFORMATION?

Christianity spread rapidly throughout the first few centuries after Christ gave the great commission to spread the Good News. Groups of Christians gathered together in homes or other meeting places to worship God, learn from His Word, and have fellowship. The church at Rome grew quickly from the beginning because it was an important economic and political center. Even during the Apostle Paul's time, he noted that the faith of the Christians at Rome was *"being reported all over the world"* (Rom. 1:8). "Before the end of the second century the church at Rome held a distinctive place in the Christian world."[3] (All dates A.D.)

A. 313: Emperor Constantine promotes Christianity after his conversion.
B. 395: Christianity becomes the only official state religion.
C   440: (circa) Leo, bishop of Rome becomes the earthly authority of the Church.[4]
D. 1054: Eastern Church rejects Pope Leo IX as authority and split begins.
E. 1350: (circa) Eastern Orthodox and Western Church clearly distinct.
F. 1517: Reformation divides Protestants from the Pope and the Church at Rome.
G. 1563: Council of Trent confirms Catholic traditionalism and Papal authority. Split deepens. The names Catholic and Protestant become attached.

When Martin Luther protested against the Church of Rome in 1517 by nailing 95 points of disagreement to the door of a church in Wittenberg, Germany, it only indicated a long and growing frustration by many Christians with Rome's teachings on the Church, the Scriptures, and tradition. The points he raised in disagreement have become the watershed issues dividing Romanism (Catholics) from Protestantism.

Today, Protestantism is a loose term for many Christian denominations / churches with distinct teachings of their own. However, there are certain elements of doctrine and belief within Protestantism as a whole that aligns it much closer to the teachings of Scripture and original Christianity than Romanism does. It is to Biblical Christianity that all believers of the Lord Jesus Christ should strive, regardless of denomination, sect, affiliation, church, etc. As Cornelius Van Til points out, it is not that Protestantism as a whole has it all together and Romanism (Catholicism) doesn't. Rather, it is simply that Protestantism is closer to *true historical Christianity*:

"It is Romanism with which we are now primarily concerned. *Romanism should be regarded as a deformation of Christianity*, in fact as its lowest deformation. And this deformation expresses itself not merely at some but at every point of doctrine. The differences between Protestantism and Romanism are not adequately indicated if we say that Luther restored to the church the true doctrines of the Bible, of justification by faith and of the priesthood of all believers. The difference is rather that Protestantism is more consistently and Rome is less consistently Christian at every point of doctrine. It could not be otherwise. Having inconsistency at one point of doctrine is bound to result in inconsistency at all points of doctrine. Rome has been consistently inconsistent in the confusion of non-Christian with Christian elements of teaching along the entire gamut of doctrinal expression."[5] (italics added)

Thinking Through The Scripture

"Now then, my sons, listen to me; blessed are those who keep my ways. Listen to my instruction and be wise; do not ignore it. Blessed is the man who listens to me, watching daily at my doors, waiting at my doorway. For whoever finds me finds life and receives favor from the Lord. But whoever fails to find me harms himself; all who hate me love death." (Proverbs 8:32-36) NIV

"He who listens to a life-giving rebuke will be at home among the wise. He who ignores discipline despises himself, but whoever heeds correction gains understanding." (Proverbs 15:31-32) NIV

Questions for discussion:
1. In the passage from Proverbs 8, Wisdom is portrayed as a type of the Lord who is giving advice. What is it? What happens when someone fails to keep the correct way? Can an entire church movement fail to keep God's way?
2. What is a "life-giving rebuke?" In what way can it be a positive thing? How should we respond if the Lord gives us a life-giving rebuke?
3. If Catholicism had listened to the life-giving rebuke that came to it in 1517, how do you think it would have changed history?
4. Since we know that God does not approve of a rebellious spirit, what is the most appropriate way for a Christian to "protest" a just cause?
5. How does God's favor relate to following His wisdom and ways?

IV. WHAT ARE THREE CRITICAL AREAS IN WHICH CATHOLICISM STRAYS FROM THE TRUTH?

  A. Their view of the Bible — Authority of Tradition equals the Scriptures

  B. Their view of the Pope — Papal Position and Infallibility

  C. Their view of Faith and Works — Salvation is a process of works

V. HOW IS CATHOLICISM STRAYING FROM TRUTH ON THE VIEW OF THE BIBLE?

  A. **Catholicism equates Tradition with the Bible.** This they have done for hundreds of years. They see the Bible as developing from the Church[6] and thus place the directives of the church (at times) in a higher authority. *This is quite serious as it undermines the Bible and what it teaches.* The contemporary situation may even be more critical than before because there seems to be a subtle underlying shift occurring which downgrades their view of both Scripture and Tradition.[7] Although, not true of all Catholics, the following diagram reflects some current thought.

Old Roman Catholic View of Scripture & Tradition	Both equally Divine as revealed from the hand of God	Both Authoritative
New Roman Catholic View of Scripture & Tradition	Both equally as revealed only by the hand of man	Both are more of a Guide

  B. **Historical Christianity places the Bible, the Logos, as supreme in authority**, but this is not so with Catholicism. Christians take comfort in the fact that the Bible is given to us as the inspired and inerrant Word of God. When we read it, we know that the Lord can speak to us out of it and that it has ultimate authority because the Lord would not violate the content or principles of His Word. Indeed, the first verse of the book of John represents God as the "Word" Himself. We know that any teaching, tradition, doctrine, etc. that contradicts or opposes what is explained in the Bible is not from God. Catholicism places the authority of tradition as equal to the Word of God. However, "*It is altogether an extraordinary piece of audacity to place anything on a par with the majesty and authority of the canonical Scripture.*"[8]

1) *Paul admonished the churches* regarding traditions when he said,
   "Be careful not to let anyone rob you of this faith, through a shal-
   low and misleading philosophy. Such a person follows human tra-
   ditions and the world's way of doing things rather than following
   Christ." (Col. 2:8) GW

2) *Jesus reproved the Pharisees* regarding traditions in this: *"And He*
   said to them, 'Rightly did Isaiah prophesy of you hypocrites, as it
   is written, This people honors Me with their lips, but their heart is
   far away from Me. But in vain do they worship Me, teaching as
   doctrines the precepts of men. Neglecting the commandment of
   God, you hold to the tradition of men.' He was also saying to them,
   'You nicely set aside the commandment of God in order to keep
   your tradition...thus invalidating the word of God by your tradi-
   tion which you have handed down; and you do many things such
   as that'." (Mark 7:6-9, 13) NASB

VI. HOW IS CATHOLICISM STRAYING FROM TRUTH ON THE VIEW
OF THE POPE?

A. **Papal Infallibility**. On November 21, 1964, Pope Paul VI proclaimed "the title of Mary as Mother of the Church".[9] To non-
Catholics this proclamation seems preposterous since the Bible
says nothing about Mary being the Mother of the Church. But the
mind of a devout Catholic would willingly accept this because it
was spoken by the Pope, who according to Catholic tradition is
the Apostle Peter's successor and speaks with infallibility regarding doctrines of faith and morals. To Catholics, the Pope is "the
Vicar of Christ and the visible Head of the whole Church."[10]

This is scary stuff for Christians because we know that the
Pope is just a man and makes mistakes - at times - in what he
thinks and says. In October of 1996, John Paul II issued a document known as a "papal bull" which clearly shows an error in his
thinking. In order to bridge the gap between Catholic teaching
and modern science, he wrote a document to the Vatican's
Pontifical Academy of Sciences stating, "Fresh knowledge leads to
recognition of the theory of evolution as more than just a hypothesis."[11] This courting of evolutionists might gain the Pope some
"brownie points" with secular scientists, but it sadly illustrates the
drift of the Vatican from the truth of God's Word.

Of course, there has been some rebuttal from within of the
Pope's infallibility over the years, but it has, to this point, been
much less than sufficient to make any real difference. While the
Council of Vatican II (1962 - 1965) sought to modify the doctrine

of Papal Infallibility by stating that the college of bishops assists the Pope, it is only a slight change and does not really alter his final decisions, as the following Vatican II document states:

"This is the infallibility which the Roman Pontiff, the head of the college of bishops, enjoys in virtue of his office, when, as the supreme shepherd and teacher of all the faithful, who confirms his brethren in their faith (cf. Lk. 22:32), he proclaims by a definitive act some doctrine of faith or morals. Therefore his definitions, of themselves, and not from the consent of the Church, are justly styled irreformable, for they are pronounced with the assistance of the Holy Spirit, an assistance promised to him in blessed Peter. Therefore they need no approval of others, nor do they allow an appeal to any other judgment."[12]

B. **The Pope as Peter**. The Bible shows a number of facts that refute Catholicism's claims of the Pope and Peter concept. Here are a few to consider:

1) Neither the word "pope" nor the office of it are mentioned in the Bible.

2) It's not clear that Peter was ever even in Rome. Paul did not mention it.

3) Jesus changing Peter's name proves nothing because he changed the names of others as well. (Mark 3:16-17; 1 Jn. 1:42)

4) Paul's work seems greater than Peter's in comparison, but he never sought ultimate leadership. Neither do we see him submitting himself to Peter. Once, he even rebuked him. (Gal. 2:11-14)

Thinking Through The Scripture

"He said to them, 'But who do you say that I am?' Simon Peter answered and said, 'You are the Christ, the Son of the living God.' Jesus answered and said to him, 'Blessed are you, Simon Bar-Jonah, for flesh and blood has not revealed this to you, but My Father who is in heaven. And I also say to you that you are Peter, and on this rock I will build My church, and the gates of Hades shall not prevail against it" (Matthew 16:15-18)

Questions for discussion:

1. What was the revelation that Simon Peter received about Jesus? Who revealed it to him? Who reveals this truth to the heart of people today?

2. What is the "rock" upon which Jesus will build His church? Is it the man Peter or is it the revelation of who Jesus is in the life of the believer?

3. The name Peter comes from the Greek *Petros and* means "a piece of a rock." The word rock comes from a similar Greek word *petra* but means "a mass of rock." Would a church be built upon a piece of rock (a pebble) or a mass of rock? Since the Catholic church was built on the succession of leaders (The Popes) representing Peter, what does this show us about their interpretation of this passage of Scripture? What was their error?

---

    5) James, the Lord's brother (Gal. 1:19) appears to be the head of the early church in Jerusalem, not Peter. Consider the following evidence of this:

        a. James was named first among the pillars of the church in Gal. 2:9.
            " James, Peter, and John, those reputed to be pillars...." NIV

        b. Peter distinguished the name of James in Acts 12:17 after he was miraculously released from prison by the angel.
            "Go, tell these things to James and the brethren."

        c. At the great Jerusalem Debate over circumcision, Barnabas, Paul, and Peter submitted to James' decision. In Acts 15:19 we see James running the meeting and deciding.
            "Wherefore my sentence is, that we trouble not them, which from among the Gentiles are turned to God." KJV

        d. Flavius Josephus (c. 93 A.D.) is considered one of the most reliable Jewish historians of all times. He was born in 37 A.D. It is remarkable that he highly regards James for his righteousness. Indeed, he speculated that the "desolation of Jerusalem" was because the Jews murdered James, but nowhere does he even mention Peter.[13]

C. **Martin Luther became convinced that the office of Pope was unscriptural.** As he stood before the Catholic council who was determined to excommunicate him for opposing the Pope and the Traditions, he boldly said,

    "I believe in neither pope nor councils alone; for it is perfectly well established that they have frequently erred, as well as contradicted themselves. Unless then I shall be convinced by the testimony of the Scriptures or by clear reason, I must be bound by *those Scriptures which have been brought forward by me*; yes, my conscience has been taken captive by these words of God. I cannot revoke anything, nor do I wish to; since to go against one's conscience is neither safe nor right: here I stand, I cannot do otherwise. God help me. Amen."[14] [italics added]

VII. HOW IS CATHOLICISM STRAYING FROM TRUTH ON THE VIEW
      OF FAITH AND WORKS ?
   A. **Some important definitions**.
      1) Justification - The act by which we are declared righteous
          through faith alone, by grace alone, in Christ alone.[15] Authors
          John Ankerberg and John Weldon give the definitions for jus-
          tification and sanctification in their book, *Protestants &
          Catholics: Do They Now Agree?*

          "Biblically, to be justified means a sinner is pardoned or
          declared legally acquitted by God from any and all punishment
          due him because of the sins he has committed."[16]
          Scripture References: Rom. 3:20-26; Titus 3:5-7; 1 Jn. 5:13;
          Rom. 5:9.
      2) Sanctification - The process by which we are made righteous
          through faith and the works of love.[17]

          "Basically there are three aspects of sanctification: one past
          (when God pronounced us justified and also sanctified us—
          that is, He set us apart to begin serving Him), one present
          ("referring to the continuing work of the Holy Spirit in the
          moment by moment life of the believer making him or her
          actually holy), and one future (after death, in heaven when
          God will complete our total sanctification)."[18]
          Scripture References: Heb. 10:10; Rom. 6:13-16; Titus 2:14; 1
          Thess. 2:12; 2 Cor. 3:18; Eph. 4:11-16; Phil. 3:21; Rom. 8:30.

Thinking Through The Scripture

*"What then shall we say that Abraham our father has found according to
the flesh? For if Abraham was justified by works, he has something to boast
about, but not before God. For what does the Scripture say? 'Abraham believed
God, and it was accounted to him for righteousness.' Now to him who works,
the wages are not counted as grace but as debt. But to him who does not work
but believes on Him who justifies the ungodly, his faith is accounted for righteousness...."* (Romans 4:1-5)

Questions for discussion:
1. What is being promoted in this passage, works or faith?
2. What made Abraham righteous before God? What justified him?
3. If works are not counted as "grace" then what does this mean for
    Catholics who are seeking salvation only through a works type of
    method?
4. How is it that some works are examples of those seeking grace while
    other works can be examples of those showing gratitude?

B. **The Revelation of Martin Luther**. One of the main Scriptures that Martin Luther brought forward to the attention of the world was *Romans 1:17 "The just shall live by faith"*. This verse opened the door to the revelation that justification for our righteousness before Almighty God had to do with faith and not works. As he searched the Scriptures, he found that this revelation was well founded throughout the Bible. Justification was not a process but a-once-and-for-all-time act. This greatly disturbed him because Catholicism was heavily indoctrinated with a work-for-salvation tradition based upon the sacraments of the church. *Catholicism teaches a justification that includes works of merit for salvation.*

C. **The Problem of the Catholic "anathemas" at the Council of Trent (1545- 1563)**. The reaction of Rome to the Protestant Reformation was severe to the point that they created statements called Canons to state their position against any who did not hold their view. The word anathema which literally means "let them be damned" or *"let them be eternally condemned" is pronounced against any who don't hold their view on many doctrines, including justification.* An example is Canon 9. As you read it, remember that this is still a part of their official statement of modern Catholicism.

"Canon 9. If anyone says that the sinner is justified by faith alone…, meaning that nothing else is required to cooperate in order to obtain the grace of justification, and that it is not in any way necessary that he be prepared and disposed by the action of his own will, let him be anathema."[19]

Thinking Through The Scripture

"I am amazed that you are so quickly deserting Him who called you by the grace of Christ, for a different gospel; which is really not another; only there are some who are disturbing you, and want to distort the gospel of Christ. But even though we, or an angel from heaven, should preach to you a gospel contrary to that which we have preached to you, let him be accursed. As we have said before, so I say again now, if any man is preaching to you a gospel contrary to that which you received, let him be accursed." (Galatians 1:6-9) NASB

Questions for discussion:
1. The Apostle Paul reprimanded the Galatian church for a "works" gospel. By what does the Apostle say they were called? What does "grace" mean? What are they doing to Him who gave this grace? Who is the "Him?"
2. Consider the words "different, distort, and contrary" in this passage. What main word (noun) are they each relating to? What is the author trying to get across?

3. The *anathemas* of the Catholic Church make strong statements against those who rely on "faith alone," but what does the Bible say about those who preach a gospel other than grace? How does this apply to Catholicism?

VIII.   WHAT ARE THE PROBLEMS WITH THE SEVEN SACRAMENTS?
  A.   Through their sacraments, Catholics are - in effect - working their way to heaven. However, even with these works they think they will have to spend time in purgatory before entering heaven. They teach that "grace" is given through the sacraments. "What Catholicism offers its one billion members is, in effect, a priestly or a 'sacerdotal' religion. In such a system, salvation is mediated through the functions of the priesthood (in this case through the Catholic Sacraments). Only Catholic priests and those above them can perform the sacraments."[20] The seven sacraments are as follows:
    1) *Baptism* - cleansed of original sin, infused with sanctifying grace, and receives the gifts of faith, hope, and love as well as the gifts of the Holy Spirit. Infant baptism is common in Catholicism but not at all supported by Scripture.
        Refutation: Baptism is scriptural (Acts 2:38), of course, and should be done by all believers, but infant baptism is not, since an infant is too young to repent. Peter's words put "repentance" prior to "baptism."
    2) *Confirmation* - Theologically, Catholicism uses Acts 2:37-38; 8:17; and 19:1-7 to show the need for bestowing the Holy Spirit in a special sense after water baptism. However, their rite really centers upon "a person profess[ing] at the beginning of adolescence the religion in which he has been reared from infancy. Thus in Roman Catholicism the Catholic does for himself what was done in his behalf by others at his baptism."[21]
        Refutation: While the Scriptures mentioned can be used to demonstrate that a greater measure of the Holy Spirit (baptism) is available to the believer, this is not the thrust of the ceremony in Catholicism.
    3) *Holy Eucharist* - This is celebrated at the *Catholic Mass* and is considered the most important sacrament. To the average Christian, the ceremony would convey the idea of simple communion, hence remembering what Christ did for us on the cross and giving Him thanks. But that is a misnomer. In Roman Catholicism, the Mass is an important vehicle through which "the blessings of Christ's death are applied to believers.

Therefore, the blessings of Christ's death are not produced
solely by faith alone in what He accomplished at the cross...In
the Catholic Mass...we find *Rome's doctrine of transubstantia-
tion*. This view details that the bread and wine each literally
become the body and blood of our Lord Jesus
Christ...Furthermore, because Christ is actually present in His
entirety in the Eucharist, the Catholic Church believes that the
Eucharist should be worshiped. This is why priests and
Catholics genuflect [bow] when the host is present—because it
is really Christ present." [italics added][22] A final point to understand is that Catholics believe that "the Eucharistic sacrifice is
also offered for the faithful departed [in purgatory] who 'have
died in Christ but are not yet wholly purified,' so that they may
be able to enter into the light and peace of Christ."[23]

Refutation: The verses of Hebrews 9:12,26,28 and
10:12,14 all show us that the atoning sacrifice of Jesus Christ
was a one time event and not a continual process. To believe
that he is sacrificing Himself over and over again in a literal
sense is well beyond any scriptural reasoning. 1 Cor. 11:23-32
shows us the proper attitude for communion and the Bible says
nothing about purgatory. Communion at the Lord's supper
should be a part of a Christian's life but for the right reasons,
and not mixed with the traditions of men.

4) *Penance* - This is popularly called "confession." However, that
is only one aspect of it. "Catholicism teaches the sacrament of
penance has three parts: first, 'contrition'—a person must be
sorry for his sins; second, 'confession'—a person must fully
confess each one of his mortal sins to a priest; and third, 'satisfaction'—a person must do works of satisfaction such as fasting, saying prayers, almsgiving, or doing other works of piety
the priest gives him to do."[24]

The tradition of a confessional is understood by most people. The priest sits in a dark booth and listens to the confes-
sions of a sinner located in an adjoining booth. They speak in
whispers through a grill, a small window-like structure
obscured by curtains or a wooden or metal grate. The priest is
not suppose to know who he is talking to, although repeated
visits can make it obvious.[25] It is in John 20:23 that
Catholicism finds a basis for confession, when Jesus gives
authority to his disciples to forgive or retain someone's sins.

Catholicim sees sin in two forms, mortal and venial. Mortal
sins are not always clearly defined but include such things as

sexual immorality, murder, envy, abortion, artificial birth control, and thievery.[26] These are very serious and remove salvation and justification immediately. If someone dies in mortal sin (no confession and forgiveness), they go straight to hell. Venial sins are also mortal sins, but are not as serious. Whereas mortal sins separate one from God, venial sins do not; but they make the relationship imperfect. A sinner must do penance for a mortal sin before he or she is reinstated into God's grace and can participate in Mass and the Holy Eucharist. Catholic obligation to annual communion (Holy Eucharist) normally brings them to the confessionals at least once a year.

Refutation: While it is very good to "confess our sins to one another" (Jas. 5:16), Catholicism has made a ritual and tradition that the Scriptures never intended. Jesus Christ is our high priest (Heb. 8:1-2) and our mediator (1 Tim. 2:5) between God and man. He has called each of us to be priests (1 Pet. 2:5,9). He forgave us all of our sins (Col. 2:13) and is not impressed with our "desire or effort" to work for it (Rom. 9:12,16). While Catholicism's desire to raise a standard for morality can be commended, its assumption that it can determine the eternal state of someone's soul is quite out of character with Scripture.

5) *Extreme Unction* - This is also referred to as "anointing the sick" or "the last rites." This is based upon James 5:14-16. The priest is requested to come and minister to those on their deathbed. This is only done when the condition is serious enough that death appears imminent. Sometimes the person is unconscious or unable to respond to the priest or bishop. If a person is in mortal sin but can no longer receive the Sacrament of Penance because of his or her critical condition, then the Sacrament of Extreme Unction eradicates the grievous sin,[27] thus renewing their justification before God.

Refutation: There is nothing wrong with the elders praying for the sick and anointing them with oil. However, this goes far beyond Scripture, once again, in that it becomes a means of working out salvation. James 5:16 tells us to confess our sins and pray for the healing. Since an unconscious person cannot confess sins, it is unreasonable to assume that Extreme Unction erases any sins.

6) *Holy Orders* - This is the ordination of deacons, priests, or bishops. It is done through the laying on of hands and imparts power to administer the various sacraments. Out of the three,

the deacons have the least authority and the bishops the most, being the only ones who can ordain. All of these are ordained for life and believe that the sacred power conferred is never lost.

Refutation: The Scriptures do support the concept of the laying on of hands to be set in ministry (Acts 6:6 and Acts 13:3). Also, the impartation of some gift is scriptural (1 Tim. 4:14; 2 Tim. 1:6 and James 5:14). The problem is the concept of priests. Whereas the Bible in both the Old and New Testament speaks of elders as rulers over the flock, the concept of individual priests is an Old Testament concept. In the New Testament, all Christians are called to be priests (1 Peter 2:6,9).

Furthermore, the hierarchy of Catholicism is unscriptural. The New Testament clearly speaks of leadership roles. We see elders and deacons in many places. The elders are given more to the spiritual end and the deacons to the physical and natural needs. We also find the five offices of apostle, prophet, evangelist, pastor and teacher (Eph. 4:11-12). Elders appear to have one of these five gifts. Since the early church did not have a large hierarchical system, a possible clarifying view regarding the words elder, bishop, and pastor is in their function. They all speak of the same individual but in different aspects: elder is the character, bishop is the office, and pastor is the work.[28]

7) *Marriage* - This is considered a sacrament because it reflects Christ's marriage with His bride, the church.

Refutation: Although marriage is a very wonderful and scriptural institution, it is stretching it to say that it is a sacrament since the word literally means a visible sign of an inward grace. Furthermore, if the marriage sacrament confers grace, then why do priests and nuns need to be celibate? The priests of the Old Testament married. Peter was married.

IX. WHAT IS THE PROBLEM WITH CATHOLICISM'S VIEW OF MARY?

A. While every God-fearing individual should respect Mary, the mother of Jesus, for her virtuous life and example of servanthood, Romanism goes far beyond scriptural boundaries and exalts her almost to the position of deity. The following paragraph from the Vatican II documents (1962-1965) speaks clearly of their view of Mary:

"Finally, preserved free from all guilt of original sin, the Immaculate Virgin was taken up body and soul into heavenly glory upon the completion of her earthly sojourn. She was exalted by the Lord as the Queen of all, in order that she might be the more thoroughly conformed to her Son, the Lord of lords and the conqueror of sin and death."[29]

The fact that none of this is supported by Scripture does not seem to interfere with Rome's view of Mary's position. To say that there has been no controversy within Catholicism over this issue would not be accurate. Heated debates have raged over the exaltation of Mary when there is no scriptural support. Catholic theologians that support the above view of Mary hang all their arguments on a few misinterpreted fragments of Scripture and much assumption. Unfortunately for those Catholics who do regard Scripture highly, tradition has won out one more time.

Thinking Through The Scripture

"As Jesus was saying these things, a woman in the crowd called out, 'Blessed is the mother who gave you birth and nursed you.' He replied, 'Blessed rather are those who hear the word of God and obey it'." (Luke 11:27-28) NIV

"Whoever shall do the will of My Father who is in heaven, he is My brother and sister and mother." (Matthew 12:50) NASB

Questions for discussion:
1. What was Jesus trying to put the emphasis on in these passages?
2. Was He trying to dishonor his natural family in any way or was He trying to emphasize His spiritual family? Please explain.
3. How does one join Jesus' spiritual family? Who does He say His family is?

B. The following is a *sketch of the time line and exaltation of Mary* within Romanism: (all dates A.D.)
1) 431: Worship of Mary begins to develop; called "Mother of God"
2) 649: Doctrine of Perpetual Virginity (she never had sex)
3) 650: Feasts in honor of Mary begin.
4) 1854: Doctrine of Immaculate Conception (she was born without sin)
5) 1950: Doctrine of Bodily Assumption (raised from dead and into heaven)
6) Other Many believe and teach that she is a great mediator to whom people can pray, that she is the Mother of the Church, and that she is a Co-Redeemer, along with Jesus, of all mankind.

Refutation: The Bible clearly teaches us to worship God and Him alone (Ex. 20:1; John 4:23; and Rev. 7:9-12). There is only one mediator between God and man and that is Jesus (1 Tim. 2:5). Mary did unite with Joseph and consummate their marriage with sex after Jesus was born (Matt. 1:25) and the Scripture appears to indicate that Mary did have other children besides Jesus (Matt. 13:55). The Bible (Rom. 3:23) tells us that "all" people have original sin and does not exclude Mary. Finally, no one knows when or where Mary died. There is no early tradition regarding their view of her resurrection, ascension into heaven, or sitting as the Queen of heaven. Certainly, the Bible does not support this. Mary was a very humble woman to whom we all owe a debt of gratitude for her obedience and faith, but Romanism has idolized her deed and memory.

C. Apparitions of Mary have been reported down through the ages as a result of Catholicism's emphasis on her. Some Catholic theologians think that there have been as many as 21,000 claimed sightings of Mary in history and it is increasing. Just in the past sixty years, there have been over two hundred different sightings reported.[30] In their book *The Cult of the Virgin: Catholic Mariology and the Apparitions of Mary*, Elliot Miller and Kenneth R. Samples explain how millions of people have been drawn by sightings of Mary to places such as Mexico, France, Belgium, New York, and more.

One of the most recent and on-going sightings began in the early 1980's at Medjugorje, Yugoslavia. Several young people claim that they have had daily apparitions of the Virgin and over 1,000 messages. As with other apparition sights over the centuries, people are claiming to see miracles. Thousands stare into the sun at Medjugorje claiming that it changes colors, spins, throbs, pulsates, and throws off rainbow colors. Others see crosses spinning, rosaries turning color, fires on the hillsides that don't scorch, and physical healings.

It seems these same kinds of miracles were also seen at Lourdes, France, in 1858, and again in Fatima, Portugal, in 1917. The Vatican itself does not readily accept all apparitions. Yet, millions of Catholics (and others) rush to these sights to see what all the clamor is about. However, Miller and Samples give caution to those who would embrace these things as divine. They point out that these types of miracles could be a lure from Satan:

"It should also be recalled that the signs and wonders allegedly performed at Lourdes and Fatima could have been done by Satan.

In fact, when one analyzes many of the alleged miracles that accompany Marian apparitions, they seem to be of a kind different from those found in Scripture. This is true of Biblical miracles as a whole, as well as the miracles of Jesus' public ministry. When did Jesus ever make the sun dance or crosses spin? All of his miracles were done in the context of ministry (service to human needs for the glory of God.) Biblical miracles had a strong practical aspect. Moreover, when Jesus performed a miracle, it was not perceived by only a few people but by all who were present, even those who were against Jesus. In contrast, many of the miracles associated with Marian apparitions seem dramatic and sensational—attention-getting if you will—the kind of miracles that Jesus consistently refused to perform (Matt. 12:38-39). This is a good reason to at least suspect the source of these miracles."[31]

X. WHAT IS THE PROBLEM WITH THE ROSARY, PURGATORY, AND INDULGENCES?
    A. **The Rosary** - Legend says that the prayer beads were given to Saint Dominic by Mary herself. They became popular in the tenth century. A person uses the beads to pray both mentally and vocally. "In mental prayer the participant meditates on the major 'mysteries' (particular events) of the life, death, and glories of both Jesus and Mary. The vocal aspect involves the recitation of 15 'decades' (portions) of the 'Hail Mary' which involves contemplating 15 principal virtues that were practiced by Jesus and Mary."[32]

        However, if one is going to use repetitious prayers, it would be wiser to use the prayer that Jesus Himself gave us, "Our Father, who art in heaven…" (Mt. 6). But the real problem with the rosary is that millions of Catholics use it to maintain and increase their justification before God. It is a ritual of works for salvation.

    B. **Purgatory** - This became a required doctrine in 1438 at the Council of Florence. Among Catholics, there are different views of purgatory. However, it is definitely not a place one wants to go. They teach that after death a Christian will most likely have to be purged of all sins in the hellish fires of purgatory. It is a little less intense than hell itself and does not last forever. It completes the final stages of santification for a good Catholic. Length of stay depends on the amount of sins to be purged and the number of indulgences offered on earth by those still living.

        There is no scriptural support for this doctrine, and Catholicism must go outside the Canon to their Apocrypha (2 Maccabees 12:46) to find anything related to it. The doctrine violates the atonement work of Christ by teaching that all sins - even those forgiven - must be purged. Also, the fear of death that it places Catholics under is wrong (Heb. 2:9-15).

C. **Indulgences** - "Purgatory produced the system of indulgences—actions one could perform in order to work off the length of someone else's stay in purgatory. It is a type of time off for good behavior by a person's living relatives, and it continues to this very day. If you want to help a dead relative in purgatory try to make it to heaven, you need to have Masses said for that person. How do you have Masses said? You pay the Church. For example, if you want a certain number of Masses said and a few years off purgatory, you pay some figure like 500 dollars. If you want bigger Masses and more years taken off purgatory, you give a much larger amount, like 5000 dollars."[33] Most Catholics in the United States do not realize that this still goes on in many places around the world. Of course, it is unscriptural, but it can also be a form of manipulation and psychological abuse.

XI. WHAT IS THE PROBLEM WITH THE CATHOLIC APOCRYPHA?

A. The Catholic Bible often includes some of the "books the Jews regarded as being specifically 'outside of the canon' and therefore apocrypha, [they] are as follows: 1 Esdras; 2 Esdras; Tobit; Judith; the additions to Esther; the Wisdom of Solomon; Ecclesiasticus; Baruch; the Letter of Jeremiah; the additions to the Book of Daniel (the Prayer of Asariah and the Song of the Three Young Men; Susanna; and Bel and the Dragon); the Prayer of Manasseh; 1 Maccabees; and 2 Maccabees."[34]

B. Rene Pache points out some of the many problems with the Apocrypha in his book *The Inspiration and Authority of Scripture*. He says, "Except for certain interesting historical information (especially in 1 Maccabees) and a few beautiful moral thoughts (e.g. Wisdom of Solomon), these books contain absurd legends and platitudes, and historical, geographical and chronological errors, as well as manifestly heretical doctrines; they even recommend immoral acts (Judith 9:10,13)."[35] However, this did not stop the Council of Trent from accepting the apocryphal writings as a part of their Biblical canon.

C. Pache goes on in his book accusing Rome of simply adding the Apocrypha to lend weight to their human traditions: "Now, we must remember that it was the Jews who were called upon to compile the Old Testament. As Paul said, it was to them that the oracles of God were confided (Rom. 3:1-2). We received those oracles from their hands and no one else. Why, then, did Rome take so new and daring a position? Because confronted by the Reformers, she lacked arguments to justify her unscriptural deviations. She declared that the Apocryphal books supported such doctrines as prayers for the dead (II Macc. 12:44); the expiatory sacrifice (eventually to become the mass, II Macc. 12:39-46); almsgiving with expiatory value, also leading to deliverance from death (Tobit 12:9; 4:10); invocation and intercession of the saints (II Macc. 15:14; Bar. 3:4); the worship of angels (Tobit 12:12); purgatory; and the redemption of souls after death (II Macc. 12:42,46)."[36]

XII. WHAT CAN CHRISTIANS DO TO HELP CATHOLICS?

A. **Prayer:** Encourage Catholic Christians to be a light within the church, and pray for them. If they are truly serving the Lord then they know some of the deep problems within Catholicism but have perhaps felt lead to remain. Christians need to be cautious about judging in these cases. There are Christians within Catholicism that the Lord is using to touch others. As their brothers and sisters in the Lord, we should pray for them and lift them up. If they are in a position in which it is obvious that their Christian life is greatly hindered by their association with Catholicism then pray that the Lord will lead them out. Ask for the guidance of the Holy Spirit to give you wisdom to share this with them.

There is also a great need today for intercessors to pray down the strongholds of demons that govern the many false teachings of the church. Wouldn't it be amazing if the Pope suddenly got true revelation regarding salvation and works. It could revolutionize the entire church. There are many well-meaning Christians today who aggressively attack the Pope - some even calling him the antichrist - but who never take any time to pray for the man. James 5:16 tells us *"The effectual, fervent prayer of a righteous man avails much."*

B. **Love:** The walls between Catholicism and Protestantism are old and strong. They will not come down easily. Nor do I suggest that they all should. The ones which represent the essential doctrines of historic Christianity should never be compromised. Are there other walls, however, of pride, prejudice, ignorance, intolerance, and perhaps rebellion that need to be brought down by both sides? As Christians, our grace needs to precede truth as our mercy does judgment. They will not hear our truth if we don't show them grace, and they will not accept judgment if we don't begin with mercy.

C. **Witness:** Most Catholics think they are saved by works,[37] so share the Gospel with them. The harvest could be great since there is much of the Word already sown into their lives. There are many that are Catholics in name only. They seldom or never go to church but think that, because they are Catholic, everything is just fine between them and God. Many countries such as Italy, Spain, Mexico, the Philippines, Brazil, etc. are heavily dominated by Roman Catholics. They grow up equating being Catholic with being Italian or Spanish. They have no relationship with Jesus Christ as their Lord and Savior.

One way to witness is to ask them the two question test. First, ask them, "Have you come to the place in your life where know for sure that if you died tonight you would go to heaven?" This only requires a "yes" or "no" response but will establish whether they believe in heaven and where they think they are headed. Second, ask them, "Suppose you were to die tonight and stand before God and He was to say to you, _____ (fill in their name) 'Why should I let you into My perfect heaven?' What would you say?"

Their answer to this second question tells you whether they are putting their faith in Jesus for salvation or in works. If they give any other answer than the fact that they are saved through the substitutionary atonement of Christ dying on the cross for their sins, then they are probably trying to work their way to heaven. At this point, share the gospel with them by emphasizing that salvation is a free gift that comes through faith in Christ alone (Ephesians 2:8-9). Ask them to accept Jesus into their life as Lord and Savior and prayer with them for this.

End Notes

1   John Armstrong, general editor, *Roman Catholicism: Evangelical Protestants Analyze What Divides And Unites Us* (Chicago, IL: Moody Press, 1994), p. 269.

2. Ron Carlson and Ed Decker, *Fast Facts on False Teachings* (Eugene, OR: Harvest House, 1994), pgs. 212-213.

3. Fritz Ridenour, *So What's the Difference?* (Ventura, CA: Regal Books, 1979), p. 29.

4. *Eerdman's Handbook To The History of Christianity*, ed. Tim Dowley (Grand Rapids, MI: Wm. B. Eerd,am's Publishing Co., 1977), p. 176.

5. Cornelius Van Til, *The Defense of the Faith* (Phillipsburg, NJ: Presbyterian and Reformed Publishing Co., 1967), pgs. 71-72.

6. John L. McKenzie, *The Roman Catholic Church* (Garden City, NY: Image Books, 1971), p. 264.

7. Armstrong, p. 103.

8. Martin Chemnitz (1522- 1586), *Examination of the Council of Trent: Part 1* (St. Louis, MO: Concordia Publishing House, 1971), p. 273.

9. Walter M. Abbot, S.J., General Editor, *The Documents of Vatican II* (Chicago: Follett Publishing Company, 1966), pgs. 741-742.

10. Ibid., p. 38.

11. Mike Gendron, "The Pope and Evolution: The drift from truth continues," *Lamplighter Newsletter* produced by Lamb & Lion Ministries 18, 10 (October, 1997): 6.

12. Ibid., pgs. 48-49.

13. *Josephus: Complete Works*, trans. W. Whiston (Grand Rapids, MI: Kregel Publications, 1980), p. 639.

14. Harry Emerson Fosdick, ed., *Great Voices of the Reformation* (New York: Random House, Inc., 1952), p. 80.

15. Armstrong, p. 328.

16. John Ankerberg and John Weldon, *Protestants & Catholics: Do They Now Agree?* (Eugene, OR: Harvest House Publishers, 1995), p. 21.

17. Armstrong, p. 332.

18. Ankerberg and Weldon, p. 60.

19. John H. Armstrong, *A View of Rome: A Guide to Understanding the Beliefs and Practices of Roman Catholics* (Chicago: Moody Press, 1995), p.47.

20. Ankerberg and Weldon, p. 68.

21. McKenzie, p. 181.

22. Ankerberg and Weldon, pgs. 76-77.

23. *Catechism of the Catholic Church* (Liguori, MO: Liguori Publications, 1994), p. 345 as cited by Ankerberg and Weldon in *Protestants & Catholics: Do They Now Agree?*, p. 77.

24. Ankerberg and Weldon, p. 89.

25. McKenzie, p. 199.

26. Karl Keating, *What Catholics Really Believe—Setting the Record Straight* (Ann Arbor, MI: Servant, 1992), pp. 66-67, as cited by Ankerberg and Weldon in *Protestants & Catholics: Do They Now Agree?*, p. 51.

27. Armstrong, *Roman Catholicism*, p. 131.

28. Dick Iverson, *Present Day Truths* (Portland, OR: Bible Temple Publishing, 1975), pgs. 135-137.

29. Abbot, p. 90.

30. Elliot Miller and Kenneth R. Samples, *The Cult of the Virgin: Catholic Mariology and the Apparition of Mary* (Grand Rapids, MI: Baker Book House, 1994), p. 82.

31. Ibid., pgs. 133-134.

32. Ankerberg and Weldon, p. 95.

33. Carlson and Decker, pgs. 226-227.

34. Philip W. Comfort, editor, *The Origin of the Bible* (Wheaton, IL: Tyndale House Publishing, Inc.,1992), p. 85.

35. Rene Pache, *The Inspiration and Authority of Scripture* (Chicago: Moody Press, 1969), p. 172.

36. Ibid., p. 173.

37. Ankerberg and Weldon, p. 185.

QUESTIONNAIRE: LESSON FIFTEEN

NAME: _____   DATE: _____

1. List three similar beliefs between Catholics and Protestants:

a) _____

b) _____

c) _____

2. Fill in the blanks: The church in Rome grew quickly because it was an important _____ and _____ center. Christianity became an official state religion in _____. The Eastern Orthodox church began splitting off from the _____ Church in 1054. In 1517, Martin _____ formally protested against Rome. Today, Protestantism is a _____ term for many churches outside of Catholicism that hold certain elements of _____ and belief in common. It is not that Protestantism as a whole has it together and Catholicism doesn't. Rather, it is simply that certain elements of Protestantism are closer to true historical _____.

3. List the three critical areas in which Catholicism strays from the truth.

a) _____

b) _____

c) _____

4. Write out Mark 7:13. _____

_____

_____

5. The current Vatican II document states that a doctrine by the Popes "need no _____ of others, nor do they allow an _____ to any other judgment."

6. The office of _____ is not mentioned in the Bible.

7. It appears that it was _____ who actually was the leader of the church of Jerusalem.

8. Justification is _____

_____

9. Sanctification is _____

_____

10. Rom. 1:17 says, _____

11. List two of Catholicism's 7 sacraments and explain the aspects of them that do not line up with historical Christianity.

a) _____

_____

_____

b) _____

_____

_____

12. For many Catholics, salvation is reduced to a system of w_____, rather than f_____.

13. Worship of Mary began in _____ A.D. In 649 A.D. the doctrine of _____ Virginity said she never had sex with Joseph even after Jesus was born. Later, in 1854, the doctrine of Immaculate _____ said she was born without _____ . Then in 1950, the doctrine of Bodily Assumption said she was raised from the dead and ascended into

_____ .

Tell why the above doctrines are false: _____

_____

_____

_____

14. Catholics believe that _____ is a fiery place that completes the final stages of _____ for a good Catholic. A shorter stay can be purchased and worked out by living relatives in a system called _____.

15. What are some of the false teachings that the Apocrypha supports but that are not substantiated in the main canon of the Scriptures? _____

_____

_____

16. Consider your knowledge of Catholicism before and after this lesson. Circle the number below that indicates how equipped you felt before taking this course to witness to someone in it as to how equipped you feel now. Be honest.

BEFORE 0 1 2 3 4 5 6 7 8 9 10 AFTER 0 1 2 3 4 5 6 7 8 9 10

LESSON 16

JUDAISM

"We were taught that Christians blamed us for killing their Savior, Jesus Christ. And it was Christians, we were told, who had persecuted Jews through the centuries. The Crusades, the pogroms of Russia, the Spanish Inquisition and ultimately the Holocaust all were done in the name of Christ and Christianity. We understood that we were born Jews and that we should die as Jews. And Jews did not believe in Jesus! In fact, I had no idea that Jesus was Jewish. I thought that Jesus Christ was the son of Mr. and Mrs. Christ. I thought he was born in Rome and grew up in the Vatican. I didn't know that the apostles were Jews who were born and raised in Israel or that Paul had been a Jewish rabbi. I was shocked to learn that Abraham, Isaac, Jacob, Moses and other great patriarchs of Jewish history were mentioned in the New Testament. I had no idea how Jewish the New Testament was. I was taught that to believe in Jesus a Jew had to convert to another religion and abandon his people. In reality, this is not the case. When Jews believe in Jesus, they are not converting to another religion. Rather, they are returning to the God of Israel and the promised Messiah of the Jewish people."[1] —Messianic Jewish Rabbi Jonathan Bernis

I. WHAT ARE SOME SIGNIFICANT WORDS IN JUDAISM?
    Bar mitzvah - For boys, the coming-of-age ceremony at age thirteen.
        Bat mitzvah - For girls
    Diaspora - Refers to Jewish people who remain dispersed outside of the
        Promise Land.
    Kosher - Keeping the dietary laws, such as not mixing meat and milk at
        the same meal.

Passover - A widely observed holiday, in March or April, recounting deliverance from Egypt.

Rosh ha-Shanah - New Year observed in September or October.

Sabbath - Begins at sundown on Friday night and continues until sundown on Saturday.

Sh'ma - The unity of God. *"Hear O Israel, the Lord our God, the Lord is One"* Deut. 6:4.

Synagogue - The house of worship of a Jewish congregation.

Talmud - Approximately 36 volumes collected from the Mishnah and Gemara.

Torah - The Law of Moses: Genesis, Exodus, Leviticus, Numbers, Deuteronomy.

YHWH - The name of God as presented in the Old Testament, probably pronounced "Yahweh."

II. WHAT IS THE SIZE AND STRENGTH OF JUDAISM TODAY?
   A. According to a census taken in the early 1990's there are over 17 million Jewish people in the world,[2] but of that number only about 14 million adhere to some form of Judaism. Why? The answer is that not all Jewish people consider themselves to be religious. Some profess to be atheists, agnostics, or secular.[3] The largest population of Jewish people live in the United States, about 6 million. Israel has another 5 million which equals close to 40 percent of the world's Jews.
   B. In size of numbers, Judaism is insignificant compared to Christianity, Islam, Hinduism, and Buddhism who each have hundreds of millions. However, the strength of Judaism should not be calculated by numbers but by influence and impact. For instance, Judaism influences Christianity, thus those impacted by Christian views. Within the United States, the Jewish voice often sways political, economic, and military actions with regard to the state of Israel and its rivals.

   The impact of the state of Israel has helped cause what is referred to as the Middle East Crisis. Geographically, the Jewish state of Israel is small but strategic in location and can cause leverage against the surrounding Arab nations. Israel is also growing rapidly as Jews return to their homeland, causing more stress with its neighbors who are mainly in league against it.

   The animosity between Israel and the warring Arabs goes back thousands of years to the time of Abraham. God wanted to make a covenant with Abraham and his descendants. He and his wife, Sarah, were told to wait for a child. However, they were impatient and because of Sarah's barrenness, she caused Abraham to lie with her servant, Hagar, who bore Ishmael. Abraham asked God to form the covenant through Ishmael, but the Lord stuck to His original plan and fulfilled his promise to Abraham and Sarah when she bore Isaac in their old age. Through Ishmael's lineage, the Arab nations were birthed, but by Isaac came Israel.

There has been fighting and bloodshed over the ground of Israel since the days of the Exodus and was reignited this century when the Jews repossessed the land in 1948, once again becoming a thorn in the side of the Arab nations. The rise of Islam within the Arab nations also causes much tension. (See the chapter on Islam.) The teachings of Islam proclaim that Abraham was of their faith, a Muslim, and not a Jew or Christian.[4] However, the tension in the Middle East did not catch the Lord off guard. It is one of the Biblical prophecies foreshadowing the soon return of the Lord Jesus Christ.

Thinking Through The Scripture

"And Abraham said to God, 'Oh, that Ishmael might live before You!' Then God said: 'No, Sarah your wife shall bear you a son, and you shall call his name Isaac; I will establish My covenant with him for an everlasting covenant, and with his descendants after him." (Genesis 17:18-19)

Questions for discussion:
1. Why do you think the Lord rejected Abraham and Sarah's solution?
2. If Ishmael had not been born, how would it have affected today's setting?
3. What can we learn from this passage about our need for patience with God?

III. ARE THERE SIMILARITIES BETWEEN CHRISTIANITY AND JUDAISM?
   A. **Similarities:** Some view Christianity as the daughter religion of Judaism, but others see it as a sister where both stemmed from the same roots. One author says, "Christianity does not supplant Old Testament Judaism, it is the fruition of it."[5] No matter how one sees the relation between these two religions, there are certain things that Christians and Jews hold uniquely in common. We both believe in one God the Father and hope in His salvation. We see Him as all powerful, all knowing, and all present. We are made of dust and yet in the image of God. We are to uphold the greatest

commandments, namely to love God and our fellow man. Furthermore, we both believe in the accuracy and divine authorship of the Old Testament. While Jews look back to Abraham as their father through a natural lineage, Christians look back to Abraham as their spiritual father through faith.

B. **Degrees of Difference:** There are various movements within Christianity that vary in degree to how close they are to today's Judaism. For instance, the number of Messianic Jewish congregations is growing. These are Jews who have accepted Jesus Christ as their Messiah, and would be the closest to Judaism. Then there are the issues dividing Catholics and Protestants. (See chapter on Catholicism.) One Jewish apologist, Dr. Trude Weiss-Rosmarin, admitted that Protestants are closer to Jewish beliefs than Catholics are because of Catholicism's veneration for a pantheon of Saints, relics, and worship of Mary. However, Dr. Weiss-Rosmarin still sees a gulf of separation between historic Christianity and Judaism because of the Christian view of Jesus Christ.[6] This is accurate because all Christians, whether Messianic Jews, Catholics, or Protestants, follow Jesus as Lord.

IV. WHAT IS THE HISTORY OF THE ANCIENT JEWS?

A. **Origins:** To better understand the history of the Jews, an interested student should read the Old Testament as well as other historical sources. The origins of this people is found in the book of Genesis. The Jews actually started as Hebrews of the Semitic race. Regarding the words "Hebrew" and "Semitic," Fritz Ridenour says the following in his book *So What's the Difference?*:

"To begin with, the Jews were called 'Hebrews.' This name comes from 'Eber,' their traditional ancestor (mentioned in Gen. 10:21). We can go back even further to the name 'Shem,' a son of Noah (mentioned in the same verse). From Shem comes the word 'Semitic' which refers to a group of peoples that includes the Jews and Arabs."[7]

B. **Ancient Time Line:** The ancient dates are only approximate ones as there are various archaeological views which differ on time lines and sequence.

2000 B.C.	Abraham, a descendant of Eber, is called by God.
1400 B.C.	Moses leads the Hebrews out of Egyptian bondage.
1360 B.C.	Joshua brings Israel into the Promised Land.
1220 B.C.	Judges begin rule over the nation.
1000 B.C.	King David begins to reign.
967 B.C.	Solomon begins to build the temple.

922 B.C.	Kingdom divides into Israel (North) and Judah (South).
722 B.C.	Northern kingdom falls to the Assyrians.
586 B.C.	Destruction of Jerusalem, Babylonian exile. Diaspora
536 B.C.	Zerubbabel leads back first group of captives.
458 B.C.	Ezra leads back second group of captives.
444 B.C.	Nehemiah brings back third group and rebuilds the wall.
167 B.C.	Antiochus IV Epiphanes begins slaughter of the Jews.
164 B.C.	The Maccabaen revolt defeats the Syrians.
63 B.C.	Roman general Pompey makes Israel a vassal state.
33 A.D.	Jesus is crucified, buried, and resurrected from the dead.
70 A.D.	Rome destroys Jerusalem and many Jews are scattered.

Thinking Through The Scripture

"You are all sons of God through faith in Christ Jesus, for all of you who were baptized into Christ have clothed yourselves with Christ. There is neither Jew nor Greek, slave nor free, male nor female, for you are all one in Christ Jesus. If you belong to Christ, then you are Abraham's seed, and heirs according to the promise." (Galatians 3:26-29) NIV

"For he is not a Jew who is one outwardly, nor is circumcision that which is outward in the flesh; but he is a Jew who is one inwardly; and circumcision is that of the heart, in the Spirit, not in the letter; whose praise is not from men but from God." (Romans 2:28-29)

Questions for discussion:
1. By what means do we come to "belong" to Christ? How does this make us Abraham's seed? What is the promise?
2. What does it mean to be a Jew inwardly? Are Christians actually Jews?
3. Christians are to be circumcised in their heart. What kind of attitude should this produce in our life? Consider Ezekiel 36:26-27.

C. **Israel's Relationship with God:** God chose Israel to serve Him, to *"proclaim the good news of His salvation from day to day,"* and to *"declare His glory among the nations, His wonders among all peoples"* (Psalm 96:2-3). God desired Israel to worship Him and Him alone. The first four of the Ten Commandments (Exodus 20:1-7) are regarding how Israel should relate to God. There were times when the people were close to God and served Him in spirit and deed.

They would properly honor Him. Celebrations of praise, festive holidays, and religious ceremonies would highlight their years of dedication. They built Him a tabernacle in the wilderness and later a temple in Jerusalem. Their entire life centered on relationship with God their Creator.

At other times, they fell away, making idol images of false gods, and serving Baal, Ashtoreh, Chemesh, Milcom and others. (2 Kings 23) They would worship the sun, moon, and constellations, as well as stones and trees (Jeremiah 2:27; 3:9). Sorcery, astrology, divination, and magic charms were not uncommon and people would even burn their children to false gods. At these times, the Lord God would judge Israel and punish them to make them repent and return to Him. The picture painted for us in the Old Testament about the Jews and their relationship with God seems to show a cycle of repetition after He would deliver them from sin. It could be displayed this way: Deliverance— Holiness— Straying— Sin— Judgment— Punishment— Repentance— Deliverance, and so on.

D. **The Jewish Calendar:** Their calendar is complicated in a couple of ways. First, it is a lunar calendar rather than a solar one. It is based on the movements of the moon around the earth. It takes about 29.5 days for the moon to circle the earth and this begins a new Jewish month. In order to adjust their lunar calendar to the solar year, they must add a month to their calendar every three years. So approximately every three years they have 13 months instead of 12.

Second, the Jews have two concurrent calendar years, one is sacred and other is civil. The sacred calendar year was established when God brought them out of Egypt (Exodus 12:2) and begins with Nisan (originally called Abib) and corresponds to the months of March or April. The civil calendar was based on their agricultural season and begins in Tishri which corresponds to the months of either September or October depending on the year. Their civil New Year's Day is called *Rosh ha-Shanah*.

E. **The Religious Feasts:** Yearly, Israel celebrated three major feasts: the Feast of Passover during barley harvest in the month of Nisan (March-April), the Feast of Pentecost during wheat harvest in the month of Sivan (May-June), and the Feast of Tabernacles during the final ingathering in Tishri (September-October). Actually, these three feasts embodied seven smaller festivals because the *Feast of Passover* included: (1) Passover, (2) the week of Unleavened Bread, and (3) Firstfruits. Then came (4) the *Feast of Pentecost*. Now add to this the *Feast of Tabernacles* which consisted of (5) Trumpets, (6) the Day of Atonement, and (7) Tabernacles. Much symbolism can be drawn from these feasts in how God interacted with His people. In short, Passover portrays the peace of God, Pentecost depicts the power of God, and Tabernacles illustrates the rest of God.[8]

F. **Changes in Worship**: During their time in the wilderness, Israel's worship centered on the activities in the *Tabernacle of Moses*. This is where various sacrifices were instituted for the cleansing of sin. The high priest made atonement for the sins of all the people once a year and approached the presence of the Lord who was on the mercy seat in the Holy of Holies. In the New Testament book of Hebrews, chapters 8 - 10, we are told that the furniture of the Tabernacle, as well as the rituals and laws, were a foreshadowing of many things to come. Primarily, it foreshadowed the coming of Christ as the High Priest to offer Himself in sacrifice on behalf of our sins (Hebrews 9:11-15). The worship represented in Moses' Tabernacle was somewhat austere and focused on holiness.

The *Tabernacle of David*, which was set up during King David's reign, differed greatly from that of Moses by adding the elements of singing and musical instruments. Dancing, lifting hands, and heart felt joy were common occurrences.

When the *Temple of Solomon* was built in Jerusalem, it was thought to be a permanent place where people could come and honor the Lord. However, the continual drifting away of Israel brought God's judgment. The destruction of Solomon's Temple in 586 B.C. brought further changes to the manner of Israel's worship.

Thinking Through The Scripture

"He was despised and rejected and forsaken by men, a Man of sorrows and pains, and acquainted with grief and sickness; and as one from Whom men hide their faces He was despised and we did not appreciate His worth or have any esteem for Him." (Isaiah 53:3) Amp

"He was in the world, and the world came into existence through him. Yet, the world didn't accept him. He went to his own people, and his own people didn't accept him. However, he gave the right to become God's children to everyone who believed in him." (John 1:10-12) GW

Questions for discussion:
1. Isaiah prophesied how men would respond to the Messiah when He came. Why do you think that men would reject Him? Why would they hide from Him?

2. John used Isaiah's prophecy to relate how the world responded to Jesus. Who was John referring to when he said, "His own people" would reject Jesus?
3. Why would His own people reject Him and what exactly were they rejecting?

G. **Emergence of Synagogues and Rabbis:** During the time of the exile of Judah in Babylon, new worship centers arose. Since the temple was destroyed and could not be used as a central place of worship, prayer houses called synagogues and religious teachers referred to as rabbis were established. Even after the temple was rebuilt, during the days of Zerubbabel, the synagogue maintained its influence as a place of worship, though not of sacrifice.[9]

Religious training for rabbis developed around 200 B.C.[10] and three sects arose in Judaism, namely *the Sadducees, Pharisees, and Essenes.* The first two groups disputed over doctrines like the immortality of the soul and the resurrection, while the Essenes distanced themselves and focused on purity. The people were still required to offer animal sacrifices for their sins at the temple in Jerusalem, but it had turned into a legalistic system of money, power, and class. But God still loved His people, and so it was that into this environment Christ the Messiah was born only 5 miles from Jerusalem in a manger in Bethlehem on a cold, starry night.

V. WHAT IS THE HISTORY OF THE MODERN JEWS?
A. **Rejection of the Messiah and Birth of the Church:** The sad truth is that everyone abandoned or rejected Jesus in his hour of need. Scriptures like Psalm 22, Isaiah 53, and the Gospel accounts of the crucifixion give us a glimpse of the rejection that He felt as He hung on that cross and bore the sins of the world. Even one of his closest followers, Peter, had denied Him at the crucial moment.

Sometimes people get the erroneous notion that it was only the Jews who rejected and killed Jesus. However, the fact of the matter is that mankind, as a whole, denied Him. That is why the great truth of God's love toward us all is so amazing in the crucifixion story. Romans 5:7 says, *"But God demonstrates His own love toward us, in that while we were still sinners, Christ died for us."* On the third day after His death, Jesus rose from the dead as was prophesied in passages like Psalm 16:8-10; Psalm 49:15; and Isaiah 25:6-12. He was with his disciples for forty more days and was seen by 500 witnesses (1 Cor. 15:6). Ten days later, on the day of Pentecost, the

Holy Spirit came like a mighty rushing wind and the church was born (Acts 2).

Within a short time, thousands of Jewish people accepted Jesus as their Messiah and the church began to grow rapidly. However, many of the Jewish leaders and citizens of Israel rejected Jesus' claims to being the Messiah because He did not do what they felt the Messiah was suppose to do. Thus, they unwittingly rejected the Son of God.

B. **The Early Years:** The Jews rebelled against Rome's control, but their efforts were in vain. General Titus defeated them in 70 A.D. Other rebellions arose trying to reconquer the land. The last was the Bar Kokhva rebellion (or Second Jewish War) from 132 - 135 A.D. Rome crushed the Jews in this war, and although the Romans rebuilt Jerusalem afterwards, the Jews were forbidden to enter it. This was the final blow and the discouraged Jewish people fled to friendlier pockets of humanity, or so they thought. McDowell and Stewart point out that "When Christianity became the state religion of the Roman Empire (325 A.D.), the Jews were seen as an accursed race and the center of Jewish life soon moved to Babylonia, a non-Christian country."[11]

Not only was the Jewish homeland changing, but their religion was being impacted as well. In the first century, at Jamnia, Jewish leaders met to discuss important issues. There was a major reconstitution of Judaism. More emphasis was placed on the Torah, and Christianity was denounced as a Jewish sect, partly because of the Christians' refusal to help fight against Rome.[12] One Jewish scholar, Rabbi Phillip Sigal, believed that "had Christian Jews not been expelled from the synagogues after 90 A.D., but remained a segment of Judaism, it is well within the realm of possibility that Jesus would have secured a place" in the rabbinic teachings of Judaism.[13] This decision to separate from the Christians brought an end to any similarities that Jews and Christians thought they held in common. Rabbinic Judaism became strong and dominated Judaism until the eighteenth century.

In the twelfth century, a Spanish Jew, named Moses Maimonides, condensed basic Jewish beliefs into a statement of faith that is still followed by traditional forms of Judaism today. The thirteen-point statement stresses the need for perfect faith in the Creator, the Torah, the coming Messiah, and the future resurrection of the dead. Even though the Jews were scattered over the centuries, they were held together as a concept and people by their traditions, Jewish calendar, rabbinic teachings, creed, and sacred books.

C. **The Modern Era:** Today, everything has changed. The Jewish people have regained the nation of Israel. The man that God used to promote this return was Theodore Herzl, born in Budapest in 1860. He came to believe that the only safe place for Jews in a Gentile world was in their own nation. In 1896 he wrote *The Jewish State* and laid the groundwork for what has become known as "Zionism."[14] Later on another Jewish man, a chemist named Chaim Weizmann, helped England improve the making of explosives for WWI. The Prime Minister sought to publicly reward Weizmann, yet his real desire was not for himself but that England would grant the Jews their own home in Palestine. He was given the request, and in 1917, James Balfour, the British Foreign Secretary, created the Balfour Declaration which was then approved by the newly formed League of Nations.[15] Various waves of migration occured. However, it wasn't until after World War II that there would be a mass Exodus of the Jews back to their homeland.

The Jewish people had suffered many times over the centuries outside of their homeland. There were the Crusades in the eleventh through thirteenth centuries in which false or misguided Christians killed Moslems and hundreds of thousands of Jews. During the Spanish Inquisition of the fifteenth and sixteenth centuries came one of the darkest hours of the church. Christians were slain as heretics and many more Jews were insanely massacred. We must understand why the Jews sometimes fear Christianity. Gross atrocities have been done to them in the name of Christ.

Then came the Russian Pogroms of the late nineteenth century in which millions of Jews were forced to convert, flee westward, or starve to death. These planned massacres were brutal, uncivilized, and certainly unchristian. Yet none compared to the monstrosity of the holocaust. Hitler's final solution to what he called "the Jewish problem" was to annihilate them. The Jews had probably not faced this kind of barbarous and insane megalomaniac since the days of Antiochus IV Epiphanes in 186 B.C. But even the butchery of that tyrant paled in comparison to the systematic slaughter of Adolph Hitler's death camps. Six million Jews were tortured and killed by Germany in World War II.

After the war, the Jews began fleeing to Palestine from all over the world. Up to this time, the amount of Jews allowed to return to Palestine had been limited by Great Britain, but now the nations of the world reacted to the atrocities of the war and demanded that the United Nations partition a portion of the Holy Land just for the

Jews. On May 14, 1948, Israel proclaimed its statehood under the leadership of David Ben-Gurion.[16] Immediately, the surrounding Arab Islamic nations responded with a holy war ("jihad") to prevent the establishment of a Jewish state. Yet, Israel won that war and survived, and for the last fifty years has continued to gain a foothold in the Middle East.

The new Jewish state's length of existence, however, has not been peaceful. After the War of Independence, others followed. There were always minor skirmishes, but then in 1956, the Egyptian ruler, Abdul Nasser, prompted the first of several wars with Israel. Egypt, Jordan, and Syria joined against Israel in the Suez conflict. Israel was victorious in this war, as well as the Six Day War of 1967 and the Yom-Kippur War of 1973. In the Six Day War, Israel took control of the West Bank and the Gaza Strip and occupied the old city of Jerusalem. Amazingly, after almost two thousand years, Israel owned Jerusalem again!

Since then, wars, politics, and Arab immigrants have kept Israel in the news headlines almost every week. The Palestinian Liberation Organization (PLO) is a terrorist group bent on destroying Israel and is constantly inflicting brutality on Israeli civilians over land ownership issues. Also, Israel has not been entirely innocent in its dealings with civilian Arabs. The tension between the Islamic PLO and Israel has stifled peace negotiations by the leaders and even lead to the assassination of Israeli Prime Minister, Yitzhak Rabin, in 1995 by an Orthodox Jew. Today, the tension continues to surround the state of Israel as the world unwittingly marches towards Armageddon, but also the triumphant and victorious return of the Messiah, the Lord Jesus Christ.

Thinking Through The Scripture

"And if the first piece of dough be holy, the lump is also; and if the root be holy, the branches are too. But if some of the branches were broken off, and you, being a wild olive, were grafted in among them and became partakers with them of the rich root of the olive tree, do not be arrogant toward the branches; but if you are arrogant, remember that it is not you who supports the root, but the root supports you." (Romans 11:16-18) NASB

Questions for discussion:
1. Read Romans 11. What is represented by the holy root, natural branches, and wild olive branches? What does Christianity owe to Judaism?

2. What kind of attitude is Paul warning Christians about here? What kind of attitude should Christians have towards Jewish people?

VI. WHO IS THE GOD OF JUDAISM?

A. **The Ancient Debate:** This question has probably been asked and disputed for the past two thousand years. I'm sure some Christians would say, "the Jews follow a false God." However, this viewpoint probably errs on the part of oversimplification. Let's suppose for a minute that it is the year 125 B.C. and a Jewish man who worships YHWH (Yahweh), the God of the Old Testament, is talking to a pagan Greek who worships the goddess Diana. Of these two, which one follows the true God? The answer is obvious to a Christian today; it would have been the Jewish believer.

Now let's move up to the year 125 A.D. and a Jewish believer is talking to a Christian. The Jewish believer says He follows the God of the Old Testament and the Christian says he follows the Lord Jesus Christ. But wait a minute, isn't Jesus the Son connected to God the Father and God the Holy Spirit? Wasn't Jesus the Son also present in the Old Testament when the Jews were praying to God? Of course, He was. That is what Jesus was trying to tell the people in John 8:58 when he identified Himself as the Great I Am of Exodus 3:14. He was there in the burning bush. He was there in the beginning (John 1:1; 1:14). He was right there helping in the process of creating man.

Genesis 1:26 reads, *"Then God said, Let Us make man in Our image, according to Our likeness."* Who was the "Us" of this verse? Well, from a New Testament orthodox Christian perspective, it was God the Father, God the Son, and God the Holy Spirit. The Hebrew word for God in the verse is Elohim, meaning a plurality in unity. It is the Godhead (Colossians 2:9) that we have come to know as the Trinity.

So then, do the Jews follow a false God? To answer this, we should consider what Jesus said. He told some of the Pharisees that they were from their father the devil (John 8:44). However, at another time He told one of the scribes that answered wisely that he was not far from the kingdom of God (Mark 12:34). Therefore, some were far from the kingdom while others were near. This correlates with what Paul told us in Romans 11:5 that there is a "remnant". Today, in Judaism it would probably be valid to say that there are those far from the kingdom and those near to it. Certainly, of those who are near the kingdom, it would be unwise to say they follow a false God in the sense that Hindus, Buddhists, or Muslims

do. Rather, it is better for us to understand that the Jews are unique
in that they were God's chosen people, but today they have "a veil"
over their hearts when they read the Old Testament, and it remains
there until they turn to Christ (2 Corinthians 3:14).

B. **The Difference in Viewpoint:** To Judaism, the Christian view of
God as a Trinity is the fundamental contrast between the two religions. They say that Judaism is "committed to pure and uncompromising monotheism" whereas Christianity "subscribes to the
belief in the trinitarian nature of the Divine Being"[17] mentioned
above. Jewish scholars call their view the Unity of God doctrine or
in Hebrew, the Sh'ma, found in Deuteronomy 6:4, *"Hear, O Israel:
The Lord our God, the Lord is one!"* In a sense, they believe that God
is unknowable by mortal man. However, they believe that God can
be approached by man.

Judaism fights against the Christian idea of incarnation, that
God came in human form.[18] However, the true problem is not with
the Christian doctrine of the Trinity; it is rather that the Jews
rejected the Messiah *Yeshua* (Hebrew name for Jesus) when he
came to them as 100% man but also 100% God. 1 Timothy 3:16
tells us that "God was manifested in the flesh." Jesus came in the
form of a "person" to let us know that we can have a "personal"
relationship with God. In fact, as we see in Acts 4:10-12, there is
salvation in no other name except that of Jesus Christ of Nazareth.
The true difference between the two religions is about relationship
rather than religion.

VII. WHAT DISTURBS JEWISH PEOPLE ABOUT THE CHRISTIAN
VIEW OF JESUS?

A. **Understanding "the Way":** Jewish people say that they "can appreciate the faith of Jesus but not the faith about Jesus"[19] being the Son
of God. They can appreciate the faith of Jesus because He was a
Jewish Rabbi, and in those things that He taught which compelled
the Jews to serve the one true God and adhere to the Torah, they
agree. The Hebrew word *halakhah* means the "way" or "walk"
which in rabbinic writings refers to the correct way to act in regard
to keeping the Law (the Torah). Some Jewish scholars believe that
Jesus was committed to keeping the whole Law and that he did a
better job than anyone else.[20]

The real pain for Jewish scholars comes in those New
Testament passages in which Jesus is said to claim equality with
God. Some think that His followers misunderstood His words.
Specifically, there is often blame laid at the Apostle Paul's feet for
being an apostate and leading the Jews astray.[21]

However, it is the Jewish scholars who misunderstand. Jesus did not just come to do the law but to "fulfill" it (Matthew 5:17-18). *He did not just come to walk in the "way." He said, "I am the way, the truth and the life. No one comes to the Father except through Me"* (John 14:6). The word "way" in this verse is the Greek *hodos* and is the New Testament equivalent to the Hebrew *halakhah*. Jesus was telling the Jews that He was the Way to the fulfillment of the Law (the Torah) given by God. As a matter of fact, Paul used the phrase "the Way" in Acts 9:2; 24:14; and 24:22 to refer to the sect known as Christians. In other words, the followers of Christ were of the Way of righteousness, the only true Way.

B. **Understanding the Messiah:** It sometimes amazes Christians that Jews can be so blind as not to recognize Jesus as the Messiah. How could anyone not understand that only the True Messiah could come and do so many miracles, fulfill so many prophecies, and teach so many truths? However, the Jews see a lot of intellectual issues to be resolved before accepting Jesus as the Messiah. For one thing, they never used miracles or the lack of them as a standard for the Messiah. The fact that the Messiah performs miracles is only natural, they think, because prophets of God were often surrounded by the miraculous; but more weight is put on what a prophet says and how he lines up with the Torah.

Jesus said He was the Son of God. This throws their intellectualism for a loop. They were not expecting the Messiah to be God incarnate (in the flesh). The Sadducees and Pharisees were given to intellectual argument but had a hard time getting down to heart level because most were far from the kingdom. They wanted to debate the exact following of the way rather than recognizing the Way that stood before them in the person of Jesus Christ. It is also important for Christians to understand that the Jewish view of Messiah has gone through change as authors McDowell and Stewart illustrate in the following:

"In the course of Jewish history the meaning of the Messiah had undergone changes. Originally it was believed that God would send His special messenger, delivering Israel from her oppressors and instituting peace and freedom. However, today any idea of a personal messiah has been all but abandoned by the majority of Jews. It has been substituted with the hope of a messianic age characterized by truth and justice.

Within the history of Judaism, from the time of Jesus of Nazareth until Moses Hayyim Luztto (died A.D. 1747, there have been a least 34 different prominent Jews who have claimed to be the Messiah...Carrying on one Jewish tradition, most of these self-proclaimed messiahs promised salvation from political, economic and cultural oppression, rather than spiritual salvation. Only Jesus of Nazareth perfectly fulfilled the Old Testament passages concerning the Messiah and only He validated His claims by His victory over death, displayed in His glorious resurrection from the dead (Acts 2:22-36)."[22]

VIII. WHAT ARE THE MAIN BRANCHES OF JUDAISM TODAY?

A. **Orthodox:** This is the traditional rabbinic Judaism, and it was the main form until the eighteenth century. Orthodox Jews carefully study the holy books and strive to follow the letter of the Law. These can include the traditional ceremonial and dietary laws. While all the branches of Judaism tend to keep the Sabbath day, the Orthodox Jews will also wear phylacteries, put *mezuzah* on their door posts, and keep kosher. Phylacteries *(tefillin)* are small black boxes containing Scripture portions worn on the forehead and arm. Mezuzah are small rectangular boxes containing various Scriptures mounted on the door posts of one's home. Keeping kosher is a term meaning to keep the dietary laws. For instance, they are not to mix meat and milk at the same meal.[23] Also, the practice of rituals such as circumcision, *bar mitzvah*, weddings, and mourning rites may occur in all the branches of Judaism.

One ultra-Orthodox movement called *Hasidic Judaism* or Hasidism has grown out of this Orthodox branch. Hasidic groups are separatists that identify with a leader who strictly follows the laws of Moses and certain mystical teachings.

B. **Conservative:** This branch is more lenient. It was established in the nineteenth century as a midpoint between the Orthodox and Reform branches. It grew rapidly in Germany and the United States. It seeks to emphasize the importance of the Law, the Hebrew language, and the traditions of Judaism but not to the level of orthodoxy. It is more concerned with form than doctrinal content. One offshoot of this branch is called *Reconstructionist Judaism* and has taken hold in America. This group emphasizes the need to adjust to the social climate.

C. **Reform:** As the liberal branch of Judaism, it arose in the eighteenth century during the Enlightenment as a reaction to orthodoxy. Doctrinal and religious beliefs vary greatly. With the exception of the Sabbath, there is little observance of dietary or other laws. The main focus is on cultural (ritual) and racial heritage. There is a mixture of humanism, ethics and the precepts of the prophets. It's interesting that the three Jewish branches could be compared to the liberal-versus-conservative-elements of Christianity. However, there's no counterpart to a Biblical Christianity that accentuates personal relationship with God.

D. **Messianic:** This is a growing branch of Judaism that represents those who have accepted Jesus Christ as Messiah and Savior. Praise the Lord! In the last couple of decades, more Jewish people have come to know Jesus as their Messiah than ever before. Hundreds of Messianic congregations have sprung up. These people often celebrate the festivals and customs that are popular within Judaism, but they do so through the eyes of being "new creatures" in Christ Jesus. They have accepted the atonement of His shed blood on their behalf and the new resurrection life that comes to those who believe. They understand that Jesus is the Son of God. Although they see Christians as being their brothers and sisters in the Lord, to them the term "Christian" generally implies a converted Gentile. Therefore, they refer to themselves as messianic—as Jews who have had the veil removed from their hearts (2 Corinthians 3:16).

Thinking Through The Scripture

"The next day John saw Jesus coming toward him, and said, 'Behold! The Lamb of God who takes away the sin of the world!'" (John 1:29)

"Then Moses called for all the elders of Israel, and said to them, 'Go and take for yourselves lambs according to your families, and slay the Passover lamb.'" (Exodus 12:21) NASB

Questions for discussion:
1. Why did John the Baptist call Jesus the Lamb of God?
2. Consider Hebrews 9:22. Why was it necessary for Christ to die for us?
3. Paul said, "I die daily" (1 Corinthians 15:31). Does this relate to sin or sin nature?

IX. WHAT ARE THE HOLY BOOKS OF JUDAISM?
A. **The Sacred Text:** The Old Testament or "Hebrew Bible" contains: 1) The Law which they call *the Torah,* 2) *the Prophets,* and 3) *the Writings.* "These books were originally written in Hebrew, except for parts of Daniel and Ezra and a verse in Jeremiah which were composed in Aramaic. These books are synonymous with the 39 books of Christianity's Old Testament. Their composure was over a period of some one thousand years, from 1400-400 B.C."[24]

Although, the Christian Old Testament has the same parts as the Hebrew Bible, the books have been rearranged and some divided. For example, the Hebrew Bible ends with Chronicles, whereas the Christian Old Testament ends with Malachi. (See the chapter on the Bible's Authenticity, sections VII - X.) The Jews consider the Torah (the Law of Moses or first five books of the Bible) to have the most divine authority and inspiration. This is followed in importance by the Prophets and finally the Writings. The importance of the Torah to the Jews cannot be overestimated. As Christians find God through Jesus, the Jewish people believe they find God through the Torah and love it. Trude Weiss-Rosmarin wrote this:

"But the awe and respect in which the Law is held does not diminish the love Israel has for it, a love that makes the Torah appear as the most beautiful bride possessed of ravishing charms and full of kindly tenderness. Thus the Torah is likened to the refreshing, life-restoring goodness of water, the sweetness of honey and milk, the joy and strength contained in wine, and the tender healing power of oil. It is an 'elixir of life' that brings healing to all men and affords protection against all evils. It is a white-hot fire which, though it does not consume its guardians, burns in eternal strength and majesty."[25]

B. **The Talmud:** The Talmud actually consists of the *Mishnah which was* compiled around 200 A.D. and the *Gemara* which was assembled about 550 A.D. The Mishnah contains about 1,000 pages of instruction for daily living. It is known as the *Halakah* (the way or walk). The Gemara is a commentary on the Mishnah and together they contain about 36 volumes. The Torah and Talmud are used heavily by the Orthodox branch of Judaism.

X. WHAT ARE SOME OF THE FALSE DOCTRINES OF JUDAISM?

A. **No Original Sin:** Judaism teaches that man is basically born good but then chooses to commit acts of sin or not. Christianity teaches that because of the transgression of Adam, all human beings are born with a sinful nature (Romans 5:12-21). This concept is not limited to the New Testament either (1 Kings 8:46). Even King David said that he was conceived in sin (Psalm 51:5).

B. **No Savior:** Since they don't understand that men are born with a sinful nature, they see no need for a Savior. When they hear Christians speak of being saved so that they won't go to hell in the afterlife, it is hard for them to relate because they are focused on how to live in "the right way" here and now. When witnessing, it is helpful to use the terms "redemption" and "redeemer" or "Messiah" because they are more familiar with these concepts.

Richard Robinson writes in *The Compact Guide to World Religions*,
"You can explain that as God freed the Israelites from slavery in
Egypt, so He wants to free us from the slavery to sin in our own
lives (Matthew 20:28; Titus 2:14)."[26]

C. **Atonement by Work**: Because they don't have a Savior, they think
    they must atone for their own sins through prayer, repentance, eth-
    ical behavior, good deeds and a measure of God's grace. It's not that
    they don't believe in God's mercy and grace; they do. Rather, it is
    that they underestimate God's Holiness and overestimate man's
    goodness. They don't realize what sinners they really are before a
    Holy and Righteous God. They still have a little of the mind set of
    the Old Testament in which Israel offered sacrifices to atone for
    their sins. Even though the ritual of sacrifice has been eliminated
    from Jewish worship, they still think they can make personal
    atonement through various acts.

    However, they missed the truth of what God was trying to tell
    them. It is a heart issue. While there was a season in history in
    which God accepted burnt offerings and blood sacrifice as a fore-
    shadowing of Christ dying on the cross (John 1:29), He eventually
    responded to their calloused hearts, in prophecy through Isaiah,
    and said, *"I have had enough of burnt offerings of rams and the fat of
    fed cattle. I do not delight in the blood of bulls, or of lambs or goats"*
    (Isaiah 1:11). He goes on to tell them that none of their rituals—
    New Moons, Sabbaths, assemblies, or appointed feasts—are
    accepted by Him because of the sin in their hearts. Later on in the
    book of Isaiah, we see that sin separates people from God (Isaiah
    59:2). To this day, Judaism still continues to focus on atonement
    for specific sins instead of the root of all sins, namely, the sin nature
    that we are all born with.

XII. WHAT ARE THE HOLIDAYS OF JUDAISM?
A. **The Sabbath**: The holy day of rest that lasts from sundown on
    Friday until sundown on Saturday. Traditional Jews refrain from
    work, driving, and household chores.
B. **Rosh Hashanah**: This Jewish New Year, celebrated in September or
    October, begins a ten-day period of High Holy Days. Traditionally,
    it was the beginning of Tabernacles which encompassed: Trumpets,
    Day of Atonement, and Tabernacles. In Richard Booker's insightful
    expose called *Jesus in the Feast of Israel*, he tells that on this day,
    they blew trumpets "extra long and extra loud, and they blew them
    all day. The type of trumpet blown was the ram's horn, for which
    the Hebrew word is *shofar*. The shofar was blown in remembrance
    of the ram that was sacrificed in place of Isaac (Genesis 22:13)."[27]

C. **Yom Kippur:** This Day of Atonement is celebrated ten days after Rosh Hashanah in September or October. It's the holiest day of the year. It is spent in fasting, confession of sins, forgiveness, and reconciliation with God. Some people read Isaiah 58:5-7 on this day in ritual.

D. **Sukkot:** The *Feast of Tabernacles* or Booths is celebrated five days after Yom Kippur in September or October and commemorates the ingathering of harvest (Leviticus 23:39-44). This is not currently observed by many Jewish people.

E. **Hanukkah:** This festive holiday lasts for eight days in November or December and commemorates the victory of the Maccabbees over the Syrian armies of Antiochus Epiphanes around 164 B.C.[28] The Menorah, a nine-branched candlestick, is a part of the ritual. One of the branches holds the "servant" candle used to light the other eight. Tradition says that when the temple was cleansed of the idolatrous acts of the Syrians, there was found only enough oil to light the lamp for one night. However, it burned for eight days. The Jews took this as a miraculous sign of God's blessing on the cleaning of the temple. Hanukkah has also borrowed the concept of gift-giving from Christmas.

F. **Purim:** This holiday is celebrated in February or March to recount the story of the book of Esther. The book of Esther is read aloud and there are often plays enacting the entire story.

G. **Passover:** This most popular of all Jewish holidays is celebrated in March or April and lasts a week. On the first two nights, there is a "Thanksgiving-like" atmosphere around a ceremonial dinner called a *seder.* The events of the book of Exodus are retold at the seder which symbolizes the *Feast of Passover.* People eat unleavened bread the entire week (Exodus 12).

H. **Shavout:** The Feast of Weeks comes in May or June, seven weeks after the Passover, and commemorates the giving of the Ten Commandments. It is also known as the *Feast of Pentecost* (Feast of Harvest, and Day of First Fruits) because it literally comes fifty days after the Feast of Passover (Lev. 23:15-21). Pentecost means "50."

I. **Jubilee:** God told Israel that every fiftieth year was a very special time of rejoicing (Leviticus 27). In the year of Jubilee, the prisoners were set free, property was returned to the original owners, and the land was given a break from being worked. Liberty was proclaimed throughout the land. Today, much speculation is being done regarding the return of the Lord because the new nation of Israel has crossed her fifty year mark.

XIII. WHAT WAS THE TEN-POINT PROPHESY MADE BY MOSES?

A. Long before the Jews were driven from their land, Moses prophesied what would happen to them. The passages of Deuteronomy 4:23-31 and 30:1-6 form the points of the prophecy. This is well laid out in Richard Booker's book entitled *Blow the Trumpet in Zion*. It appears that the first seven points have already occurred. The last three points can only be concluded through speculation. Look up these passages in the Bible and consider the following points:[29]

  1) The Jews will break the covenant. Deut. 4:23-25
  2) God will drive them from their land. Deut. 4:26
  3) God will scatter them among the nations. Deut. 4:27
  4) Jews will be few in number among the nations. Deut. 4:27
  5) Jews will serve other gods. Deut. 4:28
  6) God will preserve a remnant for the latter days. Deut. 30:1-2
  7) God will bring the Jews back to their land. Deut. 30:3-6
  8) The Jews will go through distress ("tribulation?") Deut. 4:30
  9) The Jews will return to God. Deut. 4:30
  10) God will remember His covenant. Deut. 4:31

Thinking Through The Scripture

"For I do not want you, brethren, to be uninformed of this mystery, lest you be wise in your own estimation, that a partial hardening has happened to Israel until the fullness of the Gentiles has come in; and thus all Israel will be saved; just as it is written, 'The Deliverer will come from Zion, He will remove ungodliness from Jacob.' 'And this is My covenant with them, when I take away their sins.'" (Romans 11:25-27) NASB

Questions for discussion:
1. What do you think is meant by the "fullness of the Gentiles"? (Consider Luke 21:24; John 10:16; and Romans 11:12.)
2. Will Israel really be saved? Were these words by Paul a hope or a prophecy?
3. God is faithful to His covenant. What is your covenant with Him?

XIV. HOW CAN WE WITNESS TO THEM?

A. **Prayer:** The Bible exhorts us to *"Pray for the peace of Jerusalem"* (Psalm 122:6). Christians around the world should be praying for the Jews to gain true peace by turning to the Messiah Jesus. There are strong Biblical links between the Jews turning to the Lord and His return. We should be praying for Messianic Jewish congregations to grow and impact modern day Judaism. We should be praying that the veil is removed from their hearts (1 Corinthians 3:14-16).

B. **Love:** The Jewish people have suffered at the hands of many over the centuries, including Christians. As Romans 11:28 insinuates, it seems that sometimes they are "enemies" because they rejected Jesus, but we must remember it also tells us that they are "beloved" because of the heritage they gave us. As Christians, we must reach out in love to the Jews.

One author says, "True Christians are the only real allies that the Jews have today"[30] and this should be true because we understand the desire of God for them to return to the fold. There have been those who are not "true Christians" but disguise themselves as such and promote hatred, bigotry, and anti-Semitism. True Christians will show true Christian love.

C. **Witness:** Don't try to convert them to "Christianity." Rather, convert them to the Messiah Yeshua (Jesus). Be careful about using Christian slang. Use "Yeshua" instead of Jesus, and "Redeemer" instead of Savior. Point out the "Jewishness" of the New Testament Gospels. Show the fulfillment of Old Testament prophecies in the New Testament Christ. Use the Old Testament images that point to the New Testament suffering of the Messiah (For instance, Isaiah 53). Have them read one of the Gospels. Also, there might be an occasion to use the book of Galatians to show them God's plan for Jews and Gentiles.

If a Jewish friend invites you to a special holiday, do it. Besides just being a friendly thing to do, there is often symbolism in those ceremonies that point to the truth of Jesus Christ through which you can witness. If you are a pastor or Christian leader, consider emphasizing various Jewish holidays or ceremonies like the Passover meal and invite Jewish people in the community. Various Messianic Jewish organizations (such as Jews for Jesus) will come to your community and put on a Passover meal. They will use the ritual to reveal the truths of the Gospel and the Trinity concepts hidden under the veil of ritual.

End Notes

1. Jonathan Bernis, "Have You Hugged a (Messianic) Jew Lately?" *Charisma and Christian Life,* April 1997, pgs. 63-64.
2. George A. Mather and Larry A. Nichols, *Dictionary of Cults, Sects, Religions and the Occult* (Grand Rapids, MI: Zondervan Publishing House, 1993), p. 171.
3. Richard Robinson, "Judaism and the Jewish People," *The Compact Guide to World*

Religions, ed., Dean C. Halverson (Minneapolis, MN: Bethany House Publishers, 1996), p. 121.

4. *The Koran*, Sura 3:60.

5. Josh McDowell and Bill Wilson, *The Best of Josh McDowell: A Ready Defense* (Nashville, TN: Thomas Nelson Publishers, 1993), p. 296.

6. Trude Weiss-Rosmarin, *Judaism and Christianity: The Differences* (Middle Village, NY: Jonathan David Publishers, Inc., 1993), pgs. 24-25.

7. Fritz Ridenour, *So What's the Difference?* (Ventura, CA: Regal Books, 1979), p. 55.

8. Richard Booker, *Jesus in the Feasts of Israel* (Shippensburg, PA: Destiny Image Publishers, 1987), pgs. 11-12.

9. Josh McDowell and Don Stewart, *Handbook of Today's Religions: Understanding Non-Christian Religions* (San Bernadino, CA: Here's Life Publishers, Inc., 1982), p. 134.

10. Robinson, p. 122.

11. McDowell and Stewart, p. 135.

12. Mather and Nichols, p. 167.

13. Phillip Sigal, *The Halakhah of Jesus of Nazareth According to the Gospel of Matthew* (Lanham, MD: University Press of America, 1986), p. 159.

14. Richard Booker, *Blow the Trumpet in Zion* (Shippensburg, PA: Destiny Image Publishers, 1985), pgs. 95-96.

15. Ibid., p. 97.

16. David Dolan, "The Lord Will Dwell In Zion," *Charisma and Christian Life*, May 1998, p. 44.

17. Trude Weiss-Rosmarin, p. 15.

18. Ibid., pgs. 22-23.

19. Harvey Cox, *Many Mansions: A Christian's Encounter with Other Faiths* (Boston, MA: Beacon Press, 1988), p. 102.

20. Leonard Swidler, Lewis John Eron, Gerald Sloyan, and Lester Dean, *Bursting The Bonds? A Jewish- Christian Dialogue on Jesus and Paul* (Maryknoll, NY: Orbis Books, 1990), pgs. 56-57.

21. Ibid., p. 126.

22. McDowell and Stewart, pgs. 142-143.

23. Robinson, p. 128.

24. McDowell and Stewart, p. 144.

25. Trude Weiss-Rosmarin, pgs. 89-90.

26. Robinson, p. 136.

27. Booker, *Jesus in the Feasts of Israel*, p. 77.

28. Booker, *Blow the Trumpet in Zion*, p. 39.

29. Booker, p. 152.

QUESTIONNAIRE: LESSON SIXTEEN

NAME: _____   DATE: _____

1. There are approximately _____ million Jewish people. _____ % of them live in Israel.

2. Jews, Christians, and Muslims all look back to _____, a man in the Old Testament who was called by God about 2,000 B.C., as their father in faith.

3. List some similarities between Judaism and Christianity: _____

_____

_____

_____

4. The Jewish people have had an amazing history. Moses led the Hebrews out of Egyptian bondage about 1400 B.C. and then Joshua led them into the _____ Land. God chose Israel to _____ Him and have a close relationship with Him. There were times when they would properly honor Him. He was the center of their life. However, at other times they strayed far from God and made images of false _____, such as Baal and Ashtoreh. They would worship the sun and moon and practice sorcery and _____. Finally, God judged their sin and took them into captivity by the hand of the Assyrians and Babylonians. The Temple of _____ was destroyed in 586 B.C. Eventually, between the years of 536 B.C. and 444 B.C., the Lord allowed them to return to Israel and rebuild the walls and temple. During this time and the years that followed, worship centers called _____ and religious teachers known as _____ emerged to help shape Judaism. After the Messiah _____ rose from the dead and ascended into heaven, He sent the Holy Spirit on the day of Pentecost, and the _____ was born. Thousands of Jewish people believed in Him and were saved; but many did not and rejected Him. In 70 A.D. the Jews were defeated by the _____, and they were once again driven from Jerusalem. Although, this time they were also scattered throughout the world. Terrible persecution has followed them many times throughout the generations. Sometimes even misguided Christians have been to blame. However, the worst tyranny and mistreatment done to them was during WWII when in Hitler's death camps _____ Jews were killed. After the war, many Jews fled back to Palestine to once again establish a Jewish nation. On May 14, _____, Israel once again became a nation. The modern tension and wars with the surrounding Islamic Arab nations are a foreshadowing of the Biblical prophecy regarding the soon _____ of the Lord Jesus Christ.

5. They use a _____ calendar creating the need to add a _____ every three years.

6. What is the name of God according to Jewish people? _____

7. Write out 2 Corinthians 3:14-16: _____

_____

_____

_____

_____

8. What was the Hebrew name for Jesus? _____

9. Jesus did not just come to walk in the way. He said, *"I am the _____."*

10. The most sacred text of Judaism is the Law or _____. Besides the Law, the Prophets, and the Writings, the Orthodox Jews also look to the Talmud as an instruction book for _____ _____. This is known as the Halakah.

11. How has the Jewish view of "Original Sin" messed up their theology?

_____

_____

_____

12. Although _____ is the most popular holiday, it is _____ that is considered the holiest.

13. List the three prophecies of Moses regarding the Jews that still need to be fulfilled.

a) _____

b) _____

c) _____

14. The Bible tells us to pray for the peace of _____ in Psalm 122:6. True Christians should show true love for the Jewish people. We should probably use the name _____ instead of Jesus and _____ instead of Savior when witnessing.

15. Consider your knowledge of Judaism before and after this lesson. Circle the number below that indicates how equipped you felt before taking this course to witness to someone in this religion as compared to how equipped you feel now. Be honest.

BEFORE 0 1 2 3 4 5 6 7 8 9 10 **AFTER** 0 1 2 3 4 5 6 7 8 9 10

ISLAM

"'It was Mr. Wilson's tears that led me to become a Christian,' said Abbas Abhari. Abbas was a Muslim cleric in the town of Damghan. When the Rev. Ivan Wilson, a missionary in Teheran, came to this little town and began to distribute Christian literature and talk with people about Christ, Abbas came one night to call on him. His purpose was not to become a Christian, or even to learn what the Christian teaching is, but to demonstrate the superiority of Islam to Christianity, and to humiliate the missionary. Mr. Wilson talked kindly to the Muslim caller, and explained the doctrines of the Bible to him. But Abbas made the usual response. No, Jesus was not God's Son, he did not die on the cross, and he foretold the coming of Muhammad. Also the Christian Scriptures have been corrupted, and Christians worship three gods. The missionary patiently tried to explain the misunderstandings and answer the arguments of the Muslim, but all to no avail. Abbas began to feel very proud of himself that he had defeated the Christian teacher in argument, when he saw a strange sight. The missionary began to weep! [Years later in an interview with Abbas] 'Mr. Wilson came here, he talked with me and argued with me, but I felt I had overcome him, and I was feeling very proud of myself. Then that man of God felt so sorry for me in my unbelief and pride that he began to weep. His tears did for me what his arguments did not do. They melted my heart, and I believed and became a Christian. Later I was baptized'."[1] —William Miller

I. WHAT ARE SOME IMPORTANT DEFINITIONS?
    A. *Allah* - God of Islam. Prior to Muhammad, Allah was considered a moon deity.

B. *Hadith* - It means "tradition". One of Islam's holy books.

C. *Islam* - It means "submission" (to Allah, the God of Muhammad who founded this religion).[2] It is sometimes incorrectly referred to as Mohammedanism.

D. *Mecca* - City in Saudi Arabia and birthplace of Muhammad, holy place of Islam.

E. *Muhammad* - The prophet and originator of Islam. There are various spellings.

F. *Muslim* - It means "one who is submitted" to God. A follower of Muhammad.

G. *Quran* - Recite. The holy book of Islam. Often spelled Koran, Qur'an, or other.

II. WHAT IS THE SIZE AND STRENGTH OF ISLAM TODAY?

A. Islam is the second largest religion in the world, second only to Christianity.[3] There are approximately 1.2 billion Muslims in the world, almost one-sixth of the world's population. The religion dominates 52 countries of the world.[4] While Bible-Believing Christianity is the fastest growing religion,[5] the following shows the threat of Islam. Author George Otis Jr. shows the strength and potential conflict between Christianity and Islam in his book *The Last of the Giants*:

"Of all the spiritual superpowers facing the Church...the strongest, and certainly the most visible, of these is Islam...Islam is predicted to double in size somewhere around the year 2020...One Islamic researcher reckons there are some 50 million new Muslims each year."[6]

B. There are approximately 5 to 6 million Muslims in the United States and the number is rapidly increasing. Each year about 100,000 Muslim immigrants enter the U.S. legally and about 45,000 illegally. Other factors adding to the increase are high birth rates among Muslims, marriage between Muslim men and American women, and the rise of conversions in America. It is figured that there are more than 25,000 conversions to Islam in the U.S. each year.[7] The following gives an example of how broad the Islamic influence is in the U.S. As author Ron Peck implies, we should not underestimate Islam's plan to evangelize the United States:

"Today there are more than 1,200 mosques in America—at least 1 in every state. Eighty percent are believed to have been founded during the last 10 years. Many have been built with funds received from Islamic nations. There are also 165 Islamic schools, 426 Islamic associations, and about 90 Islamic publications. Again, the majority of these endeavors are funded by Saudi Arabia, Kuwait, and other oil-rich Islamic nations, whose ultimate goal is to *Islamise the United States.*"[8] (italics added)

III. WHAT ARE SOME SIMILARITIES & DIFFERENCES WITH CHRISTIANITY?

A. **Similarities:** Even though it often appears that Christians and Muslims have nothing in common, this is not entirely accurate. As Phil Parshall points out in *The Cross and the Crescent*, "Christianity and Islam are similar in many ways. The unity of God is a great foundational truth discernible within both. Allah, like the Christian God, is a deity of mercy, truth, and judgment. The ninety-nine names ascribed to Allah are, for the most part, in harmony with the Biblical description of God.

In Islam, Jesus is described as virgin-born and performer of miracles. He is alive in heaven today and will return to earth in the end times. Muslim ethics, with few exceptions, parallel those of Christianity. The ethical distinctives of Islam that are in conflict with the New Testament are generally in harmony with those of the Old Testament."

B. **Differences:** Phil Parshall goes on to talk about the contrast between the world's two largest religions. "Yet much separates the world's two largest monotheistic religions. Sin, to Muslims, is a choice, not an inheritance, whereas in Christianity it is both. For Muslims, God is a force, not a friend. The Quran, not the Bible is the inerrant, syllable-by-syllable, dictated word of Allah. Jesus Christ was not crucified. And most importantly, Christ is neither Savior nor Son of God."[9]

C. **Knowing God.** In Christianity, we have the privilege of serving a God who desires for us to know Him and have a Father - child relationship with Him. However, as Norman Geisler and Abdul Saleeb point out in *Answering Islam: The Crescent in the Light of the Cross*, "The Islamic view of God involves a form of agnosticism. Indeed, the heart of Islam is not to know God but to *obey* him. It is not to meditate on his essence but to submit to his will."[10]

Thinking Through The Scripture

"Father, the hour has come. Glorify Your Son, that Your Son also may glorify You, as You have given Him authority over all flesh, that He should give eternal life to as many as you have given Him. And this is eternal life, that they may know You, the only true God, and Jesus Christ whom You have sent." (John 17:3)

Questions for discussion:
1. Who has been given authority over all flesh? Who gives eternal life?
2. What is eternal life? Is it possible to have eternal life without knowing
    God and to have a personal relationship with the Lord Jesus Christ?

IV. WHO WERE HAGAR AND ISHMAEL?
A. **Hagar, the mistress (servant) of Sarai.** In Genesis 16 the story is
    told of Abram and Sarai, his wife. Sarai felt bad because she was
    barren. She told her husband to take her servant, Hagar, and con-
    ceive a son through her as was the custom in those days when a
    woman was barren. Abraham did as Sarai requested and Hagar con-
    ceived a son when Abram was eighty-six. Sarai and Hagar had great
    difficulties with each other at this time.

    Hagar fled from Sarai's jealousy, and she cried in the wilder-
    ness. God heard her. He told her to return to Sarai and submit to
    her authority. He also told Hagar to name her son Ishmael ("God
    will hear") and that his descendants would be too many to count.
    She also received a prophecy regarding Ishmael's character: *"And he
    will be a wild donkey of a man. His hand will be against everyone, and
    everyone's hand will be against him; and he will live to the east of all
    his brothers."* So Hagar returned to Sarai and Abram.

B. **Ishmael, son of Abram.** In Genesis 17, God changed Abram's name
    to Abraham and Sarai to Sarah. He told Abraham that Sarah would
    conceive a son in about a year, the son of promise. Abraham would
    be a hundred years old and Sarah ninety. This was to be the son
    through whom God would keep his covenant with Abraham. His
    name was to be called Isaac ("laughter"). At one point Abraham
    was struggling with the concept that he and Sarah would have a
    son in old age, and he sought God that Ishmael might be the one.
    The conversation recorded in Genesis 17:18-21 goes like this:

    *"And Abraham said to God, 'Oh, that Ishmael might live before You!'
    Then God said: 'No, Sarah your wife shall bear you a son, and you shall
    call his name Isaac; I will establish My covenant with him for an ever-
    lasting covenant, and with his descendants after him. And as for Ishmael,
    I have heard you. Behold, I have blessed him, and will make him fruit-
    ful, and will multiply him exceedingly. He shall beget twelve princes, and
    I will make him a great nation. But My covenant I will establish with
    Isaac, whom Sarah shall bear to you at this set time next year."*

C. **A Great Nation.** The Bible indicates that Ishmael's descendants
    would become a great nation. This is confirmed in chapter 21. In
    Genesis 25:13 we are told the names of Ishmael's twelve sons and

the location of their habitation to the east of Isaac's descendants (the Hebrews). Ishmael's descendants were called Ishmaelite's (Gen. 27:35) and became nomadic tribes wandering throughout northern Arabia. Even the Jewish historian, Josephus, states that "they are an Arabian nation."[11]

Today, there is a controversy over just how great a nation Ishmael's descendants have become. Many Muslims claim Ishmael as their direct ancestor and all of Arabia as descended from him. Others, more accurately, see many people groups that came together to comprise Arabia and especially Islam which includes many nations. Islam makes much of this ancestry because it links them to Abraham. This is important because they believe that Islam was the original religion of mankind and that "every new-born human being is a Muslim by birthright."[12]

It is their belief that the Jews and the Christians violated their covenant with Allah, and therefore he raised up Muhammad the prophet to return people to the original religion. Their holy book, the Quran, states that Abraham was a Muslim. It says in Sura 3:60, "Abraham was neither Jew nor Christian; but he was sound in faith, a Muslim."[13]

Thinking Through The Scripture

"For they are not all Israel that descended from Israel; neither are they all children because they are Abraham's descendants, but: 'through Isaac your descendants will be named.' That is, it is not the children of the flesh who are children of God, but the children of the promise are regarded as descendants." (Romans 9:6-8) NASB

"You are all sons of God through faith in Christ Jesus, for all of you who were baptized into Christ have clothed yourselves with Christ...If you belong to Christ, then you are Abraham's seed, and heirs according to the promise." (Galatians 3:26,29) NIV

Questions for discussion:
1. What does is mean "neither are they all children because they are Abraham's descendants"? Whose line do the descendants come through? What does this imply regarding Ishmael?
2. If God's children are not according to the flesh then how are we able to become descendants of His? What is the promise?
3. Through what means do we become sons of God? What is an heir?

D. **The Problem with Ishmael**. Although many Muslims look to Ishmael and Abraham as their biological ancestors, God's covenant was with Isaac and his descendants. God does not change (Mal. 3:6) his ultimate plans and purposes. Therefore, it was through the line of Isaac that Christ the Messiah was born. This was the seed of promise prophesied in the garden to Adam and Eve (Gen. 3:15). Jesus gained the victory when He died on the cross and rose from the dead. (Heb. 2:14-15) It is through His name, and no other, that there is salvation (Acts 4:12). The great truth of Christianity is that eternal life is a free gift from God (Rom. 6:23) by faith alone (Rom. 1:17) and not of any works (Eph. 2:8-9).

One of the problems with Islam is that it ends up being a system of works to gain favor with Allah in exchange for eternal life. Although any system outside of Christ could be accused of the same charge, the Bible specifically uses Hagar and Ishmael to make the point that there is freedom in Christ but bondage under a law of works. In Galatians 3:21-31, the Apostle Paul shows us that Ishmael was born through the flesh but Isaac through the promise. *He makes an allegory to show that Sarah represents a free woman and Hagar a slave. His point is that Christians are born of the free woman and thus children of promise.* According to Scripture, the real issue is not so much one of ancestry to Abraham as it is faith in Jesus Christ and sonship to God.

V. WHAT IS THE PROBLEM WITH ISLAM IN REGARD TO THE SEVENTH CENTURY?
   A. **Because the religion and culture are one**. In Robert Morey's excellent work entitled *The Islamic Invasion* he states, "Islam is actually the 'deification' of the seventh-century Arabian culture. In a very profound sense, Islam is more cultural than it is religious."[14] Westerners find this concept difficult since we are use to a secular society with many religious options that are different from the secular.
   B. **Because the religion holds back progress**. Authors Ron Carlson and Ed Decker clearly illustrate the cultural stagnation of Islam when they say, "Islam imposes its seventh-century Arabian culture in its political expression, in its family affairs, in its dietary laws, in its clothing, in its religious rites, and in its language. Muslims are religiously compelled to impose seventh-century Arab culture on the rest of the cultures in the world. Muhammad took the political laws which governed seventh-century Arabian tribes and literally made them the laws of Allah, their God...Because there was no

concept of personal freedom or civil rights in the tribal life of seventh-century Arabia, Islamic law today does not recognize freedom of speech, freedom of religion, freedom of assembly, or freedom of the press. This is why non-Muslims (such as Christians) are routinely denied the most basic of human rights and are often physically attacked or jailed."[15]

VI. WHY DOES ISLAM HAVE A PROBLEM WITH PRE-ISLAMIC INFLUENCE?

Note: Muslims consider it blasphemous to even suggest that Muhammad's teachings and the Quran have their source in anything other than direct revelation from Allah.

A. **Islam teaches that the Quaran is from heaven.** Supposedly, Muhammad was illiterate and the revelations of the Quaran were new. Islamic tradition emphasizes that the Quaran was a miracle from Allah since Muhammad could neither read nor write. They contend that God revealed the truths of the Quaran to an illiterate Muhammad so that everyone would know that God was the real author rather than man. However, Muhammad was not as illiterate as Islamic tradition suggests. Archaeology proves that the Quaran was constructed by Muhammad from pre-existing written material and oral stories from the Arabian culture. In other words, much of what was considered new revelation in the Quaran was actually gleaned from previous writings by Muhammad. This creates doubt as to whether Muhammad received any revelation from a heavenly source.

B. **The name "Allah" and the name "Islam" were not new revelations.** Allah was a pagan moon god represented by a black stone in the Kaaba (temple) of Mecca before Muhammad was even born. There were 360 idols in the Kaaba and Allah was only one of them. The tribe into which Muhammad was born was devoted to Allah. The crescent moon was the pre-Islamic symbol of Allah. The word "Islam" had to do with an attribute of manliness. The meaning slowly developed into submission.[16]

VII. WHAT IS A SIMPLE TIME LINE OF MUHAMMAD'S LIFE?
(All the dates are A.D.)

A. **In Mecca:**

1)	Birth	570......	Raised by grandfather after parents' deaths.
2)	First Marriage	595......	To Khadijah, 40 year old, rich, widow.

| 3) | First Vision | 610...... | Supposedly by Gabriel in a cave near Mecca. |
| 4) | Sorrows | 619...... | Death of Khadijah; Muhammad's dream—ascension from Dome of the Rock. |

B. In Medina

1)	Emigration	622......	Muhammad left Mecca. Islamic calendar starts.
2)	Three Battles	624-625......	Established Muhammad's power
3)	Mecca Treaty	628......	Lasted one year then Mecca attacked his troops.
4)	Siege of Mecca	629......	Mecca surrenders. Islam controls most of Arabia.
5)	Death	632......	Muhammad died without warning.

VIII. WHO WAS MUHAMMAD AND WHAT IS THE ORIGIN OF ISLAM?

A. **Early Years.** Muhammad was born in A.D. 570 in Mecca to Abdullah (Abd-Allah) and Aminah. The tribe of Quraysh to which he belonged was in control of Mecca and watched over the Kaaba. They were devoted to Allah, the moon deity. Muhammad's father died before he was born, and his mother passed away when he was only six. He was passed around from grandparents to a rich uncle and finally to a poor uncle.

He grew up and worked as a camel driver until age twenty-five. At this time he married, Khadijah, a rich widow who was fifteen years older. She owned a fruit business in Mecca. Muhammad ran the business for fifteen years. It was at the age of forty that he claimed to receive revelations from heaven. This began his life as a prophet. The revelations were written down, but not until many years later. These became the Quran (Koran).

B. **A Prophet to the people.** There are four contradictory accounts of the first revelation and his call to prophethood. They are as follows: 1) Allah personally appeared to Muhammad in Sura 53:2-18 and Sura 81:19-24 , 2) The Holy Spirit did it in Sura 16:102 and Sura 26:192-194, 3) It was angels in Sura 15:8, and 4) finally, this was later amended to just one angel in Sura 2:97, the angel Gabriel.[17] Muslims subscribe to the view that says Muhammad was visited by the angel Gabriel. Since Mecca was a hub of many religions, including Judaism and Christianity, these influenced Muhammad. At times he even tried to be accepted by them as an apostle.

When Muhammad would receive a revelation, he would go into *an epileptic seizure*. He feared that he might be *demon-possessed* and even sought to take his own life once. However, he had another seizure and was told not to commit suicide. At first only his family believed him. His wife, Khadijah, encouraged him in the visions. Eventually, his following grew, but there was "opposition from disbelieving members of the Quraysh".[18] In order to appease the tribe, he claimed to have had a revelation that it was all right to worship the three idol daughters of Allah: Al-Lat, Al-Uzza, and Manat. The verses in Sura 53 revealing this compromise eventually came to be known as the "satanic verses" because Muhammad gave into the temptation of Satan through the pressure of people. Soon, some of his followers convinced him to reverse this view, so he did, and the tension grew more. [After Muhammad's death the verses were excluded from the Quran.]

By A.D. 622, three years after his wife and uncle had died, the opposition to Muhammad was so great in Mecca that he decided to move. First, he went to Taif, but he found no converts there and returned to Mecca. Suras 46:29-35 and 72:1-28 tell us that on his way back to Mecca he preached to the jinns (genies) and converted them to Islam. These spirits in turn preached Islam to the people coming under submission to Muhammad. This is probably fictitious, but it is also shamanism[19] (spirits who are directed by a wizard).

C. **Move to Medina.** Robert Morey estimates the significance of the move to Medina by the prophet with this insight: "The people of Yathrib had expressed interest and openness to Muhammad and his followers, so they secretly left Mecca and established themselves in Yathrib, renamed Medina. This move was of great significance in the development of Islam. Muslims use the date of the migration, the Hijra, as the start of the Muslim era [calendar]...The people were united into one single community, a brotherhood, called the Umma. The unity was no longer based on tribe, clan or blood relationships but on their status as believers, united by faith in the one God and Muhammad his apostle."[20]

D. **Three Battles.** During the years that Muhammad ruled in Medina, several battles with the Meccans helped established Islam in Arabia. After a successful raid on a caravan by his men, Muhammad got in the action and defeated a large caravan of Meccans who were threatening Medina in what is known as *the Battle of Badr*. In the next one, *the Battle of Uhud*, the Meccans attacked the Muslims. At first, it appeared the Muslims would win, but then the Meccans counter-attacked. The Muslims fell apart. Muhammad was almost killed having been stabbed in the mouth by a sword. The Muslims narrowly escaped.

In *the Battle of Ahzab*, the Meccans joined forces with strong Jewish tribes in the area and marched to attack Medina. However, the city had dug a large trench to protect itself.[21] The Muslims attacked and put them on the run. Muhammad repaid the Jewish settlements by looting and killing. "After one Jewish town had surrendered, 700 to 1,000 men were beheaded in one day while all the women and children were sold into slavery."[22]

E. **Siege of Mecca.** After the battles, a treaty between Mecca and Muhammad was suppose to protect the interests and religious beliefs of both for ten years. However, Muhammad broke the treaty and marched on Mecca within one year. By this time Muhammad had a great army of men and Mecca submitted to him. He entered into the city peacefully and most of the people became Muslims. The 360 idols in the Kaaba were destroyed with exception of the black stone representing Allah. With Muhammad now the undisputed leader, Arab tribesmen flocked to him and Islam swept through Arabia. He returned to Medina and lived there until his sudden death in A.D. 632 at the age of sixty-two.

F. **Character Problems.** Although Muslims don't like to admit it, Muhammad had some serious character problems. His greed was displayed in the large booty he amassed from raids on innocent towns and caravans. His quick temper would fly against any who disagreed. Those who opposed his religious views or showed the fallacy of his claims usually ended up dead.

As he rose to power, so did his harem of women. He had at least sixteen wives, two slaves, and four mistresses. One of the slaves, Mary, was a Christian and refused to marry him and so remained a slave. He lusted after his adopted son's wife and so took her by force, claiming a revelation from Allah that permitted it. One of his wives was only eight or nine years old when Muhammad took her to bed. He did all of this against his own supposed revelation from Allah that allows a man to marry no more than four women (Sura 4:3).

IX WHAT IS THE CREED OF ISLAM?

A. *There is no god but Allah and Muhammad is Allah's Apostle* is the creed of Islam.

B. Islam has the shortest creed of any religion in the world, and it is the best known by its followers. "This is the motto of the Muslim's family life, the ritualistic formula that welcomes the infant as a believer, and the final message that is whispered in the ear of the dying. By repeating these words, the unbeliever is transformed into a Muslim and the backslider is welcomed back into a spiritual brotherhood. By this creed the faithful are called to prayer five times daily, and it is the platform on which all the warring sects of Islam unite. It is the very foundation of the Islamic religion."[23]

C. **What about Jesus?** This creed exalts Allah, a moon deity, and Muhammad. Little room is made in Islam regarding Jesus as anything other than a prophet. Jesus is only considered one of many prophets who tried to persuade people about the truth of Allah.

This is a difficult issue for Muslims because of certain verses in the Quran. According to Muhammad, much of the New Testament and information about Jesus has been corrupted. Yet, even Muhammad admitted in Sura 3:40-50 that Jesus was the Messiah, born of the virgin Mary, a proclaimer of God's truth, a performer of miracles, an apostle, and one who makes disciples. It even has God saying, "I will place those who follow thee above those who believe not, until the day of resurrection."[24] Muhammad mentions the Gospel here but not the true Gospel. To Muhammad Jesus was not God and Savior. He did not die on the cross. Islam teaches that Judas actually died on the cross.

Thinking Through The Scripture

"But even though we, or an angel from heaven, should preach to you a gospel contrary to that which we have preached to you, let him be accursed. As we have said before, so I say again now, if any man is preaching to you a gospel contrary to that you received, let him be accursed. For am I now seeking the favor of men, or of God? Or am I striving to please men? If I were still trying to please men, I would not be a bond-servant of Christ. For I would have you know, brethren, that the gospel which was preached by me is not according to man. For I neither received it from man, nor was I taught it, but I received it through a revelation of Jesus Christ." (Galatians 1:8-12) NASB

Questions for discussion:

1. In this passage, the Apostle Paul tells how he received the gospel. By what manner did he receive the gospel? Who delivered it to him?
2. What does he mean "the gospel which was preached was not according to man?" How does Muhammad's teaching of the gospel line up with Paul's?
3. What is the sad truth about Muhammad and his teaching of the gospel?

X. WHAT ARE THE SIX MAJOR DOCTRINES OF ISLAM?
   A. **God:** There is one true God, named Allah, who is all-seeing, all-knowing, all- powerful.
   B   **Angels:** "The chief angel is Gabriel, who is said to have appeared to Muhammad. There is also a fallen angel named Shaitan (from the Hebrew, Satan), as well as the followers of Shaitan, the djinn (demons)".[25]
   C. **Holy Books:** Five holy books are mentioned in the Koran: 1) The scrolls of Abraham (now lost)[26], 2) The Tawrat (the Torah) given to the prophet Moses, 3) The Zabur (the Psalms) given to the prophet David, 4) The Injil (the Gospel) given to the prophet Jesus, and 5) The Quran revealed to the prophet Muhammad. Muslims believe that the books of the Bible are badly corrupted and that the Quran supersedes all previous revelations and is Allah's final revelation.
   D. **The Prophets:** Muhammad is the greatest of 28 prophets to which the Quran refers.
   E. **The End Times:** There will be a day of judgment on which Allah will reward or punish people according to their deeds. The results are heaven or hell. Heaven will be a place of eternal sensual pleasure.
   F. **Predestination:** Orthodox Islam is locked into fatalism which produces a very pessimistic view of life. Devout Muslims constantly make the comment "If Allah wills it" on most decisions because "Orthodox Islam teaches the absolute predestination of both good and evil, that all our thoughts, words and deeds, whether good or evil, were foreseen, foreordained, determined and decreed from all eternity, and that everything that happens takes place according to what has been written for it."[27]

   The ability to freely choose or reject Allah has been denied in Islam. This extreme view of predestination causes a lot of theological controversy even among Muslims because it creates natural contradictions within the Quran, eliminates human responsibility, makes God the author of good and evil, and gives rise to pantheism.

XI. WHAT ARE THE FIVE PILLARS OF ISLAMIC DUTY?
   A. **Affirmation:** Publicly repeat the *Shahadah - There is no god but Allah and Muhammad is Allah's Apostle.* This is recited constantly by devout Muslims.
   B. **Prayers:** Five times a day, Muslims must kneel and bow in the direction of Mecca. These are: Dawn, after midday, late afternoon, just after sunset, and before midnight.
   C. **Almsgiving:** One-fortieth (2.5%) of a Muslims' income must be given to the poor.

D. **Fast During Ramadan:** The highest of holy seasons is the Muslim's ninth month. Fasting is required every day during sunlight hours.

E. **Pilgrimage to Mecca:** Muslims are expected to go to Mecca at least once in their life time and pay homage to Allah at the temple. *Hajj* is a title for those who go to Mecca on this pilgrimage.

F. **The Holy War:** *(The Jihad)* Some add this as a sixth pillar of faith because in early Islam and even with some factions today, the religion is spread by force. It must be noted, however, that many Muslims consider the great jihad as "the struggle with one's own heart, the attempt to bring oneself in accord with the will of God. The various means appropriate to this struggle are prayer, study, and various forms of...inner-worldly asceticism."[28] Others today, interpret Jihad as the militant use of arms. "However, it has to be tempered by an approach which is merciful."[29]

Thinking Through The Scripture

"Therefore no one will be declared righteous in his sight by observing the law; rather, through the law we become conscious of sin. But now a righteousness from God, apart from law, has been made known, to which the Law and the Prophets testify. This righteousness from God comes through faith in Jesus Christ to all who believe. There is no difference, for all have sinned and fall short of the glory of God, and are justified freely by his grace through the redemption that came by Christ Jesus. God presented him as a sacrifice of atonement, through faith in his blood." (Romans 3:20-25) NIV

Questions for discussion:

1. The Muslims do many religious activities and keep their law, but what does the Bible say is revealed by the law? What can't we gain through keeping the law?

2. How does true righteousness from God come to us?

3. Is there a distinct difference to God between Jew, Muslim, or Gentile? Why?

4. How does the thought that we are "justified freely by his grace" line up with the Muslim's laws and works? What do they need to do for justification?

XII WHAT ARE THE QURAN AND THE HADITH?

A. **The Quran:** (Koran) This is the Bible of Islam. There are 114 Suras (chapters) contained in two major sections. There is the Meccan period with eighty-six Suras and the Median period with twenty-eight Suras, both corresponding to when the revelations were given to Muhammad. Muslims believe that the Quran is the greatest miracle ever and that it authenticates Muhammad's claim of being a prophet.

They believe that he was completely illiterate and that God divinely sent down this representation of the "preserved Eternal Tablet"[30] through an illiterate man to demonstrate his glory. "Muhammad did not write down his revelations but gave them orally. Shortly after his death, it became necessary to collect all the scattered pieces and chapters of his revelations into one book for use in the Muslim community."[31] Many had memorized sections of revelation. However, much of it was collected from Muhammad's scribes who wrote the revelations on "pieces of paper, stones, palm-leaves, shoulder blades, ribs, and bits of leather."[32] At first, there was much controversy over accuracy and authenticity of the various Suras collected. Many revisions took place. The Muslims considered the Judao-Christian Bible to be completely authentic until they came to realize that it contradicted the Quran. Therefore, they reasoned that it must be corrupted by man since the Quran was not.

B. **Four Things the Quran Means to Muslims:**
   1) It is to Muslims what Jesus is to Christians. It is the self-disclosure of God's commandments as compared to the self-disclosure of Jesus as God.
   2) The revelation was a miracle itself since Muhammad could not read or write.
   3) It was revealed in Arabic, therefore that is essential to understanding it .
   4) It is a call to worship and surrender, therefore the contradictions and lack of chronological order are not important. It is not an historical account.[33]

C. **The Hadith:** These are the collected traditions accumulated approximately 200 years after Muhammad's death. The Sunnite sect had six volumes while the Shia'ite sect has only three.[34] The Hadith records possible words and actions of Muhammad that are revered by Muslims. It is basically considered the other Islamic Bible besides the Quran.

To the Western mind, it is filled with inconsistencies, contradictions, and seventh-century superstition and idealogy, but to Muslims it is the standard by which to live. If Muhammad did it, they should do it—even though it might be unsanitary or even rude in many modern cultures. The volumes include thousands of sayings and actions.

XIII. WHAT ARE THE VARIOUS SECTS OF ISLAM?

A. **The Sunnites:** It is estimated that five out of six Muslims are Sunni. One of the main differences between Sunni and Shia'ite is centered on who would rule after Muhammad. The Sunni accepted the four Caliphs (Arabic for leader) that succeeded Muhammad. At the time, these were considered the best men in the community to lead it. Their position was not based upon kinship with Muhammad. Sunnites are considered moderate.

B. **The Shia'ites:** From the earliest days, a smaller group of Muslims "held that only a member of his [Muhammad's] family should succeed him. And since he had no son who survived him, it was thought that the only rightful successor was Ali, the husband of Fatima, the daughter of Muhammad."[35] The special appointed family leaders were called Imans and were considered by Shia'ites as the rightful political and spiritual rulers of Islam. The Shia'ites are more militant and fanatical than the Sunnites and take the Quran more literally. The majority of Iran is Shia'ite.

C. **The Sufi:** (Folk Islam) This is the mystical sect of Islam. They are rejected by many conservative Muslims for their beliefs. Sufi are not concerned so much about traditional Islam or monotheism. They often practice animism and spiritism. While formal orthodox Islam is concerned about ultimate truth about the nature of reality and the way to heaven, folk Islam is not. It is more concerned about day to day living and will use whatever it thinks might work. An example could be "A father with a sick son will ask the mullah to pray to God for him, tie an amulet to his arm to drive off evil spirits and give him modern medicine to kill the germs, all at the same time."[36]

XIV. WHAT IS THE BLACK MUSLIM MOVEMENT?

A. **The Nation of Islam:** Within the United States is a group known as *The Nation of Islam,* but this cultic organization is condemned by orthodox Islam who does not want to be identified with it, and rightfully so. The cult originated back in the 30's when an Afro-American named Elijah Poole (Elijah Muhammad) came under the influence of a white man named Wallace D. Fard. The two worked together for awhile and drew a following from the Afro-American population. Fard taught that the white man was to be hated because he was the devil, even though Fard was one himself. Eventually, Fard disappeared and Elijah Muhammad took over.

   The group has been connected with some terrorist activity. It was brought under public scrutiny when in February of 1965 Malcolm X, one of its former members, was assassinated by a black

Muslim death squad for publicly renouncing the teachings of W.D. Fard and Elijah Muhammad. When Elijah Muhammad died in 1975, the group was taken over by Louis Farrakhan who claims to be Allah in human form.

The teachings come from a mixture of Mormonism, Jehovah's Witnesses, New Age, Islam, and even Christianity. Some of them include that Christianity is a white man's religion, Jesus was a black African and only mortal, there is one temporary god for this world at a time, the concept of soul sleep, and that Master Elijah Muhammad is on a space ship.[37]

B. **Louis Farrakhan:** The organization has much money since it is funded by certain Middle East leaders who want to see the United States crumble. Farrakhan voices his message through radio, speeches, and the cult's newspaper, *The Final Call*. He drew about four hundred thousand Afro-Americans to his "One Million Man" march in Washington D.C. in October of 1995. However, the actual growth in his organization has been slight since the "membership in the Nation of Islam totals only 16,000."[38] As *Charisma* Magazine points out, Farrakhan changes his color like a chameleon in order to speak a message that will gain him public momentum:

"From 1970 to 1990, Farrakhan was generally rejected by mainstream black Christianity because of his condemnation of the Bible as a book written by 'the white man' and Christianity as 'the white man's religion.' But over the last few years, he has very cleverly and deceptively changed his strategy by adjusting his messages when addressing non-Muslim black audiences. He has begun to speak of Jesus in glowing terms, quoting the parables of Jesus and the epistles of Paul—with virtually no mention of Mohammed or the Koran. As a result, black Christians have begun to flock to his meetings, black Christian ministers have begun to invite him to speak in their pulpits and a million black men—many of them Christians—showed up for his 'day of atonement.' The fact is, Farrakhan is an Antichrist and a cult leader. I base this on his own recently revealed claims of being the Messiah. He actually claims to be Jesus."[39]

XV. WHAT IS THE SAD TRUTH ABOUT ISLAM?

A. **There is no Salvation in Islam:** An interesting account of a young convert to Christianity is given in *Ishmael my brother: A Christian Introduction to Islam*. It goes like this, "A Muslim man had been talking to the nurse working in the doctor's surgery. Suddenly he said, 'You know our language. You have worked in our country. You are a religious person...Why don't you become a Muslim? Quickly an answer came to her mind, 'Because there is no salvation in Islam'. The man thought for a minute, then he said, 'No, we cannot know about salvation.' The nurse was able to answer in this way because she remembered...a young Muslim girl who had become a disciple of Jesus. On one occasion [the girl] stood in front of a Muslim judge in a Muslim court. The judge asked her, 'Why did you leave Islam?' She answered, 'Because there is no salvation in Islam.' The judge turned to his advisors, experts in Islamic law, and asked them, 'Is this true?' After consulting together they answered, 'It is true.' The judge turned to [the girl] and said, 'There is no case. You are free to go'."[40]

B. **They have a False concept of Christ:** According to Geisler and Saleeb, "Most Muslims do not believe Jesus died on the cross, and none believe he paid the penalty for the sins of the world there. Further, while Islam teaches the resurrection of Christ, it is usually only viewed as part of the general resurrection on the last day. Thus while they hold that Jesus ascended into heaven after his time on earth, most do not believe that he was resurrected before his ascension. And none believe he was resurrected three days after his crucifixion...Further, for Muslims, Christ's second coming is not, as Christians believe, to set up a kingdom on earth but to tell Christians to follow Muhammad."[41]

XVI. WHAT ARE SOME POINTS TO REMEMBER WHEN WITNESSING TO MUSLIMS?

A. **Prayer:** F. B. Meyer once said, "The great tragedy of life is not unanswered prayer, but unoffered prayer." At times, it seems somewhat discouraging to see the growth of Islam in the world. There are times when even missiologists wonder how are we going to fulfill the Great Commission of Jesus (Matt. 28:19-20). However, they have discovered a "secret weapon" - prayer.

God is doing tremendous things around the world as a result of His people joining together in prayer. One example of this is the United Prayer Track of A.D. 2000 and Beyond. Millions of Christians have responded to a call to pray for the heathen nations and the gateway cities within the 10 / 40 Window. This is a strip of the world that is north of the equator from 10 degrees to 40 degrees latitude, and whose width extends from Northwest Africa eastward all the way to the Pacific Ocean. It includes the many nations of Northern Africa, the Middle East, and Southern Asia.

The fact is that more Muslims are coming to the Lord today than at any time in history. The reason is prayer. Prayer is pulling down the strongholds. Prayer is opening nations to receive the gospel message. Prayer is even responsible for an outpouring of heavenly visions, dreams, and miracles among heathen cities and nations. As a result, many are coming to know Jesus as Lord.

B. **Love:** Even though it might appear at times that Muslims are unmovable because of their strict adherence to Islamic law and customs, we should never underestimate the simple power that comes in love.

Shahrokh Afshar now pastors a Christian church for Iranians in Los Angeles. However, when he first came to the states he would argue his position with Christians. It was the love he saw in their lives that melted him. A Christian friend invited him to Thanksgiving dinner, and he was touched by the simple prayer of a father saying grace.[42] Simple acts of Christian charity may be the best way to approach Muslims. Their world view makes life a drudgery, so when they see the simple joy, peace, and love in a Christian's life it can be quite appealing.

C. **Witness:** Here are some tips for witnessing:

1) Always show positional respect for the Bible, i.e., don't set it on the floor.

2) Locate a Quran and find the passages that support the accuracy of the Bible and use it to demonstrate the Bible's authenticity. (Sura 5:50; 10:94). Also, use it to show that no other man ever did what Jesus did (Sura 3:40-50 - miracles; Sura 4:158 - ascension; Sura 43:61 - future sign of judgment.)

3) Order the book *Al-Masih: The Anointed One* from the Center for Ministry to Muslims located at 1445 Boonville Avenue, Springfield, MO, 65802. It uses the Koran and the Bible to present Jesus and the Gospel to Muslims.

4) Answer their questions regarding the Trinity. Show them that we believe in one God (Deut. 6:4; Eph. 4:6) who manifests Himself as three persons: God the Father, God the Son, and God the Holy Spirit (Gen. 1:26; Mt. 28:19; Mt. 3:16-17; Is. 9:6; Jn. 1:1,14,).

5) Be careful of cultural insults such as crossing legs and pointing the sole of your shoe at them.

6) Get them a Bible. It can change lives all by itself as the following true story from William Miller illustrates it so well:

"One day a shoemaker in Meshed brought home for his lunch some cheese which the grocer had wrapped in a page of the New Testament, which he was using for wrapping paper. After eating his lunch Qasim picked up the piece of paper and read the story of the man who hired laborers for his vineyard, and at the end of the day paid all the laborers the same wage, whether they had worked twelve hours or one. Qasim liked the story, and next day went again to the grocery store and bought cheese, asking that it be wrapped 'in another page of that book.' Finally, on the third day he bought what remained of the New Testament and showed it to his brother. The two of them then went to the missionary, who gave them a complete copy, and also gave them regular instruction in the Word of God. Both men were later baptized and were among the first believers in Meshed."[43]

End Notes

1. William M. Miller, *A Christian Response To Islam* (Phillipsburg, NJ: Presbyterian and Reformed Publishing Company, 1976), pgs. 125-126.
2. Fritz Ridenour, *So What's the Difference?* (Ventura, CA: Regal Books, 1979), p. 65.
3. Robert Morey, *The Islamic Invasion* (Eugene, OR: Harvest House Publishers, 1992), p. 5.
4. Ron Carlson and Ed Decker, *Fast Facts on False Teachings* (Eugene, OR: Harvest House, 1994), p. 100.
5. Bob Sjogren, Bill and Amy Stearns, *Run With the Vision* (Minneapolis, MN: Bethany House, 1995), p. 50.
6. George Otis, Jr., *The Last of the Giants* (Tarrytown, NY: Chosen Books, 1991), pgs. 58, 61.
7. Ron Peck, *The Shadow of the Crescent: The Growth of Islam in the U.S.* (Springfield, MO: Center for Ministry to Muslims, n.d. [probably 1994]), pgs. 10-11.
8. Ibid., p. 13.
9. Phil Parshall, *The Cross and the Crescent* (Wheaton, IL: Tyndale House Publishers, Inc., 1989), pgs. 13-14.
10. Norman L. Geisler and Abdul Saleeb, *Answering Islam: The Crescent in the Light of the Cross* (Grand Rapids, MI: Baker Book, 1993), p. 137.
11. *Josephus: Complete Works*, trans. W. Whiston (Grand Rapids, MI: Kregel Publications, 1980), p. 36.
12. Parshall, p. 204.
13. *The Koran*, trans. J. M. Rodwell (Rutland, VT: Charles E. Tuttle Co. Inc., 1994), p. 37.
14. Morey, p. 20.
15. Carlson and Decker, pgs. 101-102.
16. Morey, p. 37.
17. Ibid., p. 76.
18. Anne Cooper, compiler, *Ishmael my brother: A Christian Introduction to Islam* (Tumbride Wells, Great Britain: Monarch Publications, 1993), p. 106.
19. Morey, p. 80.
20. Ibid., pgs. 106-107.
21. Cooper, p. 108.
22. Morey, p. 83.
23. Geisler and Saleeb, p. 13.
24. *The Koran*, p. 36.
25. Ridenour, p. 68.
26. Cooper, p. 81.

27. Annemarie Schimmel and Abdoljavad Falaturi, *We Believe in One God* (New York: The Seabury Press, 1979), p. 85, as cited in Geisler and Saleeb, p. 28.

28. John Kelsay, *Islam and War: A Study in Comparative Ethics* (Louisville, KY: Westminster/ John Knox Press, 1993), p.34.

29. Bill A. Musk, *Passionate Believing* (Tunbridge Wells: Monarch Publications, 1992), p. 97.

30. Cooper, p. 80.

31. Geisler and Saleeb, p. 89.

32. Ibid., p. 90.

33. Cooper, p. 93.

34. Musk, p. 167.

35. Miller, p. 54.

36. J. Dudley Woodberry, ed., *Muslims & Christians on the Emmaus Road* (Monrovia, CA: MARC Publications, 1989), p. 49.

37. Morey, chapter 11.

38. Herbert Toler, "Marching To A Different Drum," *Charisma & Christian Life*, (May 1996): 31.

39. Ibid., p. 35.

40. Cooper, pgs. 293-294.

41. Geisler and Saleeb, p. 272.

42. "Escape From False Gods," *Charisma & Christian Life* (October 1997): 59.

43. Miller, pgs. 113-114.

QUESTIONNAIRE: LESSON SEVENTEEN

NAME: _____ DATE _____

1. Islam is the _____ largest religion in the world with about _____ million people.

2. The heart of Islam is not to _____ God but to _____ him.

3. Hagar was the mistress of _____ and the mother of _____. The father of the child was _____. When Hagar fled to the wilderness, she cried out and the Lord heard her. He told her to name her son Ishmael and that his descendants would be too many to _____. He also told her that he would have enmity with everyone and live to the _____ of his brothers. When Abram and Sarai were old, God changed their names to _____ and _____ and told them it was time for Him to fulfill his promise to them of a son. Abraham pleaded that it might be Ishmael that lived before the Lord, but the Lord said, "No". It was to be Abraham and Sarah's son, _____, that received the promise from the Lord. However, God did tell Abraham that Ishmael would become a _____ nation. Today, we can look back and see how God's plan unfolded. He knew why the promise needed to come through Isaac. Christians look to Abraham as their spiritual father. Also, Galatians chapter three shows us that we want to choose Sarah who represents a _____woman rather than Hagar the _____.

4. Islamic culture seems ancient because it represents which century?_____

5. Allah was a _____ moon god represented by a black stone prior to Islam.

6. The founder of Islam was _____. He received his first revelation when he was _____ years old. There are four different accounts of how he received the first revelation. The one that most Muslims adhere to is the one in which he was visited by the angel _____. Islam gained real control after Muhammad took siege of _____. He had some major character problems, one of which involved women. According to his own religion, he was only suppose to have _____ wives, but in his harem there were at least _____ women.

7. Write a paragraph on what you see as the fundamental problem displayed in Islam's creed. _____

_____

_____

_____

8. Why does the doctrine of Predestination create problems for Islam?

_____

_____

9. Christians know that their righteousness comes from _____ alone.

10. The Quran is the _____ of Islam. It is a collection of the revelations of Muhammad.

11. The Quran is to Muslims what _____ is to Christianity because they see it as the disclosure of God's commandment to men and Christians see Jesus as God's disclosure of Himself to man.

12. The _____ are the collected traditions held sacred by Muslims.

13. Tell a little about the three main sects of Islam:

a) _____ : _____

b) _____ : _____

c) _____ : _____

14. Who is the current leader of the Black Muslim movement in the U.S.?

_____

15. Although Muslims believe some things about Jesus, most do not believe that He died on the _____ or paid the penalty for the _____ of the world. The sad truth is that there is no _____ through faith in Jesus Christ in Islam.

16. What is the thing that you find the most interesting or upsetting about Islam? _____

_____

_____

17. List two points to remember when witnessing to Muslims:

a) _____

b) _____

18. Consider your knowledge of Islam before and after this lesson. Circle the number below that indicates how equipped you felt before taking this course to witness to someone in this religion as compared to how equipped you feel now. Be honest.

BEFORE 0 1 2 3 4 5 6 7 8 9 10 **AFTER** 0 1 2 3 4 5 6 7 8 9 10

LESSON 18

BAHA'ISM

"There is very little indeed that a true Christian can have in common with the faith of Baha'i. There is simply no common ground on which to meet or to talk once the affirmations have been made on both sides of Jesus Christ, as opposed to Baha'u'llah. Of course, there is the common ground of Scripture upon which we can meet all men to proclaim to them the indescribable gift of God in the Person of Christ, but there can be no ground for fellowship with the Baha'i World Faith, which is, at its very core, anti-Christian theology... No Christian can refute the perversions of the Baha'i World Faith unless he is first aware of their existence and of their conflict with the doctrines of the Bible. We must therefore be prepared to understand the scope of the teachings of the Baha'is, their basic conflict with the Gospel and the means by which we may refute them as we witness for Christ."[1] —Walter Martin

I. WHAT ARE SOME SIGNIFICANT WORDS IN BAHA'ISM?

Abdu'l Baha - Formerly known as Abbas Effendi,[2] the son of Baha'u'llah.

Bab - Means "Gate." The founder of Baha'ism.

Babists - Followers of the Bab.

Baha'i - A follower of Baha.[3] The movement is called Baha'i or Baha'ism.

Baha'u'llah - Means "The Glory of God." Co-Founder of Baha'ism.

Hajj - Pilgrimages to the cite where the Bab's house stood and to Baha'u'llah's house.

Imam - Name of the spiritual leader of a Muslim Shia'ite sect.

Madhi - The Promised Messiah or him whom God should manifest.

Qibla - Prayer direction to the tomb of Baha'u'llah near Acre in Palestine.

Salat - Ritual prayer.

Sawm - Annual fasting.

Shia'ites - A Muslim sect who looks to leadership in the family line of Muhammad.

Shoghi Effendi - Twentieth Century leader of Baha'i after the death of Abdu'l Baha.

Siyyid - A title referring to the descendants of Muhammad.

Ziyara - Lesser pilgrimage to the tombs of the Bab and Baha'u'llah.[4]

II.   WHAT IS THE SIZE AND INFLUENCE OF BAHA'ISM TODAY?

     A.   To some, Baha'i is a sect of Shia'ite Islam. To Muslims, it is an aberrant cult that should be stamped out, but to others, it is an emerging world religion with its own distinctives. Statistics are somewhat conflicting, but it appears to have about 5 million members worldwide in over 205 countries with more than 100,000 members in the U.S.A.

         Baha'ism which began in Iran in 1844 would have probably become just another Islamic sect, "but in 1894, the movement became one of the first missionizing Eastern religions to reach the West."[5] It has vigorously sought for converts in Africa, India, parts of South America, East Asia, and the Pacific Islands. The writings of Baha'u'llah, which Baha'is revere as Scripture, have been translated into hundreds of languages.

     B.   Although the most important Baha'i community is still in Iran,[6] the World Center of Baha'i Faith is located in Haifa, Israel. However, there are temples in other places as well, including the United States. In the Chicago suburb of Wilmette is the national headquarters for the U.S. It has "nine sides to the building, nine pillars, nine arches, nine gates, and nine fountains"[7] to represent the nine manifestations or prophets of Baha'i.

         The United States is not just another country to them. Abdu'l Baha, the son of Baha'u'llah, indicated that it would become the "cradle" of the administrative order and also that the West would replace the East in the importance of radiating the divine guiding light.[8]

     C.   Baha'ism has an appeal for "those who long for world peace and elimination of religious divisions over peripheral doctrines."[9] It overlaps somewhat with the beliefs of Theosophy, Spiritism, Freemasonry,[10] Hinduism, and the New Age movement in that they all see, to varying degrees, similar elements in all religions and an underlying force moving them into one world order. Some of those drawn to Baha'ism have been Count Leo Tolstoy; the daughter of Woodrow Wilson; Crosby, Stills, Nash, and Young; Jimmy Seals and Dash Croft, as well as "Maurice Strong, secretary general of the United Nations Conference on Environment (UNCED), more popularly known as the Earth Summit."[11]

III. WHAT IS SYNCRETISM?
   A. **In religion:** It is the attempted union of different or even opposing elements of various religions into a single new religion. For example, voodoo on the island of Haiti is syncretic in that it combines elements of Roman Catholicism with ancient African polytheistic beliefs.

   In his book *Christianity and World Religions: The Challenge of Pluralism*, author Norman Anderson says, the "syncretic approach may be defined as the view which holds that there is no unique revelation in history, that there are many different ways to reach the divine reality, that all formulations of religious truth or experience are by their very nature inadequate expressions of that truth and that it is necessary to harmonize as much as possible all religious ideas and experiences so as to create one universal religion for mankind...Baha'ism represents a syncretic religion which combines elements drawn from several faiths in a novel synthesis."[12]

   B. **The Need for Separation:** For Christians, there can be no syncretic compromise when it comes to serving the one true God. The central teaching of the Old and New Testaments are that the Lord God created man (Genesis 1 - 3) who fell away from Him and served himself rather than his Creator (Romans 1:18-25). He desires for us to have no other gods before Him (Exodus 20:3). One of the main faults of Israel was syncretism. They would serve Baal (Judges 2:11), Ashtoreth (1 Kings 11:5), Molech (Jeremiah 32:35), and others.

   God judged them for their syncretic ways, but His overall plan was to redeem men from their fallen state of death and bring salvation to the nations (Psalm 95). In His mercy, He sent His only Son, Jesus, to show us the way and to be the propitiation for our sins (Isaiah 53) by dying on the cross for us (1 Peter 2:24). He rose from the dead on the third day as the prophecies predicted (1 Cor. 15:1-8) and eventually ascended into heaven in the sight of many witnesses. The basic understanding of the Scriptures is that Jesus Christ is God. He came to set us free from sin, bondage, and death. He loves us, but wants us to know the truth about Him and worship only Him.

IV. WHAT WERE THE ROOTS OF BAHA'I?
  A. Baha'i emerged out of the Islamic or Muslim faith[13] in the mid-nineteenth century. Muslims follow the teachings of their prophet Muhammad from their holy book, the Koran, and revere Allah as God. Allah was simply a pagan moon deity that Muhammad's clan revered. When Muhammad took control of Arabia in the seventh century (630 A.D.), he forced all the people to worship Allah. After Muhammad died just two years later, there was division over who would succeed him. This created the Sunni Muslims and the Shi'ite Muslims.
  B. The Shi'ites looked to a direct descendant of Muhammad, through his daughter Fatima, as their spiritual leader. The title of this position was Imam. In 878 A.D., the twelfth Iman mysteriously disappeared. He was called the Madhi (the rightly guided or promised one), and the Shi'ites have awaited his return ever since. Since Iran was the center of the Shi'ite sect of Islam, it was in this country that the return of the Madhi was expected. On May 23, 1844, in the town of Shiraz, Iran, a young man named Siyyad (a title referring to the descendants of Muhammad) Ali-Muhammad (or Mirza' Ali-Muhammad[14]) claimed that he was the Promised One. Siyyad Ali-Muhammad referred to himself by the traditional Muslim title of "the Bab," meaning the gate. This was the beginning of the Babi faith and his followers became known as Babists.[15] Eventually, this turned into the Baha'i faith.

V. WHAT IS A SHORT SKETCH OF THE HISTORY OF BAHA'I?
  A. 1844   The Bab proclaims he is the twelfth Iman. Tension with the Shah.
  B. 1850   The Bab executed by firing squad in Tabriz, Iran.
  C. 1863   Baha'u'llah proclaims he is the Promised One whom the Bab prophesied.
  D. 1892   Baha'u'llah died in exile in Palestine. His son, Abdu'l-Baha succeeds him.
  E. 1894   Baha'i becomes a missionizing religion. First Western converts.
  F. 1907   First U.S. Baha'i convention.
  G. 1912   Abdu'l-Baha traveled in the U.S. and dedicated the building site in Wilmette.
  H. 1921   Death of Abdu'l-Baha. His grandson, Shoghi Effendi takes control.
  I. 1937   Shoghi begins the first 7 year plan of missions to establish spiritual assemblies.

J.   1953   Baha'i temple formally dedicated in Wilmette near Chicago.
K.   1957   Shoghi Effendi dies without leaving a successor.
L.   1963   National Assemblies elects the first Universal House of Justice.
M.   1974   Five-year missionary plan increased size by forty percent.
N.   1990's   5 million members in over 205 countries. Books in many languages.

Thinking Through The Scripture

"Then Jesus said to them again, 'Most assuredly, I say to you, I am the door of the sheep. All who ever came before Me are thieves and robbers, but the sheep did not hear them. I am the door. If anyone enters by Me, he will be saved, and will go in and out and find pasture. The thief does not come except to steal, and to kill, and to destroy. I have come that they may have life, and that they may have it more abundantly. I am the good shepherd. The good shepherd gives His life for the sheep." (John 10:7-11)

Questions for discussion:
1. What architectural type does Jesus say He represents? Who do the sheep hear? Where do they enter in? What do they gain by entering in through Jesus? What does He give us abundantly?
2. Siyyad Ali-Muhammad said that he was "the gate" (the Bab). Even though the Baha'i faith focuses more on Baha'u'llah today, the Bab proclaimed that he was the Promised One. How does this line up with what Jesus said? Does the Bible teach that there is any other door to salvation than Jesus?

VI HOW DID BAHA'I BEGIN AND WHO ARE THE FOUR MAIN FIGURES?
A. **The Bab**: Siyyad Ali-Muhammad was born in Shiraz, Iran, on October 20, 1819, to descendants of the Prophet Muhammad. After his father died, his uncle raised him. He worked in his uncle's business and married Khadijih while in his early twenties. When Siyyad proclaimed a couple of years later, in 1844, that he was the long awaited Madhi, curiosity seekers came from all over to hear him. Within a few weeks, the Bab had eighteen disciples whom he called the "Letters of the Living."[16] He commissioned these to go throughout Iran and announce that the Day of God, spoken about in the Koran, had dawned.

The next six years brought growth to his movement but also much opposition by Islamic fundamentalists. It was one thing for Siyyad to claim to be the twelfth Imam, but he claimed to be the "Primal Point", a title reserved for Muhammad alone.[17] Thousands of the Babists were killed for their beliefs, and Siyyad spent about three years in prison before he was sentenced to death. He was executed by firing squad on July 8 or 9, 1850, in the town of Tabriz.[18]

The Baha'is claim that a miracle took place at this time. Supposedly, 750 Armenian Christian troops fired on the Bab. When the smoke cleared, the Bab was gone. The bullets had cut through the ropes that held him. They found him back in his cell giving final instructions to a disciple. The troops refused to fire on him again, so a fresh batch were called in and the execution was completed. Some of those in Baha'i try and compare this supposed miracle (which lacks substantial historical support) to the death and resurrection of our Lord Jesus Christ. They call it a "second Calvary,"[19] but there is no real comparison to Jesus who rose from the dead.

B.   **Baha'u'llah**: Baha'is claim that the Bab was actually a herald of Baha'u'llah in the same way that John the Baptist heralded Jesus. According to J. K. Van Baalen in *The Chaos of Cults*, Baha'ism teaches that the Bab "constantly pointed to a divine prophet who was shortly to succeed him. Before his death he sent his signet rings and writings to one of his friends and foremost supporters, one Mirza Husayn 'Ali, his senior by two years. The two had never met, and were not related."[20]

Baha'is "believe that the Bab and Baha'u'llah were Co-Founders of their Faith,"[21] both being manifestations of God's Messenger to men. Mizra Husayn 'Ali Baha' Allah was born in 1817 to a noble family in the province of Mazindaran. His parents were wealthy and influential. He turned down a position as chief minister of the province to become a Babist. Many of the Bab's followers were peasants, so Mizra Husayn 'Ali, with his wealth, education, and social position, stood out as a Babist leader even though he never met the Bab in person. They corresponded through letters and messengers.[22]

The Bab was killed in 1850. Thirteen years later, in 1863, Mizra Husayn 'Ali proclaimed that he was Baha'u'llah (The Glory of God), the Madhi and Promised One to whom the Bab had referred. However, there was much controversy over the issues of who was to succeed the Bab and over certain doctrines, as author Denis Maceoin points out in his chapter on Baha'ism:

"Leadership of this group initially fell to the son of an Iranian state official, Mirza Yahya Nuri Subh-i Azal (c. 1830-1912), regarded by many as the Bab's appointed successor...The question of authority was concentrated by the early 1860's in *a growing power struggle between Yahya and his half-brother, Mirza Husayn 'Ali Baha' Allah,* who had by then become the de facto leader of a large section of the Baghdad community. Whereas the Azali faction was essentially conservative, seeking to preserve the late doctrines and laws of the Bab, *the Baha'i sect sought for radical modifications in doctrine and practice.* In his early writings, Baha' Allah effectively reconstructed the Bab's highly complex system, simplifying it and preaching tolerance and love in place of the legalism and severity of the later Babi books."[23] [italics added]

Baha'u'llah was eventually banished from Persia for his potential threat to the Shah. He was exiled to Palestine where he spent the last 24 years of his life writing extensively and creating various ordinances for the community of Iranian followers that surrounded him. He wrote letters to the kings of the earth trying to convince them to except his one new overall religion for mankind. He died on May 29, 1892, having spent much of his life imprisoned. Baha'is consider Baha'u'llah the Lord of Hosts, the Prince of Peace, and the Everlasting Father[24] who was prophesied by Isaiah to come into the world. They teach that there was a great outpouring of the Holy Spirit through Baha'u'llah.[25] Indeed, he even taught that he was "the Spirit of Truth"[26] of whom Jesus prophesied (John 16:13) would come.

Thinking Through The Scripture

"*This is He who came by water and blood—Jesus Christ; not only by water, but by water and blood. And it is the Spirit who bears witness, because the Spirit is truth…If we receive the witness of men, the witness of God is greater; for this is the witness of God which He has testified of His Son. He who believes in the Son of God has the witness in himself; he who does not believe God has made Him a liar, because he has not believed the testimony that God has given of His Son. And this is the testimony: that God has given us eternal life, and this life is in His Son.*" (1 John 5:6,9-11)

Questions for discussion:
1. Of whom did the Spirit of God bear witness? What are some of the things that happened in Jesus' life that bear the Witness of the Spirit that He was the Son of God? What happens to him who believes in the Son of God? If someone does not believe in God's witness, what is that person really saying?
2. What is the testimony of God regarding the Son? To whom has eternal life been given? In Whom do we find that life? Is there life in any other?

C. **Abdu'l-Baha**: Born in 1844, the son of Baha'u'llah assumed leadership after his father's death in 1892. He was called the "Great Branch" by his father, referring to the prophecy in Isaiah 11. Baha'u'llah had solidified a covenant with his followers before he died which "made it clear that Abdu'l-Baha was to be regarded not as a prophet or divine messenger, but rather as the perfect human example of Baha'u'llah's teachings."[27] Abdu'l-Baha was instrumental in establishing the Baha'i faith in Europe and North America. He pushed for missions.

A man named Kheiralla preached Baha'ism in Chicago, and one of his converts, Louisa Getsinger, lectured throughout the United States. A rich philanthropist named Phoebe Hearst took fifteen Americans on the first U.S. pilgrimage to Acre in Palestine where Baha'u'llah died. By 1907, when the first U.S. Baha'i convention was held, there were a number of believers. Abdu'l-Baha toured the U.S. in 1912 and dedicated the building site of what was to become the U.S. Baha'i Center near Chicago in Wilmette.

There was a power struggle in Abdu'l-Baha's life as a younger half-brother, Muhammad-'Ali, and Kheiralla rose up to each take control, but Abdu'l-Baha prevailed. He died in 1921 leaving Shoghi Effendi, his grandson, as successor. However, there is much controversy within Baha'ism about whether or not he really selected Shoghi. Abdu'l-Baha was a respected leader for his humanitarian views. However, he erroneously taught that the "Christian cycle" had ended and that in the Baha'i cycle the prophecy of Isaiah 11 would come to pass as the whole world "will become one religion, one faith, one race, and one single people, and will dwell in one native land which is the terrestrial globe."[28]

Thinking Through The Scripture

"Take heed that no one deceives you...For nation will rise up against nation, and kingdom against kingdom...Then many false prophets will rise up and deceive many. And because lawlessness will abound, the love of many will grow cold. But he who endures to the end shall be saved." (Matthew 24:4,7,11-13)

Questions for discussion:
1. Abdu'l-Baha taught that the prophecy of Isaiah 11 was beginning and that the Baha'i cycle would usher in peace and oneness. However, Jesus told us that other things would happen in the last days? What were some of those things?
2. When you look at the world today, do you see nation rising against nation? Do you see false prophets rising to deceive many? Is lawlessness abounding?

3. The word love is from the Greek *agape* meaning "godly love." Do you see people's love for God growing cold? Why is this so?
4. What is the promise for Christians who endure until the end? In regard to love, what do we need to protect against?

D. **Shoghi Effendi**: The advancement of Baha'i into an emerging world religion certainly owes much to this man. Shoghi (1897 - 1957) helped westernize Baha'i bringing a great deal of organization to it. Basic Baha'ism teaches that Abdu'l-Baha appointed Shoghi to be the "Guardian" of the faith in his Will and Testament. The two important responsibilities of the Guardian were the interpretation of Baha'i teachings and the guidance of the community. Shoghi did not interpret the teachings or guide the community in the way that many Baha'i thought he should.

There have been splits occur within Baha'ism. However, any Baha'i loyal to the current organization would say that these haven't really been splits. Rather these were "covenant breakers" who tried to gain power and lead others away. One Baha'i said that these "covenant breakers" are no more representative of true Baha'ism than David Koresh is of true Christianity. While I agree with the fact that some are wolves in sheep's clothing, there are faction groups within Baha'ism who simply disagree with the way some things have been done. One such group caused a split and are know as "Free Baha'is."[29] Free Baha'is believe that Shoghi forged Abdu'l-Baha's Will and Testament to make a position for himself. They teach that he mistranslated Baha'u'llah's words and misinterpreted much of Baha'i teaching for his own gain. What developed they refer to as "Political Shoghism," and they compared Shoghi to Judas.[30] Shoghi excommunicated any who held to this belief, including some of Abdu'l-Baha's own family. Shoghi died unexpectedly in 1957 of a heart attack while in the middle of a crusade. He had not appointed a successor.

In 1963, The Universal House of Justice was elected at the International Convention by the National Spiritual Assemblies. They in turn are elected by the Local Spiritual Assemblies. The movement continues to grow and evangelize all other religions.

VII. WHAT ARE SOME OF THE FALSE TEACHINGS OF BAHA'I?
   A. **Nine Prophets of God**: They teach that there have been nine messengers or "sanctified Mirrors"[31] shining forth the word of God. Mather and Nichols in their dictionary on cults tell us that some

Baha'is teach that these nine messengers are Moses, Buddha, Zoroaster, Confuscious, Jesus, Muhammad, Hare Krishna, Bab, and Baha'u'llah.[32] Others put the emphasis on Adam, Noah, Abraham, Moses, Zoroaster, Buddha, Jesus, Muhammad, and Bab, with Baha'u'llah being considered the Universal Manifestation of all times.[33]

However, this list is contradictory and confusing to say the least. Many of these are from the Christian religion and would point to Jesus Christ as the Son of God, who cannot be compared to the others. Zoroaster was a dualist, Buddha avoided the subject of God, Confuscious was simply a Chinese Philosopher, Muhammad followed a Moon deity and wondered if he was demon possessed, and so little is known about Krishna that he might only be a legend. Of course, the Bab and Baha'u'llah both proclaimed to be the Promised Ones, but so do Sun Myung Moon, Joseph Smith Jr., Marshall Applewhite (Heaven's Gate cult), and a host of other modern-day false prophets and false Christs.

The fact is, that of all these, only Jesus Christ rose from the dead. Only Jesus Christ walked among the people healing the sick, casting out demons, miraculously feeding thousands, raising the dead to life, walking on water, and proclaiming to be God.

Thinking Through The Scripture

"He is the image of the invisible God, the firstborn over all creation. For by Him all things were created that are in heaven and that are on earth, visible and invisible, whether thrones or dominions or principalities or powers. All things were created through Him and for Him. And He is before all things, and in Him all things consist. And He is the head of the body, the church, who is the beginning, the firstborn of the dead, that in all things He may have the preeminence. For it pleased the Father that in Him all the fullness should dwell, and by Him to reconcile all things to Himself, by Him, whether things on earth or things in heaven, having made peace through the blood of His cross." (Colossians 1:15-20)

Questions for discussion:
1. Who is the "image of the invisible God"? How does this compare to the teaching of Baha'i that certain messengers were "sanctified mirrors"?
2. Look up John 1:1,14. Baha'i teaches that these sanctified mirrors shine forth God's word. In contrast, who does the Bible say the Incarnate Word was?
3. Even if these other men - that Baha'ism reveres - had important messages, whom does the Bible revere as the Firstborn of the dead? Have

any of these others risen from the dead? Why is the Lord Jesus in a class all by Himself? What does "all the fullness" mean?

B. **Man is basically good:** Baha'i denies the doctrine of original sin and the doctrine of a devil. This is a naive view of mankind that is not even supported by many of their supposed prophets. Of course, they teach that Baha'u'llah's writings have the most authority because they are the most recent revelation. But eventually the Baha'is noble goals will fall quite short because of the sin nature within men. The Bible says that man fell into sin in the garden of Eden after eating of the tree of the knowledge of good and evil (Gen. 3). Man is now born in sin (Psalm 51:5). The Bible tells us to repent (Matt. 4:17) and accept the free gift of salvation that comes through Jesus Christ our Lord (Rom.5). The devil tricked man in the garden and continues to deceive him. He *"walks about like a roaring lion, seeking whom he may devour"* (1 Pet. 5:8).

C. **A New World Order:** Like many modern-day cults, Baha'i is convinced that there is a new order of things emerging and that their religion will eventually be the one that gathers all others under its canopy. Their dictum reads that "the earth is but one country and mankind its citizens."[34] They teach that unity and brotherhood are more important than any religion's doctrine.

   Although they proclaim that people can remain Christians or Muslims or Buddhists and become Baha'is, this makes no sense. Christianity ceases to be Christianity if we accept any other Savior besides Christ. Baha'i's chief goal of uniting all faiths cannot be realized because it really means the annihilation of other religions. However, there is a push towards a New World Order and some are using Baha'i to help draw elements of various religions into a syncretic New-Age religion. In his book *Saviors of the Earth?*, author Michael S. Coffman gives the example of Maurice Strong, the secretary general of the United Nations Conference on Environment (known as "Earth Summit"):

   "It should surprise no one that Strong is a New Age mystic, and a member of the Baha'i World Faith which proclaims the unity of all religions, the oneness of all people, and the coming of A Promised One. Strong calls his New Age center and ranch in the Baca Grande of Colorado 'The Valley of the Refuge of World Truths, where Strong claims 'we feel a sense of unity with the cosmos.' Strong's wife, Hanah, reportedly believes that her grandson is the reincarnation of an eleventh-century Tibetan Buddhist monk named Rechung Dorje Drakpa. Strong is a personal friend of William Thompson, founder of the Lindisfarne Association. The Lindisfarne Association built a great temple to the sun god at Strong's Baca Ranch. The Baca Grande Ranch has become an ecumenical mini-U.N. with a monastery, ashram, Zen center, according to E Magazine reporter Anne Wingfield Semmes. Strong believes that the only way of saving the world will be for industrial civilization to collapse."[35]

Of course, not all Baha'i are new age mystics or have temples built to sun gods like Maurice Strong. A Baha'i man named David observed that every religion can have people like Strong who do not really represent the heart of the Baha'i faith. This is true. There are many Baha'i who are dedicated to Baha'u'llah because they sincerely think that he represents Christ, and they are also dedicated to Baha'ism because they think it is the best model for a New World Order of peace and equality for all men. However, this does not negate the fact that Baha'ism is a syncretic religion which includes bits and pieces from many other religions thus becoming a magnet for people with world views similar to Strong's.

D. **Denial of Central Christian Doctrines**: They teach that the Biblical doctrines of resurrection, judgment, paradise, and hell should not be taken literally. Like so many other modern-day humanists, Shoghi Effendi taught that religious truth is relative and not absolute. But for Christians, Jesus Christ is *"the way, the truth, and the life"* (John 14:6), and we must take Him literally as well as what He taught, including the above doctrines.

Jesus told us, *"My doctrine is not Mine, but His who sent Me. If anyone wills to do His will, he shall know concerning the doctrine"* *(John 7:16-17)*. The Bible tells us that Jesus taught us doctrine that came from the Father and that we will know that this is God's will when we determine to line our will up with His. In the end, it boils down to faith. I would much rather put my faith in Jesus, who not only taught these things but then proved who He was by rising from the dead, than in Baha'u'llah who is still in the grave.

E. **Evolution**: Abdu'l-Baha taught that man has evolved from a lower form of physical existence that resembled some animals in superficial ways, but yet was always superior.[36] Although, Baha'i does not hold to reincarnation, Baha'u'llah taught that when a soul is born on earth, it continues to progress - even after death - until it attains the presence of God. Prayers for the dead help the deceased along their path. He also taught that the universe is without beginning or end and held to the somewhat Hinduistic concept that there are various cycles. The current Baha'i cycle is to last 500,000 years.

Of course, historical Christianity does not hold to any of this. God created the heavens and the earth, as well as man and other life in their completed forms (Gen. 1). Furthermore, the second law of thermodynamics refutes their views because it teaches that everything loses energy and becomes increasingly disorganized. The theory of physical and spiritual evolution assumes an increase in organization, even if by chance. Today, more and more scientists are reevaluating their views of evolution. Many are jumping into the camp of a special creation because it makes the most sense, just as Christianity has maintained all along.

VIII.   WHAT ARE THE PRINCIPLES OF BAHA'I?
   A.   Since the faith of Baha'i is centered on the unity and brotherhood of mankind, the following principles often have noble sounding goals:
      1)   The Oneness of God: one God whether we call him Allah, Yahweh, or Brahma.
      2)   The Oneness of Humankind: one evolved species in one society.
      3)   The Oneness of Religion: all revealed religions are a part of God's divine plan.
      4)   Independent Investigation of Truth: each must search for revealed religious truth.
      5)   Abandoning Prejudice and Superstition: religious, race, class, personal.
      6)   The Unity of Religion and Science: religious and scientific truth must agree.
      7)   The Equality of Men and Women: equal education and social opportunities.
      8)   Universal Education: for all children, women, and men.
      9)   Abolishing the Extremes of Poverty and Wealth: Levels of income established.
      10) Spiritual Foundation of Society: all of life must be lived from a spiritual view.
      11) Auxiliary International Language: a common language for all people.[37]
   B.   While some of these principles sound noble and actually have their roots in Christianity, many of them are simply man made humanistic ideals. For instance, the principle of the oneness of God is completely unbiblical. In **Isaiah 46:5** the God of the Bible says, "*To whom will you liken Me, and make Me equal and compare Me, that we should be alike?*"

Yet, in Baha'i, they say that Yahweh (God of the Bible) is just another name for Allah or Brahma or others. But this is ridiculous since Allah was a moon deity that Muhammad exalted and Brahma is but one of many Hindu idols that are in Indian homes. Another example of humanistic idealism is their principle of oneness of religion. Of the nine "revealed religions" that they suggest, many of them are in complete contradiction to one another. The essential doctrines of Christianity contradict the doctrines of Islam, Hinduism, Buddhism, etc.

Thinking Through The Scripture

"The god of this age [the devil] has blinded the minds of unbelievers, so that they cannot see the light of the gospel of the glory of Christ, who is the image of God." (2 Corinthians 4:4) NIV

Questions for discussion:
1. Who are the unbelievers whose eyes the devil has blinded?
2. In what way are they blind? What can't they see?
3. What is the gospel (good news) to which this passage is referring?
4. Why is it impossible for Christianity to be compatible with religions like Islam, Hinduism, Buddhism, or Baha'i?

IX. WHAT ARE THE HOLY BOOKS OF BAHA'I?
   A. The many books of Baha'u'llah are considered inspired Scripture by Baha'is. A few of his over one hundred books include *al-kitab al Aqdas* (The Most Holy Book) containing the laws governing Baha'i, *ketab-e Iqan* (The Book of Certitude), *The Hidden Words*, and *The Seven Valleys*. Baha'i also values the sacred books of the major religions, such as the Bible or the Koran, but maintain that the latest revelations by Baha'u'llah supersede them and are to be more revered. It should be noted that Baha'u'llah was very influenced by the Bible and quoted the New Testament extensively in his writings.

X. WHAT ARE SOME OF THE ASPECTS OF BAHA'I LIVING?
   A. **A Paradox:** Baha'i thinking is somewhat contradictory. The whole movement is supposedly progressive in that they identify with one world government, one world language, racial harmony, and religious unity, and yet they refuse to get involved in the politics of human rights, disarmament, or anti-racism efforts.
        One Baha'i informed me that Baha'is are encouraged to vote and participate as citizens of whatever country they reside in, but they are not allowed to join political parties because of the strong divisive,

adversarial, and antagonistic goals of those parties. While I agree that political parties can be like that, it doesn't eliminate the paradox within Baha'ism. They are encouraged to vote, but in order to vote in most primary elections (at least in the United States), one must belong to that political party. Since this is the level at which the party platform is developed, this stand by Baha'ism becomes contradictory.

B. **Religious Activities:** Since the roots of Baha'i are Islamic, many of the religious rituals parallel Islam. For instance, each has daily prayer, a month of fasting, and the requirement of a pilgrimage to their holy places. In their ritual called salat, Baha'is pray three times a day. Qibla is the prayer - direction towards the tomb of Baha'u'llah near Acre. In their month called 'Ala' (March 2 to March 20), they fast from sunrise to sundown for nineteen days. This annual fasting is called sawm. Their calendar has nineteen months of nineteen days.

The main communal gatherings are in private homes or rented halls on the first day of each month. These are "feast" days. They consist of sacred readings, business, and sharing food. They also gather on the nine principle holy days of their year. There is no priesthood or clergy, so their gatherings are somewhat informal. There rites of passage are limited to marriage and funeral rites. The Baha'i men are suppose to take two pilgrimages, the hajj and the ziyara. The hajj is a pilgrimage to the homes of the Bab and Baha'u'llah. However, the Bab's home was destroyed in 1979 following the Iranain revolution. The ziyara, or lesser pilgrimage, is to the tombs of the Bab and Baha'u'llah. Pilgrimages are difficult, to say the least, since a part of the pilgrimage is to Iran and it is against the law to be a Baha'i in Iran.[38]

Thinking Through The Scripture

"For I bear them witness that they have a zeal for God, but not according to knowledge. For they being ignorant of God's righteousness, and seeking to establish their own righteousness, have not submitted to the righteousness of God. For Christ is the end of the law for righteousness to everyone who believes." (Romans 10:2-4)

Questions for discussion:
1. The Apostle Paul made this statement regarding the Jews, but it could be said to apply to Baha'ism today, as well. In what way does it apply?
2. How do they try to establish their own righteousness? What are some of the noble goals they have? What are some of their good works?

3. How is it possible for people to do good works and yet not be submit-
    ted to the righteousness of God? What does it take to gain God's righ-
    teousness?

XI. WHY IS BAHA'I NOT COMPATIBLE WITH CHRISTIANITY?
    A. It is not possible for Christianity to really be incorporated under
        the umbrella of Baha'ism. Christianity is exclusive! It doesn't leave
        room for any religion which does not focus upon the Lord Jesus
        Christ. To the Baha'is, Jesus is but one of nine manifestations of
        God, but to Biblical Christianity He is the one and only true God.

        To accept Baha'ism is to reject the Lordship of Jesus Christ. To
        accept Baha'ism is to mix Biblical Christianity with the teachings of
        various religious leaders who never claimed be God, nor did
        incredible miracles, nor rose from the dead. Jesus alone did these!
        Baha'ism is syncretic and weaves its unity of religion upon a few
        threads of similarity that run through all the major religions.
        However, it is naively blind to the fundamental, and even contra-
        dictory, differences within the religions that it tries to embrace
        under its umbrella.

        It is like trying to take pieces from various puzzles and make a
        new picture, but all the cuts are different and impossible to blend.
        Baha'ism places their latest prophet, Baha'u'llah, above all the oth-
        ers, but this is not compatible with Biblical Christianity because
        the Bible says that Jesus *"is far above all rulers, authorities, powers,
        lords, and all other names that can be named, not only in this present
        world but also in the world to come. God has put everything under the
        control of Christ. He has made Christ the head of everything for the
        good of the church. The Church is Christ's body and completes him as
        he fills everything in every way."* (Ephesians 1:21-23) GW

XII. WHAT IS THE SAD TRUTH ABOUT BAHA'I?
    A. Baha'ism is like the picture of a boy who sees other boys in a great
        controversy over who is right. The boy steps into the struggle and
        says, "Listen, don't disagree. You are all saying basically the same
        thing. All of you were right at one time, but now I am the most right.
        So stop competing and join my team, for God is on my team." There
        is great irony in this picture because he simply becomes one more
        boy trying to say that he is right. Perhaps, however, the greater irony
        is that he thinks that he is being noble in his efforts to unite all the
        other boys under his banner, but in reality he is deceived. One of the
        other boys was right after all, the one that followed Christ.

B. Many good works can be laid at the feet of those who follow Baha'
    u'llah, but the same could be said for those who follow Christ. The
    question is not really about goods works, but about salvation. We
    are told in Acts 4:12 that there is no other name besides the name
    of Jesus Christ that produces salvation.

    The Baha'is are working hard towards world harmony and unity,
    but it is like putting a bandage on cancer. The real issue is not the
    sore on the surface of the skin, but the rottenness underneath. It is
    sad that the Baha'is love the portions of the Bible that support their
    theories, but reject the portions that refute what they say. Much of
    their religion is built upon the truths found in Judaism and
    Christianity, but it is mixed with unbelief and idolatry.

C. Despite what the Baha'i may say there are factions happening in the
    movement. As mentioned previously, there has been a certain level
    of power struggle from the beginning, but a lack of access to infor-
    mation kept most Baha'i blinded to it. Today, however, one needs
    to merely surf the internet to find an array of information on the
    Baha'i. There are splintering groups that probably resemble what
    happens to any growing religion. Yet, with this one it is truly to
    their detriment as they themselves think that Baha'ism is the
    umbrella underneath which all other religions will eventually
    come. But there are gaping holes in their umbrella and the rain is
    coming in. There are now a number of ex-baha'i as well as dis-
    gruntled members, and they are not all passive about it.

    I spoke to one couple, Bob and Cathryn, who recently left the
    Baha'i Faith in northern California. They were extremely upset
    about every aspect of the movement. Cathryn felt coerced into
    attending the first meeting called a Fireside, and then they both felt
    tricked as they were required to sign a membership commitment
    form before they were allowed to attend the actual main monthly
    communal feast gathering. It was as though they had to buy into
    the religion and the group before they really knew what it was
    about. After they were involved for awhile, they began having
    problems with the character of certain individuals as well as doc-
    trines that they considered hypocritical. One example of hypocrisy
    is that women and men are suppose to be equal but women cannot
    hold office. When Bob and Cathryn starting having some doubts
    about Baha'u'llah himself and the truth of the religion, they said
    that they were ostracized and shunned.

    The story of this couple is not unique. However, the really sad
    thing is that Baha'i seem to be oblivious to the fact that there truly
    are splinter groups, disgruntled members, and ex-baha'i who have
    been mistreated even by leadership.

XIII. HOW CAN WE WITNESS TO BAHA'I?

A. **Prayer:** As discussed in the many other studies of this book, prayer can be a powerful tool for pulling down the strongholds that trap people within Baha'ism. Of course, each cult and world religion is unique in certain ways. Baha'i actually started as a cult of Islam and has now moved into a place of prominence. Because they are persecuted by the religion of Islam at times, they seem to carry somewhat of a martyr's complex. Because they promote the unity of religions, this appeals to humanistically educated people. The computer Internet gives quite a few websites for Baha'i groups and Baha'i readings.

They seem to have a waft of superiority about them. Although, this could probably be said of most religions, including Christianity, there appears to be something about the Baha'i world view that comes across as though they have arrived. This might be offensive to a Baha'i reading this, (and that is not my goal) but I sense a lack of humility in what I have read thus far from Baha'i authors.

I think then that these are some of the strongholds in Baha'i which Christians need to pray about. We need to pray that God will expose them to their need for true openness and humility. They need to realize that they have not arrived, and that they are merely people who can and do make mistakes in reasoning. Also, there needs to be prayer that they would see that their roots started in a religion (Islam) that was already off track. Perhaps their views are miles ahead of Islam, but that doesn't make their world view necessarily accurate.

In John 17:20-21, Jesus prayed that his followers would be "one" in Him and the Father. True oneness only comes in Christ as we look to Him as the Head of the body. The Baha'is reach for an illusion of oneness that can never come among the religions of the world. Pray that God will open their eyes to the truth of Jesus.

B. **Love:** Christians are quite often very nice people, but then again so are Baha'is. When making contact with Baha'is and witnessing, it is important that the event does not just become one big "I'm nicer than you, therefore I am correct" type of competition. Although Christians should be courteous, they should also be somewhat aggressive with Baha'is as the Baha'is themselves are out to evangelize. Also, love must be genuine, so be careful about attitude. If the Baha'i starts getting that superior mind set, be careful about getting into a spirit of competition. That will not produce good fruit.

As Christians, it can be frustrating when others don't see the simple, obvious truth about Jesus Christ as Lord and Savior, but we must be careful that we don't slip into a contest of superiority in the dialog. We must be humble before God and remember that love *"does not envy, love does not parade itself, is not puffed up; does not behave rudely, does not seek its own, is not provoked, thinks no evil, does not rejoice in iniquity, but rejoices in truth"* (1 Corinthians 13:4-6).

C. **Witness:** Baha'i's are often intelligent and well read in the various religions that they revere, including Christianity. The problem is that they only regard a portion of the Scriptures and think that the new writings of Baha'u'llah supersede the Bible. So be cautious about making the general context of the Bible the main focus.

Make Jesus the main focus. He is the best bridge that Christians have to those of the Baha'i faith. Even though Baha'is don't regard Him as Christians do, they still make room for Him as a prophet and many are drawn to Him because of the power of His character. The main focus of witnessing should be on the distinctiveness of Jesus Christ as compared to the other prophets they revere. Although many Baha'is will disregard some of the Bible stories about Jesus, they will find it difficult to deny that there are some distinctions. For instance, consider emphasizing the following areas that set Jesus apart from the other men that Baha'is revere.

1) **Jesus claimed to be God:** None of the others claimed such a station for themselves. Buddha did not claim to be God even though his followers have called him such. Some of the Baha'i faith call Baha'u'llah, God, but he never claimed to be. He taught that he was not God.

2) **Jesus did miracles:** The Baha'is might try to compare the supposed miracles of Muhammad with Jesus, but there is no comparison. Most of what Muslims call Muhammad's miracles are superstitious nonsense. For example, it is said that he took his sword and sliced the moon in half. Right! No one has ever done the incredible miracles that our Lord did while on earth.

3) **Jesus rose from the dead:** Some Baha'is might believe this while the others do not. The important thing is that none of the other men they revere come close to this distinction. They might say that the Bab miraculously escaped from the execution by the firing squad. Even if this took place - and it is doubtful that it did - what comparison is there? The Bab died the next time around and never rose from the dead. Jesus proclaimed that He would die and rise from the dead (Mark 9:31). Afterwards, He ascended to heaven in front of witnesses (Acts 1:9).

Finally, remember that those of the Baha'i faith are involved in a religion that consumes their lives. It is much like Islam in that it impacts every strata. Most things in their lives revolve around their religion, whether it is ethical, legal, or social issues. It has been noted that the children raised in Baha'ism are actually more open to conversion because they did not choose it for their lives. The Christian that is witnessing must have a mind set of "planting seeds." As in the case of certain cults, you probably won't see the fruit of your efforts, but don't concentrate on that. Plant the seeds. Let the Lord bring those that will water and harvest the fruit of your labors. Your job is to love them, pray for them, and witness to them.

End Notes

1. Walter Martin, *The Kingdom of the Cults* ((Minneapolis, MN: Bethany House Publishers, 1985), p. 278.
2. John Butterworth, *Cults and New Faiths* (Elgin, IL: David C. Cook Publishing, 1981), p.45.
3. Shoghi Effendi, trans. *Gleanings From The Writings of Baha'u'llah* (Wilmette, IL: Baha'i Publishing Trust, 1976), p. v.
4. John R. Hinnells, ed. *A Handbook of Living Religions* (Harmondsworth, England: Penguin Books, 1985), p. 489.
5. Ibid., p. 475.
6. Ibid., p. 476.
7. George Mather and Larry Nichols, *Dictionary of Cults, Sects, Religions and the Occult* (Grand Rapids, MI: Zondervan Publishing Company, 1993), p. 33.
8. William S. Hatcher and J. Douglas Martin, *The Baha'i Faith: The Emerging Global Religion* (San Francisco: Harper & Row, Publishers, 1984), pgs. 66-67.
9. Bob Larson, *Larson's Book of Cults* (Wheaton, IL: Tyndale House Publishers, 1988), p. 264.
10. J. K. Van Baalen, *The Chaos of Cults* (Grand Rapids, MI: Wm. B. Eerdmans Publishing Company, 1962), pgs. 154-156.
11. Michael S. Coffman, *Saviors of the Earth?* (Chicago: Northfield Publishing, 1994), pgs. 196-197.
12. Norman Anderson, *Christianity and World Religions: The Challenge of Pluralism* (Downers Grove, IL: Inter-Varsity Press, 1984), pgs. 17,67.
13. Hatcher and Martin, p. 1.
14. Walter Martin, p. 271.
15. Ibid., pgs. 6-7.
16. J. E. Esslemont, *Baha'u'llah and the New Era* (Wilmette, IL: Baha'i Publishing Trust, 1950), p. 19.
17. Ibid., p. 21.
18. Hinnells, p. 481.
19. Ruth Tucker, *Another Gospel: Alternative Religions and the New Age Movement* (Grand Rapids, MI: Zondervan Publishing House, 1989), p. 288.
20. Van Baalen, p. 147.
21. Esslemont, p. 26.

22. Hatcher and Martin, pgs. 28-29.

23. Hinnells, p. 481.

24. Esslemont, pgs. 261-263.

25. Tucker, p. 286.

26. Esslemont, p. 154.

27. Hatcher and Martin, p. 50.

28. Esslemont, p. 267.

29. Hermann Zimmer, *A Fraudulent Testament Devalues the Bahai Religion into Political Shoghism* (Waiblingen / Stuttgart, Germany: World Union for Universal Religion and Universal Peace, 1973), p. 34,

30. Ibid., pgs. 15, 29, 30, 44, 58, 80, 104.

31. Effendi, p. 47.

32. Mather and Nichols, p. 33.

33. Hinnells, p. 480.

34. Larson, p. 262.

35. Coffman, p. 197.

36. Hatcher and Martin, p. 107.

37. Ibid., pgs. 74-95.

38. Hinnells, pgs. 489-490.

QUESTIONNAIRE: LESSON EIGHTEEN

NAME: _____ DATE _____

1. Baha'ism has approximately _____ members worldwide with about _____ in the United States.

2. The most important Baha'i community is in _____, but the World Center of Baha'i Faith is located in Haifa, _____.

3. Explain why there can be no syncretic compromise for Christians:

_____

_____

_____

_____

4. Baha'i emerged out of the _____ faith in the mid-nineteenth century. Ever since 878 A.D., the Shi'ite Muslims had been expecting the return of the twelfth _____. On May 23, 1844, in Shiraz, Iran, a young man named Siyyad Ali-Muhammad claimed that he was the _____ One. He gave himself the title of _____, meaning "the gate." His followers referred to themselves as Babists. The Bab was executed six years later. Then in 1863, Mizra Husayn 'Ali proclaimed that he was the other Promised One to whom the Bab had referred. He called himself _____, meaning the glory of God. It was through him that his followers became known as Baha'is. The group grew but faced terrible persecution in Iran. Baha'u'llah was eventually exiled to _____ where he spent the last 24 years of his life in and out of prison. Many followers surrounded him. He wrote extensively and created ordinances for the new religion. His son, _____, assumed leadership in _____ and pushed missions and evangelism. It was during his visit to the United States in 1912 that the vision for U.S. Baha'i Center was planned in Wilmette, Illinois, near the city of _____. After Abdu'l-Baha died, his grandson, Shoghi Effendi lead Baha'i to become an emerging world religion. He helped _____ Baha'i bringing a great deal of organization to it. After his unexpected death in 1957, the National Spiritual Assemblies elected The Universal _____ in 1963. This group now leads the Baha'i religion.

5. List the Nine prophets of Baha'i:

1. _____   4. _____   7. _____

2. _____   5. _____   8. _____

3. _____   6. _____   9. _____

6. Give various reasons of why their list of prophets is incompatible and why Jesus Christ is in a league all by Himself. _____

_____

_____

_____

7. Read Acts 4:10-12. Who is verse 10 talking about? _____

Write out verse 12. _____

_____

_____

_____

8. List the first three principles of Baha'i.

1. _____

2. _____

3. _____

9. Explain why these are unbiblical and unreasonable. _____

_____

_____

_____

10. Have you ever met a Baha'i or been involved with Baha'ism yourself? _____. If so, please take a moment to explain: _____

_____

_____

11. When witnessing to Baha'is, you make _____ the main focus. He is the best bridge for Christians. We need to show the Baha'i the _____ of Jesus Christ as compared to the other prophets they revere. Only Jesus claimed to be _____, did the incredible _____, and rose from the _____.

12. Consider your knowledge of Baha'ism before and after this lesson. Circle the number below that indicates how equipped you felt before taking this course to witness to someone in this religion as compared to how equipped you feel now. Be honest.

BEFORE 0 1 2 3 4 5 6 7 8 9 10 AFTER 0 1 2 3 4 5 6 7 8 9 10

LESSON 19

HINDUISM

"In July, right as I was getting more deeply involved with the ashram, I had a very extraordinary experience. On one of those hot, humid Indian nights filled with mosquitos, I was sitting in my hotel room and reading Rabi Maharaj's book, Death of a Guru. Suddenly I saw a brilliantly shining being standing in the hotel room, and He said to me with a mighty voice, 'I want you to become my disciple.' I immediately understood that Jesus had called me, yet I really didn't know what to do with it. I went to Rajneesh and told him what had happened to me. As I was talking to him about this experience, I could feel a kind of very warm energy or light radiating from me and I saw that Rajneesh was very irritated, and even startled as he looked at me. He was unable to speak. At that moment I could see that he was not a master like Jesus Christ, as he claims. It was at this time I decided to become a disciple of Jesus."[1] —Eckart Flother

I. WHAT ARE SOME SIGNIFICANT WORDS IN HINDUISM?

Atman - The soul or self; innermost reality of a person; spiritual principle of life.

Avatar - Descent of a deity from heaven; one of the many incarnations of God.

Bhagavad Gita - Most popular holy book; story of Krishna and the warrior, Arjuna.

Bhakti - Attachment and devotion to a personal god.[2]

Brahman - Universal soul; ultimate divine; absolute "reality comprehended objectively."[3]

Caste - System of social classes in India; five major castes with many subdivisions.

Dharma - Divine Hindu law governing spiritual beings; justice, righteousness, & morality.

Guru - A teacher of religion; and a spiritual guide.

Jnana - Knowledge. Noncognitive, intuitive knowledge of Brahman.

Karma - Hindu law of activity governing physical beings; consequence and fruit of actions.

Krishna - One of ten incarnations of the god, Vishnu. Main deity of Hare Krishna (ISKON).

Mantra - A sacred word or sound for meditation, representing one of Hindu's many gods.

Maya - Illusion of the physical world that must be overcome in order to reach Brahman.

Moksha - Enlightenment; Liberation from maya and samsara to unite with Brahman.

Om - Krishna representing himself as "the eternal syllable OM"[4] in the Bhagavad-Gita.

Reincarnation - Hindu belief of endless rebirth until one overcomes maya into moksha.

Samsara - Wheel of life through cyclical reincarnation until the soul gains moksha.

Trimutri - "Three-in-one-God" [5] represented as Brahma, Vishnu, and Shiva.

Upanishads - Ancient philosophical & theological holy books that synthesized the Vedas.

Vedas - Ancient holy writings of hymns and prayers. Veda means "wisdom" or "knowledge".

Yoga - Discipline of mind, soul, and body used "for transcending this world of illusion".[6]

II.   WHAT IS THE SIZE AND STRENGTH OF HINDUISM TODAY?

A.   There are approximately 811 million Hindus comprising 13 percent of the world's population. Its impact is felt in 88 countries around the world including those in Europe and North America.[7] Although modern Hinduism allows for millions of gods, the majority of Hindus, about 79 percent, worship Vishnu while "other millions worship Shiva, the god of fertility, whose rituals are as evil as those of the Canaanites whom God commanded the children of Israel to destroy."[8]

There are   The United States has been more impacted by various persuasions of Hinduism in the last century than any other eastern religion. Groups such as the Vedanta Society, ISKON, Theosophy, the Divine Light Mission, Rajneeshism, and Transcendental Meditation have swayed millions of people. The New Age Movement also finds many of its roots in Hinduism.

My own life, as well as that of many friends, was impacted by various aspects of Hindu teaching in the late sixties and early seventies. As the young people of the United States tried to make sense out of a world that suddenly seemed to be turned upside down by the Vietnam War, the Civil Rights Movement, technological future shock, and corruption at the highest levels of political office, many reached out to embrace whatever truth seemed to present itself from other world views.

Thinking Through The Scripture

"Come here, you refugees from the nations. Ignorant people carry wooden idols and pray to gods that cannot save anyone. Speak and present your case. Yes, let them consult one another. Who revealed this in the distant past and predicted it long ago? Wasn't it I, the Lord? There is no other God except me. There is no other righteous God and Savior besides me. Turn to me and be saved, all who live at the ends of the earth, because I am God, and there is no other." (Isaiah 45:20-22) GW

Questions for discussion:
1. Who is God calling to come and be saved? What does "turn to me" imply?
2. What does He call these people? Why does He call them that? What do they do that shows a lack of understanding?
3. How many other Gods and Saviors are there?

III. WHAT ARE THE FOUR PERIODS OF HINDU HISTORY?
   A. **Pre-Vedic Period** (3000 - 1500 B.C.) - Dravidians, the earliest known settlers of the Indian Peninsula practiced animism. Form of idol worship similar to witchcraft.
   B. **Vedic Period** (1500 - 500 B.C.) - Aryan invaders brought their religion known as Vedism.
      1) *Oral texts written in the Vedas:* the most famous was the Rig-Veda composed around 1000 B.C. It is a collection of 1,028 hymns, prayers, and chants.
      2) *Emphasis of polytheism:* many superhuman deities of this world in the Vedas.

3) *Emergence of the Social Caste System:* (outlawed in 1949, but still a problem) The system was developed from one of the later Vedic hymns based upon the head, arms, thighs, and feet of Brahma, the creator god. "The first three classes can take full advantage of all the Hindu religion has to offer, but the Sudras [and the Hariyan] are not even allowed to hear the Vedas or to use them to try to find salvation."[9] Salvation is based upon completion of a rigid system of life time development and life time goals that only the upper three castes can attain.
   a. Brahmans - priests / scholars
   b. Kyhatriyas - warriors / soldiers
   c. Vaishyas - farmers / merchants
   d. Sudras - peasants / servants
   e. Hariyan - outcasts / untouchables

C. **Upanishadic Period** (700 - 200 B.C.) - Rebellion against the Brahman caste and the Vedic system of salvation.
   1) *The Upanishad writings:* 108 poems written by sages synthesize the Vedas by emphasizing certain aspects of them but ignoring others.
   2) *Emphasis of philosophic monism:* deities no longer perceived to be of-this-world but now they are believed to be of-the-other-world.[10]
   3) *Emergence of Guru / disciple relationship.*
   4) *New Salvation System Developed:* Teachings of Karma, Dharma, Transmigration (similar to reincarnation except one might return as an animal instead of a person), Samsara, and Moksha tell the people that everyone, regardless of caste or position of birth, can attain salvation and unite with Brahman.

   In his book *The Philosophy of Upanishads*, author Balbir Singh of India tells us what the Upanishads teach. He states, "If [man] has the requisite power of spiritual determination he can raise himself above his animal ancestry and attain true peace. The whole teaching of the Upanishads centers on this point. Every man must cultivate the requisite power of discrimination (viveka) and so discipline his will that it issues forth in the determination of all activity by dharma. He must ever strive to realize the supreme divine vision. It is in this way that he can free himself from the bondage of the realm of good and evil and discover his affinity with God."[11]

D. **Revival of Vedantic Literature** (200 BC - 200 AD) - old theology and new theology mixed together in new teachings and literature.

1) *Formation of the Trimutri:* Three gods arise from the literature to take dominance over the lesser deities. Brahma the creator, Vishnu the preserver, and Shiva the destroyer. Each of these gods have their own followers in Hinduism, but it is Vishnu that gains the most followers.

Hinduism teaches that Vishnu has appeared to men in nine different incarnations at various times and that there is one more coming. It was when he was supposedly incarnated as the Lord Krishna that captured the heart of most Hindus. It is the Lord Krishna (Sri Krishna) then that actually has become the main deity of Hinduism.

2) *The Bhagavad-Gita:* This was created as a portion of a larger work called the *maha bhanta.* The Gita is considered the most revered book of Hinduism. Basically, it is a long poem explaining a lengthy conversation between the warrior Arjuna and his charioteer, Krishna. Arjuna is perplexed because he is pitted against his own kinsmen in the battle.

Arjuna explains to Krishna that he has decided not to kill his kinsmen in war, but "Krishna proceeds to exhort him to forsake personal feelings and do what is right (DHARMA). The overarching motif in the Bhagavad Gita is intense spiritual devotion, an idea most prevalent in Hinduism today."[12] This spiritual devotion to Krishna is called bhakti and is one of the main paths of salvation in Hinduism.

IV. WHY DO WESTERNERS HAVE DIFFICULTY UNDERSTANDING HINDUISM?

A. **Because Hinduism has a fundamental difference in thinking and world view.** The western mind places importance upon this life and its surroundings. The world and the universe have a purpose. Logic and science are important. Western Civilization has been impacted by Biblical truth. Life has purpose and meaning. There is a set order to the reality in which we live. The Westerner often strives to impact the world and make changes for the betterment of mankind and future generations.

In his classic book *So What's the Difference?*, Fritz Ridenour points out the contrast in that the Hindu's religion teaches "him that all things that exist in the universe, including himself, are of no importance because they are temporary. He believes that the only important thing is the realm that exists out and beyond this world. He wants to reach this realm, and he thinks he can reach it only by completely denying the world around him."[13]

Hinduism teaches that the world around us is *maya*, an illusion. Author and religion expert Bob Larson explains how this type of thinking has impacted modern India:

"Maya, in all its ramifications, is the explanation the Westerner is given when he sees the suffering and poverty of India. This author has walked the streets of Indian cities where millions sleep on sidewalks and naked children bathe in gutters. Even as a writer, words seem inadequate to describe the sight of lepers and the congenitally deformed banging on taxi windows to beg for 'buckshesh' (handouts), and wretched waifs with crippled bodies rummaging through garbage for morsels of food.

The Hindu has inoculated himself against any empathy for his fellow man. All of the universe is lila, God's cosmic game. And pain and pleasure are not absolutes but an illusion. The suffering one sees is not real, it is *maya* and therefore unworthy of any efforts to alleviate. Furthermore, to extend kindness to those who are less fortunate would be to disobey the law of karma. That poor creature is suffering because of his sins in a past life and lending any assistance to his state would violate the principle of divine vengeance."[14]

B. **Because Hinduism sees time as cyclical rather than linear.** The Westerner sees time in a straight line. It has a beginning and continues along a continuum into the future. This is not so with Hindus. They see life and time in cyclical patterns. Just as they believe that people are caught up in Samsara until they break out of the cycle, so they believe that time itself cycles through an endless progression.

Since its beginning, the present world cycle is approximately 4 million years old. It will eventually come to an end and the process will begin again. Even then, these gods can only maintain their place in moksha for a certain amount of cycles until they must reenter the cycle of births themselves. However, some hold that Vishnu is eternal and does not re-enter Samsara.[15]

C. **Because Hinduism has no single concept of God.** In a sense, Hinduism is more a philosophy of religious living than it is a religion itself. Because it seeks to encompass every aspect of human life, it has become more of a conglomeration of views rather than the development of religious doctrine. There is no pure theology or doctrine in Hinduism in the sense that there is in most Western religions.[16]

As Walter Martin observed in *The Kingdom of the Cults*, "There is no single Hindu idea of God. Hindu concepts of deity can include any of the following: monism (all existence is one substance); pantheism (all existence is divine); panentheism (God is in creation as a soul is in a body); animism (God or gods live in nonhuman objects such as trees, rocks, animals, etc.); polytheism (there are many gods); henotheism (there is one god we worship among the many that exist); and monotheism (there is only one God)."[17]

D. **Because Hinduism strives to encompass all religions under its canopy.** Since the heart of Hinduism is more of a philosophical view of the universe and life, it seeks to place all religions under its canopy. This view is completely opposite that of Christianity and is rejected by the Lord Jesus Christ when he said, *"Enter by the narrow gate; for the gate is wide, and the way is broad that leads to destruction, and many are those who enter it" (Matt. 713) NASB.* The famous scholar and [18] author C. S. Lewis "wisely observed that at the end of all religious quests one must choose between Hinduism and Christianity; the former absorbs all others and the latter excludes them." To better understand their view, however, the following illustration by Paul Clasper in his book *Eastern Paths and the Christian Way* gives added insight to their philosophical perspective of various religions:

"The Hindu viewpoint is generous in its appreciation of the many paths that lead to Moksha—deliverance. This broad tolerance is possible because of the belief in the essential oneness of all the diverse paths. A favorite figure for the essential unity of religions is that of the large tree, with roots deep in the soil and its widely extended branches. This giant tree draws from the rich soil of human experience; it is nourished by the sun, the wind, and the rain of the divine Spirit. The trunk is strong; the large branches reach out and eventually divide into smaller branches. New shoots and leaves come in their seasons.

The larger branches are the major religions such as Hinduism, Buddhism, Taoism, Christianity, and Islam. Large branches like Christianity divide again into branches such as Roman Catholicism, Eastern Orthodoxy, and Protestantism. The last again continually subdivides. But all of these, says the Hindu, are drawing from the same source. Religious differences are due to such factors as climates, culture, politics, and psychology. It is not surprising that similar phenomena can be found in all of the branches of religion. Prayer, meditation, the reading of selected Scriptures, special festival days, the lives of saints and reformers, and the religious heritage.

Much can be learned from other traditions! But there is little point in trying to 'convert' a person from one branch to another.

Hindus are not trying to make Hindus out of Christians and Buddhists! Rather the Hindu seeks to deepen whatever religious life exists in any person; he knows that at the deepest levels all are nourished by the same source."[19]

Thinking Through The Scripture

"I am the way, the truth, and the life. No one comes to the Father except through Me. (John 14:6)

Questions for discussion:
1. Jesus used three different illustrations to make a point. How do these each reveal a different aspect of His ministry in the experience of the believer?
2. How does this proclamation contrast with the central Hindu teaching that "all paths lead to God?" Is there any path to God that does not go through Jesus?

V. WHAT MIGHT A TOURIST SEE IN INDIA REGARDING IDOL WOR-SHIP?
   A. **Pictures and statues of idols everywhere:** On almost every car and truck a tourist would see a little picture of a deity, often decorated with fresh flowers. Driving in the country or city one might see a tree dividing the road. The tree probably has an image of a god on it. It is sacred. The road must give way. He will see the old and sick lining up to enter famous sanctuaries and many others faithfully bathing in the brown polluted waters of the Ganges hoping for purification of body and soul. In the early morning he can see the Hindus offering water to the rising sun and begging for enlightenment.

   The upper three classes of the caste system are united across India daily as they reverently offer a prayer from Rig-Veda.[20] In their way of thinking, only the upper three classes can attain salvation.

   One visitor near the Ganges heard a wail of grief pierce the still, morning air. Not far away, an Indian woman writhed in agony at the feet of a six-foot-tall stone idol—Hanuman, the monkey-god. Half human with a monkey's head, the lifeless statue was oblivious to the penitent's desperate pleas. Though her god failed to respond, she persisted in her cry for assistance, pressing herself against its cold, limestone legs.[21]

B. **Reverence of animals**: Cows are sacred in India along with rats, cobras and other living things. To many these are gods. The cow might be someone's mother or cousin. The Hindu believes that after death a person might be transmigrated as an animal which is to be worshipped because the animal might be closer to breaking out and into moksha.

Thinking Through The Scripture

"When the philistines took the ark of God, they brought it into the house of Dagon and set it by Dagon. And when the people of Ashdod arose early in the morning, there was Dagon, fallen on its face to the earth before the ark of the Lord. So they took Dagon and set it in its place again. And when they arose early the next morning, there was Dagon, fallen on its face to the ground before the ark of the Lord. The head of Dagon and both the palms of its hands were broken off." (1 Samuel 5:2-4)

Of what value is an idol, since a man has carved it? Or an image that teaches lies? For he who makes it trusts in his own creation; he makes idols that cannot speak. Woe to him who says to wood, 'Come to life!' Or to lifeless stone, 'Wake up!' Can it give guidance? It is covered with gold and silver; there is no breath in it. But the Lord is in his holy temple; let all the earth be silent before him." (Habakkuk 2:18-20) NIV

"Do not turn to idols, nor make for yourselves molded gods: I am the Lord your God." (Leviticus 19:4)

Questions for discussion:
1. What happened when the Philistines brought the ark of God into Dagon's temple? How does this apply to the life of an individual? What happens when the presence of the Lord comes in?
2. Habakkuk asks a rhetorical question. Does an idol have value to the one who fashioned it? How does the image teach lies? What happens when people put their trust in idols? If your children went out and made an image of you and called it Father or Mother, how would it make you feel?
3. Why do men "turn to idols" and away from the Lord God? Is it hard for men to simply face the truth? Does it have to do with control?

C. **Idols in the home**: Hans Kung tells of the strange idol worship that occurs daily in many Hindu homes. In his book *Christianity and the World Religions* he states, "The object venerated with the sixteen rituals is a little bronze statue of a god, found in practically every house (or, if one cannot afford bronze, at least a cheap print of the deity). That is enough to bring the god to mind and to enter into a dialogue with him. The sixteen rituals have regional variants, but in essence they are as follows: [They do these things to the little bronze statute] (1) The deity is led in, (2) offered a seat; and since the guest has traveled far, he is (3) offered water to wash his feet, (4) face and hands, as well as (5) water to rinse his mouth. Each of these actions is naturally accompanied by pertinent ritual sayings and gestures. If now one would happen to offer the deity (5a) a little sweet refreshment, then he is also given (5b) some more water to rinse his mouth. Then the deity is (6) bathed, (7) dressed, (8) furnished with the sacred cord carefully decorated, and (9) rubbed with aromatic ointments—usually sandalwood paste, camphor, and saffron. The god receives (10) blossoms from his favorite flowers and trees, (11) incense, and (12) light from a lamp burning sesame oil or melted butter. Then a sacrificial meal (13) is set before the god and after that some betel nuts (14). Only when the guest has dined is he given a present (15), and the ritual ends (16) with a reverential circumambulation [ceremony of walking around it] of the deity."[22]

VI. WHAT IS KARMA?

A. It is the law of retributive justice.[23] It determines one's place in samsara. In other words, the actions of this life, good and bad, will determine what a Hindu will be in the next life, whether a brahman, an outcast, a pig, a cow, a frog, or actually breaking out into moksha, which is the triumphant merging with the universal oneness that the Hindu hopes to gain. The Bhagavad Gita tells us the salvation work's aspect of karma. In 14:18 it says, "Men who are lucid go upward; men of passion stay in between; men of dark inertia, caught in the vile ways, sink low."[24]

In a restricted sense it is like the Biblical principle that says *"you reap what you sow"* (Gal. 6:7-9). But whereas the Bible teaches that we only have one life (Heb. 9:27) and that we will then stand before the judgment seat of Christ (Rom. 14:10), Hinduism says we have countless lives here on earth either digressing or progressing because of previous actions.

VII. WHAT IS THE GURU AND DISCIPLE RELATIONSHIP?

A. Gurus are suppose to be spiritual masters, teachers, and guides. In Hinduism the selection of a guru is more important than choosing a mate.[25] In principle the pupil is free to choose his guru and the guru the pupil. However, gurus do not just take anyone as it has karmic impact upon their future, as well as the pupil's. When both guru and pupil are in agreement, the relationship is sealed with an initiation ceremony in which the guru imparts a secret mantra and certain instructions. Instruction is aimed at the pupil's competence and stage of development. The goal is to help the pupil discover true self-identity (self- realization) and thus break out of samsara. Disciples often go and live with their gurus.

Many times disciples honor and serve their gurus as a god. To them "the true guru's the true hero".[26] But the Bible says that it is the Holy Spirit that *"will guide you into all truth"* (Jn. 16:13) and that we need to avoid those who are *"always learning and never able to come to the knowledge of the truth"* (2 Tim. 3:7).

VIII.   WHICH ARE THE THREE MAJOR PATHS OF HINDU SALVATION?

A. **Jnana Marga (The Path of Knowledge)** - Thinkers can look deeply into the mysteries of life and through mystical insight and intuitive awareness, gain self-realization. The way of knowledge was taught by the Upanishads and is suppose to bring one to the ultimate realization of the universal being of Brahman so that moksha can be attained.

B. **Karma Marga (The Path of Works)** - Doers can upgrade their caste positions in future lives by faithfully following their dharma or duty in life. Dharma is the divine law behind the scene that governs the proper works of justice, righteousness, and morality for each person's station in life. As Richard Kyle points out, "Each person is born into a particular class and thus acquires a birthright, a set of prescribed obligations and actions. The religious way of action [or path of works] taught that each person must live according to the law for his or her caste. The faithful performance of the duties required by one's state in life, called karma, will lead to a rebirth in a higher state in the next lifetime."[27]

Thinking Through The Scripture

"When the kindness and love of God our Savior appeared, he saved us, not because of righteous things we had done, but because of his mercy. He saved us through the washing of rebirth and renewal by the Holy Spirit, whom he poured out on us generously through Jesus Christ our Savior, so that, having been justified by grace, we might become heirs having the hope of eternal life." (Titus 3:4-7) NIV

Questions for discussion:
1. Contrast the type of love in this passage with that of Bhakti Marga. How do they differ? What did we do to deserve God's love? How does God's mercy compare to any in Hinduism? Is there any prominent mercy in Hinduism?
2. If we worked our way to God's love, why would that not be sufficient?

C. **Bhakti Marga (The Path of Devotion)** - Lovers can achieve self-realization through ritualistic sacrifice, discipline, and a close adherence to one or more gods. Bhakti is the path that Krishna most emphasized in the Bhagavad-Gita. Of the three paths, it is considered the one to have the most emotion with it.

Bhakti emotion is likened unto the emotion of 1) a worshiper, 2) a servant, 3) a parent or brother, 4) a friend, or 5) a lover.[28] This "way especially appeals to the lower classes (the vast majority of Indians) because it offers an easy way for their souls to make it to a higher class—and eventually moksha."[29]

IX. WHAT IS YOGA?
A. **The history and goal.** The teachings and techniques of yoga were incorporated into the Hindu religion about 100 BC by Patanjali in the Yoga Sutras. Yoga became one of six schools of thought regarding salvation through the path of knowledge (Jnana Marga). Each of the six schools have their peculiar views on the best way to attain knowledge. Yoga, along with the closely related school of Samkhya are dualists (seeing spirit and matter at war with each other). Their ultimate goal is isolation from "evil" matter by entering into moksha and becoming like God in his timeless unity who is never affected by matter or nature.[30] Yoga means "yolk or union with God." God is the Impersonal All and Universal Soul to which they want to yolk themselves.

Thinking Through The Scripture

JESUS SAID: *"Come to Me, all you who labor and are heavy laden, and I will give you rest. Take My yoke upon you and learn from Me, and you will find rest for your souls. For My yoke is easy and My burden light."* (Matthew 11:28-30)

Questions for discussion:
1. In light of this passage, what is the opposite of work? Is this something we do or something He gives when we come to Him? What kind of

attitude should we have then when we come to Him? Do we take or receive?

2. How does the yolk of Jesus contrast with the yoga of Hinduism? How is it that we can find "rest" in taking the yolk of Jesus? What are the other aspects?

B. **The Process.** In the Western world, yoga is often thought of as simple isometric exercises, but it is much deeper than that. Yoga has become the leading method for Hindus to learn to transcend this world of illusion. The union with their god that a yogi (one who practices yoga) hopes to achieve is supposedly reached only after living a moral life, gaining inner and outer purity, and training the body through various exercises and postures.

Yoga is actually an eight-step process. The first five are called "Hatha Yoga" and deal primarily with isometric and breathing exercises whose aim is to help the mind overcome the illusion of maya. The last three steps are called "Raja Yoga" and work through the steps of dharama (concentration), dhyana (meditation), and samadhi (absorption).[31] It is said that at this last stage the yogi has an overwhelming sense of radiant light and disconnects with maya to unite his soul (atman) with the universal soul Brahman in what is called "Brahman-Atman."

X. WHAT THREE WAVES OF HINDUISM CAME TO THE UNITED STATES?

A. **The Vedanta Society** (1895) - Swami Vivekananda (1863-1902) introduced Hinduism's monistic philosophy to the United States in 1891 at the World's Fair of Religions in Chicago. Swamis are learned, ascetic, and often celibate monks. Vivekananda had been the prime disciple of Sri Ramakrishna, a priest in the Kali Temple of India. At the fair, Vivekananda taught Westerners about transmigration, the Hindu concept that one can come back as a person or lower life form, such as a snail or dog. This was not received well by Westerners, so Vivekananda changed the concept and called it reincarnation, meaning that a person always returned as another person. This was more acceptable.

The Vedanta Society leaned heavily on the Vedas and taught salvation through an intellectual path of knowledge that saw all religions leading to the same goal. The main headquarters in the U.S. today are in Hollywood. From one of his trips to India, Bob Larson tells of the results of this type of religious thinking upon India:

"Those who favorably view Vivekananda's influence on Western religious thought might do well to visit personally both Kali Temple and the Ramakrishna Mission in Calcutta. Kali, the blackened goddess of death, stands draped in a necklace of human skulls and holds a bloody severed head in one hand. Near the entrance of Kali temple, I witnessed bloody goat sacrifices before a phallic lingam (genital replica). Not far away, at the Ramakrishna Mission Temple, I watched poor peasants bow before an idol, offering the deity the little money they had."[32]

B. **The Self-Realization Fellowship** (1920) - Paramahansa Yogananda (1893-1952) became the first Hindu master to teach in the U.S. for such a long period. For over thirty years, he taught yoga as the best tool for the path of knowledge. This Yogi founded the fellowship in Los Angeles which has impacted hundreds of thousands of lives since then.

Thinking Through The Scripture

"The Spirit clearly says that in later times some will abandon the faith and follow deceiving spirits and things taught by demons...They forbid people to marry and order them to abstain from certain foods, which God created to be received with thanksgiving by those who believe and know the truth. For everything God created is good, and nothing is to be rejected if it is received with thanksgiving, because it is consecrated by the word of God and prayer." (1 Timothy 4:1-5) NIV

Questions for discussion:

1. In regard to this passage, what type of things did Swami Prabhupada teach that verify its accuracy? What does this imply about the source of his doctrine?

2. What kind of influence upon nominal Christians does the Spirit show that these types of teachings may have? Why? Why would demons not want people to marry and / or eat certain foods? Even though abstaining from marriage or certain foods is not in and of itself wrong, how could it impact a human life and change world view and thinking? What level of control should we allow others to have in these personal areas of our life?

C. **The International Society for Krishna Consciousness, ISKCON** (1965) - This cult, also known as Hare Krishna came to the U.S. through the teachings of Swami Prabhupada (1896-1977) who emphasized the attainment of self-realization by the path of devotion (bhakti) to Krishna represented in the Bhagavad-Gita.

ISKCON reverses roles between Vishnu and Krishna. Krishna is supreme and Vishnu the avatar. He taught disciples to chant "Hare Krishna" which means "O energy of God, O God [Krishna], please engage me in your service."[33] He avidly opposed the killing of animals and the eating of meat, especially cows which are thought to be reincarnated people. He also stressed celibacy although he did allow for marriage. His followers shaved their heads, wore orange robes, lived by strict rules, and stood for hours in public places chanting, proselytizing, and seeking donations. Their organization was hurt in 1992 when a Supreme Court ruling forbid religious groups to panhandle money in airports. Their main headquarters are located in Los Angeles.

XI. WHAT ABOUT TRANSCENDENTAL MEDITATION?

A. Many other gurus have sought a following in America. Dozens of Hindu-related groups have sprung up in the twentieth century. One of the more prominent teachers of the last few decades has been Maharishi Mahesh Yogi who expounds on the meditation techniques of his former master, Guru Dev. These meditative techniques are commonly called Transcendental Meditation (TM). Maharishi made a big splash on the American scene in the 1960's with the founding of his organization called Spiritual Regeneration Movement. Many celebrities such as the Beatles, the Rolling Stones, Shirley MacLaine, Mia Farrow, and Joe Namath tried TM making Maharishi well-known.

In the early 1970's, however, the Beatles lost faith in him - calling him a fraud - and so he returned to India for a while to reorganize. He changed strategy and names. He now called his teaching "The Science of Creative Intelligence" (SCI) and tried to pass off TM as a science rather than religion. In 1974, Maharishi bought an old Presbyterian college in Iowa and started Maharishi International University. He actually got quite a following among government agencies during this time, even getting the U.S. Army involved with it as an instrument to combat drug and alcoholism. In 1977 the New Jersey Federal Court ruled that TM was a religion and threw it out of the New Jersey public schools. The U.S. government now sees TM as a religion.

Today, the organization is called the World Plan Executive Council and the technique is referred to as the "Maharishi Technology of the Unified Field." Over one million Americans have paid their money and been initiated. The initiate brings six flowers, three pieces of fruit, and a white handkerchief to the ceremony. He bows before a picture of Guru Dev and sings a hymn of worship to him (Dev, represents Brahman). The initiate is given his or her mantra at this time. The techniques of TM include relaxation by sitting in a prescribed position twice a day for twenty minutes while meditating on and repeating one's mantra over and over again. The mantra is the key to TM. The following definition of a mantra by K. W. Morgan in his book *The Religion of the Hindus* shows the direct connection to the Hindu monistic philosophy of life:

"A mantra is not a mere formula or a magic spell or a prayer; it is an embodiment in sound of a particular deity. It is the deity itself. And so, when a mantra is repeated, the worshiper makes an effort to identify himself with the worshiped, the power of the deity comes to his help. Human power is thus supplemented by the divine power."[34]

Thinking Through The Scripture

"And when you are praying, do not use meaningless repetition, as the Gentiles do, for they suppose that they will be heard for their many words. Therefore do not be like them; for your Father knows what you need, before you ask Him. Pray, then, in this way: 'Our Father who art in heaven, Hallowed be Thy name. Thy kingdom come. Thy will be done, on earth as it is in heaven. Give us this day our daily bread. And forgive us our debts, as we also have forgiven our debtors. And do not lead us into temptation, but deliver us from evil. For Thine is the kingdom, and the power, and the glory, forever. Amen.'" (Matthew 6:7-13) NASB

Questions for discussion:
1. How do the words "meaningless repetition" describe the activity of a mantra? What does Jesus tell us about this type of endeavor? How much good do these repetitions really do?
2. The Lord's prayer has substance and gives direction. To whom is it prayed? Jesus told us that the Father knew what we needed even before prayer. How is this view represented in the words of the prayer? What are some of the distinctives of the prayer that show its depth and breadth?

XII. WHAT ABOUT REINCARNATION?
   A. The Bhagavad-Gita teaches "Never have I not existed, nor you, nor these kings; and never in the future shall we cease to exist. Just as

the embodied self enters childhood, youth, and old age, so does it enter another body...." (2:12-13).

The doctrine of reincarnation (called transmigration in India) is a major cornerstone of their faith. Without it, the entire system of Hinduism would shatter into meaningless unrelated pieces. The theory of a soul progressing through successive bodies to reach enlightenment, self-realization, and actual godhood is also important in a lot of cults, including the New Age Movement. The fact that there is no legitimate proof of it does not seem to bother those who espouse it.

The luring temptation to believe it is the same one that the serpent used in the garden of Eden (Gen. 3:4) and the result of biting into it is death. In deed! It is this very type of thinking that caused man to fall from grace in the first place. The thrust of the Bible is that man *is dead and lost until he is "born again"* (Jn. 3:3) into the Kingdom of God, that comes through accepting the free gift (Rom. 6:23) of eternal life by placing our trust in Jesus Christ alone (Eph. 2:8-9).

The whole idea of reincarnation and karma is simply a glorified system of works that plays into the hands of humanism. The Bible teaches that reincarnation is a false doctrine in many places. In Phil. 1:21, 2 Cor. 5:8, and Acts 7:59 we see that dying brings one into the presence of Christ. Luke 23:43 shows the thief going into paradise instead of a bad karma situation for his sins. 1 John 3:2 shows that when we do meet God he will be a personality and not some nebulous impersonal force in the universe. John 9:1-3 shows a blind man who was blind not due to any past karma, but so that the power of God could be manifest in healing. Heb. 9:27 tells us that we only die once [physically] before facing the judgment, and in Heb. 6:2 we find that the judgment is eternal. Christians believe in resurrection freedom not reincarnation bondage.

XIII. HOW DOES KRISHNA COMPARE TO CHRIST?

A. What many Westerners do not often realize is that Hindus look to Krishna as an historical figure. They go on pilgrimages to places he once lived.[35] Very little is known about his true character or life because he has been shrouded in legends. The name Krishna means "black" and was often given to dark children. There is a reference to a Krishna as far back as the Upanishadic writings. It is thought that he was a hero or a king that was later elevated to godhood by the people. Near the city of ancient Mathura resided a Krishna-worshiping people. There, religion converged with those of other local sun worshiping groups and came to be known as the "Bhagavata". The many legends of Krishna united the groups and inspired the writing of the Bhagavad-Gita, and a major religion was born.

B. The Bhagavad-Gita presents a beautiful poem about a legendary Krishna. However, the Bible presents eye-witness accounts documenting the historical Christ. There are more than 24,000 manuscript copies or portions of the New Testament alone that accurately concur and verify the historicity of Christ. Many other ancient historical accounts confirm his life. Jesus Christ is not an amalgamation of myths and legends. Nor is he one revelation or god among many as Krishna is projected to be. He is not the son of Krishna, but He is the only begotten Son of the Living God, the second person of the Trinity, the risen Savior, the Great I Am, and the coming King. Jesus Christ is God! Hallelujah!

XIV. WHAT ARE JAINISM AND SIKHISM?

A. Hinduism gave birth to three religious factions: Jainism, Buddhism, and Sikhism. The next chapter is devoted to the subject of Buddhism.

B. **Jainism:** This offshoot of Hinduism has many similarities but also some striking differences. It began with its founder Vardhamana Mahavira, a contemporary of Buddha, who lived from 599 to 527 B.C. At thirty years of age, he left his life as a member of the Hindu warrior class (Kyhatriyas) and became a beggar who refused to own any possessions. After more than twelve years of renunciation and detachment from physical needs and comforts, he claimed complete understanding of the nature of the universe. Although Mahavira opposed the worship of a supreme being, his followers later deified him. Some of his doctrinal differences with Hinduism are that he taught (1) the independence and autonomy of the individual soul, (2) the need for a casteless, democratic society, (3) an emphasis on harmlessness toward all living things, and (4) rigid asceticism. Today, Mahavira is worshiped by Jains as the 24th Tirthankara, the last and greatest of the savior beings. Jainism has monks and nuns who are very ascetic but also a lay community who are not as strict. Mostly, Jainism is found in India today where there are several million followers. However, some Jain influence came to the United States through Bhagwan Rajneesh who had a commune in Oregon in the 1980's. Rajneesh did not stick with strict Jainism but incorporated sexual promiscuity and elements from many religions to create his own synthetic religion. He was deported from the United States in 1985 back to India and died in 1990.

C. **Sikhism:** This strange mixture of Hinduism and Islam was begun by an Indian named Nanak who was born in 1469 A.D. in the village of Talwandi (now called Sahib). When he was thirty-three, he wandered off into the woods for three days where he supposedly had a revelation of God, the primal Brahma, who gave him a cup of nectar to drink and pronounced that Nanak was the divine Guru. When he returned home, Nanak pronounced, "There is neither Hindu nor Muslim, so whose path shall I follow? I shall follow God's path. God is neither Hindu nor Muslim and the path which I follow is God's." Nanak's religion gained a following in Punjab where people became his Sikhs (disciples). He died at age seventy at which time Guru Angad became his successor. Eight other gurus succeeded Angad. The teachings of Sikhism are a syncretism of the doctrines of Islam and Hinduism. Their holy book, Guru Granth Sahib, was composed by several dozen Sikhs and includes different languages and dialects all in the same book. The most distinctive teaching of Sikhism is its doctrine of guru-ship. They teach that all people need to learn from gurus, but especially from the greatest guru who is God. Yet, their God is not considered personal but an abstract principle of eternal truth or reality that gives inner guidance. Other doctrines include karma and transmigration, a salvation through submission to God which breaks the cycle of karma and transmigration in the individual, the importance of repeating prescribed prayers, and reverence for their Scripture. Today, there are about 23 million Sikhs in India and throughout parts of the world.

XIV. WHO IS JESUS CHRIST TO THE HINDU?
   A. **To Formal Hinduism** - Jesus Christ was a guru, a teacher, or even an avatar of Vishnu.
   B. **To Hare Krishna** - Jesus Christ was an enlightened vegetarian teacher who taught meditation. Some say he was the son of Krishna.
   C. **To Transcendental Mediation** - Jesus Christ simply discovered his higher self, most others have not.
   D. **To the Vedanta Society** - Jesus Christ is the "special manifestation of the Absolute". But he is still only one of the many.
   E. **To the Self Realization Fellowship** - Jesus Christ is a past yoga master.

XV. WHAT IS THE SAD TRUTH ABOUT THOSE WHO EMBRACE HINDUISM?
   A. They view life as illusion and do little to improve themselves.
   B. They starve in the streets of India while the animal "gods" eat like royalty.

C. They seek "rebirth" in carnal life when true "rebirth could be theirs now (Jn. 3:3).

D. They forsake the one life God gave them for future lives that do not exist.

E. They seek help from a mythical hero when the real hero came to save them.

F. They take on the "yolk" of works when a yolk of rest could be theirs.

XVI. WHAT ARE SOME CONSIDERATIONS WHEN WITNESSING TO A HINDU?

A. **Prayer:** In a little book called *The Kneeling Christian* by an unknown Christian, it gives advice to Christians about praying for the outpouring of the Holy Spirit:

"God promised that He would 'pour out the Spirit of grace and supplication upon all flesh' (Joel 2:28). How much of that Spirit of 'supplication' is ours? Surely we must get that Spirit at all costs? Yet if we are not willing to spend time in 'supplication,' God must perforce withhold His Spirit, and we become numbered amongst those who are 'resisting the Spirit,' and possibly 'quenching' the Spirit. Has not our Lord promised the Holy Spirit to them that ask? (Luke 11:13). Are not the very converts from heathendom putting some of us to shame?

A few years ago, when in India, I had the great joy of seeing something of Pandita Ramabai's work. She had a boarding-school of 1,500 Hindu girls. One day some of these girls came with their Bibles and asked a lady missionary what St. Luke 12:49 meant—'I came to cast down fire upon the earth; and what will I, if it is already kindled?' The missionary tried to put them off with an evasive answer, not being very sure herself what those words meant. But they were not satisfied, so they determined to pray for this fire. And as they prayed—and because they prayed—the very fire of heaven came into their souls. A very Pentecost from above was granted them. No wonder they continued to pray!

A party of these girls upon whom God had poured the 'Spirit of supplication' came to a mission house where I spent some weeks. 'May we stay here in your town and pray for your work?' they asked. The missionary did not entertain the idea with any great enthusiasm. He felt that they ought to be at school, and not 'gadding about' the country. But they only asked for a hall or barn where they could pray; and we all value prayers on our behalf. So their request was granted, and the good man sat down to his evening meal, thinking.

As the evening wore on, a native pastor came round. He broke down completely. He explained, with tears running down his face, that God's Holy Spirit had convicted him of sin, and that he felt compelled to come and openly confess his wrongdoing. He was quickly followed by one Christian after another, all under deep conviction of sin. There was a remarkable time of blessing. Backsliders were restored, believers were sanctified, and heathen brought into the fold—all because a few mere children were praying."[36]

B. **Love:** Hindus are impressed about various aspects of Jesus' ministry, one of which was his ministry to the poor. Such charity draws them. Since their world view includes a you-get-what-you-deserve mentality, it amazes them when someone reaches out with Christian love. Everybody likes it when "good fortune" smiles upon them. Therefore, the Hindus—like most of us—respond with openness to love and the charity of good works. In 1 John 4:19 we read, *"We love Him because He first loved us,"* and in Romans 2:4 it says, *"the goodness of God leads you to repentance."* God desires them to turn away from idols to His rich mercy and truth. It will take time, however, for them to mentally process the truths of Christianity because Hinduism is so very different.

This is not to say that Hinduism has no truth in it. Christians need to appreciate the nuggets of truth found in some of the wisdom and philosophy of Hinduism while - at the same time - sharing with Hindus the tremendous love that is in Christ Jesus. He loves them so much that He came to set the captives to maya and samsara free, really free! He came to set them free from the concept of little gods.

Because of the Hindu view of little gods, Christians need to make sure that the Hindu does not just see or accept Jesus as the little-god-of-love or the little-god-of-miracles. Some of them think that Christians in the West have many gods such as Jesus, Santa Claus, the Easter Bunny, and so on. Because of their world view, they think that our holidays all represent some type of little god. So, as you present the love of the Lord Jesus Christ realize that it will take time for them to process how the Bible represents the one true God and Savior.

C. **Witness:** Here are some tips:

1) Use the teachings of Christ, specifically the Sermon on the Mount and the Laws of love, because the philosophic emphasis of devotion (*bhakti*) to God and man is very important to Hindus. Even Ghandi was moved by the beauty of the Sermon on the Mount.

2) Hindus are often fascinated by the suffering of Christ, not so much as an historical reality but as a principle for which to live day by day. Use it as common ground to introduce the victorious resurrection life that can be theirs.

3) Use 1 Corinthians 8:4-6 to show that the little "gods" are illusion, but Jesus is reality:

> "We know that an idol is nothing in the world, and that there is no other God but one. For even if there are so-called gods, whether in heaven or on earth (as there are many gods and many lords), yet for us there is one God, the Father, of whom are all things, and we for Him; and one Lord Jesus Christ, through whom are all things, and through whom we live."

End Notes

1. Walter Martin, *The Kingdom of the Cults* (Minneapolis, MN: Bethany House, 1985), p. 360.
2. Philip H. Ashby, *Modern Trends in Hinduism* (New York: Columbia University Press, 1974), glossary.
3. T W. Organ, *Hinduism: Its Historical Development* (Woodbury, NY: Barron's Educational Series., 1974), p. 256.
4. Barbara S. Miller, translator, *The Bhagavad-Gita: Krishna's Counsel in Time of War* (New York: Columbia University Press, 1986), p. 92.
5. Richard Kyle, *The Religious Fringe: A History of Alternative Religions in America* (Downer's Grover, IL: InterVarsity Press, 1993), p. 130.
6. Ron Carlson and Ed Decker, *Fast Facts on False Teachings* (Eugene, OR: Harvest House, 1994), p. 91.
7. George A. Mather and Larry A. Nichols, *Dictionary of Cults, Sects, Religions and the Occult* (Grand Rapids, MI: Zondervan Publishing House, 1993), p. 121.
8. Fritz Ridenour, *So What's the Difference?* (Ventura, CA: Regal Books, 1979), p. 78.
9. Ibid., p. 75.
10. Mather and Nichols, p. 117.
11. Balbir Singh, *The Philosophy of Upanishads* (New Delhi, India: Arnold-Heinemann, 1983), p. 73.
12. Mather and Nichols, p. 117.
13. Ridenour, p. 74.
14. Bob Larson, *Larson's Book of Cults* (Wheaton, IL: Tyndale House Publishers, Inc., 1988), pgs. 73-74.
15. Hans Kung, *Christianity and the World Religions* (Garden City, NY: Doubleday & Co., 1986), p. 186-187.
16. Milton Singer, editor, *Krishna: Myths, Rites, and Attitudes* (Honolulu, HI: East- West Center Press, 1966), pgs, 139-140.
17. Martin, p. 353.
18. Ibid., p. 363.
19. Paul Clasper, *Eastern Paths and the Christian Way* (Maryknoll, NY: Orbis Books, 1980), pgs. 28-29.
20. Kung, pgs. 242-243.
21. Larson, p. 14.
22. Kung, pgs. 244-245.
23. Mather and Nichols, p. 172.
24. Miller, p. 123.
25. Organ, p. 57.

26. Wendy Doniger O'Flaherty, ed., *Textual Sources For The Study Of Hinduism* (Chicago: The University of Chicago Press, 1990), p. 142.

27. Kyle, p. 131.

28. Singer, p. 49.

29. Ridenour, p. 78.

30. Sir Norman Anderson, *Christianity and World Religions: The Challenge of Pluralism* (Downers Grove,IL: InterVarsity Press, 1984), p.90.

31. Carlson and Decker, p. 92.

32. Larson, p. 395.

33. A. C. Bhaktivedanta Swami Prabhupada, *The Science of Self Realization* (Los Angeles: The Bhaktivedanta Book Trust, 1984), p. 126.

34. Carlson and Decker, p. 254, quoting from K. W. Morgan, *The Religion of the Hindus*, p. 24.

35. Kung, p. 277.

36. *The Kneeling Christian* (Grand Rapids, MI: Zondervan Publishing House, 1971), pgs. 32-33.

QUESTIONNAIRE: LESSON NINETEEN

NAME: _____ DATE _____

1. Hinduism comprises approximately _____ % of the world's population in _____ countries.

2. List the four periods of Hindu history and name one thing that happened in each.

a) _____

b) _____

c) _____

d) _____

3. Who are three main deities of Hinduism?

1) _____ 2) _____ 3) _____

4. Who is the main incarnation of Vishnu that many Hindus worship?

_____

5. The _____ is a long poem about the warrior _____ and his charioteer _____. It is the most _____ of Hinduism.

6. The Westerner has difficulty understanding Hinduism. To the Western mind life has _____ and meaning, but to the Hindu all of the universe, including himself, is of no practical importance because it is only _____. To them the world is nothing but _____ (an illusion). Rather than time being linear along a continuum, they see it as cyclical just like the seasons. People, they think, are caught up in an endless cycle of rebirths in a system called _____ (wheel of life). The goal is to break out of Samsara into _____ (enlightenment with Brahman). There are many gods in Hinduism and many views of God. It places all religions under its canopy because, in some sense, the heart of Hinduism is more of a _____ view of life than a formal religion. However, in the end all religious quests must choose between Hinduism and Christianity because the former _____ all others and the latter _____ them.

7. Explain what a tourist might see in India: _____

_____

_____

_____

8. The doctrine of _____ teaches Hindus that their good and bad actions in this life will determine their future place in _____, but the Bible teaches we only have one life.

9. Write our Hebrews 9:27. _____

_____

_____

10. Hinduism teaches that salvation (attainment of a better life in rebirth) can be gained through the paths of 1) _____, 2) _____, or 3) _____, but Acts 4:12 tells us that there is salvation in no other name but the name of _____.

11. Yoga is a method for supposedly reaching salvation through the path of _____. It is an _____ step process for breaking out of maya and uniting with _____.

12. What three organizations ushered Hinduism into the United States?

a) _____

b) _____

c) _____

13. Explain what Transcendental Mediation really is: _____

_____

_____

14. Write out one Scripture that refutes the theory of reincarnation. _____

_____

_____

15. Who was Jesus to Hindus?_____

16. List two sad truths about Hinduism.

a) _____

b) _____

17. What's a good Scripture to use when witnessing to Hindus?_____

18. Consider your knowledge of Hinduism before and after this lesson. Circle the number below that indicates how equipped you felt before taking this course to witness to someone in this religion as compared to how equipped you feel now. Be honest.

BEFORE 0 1 2 3 4 5 6 7 8 9 10 **AFTER** 0 1 2 3 4 5 6 7 8 9 10

LESSON 20

BUDDHISM

"[W]hen I was a Buddhist, it was like I was drowning in a big lake and I didn't know how to swim. I was going under for the third time when Buddha walked up to the edge of the lake and began to teach me how to swim. Buddha said, 'start moving your hands and kicking your legs, but you have to make it to shore yourself!' Then Jesus Christ walked up to the edge of the lake, but He did not stop there! He dove into the lake, swam out, rescued me, and brought me to shore. After He brought me to shore, then He taught me how to swim, so I could go back and rescue others!"[1] —Former Buddhist from Thailand

I. WHAT ARE SOME SIGNIFICANT WORDS IN BUDDHISM?

Anatta - No self; doctrine in Theravada Buddhism that no continuous self exists.

Anicca - Everything is impermanent; the doctrine that everything changes.

Arhat - Holy one in Theravada; "one who has conquered all lust, hatred, and delusion."[2]

Bodhi - Enlightenment or the wisdom that attains enlightenment.

Bodhisattva - In Mahayana Buddhism, one who postpones gaining nirvana to help others.

Buddha - Awakened or enlightened one; Siddhartha Gautama.

Dharma - Something firmly established in the universe; path taught by Buddha.

Duhkha - Suffering; one of Buddhism's three characteristics of existence.

Hinayana - The Little Vehicle; branch of Buddhism teaches nirvana only open to monks.

Karma - Law of activity governing physical beings; consequence & fruit of actions.

Mahayana - The Great Vehicle; branch of Buddhism teaching nirvana open to all.

Mantra - a word, sound, thought form or even magical incantation for meditation.[3]

Nirvana - To extinguish all lust, hatred, and delusion; highest spiritual plain; bliss & peace.

Samsara - World system of birth, suffering, death, and rebirth caused by karma.

Sutra - Text that contains the words of Buddha.

Tantra - Ritual manual used in Tibetan Buddhism.

Tantrayana - The Vehicle of specialized ritual; Tibetan sub-development of Mahayana.

Theravada - (Another name for Hinayana); the way of the elders.

Tripitaka - The three baskets (texts) that form the canon of sacred Buddhist writings.

Zen - Mediation; Japanese sect of Mahayana Buddhism.

II. WHAT IS THE SIZE AND STRENGTH OF BUDDHISM TODAY?

A. Buddhism is the world's fourth largest religion following Christianity, Islam, and Hinduism. Approximately 360 million people adhere to one form of Buddhism or another. This is 6 percent of the world's population.[4] Theravada (or Southern) Buddhism developed in Sri Lanka, Burma, Thailand, Cambodia, and Laos, while the largest branch of Buddhism, Mahayana (or Northern) Buddhism, took hold in Nepal, Tibet, China, Japan, Hong Kong, Viet Nam, and Korea.

B. In the Uni ted States, the greatest impact from Buddhism has occurred since World War II.[5] Although it is not very missionary-minded like Christianity or Islam, Buddhism has seen large growth in the U.S. during the 60's and 70's as "truth" seekers turned to meditation.

In the early 1980's, American Buddhism had some major problems as it mixed with New Age philosophy and secular modernism. One of those problems was in sexual misconduct. In 1983, for instance, it was discovered that the "majority of U.S. teachers, both foreign born and American, had abused their authority by sleeping with their disciples."[6]

Buddhism broke down into various sects over the generations, and it appears that all of them have a following in America today. In *Buddhism: The Path to Nirvana*, author Robert Lester claims:

"All of the major traditions of Asian Buddhism—Pure Land, Zen, and Nichiren Mahayana, Theravada and Tibetan Tantrayana—have a following in the United States. Indeed, one can find a list of 'Buddhist churches' in the yellow pages of the telephone directories of most major cities. *It is estimated that there are about five hundred thousand American Buddhists*, mostly of non-Asian descent, active in more than three hundred places of worship and meditation."[7] [italics added]

Today, Buddhism is impacting the United States. Various dens of dharma are being established where people can meditate individually or in groups. There are meditation walks and various exercise classes that incorporate Buddhist teachings. A punk rap group named the Beastie Boys creates songs like *Bodhisattiva Oath*. Coach Phil Jackson (former coach of the Chicago Bulls) calls himself a Zen Christian. Fans flock to talks by various Buddhists teachers, such as Thich Nhat Hanh, a Vietnamese monk who wrote *Living Buddha, Living Christ*. English language Buddhist teaching centers have jumped from 429 in 1988 to 1,062.

Hollywood has helped the recent interest in the subject. The 1997 movie *Seven Years in Tibet*, staring Brad Pitt, glorifies the life of the Dalai Lama, a Tibetan Buddhist. Actors Steven Seagal and Richard Gere are both actively involved in promoting Buddhism in the United States. Gere, who is a primary disciple of the Dalai Lama recently said, "There has been not enough time to ferment and intoxicate the culture of America...But our approach, because we're so new at it, has a certain eagerness and excitement that you don't see in the Tibetans."[8] Perhaps they felt some of this sensation on August 15, 1999, as Gere introduced the Dalai Lama, who was on a U.S. tour, to more than 40,000 at Central Park in New York.

Thinking Through The Scripture

"He who believes in the Son has everlasting life; and he who does not believe the Son shall not see life, but the wrath of God abides on Him." (John 3:36)

Questions for discussion:
1. What are the results of believing or not believing? If they don't believe, will Buddhists really "see life"? What does it mean to "see life"? What life?
2. Consider the verses in Romans 1:18 and Ephesians 2:3 dealing with "the wrath of God." Who is under wrath? How does it get removed? Read Ephesians 2:4-9. How can Buddhists remove wrath and find God's grace?

III. WHO WAS BUDDHA AND WHAT WAS THE BEGINNING OF BUD-
DHISM?

   A. **Siddhartha Gautama became known as Buddha.** According to
   David J. Kalupahana in his book *A History of Buddhist Philosophy:
   Continuities and Discontinuities* much of what is actually known
   about Siddhartha is "enshrined in all forms of myths and legends."[9] Whereas the texts containing the words of Jesus were
   written down in the New Testament within a couple of decades
   after His ascent into heaven, the texts containing the words of
   Buddha were written anonymously about two centuries after his
   death. There were some earlier biographies written about
   Buddha, but these "do not tally with Buddha's historical career"[10]
   in the later texts. We can only guess as to the accuracy of the
   accounts.

   That being said, however, there are strong oral traditions in
   India regarding Buddha, and it is good to remember that "his biog-
   raphy becomes a kind of commentary on his teaching."[11] In other
   words, the oral traditions give us a character sketch of Buddha
   based upon what they say he taught. Author Fritz Ridenour writes
   the following summary of Siddhartha's life:

   "The man who formulated Buddhism was Siddhartha
   Gautama, who was born a Hindu about 560 B.C. at Lumbini in
   what is now Nepal, near the border of India. Tradition says that
   when Gautama was born, a seer prophesied that he would become
   the greatest ruler in human history. The seer added that if Gautama
   were to see four things: sickness, old age, death, and a monk who
   had renounced the world, the boy would give up his earthly rule
   and discover a way of salvation for all mankind. Gautama's father,
   wanting him to become a great earthly ruler, built a palace for his
   son. He gave orders that neither the sick, the old, a dead body nor
   a monk could be allowed near the palace. Gautama grew up in this
   way, protected from the world. He later married a beautiful girl,
   Yasodhara, who bore him a son.

   But the gods had other plans for Gautama. One day as he rode
   through the park that surrounded his palace, he saw a man covered
   with terrible sores, a man tottering with age, a corpse being carried
   to its grave, and a begging monk who appeared peaceful and happy.
   That night, as Gautama reported later, he began to think about the
   look of peace on the face of the monk. He began to wonder if there
   was more to life than the luxuries of his palace. Late that night he
   took a last look at his sleeping wife and child, then left the palace
   forever.

Gautama, 29 years old, was determined to solve the riddle of life. He shaved his head, put on a yellow robe and wandered the countryside as a beggar monk. First he studied the Upanishads with the finest teachers, but he could find no satisfaction in these writings. Then he tried to find salvation through self-denial. He starved himself until he was a walking skeleton, but this brought him no happiness either. Finally, he sat under a tree for 40 days and nights. He swore that he would not move until he found what he was searching for. During this time, Mara (the evil one) tried to make him give up his quest. Then, at the end of the 40 days he experienced nirvana (the final state). He felt he had found salvation.

From then on, he was known as 'Buddha' or the 'enlightened one.' After this experience, Gautama Buddha went back to the world of man. He began to preach and teach about the meaning of life and his way of salvation. Soon, he founded the Sangha, an order of monks. By the time Gautama Buddha died, 45 years later, many thousands had accepted his religion."[12]

IV. WHAT IS A POSSIBLE TIME SKETCH OF BUDDHA'S LIFE? (Dates are B.C.)

A. **563 His birth:** Siddhartha was born in the Kshatriya (soldier) caste to a rich ruler. His father was Suddhodana and his mother Maya,[13] but she died shortly after his birth. A seer gave a prophecy that Siddhartha would help mankind find salvation.

B. **547 His marriage:** At 16, he married Yasodharma who bore Rahula, their son.

C. **534 Great Renunciation:** At 29, Siddhartha is affected by various sights of suffering. After seeing sickness, old age, death, and poverty with bliss, he leaves his wife and child and renounces the throne to discover the reason for suffering.

D. **528 Attaining Nirvana:** After six years of searching through the teachings of Hinduism and then the asceticism of the monks, Siddhartha sat under a Bodhi tree in a city called Bodh Gaya for a period of time (accounts vary from 1 to 49 days) to attain enlightenment. After resisting the temptation of Mara (death; feminine Buddhist tempter of sensual pleasure; "the personification of all evils and passions"[14]), he attained nirvana.

Dean Halverson explains in *The Compact Guide to World Religions* that "Buddha called his path to enlightenment the Middle Way, because it avoided the extremes of both affluence and asceticism, both of which had only caused him to suffer. Shortly after his enlightenment, Buddha traveled to Benares, and in the Deer Park there he preached his first sermon—the contents of which have come to be known as the Four Noble Truths. Eventually, he won thousands of followers, who formed communities called sanghas."[15] Thus, Buddha supposedly fulfilled the seer's prophecy bringing a type of salvation to mankind.

Thinking Through The Scripture

"You worship that which you do not know; we worship that which we know; for salvation is from the Jews." (John 4:22) NASB

"And behold, there was a man in Jerusalem whose name was Simeon, and this man was just and devout, waiting for the Consolation of Israel, and the Holy Spirit was upon him. And it had been revealed to him by the Holy Spirit that he would not see death before he had seen the Lord's Christ. So he came by the Spirit into the temple. And when the parents brought in the Child Jesus, to do for Him according to the custom of the law, he took Him up in his arms and blessed God and said: 'Lord, now You are letting Your servant depart in peace, according to Your word; for my eyes have seen Your salvation which You have prepared before the face of all peoples, a light to bring revelation to the Gentiles, and the glory of Your people Israel." (Luke 2:25-32)

Questions for discussion:
1. According to these Scriptures, from what group did salvation arise? What individual in that group brings salvation? To whom does He bring it?
2. What does this indicate about the seer's prophecy, Buddha, and Buddhism?

E. **483 Buddha's death:** Buddha died at the age of 80, probably as a result of food poisoning. There is speculation about some of his last actions and words. In the book *Eastern Paths and the Christian Way*, author Paul Clasper tells us that Buddha's last recorded words to his disciples were "Be ye lamps unto yourselves. Betake yourselves to no external refuge. Hold fast to the truth as a lamp. Hold fast as a refuge to the truth. Look not for refuge to anyone besides yourselves. Behold now, brethren, I exhort you saying: Decay is inherent in all component things! Work out your salvation with diligence."[16]

Archaeologists believe they recently discovered Buddha's mortal remains within a sandstone coffin. On the casket is inscribed "Be a lamp unto yourself".[17] Even though Siddhartha Gautama was probably a great and virtuous man who sought answers to the deep questions of suffering, his corpse is still in the grave. Since then, many of his followers worship him as God[18] even though "[s]uch veneration of the Buddha is against the basic teachings of Buddha himself."[19]

But the Bible tells us that Jesus is the "light of the world" (Jn. 8:12) and that it is through Him that we have light (Jn. 1:9). It is through Him that we have the right to become the children of God (Jn. 1:12-13). Although Buddha's body is still in the grave, it is not so with Jesus; He has risen from the dead (Mt. 28:6) and ascended into heaven (Acts 1:9-11). Furthermore, while we should follow Buddha's advice regarding holding fast to the truth, his advice about not putting trust in external refuge is faulty regarding God. The Bible says, "God is our refuge and strength, a very present help in trouble" (Ps. 46:1).

V.   WHAT WERE THE TEACHINGS OF BUDDHA?

A. **Denial and Discovery**: Buddha denied the inspiration of the Vedas and Upanishads, the authority of the Brahmins (priestly caste), and certain doctrines. His intent, however, was not to start a new religion but to reform Hinduism. Fernando and Swidler reveal in *Buddhism Made Plain: An Introduction for Christians and Jews* that Buddha's basic goal was to clearly define the purpose of religion:

"The simple aim of the Four Noble Truths is to define religion with regard to its primary purpose. Religion as he [Buddha] saw it had to be an answer to a concrete human problem. It had to be a medicine to a definite human ailment. To put it more technically, it had to bring about a liberation. A religion that did not offer liberation was for him no religion at all. To liberate human beings was for him the primary function of religion."[20]

Buddha saw in Hinduism the bondage of the caste system, the denial of suffering, and the false hope of attaining moksha (liberation) in some future life after endless rebirths. He sought to find a remedy for relieving people's suffering here and now and not in some future place on which could only be speculation. While he held to the Hindu doctrines of karma, transmigration, and samsara, he felt they were distorted because of the Hindu view of the world. The Hindu concept that the physical world is illusion (maya), he felt did not go far enough. Not only the world is illusion, but the body and soul as well. Thus the illusion of rebirth itself needs to be overcome, as we see in William de Bary's work, *The Buddhist Tradition in India, China, and Japan*:

"In an illusory world, rebirth is also illusory. The things a man craves for have no more reality than a dream, but he craves nevertheless, and hence his illusory ego is reborn in a new but equally illusory body...[T]he importance of the last conscious thought before death...plays a very decisive part in the nature of the rebirth."[21]

B. **The Sermon of the Four Noble Truths:** Under the Bodhi tree, Siddhartha Gautama claims he received the revelation of the four noble truths, attained nirvana, and became the Buddha. He returned to the five ascetic monks he had once lived with and told them he was liberated and that they could be also. He taught about the middle path by explaining the four noble truths. The monks then taught others and Buddhism was born. In the Buddhist text called the Vinanya Pitaka, his sermon to the monks is written below. Remember this was oral tradition written two hundred years later. William de Bary tells us that Buddha taught the following sermon:

"Two extremes, monks, are not to be approached by him who has withdrawn from the world. Which two? One is that which is linked and connected with lust, through sensuous pleasures, because it is low, of the uncultured, of the mediocre man, ignoble and profitless. The other is that which is connected with mortification and asceticism, because it is painful, ignoble, incapable of achieving the target. Avoiding both brings knowledge, and leads to tranquility, to full knowledge, to full enlightenment, to Nirvana.

And monks, what is this Middle Path that leads to Nirvana? It is indeed, the Noble Eightfold Path, namely right understanding, right thought, right speech, right action, right livelihood, right effort, right mindfulness, right concentration. The Middle Path leads to Nirvana. Now monks, this is the Noble Truth as to sorrow. Birth (earthly existence) indeed is sorrowful. Disease, death, union with the unpleasing, separation from the pleasing is sorrowful; in brief, desirous transient individuality (five grasping aggregates) is sorrowful. Again, monks, this the Noble Truth as to the origin of sorrow. It is the recurring greed, associated with enjoyment and desire and seeking pleasure everywhere, which is the cause of this sorrow.

In other words, it is the greed for sense-pleasure, greed for individual existence, and the greed for non-existence. Again, monks, this the Noble Truth as to the cessation of sorrow...the complete cessation, giving up, abandoning, release and detachment from greed. And this once more, monks, is the Noble Truth as to the path to the cessation of sorrow. It is indeed that Noble Eightfold Path: right understanding, right thought, right speech, right action, right livelihood, right effort, right mindfulness, right concentration.

The Middle Path, monks, leads to Nirvana. As soon, monks, as my knowledge and sight concerning these four Noble Truths became complete, I knew that I had attained supreme and full enlightenment. I became aware and fully convinced that my mind was liberated, that existence in its unhappy form had ended, that there would no longer be an unhappy survival."[22]

C. **What Buddha taught in a nutshell:**

The Four Noble Truths:

1) *Life consists of suffering* (dukkha) *in an illusory existence.*
2) *Suffering is caused by selfish desire for illusory things.* ("clinging to the five aggregates of the personality—body, feeling, perception, disposition, and consciousness—as possessions of 'my self' is suffering")[23]
3) *Liberation comes through elimination of all these desires.*
4) *Desires are eliminated by following the Eight-Fold path* (The Middle Way).

The Eight-Fold Path:

1.	Right Understanding	5.	Right Livelihood
2.	Right Thought	6.	Right Effort
3.	Right Speech	7.	Right Awareness
4.	Right Action	8.	Right Meditation

Thinking Through The Scripture

"Not only was the Teacher wise, but also he imparted knowledge to the people. He pondered and searched out and set in order many proverbs. The Teacher searched to find just the right words, and what he wrote was upright and true. The words of the wise are like goads, their collected sayings like firmly embedded nails—given by one Shepherd. Be warned, my son, of anything in addition to them. Of making many books there is no end, and much study wearies the body. Now all has been heard; here is the conclusion of the matter: Fear God and keep his commandments, for this is the whole duty of man. For God will bring every deed into judgment, including every hidden thing, whether it is good or evil." (Ecclesiastes 12:9-14) NIV

Questions for discussion:
1. The author of this passage was most likely Solomon. Much like Buddha, he pursued pleasure, attainment, and wisdom. He studied

suffering and labor, and deduced that much of life is vanity. In the end, he concluded the passage above. What does he say the words of the wise are like? From whom do these words originate? What warning does he give the reader and why?

2. What is his actual conclusion for how we should live? How does it contrast with Buddha's teachings? What does he mean "the whole duty of man"?

3. The Bible tells us that Solomon was the wisest man who ever lived (1 Kings 3:12). Though Buddha may have had wise advice regarding certain matters, how should we view his teachings that contradict Solomon's wisdom?

D. **Right Understanding - The Doctrine of the No-Self:** The foundation to the Eight-Fold path is the first step, that of right understanding. There are three parts to right understanding. They are anicca, dukkha, and anatta. 1) Anicca is the doctrine or teaching that everything is changing and impermanent. Desire changes and pleasure is fleeting. 2) Because of this, man is constantly suffering (dukkha). 3) Our only hope is to gain anatta, which is no-self. The term is confusing, to say the least. It has caused major divisions within Buddhism and various sects have arisen over disputes. Theravada Buddhism takes this to mean that people have no soul, whereas Mahayana Buddhism teaches the theory that everything is empty or has "non-ego".[24]

But the Bible teaches that everyone has sinned (Rom. 3:23) and abides in a state of death (Rom. 6:23) until they accept the free gift of eternal life through Jesus Christ our Lord. Buddha sees man's selfish desire and blames suffering upon this. But the truth is that men are much worse than just those who have selfish desire. Mankind not only ate the forbidden fruit (Gen. 3:6), but in doing so rejected God.

Buddha might have been a great psychologist of self helps, but he did not deal with the root problem, namely sin. He did not teach about sin because he did not believe in sin. But the Bible says, *"If we say that we have no sin, we deceive ourselves, and the truth is not in us"* (1 Jn. 1:8).

Although, there is a measure of accuracy in Buddha's words, they fall short of complete truth because he misunderstood man's real problem of alienation from God our Creator. Also, the Bible clearly shows that some desire is appropriate. (Ps. 145:19; Pr. 10:24). Finally, Buddhism teaches that "ignorance is the root of all evil,"[25] but actually 1 Tim. 6:10 teaches us that the *"love of money is a root of all kinds of evil."*

E. **Buddha's Goals:** World religion expert, Dean Halverson, says, Buddha's "immediate goal was to eliminate the cause of suffering. His ultimate goal, though, was to become liberated from the cycle of death and rebirth (samsara) by teaching how we can cease craving and thereby eliminate our attachment to and beliefs in the existence of the illusory self. As we are successful in eliminating such attachment, then the effects of karma will have nothing to attach themselves to, which releases the individual from the realm of illusion. At that moment of enlightenment, the person achieves the state of nirvana—the ultimate goal for the Buddhist, and Buddhism's equivalent of salvation."[26]

But the Bible does not indicate that life or these bodies are at all an illusion. Our bodies are a part of the plan of the creation of God, and they are good because God created everything and called it good (Gen. 1). Psalm 139:14 tells us that these bodies are "fearfully and wonderfully made" by the great Creator God of the universe. We are born, live, die, and then come to the judgment (Heb. 9:27).

There is no endless cycle of rebirths, no cosmic karma guiding each life, and no nirvana in which to escape from this reality, which Buddha calls an illusion. Buddha might have been so self-disciplined that he came to a mental place in which he was able to step out of his body (much like astral projection) into a supposed state of bliss. But his spirit came back to his body and stayed there until he died, and then it came no more. If rebirth (according to Buddha) is a part of the illusion, then why did he die of food poisoning? Why didn't he stick around a long time to really show the illusion of it all?

VI. WHAT ARE THE DIFFERENCES BETWEEN THERAVADA AND MAHAYANA?

Two Main Branches

A. **How they view man**
    1. Theravada: Individual; must help self
    2. Mahayana: Not alone; others can help
B. **How they view God**
    1. Theravada: Atheists; or topic unimportant
    2. Mahayana: Polytheists
C. **How they view Buddha**
    1. Theravada: Saint; only one

   2. Mahayana: Savior; but there have been many manifestations;
      avatars
D. **How they view religion**
   1. Theravada: Full time job / must be monk
   2. Mahayana: Relevant to life / for everyone
E. **What is key virtue**
   1. Theravada: Wisdom
   2. Mahayana: Compassion
F. **Striving to become**
   1. Theravada: Arhat
   2. Mahayana: Bodhisattva
G. **Which Scriptures**
   1. Theravada: Tripitaka - main ones
   2. Mahayana: Hundreds of books
H. **Ritual**
   1 Theravada: Avoid
   2. Mahayana: Embrace
I. **Solution to life**
   1. Theravada: "To cease all desire in order to realize the nonexis-
      tence of the self, thus finding permanence"[27]
   2. Mahayana: Awareness of Buddha-nature within. All plants and
      animals have Buddha-nature and will eventually gain
      Buddhahood[28]
J. **Means to get there**
   1. Theravada: "Self-reliance. We must follow the Middle Path and
      accrue karmic merit"[29]
   2. Mahayana: "Self-reliance. The means vary from that of follow-
      ing the Eightfold Path, to emptying the mind, to accruing merit
      by performing rituals, to realizing the Buddha-nature within, to
      depending on the merits of a bodhisattva."[30]
K. **Persuasion**
   1. Theravada: Conservative - consider themselves truer to
      Buddha's written teachings & doctrine
   2. Mahayana: Liberal - consider themselves closer to Buddha's
      true heart for all people to gain nirvana

VII. WHAT ARE THE VARIOUS SECTS OF MAHAYANA BUDDHISM?
A. **Pure Land Buddhism** - Started in the thirteenth century by Shinran,
   today it is the largest sect of Buddhism in Japan. Author and histo-
   rian Richard Kyle noted that it teaches "faith in a Buddha called
   Amida Buddha. When he experienced enlightenment and became a
   Buddha, Amida took steps to fulfill his previous bodhisattva vows

to establish a paradise or 'western kingdom.' By trusting in Amida, people could enter the Pure Land after death and there attain enlightenment.

To experience this enlightenment, one did not need to develop great meditation techniques or to reach a sinless state. Rather, one had to show gratitude to Amida by calling on him in the formula 'Hail to Amida Buddha'. Pure Land Buddhism relied on the 'other power' of Amida to attain enlightenment, not the 'self power' emphasized by Theravada and other types of Buddhism."[31]

This Amida Buddha personifies the "compassion" aspect of the bodhisattvas in Mahayana Buddhism. These enlightened beings have chosen to stay and help man rather than enter into nirvana immediately. Interestingly, Amida sounds somewhat like The Lord Jesus. Historians realize that Christian missionaries probably impacted Mahayana Scriptures with the Christian stories of a suffering Savior and a people saved by faith.[32]

Thinking Through The Scripture

"Fix our eyes on Jesus, the author and perfecter of our faith, who for the joy set before him endured the cross, scorning its shame, and sat down at the right hand of the throne of God. Consider him who endured such opposition from sinful men, so that you will not grow weary and lose heart." (Hebrews 12:2-3) NIV

Questions for discussion:
1. Rather than Amida Buddha, who does the Bible tell us to fix our eyes upon?
2. How is Jesus perfecting your faith? What types of things are you going through that He has authored? Where is Jesus seated?
3. Why does it say "for the joy set before him"? How does the thought of what Jesus did for you give you the strength and heart to continue even at times when life has suffering? Have you told Jesus how much you love Him lately?

B. **Zen Buddhism** - Two schools of Zen began in Japan. Eisai originated the Rinzai sect in 1191 A.D. and Dogen founded the Soto sect in 1227 A.D. Both these schools look back to the ancient Indian Buddhist sage, Bodhi-Dharma (480-528 A.D.), who practiced "wall meditation" after going to China to influence Emperor Wu with his technique. It is said he sat in a cave for nine years and stared at a wall. The word Zen is derived from a Sanskrit word meaning "meditation". Zenists do not look to a higher "god" to save them. Zen's special flavor as compared to other sects is the idea that in Zen an awakening to a higher state of being is something quite natural and can happen at any time.

Whereas much of Buddhism places the focus of achieving "nirvana" in some future place, Zen believes that it captures Gautama Buddha's true teaching—that it can be achieved instantaneously and now.

There are five key words basic to understanding Zen. 1) Zendo is the place where meditators meet. 2) Zazen is the practice of meditation usually done by sitting in lotus position staring at some object (candle, pool, rock, flower, etc.) to capture one's attention. 3) Satori is the immediate perception of truth or enlightenment that comes to a meditator who realizes that all reality is one (pantheism) and that there is no right or wrong because truth is subjective. 4) Mondo is a form of question-and-answer format that the Zen master uses to drive the meditator deeper into subjective truth. 5) Koan is a paradoxical question designed to help the mind free itself from all objective truth and look inward. An example of this type of question is, "What is the sound of one hand clapping?"

Zen strives to use shock treatment to break us out of the mental encumbrances of daily living. Zen's greatest impact in America came through the beatniks of the 1950's. It became the symbol for the spiritual counterculture and prepared the way for LSD, astrology, and gurus.[33]

Thinking Through The Scripture

"For among them are those...always learning and never able to come to the knowledge of the truth." (2 Timothy 3:6-7) NASB

"Seek the Lord while He may be found, call upon Him while He is near. Let the wicked forsake his way, and the unrighteous man his thoughts; let him return to the Lord, and He will have mercy on him; and to our God, for He will abundantly pardon. 'For My thoughts are not your thoughts, nor are your ways My ways,' says the Lord. 'For as the heavens are higher than the earth, so are My ways higher than your ways, and My thoughts than your thoughts'." (Isaiah 55:6-9)

Questions for discussion:

1. What's the difference in the first passage between "always learning" and "the knowledge of the truth"? Why aren't they able to come to the truth?

2. How does this relate to the idea of meditating on a wall, candle, or flower in a lotus position? When does learning lead to the knowledge of the truth?

3. According to Isaiah, whom should the Buddhists seek and why? Will their meditations really be able to search out God's thoughts and ways?

C. **Nichiren Shoshu Buddhism** - On April 18, 1253, Nichiren Daishonin of Japan chanted the words "Nam-Myoho-Renge-Kyo" meaning "Hail to the Lotus Sutra" and supposedly fulfilled a prophecy by Buddha that a special teacher would come forth in the thirteenth century A.D. This form of true Buddhism is suppose to eventually unite the world and bring peace to all mankind.

Nichiren taught that this new chant, never before heard, was to replace the Pure Land Buddhism chant "Hail to Amida Buddha". Although his teaching had little impact in the thirteenth century, it has had a dramatic one in the twentieth with the formation of *Soka Gakkai* (Value Creation Society) in 1930. Arriving in the United States after WWII, this has grown to become the largest Buddhist body in the country. One of the celebrities of this form of Buddhism is rock 'n' roll star Tina Turner, who chants the Buddhist mantras of Soka Gakkai.

This form of Buddhist idolatry has no problem merging with American materialism. The practice of this idolatry happens before a black box (butsodon) containing a sacred scroll (Gohonzon) and chanting "Hail to the Lotus Sutra" while fingering 108 beads on a rosary. The ultimate goal is for the devotee to merge with the one essence of Buddha (monism). Nichiren says the Lotus Sutra was written by Buddha himself, but it was actually written much later around 200 A.D. The primary purposes of the Nichiren Shoshu of America (NSA) are to chant, attain one's personal life goals, evangelize, and bring about world happiness and peace. This group evangelizes heavily.

I had an acquaintance through work in the mid 1970's who would chant before the black box. It was positioned as a shrine near a wall in his apartment that was arranged with tapestries and candles. Amidst the smell of incense, he would sit in lotus position meditating on the black box, handling the rosary, and chanting. He showed off his meditation center with pride hoping that others would get involved. However, as I recall, the black box chants were not able to help him fix a broken marriage, nor deliver him from drugs, poor work habits, and illicit sex. This idol worship also gave him a false sense of superiority that would war against any Biblical truth.

D. **Tantra Buddhism** - Started in Tibet by Padina Sambhava in 747 A.D. Tibetan Buddhism is only partially related to Mahayana in certain aspects. It is considered an entirely different branch of Buddhism by some because of its emphasis upon occultic technique to gain spiritual power. It is called Vajrayana (Vehicle of the Thunderbolt) or Tantrayana (Vehicle of specialized ritual). The Dhali Lama is the current leader and thought to be the fourteenth incarnation of a famous bodhisattva. One of the major Tibetan Buddhist texts is *The Tibetan Book of the Dead* which emphasizes demons, spirits, and powers of witchcraft. These agents of the darkness are to be avoided and appeased. Bob Larson gives the following account of what one form of Tantra Buddhism is all about:

"Padina Sambhava, a famed pagan exorcist, introduced Buddhism to Tibet in A.D. 747. His reputation so impressed the king, that the entire land soon was following his blend of Hindu / Buddhist beliefs with spells and secretive tantric ceremonies. Devotees preceded acts of sexual union with the ritualistic consumption of wine, meat, fish, and parched grains.

They instituted a priesthood of lamas ("superior ones") and designed prayer wheels with inscribed litanies. Mantras and mandalas, mystic diagrams, were also adopted. The former was believed to possess a sound able to induce transcendent experiences. Mandalas, circular cosmograms of the universe, were also used as an aid in worship. (The center of the mandala was thought to be a focal point of the universe.) Adherents of Tibetan Buddhism were taught that merely glimpsing a mandala could start one on the road to nirvana. They also developed the legend of Shambhala, an imaginary kingdom of enlightened citizens. This central Asian civilization was said to be the spiritual inspiration of the entire world. Their 'warriors' were people of compassion and awareness who still serve as models of Tibetan Buddhist aspirations."[34]

E. **Folk Buddhism** - Like folk Hinduism and folk Islam, there is also a folk Buddhism that is animistic. The term "folk" applies to animists. Involvement in folk Buddhism can be very different than formal Buddhism.

Animism is the idea that all things in the universe are inherently invested with a life force, soul or mind, even things like a stone or a tree, etc. In animism, things like accidents, sickness, or problems don't just happen; there is a spiritual reason behind all of it. Although an animist might believe in a Supreme God (like folk

Islam), he sees God as someone in the distant background who is not involved in daily affairs. He is mainly concerned with the local spirits (demons) that need to be appeased.

An animist might belong to a world religion, but lives in fear of offending a local powerful spirit or dead ancestor. Animists might use any variety of divinations to find out why they are having a problem, who threw the curse at them, how they can counter-curse, and how to resolve the problem they are having. They often see objects as having magical powers (charms). They might wear these for protection against spirits or perform rituals of homage to keep the spirits happy. Some experts estimate that 40 % of the world's population have animistic tendencies.[35]

VIII. WHAT ARE THE HOLY BOOKS OF BUDDHISM?
  A. **Theravada Buddhism**: The Tripitaka (three baskets) are three groups of writings considered holy scripture in the Pali canon. 1) The Vinaya Pitaka (discipline basket) contains rules for monastic life and the ten commandments of Buddha: no killing, stealing, adultery, lying, drinking intoxicating liquor, eating after midday, being present at any dramatic or musical performance, using perfume, sleeping on a comfortable bed, or owning silver or gold. 2) The Sutra Pitaka (teaching basket) contains the sermons and parables of Buddha. 3) The Abidhamma Pitaka (metaphysical basket) contains Buddhist theology and interpretation of Buddha's teachings. The Tripitaka size = 70 x's the Bible.
  B. **Mahayana Buddhism**: The canon of Mahayana is so large that it is estimated to be over 5,000 volumes. This is because their canon remains open to Indian, Chinese, Japanese, and Tibetan scriptures. Most Mahayana sects have chosen favorite books that they refer to exclusively. Two of the most popular Mahayana scriptures are the Lotus Sutra and the Perfection of Wisdom, which includes the Diamond Sutra and the Heart Sutra. Generations of Buddhists revere these. It is said that the Diamond Sutra is the "Perfection of Wisdom that cuts like a thunderbolt," and that the Heart Sutra "formulates the very heart, core, or essence of wisdom." These are heavily emphasized in Zen monasteries in Japan and lamaseries of Tibet.[36]

IX. WHAT IS THEIR WORLD VIEW CONCERNING KARMA AND SAMSARA?
  A. Although Buddha himself concentrated on the here and now, much of Buddhism has evolved into a complex system of theology which says the universe is 432 billion years old, expanding and

declining at various times. Lesser phases are 432 million years and each have four ages. The universe is made up of one billion world systems. Author Robert Lester says their view of karma and rebirth is as follows:

"While they recognize these great cycles of time and the numerous world-cycles, the teachings of Buddhism focus on the repeated cycling (samsara) of life forms in this world system by reason of karma. Karma, the force or energy created by human thoughts, words, and deeds, causes the various life forms that inhabit our world system—their physical and mental capacities, sex, and social circumstances. There are gods who reside in heavens above the earth; humans, demons, hungry ghosts, and animals who live on or near the earth; and hell dwellers whose abode is below the earth. Karma is of two kinds: meritorious (punya, or 'good,' karma) and demeritorious (papa, or 'bad,' karma).

Merit results in pleasure, demerit in effects must be experienced, if not in the present life, then in another. Human beings who die with greater merit than demerit are reborn as gods or again as humans. Those with greater demerit than merit are reborn as demons, hungry ghosts, animals, or inhabants of hell. The life of a god is one of great pleasure; that of a human, mixed pleasure and pain; and that of demons, hungry ghosts, animals, and hell dwellers, great pain.

Thus, it is desirable to gain heaven, or at least rebirth in a human form of high status and potential. But, even heavenly existence comes to an end when merit is exhausted; these beings must then revert to human status, or if they carry sufficient demerit from their former human existence, a lower form where they experience the result of this demerit. Therefore, the ultimate goal of the practice of Buddhism is freedom from karma and rebirth, freedom from suffering."[37]

X.   WHAT IS NIRVANA?

A.   The term is difficult to define. Nirvana is the place where karma is "blown out" or "extinguished." It is a cooling down of passions connecting one with this world's influences. It is a total reorientation to existence. In Theravada, it is up to the individual to become an arhat and attain nirvana. But in Mahayana, those close to nirvana, called bodhisattvas, can choose to not enter it until after sharing their stored up meritorious karma as benefit for others. Because of this, Mahayana is considered a more compassionate religion than Theravada.

Both of these view nirvana in a different light. While Theravada places emphasis on what is "extinguished," namely craving and vain attachments to this illusory life, Mahayana puts emphasis on what is gained, that being "the further shore, the harbor of refuge, the cool cave, the matchless, island, the holy city. It is sheer bliss."[38] The Buddha saw it as a state of liberation in which karma and samsara are overcome in this life. He did not really focus too much on future life after death.

Some compare the nirvana to the "Kingdom of God" because both can be attained now. But this is very inaccurate because the Kingdom of God also includes eternal heaven. Furthermore, the hell concept of the Bible is eternal and men spend eternity in one or the other, depending upon whether they accept the free gift of eternal life (Rom. 6:23).

XI. WHAT ABOUT BUDDHA AND GOD?

A. **Buddha's view of God:** Buddha was concerned about helping men break out of an illusory state that contained real suffering. What is actually known about him is very vague. Many of the things he supposedly taught were morally good and support the Bible. Some of the things he taught were in error. He, like all men, *"must appear before the judgment of Christ"* (2 Cor. 5:10) and give account. Whether he believed in God or not is hard so say. He normally refused to comment upon the after life or the existence of God. He preferred to bring all conversation back to the here and now. He taught people to meditate on today. One of his favorite meditation techniques was to focus upon one's breathing—breathe in, breathe out, breath in, breathe out.[39] He never claimed to be God or Savior. But his followers exalted him to a place of prominence in all of their traditions and rituals.

B. **False Idols of Buddhism:** Mahayana Buddhism, which is by far the largest religious body of Buddhism with many sects has made Buddha their god, or one of many gods. *Buddhist temples worldwide are filled with idols of Buddha.* He is celebrated at annual festivals honoring his birth, enlightenment and death. Certain countries display some of his hair or even "Buddha's finger" as his possible mortal remains.

"The largest Buddhist pagoda in the world is in Rangoon, Burma. The Shwe Dagon or Golden Pagoda contains over 3500 idols of Buddha. Every day of the year, people parade up the winding steps of the 300-foot monument to place thin pieces of gold on the shrine, light candles and incense, and pray for their dead ancestors before these wood, stone, and metal statues."[40]

A temple in Hong Kong housed 13,000 idols until July 2, 1997. The day before had marked a celebration by 40,000 Buddhists who gathered to publicly applaud the fact that Hong Kong once again belonged to China. However, the next morning at 5 a.m. on July 2, torrential rains fell (almost like a judgment) and caused massive mud slides destroying the temple and the thousands of idols within.[41]

Thinking Through The Scripture

"Everyone is senseless and without knowledge; every goldsmith is shamed by his idols. His images are a fraud; they have no breath in them. They are worthless, the objects of mockery; when their judgment comes, they will perish. He who is the Portion of Jacob is not like these, for he is the Maker of all things, including Israel, the tribe of his inheritance—the Lord Almighty is his name." (Jeremiah 10:14-16) NIV

Questions for discussion:
1. How would a goldsmith become shamed by his idols? In what way are the images fraudulent and worthless?
2. What kind of judgment might come upon them?
3. In what ways is the "Portion of Jacob" not like these? If He is the Maker of all things, why doesn't He just quickly destroy all these idols?

XII. HOW CAN WE HELP THESE PEOPLE FIND THE TRUTH ABOUT JESUS?
   A. **Prayer:** *The key to mobilizing evangelism today is prayer.* It is not the only thing to do, but it is the first thing to do. There are many books on prayer and many teachings on prayer, but none of these replaces prayer. If we want to see the captives of Buddhism set free (or of any other religion or cult) then we must willingly commit ourselves to the task of spiritual warfare. We often employ our greatest energy to do things that only yield minimal results. We wonder why things are not going better. Well, prayer is the answer! The Lord may draw us into it, and we suddenly realize that this is what has been missing. We must submit ourselves to the Master in prayer and let Him examine our motives and ways.

   One aspect of this is touched upon in *The Kneeling Christian* when it says, "What are we out for? What is our real aim in life? Surely we desire most of all to be abundantly fruitful in the Master's service. We seek not position, or prominence, or power. But we do long to be fruitful servants. Then we must be much in prayer. God can do more through our prayers than through our preaching. A. J. Gordon once said, 'You can do more than pray, after you have prayed, but you can never do more than pray until you have prayed.'"[42]

B. **Love:** *The key to winning the right to evangelize today is love.* When we show acts of love and kindness to others it opens their hearts. It makes opportunites for them to get to know us and to perhaps listen to what we have to share. We need to show Christian love and then share the gospel. Obviously, there may be times in which the Holy Spirit leads you to spontaneously witness to someone on an airplane, in a restaurant, or in the market. However, for the most part, we share the gospel with those we know. In these situations, we can best impact through deeds and then words. As Steve Sjogren points out in his book *Conspiracy of Kindness*, first comes the deeds of love then the words of love:

"God's love must be communicated from person to person, not just from page to person. If his love could be sent through printed information alone, we could simply flood our cities with gospel tracts and then rest assured that we have done our part. Deeds of love allow us to speak into the hearts of those we serve. Even though people aren't conscious of what's happening, they are welcoming us and the God we represent into the fortress of their hearts. Deeds of love aren't enough on their own to bring someone to Christ, but they do create 'phone wires' for transmitting the spoken message...Deeds of kindness get people's attention and often cause them to ask us questions. Instead of having a forced presentation of the gospel to people who really aren't interested in what we have to say, we find people are curious and ask us to explain the message which is vital in bringing someone to Christ without taking a sales approach.

When we do speak we must be sensitive to the level of receptivity of each person and explain the words of God's love in whatever way the hearer can understand. These words are the cognitive or conscious element of our evangelism. If we don't follow our actions with words, they will only know that we are nice people, not that God loves them."[43]

C. **Witness:** *The key to setting the captives free is witness.* In the larger sense, we can say that both prayer and love are a part of witnessing. However, on a practical level the Gospel message must go forth to sow the seed in the heart of the hearer. As Romans 10:14-15 tells us, *"How then shall they call on Him in whom they have not believed? And how shall they believe in Him of whom they have not heard? And* *how shall they hear without a preacher? And how shall they preach unless they are sent? As it is written: 'How beautiful are the feet of those who preach the gospel of peace, who bring glad tidings of good things!'"*

The following is a true story of an elderly man who went from being a Buddhist lama (priest) to a Christian pastor. It shows the salvation workings of the Gospel preached:

"Some time earlier, my sister had become a Christian. She witnessed to me regularly and prayed for me daily. But my response to her was mockery and ridicule. Eventually my health began to deteriorate from spreading paralysis. From October 1982 to April 1983, I suffered complete paralysis of one arm and both of my legs. Oozing sores covered my body. For about 7 months I lay in a pool of blood and dirt. My house was a virtual shrine for scores of idols whom I hoped would cure me. I employed numerous lamas, witch doctors, and others to ward off the dreaded disease. But my condition worsened daily. As a last resort, I placed myself under the medical treatment of vaidyas (local doctors), but to no avail. In the process I spend about $250—a substantial amount for a man of my standing. Day by day I drew nearer to death. I was convinced that my end had come. Family members and neighbors silently bade me farewell.

Then on April 13, 1983, at about 1 a.m. in hopelessness I spoke the word Prabhu (Lord). Instantly a shaft of light penetrated the room. I heard a voice say, 'If you will serve Me, I will heal you.' The pain in my body subsided, and a feeling of peace swept over me. Strength and mobility were restored. The next day I walked 6 miles from my village to the city of Darjeeling where I met the Assemblies of God pastor, Claude Barua. When I accepted the Lord Jesus Christ as my Savior, I discarded my idols and forsook Lamaism…About half of my family members joined me in baptism on August 1, 1983. Since then the rest of my family has converted, and we are all leading new lives. In less than 1 year, 98 tormented souls in my neighborhood were saved and have witnessed the miraculous word of the Lord Jesus Christ. Our old Lamaist village has become a Christian village."[44]

D. Tips for witnessing:
   1) Do a little probing to find out which school of Buddhism they follow.
   2) Share your experience with them about our personal God, but realize that in Buddhism emotions are something to escape. When Christians speak of a personal God who shows love,

anger, hope, faith, etc., it might confuse them. Go slowly through the concepts.

3) Regarding their doctrine that says everything is changing, point to Jesus Christ, *"the same yesterday, today and forever"* *(Heb. 13:8)*.

4) Most Buddhists have never really understood the Gospel; explain it to them.

5) For Mahayana Buddhism use the concept of bodhisattva as a "bridge to the Gospel".[46] If they believe that a bodhisattva can use extra karmic merit to benefit others who believe in him, then explain what Christ did for us on Calvary, using Isaiah 53.

6) Explain that suffering is a part of the curse, but that true peace can be found today through Jesus Christ our Lord. They do not have to wait for nirvana someday.

End Notes

1. Ron Carlson and Ed Decker, *Fast Facts on False Teachings* (Eugene, OR: Harvest House, 1994), p. 29-30.

2. Robert C. Lester, *Buddhism: The Path to Nirvana* (San Francisco: Harper & Row, 1987), p. 150.

3. Edward Conze, ed., *Buddhist Wisdom Books: The Diamond Sutra and the Heart Sutra* (London: George Allen & Unwin, 1975), p. 102.

4. Dean Halverson, ed., *The Compact Guide To World Religions* (Minneapolis, MN: Bethany House, 1996), p. 54.

5. Richard Kyle, *The Religious Fringe: A History of Alternative Religions in America* (Downers Grove, IL: InterVarsity Press, 1993), p. 135.

6. David Van Biema, "Buddhism in America," *Time Magazine* (October 1997): 80.

7. Lester, p. 140.

8. Van Biema, p. 77.

9. David J. Kalupahana, *A History of Buddhist Philosophy: Continuities and Discontinuities* (Honolulu: University of Hawaii Press, 1992), p. 22.

10. Hans Kung, *Christianity and the World Religions* (Garden City, NY: Doubleday & Company, Inc., 1986), p. 319.

11. Antony Fernando and Leonard Swidler, *Buddhism Made Plain: An Introduction for Christians and Jews* (Maryknoll, NY: Orbis Books, 1985), p. 9.

12. Fritz Ridenour, *So What's the Difference?* (Ventura, CA: Regal Books, 1979), pgs. 83-84.

13. Bob Larson, *Larson's Book of Cults* (Wheaton, IL: Tyndale House Publishers, 1988), pgs. 83-84.

14. Edward Conze, ed., *Buddhist Texts Through the Ages* (New York: Philosophical Library, Inc., 1954), p. 317.

15. Halverson, pgs. 55-56.

16. Paul Clasper, *Eastern Paths and the Christian Way* (Maryknoll, NY: Orbis Books, 1980), pgs. 45- 46.

17. Larson, p. 89.

18. Balbir Singh, *The Philosophy of Upanishads* (New Delhi, India: Arnold-Heinemann, 1983), pgs. 135-136.

19. Josh McDowell and Don Stewart, *Handbook of Today's Religions: Understanding Non-Christian Religions* (San Bernardino, CA: Here's Life Publishers, 1982), p. 53.
20. Fernando and Swidler, p. 98.
21. William de Bary, ed. *The Buddhist Tradition in India, China, and Japan* (New York: Vintage Books, 1972), p. 98.
22. Ibid., pgs. 18-19.
23. Kalupahana, p. 86.
24. Beatrice Lane Suzuki, *Mahayana Buddhism: A Brief Outline* (New York: Collier Books, 1963), p. 153.
25. Mather and Nichols, p. 45.
26. Halverson, p. 59.
27. Ibid., p. 61.
28. Suzuki, p. 141.
29. Halverson, p. 59.
30. Ibid.
31. Kyle, p. 138.
32. de Bary, p. 83.
33. Kyle, p. 228.
34. Larson, p. 89-90.
35. Halverson, p. 38.
36. Conze, *Buddhist Wisdom Books: The Diamond Sutra and the Heart Sutra*, p. 10.
37. Lester, p. 58.
38. Sir Norman Anderson, *Christianity and World Religions: The Challenge of Pluralism* (Downers Grove, IL: InterVarsity Press, 1984), p. 91.
39. Fernando and Swidler, p. 90.
40. Carlson and Decker, p. 26.
41. *Charisma Magazine*, (January 1998): 40.
42. *The Kneeling Christian* (Grand Rapids, MI: Zondervan Publishing House, 1971), p. 30.
43. Steve Sjogren, *Conspiracy of Kindness* (Ann Arbor, MI: Servant Publications, 1993), pgs. 22-23.
44. James D. Sherpa, *"From Buddhist Priest to Pastor,"* *Mountain Movers* (April 1997): 16-17.
45. Halverson, p. 66

QUESTIONNAIRE: LESSON TWENTY

NAME: _____ DATE _____

1. Buddhism comprises _____ % of the world's population and _____ million people.

2. The United States has approximately how many Buddhists? _____

3. Fill in the following: The story of _____ Gautama is that he was born in _____ in the Kshatriya caste to a rich ruler named Suddhodana and Maya, his mother. A seer prophesied at his birth that he would become a great ruler. He added that if Siddhartha saw four things: sickness, old age, death, and a _____ who had renounced the world that he would discover a way of _____ for all of mankind. His father wanted him to rule the kingdom, so he tried to protect his son against the visions. When Siddhartha was _____ years of age he married and together they had a son. He lived happily until he was twenty-nine years old, not realizing all the suffering in the world. Then one day he went outside the palace walls and saw _____, _____, _____, and a begging monk who appeared peaceful and happy. After he encountered the foretold visions, he decided to search for the reason of suffering. He left his wife and son and became a wandering monk. First, he learned from the finest teachers of the Upanishad writings and then he became an ascetic. He did not find his answer in either one even after searching for six years. One night he decided to sit under a _____ until he found what he was searching for. After _____ days he found _____ and from that time on was known as _____ or the enlightened one. Buddha went and told the monks what he had discovered. They spread the word and Buddhism was born. Buddha died at the age of 80 as a result of _____ poisoning.

4. Write one paragraph describing your thoughts about Buddha: _____

_____

_____

_____

5. List the Four Noble Truths of Buddha's Sermon:

1. _____

2. _____

3. _____

4. _____

6. What is the problem with Buddha's teaching of No-Self according to the Bible? _____

_____

_____

7. What is the problem with Buddha's goal according to the Bible? _____

_____

_____

_____

8. What are the main two branches of Buddhism? _____ and

_____

9. List three of the various sects of Mahayana and tell a little about each one:

a) _____ : _____

b _____ : _____

c) _____ : _____

10. The _____ of Theravada contains the rules for monastic life and the ten commandments.

11. The _____ of Mahayana is said to formulate the very core of wisdom.

12. According to Buddhism a person's karma can make him be reborn as one of six things. These include: 1) _____, 2) _____, 3) _____, 4) hungry ghosts, 5) _____, or 6) hell dwellers.

13. What are the three keys needed today for witnessing to those in cults and false religions?

a) _____

b) _____

c) _____

14. Consider your knowledge of Buddhism before and after this lesson. Circle the number below that indicates how equipped you felt before taking this course to witness to someone in this religion as compared to how equipped you feel now. Be honest.

BEFORE 0 1 2 3 4 5 6 7 8 9 10 AFTER 0 1 2 3 4 5 6 7 8 9 10

HOW TO LEAD SOMEONE
TO THE LORD

Leading someone to the Lord is one of the most exciting privileges we have as Christians. Much of this book is about the prayer, love, and witness that we as Christians can offer those ensnared in the cults and non Christian religions. It is our dearest hope that they will be delivered from deception and come to know the *real* Jesus Christ as their Lord and Savior; for there is salvation in no other. However, once they come to that point of wanting to accept Jesus, what then? How do you lead someone to the Lord? Since salvation is something that happens in the heart between the believer and Jesus, there are no certain rules regarding method. Yet, there are principles found within various Scriptures that can help you lead the seeker to the Lord. Below is a format for leading someone to the Lord that incorporates two questions and ten steps. The steps have various Scriptures that can be used to show them the concept in the Word of God. Once they accept the Lord, there are follow up suggestions:

A. USE THE TWO QUESTION TEST.
1. Ask, "Have you come to a place in your life where you know for sure that if you died tonight you would go to heaven?"
    This establishes whether they believe in heaven and where they think they might go when they die. It does not necessarily establish whether they believe in hell, however.
2. Ask, "Suppose you died tonight and stood before God and He asked you why He should let you into His Heaven - what would you say?"

This establishes why they think they will spend eternity with God. They normally respond with a works type of answer such as, "I go to church," or "I obey the commandments," or "I was baptized as a baby," or "I do good deeds," or "I'm a good person," etc. If their answer is anything other than that they have a personal relationship with Jesus Christ as Lord and Savior because He died for their sins, has forgiven them, and now lives in their heart by faith, then they are probably not yet born again. Go through the ten steps focusing on the fact that works and goodness do not pay our way into heaven.

B. FOLLOW THESE TEN STEPS OF EXPLANATION.
1. In God's eyes all have sinned and are far from His glorious presence.
    "for all have sinned and fall short of the glory of God." **Romans 3:23**
2. This sin can potentially separate us from God forever.
    "But your iniquities have separated you from your God." **Isaiah 59:2**
3. The final outcome of sin is eternal death and separation from God.
    "For the wages of sin is death..." **Romans 6:23**
4. God's wrath is revealed from heaven against the ungodlessness of sin.
    "For the wrath of God is revealed from heaven against all ungodliness..." **Romans 1:18**
5. However, God does not want men to perish, but He wants all to be saved.
    "who desires all men to be saved and to come to the knowledge of the truth." **1 Timothy 2:4**
    "not willing that any should perish but that all should come to repentance." **2 Peter 3:9**
6. He sent His Son to pay the penalty for our sins.
    "who Himself bore our sins in His own body on the tree, that we, having died to sins, might live for righteousness—by whose stripes we are healed. For you were once like sheep going astray, but have now returned to the Shepherd and Overseer of your souls." **1 Peter 2:24-25**
7. The Gospel is this: 1) Jesus died on the cross for our sins, 2) Jesus was buried, and, 3) Jesus rose from the dead on the third day victorious over death.
    "Moreover, brethren, I declare to you the gospel which I preached to you, which also you received and in which you stand, by which

also you are saved, if you hold fast that word which I preached to you—unless you believed in vain. For I delivered to you first of all that which I also received; that Christ died for our sins according to the Scriptures, and that He was buried, and that He rose again the third day according to the Scriptures." **1 Corinthians 15:1-4**

8. God gives everyone the choice to accept Jesus Christ as Lord and Savior and through Him receive the gift of eternal life, or to reject Jesus and to remain under the wrath of God headed for eternal death.

    "For God so loved the world that He gave His only begotten Son, that whosoever believes in Him should not perish but have everlasting life." **John 3:16**

    "He who believes in the Son has everlasting life; and he who does not believe in the Son shall not see life, but the wrath of God abides on him." **John 3:36**

    " the gift of God is eternal life in Christ Jesus our Lord." **Romans 6:23**

9. For those seeking salvation, God requires: 1) *Repentance* - a turning away from sins, unbelief, and dead works, to Jesus Christ, and 2) *Faith* in the substitutionary atonement of Christ alone. It is what He did for us on the cross that counts. We cannot be good enough or do enough works to deserve salvation and eternal life.

    "God...now commands all men everywhere to repent." **Acts 17:30**

    "For by grace you have been saved through faith, and that not of yourselves; it is the gift of God, not of works, lest anyone should boast. **Ephesians 2:8-9**

10 Prayer for salvation: It comes through confession and belief. Lead them in it.

    "if you confess with your mouth the Lord Jesus and believe in your heart that God has raised Him from the dead, you will be saved. For with the heart one believes unto righteousness, and with the mouth confession is made unto salvation." **Romans 10:9-10**

The person asking the Lord for salvation should pray. Below is a possible prayer to lead them through unless they want to make up their own words. Often, people don't know how to pray and so it would help if you ask them to follow along with you in prayer. Tell them that prayer is communication with God. As they follow along, they should direct their prayer to God. Pray these words and ask them to follow:

"Dear Heavenly Father, I am sorry for my sin and unbelief. Please forgive me. I thank you for sending your Son to die for me on the cross at Calvary. Lord Jesus, I accept your sacrifice on behalf of my sins. I accept the atonement of your blood that cleanses all my sins and creates in me a clean heart. I place my complete trust and faith in you for salvation. I know that I can't work my way to heaven and that I am not good enough. Jesus, I want to know you as my Lord and Savior. I need your help and the guidance of the Holy Spirit. Your plan is for me to live for God and to spend eternity with you. Please come into my life and give me life everlasting. I want to be with you from this moment on and forever. Thank you for saving me from a path that leads to death and destruction. Thank you for loving me. Thank you for seeking me. Thank you for finding me. I ask these things in the name of Jesus Christ. Amen."

Take time afterwards and do a Bible study on the Book of Life. Let them know that their name is now written in the Lamb's Book of Life: Philippians 4:3; Revelation 3:5, 13:8, 17:8, 20:12, 20:15, 21:27; Exodus 32:32; Psalm 69:28; Luke 10:20.

C. HELP THEM GET ESTABLISHED IN THEIR NEW CHRISTIAN LIFE.
   1. Through developing a habit of daily prayer.
   2. Through developing a habit of reading the Bible.
   3. Through finding a good Christ-centered and Bible-centered home church.
   4. Through learning to fellowship with other Christians.
   5. Through taking steps to get water baptized.
   6. Through seeking the baptism of the Holy Spirit.
   7. Through taking discipleship courses.
   8. Through learning to share their faith in Christ with others.

ANSWER KEY FOR CHAPTER QUESTIONNAIRES

Scoring Key Answers will be of several types: 1) Specific answers will be *italicized*, 2) General ideas for answers will be in normal font (non italicized), 3) Some will say "answer varies" because they are a matter of one's opinion, personal experience, or can have varying answers, and 4) Some will refer back to the lesson because the length of answer is too long.

Chapter One: Christian Apologetics and Doctrine

1. *"I will build My church and the gates of Hades shall not prevail against it."*
2. Lawlessness and a loss of love / Spiritual Degeneration / False Teaching and Deception.
3. *Defense / proof / faith / contend.*
4. Compare with the definition of "cult" in the lesson.
5. *No*
6. *No*
7. Pseudo-Christian: Jehovah's Witness, Oriental: Hare Krishna, New Age: Mind Sciences, Occult—Spiritualistic: Satanism, Apocalyptic: Solar Temple.
8. *No / Yes*
9. Answer varies.
10 Check in lesson for the eight essential doctrines.
11. Personal answer.
12. Answer varies.
13. 1) Jesus died on the cross for our sins, 2) He was buried, and 3) He rose on the third day.

Chapter Two: The Bible's Authenticity

1. See answer at the beginning of the chapter.

2. Because Christianity is built on faith / The Bible is all about faith and faithful-
    ness / It is important to mix the Word with faith.
3. See Isaiah 40:8
4. Answer varies.
5. *Approximately 24,600*
6. Answer varies.
7. *The Law / The Prophets / The Writings.*
8. *Yes.*
9. Luke 24:44 / Matthew 23:35 / Luke 11:51.
10. *Chronicles.*
11. *The Septuagint.*
12. *gradual collection / writings / standard.*
13. *A. D. 367.*
14. *Apostolic authorship / Recognized and used by leading churches or the majority of
    them / A conformity to the standards of sound doctrine as from the Lord.*
15. Answer varies.
16. Answer varies.
17. Not giving the author the benefit of the doubt / failing to distinguish between
    a contradiction and a difference / forgetting the limitations of translation.

Chapter Three: Mormonism - Part One

1. *"Pillar of light." 2 Corinthians 11:14.*
2. *No.*
3. Answer varies.
4. Door-to-door witnessing / A massive advertising campaign / Friendship
    Evangelism / or Emphasis to Native Americans.
5. Because they have perverted the true teaching [doctrine] of Christ by teach-
    ing that He is only one among a multitude of gods.
6. *"The fraud capital of the world."*
7. *The evolution of God.* Answer varies on the Scriptures used.
8. *No.*
9. He was a treasure seeker / well known for his storytelling / a very controver-
    sial figure / founded a whole new religion / died in a shoot out.
10. Answer varies.
11. Personal answer.
12. *No.* Scripture varies.
13. The Bible teaches that there has been and only ever will be one God. Isaiah
    43:10-11.
14. *Faith + baptism + obedience to the laws and ordinances + membership in the
    Mormon church.* Other answer varies.
15. That they have turned away to fables / That they have exchanged the truth of
    God for a lie / That they have been working hard, but not for God's righ-
    teousness.

Chapter Four: Mormonism - Part Two

1. Get educated about the arguments and issues / don't get shaken up by calcu-
    lated attacks / let the love of Christ shine through you.

2. *Approaches.*
3. Answer varies.
4. Answer varies. Twenty examples given in the lesson.
5. Answers could include: that archaeologists deny the existence of Lamanites or Nephites in America, the problem with the language and terminology expressions, the problem with blood factors, the Smithsonian Institute's refutation, etc.
6. Answers could include: the excessive amount of King James usage, the problem with the reformed Egyptian Hieroglyphics coming out in King James, the grammar issue, etc.
7. *Ethan / Spaulding / Bible.*
8. Answers could include: that the book is not polytheistic and yet Mormonism is, that the book denounces polygamy and yet Smith embraced it, the racial issue, the problem with their own professors and theologians, etc.
9. *Confusion.*
10 - 13 Answers vary.

Chapter Five: Jehovah's Witnesses - Part One

1. *Charles Russell.*
2. *Isaiah 43:10.*
3. Door-to-door witnessing / Massive Publication.
4. Answer varies.
5. Answer varies. Any three of the five listed in the lesson.
6. *Jesus Christ.*
7. Denial of the Trinity and the Deity of Christ.
8. Scriptures vary.
9. If a person reads the Bible without reading the *Studies in the Scriptures*, he will go into darkness within two years. Yet, the *Studies in the Scriptures* is sufficient without reading the Bible.
10. Through the scholarly authorities they cite who are actually in disagreement with the Watchtower. Also, through their refusal to give the names of those in their organization who supposedly were the Hebrew and Greek experts who translated it.
11. *1874 / 1914 / invisibly / spiritually.*
12. *Theocratic / character* (or one of the specific problems).
13. *That within the nature of the one God, there are three eternal and co-equal persons: God the Father, God the Son, and God the Holy Spirit.*
14. *Jesus / Holy Spirit.*
15. *"it is I Myself."*
16. *"all."*
17. Answer varies.
18. Answers can include any four of the doctrines in the lesson.
19. Personal answer.

Chapter Six: Jehovah's Witnesses - Part Two

1. They never get saved or leave the organization / They know their Bible well / They are always antagonistic.

2. Answer varies.
3. Answers could include: failures in the prophecies of 1874, 1914, 1918, 1925, 1976, etc.
4. Answers could include: the issues of scholars cited, the issue of scholars within the organization, the problem with Johannes Greber, the example of Luke 23:43, etc.
5. Answer varies. Look in the lesson.
6. *"Father."*
7. *"I Am Who I Am." / "Before Abraham was born, I am."*
8. Answers could include stands on divorce, transplants, or Acts 20:20.
9. *Heaven / devil.*
10. Answer varies.
11. Answer varies.
12. Revelation 1:8, 21:5-7, 22:13, and 1:17-18.
13. Because it shows that Jehovah died. Therefore; Jehovah and Jesus are one.

Chapter Seven: The Evolution Deception

1. Answer varies.
2. The deception of it has created a foundation for humanism / many false religions accept it / many atrocities have occurred by it / evolution actually comes across as a religion.
3. Personal answer.
4. The view that both the Bible and evolution can work together by believing that God created the first protozoa and evolution took over from there.
5. *No.*
6. Answer varies.
7. It is the foundation that adds meaning to our lives. It gives a true and reliable account of the origins of all the basic entities of the universe and of life.
8. Answer varies.
9. Spontaneous generation teaches that life only originates from life / Reproduction only occurs with the presence of a metabolic motor / The probability of life arising from non life is astronomical / The second law of thermodynamics teaches that energy is running down / The fossil record has not unveiled the transitions as Darwin said it should.
10. Answer varies.
11. See Genesis 1:27.
12. Answers could include: Flood accounts from numerous cultures including Babylonia clay tablets / fossil graveyards indicate a quick death / tree fossils indicate a quick burial /mammoth remains in Northern Siberia.
13. *Yes / Yes /* Scriptures vary.

Chapter Eight: The New Age Movement

1. *No.*
2. Information and Scriptures vary.
3. *Embraced By The Light.*
4. *evolving / avatars / monistic / God / illusion / deity / evolved guides.*
5. Consciousness Renaissance: certain individuals are stepping into godhood /

Quantum Leap of Consciousness: the whole world must ready itself to enter into godhood.

6. *Harmonic Convergence.*
7. *Holistic.*
8. *Transpersonal.*
9. India has been a land dominated for thousands of years by a holistic world view. If a holistic world view supposedly produces social evolution then why has India not overcome its tremendous problems with hunger, violence, over-population, and the caste system?
10. *Iron Mountain.*
11. There really is a conspiracy / Theories about it generally begin in fear and end in rationalization / The theories tend to be diversions, even when factually accurate.
12. *Ramtha.*
13. Look up Deuteronomy 18:10-12.
14. *Mysticism / science.*
15. Answer varies.

Chapter Nine: The Mind Sciences

1. *Metaphysical.*
2. *Cults / Mind Science.*
3. *Phineas P. Quimby.*
4. *Mary Baker Eddy - 1879 / Charles Fillmore - 1887 / Nona Brooks - 1889 / Ernest Holmes - 1927 / Evans & Dresser - 1895.*
5. *Science and Health with Key to the Scriptures*
6. Answers could include: doctor's denial of her claims of having a life-threatening condition / her plagiarism of other books / repeated drug use / her emotional instability / or her excessive riches.
7. *hundreds / thousands.*
8. *Reality.*
9. Answer varies.
10. *Truths / personal /* See 2 Timothy 3:16; Exodus 2:24-25; and 1 John 2:22.

Chapter Ten: The Unification Church

1. *South Korea / 30,000 / New Yorker Hotel.*
2. *Sun Myung Moon / Yong Myung Moon / 16.*
3. Refer to "Pikaruna" in the lesson.
4. *Fletcher /* Moon would be the front runner of the New Age Movement.
5. See Leviticus 19:31.
6. Refer to "dualism" in the lesson.
7. *The Divine Principle.*
8. The Divine Principle adds to the Bible and contradicts it / Eve did not have sex with Satan in the Garden of Eden / the cross is a sign of victory rather than failure / Jesus Christ is God / Moon is a false Messiah / The Holy Spirit is not the feminine counterpart to the Father. Various Scriptures may be used.
9. *Indemnity.*
10. Answers could include: Inviting people to workshops, heavenly deception, or love-bombing.

11. Answers could include: Independence from family / successful relationship with the opposite sex / an occupation for personal support / a meaningful and workable philosophy of life.
12. Answer varies.

Chapter Eleven: Freemasonry

1. *Secret.*
2. Answer varies.
3. *June 24, 1717.*
4. *6 million / 4 million.*
5. Answer varies.
6. *The Antimasonic Party.*
7. *Scottish / de-Christianize.*
8. *Temple.*
9. *Worshipful Master.*
10. *Entered Apprentice / Fellow Craft / and Master Mason.*
11. *33rd.*
12. Personal answer.
13. Answer varies.
14. *God / Hiram.*
15. *Jabulon.*
16. Answer varies.
17. *Yahweh / Baal / Osiris.*
18. See Revelation 9:11.
19. *Fezzes / sword / Fez / Islamic / Allah.*
20. Answer varies.

Chapter Twelve: Scientology

1. Answer varies.
2. *L. Ron Hubbard / David.*
3. Answer could include: being tutored by Mayo / graduate of George Washington University / a legitimate Ph.D / a war hero / battle wounds, etc.
4. *Dianetics / Scientology / Los Angeles / Orgs / thetans / MEST / engrams / auditors / meter / Clear.*
5. *Fruit /* Answer varies.
6. Answer could include: science fiction, psychology, religion, or the occult and their definitions from the lesson.
7. We can be as gods.
8. *Once / eternal.*
9. We cannot work our way to salvation or we could boast about it.

Chapter Thirteen: The Occult - Part One

1. *hidden / secret.*
2. Answer varies.
3. It is an attempt to foretell the future or gain "secret knowledge" from occultic methods such as astrology, crystals balls, dreams and predictions by secular prophetic figures, I Ching, numerology, omens, Ouiji board, palm reading, tarot cards, etc.

4. Answer varies.
5. Answer varies.
6. Personal answer.
7. The serpents of the magicians were all eaten by the serpent of Moses.
8. Answer varies.
9. *No.*
10. Answer should include the significance of their impact, their secrecy, and their subtleness.
11. They admitted that the rapping noises were an artificial gimmick.
12. *Brazil, France, and England.*
13. The story of King Saul in 1 Samuel 28 contacting the spirit of Samuel.
14. See Leviticus 19:31.
15. He was a false prophet / he turned men from the faith / he was full of deceit and fraud.
16. *Predict fortunes.*
17. Answer varies.
18. *No.*
19. Answer varies.

Chapter Fourteen: The Occult - Part Two

1. *Blame shifting / extremism.*
2. Personal answer.
3. Answer varies.
4. The devil and his angels.
5. Aleister Crowley impacted modern Satanism by his writings and teachings. He wrote *The Book of the Law* with the central theme of "Do what thou wilt shall be the whole of the Law." He violated every moral law possible.
6. *Authentic Satanism / sex club / gang club / The Satanic Church.*
7. *Anton LeVey.*
8. *Control.*
9. *The blood of the Lamb / the word of their testimony.*
10. They both share magical world views / Some Satanists openly identify with witchcraft.
11. *Christianity / independent / Satanism.*
12. *Gerald Garner.*
13. The Great Mother Goddess (known by Artemis, Astarte, Diana, Isis, etc.)
14. *Wiccan Rede / "That ye harm none, do what you will."*
15. *Magic.*
16. See Leviticus 19:31.
17. Answer varies.
18. Answer varies.

Chapter Fifteen: Roman Catholicism

1. Answers could include: The Apostle's Creed, similar doctrines, songs, prayers, etc.
2. *Economic / political / A.D. 395 / Catholic / Luther / loose / doctrine / Christianity.*
3. *Their view of the Bible / their view of the Pope / their view of faith and works.*

4. See Mark 7:13.
5. *Approval / appeal.*
6. *Pope.*
7. *James.*
8. Justification is the act by which we are declared righteous through faith alone, by grace alone, in Christ alone.
9. Sanctification is the process by which we are made righteous through faith and works of love.
10. *"The just shall live by faith."*
11. Answer varies.
12. *works / faith.*
13. *431 A.D. / Perpetual / Conception / sin / heaven.* Answer varies.
14. *Purgatory / sanctification / indulgences.*
15. Answer varies.

Chapter Sixteen: Judaism

1. *17 million / 40 %.*
2. *Abraham.*
3. Answer varies. Look in the lesson.
4. *Promise / serve / gods / divination or astrology / Solomon / synagogues / rabbis / Jesus / church / Romans / six million / 1948 / return.*
5. *Lunar / month.*
6. *YHWH or Yahweh.*
7. See 2 Corinthians 3:14-16.
8. *Yeshua.*
9. *Way.*
10. *Torah / daily living.*
11. Since they don't believe in the doctrine of original sin, they see no need for a Savior to bring atonement. Each can atone for his own sins, they think. So, while they might understand that people can commit sin, they miss the concept of a deep sin nature that needs atoned for by God alone.
12. *Passover / Yom Kippur.*
13. *The Jews will go through tribulation / the Jews will return to God / God will remember His covenant.*
14. *Jerusalem / Yeshua / Redeemer.*

Chapter Seventeen: Islam

1. *Second / 850 million.*
2. *know / obey.*
3. *Sarai / Ishmael / Abram / count / east / Abraham / Sarah / Isaac / great / free / slave.*
4. *7th.*
5. *Pagan.*
6. *Muhammad / 40 / Gabriel / Mecca / four / sixteen.*
7. Answer varies.
8. It causes theological controversy even among Muslims because it creates natural contradictions within the Koran, eliminates human responsibility, makes God the author of good and evil, and gives rise to pantheism.

9. *Jesus Christ.*
10. *Bible.*
11. *Jesus.*
12. *Hadith.*
13. The Sunnites: five out of six Muslims / The Shia'ites: the most radical / The Sufi: folk Islam, the mystical sect of Islam.
14. *Louis Farrakhan.*
15. Cross / sins / salvation.
16. Answer varies.
17. Answer varies.

Chapter Eighteen: Baha'ism

1. *5 million / 100,000.*
2. *Iran / Israel.*
3. We cannot mix Christianity with anything that detracts from Jesus Christ. He alone is God and there can be no other.
4. *Islamic / Imam / Promised / Bab / Baha'u'llah / Palestine / Abdu'l-Baha /1892 / Chicago westernize / House of Justice.*
5. *Moses / Buddha / Zoroaster / Confuscious / Jesus / Muhammad / Hare Krishna / Bab / and Baha'u'llah.*
6. Answer varies.
7. *Jesus Christ of Nazareth / Look up Acts 4:12.*
8. *The Oneness of God / the Oneness of Humankind / and the Oneness of Religion.*
9. Answer varies.
10. Personal answer.
11. *Jesus / distinctiveness / God / miracles / dead.*

Chapter Nineteen: Hinduism

1. *13 percent / 88.*
2. Pre-Vedic: Dravidians practiced animal worship / Vedic: the Vedas were written / Upanishadic: the Upanishad writings / Revival of Vedantic: The Bhagavad-Gita written.
3. *Brama, Vishnu, and Shiva.*
4. *Lord Krishna.*
5. *Bhagavad-Gita / Arjuna / Krishna / revered.*
6. *Purpose / temporary / maya / Samsara / moksha / philosophical / includes / excludes.*
7. Answer varies.
8. *Karma / Samsara.*
9. Look up Hebrews 9:27.
10. *Knowledge / works / devotion / Jesus Christ.*
11. *Knowledge / eight / Brahman.*
12. *The Vedanta Society / the Self-Realization Fellowship / ISKCON.*
13. Supposed meditation techniques that end up as worship to Guru Dev.
14. Scriptures vary.
15. Answer could include: a guru, teacher, avatar, yoga master, etc.
16. Answer varies.
17. 1 Corinthians 8:4-6

Chapter Twenty: Buddhism

1. *6 % / 311 million.*
2. *five hundred thousand.*
3. *Siddhartha / A.D. 563 / monk / salvation / 16 / sickness / old age / death / Bodhi / 40 days / nirvana / Buddha / food.*
4. Personal answer.
5. Life consists of suffering / suffering is caused by selfish desire for illusory things / liberation comes through elimination of all these desires / desires are eliminated by following the eight-fold path (The Middle Way).
6. Answer varies.
7. Answer varies.
8. *Theravada / Mahayana.*
9. Answer varies.
10. *Vinaya Pitaka.*
11. *Heart Sutra.*
12. *Gods / humans / demons / hungry ghosts / animals / hell dwellers.*
13. *The key to mobilizing evangelism today is prayer / the key to winning the right to evangelize today is love / the key to setting the captives free is witness.*

APPENDIX C

THINKING THROUGH THE SCRIPTURE GUIDE

If you want to locate one of the many Scriptures used in the chapter boxes entitled "**Thinking Through The Scripture**," simply locate the passage below. The chapter number is given directly after the slash. For example: Proverbs 8:32-36 / 15 = chapter fifteen. Now turn to chapter fifteen and scan the boxes until you locate the particular passage and the questions that examine that passage.

THE OLD TESTAMENT
Genesis 1:24-25 / 7
Genesis 1:27 / 7
Genesis 2:7 / 7
Genesis 3:4-6 / 8
Genesis 4:1-2 / 10
Genesis 17:18-19 / 16
Exodus 3:13-14 / 6
Exodus 7:10-12 / 13
Exodus 12:21 / 16
Exodus 20:3 / 11
Leviticus 5:4-6 / 11
Leviticus 19:4 / 19
Leviticus 19:31 / 13
Deut. 4:2 / 3
Deut. 18:10-12 / 8
Deut. 18:20-22 / 4
Judges 3:7 / 11

1 Samuel 5:2-4 / 19
1 Samuel 15:23 / 13
Job 30:2-8 / 7
Psalm 51:5 / 9
Psalm 104:30 / 7
Proverbs 8:32-36 / 15
Proverbs 8:35-36 / 1
Proverbs 11:5-9 / 12
Proverbs 12:12 / 5
Proverbs 14:7-8 / 11
Proverbs 14:12 / 1
Proverbs 15:31-32 / 15
Proverbs 30:8-9 / 9
Ecclesiastes 1:9 / 8
Ecclesiastes 12:9-14 / 20
Isaiah 9:6 / 5
Isaiah 14:12 / 3
Isaiah 19:1-4 / 8

Isaiah 43:10-11 / 12
Isaiah 44:6,8 / 12
Isaiah 45:20-22 / 19
Isaiah 47:11-15 / 13
Isaiah 53:3 / 16
Isaiah 55:6-9 / 20
Isaiah 59:2-3 / 9
Jeremiah 10:14-16 / 20
Jeremiah 23:29-32 / 5
Jeremiah 27:9-10 / 13
Habakkuk 2:18-20 / 19
Zechariah 12:10 / 4

THE NEW TESTAMENT
Matthew 1:22-23 / 5
Matthew 6:7-13 / 19, 6
Matthew 6:24 / 9
Matthew 7:13-15 / 8

Matthew 7:15-17 / 12
Matthew 7:18-21 / 5
Matthew 7:21-23 / 9
Matthew 10:26 / 4
Matthew 11:28-30 / 19
Matthew 12:50 / 15
Matthew 16:15-18 / 15
Matthew 24:4-5 / 10
Matthew 24: 4-13 / 18
Mark 13:31 / 4
Luke 1:31-35 / 10
Luke 2:25-32 / 20
Luke 8:17 / 4
Luke 8:46-47 / 9
Luke 10:18-20 / 14
Luke 11:27-28 / 15
Luke 12:2-5 / 11
John 1:1, 14 / 2
John 1:10-12 / 16
John 1:29 / 16
John 3:5 / 6
John 3:16 / 1
John 3:20-21 / 5
John 3:36 / 20
John 4 / 8-9 / 9
John 4:22 / 20
John 5:18 / 9
John 5:22-23 / 6
John 8:58-59a / 6
John 9:6-7 / 9
John 10:7-11 / 18
John 13:48-49 / 11
John 14:6 / 19
John 16:13-15 / 5, 6

John 17:3 / 17
Acts 4:10,12 / 6
Acts 19:26-28 / 12
Romans 1:18,24 / 10
Romans 1:20-25 / 4, 7
Romans 2:28-29 / 16
Romans 3:20 / 6
Romans 3:20-25 / 17
Romans 4:1-5 / 15
Romans 5:8-9 / 9
Romans 9:6-8 / 17
Romans 10:2-4 / 18
Romans 11:16-18 / 16
Romans 11:25-27 / 16
1 Corin. 1:18-21 / 13
1 Corin. 3:10-13 / 11
1 Corin. 11:27-29 / 11
1 Corin. 14:33 / 4
1 Corin. 15:1-4 / 1
2 Corin. 3:17 / 6
2 Corin. 4:4 / 18
2 Corin. 5:8-10 / 9
2 Corin. 6:14-15,17 / 9
2 Corin. 10:4-5 / 1
2 Corin. 11:3-4 / 1
2 Corin. 11:13-15 / 3, 5
Galatians 1:6-9 / 3, 15
Galatians 1:8-12 / 17
Galatians 3:26-29 / 16
Galatians 3:26, 29 / 17
Ephesians 2:8-9 / 6
Colossians 1:15-20 / 18
Colossians 1:18 / 5
Colossians 2:6-8 / 7

Colossians 2:8-10 / 5
2 Thess. 2:3 / 5
2 Thess. 2:10b-12 / 3
1 Timothy 2:3-4 / 1
1 Timothy 4:1-5 / 19
1 Timothy 6:6-10 / 9
2 Timothy 2:24-26 / 1
2 Timothy 3:6-7 / 20
2 Timothy 3:16-17 / 2
2 Timothy 4:3-4 / 4
Titus 3:4-7 / 19
Hebrews 4:12 / 2
Hebrews 9:27 / 9
Hebrews 12:2-3 / 20
1 Peter 1:18-19 / 3
2 Peter 1:20-21 / 2
2 Peter 2:1-3 / 4, 11
2 Peter 3:15-16 / 2
1 John 1:7,9 / 3
1 John 2:22 / 9
1 John 2:26-27 / 5
1 John 4:1-3 / 1
1 John 4:4-8 / 14
1 John 4:15-17 / 13
1 John 5:6, 9-11 / 18
2 John 7-10 / 3
Jude 3-4 / 10
Jude 14-16 / 12
Revelation 9:11 / 11
Revelation 12:10-11 / 14
Revelation 19:13 / 2
Revelation 20:10 / 14
Revelation 21:8 / 14
Revelation 22:18-19 / 3

APPENDIX D

RESOURCE GUIDE

American Family Foundation
PMB 313
P.O. Box 413005
Naples, FL 34101-3005
Phone: (941) 514-3081
Fax: (941) 649-2267
(Psychological abuse cults - newsletter)

Berean Christian Ministries
John Farkas
1297 Mill Creek Run
Webster, N.Y. 14580-9550
Phone: (716) 872-4033
(Mormonism - newsletter)

Christian Liberty Outreach
P.O. Box 8552
Independence, MO 64054
(RLDS - Reorganized Church of Jesus
Christ
of Latter Day Saints)

Christian Ministries International
Dr. Ron Carlson
7601 Superior Terrace
Eden Prairie, MN 55344
Phone: (612) 937-1385
(General cults and false teachings ,
Creation Science - audio cassettes /
video teachings / books)

Christian Research Institute
P.O. Box 7000
30162 Tomas
Rancho Santa Margarita, CA 92688
Phone: (949) 858-6100
Fax: (949) 858-6111
(General - books, pamphlets, and
audio cassettes)

Institute for Creation Research
Dr. John Morris
P.O. Box 2667
El Cajon, CA 92021
Phone: (619) 448-0900
Fax: (619) 448-3469
(Creation Science - books, videos,
audio cassettes)

Jeremiah Films
P.O. Box 1710
Hemet, CA 92546-1710
1 (800) 828-2290
(Cults and the Occult - videos)

Jews for Jesus
60 Haight Street
San Francisco, CA 94102-5895
Phone: (415) 864-2600
(Jews - newsletter, books)

The John Ankerberg Show
John Ankerberg
P.O. Box 8977
Chattanooga, TN 37414
Phone: (423) 892-7722
(Cults - books, videos)

MacGregor Ministries
Lorri MacGregor
Box 454 Metaline Falls, WA 99153
Box 294 Nelson B.C. V1L5P9
(Jehovah's Witnesses - videos)

Saints Alive in Jesus
Ed Decker
P.O. Box 1347
Issaquah, WA 98027
Phone: (425) 888-3904
1 (800) 861-9888
(Mormonism, Freemasonry - newsletter, books, cassettes, and videos)

Spiritual Counterfeits Project
P.O. Box 4308
Berkeley, CA 94704
Phone: (510) 540-0300
Fax: (510) 540-1107
(General - books)

Utah Lighthouse Ministry
Jerald & Sandra Tanner
P.O. Box 1884
Salt Lake City, UT 84110
Phone: (801) 485-8894
Fax: 484-0312
(Mormonism - pamphlets, books)

Watchman Fellowship
P.O. Box 530842
Birmingham, AL 35253
Phone: (205) 871-2858
Fax: (205) 871-2881
(General - magazine, newsletter, books, and videos)

With One Accord
P.O. Box 457
Dubuque, IA 52004-0457
Phone: (319) 583-5473
Fax: (319) 583-2998
(Catholicism, Freemasonry, Mormonism, Satanism - books, audio cassettes, videos)

To order additional copies of:

Gate Breakers

send $16.99 plus $3.95 shipping and handling to:

Books, Etc.
PO Box 4888
Seattle, WA 98104

Or have your credit card ready and call toll free:

877-537-8836

CPSIA information can be obtained at www.ICGtesting.com
Printed in the USA
BVOW07s0208090813

328264BV00001B/12/A

9 781589 300989